Further praise for

CULTURAL COHESION

"Clive James is in the tradition of Hazlitt, Bagehot, and Edmund Wilson, with a gusto to succeed theirs."
—John Bayley

"[Clive James's] outstanding talent is as a cicerone, guiding the ignorant traveler with patience, knowledge, and wit round some favorite literary edifice and communicating his own admiration of it to the goggling and fascinated visitor."
—*Times Literary Supplement*

"The timelessness, acuity, and humanism of James' criticism is everywhere evident in this scintillating collection."—Donna Seaman, *Booklist*

Praise for Clive James

"James's prose is . . . comic, inventive, above all, energetic."
—*New York Times Book Review*

"Clive James is a brilliant bunch of guys."
—*The New Yorker*

"[James] writes like a prophet and he can satirize folly in high places with a touch as elegant as Oscar Wilde."
—*Daily Mail*

"In a world where knowledge is becoming more fragmentary and specialized every day, Clive James can write about the high, the middle and low alike with astonishing facility and erudition."
—*Times Literary Supplement*

Autobiography

The Blaze of Obscurity
North Face of Soho
May Week Was in June
Falling Towards England
Unreliable Memoirs

Fiction

The Silver Castle
The Man from Japan
The Remake
Brilliant Creatures

Verse

Nefertiti in the Flak Tower
Opal Sunset: Selected Poems, 1958–2008
Angels over Elsinore
The Book of My Enemy: Collected Verse, 1958–2003

Criticism

A Point of View
The Revolt of the Pendulum
Cultural Amnesia
The Meaning of Recognition
Even as We Speak
Reliable Essays: The Best of Clive James
The Dreaming Swimmer
On Television
Snakecharmers in Texas
Glued to the Box
From the Land of Shadows
The Crystal Bucket
First Reactions
At the Pillars of Hercules
Visions Before Midnight
The Metropolitan Critic (new edition, 1994)

Travel

Flying Visits

CLIVE JAMES

THE *Essential* ESSAYS, 1968–2002

CULTURAL

COHESION

W. W. NORTON & COMPANY

NEW YORK AND LONDON

TO THE MEMORY OF

SARAH RAPHAEL

"The Dreaming Swimmer," "Snakecharmers in Texas," "Primo Levi's Last Will and Testament," "Mark Twain, Journalist," "Casanova Comes Home Again," Hitler's Unwitting Exculpator," "Bertrand Russell Struggles After Heaven," "Pier Paolo Pain in the Neck," "Mondo Fellini," and "Who Was that Masked Man" were originally published in *The New Yorker.*

"Go Back to the Cold!" reprinted with permission from the *New York Review of Books*. Copyright © 1977 NYREV, Inc.

"Castalia" reprinted with permission from the *New York Review of Books*. Copyright © 1980 NYREV, Inc.

"Waugh's Last Stand" reprinted with permission from the *New York Review of Books*. Copyright © 1980 NYREV, Inc.

"Sherlockology" reprinted with permission from the *New York Review of Books*. Copyright © 1975 NYREV, Inc.

Manufacturing by the Haddon Craftsmen, Inc.
Book design by Jam Design
Production manager: Julia Druskin

The Library of Congress has cataloged the hardcover edition as follows:

James, Clive, 1939–
As of this writing: the essential essays, 1968–2002 / by Clive James
p.m.
Includes index
ISBN 0-393-05180-3
I. Title.

PR9619.3.J27A6 2003
8298'.914—dc21
2003041257

ISBN 978-0-393-34636-7 pbk.

W. W. Norton & Company, Inc., 500 Fifth Avenue, New York, N.Y. 10110
www.norton.com

W. W. Norton & Company Ltd., Castle House, 75/76 Wells Street, London W1T 3QT
1 2 3 4 5 6 7 8 9 0

Barbarism is not the prehistory of humanity but the faithful shadow that accompanies its every step.

— ALAIN FINKIELKRAUT,
Le mécontemporain

CONTENTS

A NOTE ON THE TEXT

Over the years I have made it a practice, which I continue here, of leaving an article virtually untouched when collecting it into a book. Sometimes I was glad to reinsert a sentence or two which I had thought particularly clever and an editor had taken out, probably for that very reason; and occasionally there were simple factual errors which should have been caught at the time. But on the whole it seemed best to leave things unimproved. If you start updating a piece in the light of subsequent developments, the result is a tacit claim to a congenital infallibility of judgement: an attribute which, were one to possess it, would remove the whole point of critical journalism at a blow. Aspiring to permanence only by the measure with which it illuminates the ephemeral, such writing can be pertinent or not, but either way it has to be contingent: if it tries to cut itself free from time and chance, it removes itself from life.

So each piece is marked with its provenance, not as a claim to automatic importance but as a reminder that it was written at a specific moment of modern history by a specific person, who was younger and less wary than the codger carrying the same name now. When the expressed sentiments cry out to be updated, the necessary work is done in a postscript. Some of the postscripts date from 1992, when I reissued my debut book of pieces *The Metropolitan Critic*, which had been originally published in 1974 and was so full of stylistic excesses that my only choice seemed to be between rewriting it and forgetting it. Conceit ruled out the second course, and a new, sudden and strange access of humility ruled out the first. Hadn't my young clumsiness been a true testimony, and wouldn't an airbrushed refurbishment be a false one? Better to admit the absurdities, and say how they had come to be perpetrated. Thus I hit on the scheme of commenting on my own commentary.

More recently, in the year 2001, a "best of" selection called *Reliable Essays*—drawn from half a dozen separate collections—was published in Britain, and I added more postscripts where they seemed appropriate. Some of them are here, marked with that date. Other postscripts were written especially for this selection, the initiative for which I owe Robert Weil, along with the rare combination of enthusiasm and selectivity he brought to the task of convincing the author that one or two things might just possibly make their best contribution by being left out, so as not to dim the light of all the coruscating stuff that was demanding to be put in.

—CLIVE JAMES
London
2003

FOREWORD

Though it would please their author if the pieces in this book were to be called essays, there is no denying that most of them had their first life as literary journalism. If we take it for granted that a writer is posturing if he calls himself an essayist, just as he would be preening if he called himself a wit, it is partly because the essay had its origins in a low trade whose practitioners awarded distinction to each other only on performance, and never on mere membership. As a form in the English language, the essay had its true beginnings in the London coffee houses, where it depended for its energy on a seeming paradox: contributing to a periodical designed to be thrown away, the essayist composed his piece as if it were meant to be kept. There was always the chance that he might be the only one to keep it, but if he failed in his aim of bringing permanence to ephemerality, he could always congratulate himself on having respected his disrespectable work by devoting his best efforts to it. I hope I can plausibly claim that much—that these pieces are workmanlike—because when I add up the time it took to write them, the sum accounts for a large part of my life.

For almost forty years I have been writing literary journalism in London, and London is probably where I will go on writing it until the pen drops from my fingers. Actually, of course, although I still write my first and second drafts in a notebook, the dropped pen no longer applies as a token of weary death. More likely, when it comes to the last word, I will multi-punch the laptop's keyboard with my face, my fingers only halfway through the sequence that activates the most sadly beautiful of all modern rubrics, Windows Is Shutting Down. And English grammar are checking out. When the time comes to follow it into oblivion, my exit will probably owe more to old age than to malnutrition. As a slow writer who got slower still the more he had to say, I could never have earned a living from literary journalism alone. It was always amateur night, and I made my eating money by other means, first as a television critic, then as a television performer. There are reasons for thinking that in the field of literary journalism, full professionalism in the economic sense is not necessarily a desirable object. On the other hand, it doesn't hurt to get paid something, and luckily I always was. But it never added up to a fortune—which raises the question of whether I might not have set out my stall in the wrong town. Shouldn't I have been in New York? By American standards, London and low wages go together, like London and a malfunctioning subway system. But there is something else that goes with London, too; something vital to the life of the mind, or to my mind at any rate. London isn't in America.

America is magnetic in its power, drawing all the world's activities towards it for their validation, with the possible exception of football with a round ball; and even then, Brazil's great Edison Arantes do Nascimento, later known as Pele, probably counted it as one of the highlights of his life when he showed President Ford how to bounce the ball on his foot, and President Ford showed him how not to. Good foreign movies are drawn towards Los Angeles, where they are remade as bad ones for their only chance at the world market. Japan's black-belt sushi cooks are drawn towards the restaurants of Aspen, Russia's most gorgeous young female tennis players towards the sports-babe nurseries of Florida. When the suicide pilots were drawn towards the twin towers of New York, their unerring flight was a confirmation as much as it was a criticism. They were making their mark where the whole planet would see it. To be famous throughout the world, you must first be famous in America. Shakira's contrapuntally undulating stomach muscles are famous in Latin America, but when they are famous in the real America they will be famous in Iceland. If it hasn't happened in America, it hasn't happened. Foreign media personnel, especially if they stem from the Left, are apt to decry this assumption; but they are just as apt, and especially if they stem from the left, to succumb to it when their moment comes. Given the chance, they go for the green card. Should writers do the same?

I know several that have. Even if they forgo the card, each has shifted the powerhouse of his mentality—the centre of his attention—out of London and into New York. They have probably done the right thing. As a world figure, Salman Rushdie feels more at home in the centre of events than he ever did at home—the home which was already his second home, India having been the first. Rushdie, like Nirad Chaudhuri and other subcontinental masters of the English language before him, knows that there is a sense in which the phrase "England made me" is undeniable. But he also knows that when the British government sensibly decided to pay for his protection as the cheapest way of fighting the war which Iran had declared by pronouncing a death sentence on a British resident, the decision was not unanimously approved by his fellow men of letters. Some of them thought he should pick up the tab, and among those there were a vocal few who clearly believed that it would be no bad thing if he paid for his fame with his life. In America, he thought, nobody who mattered would speak that way. John Lennon no doubt thought the same, and had not been entirely wrong: the man who killed him did not matter except for a moment. So Rushdie went to the centre of the magnetic field.

So did Martin Amis, when he declared that Britain no longer leads the world in anything, except in decline. For those of us who stick with Britain, or at any rate are stuck with it, this might have seemed a large statement, but only a churl could blame him for making it. Some of the British journalism written to spite his success has to be read to be believed. In most cases it is written by people who would like to be him: you can tell by the way they ape his epithets without possessing the talent to ape an ape. In London he is besieged by carping graduates in media studies—mad on America even when they are mad against it—who measure his achievement only in terms of money and success: their key concepts of value sound like the titles he gives his novels. In New York he can at least meet that kind of materialism at first hand. If the Moronic Inferno is your adversary, you might as well go up against it in the main furnace, rather than in some subsidiary steam-room rattling with rusty pipes. The main furnace powers the magnet. For Christopher Hitchens, the adversary was the capitalist conspiracy against the wretched of the earth. Somewhere around the time that Prince Charles married Lady Diana Spencer and the people danced in the streets instead of greasing the wheels of the tumbril, Hitchens decided that Britain was the wrong place to fight the battle. To the dismay of his friends, but with their heartfelt understanding, Hitchens subtracted his brilliance from London and took it to America, there to beard the adversary in his den. When the planes hit the towers, Hitchens bravely faced the unsettling fact that some of the wretched of the earth might be adversaries too, but there is no sign that he has wavered in his choice of platform, and every sign that his platform revels in its choice of him. With a neigh of pleasure, America has taken Hitchens over as its licensed horsefly. When Dwight Macdonald assailed America's conduct of World War II, he had to do it in magazines of small circulation, usually under his own editorship. When Hitchens calls for the indictment of Henry Kissinger as a war criminal, he can do it in *Vanity Fair*: angelically phrased invective on double-coated art paper, closely supported by radiant images of Gwyneth Paltrow. Even at the heart of the magnetic field, his wit, instead of being flattened, dances for the delight of all, with the possible exception of Kissinger. For Hitchens, as for Rushdie and Amis, the centre of the attraction is the heart of the action.

There is only one disadvantage I can think of, but I have thought of it often, and in the long term I have staked my life on it. The centre of the magnetic field is the wrong place to see the distortions it creates. This might not matter for novelists like Rushdie and Amis, or for a globe-girdling political commentator like Hitchens, but for a literary journalist it should be a consideration, because literary journalism is weakened when allied to power, which breeds power within itself, and thus reinforces specialization. In New York, one woman writing for the *New York Times* can decide the commercial fate of a novel. She exercises her power with independence and integrity, but it is an awful lot of power to have. In London nobody ever had it, not even Cyril Connolly when he was reviewing for the *Sunday Times* every week. The master of writing a review you cared about of a book he scarcely cared about at all, he had influence but not power, and there is a difference. In New York, prominent members of the Fourth Estate behave as if they were part of the government of the country, encouraged in that belief by the publications they write for. The publications behave like journals of record. I don't know what happens at *Hustler*, but at any other American paper or magazine of which I have knowledge, the contributor is likely to find himself edited as if he speaks for the publication before he speaks for himself.

In London, none of this happens. There is editing, but it is done by agreement, and to help you to sound more like yourself, not less. Otherwise there is little intervention, even in fact checking. I don't deny that a light hand in that department can leave a writer feeling lonely. Unless the editor knows the difference, if you attribute the *Goldberg Variations* to Beethoven instead of Bach the mistake will go straight into print, to make you a laughing stock for a month. More seriously, it would be very difficult in London to pull off a triumph like Nicholson Baker's initial *New Yorker* article about the junking of library cards (the article served as the precursor for his marvellous book *Double Fold*, in which the world's great libraries emerge as remorseless engines for destroying books in the name of their preservation) because no London publication has the staff whose busy surveillance would automatically provide a free source of additional research. Most of the London editors work on the assumption that if a blunder is committed, it will be pointed out in the letters column. (It's the main reason that the letters columns of the London publications are so much more informative than the equivalent forums in New York, where a typical letter either lauds the "insightful" richness of some piece in the previous issue or damns it to hell.) And as for the style, the piece is much more likely to go into the paper pretty much as written, with the writer's allusions left unflagged and all his quirks intact. The late Anthony Burgess got so used to this that when he contributed to American magazines, and found an American editor calling him to order on the transatlantic telephone, Burgess would bark, "Just print it." More often than not, the editor just didn't. Even though the conversation was in English, contributor and editor were speaking two different languages. Burgess thought his manuscript was the finished product. His American editor thought it was only the raw material.

Admittedly, London publications can overdo their respect for individuality. In recent years, with the collapse of the Left, the *New Statesman* has yielded its position of the weekly "everybody reads" to the *Spectator*. Politically, the *Spectator* is chiefly concerned with restoring credibility to the Conservative Party, a victim of the collapse of the Right. Since the only politics that matter are now in the centre, anybody can write for the *Spectator* with a clear conscience; but it can be disturbing, when you send the magazine your latest poem, to contemplate the possibility that it might make its appearance framed by the chill prose of Diana Mosley. Nevertheless, the tolerance for a wide range of political affiliation is a good thing for literary journalism. The conversational tone can become sibilant and even waspish, but there are not really any separate tables. In London, the *Times Literary Supplement* and the *London Review of Books* could never go to war against each other as the *New York Review of Books* and *Commentary* once did. In London, the annual parties thrown by the literary magazines still matter more than any book launch, and to each of those parties everybody comes. There is a sense of community, even when opinions differ. It could be said that this is only because nobody's opinion is felt to matter very much, but that would not be quite true. The writers have their pride. But they know that they have no power. Prestige is acquired not from position, but from the possession of a personal style.

Ideally, it should be an inclusive style, but there is room for the cranky, the narrow, the wilfully provocative. Room for manoeuvre was a big help when it came to establishing the tradition of providing a supplement and a corrective to the academic study of literature. This tradition is still known under the bewildering title of Grub Street, as if it were a place: but really it is a spirit, and one that has flourished since the time of Johnson and Pope, who were never afraid to chide the scholars. At the beginning of my career in Grub Street I praised Edmund Wilson as the arch example of the Metropolitan Critic, the critic who operates in the vital space between the hack reviewers of the periodicals and the dust contractors of the universities. Looking back on it, I can see now that I was seeking an American endorsement for something that Britain had always had. Nowadays it has more of it than ever, and largely because no American endorsement is needed, even if it might be wanted. The London literary journalists might dream of an American stipend, but they are lucky not to have it, because the price is high. The price of achieving prominence as a literary journalist in America is to play an enforced role as an arbiter of success, and the price of not achieving it is to be marginalized. In America, the excellent literary essays of Howard Nemerov are collected in a book published by the University of Missouri Press, a solitary copy of which I lately happened on in a Bloomsbury remainder shop. Some of the essays appeared in the *Sewanee Review*. In Britain, all of them would have appeared in periodicals available to the general reader; I would have seen them years ago, and perhaps drawn upon their opinions to modify mine. The Edward Mallinckrodt Distinguished University Professor of English at Washington University in St. Louis would have had a different audience, and I would have been glad to be part of it.

To write in London is a better way to be marginalized. One might not be a Distinguished Professor, but one occupies a more advantageous margin. Placed at the perimeter, one can see in, and can comment more surely on what comes out, and on how far it comes: the field of attraction. As of this writing, there is concern in London about the proposal to accept American sponsorship of the Booker Prize, with the likely corollary of opening the competition to American novels. The question is thought to turn on whether or not this prospective Americanization will leave the way open for non-American novelists in English to be blown off the court as if by a Dream Team of American basketballers: seven-foot-tall All-Stars wearing Air Jordans. Roth! Bellow! Donna Tartt! Forget about it! But London, and not New York, is the best place in which to realize that the Booker Prize was Americanized from the jump. The Booker Prize is a marketing tool. And the market is part of the magnet.

Some subjects have no market value. They only have value. Literary journalism is one of them. The demand for it will never increase. Nobody who practises it will get rich. When Hollywood makes the movie about Edmund Wilson's passion for Edna St. Vincent Millay, it could well mean Oscars for Ben Affleck and Kirsten Dunst, but the box office returns will come too late to help Wilson with his tax problem. Literary journalism is a branch of humanism, and humanism is not utilitarian: it must be pursued for its own sake. In America this is a hard principle to stick to, but there are many Americans who are glad to be reminded it exists, because they know that America is not the whole world, and would be impoverished if it were. By that reckoning, the best way to serve America is to stay out if it, and send in messages along the lines of magnetic force. They can be messages of admonition, or messages of appreciation, or both. But unless some of us stay away from the magnet, the messages cannot be sent.

INTRODUCTION TO THE
PAPERBACK EDITION

Under the title *As of This Writing*, this anthology of my work as an essayist was first published in 2003 and attracted a certain amount of attention from the American critics. Four years later another book, *Cultural Amnesia*, attracted much more attention from those same critics and also won a following among the public. Eventually it went to a paperback edition, which continues to do gratifyingly well: enough for my publishers to make it clear that if I wanted to write a sequel they might put it into print. I thought of calling the sequel *Cultural Amnesia II: The Quest Goes On*, so as to give the flavour of a movie franchise. The cover could feature artwork of myself in a Harrison Ford pose, with a ray-gun, and perhaps an intergalactic female aristocrat clinging to my waist. But over the past two and a half years my health has been too fragile to permit my making a start on it.

Frustrated in my intentions to write a sequel, I was a good while thinking of an alternative means of procedure, namely a prequel. In all but name, *As of This Writing* had been the predecessor to *Cultural Amnesia*. With a new title, its continuity with that later book might be made explicit. Over the long period in which I wrote the pieces in this volume, I was working towards, but had not yet reached, the conclusion that *Cultural Amnesia* would depend on: the conclusion, that is, that a culture is not a coherent whole, but a multiform and expanding mass of creative activities held together by lines of connection that can be described only on the understanding that the description must be incomplete.

Earlier on, between the years 1968 and 2002—the working years covered by this volume—I had proceeded on the assumption that the culture I had been born into, and which I had set out to operate within as a cultural critic, was all of a piece. There was poetry and there was prose, and there were high and low versions of each. Things like painting and music came at various levels of intensity: levels which could safely be identified as either worthy or trivial. As the reader will soon see, I had doubts myself about the self-containment of these categories. To take an extreme example, I was already wondering whether the creations of Judith Krantz might not be more alive than half of the putatively serious novels I was reading. Back in the 1970s and 1980s, she was a big name among popular novelists: her books sold in millions. With *Princess Daisy* she hadn't written *Tess of the d'Urbervilles*, but she had raised the question of whether dullness should be put up with. My essay about her, which the reader will find here under the title of "A Blizzard of Tiny Kisses," made it all the way to the *Oxford Book of Essays*. I found it hard to convince myself that I could have got there without her.

To put it briefly, I already knew that things were more complicated than I had thought. But for a long while they were complicated enough. There was so much first-rate stuff to be praised. In poetry, Philip Larkin published important new poems during my time as a critic. (I actually reviewed his collection *High Windows* when it came out.) In prose, the whole of George Orwell was reissued in one go. Critics could occupy their time impeccably by dealing with nothing except books written in English. But finally I noticed, from my own behaviour, that paying attention to Solzhenitsyn and to Primo Levi meant that there was a larger and less harmonious cultural world. The forces of disintegration that those two great writers had helped to define were part of our culture too, or at any rate their consequences were. Cultural stability was an illusion. It was coming apart all the time. It was like the universe: its edges all fled away from you no matter where you stood.

But this chilling realization was for a later volume. In the volume before you now, confidence reigns. The critic thinks that he knows exactly what he is doing, and has a wonderful time doing it. As I read the text again, I find that I inadvertently wrote a happy book. Even when I tell John le Carré to stop being so pompous, I sound just as intent on having fun as on correcting his taste. (He thought I was conducting a vendetta, but that reaction was an example, I thought, of the very pomposity I was talking about.) I don't say that the book comes from a more innocent era. But it does come from a more innocent writer. Once, I thought that a culture could stave off the world's evil. Now I think that a culture must take continual account of the irrationality that would like to destroy it. I hope my later view is the more mature, but perhaps I have just grown old.

—CLIVE JAMES
Cambridge
2013

PART

I

POETRY

I

ON AUDEN'S DEATH

For a long time before his death, the fact that a homosexual was the greatest living English poet had the status of an open secret: anybody with better than a passing knowledge of W. H. Auden's writing must have been in on it, and in his later essays (one thinks particularly of the essays on Housman and Ackerley) he was teetering on the verge of declaring himself outright. During E. M. Forster's last decades the intelligentsia was similarly privy to covert information. At Forster's death, however, the obituaries— many of them written by old acquaintances—didn't hesitate to let the cat spring from the bag and dash about among a wider public. It isn't recorded that anybody died of shock at this revelation. One would have thought that a precedent for plain dealing had at long last been set. With Auden's demise, though, there has been a retreat into coy mummery— perhaps to protect his dedicatees still living, but more probably because no respectable literatus wants the responsibility of firing the gun that will set the young scholars off on their plodding race to re-explicate what any sensitive reader has long since seen to be one of the more substantial poetic achievements of the modern age. Poor scorned clericals, they will find that their new key turns with bewitching ease, but that it might as well be turning in a lake as in a lock. Auden is a long way beyond being a crackable case.

Nevertheless, the truth helps. It was an often-stated belief in Auden's later essays that knowledge of an artist's personal life was of small relevance in understanding his work. Insatiably and illuminatingly inquisitive, Auden transgressed his own rule on every possible occasion. The

principle was the right one, but had been incorrectly stated. He was saying that to know the truth will still leave you facing a mystery. What he
should have said was that to know the truth will leave you with a better
chance of facing the *right* mystery. And it quickly becomes evident, I
think, that to accept the truth about Auden's sexual nature does nothing to diminish his poetry—quite the opposite. Acceptance leads in the
very short run to the realization that the apparent abstractness of
Auden's expressed sensuality is really a lyricism of unique resonance,
and in the long run to the conviction that Auden's artistic career, taken
as a whole, is a triumph of the moral self living out its ideal progress as
a work of art.

Auden's first poems instantly revealed an unrivalled gift for luminous
statement. Simply by naming names he could bring anything to life:

> Who stands, the crux left of the watershed,
> On the wet road between the chafing grass
> Below him sees dismantled washing-floors,
> Snatches of tramline running to the wood
> An industry already comatose. . . .

After the withering of 1930s illusions it became fashionable to laugh at
"Pylon" poetry, but even though intentions do not make deeds there was
always something honourable in the intention of domesticating a tech-
nological imagery, and anyway Auden himself had only to intend and the
deed was done. So formidable a capacity to elevate facts from the prosaic
to the poetic had been seen rarely in centuries, and such fluent gestures
in doing it had almost never been seen. Auden's poetry possessed the
quality which Pasternak so admired in Pushkin—it was full of *things*. And
yet in an epoch when homosexuality was still a crime, this talent was the
very one which could not be used unguarded to speak of love.

For that, he was forced from the concrete to the abstract, and so
moved from the easy (for him) to the difficult. As Gianfranco Contini
definitively said when talking of Dante's dedication to the rhyme, the
departure point for inspiration is the obstacle. The need to find an
acceptable expression for his homosexuality was the first technical obstacle to check the torrential course of Auden's unprecedented facility. A

born master of directness was obliged to find a language for indirection, thus becoming immediately involved with the drama that was to continue for the rest of his life—a drama in which the living presence of technique is the antagonist.

> Doom is dark and deeper than any sea-dingle.
> Upon what man it fall
> In spring, day-wishing flowers appearing,
> Avalanche sliding, white snow from rock-face,
> That he should leave his house,
> No cloud-soft hand can hold him, restraint by women;
> But ever that man goes
> Through place-keepers, through forest trees,
> A stranger to strangers over undried sea,
> Houses for fishes, suffocating water,
> Or lonely on fell as chat,
> By pot-holed becks
> A bird stone-haunting, an unquiet bird.

In this first stanza of Poem II in *Poems* (it was entitled "The Wanderer" only later, in *Collected Shorter Poems 1930–1944*), the idea of the homosexual's enforced exile is strongly present, although never explicit: the theme lies hidden and the imagery is explicit instead, thereby reversing the priorities of the traditional lyric, and bodying forth an elliptical suggestiveness which rapidly established itself as the new lyricism of an era. But already we are given a foretaste of the voyage that came to an end in Oxford forty years later—a wanderer's return to the Oxford of *Another Time*, the centre of anger which is the only place that is out of danger. Auden never looked for cloistered safety until very late on the last day. The danger and fatigue of his journey were too much of an inspiration.

> There head falls forward, fatigued at evening
> And dreams of home,
> Waving from window, spread of welcome,
> Kissing of wife under single sheet;
> But waking sees
> Birds-flocks nameless to him, through doorway voices
> Of new men making another love.

Only tiredness could make the doomed traveller dream the banalities of hearth and wife: awake, he is once again involved with real love. And real love is a new love, with all political overtones fully intended. Auden's radicalism, such as it was, was at one with his sexuality, with the piquant result that he spent the 1930s experiencing communism as sensual and sex as political.

.   .   .

As Brecht found his politicized lyricism in sophistication (*In der Asphaltstadt bin ich daheim*), Auden found his in innocence: masturbation in the dormitory, languishing looks between prefects and blond new boys, intimate teas and impassioned lollings on grassy hillsides. The armies and the political parties of the 1930s were the thrillingly robust continuation of school rugger and cricket teams, being likewise composed of stubborn athletes and prize competitors. Bands apart, they were all-male and Hellenic—and the neo-Hellenism of the 1930s was all Teutonic. Auden's political and intellectual spectrum in the 1930s is mainly German, and it's harder than the gullible might think to pick his emotional allegiance between the two sets of muscle-packed shorts, Communist or Nazi. Intellectually, of course, he didn't fool with Fascism for a moment; but to his sexual proclivities the blond Northern hero made an appeal which only a poetic embodiment could resolve—it took pearl to silence the irritation set up by those vicious specks of grit.

> Save him from hostile capture
> From sudden tiger's leap at corner;
> Protect his house,
> His anxious house where days are counted
> From thunderbolt protect,
> From gradual ruin spreading like a stain;
> Converting number from vague to certain,
> Bring joy, bring day of his returning.
> Lucky with day approaching, with leaning dawn.

Towards the glamour of the opposing teams—the chaps—Auden's feelings were ambiguous. So were his feelings towards his own homosexuality. Like many homosexuals he seems to have experienced homosexual congress as the only clean kind, and thus had no reason to hesitate in identifying homosexuality with a new political order. Nevertheless guilt remained. In the 1930s it was a cultural residue (later on, when Auden returned to Christianity, it became a religious precept), but was no less powerful for that. Just as, in another poem, the "ruined boys" have been damaged by something more physical than the inculcation of upper-class values which left-wing readers delightedly assumed, so in this last stanza of "The Wanderer" the spreading ruin is something closer to home than the collapse of Europe. There was fear in Auden's pride about his condition. Fear of the police and fear that the much-trumpeted corruption might be a fact. He thought that heterosexual people could enjoy security but that only homosexuals could enjoy danger; that the intensity of the homosexual's beleaguered experience was the harbinger of a new unity; but that, nevertheless, the homosexual was unlucky. In the last line of this most beautiful of young poems, he doesn't really expect luck to be granted or his kind of day to dawn. It's yet another mark of Auden's superiority that whereas his contemporaries could be didactic about what they had merely thought or read, Auden could be tentative about what he felt in his bones. (It was marvellous, and continues to be marvellous, that the *Scrutiny* critics never detected in Auden his unwearying preoccupation with the morality of his art, nor realized that a talent of such magnitude — the magnitude of genius — matures in a way that criticism can hope to understand but not prescribe.)

It will be useful, when the time comes, to hear a homosexual critic's conjectures about the precise nature of Auden's sexual tastes. It seems to me, who am no expert, that Auden's analysis of Housman's guilt feelings (he said Housman was so convinced a Hellenist that he felt ashamed of being passive rather than active) was an indirect admission that Auden was passive himself. Even in the earliest poems he seems not to be taking the lead. All too often he is the forsaken one, the one who loves too much and is always asking his beloved to share an impossibly elevated conception of their union.

> You whom I gladly walk with, touch,
> Or wait for as one certain of good,
> We know it, we know that love
> Needs more than the admiring excitement of union,
> More than the abrupt self-confident farewell,
> The heel on the finishing blade of grass,

> The self-confidence of the falling root,
> Needs death, death of the grain, our death,
> Death of the old gang . . .

But as Auden half-guessed that it might turn out, the old gang would-n't go away: oppression would always be a reality and homosexual lovers would continue to live in fear and fragments. Out of this insecurity as a soldier in a lost army, it seems to me, emerged Auden's unsettling obses-sion with the leader principle—a version of *führerprinzip* which was in fact no more Hitlerite than Stalinist, but was simply Auden's dream of a puissant redeemer.

> Absence of fear in Gerhart Meyer
> From the sea, the truly strong man.

The Truly Strong Man, the Airman, the Tall Unwounded Leader of Doomed Companions—he occurs and recurs throughout Auden's younger work, forever changing form but always retaining the magic power to convert fear into peace. A tall white god landing from an open boat, a laconic war-bitten captain, the Truly Strong Man is a passive homosexual's dream of equitable domination. He is the authentic figure of good in early Auden just as his half-brother, the Dictator, is the authen-tic figure of evil, the man swifter than Syrian horses who can throw the bully of Corinth and is seeking brilliant Athens and us.

In the Strong Man's embrace Auden achieves release from terror and a respite from his own admitted ugliness—his post-coital death at the hands of his Hellenic aggressor would appear to have a close visual affin-ity with the Dying Warrior.

> Acquire that flick of wrist and after strain
> Relax in your darling's arms like a stone.

In this Owenesque half-rhymed couplet the schoolboy vocabulary of mutual masturbation snuggles up with dainty boldness to the image of the narrator coiled in the tall leader's massive embrace. We could be excused for assuming that Auden spent half of his most productive decade fainting dead away: he returns to the image of orgasm over and over, as the lolling bridegroom droops like a dying flower or lapses into a classic fatigue.

Auden's butch hero flying fast aeroplanes or roping his weaker companions up F6 bears an ineluctable resemblance to the Aryan demigod breaking records in his BF 109 or pounding skyward at 45 degrees into the white hell of Pitz Palu. As with heterosexuals, so with homosexuals, sexual fantasizing is the mind's dreariest function. The scholars, when they finally do get started on this tack, would do well to refrain from waxing ecstatic when nosing truffles of ambiguity. Auden started supplying a sardonic critique of his physical ideal almost from the moment of its creation. All generalized desire leads to banality. Auden staved off bathos by transcendence on the one hand and by foolery on the other. It needs always to be understood that the British schoolboys of his generation saw too much homosexuality ever to think of its mere mechanism as a mystery. Auden planted an abundance of gags for the lads.

> Out of the reeds like a fowl jumped the undressed German,
> And Stephen signalled from the sand dunes like a wooden madman. . . .

Those were the days. Penned during his early time as a schoolmaster, frolicsome lovesick odes to the rugger team are similarly self-aware. Their presence in *Poems* edifyingly reminds us that Auden's exaltation of the third sex (soon to have its internationalism recognized by being sneeringly branded "the homintern") as a political paradigm was innocent only politically — sexually it was self-analytical to an extent that made Auden's achievement of chaste lyricism a double triumph.

In *Look, Stranger!*, the wonder book of Auden's poetry, the lyricism was carried to its height. On the one hand, there was the perfection of his abstract sweetness — *dolcezza* so neutralized that it could be sung as plighting music for lovers everywhere.

> Moreover, eyes in which I learn
> That I am glad to look, return
>   My glance every day;
> And when the birth and rising sun
> Waken me, I still speak with one
>   Who has not gone away.

On the other hand, there was a deepening admission of vulnerability, of a fateful strangeness which no amount of bravado could usher into its inheritance.

> Whispering neighbours, left and right,
> Pluck us from the real delight;
> And the active hands must freeze
> Lonely on the separate knees.

All lust, Auden now complains, is at once informed on and suppressed: the new political forces will offer outlaws no place. Throughout *Look, Stranger!* the heterosexuals are characteristically pictured as the tireless sentries guarding those lonely roads on which lovers walk to make a tryst, unpitying soldiers

> Whose sleepless presences endear
> Our peace to us with a perpetual threat.

It's the threat which makes the homosexual's peace more poignant than the heterosexual's freedom, as Auden had already stated in *Poems*, XXVI:

> Noises at dawn will bring
> Freedom for some, but not this peace
> No bird can contradict: passing, but is sufficient now
> For something fulfilled this hour,
>   loved or endured.

In *Look, Stranger!*, with the 1930s barely half over and the big battles yet to be fought, Auden already knew that for him and his kind the new age, if it ever came, would not come easily. Love would go on being a thing of glances meeting in crowded pubs, risky whispers in lavatories, one night stands in cheap rooms, partings on railway stations, persecution and exile. Rhetorically he still proclaims his confidence; realistically he hints at a maturing doubt; poetically he creates from this dialectic some of the great love poetry of the century. To Poem IX in *Look, Stranger!* (called "Through the Looking Glass" in *Collected Shorter Poems 1930–1944*) only Lorca's *Llanto por Ignacio Sánchez Mejías* is even an approximate rival. For his compactness, for his mastery of lyricism as a driving force rather than a decoration, for his unstrained majesty of movement, Auden in this phase of his writing is without an equal. The poetry happens like an event in nature, beautiful because it can't help it.

> Your would-be lover who has never come
> In the great bed at midnight to your arms. . . .

Imperfect, ruggedly rounded out, and in places appearing almost uncorrected, the poem creates its effects with a monstrously skilled carelessness that is in every sense superb, as if the mere details had been left to a team of assistants and the haughty master's attention reserved for passages like

> Such dreams are amorous, they are indeed:
> But no one but myself is loved in these,
> And time flies on above the dreamer's head
> Flies on, flies on, and with your beauty flies.

How can we tell the intoxicator from the intoxicated? Lines like these are the loose scrawl of genius in its cups, the helpless, incandescent finale of Auden's meteorite making contact with the atmosphere of realism. Gorgeous fires of defeat.

But Auden's prescient withdrawal into loneliness was pained as well as plangent, as we see in the hard-edged bitterness of *Look, Stranger!*, XXVIII:

> Dear, though the night is gone
> The dream still haunts today
> That brought us to a room,
> Cavernous, lofty as
> A railway terminus

In this enormous room crowded with beds, Auden's lover turns towards someone else. The clarity of the setting belongs less to Lorca's branch of surrealism than to something colder and more northern. The presiding spirits at Lorca's lament are those of Buñuel and Dalí. With Auden, it's Magritte.

Poem XXX in *Look, Stranger!* starts with the famous line "August for the people and their favorite islands" and is dedicated to Christopher Isherwood. In *Collected Shorter Poems 1930–1944* it is called "Birthday Poem," and in *Collected Shorter Poems 1927–1957* it does not appear at all—one of that volume's several shattering omissions. The line about the spy's career gains luminosity once we have accustomed ourselves to the close identification in Auden's mind of homosexuality with clandestine activity and all its apparatus of codes and invisible inks. There are lines between the lines of Auden's younger poems which will come to life in the mild heat of knowledge. Beginning far back in the schoolboy mythology of Mortmere, such symbolic cloak-and-dagger men as the Adversary and the Watcher in Spanish defeat all scholarly attempts to place them as political exemplars, but are easily apprehended as madly camp star turns at a drag ball. They are there to brighten the lives of secret men. As Auden wrote years later in "The Fall of Rome," all the literati keep an imaginary friend. Auden's artistic indulgence in the 1930s vocabulary of espionage—a vocabulary which was a matter of life and death to those from whom he borrowed it—seemed then, and can still seem now, trivial beyond forgiveness. It's worth remembering, though, that Auden was in a war too, and needed to hide himself just as deep. And his war had been going on since time out of mind.

To use his own phrase, the wicked card was dealt: in the face of totalitarianism, homosexuality was no longer a valid image for collective action. The world was not a school and adolescence was at long last over. Auden's exile began in earnest. In *New Year Letter* we learned that those hunted out of ordinary life are "wild quarry," but are granted the privilege of themselves becoming hunters—hunters of the past. *New Year Letter* is one of the synthetic works by which Auden accepted the responsibility of comprehending European culture—an acceptance which was to lead him in the course of time to his position as the most variously erudite poet since Goethe. The Strong Man had faded out and the Dictator was in control, leaving

> Culture on all fours to greet
> A butch and criminal elite

which is as clear, and personal, an image of violation as you could wish. The innocence of young love retained its purity through knowledge,

of itself and of the multiple past which justified the pluralist political
dream—now solely an ideal, and more radiant for that—of the Just City.

> White childhood moving like a sigh
> Through the green woods unharmed in thy
> Sophisticated innocence
> To call thy true love to the dance.

In *Another Time*, his collection of lyrics from that period, Auden ush-
ered in the new decade with a reiteration of his solitude:

> Ten thousand soldiers marched to and fro:
> Looking for you and me, my dear, looking for you and me.

The sentries were still walking the ridges. During the long decade of warfare and recovery they gradually and mysteriously grew fewer and less
imbued with missionary zeal. In the decade between *Another Time* and
Nones Auden seems to have faced the fact that art, politically speaking,
has no future, only a past. Whatever Auden the person was up to, Auden
the poet had begun to accept and love the world. He no longer thought
of homosexuality as newness—just a permanent apartness. From *Nones*
the diligent stylistic analyst will deduce that the poet's studies of *The
Oxford English Dictionary* had got as far as the letter C. The lover of his
poetry will find that the period of dialectical tension has come to an end.
Often taken as a gratuitous glibness, Auden's later insistence that all his
poetry put together had not saved a single Jew was already a plain fact.
Poetry, he had said even before the 1930s were over, makes nothing happen. In *Nones* there was sardonic realism about love but any idealism
about it had been banished. What idealism there was was all about art,
and the eternal order which art formed outside history.

As a mind, Auden curved away from the purely Germanic culture
and developed a growing kinship with the all-embracing Latin one, of
which he is indeed the true modern representative in English after Eliot.
Despite his domicile in Austria and his involvement with German opera,
his final affinity appears to have been with the thought of Valéry—whose
shelf of Gallimard paperbacks is the closest contemporary parallel to
Auden's preoccupations with the aphorism and the ideal order of creativity.

In Christianity Auden found forgiveness for sin. But to redeem the luxuriance of his early cleverness he had to work out his own cure, and as with Dante the cure was *technical*. Holding his art to be a sacrament, Dante acted out his penitence in the form of technical behaviour. For the early sin of rhyming Christ's name with a dirty word he makes recompense in *The Divine Comedy* by never rhyming it with anything except itself—the only word to be so treated. The triadic symmetries of *The Divine Comedy* are a set of disciplines so strict that lyricism has no freedom to indulge itself: when it happens, it happens as a natural consequence of stating the truth. For the educated man, there is a moment of his early acquaintanceship with Dante when he realizes that all he has slowly taught himself to enjoy in poetry is everything that Dante has grown out of. A comparable moment of fear is to be had with Auden, when we understand that his slow change through the 1940s entails a renunciation of the art-thrill, and that the Audenesque dazzle is forever gone. For a poet to lose such a talent would have been a misfortune. For a poet to give it up was an act of disciplined renunciation rarely heard of in English.

A brief recapitulation of Auden's innovations in technical bravura is worth making at this point. Unlike Brecht, who wrote both *Die Moritat von Mackie Messer* and *Die Seeräuber-Jenny* in the year of Auden's first privately printed booklet, Auden never met his Kurt Weill. He met Britten, but the results were meagre. It is no denigration of Isherwood to say that if, of his two admired artistic types, Auden had teamed up with the Composer instead of the Novelist, modern English musical history would have been transformed. As it was, Auden's talent as a lyricist was never developed: the songs for Hedli Anderson had the melody-defeating line-turnovers of ordinary poems, and his activities as a librettist—whether writing originals for Stravinsky or translating *The Magic Flute*—seem to me frustrating in the recognizable modern English manner. Auden had command of a linear simplicity that would have suited the lyric to perfection. As it was, however, he stuck mainly to poetry: and anyway it's probable that the pressure of his homosexual indirectness would have distorted his linear simplicity as thoroughly as, and less fruitfully than, it dislocated his pictorial integrity. Alone with pencil and paper, Auden was free to explore his technical resources. They were without limit, Mozartian. Auden mastered all the traditional lyric forms as a matter of course, bringing to some of them—those which had been imported from rhyme-rich languages and for good reasons had never flourished—the only air of consummate ease they would ever possess. At the same time he did a far more thorough job than even *vers libre* had done of breaking down the last vestiges of the artificial grip the lyric still had on the written poem. He produced apprehensible rhythmic unities which were irregular not only from line to line but within the lines themselves. Finally he penetrated within the word, halting its tendency towards slur and contraction, restoring its articulated rhythmic force. This is the technical secret behind his ability to sustain the trimeter and tetrameter over long distances, driving them forward not along a fixed latticework of terminal and internal rhymes but with an incessant modulation across the vowel spectrum and the proliferating concatenated echoes of exploded consonantal groups.

Hazlitt said that Burke's style was as forked and playful as the lightning, crested like the serpent. Everybody sensitive to poetry, I think, has known the feeling that Auden's early work, with its unmatched technical brilliance, is an enchanted playground. The clear proof of his moral stature, however, is the way he left the playground behind when all were agreed that he had only to keep on adding to it and immortality would be his.

Auden's later books are a long—and sometimes long-winded—penitence for the heretical lapse of letting art do his thinking for him. In *Homage to Clio*, *About the House*, *City Without Walls*, and *Epistle to a Godson* he fulfils his aim of suppressing all automatic responses. A blend of metres and syllabics, his austere forms progressively empty themselves of all mesmeric flair. Auden conquers Selfhood by obliterating talent: what is left is the discipline of mechanical accomplishment, supporting the salt conclusions of a lifetime's thinking—cured wisdom. At the same time, Auden claimed the right to erase any of his early works he now thought were lies. A generation's favourites fell before his irascible, Tolstoyan scythe. His friend Louis MacNeice had once written that after a certain time the poet loses the right to get his finished poems back. Auden didn't agree with MacNeice's humility, just as he had never agreed with Mac-Neice's sense of usefulness: MacNeice had tired himself out serving the BBC instead of the Muse.

It is a common opinion among the English literati that Auden's later work is a collapse. I am so far from taking this view that I think an appreciation of Auden's later work is the only sure test for an appreciation of Auden, just as an appreciation of Yeats's earlier work is the only sure test for an appreciation of Yeats. You must know and admire the austerity which Auden achieved before you can take the full force of his early long-ing for that austerity—before you can measure the portent of his early brilliance. There is no question that the earlier work is more enjoyable. The question is about whether you think enjoyability was the full extent of his aim. Auden, it seems to me, is a modern artist who has lived out his destiny as a European master to the full, a man in whom all cultural his-tory is present just as the sufferings of all the past were still alive in his lover's eyes:

> A look contains the history of Man,
> And fifty francs will earn the stranger right
> To warm the heartless city in his arms.

Famed stranger and exalted outcast, Auden served a society larger than the one in which he hid. In his later work we see not so much the ebbing of desire as its transference to the created world, until plains and hills begin explaining the men who live on them. Auden's unrecriminating generosity towards a world which had served him ill was a moral triumph. Those who try to understand it too quickly ought not to be trusted with grown-up books.

.   .   .

I was born in the month after Auden wrote "September 1, 1939" and saw him only three times. The first time, in Cambridge, about five years ago, he gave a poetry reading in Great St. Mary's. The second time, on the Cambridge-to-London train a year later, I was edging along to the buffet car when I noticed him sitting in a first-class compartment. When the train pulled in I waited for him at the barrier and babbled some nonsense about being privileged to travel on the same train. He took it as his due and waved one of his enormous hands. The third time was earlier this year, in the Martini Lounge atop New Zealand House in London, where a reception was thrown for all of us who had taken part in the Poetry International Festival. Auden shuffled through in a suit encrusted with the dirt of years—it was a geological deposit, an archaeological pile-up like the seven cities of Troy. I don't think anybody of my generation knew what to say to him. I know I didn't. But we knew what to think, and on behalf of my contemporaries I have tried to write some of it down here. I can still remember those unlucky hands; one of them holding a cigarette, the other holding a brimming glass, and both trembling. The mind boggled at some of the things they had been up to. But one of them had refurbished the language. A few months later he was beyond passion, having gone to the reward which Dante says that poets who have done their duty might well enjoy—talking shop as they walk beneath the moon.

Commentary, October 1973; later included in
At the Pillars of Hercules, 1979

POSTSCRIPT

Reading this piece again after thirty years, I itch to tone it down. To write it, I re-read the whole of Auden's poetry all at once: so a previous encephalitic fever that I had suffered in instalments recurred as a single rush of enthusiasm to the head, and hence to the style. The word "immediately" is used twice, which is twice too often: intensifying adverbs, and especially that one, are a bad way of generating an air of immediacy. Nor is "it seems to me" often advisable, because the usage does little to make an opinion sound tentative, and too much to make the user sound self-absorbed. The phrase snuck in out of a semi-conscious recognition that my Delphic assertions of Auden's greatness might sound extravagant. But (it seems to me) they weren't, and still aren't. As a field of scholarship, Auden continues to grow, like an industrial estate: people as clever as Edward Mendelson can give their whole lives to him, and with a clear conscience. But there is still room for the critical view that tries to transmit the pristine, delighted response: room and necessity, because as Auden's poetry becomes a posthumous institution it tends towards the daunting, and it should never be allowed to be that. Thick collected editions don't help. Learned commentary and chronological reordering are sometimes valuable, but more often they dampen the fugitive spirit of the original slim volumes, which were sent into the world as single spies, not as a battalion. The comparatively brief critical article has a better chance than the proliferating scholarship of directing the general reader towards the source of the thrill. For some of us, the thrill of Auden never stops, and we find ourselves composing critical pieces as our natural way of being thankful for it. At the moment, and with nobody asking me to do so, I am ordering the notes I have just made on my hundredth reading of "Letter to Lord Byron." (I hardly need to read it; there are whole stretches of it I can recite; but it never hurts to go back to the text and find out if loving memory has played tricks.) The spaces between the notes are filling up with linking commentary. Preserved by negligence through one reprinting after another, there are typesetter's blunders which (it seems to me) need to be distinguished from the liberties Auden deliberately took with his rhyme scheme. And just how inextricably is *The Age of Anxiety* entrapped by its throwback disciplines of alliteration, its Beowulfian barriers of barbed wire? Doesn't his lyrical genius fight its way out anyway, and all the more fascinatingly for being starved and scarred? A critic who is finished with Auden is finished with criticism. He might have attained a dignified indifference, but he has forgotten the essential sobriety of his job, which is to restore poetry to those readers capable of being astonished. The sobriety means nothing without the initial capacity to get drunk, so I have left the piece with all its spasms intact, as a token of how drunk I could once get.

2003

2

ON SEAMUS HEANEY

Door into the Dark by Seamus Heaney

Of all the newer tight-lipped poets Mr. Heaney is the hardest case, and the tight-lipped critics whose praise is not usually easy to get have been sending quite a lot of approbation his way. His technique is hard-edged: a punchy line travels about two inches. The subject matter is loud with the slap of the spade and sour with the stink of turned earth. Close to the vest, close to the bone and close to the soil. We have learnt already not to look to him for the expansive gesture: there are bitter essences to compensate for the lack of that. *Door into the Dark* confirms him in his course, its very title telling you in which direction that course lies. I will show you fear in a tinful of bait. It should be said at the outset that poetry as good as Mr. Heaney's best is hard to come by. But it is all pretty desperate stuff, and in those poems where we don't feel the brooding vision to be justified by the customary dense beauty of his technique we are probably in the right to come down hard and send our criticism as close as we can to the man within. The man within is at least in some degree a chooser. If he chose to be slick, to let his finely worked clinching stanzas fall pat, there would be a new kind of damaging poetry on the way — squat, ugly and unstoppable.

But first let us demonstrate the quality of the poetic intelligence with which we have to deal. This is the first stanza of his two-stanza poem "Dream": it should be quickly apparent that his virtuoso kinetic gift can find interior equivalents in language for almost any movement in the exterior world, so that the mere act of sub-vocalizing the poem brings one out in a sweat.

> With a billhook
> Whose head was hand-forged and heavy
> I was hacking a stalk
> Thick as a telegraph pole.
> My sleeves were rolled
> And the air fanned cool past my arms
> As I swung and buried the blade,
> Then laboured to work it unstuck.

All the correct chunks and squeaks are caught without being said. But where does it get us? It gets us to the second stanza.

> The next stroke
> Found a man's head under the hook.
> Before I woke
> I heard the steel stop
> In the bone of the brow.

He had a dream, you see, and his skill brings you close to believing it— but not quite. This deadfall finish is really a conventional echo of the professional toughies, "realistic" about violence, who have been giving us the jitters for some time. Most of the other symptoms in the syndrome are manifest somewhere or other in the book. Human characteristics tend to be referred back to animals and objects. As with Ted Hughes, it takes a visit to the zoo, the game reserve, or an imaginary dive below the sod before the idea of *personality* gets any showing at all. The people themselves are mostly clichés disguised in heroic trappings. A stable vacated by a horse ("Gone") offers more character than the smithy still occupied by the smith ("The Forge"). This latter poem is surely fated to be an anthology piece for the generations to come.

> All I know is a door into the dark.
> Outside, old axles and iron hoops rusting;
> Inside, the hammered anvil's short-pitched ring,
> The unpredictable fantail of sparks
> Or hiss when a new shoe toughens in water.
> The anvil must be somewhere in the centre,
> Horned as a unicorn, at one end square,

Sometimes, leather-aproned, hairs in his nose,
He leans out on the jamb, recalls a clatter
Of hoofs where traffic is flashing in rows;
Then grunts and goes in, with a slam and flick
To beat real iron out, to work the bellows.

The numbered questions in the back of the school anthology are obvious. What is the attitude of the smith to modern civilization? Is it the same as the poet's attitude? And (for advanced students) would you consider the Leavisite views on the organic relationship of work to life relevant? But it should also be obvious that the interest of the poem drops considerably when the human being replaces the object at stage centre. Those hairs in his nose don't do much to establish him, except as a character actor sent down at an hour's notice from Central Casting. If he were more real, his attitudes towards mechanized culture might not fall so pat. Get through that doorway in the dark and you might find him beating out hubcaps or balancing the wire wheels on a DB6—both jobs which can be done with as much love as bending your millionth horseshoe. There is no conflict here: there is just a received opinion expressed in hints and cleverly overblown in unexpected places—that altar, and the unicorn's horn, which ought to be a rhino's only that's too easy. On the page the refined poem has its attractive spareness: it's the implication, the area of sugges-tion, that worries the reader through the ordinariness of its assumptions about culture. Self-employed artisans are usually tough enough to see reality straight: given the chance, the leather-aproned subject might well remind Mr. Heaney that there ain't no pity in the city.

Things live; animals almost live; humans live scarcely at all. The inverse progression holds disturbingly true in well-known efforts like the poem about the frozen pump, "Rite of Spring."

That sent the pump up in flame.
It cooled, we lifted her latch,
Her entrance was wet, and she came.

It's a roundabout way for passion to get into print. The obverse poems to this are "Mother," in which the lady ends up wanting to be like the pump, and "The Wife's Tale," a brilliantly tactile poem in which you touch everything—cloth, stubble, grass, bread, seed and china cups—except flesh.

Mr. Heaney's "A Lough Neagh Sequence" forms an important section of the book and could well be pointed to if one were asked to isolate a thematic area absolutely his.

> They're busy in a high boat
> That stalks towards Antrim, the power cut.
> The line's a filament of smut
>
> Drawn hand over fist
> Where every three yards a hook's missed
> Or taken (and the smut thickens, wrist-
>
> Thick, a flail
> Lashed into the barrel
> With one swing). Each eel
>
> Comes aboard to this welcome:
> The hook left in gill or gum,
> It's slapped into the barrel numb
>
> But knits itself, four-ply,
> With the furling, slippy
> Haul, a knot of back and pewter belly
>
> That stays continuously one
> For each catch they fling in
> Is sucked home like lubrication.

Evocation could go no further: the eels ("hatched fears") are practically in your lap. Similarly in poems like "Bann Clay" and "Bogland" his grating line, shudderingly switched back and forth like teeth ground in a nightmare, finds endless technical equivalents for the subject described: he really is astonishingly capable. And in "Bogland" there is an indication that he can do something even more difficult—state the open statement, make the gesture that enlivens life.

They've taken the skeleton
Of the Great Irish Elk
Out of the peat, set it up
An astounding crate full of air.

The spirits lift to the flash of wit. There ought to be more of it. Nobody in his right mind would deny that Mr. Heaney's is one of the outstanding talents on the scene, or want that talent to settle in its ways too early.

Times Literary Supplement, 1969

POSTSCRIPT (I)

One of my earliest notorieties was obtained by mentioning Seamus Heaney in the same breath as Yeats. I was right not to regret it, because sooner rather than later everyone was doing it. More commendably, this piece paid Heaney the compliment of careful writing on the reviewer's part. By using "symptom" and "syndrome" in the same sentence to show that they did not mean the same thing (strictly, a syndrome is a group of symptoms) I pioneered a technique which I have been using ever since in the attempt to do my share of saving useful distinctions threatened with decay through misuse. As a TV critic, writing every week, I would frequently form a sentence around such paired words as "disinterested" and "uninterested," or "mitigate" and "militate," in order to prove that the precision conferred by using them correctly was worth preserving. If the campaign had succeeded I could be more modest about it. It failed completely. As Kingsley Amis has pointed out, there is an iron law operating which dictates that anyone working in the media who makes such errors somehow never gets to read articles deploring them.

The Metropolitan Critic, 1994

POSTSCRIPT (II)

To hitch a ride on the coat-tails of a comet is a bad ambition, but can be gratifying if it happens accidentally. I was lucky enough to be the first critic into print with the nerve, or the naivety, to suggest that Heaney might have a Yeatsian gift. For some time afterwards the comparison was cited by my detractors as clear evidence of hysteria. Later on it was called a boldly premature tip that turned out to be right, and still later everyone forgot that I had ever said it. But it was fun while it lasted. With another flight of fancy I was less lucky. In my mock epic poem *Peregrine Prykke's Pilgrimage* I fielded a Guinness-voiced character called Seamus Feamus. The nickname caught on, but I never got the credit for it. In profiles about Heaney, its coinage (but with the second name spelt "famous," which loses half the point, one would have thought) is usually ascribed to his old literary chums in Ireland. This might very well have been so: it was an idea begging to be had, so anything less than multiple authorship would have been surprising. Fortunately it is not possible to copyright a coinage, or else professional jealousy would spawn a million lawsuits. If you invent a word or a phrase, you should be ready to see other people lift it without acknowledgement; why else did you invent it, except to get it into the language? In the best critics of any medium there is always a poetic urge, and in the critic of poetry it can lead to a professional defor- mation. Almost always he is, or has been, a poet himself, and when faced with a brilliant new arrival he needs to guard himself against his own envy. The best way is to admit it. From his first book, it was obvious that Heaney commanded, as a natural dispensation, a vocal register well fitted for grandeur—rather more grandeur, in fact, than the emergent Yeats, who spent a long time trilling lightly near the top of the stave before his voice finally broke. The comparison was elementary. Yet one poet of my acquaintance—famous himself later on, although not quite *Seamus* famous—spent years telling me that it was the silliest thing he had ever heard.

Reliable Essays, 2001

3

ROBERT LOWELL'S
MARBLE CHIPS

Of the three new books by Robert Lowell—all of them consisting, like their antecedent *Notebook*, of unrhymed sonnets—only *The Dolphin* contains entirely fresh material. It is dedicated to Lowell's new consort Caroline, and deals with the life they are now leading together. *For Lizzie and Harriet* deals exclusively with the life Lowell has left behind: it isolates and reworks those poems concerning his ex-wife and daughter which were earlier scattered through *Notebook*. The central and bulkiest volume of the current three, *History*, is an extensive reworking and thoroughgoing reordering of all the remaining poems in *Notebook*, with eighty extra ones mixed in.

When we consider that *Notebook* itself had two earlier versions before being published in Britain, it is clear that there is a great deal going on. If mere bustle were creativity, then later Lowell would be the most creative thing in modern poetry. Daunted, the critic is tempted to hand the whole problem directly to the scholar and get the work of collating done before any judgements are hazarded. Unfortunately judgement will not wait—not least because these recent works offer an invitation to scholarship to start up a whole new branch of its industry, an invitation which will be all too eagerly accepted if criticism neglects to mark out the proper, and reasonably discreet, size of the job. Lowell is a giant, but his perimeter is still visible: there is no need to think that he fills the sky.

In so far as it had one, *Notebook*'s structure was rhapsodic—an adjective which, in its technical sense, we associate with the Homeric epic. As the poet stumbled in circles of crisis and collapse, digressions could occur in any direction, sub-sequences of the proliferating sonnets form around any theme. These sequences constituted rhapsodies, and it was easy to sense that the rhapsodies were intent on forming themselves into an epic. At that stage, the Lowell epic resembled John Berryman's *Dream Songs*: its digressions had shape, but there was no clear line of progress initiating them—no simple story for which they could serve as complications. The story was mixed in with them. All of human history was there, and Lowell's personal history was there too. Both kinds of history jumped about all over the place.

The new books have simplified everything, while simultaneously making a claim to universality that takes the reader's breath away. "My old title, *Notebook*, was more accurate than I wished, i.e., my composition was jumbled," writes the poet in a foreword. "I hope this jumble or jungle is cleared—that I have cut the waste marble from the figure." Cutting away the marble until the figure is revealed is an idea that reminds us—and is probably meant to remind us—of Michelangelo. As we realize that not even these new books need bring the matter to an end, the idea that the figure need never fully emerge from the marble also reminds us of Michelangelo. Lowell seems intent on having us believe that he is embarked on a creative task which absolves his talent from wasting too much time polishing its own products. He does a lot to make this intention respectable, and we soon see, when reading *History*, that although thousands of details have been altered since *Notebook*, the changes that really matter are in the grand structure. It is at this point that we temporarily cease thinking of marble and start thinking about, say, iron filings. *Notebook* was a random scattering of them. In *History* a magnet has been moved below, and suddenly everything has been shaken into a startling linear shape.

As rearranged and augmented in *History*, the sonnets begin at the dawn of creation and run chronologically all the way to recent events in the life of the poet. We have often thought, with Lowell, that history was being incorporated into the self. Here is the thing proved, and the pretension would be insupportable if it were not carried out with such resource. The information which Lowell commands about all cultures in all ages found a ragged outlet in *Notebook*. Deployed along a simple line of time, it gains in impressiveness—gains just enough to offset the realization that it is Lowell's propensity for reading his own problems into anything at all which makes him so ranging a time traveller. *History* is the story of the world made intelligible in terms of one man's psychology. It is a neurotic work by definition. Nobody reasonable would ever think of starting it, and the moment Lowell begins to be reasonable is the moment he will stop. There is no good cause to assume, however, that Lowell any longer thinks it possible to be reasonable about history. Stephen Dedalus said history was a nightmare from which he was trying to awake. Raising the stakes, Lowell seems to believe that history is something you cannot appreciate without losing your sanity. This belief releases him into realms of artistic effect where reason would find it hard to go. That the same belief might bring inhibition, as well as release, is a separate issue.

Broadly, *History*'s progression is first of all from Genesis through the Holy Land to the Mediterranean, ancient Greece and Rome, with diversions to Egypt at the appropriate moments. Medieval Europe then gives way to the Renaissance and the Enlightenment, tipping over into the French Revolution. Through the complexities of the nineteenth century, strict chronological sequence is manfully adhered to, whether in painting, letters, music or ante- and post-bellum American politics. French symbolism sets the scene for the twentieth-century arts, while the First World War sets the tone for the modern politics of crisis and annihilation. The Russian Revolution throws forward its divisive shadow, which later on will split the New York intelligentsia. By this time Lowell's family history is active in all departments, and soon the poet himself arrives on stage. Everything that has happened since the dawn of humanity has tended to sound like something happening to Lowell. From here on this personal tone becomes intense, and those named—especially if they are artists—are mainly people the poet knows. By now, unquestionably, he is at the centre of events. But the book has already convinced us that all events, even the vast proportion of them that happened before he arrived in the world, are at the centre of him.

History is a long haul through places, things and, preeminently, names. Helen, Achilles, Cassandra, Orestes, Clytemnestra, Alexander, Hannibal, Horace, Juvenal, Dante, Villon, Anne Boleyn, Cranach, Charles V, Marlowe, Mary Stuart, Rembrandt, Milton, Pepys, Bishop Berkeley, Robespierre, Saint-Just, Napoleon, Beethoven, Goethe, Leopardi, Schubert, Heine, Thoreau, Henry Adams, George Eliot, Hugo, Baudelaire, Rimbaud, Mallarmé, Lady Cynthia Asquith, Rilke, George

Grosz, Hardy, Al Capone, Ford Madox Ford, Allen Tate, Randall Jarrell, John Crowe Ransom, F. O. Mattheissen, Roethke, Delmore Schwartz, T. S. Eliot, Wyndham Lewis, MacNeice, William Carlos Williams, Robert Frost, Stalin, Harpo Marx, Che Guevara, Norman Mailer, Dwight Macdonald, Adrienne Rich, Mary McCarthy, Eugene McCarthy, Elizabeth Schwarzkopf, Martin Luther King, Robert Kennedy, De Gaulle, Lévi-Strauss, R. P. Blackmur, Stanley Kunitz, Elizabeth Bishop, I. A. Richards, John Berryman, Robert Lowell and many more: a cast of thousands. The range they cover, and the pertinent information Lowell is able to adduce when treating each one — these things are little short of astonishing. But they were already startling in *Notebook*. What makes these qualities doubly impressive now is the new effect of faces succeeding faces in due order. Leaving, of course, a thousand gaps — gaps which the poet seems understandably keen to set about filling.

Lizzle and Harriet's retributive presence in *Notebook* has been eliminated from *History* and given a book of its own. *The Dolphin* likewise enshrines a portion of Lowell's experience which is plainly not going to be allowed to overbalance the future of *History*. It is possible to suggest, given the dispersal of foci represented by these three volumes, that Lowell's "confessional" poetry is no longer his main thing. The *History* book now embodies his chief effort, and in relation to this effort the ordinary people inhabiting his life don't make the weight. *History* is full of public names, rather than private ones: public names united not so much by prestige as in their undoubted puissance in shaping, exemplifying or glorifying historic moments. In *History* Lowell, alone, joins the great.

And the number of the great grows all the time. Instructive, in this respect, to take a close look at the *History* poem called "Cleopatra Topless," one of a short sequence of poems concerning her. Where have we seen it before? Was it in *Notebook*? But in *Notebook* it is untraceable in the list of contents. Where was it, then? The answer is that the poem is in *Notebook* but is called simply "Topless" and has nothing to do with Cleopatra. In the *Notebook* poem she's just a girl in a nightclub:

> She is the girl
> as Renoir, Titian and all full times have left her

To convert her into Cleopatra, it is only necessary to get rid of the inappropriate Renoir and Titian, filling the space with a line or so about what men desire. Throughout *History* the reader is continually faced with material which has apparently been dragged in to fill a specific chronological spot. Nor does this material necessarily have its starting point in *Notebook*: the fact that it appears in that volume, if it does appear, doesn't preclude its having begun its life in an earlier, and often far earlier, Lowell collection. For example, a version of Valéry's "Hélène" is in *Imitations*, with the inspiration for it credited to Valéry. By the time it arrives in *History*, it is credited to no one but Lowell. It is true that the drive of the verse has been weakened with over-explanatory adjectives:

> My solitary hands recall the kings
> (*Imitations*)
> My loving hands recall the absent kings
> (*History*)
> Mes solitaires mains appellent les monarques
> (Valéry)

But this is incidental. As we can see abundantly in other places, Lowell's minor adjustments are just as likely to impart point as detract from it. Fundamentally important, however, is the way the imitation has been saddled with extraneous properties (Agamemnon, Ulysses) in order to bolster it for the significance it is being asked to provide in its new slot. Though making regular appearances in the early sections of *History*, Agamemnon and Ulysses are nowhere mentioned in Valéry's poem. But then, the poem is no longer Valéry's: in *History* the source is uncredited.

Trusting to the itch of memory and ransacking the library shelves in order to scratch it, the reader soon learns that Lowell has been cannibalizing his earlier works of translation and imitation—cutting them up into fourteen-line lengths and introducing them with small ceremony first of all into *Notebook* and later, on the grand scale, into *History*. Usually the provenance of the newly installed sonnet is left unmentioned. There are exceptions to this: the "Le Cygne" of *Notebook*, which the gullible might have attributed to Lowell, has a better chance of being traceable to its origins now that it is called "Mallarmé I. Swan." It is in fact the second of the "Plusieurs Sonnets" in *Poésies* and is called—after its first line—"Le vierge, le vivace et le bel aujourd'hui." In *Notebook* Lowell had "blind" for *vivace*, an inscrutable boldness which in *History* has been softened to "alive." Other improvements in the new version are less welcome: "the horror of the ice that ties his wings" is a reversal of Mallarmé's sense, which in the *Notebook* version had been got right. Mallarmé is saying that the swan *accepts* the ice. Here Lowell seems to have been improving his first version without reference to the original. On the other hand, he has now substituted "wings" for "feet" and thereby humbly returned much closer to *plumage*. The key phrase, *l'exil inutile*, which is ringingly present in the *Notebook* version, is now strangely absent. Anyone who attempts to trace poems back through *Notebook* to their sources in foreign literatures is fated to be involved in these niggling questions at all times. But at least, with such a clear signpost of a title, there is a hint that this particular poem *has* such a history. In many cases even this tenuous condition does not obtain.

When a bright young American scholar produces a properly indexed Variorum Lowell—preferably with a full concordance—it will be easier to speak with confidence about what appears in *History* that is not in *Notebook*. A good few poems appear in both with different titles, and it is difficult for even the keenest student to hold the entire mass of material clearly in his mind. But if *History*'s "Baudelaire 1. The Abyss" is not in *Notebook*, it was in *Imitations*, where it was billed as a version of "Le Gouffre." There, it reduced Baudelaire's fourteen lines to thirteen. Now it is back to being a sonnet again, and the *Etres* are now rendered as "being" instead of "form," which one takes to be a net gain. One is less sure that the poem's provenance would be so recognizable if it were not for the memory of the *Imitations* version. The question keeps on cropping up—are we supposed to know that such material started out in another poet's mind, or are we supposed to accept it as somehow being all Lowell's? Is it perhaps that Lowell is putting himself forward as the representative of all past poets? It should be understood that one is not questioning Lowell's right to employ allusion, or to embody within his own work a unity of culture which he feels to be otherwise lost. The ethics are not the problem; the aesthetics are. Because none of these poems carries the same weight, when presented as ordinary Lowell, as it does when its history is clearly seen to be still surrounding it.

"Baudelaire 2. Recollection" was called "Meditation" in *Imitations* and is thus a revision of a version of "Recueillement." It is interesting to see that *va cueillir des remords* now means "accumulating remorse" rather than the previous and unfathomable "fights off anguish." Minor satisfactions like that can be clung to while the reader totals "Baudelaire 1. The Abyss" and "Baudelaire 2. Recollection" and glumly reconciles himself to the fact that that's his lot on Baudelaire—two revamped imitations.

Rimbaud does better. Five sonnets. But all five turn out to have been in a sequence of eight versions printed in *Imitations*. "Rimbaud 1. Bohemia" was called "On the Road" and is a version of "Ma Bohème"; "Rimbaud 2. A Knowing Girl" was called "A Knowing Girl" and is a version of "La Maline"; "Rimbaud 3. Sleeper in the Valley" was more expansively called "The Sleeper in the Valley" and is a version of "Le Dormeur du Val"; "Rimbaud 4. The Evil" was less expansively called "Evil" and is a version of "Le Mal"; "Rimbaud 5. Napoleon after Sedan" was called "Napoleon after Sedan," is a version of "Rages de Césars," and was the only one of the five to have made an intermediary appearance in *Notebook*, where it was called "Rimbaud and Napoleon III." With this last poem, then, we have three separate texts to help send us cross-eyed, but if we can concentrate long enough we will see a characteristic change. The *Imitations* version is shaped like the original and confines itself to the original's material, plus a few scraps of interpolated elucidatory matter (where Rimbaud just said "Compère" Lowell tactfully adds some explanatory horses) and of course the inevitable intensifying of the verbs. The *Notebook* version is no longer readily identifiable as an imitation: the stanza breaks have been eliminated, the first four lines are a piece of scene setting which have nothing to do with the original, and Robespierre's name has been introduced, answering a question—"quel nom sur ses lèvres muettes/Tressaille?"—which Rimbaud had left unanswered. The *History* version gets the fidgets, throwing out Compère but leaving the horses. By this time, you would need to be pretty thoroughly acquainted with Rimbaud if you were to spot the poem as anything but neat Lowell.

Of the other Rimbaud poems, "La Maline" is now closer to the way Rimbaud wrote it than the *Imitations* version, but Lowell's "Ma Bohème" misses by just as far as it used to, though in a different way:

> September twilight on September twilight.
>   (*Imitations*)
> September twilights and September twilights
>   (*History*)

A minor alteration to a major aberration: the repetition is not in Rimbaud and does nothing for his meaning whichever way Lowell puts it.

Material which had its starting point in *Imitations* can be changed to any extent from slightly to drastically on its way to a fourteen-line living-space in *History*. Lowell's version of "L'Infinito" is squeezed by three lines but is otherwise the poem we have come to recognize as probably the least sympathetic translation of Leopardi ever committed. "Hugo at Théophile Gautier's Grave" is a rearrangement of an *Imitations* version of Hugo's "À Théophile Gautier" which had already cut the original by more than half. "Sappho to a Girl" was in *Notebook* as just "Sappho," and is a mosaic of bits and pieces which can be seen in *Imitations* still mounted in their original settings—i.e., versions of the poem to the bride Anactoria (No. 141 in *The Oxford Book of Greek Verse*) and that tiny, lovely poem to Night (No. 156) which contains the line about the Pleiads. In his *Imitations* version Lowell left the Pleiads out. In the *Notebook* version they were still out. In the *History* version he put them back in. The card player, who is in all three versions, seems not to belong to Sappho, but could conceivably belong to Cézanne.

Imitations, however, is not the only source of workable stone. *Notebook/History* is Lowell's Renaissance and like the Renaissance in Rome it doesn't question its right to use all the monuments of the ancient city as a quarry. *History*'s "Horace: Pardon for a Friend" started life, at twice the length, as a version of Horace's *Odes* II, 7, in *Near the Ocean*. In the same collection first appeared "Juvenal's Prayer," which at that stage constituted the last nineteen lines of a version of Juvenal's 10th Satire. And to return briefly to Cleopatra, "Nunc est bibendum, Cleopatra's Death" is (as the title this time allows) another imitation, or at least a fragment of one—Horace's *Odes* I, 37, which in *Near the Ocean* can be found imitated in full.

And still they come, racing out of the past to find their new home. *History*'s "Caligula 2" is part of a much longer Caligula in *For the Union Dead*. And from as far back as *Lord Weary's Castle*, "In the Cage" is an acknowledged reworking, with the attention now turning from the observed to the observer. But other material from the same early period is less easily spotted. The sonnet "Charles V by Titian," for example, was called "Charles the Fifth and the Peasant" in *Lord Weary's Castle*, where it was subtitled "After Valéry" and appeared to be a version of his "César" in which almost every property, Titian included, was an interpolation. *History*'s "Dante 3. Buonconte" goes back to a poem in *Lord Weary's Cas-*

tle called "The Soldier," which was modelled on the Buonconte da Montefeltro episode in *Purgatorio* V. Here we have a clear case of the way Lowell's wide learning has matured with the years: he nowadays quietly and correctly renders *la croce* as Buonconte's hands folded on his chest, rather than as a crucifix—a subtly rich textual point of the kind which Lowell at his best is brilliantly equipped to bring out. Restored from an unwieldy third person to the direct first person of the original, this poem is easily the best of those devoted to Dante: "Dante 4. Paolo and Francesca" is a copybook example of how Lowell's irrepressible extremism of language is unable to match the flow of lyrical Italian—and unabashed lyricism is a good half of Francesca's self-deluding personality. Lowell takes Francesca's side against the oppressors of her flesh. If it has occurred to him that Dante didn't, he doesn't say so. In the Dante rhapsody as a whole, we are able to see that below the uniform intensity of Lowell's language there is a uniform intensity of psychology—a certain monotony of feeling. Dante's love for Beatrice is presented rather as if the relationship between work and love bore strong resemblances to that same relationship in the life of Robert Lowell. Could Lowell find means, we wonder, to convey the fact that with Dante the consuming, disabling passion was just as likely to be for philosophy as for sex?

For all the examples cited above, elementary sleuthing suffices to trace the origins—either the title gives a clue or else the poem is more or less intact and can't fail to jog the reader's memory. But it's doubtful if the cannibalizing process stops there, and at this stage it's probably safer to assume that Lowell regards none of his earlier work, whether imitative or original, as exempt from requisitioning and a reconstruction ranging from mild to violent. For example, in a *History* poem called "The Spartan Dead at Thermopylae" the lines about Leonidas are lifted straight from the *Imitations* version of Rilke's "Die Tauben." Pretty well untraceable, if these lines weren't original Lowell then, they are now.

Lowell's discovery of a linear historical structure for *History* has opened the way to a poet's dream—the simple line allowing infinite complication. The sudden insatiable demand for material has sent him raiding back over all his past poetry—not necessarily just the translations—in a search for stuff that fits. A great deal does. On the other hand, isn't there something Procrustean about carving up all that past work into fourteen-line chunks? To get back to Michelangelo and the marble, it's as if Michelangelo were to pick up a power saw and slice through everything

from the Madonna of the Stairs to the Rondinini Pietà at a height of fourteen inches.

Whatever Procrustes might have thought, trimming things to fit an
arbitrary frame is not a discipline. And without its rhyme-schemes, the
sonnet is an arbitrary frame. There are many times in *Notebook/History*
when the reader thrills to the impact of an idea achieving a formal measure almost in spite of itself:

> I hear the catbird's coloratura cluck
> singing fuck, fuck above the brushwood racket.
> The feeder deals catfood like cards to the yearling
> salmon in their stockpond by the falls.

The singing power of the mimesis, the clashing couplings of the shunt-
ing assonance, the muscle of the enjambement: if there were a single sonnet wholly assembled with such care then one would not even have to set
oneself to learn it—it would teach itself. But fragments are the most we
get. Lowell's later method might allow some parts of his talent free play
but it allows his technique only child's play. "I want words meat-hooked
from the living steer," he writes in the course of rebuking Valéry for preferring six passable lines to one inspired one. He gets what he wants:
meat-hooked words and inspired lines. But what one misses, and goes on
missing until it aches, is form.

Still, within the limits he has now set for it—the liberating limits, as
he sees them—Lowell's talent is still operating, and still majestic. There
are times when nothing has happened except language yet you must
helplessly concede that the vitality of his language is unique:

> Man turns dimwit quicker than the mayfly
> fast goes the lucid moment of love believed;

And there are times when the language subsides into nothing special, but the
visualizing faculty reveals itself for the hundredth time as a profound gift:

> coming back to Kenyon on the Ohio local—
> the view, middle distance, back and foreground, shifts,
> silos shifting squares like chessmen—

What an idea! But in all the vast expanse of *Notebook/History* there are not many times when both things come together, and none at all when a poem sustains itself in the way to which Lowell once made us accustomed. There is no doubt that Lowell has abandoned his old course deliberately. Nor is there any doubt that he has opened up for himself an acreage of subject matter which could never have been reached in the old way. But we still have to decide if what we are being given is poetry or something else. Of some comfort here is that Lowell appears to be still undecided himself.

Setting aside the decisive alteration of structure which turned the circularity of *Notebook* into the linear stride of *History*, all the minor changes seem to have been made with the fidgeting lack of direction that you might expect from a writer who somehow feels compelled to refurbish the deliberately formless. Most of the attention has been expended on points of language: it's too late by now to go back to fourteen passable lines, but apparently there is still hope of drumming up the odd inspired one. All too frequently, the striving for intensity results in a further, incomprehensible compression of an idea already tightened to the limit. In the *Notebook* version of "In the Forties I":

> Green logs sizzled on the fire-dogs,
> painted scarlet like British Redcoats. . . .

Whereas the *History* version has:

> greenwood sizzling on the andirons,
> two men of iron, two milk-faced British Redcoats.

Without a knowledge of the first version, it would be hard to guess what the second might mean: the idea of the red paint has become familiar to Lowell, and he has got rid of it without pausing to reflect that we will have trouble following the idea unless it is spelled out to some extent. Scores of these changes for the worse could be adduced. Other changes are simply neutral. In *Notebook*'s "Harriet 2," the fly is like a plane gunning potato bugs. Appearing again in the sonnet "Summer, 2" in *For Lizzie and Harriet*, the fly is like a plane dusting apple orchards. The second version is perhaps preferable for its verb being the more easily appreciated, but on the other hand potato bugs have more verve than apple orchards. It's a toss-up.

Another kind of change is incontestably for the better. In *History* Robert Frost's voice is "musical and raw" rather than, as in *Notebook*, "musical, raw and raw." One had always wondered why the repetition was there, and now one finds that Lowell had been wondering the same thing. In *Notebook* Frost was supposed to have inscribed a volume "Robert Lowell from Robert Frost, his friend in the art." In *History* this becomes "For Robert from Robert, his friend in the art." Much chummier. Was Lowell, for modesty's sake, misquoting the first time? Or is he, for immodesty's sake, misquoting now? It is impossible to tell, but grappling with the implications of these minor shifts is one of the involving things about reading all these books together.

The comparison between *Notebook* and *History* could go on for ever, and probably will. Discovering that the *Notebook* poem for Louis MacNeice is reproduced in *History* with one of its lines doubled and another line dropped—a really thunderous printer's error—one wonders distractedly if anybody else knows. Does Lowell know? It's large territory to become familiar with, even for him. Finally one decides that getting familiar with it is as far as appreciation can go. To recognize details is possible; but there is small hope of remembering the whole thing. Like Berryman's *Dream Songs*, Lowell's *Notebook/History/For Lizzie and Harriet* defeats memory. Perhaps *The Dolphin* is heading back to the way things were, but on examination it starts yielding the kind of names— Hölderlin, Manet—which make us think that most of it is fated to end up in the next version of *History*. In *The Dolphin* the only human, unhistoried, unsignificant voice occurs in the quoted parts of Lizzie's letters. If Lowell wrote them, he should write more. But there isn't much point in saying "should." The outstanding American poet is engaged in writing his version of the poem that Pound, Williams and Berryman have each already attempted—The Big One. Lowell thinks he is chipping away the marble to get at the statue. It's more likely that he is trying to build a statue out of marble chips. Who cares about history, if poetry gets thrown away? Perhaps he does. And anyway the poetry was his to throw.

Times Literary Supplement August 10, 1973;
later included in *At the Pillar of Hercules*, 1979

POSTSCRIPT

In a subsequent letter, John Bayley twitted me about the Redcoat andirons. He said that the image in its revised form was not hard to puzzle out. On reflection, I decided Bayley was right, but I still wondered whether the image was improved by being made a puzzle. (Tightened, or screwed? is always a good question to ask about a poet's emendation.) At the time, the main issue raised by Lowell's final barrage of poetry collections was a journalistic one: the legitimacy, or lack of it, of his quoting Elizabeth Hardwick's letters without permission. Only slowly did the discussion shift towards the lasting critical point, which was whether or not Lowell was engaged in the distortion of his own achievement by crushing it under a heap of busywork that it took a tenured scholar to care about. From the point of view of his British publishers (who were in the front line, because Lowell had shifted his base from New York to London), their accommodation to Lowell's latter-day prolificity was a disaster. Sales of the new books were negligible, and the blight eventually affected his back catalogue. The critic's duty was clear: to remind the educated reading public that this absurd attempt to build a pyramid single-handed from within, though it looked like the work of a mad pharaoh, was the aberration of a very talented man. The critic also had the duty to remind his more gullible colleagues that the talent was not attaining an apotheosis, but consuming itself before their eyes. What happened to Lowell in London was not the final development of his confessional poetry. It was the final development of his clinical dementia, a condition for which there had never been any legislating, although there had always been a romantic critical tendency to believe that the poetry would not have been possible without the madness. In that respect, distance lent enchantment to the view. Anyone who caught the merest glimpse of Lowell's solipsistic mania knew that it was more likely to produce boredom than creative freedom. Even at his craziest, Lowell seemed to realize that himself. At the peaks of his delusion, he thought that he was Hitler, not Shakespeare. The saddest thing about the *History* book was its encouragement of the notion that his early volumes might have been precursors to its development, and can thus be safely forgotten along with it. But they'll be back. Poetry of that order always comes back.

2003

4

FOUR ESSAYS ON
PHILIP LARKIN

I. Somewhere becoming rain

Collected Poems by Philip Larkin,
edited by Anthony Thwaite

At first glance, the publication in the United States of Philip Larkin's *Collected Poems* looks like a long shot. While he lived, Larkin never crossed the Atlantic. Unlike some other British poets, he was genuinely indifferent to his American reputation. His bailiwick was England. Larkin was so English that he didn't even care much about Britain, and he rarely mentioned it. Even within England, he travelled little. He spent most of his adult life at the University of Hull, as its chief librarian. A trip to London was an event. When he was there, he resolutely declined to promote his reputation. He guarded it but would permit no hype.

Though Larkin's diffidence was partly a pose, his reticence was authentic. At no point did he announce that he had built a better mousetrap. The world had to prove it by beating a path to his door. The process took time, but was inexorable, and by now, only three years after his death, at the age of sixty-three, it has reached a kind of apotheosis. On the British best-seller lists, Larkin's *Collected Poems* was up there for months at a stretch, along with Stephen Hawking's *A Brief History of Time* and Salman Rushdie's *The Satanic Verses*. In Larkin's case, this extraordinary level of attention was reached without either general relativity's having to be reconciled with quantum mechanics or the Ayatollah Khomeini's being required to pronounce anathema. The evidence suggests that Larkin's poetry, from a standing start, gets to everyone capable of being got to. One's tender concern that it should survive the perilous journey across the sea is therefore perhaps misplaced. A mission like this might have no more need of a fighter escort than pollen on the wind.

The size of the volume is misleading. Its meticulous editor, Anthony Thwaite—himself a poet of high reputation—has included poems that Larkin finished but did not publish, and poems that he did not even finish. Though tactfully carried out, this editorial inclusiveness is not beyond cavil. What was elliptically concentrated has become more fully understandable, but whether Larkin benefits from being more fully understood is a poser. Eugenio Montale, in many ways a comparable figure, was, it might be recalled, properly afraid of what he called "too much light."

During his lifetime, Larkin published only three mature collections of verse, and they were all as thin as blades. *The Less Deceived* (1955), *The Whitsun Weddings* (1964) and *High Windows* (1974) combined to a thickness barely half that of the *Collected Poems*. Larkin also published, in 1966, a new edition of his early, immature collection, *The North Ship*, which had first come out in 1945. He took care, by supplying the reissue with a deprecatory introduction, to keep it clearly separate from the poems that he regarded as being written in his own voice.

The voice was unmistakable. It made misery beautiful. One of Larkin's few even halfway carefree poems is "For Sidney Bechet," from *The Whitsun Weddings*. Yet the impact that Larkin said Bechet made on him was exactly the impact that Larkin made on readers coming to him for the first time:

> On me your voice falls as they say love should,
> Like an enormous yes.

What made the paradox delicious was the scrupulousness of its expression. There could be no doubt that Larkin's outlook on life added up to an enormous no, but pessimism had been given a saving grace. Larkin described an England changing in ways he didn't like. He described himself ageing in ways he didn't like. The Empire had shrunk to a few islands, his personal history to a set of missed opportunities. Yet his desperate position, which ought logically to have been a licence for incoherence, was expressed with such linguistic fastidiousness on the one hand, and such lyrical enchantment on the other, that the question arose of whether he had not at least partly cultivated that view in order to get those results. Larkin once told an interviewer, "Deprivation for me is what daffodils were for Wordsworth."

In the three essential volumes, the balanced triad of Larkin's achievement, all the poems are poised vibrantly in the force-field of tension between his profound personal hopelessness and the assured command of their carrying out. Perfectly designed, tightly integrated, making the feeling of falling apart fit together, they release, from their compressed but always strictly parsable syntax, sudden phrases of ravishing beauty, as the river in Dante's Paradise suggests by giving off sparks that light is what it is made of.

These irresistible fragments are everyone's way into Larkin's work. They are the first satisfaction his poetry offers. There are other and deeper satisfactions, but it was his quotability that gave Larkin the biggest cultural impact on the British reading public since Auden—and over a greater social range. Lines by Larkin are the common property of everyone in Britain who reads seriously at all—a state of affairs which has not obtained since the time of Tennyson. Phrases, whole lines and sometimes whole stanzas can be heard at the dinner table.

There is an evening coming in
Across the fields, one never seen before,
That lights no lamps . . .

Only one ship is seeking us, a black-
Sailed unfamiliar, towing at her back
A huge and birdless silence. In her wake
No waters breed or break . . .

Now, helpless in the hollow of
An unarmorial age, a trough
Of smoke in slow suspended skeins
Above their scrap of history,
Only an attitude remains . . .

And as the tightened brakes took hold, there swelled
A sense of falling, like an arrow-shower
Sent out of sight, somewhere becoming rain . . .

How distant, the departure of young men
Down valleys, or watching
The green shore past the salt-white cordage
Rising and falling . . .

Steep beach, blue water, towels, red bathing caps,
The small hushed waves' repeated fresh collapse
Up the warm yellow sand, and further off
A white steamer stuck in the afternoon . . .

Later, the square is empty: a big sky
Drains down the estuary like the bed
Of a golïd river . . .

At death, you break up: the bits that were you
Start speeding away from each other for ever
With no one to see . . .

Rather than words comes the thought of high windows:
The sun-comprehending glass,
And beyond it, the deep blue air, that shows
Nothing, and is nowhere, and is endless.

Drawn in by the subtle gravity beam of such bewitchment, the reader becomes involved for the rest of his life in Larkin's doomed but unfailingly dignified struggle to reconcile the golden light in the high windows with the endlessness it comes from. Larkin's sense of inadequacy, his fear of death are in every poem. His poems could not be more personal. But, equally, they could not be more universal. Seeing the world as the hungry and thirsty see food and drink, he describes it for the benefit of those who are at home in it, their senses dulled by satiation. The reader asks: How can a man who feels like this bear to live at all?

Life is first boredom, then fear.
Whether or not we use it, it goes,
And leaves what something hidden from us chose,
And age, and then the only end of age.

But the reader gets an answer: There are duties that annul nihilism, satisfactions beyond dissatisfaction, and, above all, the miracle of continuity. Larkin's own question about what life is worth if we have to lose it he answers with the contrary question, about what life would amount to if it didn't go on without us. Awkward at the seaside, ordinary people know better in their bones than the poet among his books:

The white steamer has gone. Like breathed-on glass
The sunlight has turned milky. If the worst
Of flawless weather is our falling short,
It may be that through habit these do best,
Coming to water clumsily undressed
Yearly; teaching their children by a sort
Of clowning; helping the old, too, as they ought.

Just as Larkin's resolutely prosaic organization of a poem is its passport to the poetic, so his insight into himself is his window on the world.
He is the least solipsistic of artists. Unfortunately, this fact has now
become less clear. Too much light has been shed. Of the poems previously unpublished in book form, a few are among his greatest achievements, many more one would not now want to be without, and all are
good to have. But all the poems he didn't publish have been put in
chronological order of composition along with those he did publish,
instead of being given a separate section of their own. There is plenty of
editorial apparatus to tell you how the original slim volumes were made
up, but the strategic economy of their initial design has been lost.

All three of the original volumes start and end with the clean, dramatic decisiveness of a curtain going up and coming down again. The
cast is not loitering in the auditorium beforehand. Nor is it to be found
hanging out in the car park afterwards. *The Less Deceived* starts with
"Lines on a Young Lady's Photograph Album," which laments a lost love
but with no confessions of the poet's personal inadequacy. It ends with "At
Grass," which is not about him but about horses: a bugle call at sunset.

Only the groom, and the groom's boy,
With bridles in the evening come.

Similarly, *The Whitsun Weddings* starts and ends without a mention
of the author. The first poem, "Here," is an induction into "the surprise
of a large town" that sounds as if it might be Hull. No one who sounds as
if he might be Larkin puts in an appearance. Instead, other people do,
whose "removed lives/ Loneliness clarifies." The last poem in the book,
"An Arundel Tomb," is an elegy written in a church crypt which is as

sonorous as Gray's written in a churchyard, and no more petulant: that things pass is a fact made majestic, if not welcome.

As for *High Windows*, the last collection published while he was alive, it may contain, in "The Building," his single most terror-stricken— and, indeed, terrifying—personal outcry against the intractable fact of death, but it begins and ends with the author well in the background. "To the Sea," the opening poem, the one in which the white steamer so trans-fixingly gets stuck in the afternoon, is his most thoroughgoing celebration of the element that he said he would incorporate into his religion if he only had one: water. "The Explosion" closes the book with a heroic vision of dead coal miners which could be called a hymn to immortality if it did not come from a pen that devoted so much effort to pointing out that mortality really does mean what it says.

These two poems, "To the Sea" and "The Explosion," which in *High Windows* are separated by the whole length of a short but weighty book, can be taken together as a case in point, because, as the chronological arrangement of the *Collected Poems* now reveals, they were written together, or almost. The first is dated October 1969, and the second is dated January 5, 1970. Between them in *High Windows* come poems dated anything from five years earlier to three years later. This is only one instance, unusually striking but typical rather than exceptional, of how Larkin moved poems around through compositional time so that they would make in emotional space the kind of sense he wanted, and not another kind. Though there were poems he left out of *The Less Deceived*, and put into *The Whitsun Weddings*, it would be overbold to assume that any poem, no matter how fully achieved, that he wrote before *High Windows* but did not publish in it would have found a context later—or even earlier if he had been less cautious. Anthony Thwaite goes some way towards assuming exactly that—or, at any rate, suggesting it—when he says that Larkin had been stung by early refusals and had later on repressed excellent poems even when his friends urged him to publish them. Some of these poems, as we now see, were indeed excellent, but if a man is so careful to arrange his works in a certain order it is probably wiser to assume that when he subtracts something he is adding to the arrangement.

Towards the end of his life, in the years after *High Windows*, Larkin famously dried up. Poems came seldom. Some of those that did come equalled his best, and "Aubade" was among his greatest. Larkin thought highly enough of it himself to send it out in pamphlet form to his friends and acquaintances, and they were quickly on the telephone to one another quoting phrases and lines from it. Soon it was stanzas, and in London there is at least one illustrious playwright who won't go home from a dinner party before he has found an excuse to recite the whole thing.

> This is a special way of being afraid
> No trick dispels. Religion used to try,
> That vast moth-eaten musical brocade
> Created to pretend we never die,
> And specious stuff that says *No rational being*
> *Can fear a thing it will not feel*, not seeing
> That this is what we fear—no sight, no sound,
> No touch or taste or smell, nothing to think with,
> Nothing to love or link with,
> The anaesthetic from which none come round . . .

Had Larkin lived longer, there would eventually have had to be one more slim volume, even if slimmer than slim. But that any of the earlier suppressed poems would have gone into it seems very unlikely. The better they are, the better must have been his reasons for holding them back. Admittedly, the fact that he did not destroy them is some evidence that he was not averse to their being published after his death. As a seasoned campaigner for the preservation of British holograph manuscripts—he operated on the principle that papers bought by American universities were lost to civilization—he obviously thought that his own archive should be kept safe. But the question of *how* the suppressed poems should be published has now been answered: some other way than this. Arguments for how good they are miss the point, because it is not their weakness that is inimical to his total effect; it is their strength. There are hemistiches as riveting as anything he ever made public.

> Dead leaves desert in thousands . . .

He wrote that in 1953 and sat on it for more than thirty years. What other poet would not have got it into print somehow? The two first lines of a short poem called "Pigeons," written in 1957, are a paradigm distillation of his characteristic urban pastoralism:

> On shallow slates the pigeons shift together,
> Backing against a thin rain from the west . . .

Even more remarkable, there were whole big poems so close to being fully realized that to call them unfinished sounds like effrontery. Not only would Larkin never let a flawed poem through for the sake of its strong phrasing; he would sideline a strong poem because of a single flaw. But "Letter to a Friend about Girls," written in 1959, has nothing frail about it except his final indecision about whether Horatio is writing to Hamlet or Hamlet to Horatio. The writer complains that the addressee gets all the best girls without having to think about it, while he, the writer, gets, if any, only the ones he doesn't really want, and that after a long struggle.

> After comparing lives with you for years
> I see how I've been losing: all the while
> I've met a different gauge of girl from yours . . .

A brilliantly witty extended conceit, full of the scatalogical moral observation that Larkin and his friend Kingsley Amis jointly brought back from conversation into the literature from which it had been banished, the poem has already become incorporated into the Larkin canon that people quote to one another. So have parts of "The Dance," which would probably have been his longest single poem if he had ever finished it. The story of an awkward, put-upon, recognizably Larkin-like lonely man failing to get together with a beautiful woman even though she seems to be welcoming his attentions, the poem could logically have been completed only by becoming a third novel to set beside *Jill* and *A Girl in Winter*. (Actually, the novel had already been written, by Kingsley Amis, and was called *Lucky Jim*.)

But there might have been a better reason for abandoning the poem. Like the Horatio poem and many of the other poems that were held back, "The Dance" is decisive about what Larkin otherwise preferred to leave indeterminate. "Love Again," written in 1979, at the beginning of the arid last phase in which the poems that came to him seem more like bouts of fever than like showers of rain, states the theme with painful clarity.

> Love again: wanking at ten past three
> (Surely he's taken her home by now?),
> The bedroom hot as a bakery . . .

What hurts, though, isn't the vocabulary. When Larkin speaks of "Someone else feeling her breasts and cunt," he isn't speaking with untypical bluntness: though unfalteringly well judged, his tonal range always leaves room for foul language—shock effects are among his favourites. The pain at this point comes from the fact that it is so obviously Larkin talking. This time, the voice isn't coming through a persona: it's the man himself, only at his least complex, and therefore least individual. In his *oeuvre*, as selected and arranged by himself, there is a dialogue going on, a balancing of forces between perfection of the life and of the work—a classic conflict for which Larkin offers us a resolution second in its richness only to the later poems of Yeats. In much of the previously suppressed poetry, the dialogue collapses into a monologue. The man who has, at least in part, chosen his despair, or who, at any rate, strives to convince himself that he has, is usurped by the man who has no choice. The second man might well be thought of as the real man, but one of the effects of Larkin's work is to make us realize that beyond the supposed bedrock reality of individual happiness or unhappiness there is a social reality of creative fulfilment, or, failing that, of public duties faithfully carried out.

Larkin, in his unchecked personal despair, is a sacrificial goat with the sexual outlook of a stud bull. He thinks, and sometimes speaks, like a Robert Crumb character who has never recovered from being beaten up by a girl in the third grade. The best guess, and the least patronizing as well, is that Larkin held these poems back because he thought them self-indulgent—too private to be proportionate. One of the consolations that Larkin's work offers us is that we can be unhappy without giving in, without letting our wish to be off the hook ("Beneath it all, desire of oblivion runs") wipe out our lives ("the million-petalled flower/ Of being here"). The ordering of the individual volumes was clearly meant to preserve this balance, which the inclusion of even a few more of the suppressed poems would have tipped.

In the *Collected Poems*, that hard-fought-for poise is quite gone. Larkin now speaks a good deal less for us all, and a good deal more for himself, than was his plain wish. That the self, the sad, dithering personal condition from which all his triumphantly assured work sprang, is now more comprehensively on view is not really a full compensation, except, perhaps, to those who aren't comfortable with an idol unless its head is made from the same clay as its feet.

On the other hand, to be given, in whatever order, all these marvellous poems that were for so long unseen is a bonus for which only a dolt would be ungrateful. Schnabel said that Beethoven's late piano sonatas were music better than could be played. Larkin's best poems are poetry better than can be said, but sayability they sumptuously offer. Larkin demands to be read aloud. His big, intricately formed stanzas, often bridging from one to the next, defeat the single breath but always invite it. As you read, the ideal human voice speaks in your head. It isn't his: as his gramophone records prove, he sounded like someone who expects to be interrupted. It isn't yours, either. It's ours. Larkin had the gift of reuniting poetry at its most artful with ordinary speech at its most unstudied— at its least literary. Though a scholar to the roots, he was not being perverse when he posed as a simple man. He thought that art should be self-sufficient. He was disturbed by the way literary studies had crowded out literature. But none of this means that he was simplistic. Though superficially a reactionary crusader against Modernism, a sort of latter-day, one-man Council of Trent, he knew exactly when to leave something unexplained.

The process of explaining him will be hard to stop now that this book is available. It is still, however, a tremendous book, and, finally, despite all the candour it apparently offers, the mystery will be preserved for any reader acute enough to sense the depth under the clarity. Pushkin said that everything was on his agenda, even the disasters. Larkin knew about himself. In private hours of anguish, he commiserated with himself. But he was an artist, and that meant he was everyone; and what made him a genius was the effort and resource he brought to bear in order to meet his superior responsibility.

Larkin went to hell, but not in a handcart. From his desolation he built masterpieces, and he was increasingly disinclined to settle for anything less. About twenty years ago in Britain, it became fashionable to say that all the poetic excitement was in America. Though things look less that way now, there is no need to be just as silly in the opposite direction. The English-speaking world is a unity. Britain and the United States might have difficulty absorbing each other's poetry, but most people have difficulty with poetry anyway. In Britain, Larkin shortened the distance between the people and poetry by doing nothing for his career and everything to compose artefacts that would have an independent, memorable life apart from himself. There is no inherent reason that the American reader, or any other English-speaking reader, should not be able to appreciate the results.

Art, if it knows how to wait, wins out. Larkin had patience. For him, poetry was a life sentence. He set happiness aside to make room for it. And if it turns out that he had no control over where his misery came from, doesn't that mean that he had even more control than we thought over where it went to? Art is no less real for being artifice. The moment of truth must be prepared for. "Nothing to love or link with," wrote Larkin when he was fifty-five. "Nothing to catch or claim," he wrote when he was twenty-four, in a poem that only now sees the light. It was as if the death he feared to the end he had embraced at the start, just so as to raise the stakes.

The New Yorker, July 17, 1989; later included in
The Dreaming Swimmer, 1992

2. On Larkin's Wit

Larkin at Sixty, edited by Anthony Thwaite

There is no phrase in Philip Larkin's poetry which has not been turned, but then any poet tries to avoid flat writing, even at the cost of producing overwrought banality. Larkin's dedication to compressed resonance is best studied, in the first instance, through his prose. The prefaces to the reissues of *Jill* and *The North Ship* are full of sentences that make you smile at their neat richness even when they are not meant to be jokes, and that when they are meant to be jokes—as in the evocation of the young Kingsley Amis at Oxford in the preface to *Jill*—make you wish that the article went on as long as the book. But there is a whole book which does just that: *All What Jazz*, the collection of Larkin's *Daily Telegraph* jazz record review columns which was published in 1970. Having brought the book out, Faber seemed nervous about what to do with it next. I bought two copies marked down to seventy-five pence each in a Cardiff newsagent's and wish now that I had bought ten. I thought at the time that *All What Jazz* was the best available expression by the author himself of what he believed art to be. I still think so, and would contend in addition that no wittier book of criticism has ever been written.

To be witty does not necessarily mean to crack wise. In fact it usually means the opposite: wits rarely tell jokes. Larkin's prose flatters the reader by giving him as much as he can take in at one time. The delight caused has to do with collusion. Writer and reader are in cahoots. Larkin has the knack of donning cap and bells while still keeping his dignity. For years he feigned desperation before the task of conveying the real desperation induced in him by the saxophone playing of John Coltrane. The metaphors can be pursued through the book—they constitute by themselves a kind of extended solo, of which the summary sentence in the book's introductory essay should be regarded as the coda. "With John Coltrane metallic and passionless nullity gave way to exercises in gigantic absurdity, great boring excursions on not-especially-attractive themes during which all possible changes were rung, extended investigations of oriental tedium, long-winded and portentous demonstrations of religiosity." This final grandiose flourish was uttered in 1968.

But the opening note was blown in 1961, when Larkin, while yet prepared (cravenly, by his own later insistence) to praise Coltrane as a hard-thinking experimenter, referred to "the vinegary drizzle of his tone." In 1962 he was still in two minds, but you could already guess which mind was winning. "Coltrane's records are, paradoxically, nearly always both interesting and boring, and I certainly find myself listening to them in preference to many a less adventurous set." Notable at this stage is that he did not risk a metaphor, in which the truth would have more saliently protruded. In May 1963 there is only one mind left talking. To the eighth track of a Thelonius Monk album, "John Coltrane contributes a solo of characteristic dreariness."

By December of that same year Larkin's line on this topic has not only lost all its qualifications but acquired metaphorical force. Coltrane is referred to as "the master of the thinly disagreeable" who "sounds as if he is playing for an audience of cobras." This squares up well with the critic's known disgust that the joyous voicing of the old jazz should have

so completely given way to "the cobra-coaxing cacophonies of Calcutta."
In 1965 Larkin was gratified to discover that his opinion of Coltrane's
achievement was shared by the great blues-shouter Jimmy Rushing. "I
don't think he can play his instrument," said Rushing. "This," Larkin
observed, "accords very well with my own opinion that Coltrane sounds
like nothing so much as a club bore who has been metamorphosed by a
fellow-member of magical powers into a pair of bagpipes." (Note Larkin's
comic timing, incidentally: a less witty writer would have put "metamorphosed into a pair of bagpipes by a fellow-member of magical powers,"
and so halved the effect.) Later in the same piece he expanded the attack
into one of those generally pertinent critical disquisitions in which *All
What Jazz* is so wealthy. "His solos seem to me to bear the same relation
to proper jazz solos as those drawings of running dogs, showing their legs
in all positions so that they appear to have about fifty of them, have to real
drawings. Once, they are amusing and even instructive. But the whole
point of drawing is to choose the right line, not drawing fifty alternatives.
Again, Coltrane's choice and treatment of themes is hypnotic, repetitive,
monotonous: he will rock backwards and forwards between two chords
for five minutes, or pull a tune to pieces like someone subtracting petals
from a flower." Later in the piece there is an atavistic gesture towards giving the Devil his due, but by the vividness of his chosen figures of speech
the critic has already shown what he really thinks.

　　"I can thoroughly endorse," wrote Larkin in July 1966, "the sleeve of
John Coltrane's *Ascension* (HMV), which says 'This record cannot be
loved or understood in one sitting.' " In November of the same year he
greeted Coltrane's religious suite *Meditations* as "the most astounding
piece of ugliness I have ever heard." After Coltrane's death in 1977
Larkin summed up the departed hero's career. ". . . I do not remember
ever suggesting that his music was anything but a pain between the ears.
. . . Was I wrong?" In fact, as we have seen, Larkin had once allowed himself to suggest that the noises Coltrane made might at least be interesting,
but by now tentativeness had long given way to a kind of fury, as of someone defending a principle against his own past weakness. "That reedy,
catarrhal tone . . . that insolent egotism, leading to 45-minute versions of
'My Favourite Things' until, at any rate in Britain, the audience walked
out, no doubt wondering why they had ever walked in . . . pretension as
a way of life . . . wilful and hideous distortion of tone that offered squeals,
squeaks, Bronx cheers and throttled slate-pencil noises for serious consid-

eration . . . dervish-like heights of hysteria." It should be remembered, if this sounds like a grave being danced on, that Larkin's was virtually the sole dissenting critical voice. Coltrane died in triumph and Larkin had every right to think at the time that to express any doubts about the stature of the deceased genius was to whistle against the wind.

The whole of *All What Jazz* is a losing battle. Larkin is arguing in support of entertainment at a time when entertainment was steadily yielding ground to portentous significance. His raillery against the saxophonists is merely the most strident expression of a general argument which he goes on elaborating as its truth becomes more clear to himself. In a quieter way he became progressively disillusioned with Miles Davis. In January 1962 it was allowed that in an informal atmosphere Davis could produce music "very far from the egg-walking hushedness" he was given to in the studio. In October of the same year Larkin gave him points for bonhomie. "According to the sleeve, Davis actually smiled twice at the audience during the evening and there is indeed a warmth about the entire proceedings that makes this a most enjoyable LP." But by the time of *Seven Steps to Heaven* a year later, Davis has either lost what little attraction he had or else Larkin has acquired the courage of his convictions. ". . . his lifeless muted tone, at once hollow and unresonant, creeps along only just in tempo, the ends of the notes hanging down like Dalí watches . . ." In 1964, Larkin begged to dissent from the enthusiastic applause recorded on the live album *Miles Davis in Europe*. ". . . the fact that he can spend seven or eight minutes playing 'Autumn Leaves' without my recognizing or liking the tune confirms my view of him as a master of rebarbative boredom." A year later he was reaching for the metaphors. "I freely confess that there have been times recently, when almost anything—the shape of a patch on the ceiling, a recipe for rhubarb jam read upside down in the paper—has seemed to me more interesting than the passionless creep of a Miles Davis trumpet solo." But in this case the opening blast was followed by a climbdown. "Davis is his usual bleak self, his notes wilting at the edges as if with frost, spiky at up-tempos, and while he is still not my ideal of comfortable listening his talent is clearly undiminished." This has the cracked chime of a compromise. The notes, though wilting as if with frost instead of like Dalí watches, are nevertheless still wilting, and it is clear from the whole drift of Larkin's criticism that he places no value on uncomfortable listening as such. A 1966 review sounds more straightforward. "… for me it was an experience in pure duration. Some of it must have been quite hard to do."

But in Larkin's prose the invective which implies values is always matched by the encomium which states them plainly. He jokes less when praising than when attacking but the attention he pays to evocation is even more concentrated. The poem "For Sidney Bechet" ("On me your voice falls as they say love should,/ Like an enormous yes") can be matched for unforced reverence in the critical prose: "… the marvellous 'Blue Horizon,' six choruses of slow blues in which Bechet climbs without interruption or hurry from lower to upper register, his clarinet tone at first thick and throbbing, then soaring like Melba in an extraordinary blend of lyricism and power that constituted the unique Bechet voice, commanding attention the instant it sounded." He is similarly eloquent about the "fire and shimmer" of Bix Beiderbecke and of the similes he attaches to Pee Wee Russell there is no end—Russell's clarinet seems to function in Larkin's imagination as a kind of magic flute.

The emphasis, in Larkin's admiration for all these artists, is on the simplicity at the heart of their creative endeavour. What they do would not have its infinite implications if it did not spring from elementary emotion. It can be argued that Larkin is needlessly dismissive of Duke Ellington and Charlie Parker. There is plenty of evidence to warrant including him in the school of thought known among modern jazz buffs as "mouldy fig." But there is nothing retrograde about the aesthetic underlying his irascibility. The same aesthetic underlies his literary criticism and everything else he writes. Especially it underlies his poetry. Indeed it is not even an aesthetic: it is a world view, of the kind which invariably forms the basis of any great artistic personality. Modernism, according to Larkin, "helps us neither to enjoy nor endure." He defines Modernism as intellectualized art. Against intellectualism he proposes, not anti-intellectualism—which would be just another coldly willed programme—but trust in the validity of emotion. What the true artist says from instinct, the true critic will hear by the same instinct. There may be more than instinct involved, but nothing real will be involved without it.

The danger, therefore, of assuming that everything played today in jazz has a seed of solid worth stems from the fact that so much of it is tentative, experimental, private. . . . And for this reason one has to fall back on the old dictum that a critic is only as good as his ear. His ear will tell him instantly whether a piece of music is vital, musical, exciting, or cerebral, mock-academic, dead, long before he can read Don DeMichael on the subject, or learn that it is written in inverted nineteenths, or in the Stygian mode, or recorded at the NAACP Festival at Little Rock. He must hold on to the principle that the only reason for praising a work is that it pleases, and the way to develop his critical sense is to be more acutely aware of whether he is being pleased or not.

What Larkin might have said on his own behalf is that critical prose can be subjected to the same test. His own criticism appeals so directly to the ear that he puts himself in danger of being thought trivial, especially by the mock-academic. Like Amis's, Larkin's readability seems so effortless that it tends to be thought of as something separate from his intelligence. But readability *is* intelligence. The vividness of Larkin's critical style is not just a token of his seriousness but the embodiment of it. His wit is there not only in the cutting jokes but in the steady work of registering his interest. It is easy to see that he is being witty when he says that Miles Davis and Ornette Coleman stand in evolutionary relationship to each other "like green apples and stomach-ache." But he is being equally witty when he mentions Ruby Braff's "peach-fed" cornet. A critic's language is not incidental to him: its intensity is a sure measure of his engagement and a persuasive hint at the importance of what he is engaged with.

A critical engagement with music is one of the several happy coincidences which unite Larkin's career with Eugenio Montale's. If Larkin's *Listen* magazine articles on poetry were to be reprinted the field of comparison would be even more instructive, since there are good reasons for thinking that these two poets come up with remarkably similar conclusions when thinking about the art they practise. On music they often sound like the same man talking. Montale began his artistic career as a trained opera singer and his main area of musical criticism has always been classical music, but he writes about it the same way Larkin writes about jazz, with unfaltering intelligibility, a complete trust in his own ear, and a deep suspicion of any work which draws inspiration from its own technique. In Italy his collected music criticism is an eagerly awaited book, but then in Italy nobody is surprised that a great poet should have written a critical column for so many years of his life. Every educated Italian knows that Montale's music notices are all of a piece with the marvellous body of literary criticism collected in *Auto da Fé* and *Sulla Poesia*, and that his whole critical corpus is the natural complement to his poetry. In Britain the same connection is harder to make, even though Larkin has deservedly attained a comparable position as a national poet. In Britain the simultaneous pursuit of poetry and regular critical journalism is regarded as versatility at best. The essential unity of Larkin's various activities is not much remarked.

But if we do not remark it we miss half of his secret. While maintaining an exalted idea of the art he practises, Larkin never thinks of it as an inherently separate activity from the affairs of everyday. He has no special poetic voice. What he brings out is the poetry that is already in the world. He has cherished the purity of his own first responses. Like all great artists he has never lost touch with the child in his own nature. The language of even the most intricately wrought Larkin poem is already present in recognizable embryo when he describes the first jazz musicians ever to capture his devotion. "It was the drummer I concentrated on, sitting as he did on a raised platform behind a battery of cowbells, temple blocks, cymbals, tomtoms and (usually) a Chinese gong, his drums picked out in flashing crimson or ultramarine brilliants." There are good grounds for calling Larkin a pessimist, but it should never be forgotten that the most depressing details in the poetry are seen with the same eye that loved those drums. The proof is in the unstinting vitality of language.

As in the criticism, so in the poetry, wit can be divided usefully into two kinds, humorous and plain. There is not much need to rehearse the first kind. Most of us have scores of Larkin's lines, hemistiches and phrases in our heads, to make us smile whenever we think of them, which is as often as the day changes. I can remember the day in 1962 when I first opened *The Less Deceived* and was snared by a line in the first poem, "Lines on a Young Lady's Photograph Album." "Not quite your class, I'd say, dear, on the whole." What a perfectly timed pentameter! How subtly and yet how unmistakably it defined the jealousy of the speaker! Who on earth was Philip Larkin? Dozens of subsequent lines in the same volume made it clearer: he was a supreme master of language levels, snapping into and out of a tone of voice as fast as it could be done without losing the reader. Bringing the reader in on it—the deep secret of popular seriousness, Larkin brought the reader in on it even at the level of prosodic technique.

> Flagged, and the figurehead with golden tits
> Arching our way, it never anchors; it's . . .

He got you smiling at a rhyme. "Church Going" had the ruin-bibber, randy for antique, "Toads" had the pun on Shakespeare, "Stuff your pension!" being the stuff dreams are made on. You couldn't get halfway through the book without questioning, and in many cases revising, your long-nursed notions about poetic language. Here was a disciplined yet unlimited variety of tone, a scrupulosity that could contain anything, an all-inclusive decorum.

In *The Whitsun Weddings*, "Mr. Bleaney" has the Bodies and "Naturally the Foundation Will Bear Your Expenses" has the ineffable Mr. Lal. "Sunny Prestatyn" features Titch Thomas and in "Wild Oats" a girl painfully reminiscent of Margaret in *Lucky Jim* is finally shaken loose "after about five rehearsals." In "Essential Beauty" "the trite untransferable/ Truss-advertisement, truth" takes you back to the cobra-coaxing cacophonies of Calcutta, not to mention forward to Amis's nitwit not fit to shift shit. Even *High Windows*, the bleakest of Larkin's slim volumes, has things to make you laugh aloud. In "The Card-Players" Jan van Hogspeuw and Old Prijck perhaps verge on the coarse but Jake Balokowsky, the hero of "Posterity," has already entered the gallery of timeless academic portraits, along with Professor Welch and the History Man. "Vers de Société" has the "bitch/ Who's read nothing but *Which*." In Larkin's three major volumes of poetry the jokes on their own would be enough to tell you that wit is alive and working.

But it is working far more pervasively than that. Larkin's poetry is *all* witty—which is to say that there is none of his language which does not confidently rely on the intelligent reader's capacity to apprehend its play of tone. On top of the scores of fragments that make us laugh, there are the hundreds which we constantly recall with a welcome sense of communion, as if our own best thoughts had been given their most concise possible expression. If Auden was right about the test of successful writing being how often the reader thinks of it, Larkin passed long ago. To quote even the best examples would be to fill half this book, but perhaps it will bear saying again, this time in the context of his poetry, that between Larkin's humorous wit and his plain wit there is no discontinuity. Only the man who invented the golden tits could evoke the black-sailed unfamiliar. To be able to make fun of the randy ruin-bibber is the necessary qualification for writing the magnificent last stanza of "Church Going." You need to have been playfully alliterative with the trite untransferable truss-advertisement before you can be lyrically alliterative with the supine stationary voyage of the dead lovers in "An Arundel Tomb." There is a level of seriousness which only those capable of humour can reach.

Similarly there is a level of maturity which only those capable of childishness can reach. The lucent comb of "The Building" can be seen by us only because it has been so intensely seen by Larkin, and it has been so intensely seen by him only because his eyes, behind those thick glasses, retain the naive curiosity which alone makes the adult gaze truly penetrating. Larkin's poetry draws a bitterly sad picture of modern life but it is full of saving graces, and they are invariably as disarmingly recorded as in a child's diary. The paddling at the seaside, the steamer in the afternoon, the ponies at Show Saturday—they are all done with crayons and coloured pencils. He did not put away childish things and it made him more of a man. It did the same for Montale: those who have ever read about the amulet in "Dora Markus" or the children with tin swords in *Caffè a Rapallo* are unlikely to forget them when they read Larkin. A third name could be added: Mandelstam. When Mandelstam forecast his own death he willed that his spirit should be resurrected in the form of children's games. All three poets represent, for their respective countrymen, the distilled lyricism of common speech. With all three poets the formal element is highly developed—in the cases of Larkin and Mandelstam to the uppermost limit possible—and yet none of them fails to reassure his readers, even during the most intricately extended flight of verbal music, that the tongue they speak is the essential material of his rhythmic and melodic resource.

In Philip Larkin's non-poetic poetic language, the language of extremely well-written prose, despair is expressed through beauty and becomes beautiful too. His argument is with himself and he is bound to lose. He can call up death more powerfully than almost any other poet ever has, but he does so in the commanding voice of life. His linguistic exuberance is the heart of him. Joseph Brodsky, writing about Mandelstam, called lyricism the ethics of language. Larkin's wit is the ethics of his poetry. It brings his distress under our control. It makes his personal unhappiness our universal exultation. Armed with his wit, he faces the worst on our behalf, and brings it to order. A romantic sensibility classically disciplined, he is, in the only sense of the word likely to last, modern after all. By rebuilding the ruined bridge between poetry and the general reading public he has given his art a future, and you can't get more modern than that.

1981; later included in
From the Land of Shadows, 1982

3. Don Juan in Hull

I. WOLVES OF MEMORY

Larkin collections come out at the rate of one per decade: *The North Ship*, 1945; *The Less Deceived*, 1955; *The Whitsun Weddings*, 1964; *High Windows*, 1974. Not exactly a torrent of creativity: just the best. In Italy the reading public is accustomed to cooling its heels for even longer. Their top man, Eugenio Montale, has produced only five main collections, and he got started a good deal earlier. But that, in both countries, is the price one has to pay. For both poets the parsimony is part of the fastidiousness. Neither writes an unconsidered line.

Now that the latest Larkin, *High Windows*, is finally available, it is something of a shock to find in it some poems one doesn't recognize. Clipping the poems out of magazines has failed to fill the bill—there were magazines one hadn't bargained for. As well as that, there is the surprise of finding that it all adds up even better than one had expected: the poems which one had thought of as characteristic turn out to be more than that—or rather the *character* turns out to be more than that. Larkin has never liked the idea of an artist Developing. Nor has he himself done so. But he has managed to go on clarifying what he was sent to say. The total impression of *High Windows* is of despair made beautiful. Real despair and real beauty, with not a trace of posturing in either. The book is the peer of the previous two mature collections, and if they did not exist would be just as astonishing. But they do exist (most of us could recognize any line from either one) and can't help rendering many of the themes in this third book deceptively familiar.

I think that in most of the poems here collected Larkin's ideas are being reinforced or deepened rather than repeated. But from time to time a certain predictability of form indicates that a previous discovery is being unearthed all over again. Such instances aren't difficult to spot, and it would be intemperate to betray delight at doing so. Larkin's "forgeries" (Auden's term for self-plagiarisms) are very few. He is more original from poem to poem than almost any modern poet one can think of. His limitations, such as they are, lie deeper than that. Here again, it is not wise to be happy about spotting them. Without the limitations there would be no Larkin—the beam cuts *because* it's narrow.

It has always seemed to me a great pity that Larkin's more intelligent critics should content themselves with finding his view of life circumscribed. It is, but it is also bodied forth as art to a remarkable degree. There is a connection between the circumscription and the poetic intensity, and it's no surprise that the critics who can't see the connection can't see the separation either. They seem to think that just because the poet is (self-admittedly) emotionally wounded, the poetry is wounded too. There is always the suggestion that Larkin might handle his talent better if he were a more well-rounded character. That Larkin's gift might be part and parcel of his own peculiar nature isn't a question they have felt called upon to deal with. The whole fumbling dereliction makes you wonder if perhaps the literati in this country haven't had things a bit easy. A crash course in, say, art criticism could in most cases be recommended. Notions that Michelangelo would have painted more feminine-looking sibyls if he had been less bent, or that Toulouse-Lautrec might have been less obsessive about Jane Avril's dancing if his legs had been longer, would at least possess the merit of being self-evidently absurd. But the brainwave about Larkin's quirky negativism, and the consequent trivialization of his lyrical knack, is somehow able to go on sounding profound.

It ought to be obvious that Larkin is not a universal poet in the thematic sense—in fact, he is a self-proclaimed stranger to a good half, *the* good half, of life. You wonder what a critic who complains of this imagines he is praising when he allows that Larkin is still pretty good anyway, perhaps even great. What's missing in Larkin doesn't just tend to be missing, it's glaringly, achingly, unarguably *missing*. But the poetry is all there. The consensus about his stature is consequently encouraging, even if accomplished at the cost of a majority of its adherents misunderstanding what is really going on. At least they've got the right man.

.   .   .

The first poem in the book, "To the Sea," induces a fairly heavy effect of *déjà lu*. Aren't we long used to that massive four-stanza form, that conjectural opening ("To step over the low wall . . .") in the infinitive? Actually we aren't: he's never used them before. It's the tone that's reminiscent, and the tactics. The opening takes us back to the childhood and the lost chance of happiness, the shots that all fell wide—

> The miniature gaiety of seasides.

In the familiar way, sudden brutalities of diction bite back a remembered sweetness—

> A white steamer stuck in the afternoon.

Alienation is declared firmly as the memories build up—

> Strange to it now, I watch the cloudless scene:

Details well up in the mind with Proustian specificity—

> . . . and then the cheap cigars,
> The chocolate-papers, tea-leaves, and, between
> The rocks, the rusting soup-tins . . .

The mind, off guard, unmanned by recollection, lets slip the delicately expressed lyrical image—

> The white steamer has gone. Like breathed-on glass
> The sunlight has turned milky.

Whereupon, as in "Church Going" or "The Whitsun Weddings," the poem winds up in a sententious coda.

> . . . If the worst
> Of flawless weather is our falling short
> It may be that through habit these do best,
> Coming to water clumsily undressed
> Yearly, teaching their children by a sort
> Of clowning; helping the old, too, 1p7.33as they ought.

The happiness we once thought we could have can't be had, but simple people who stick to time-honoured habits probably get the best approximation of it. Larkin once said that if he were called in to construct a religion he would make use of water. Well, here it is, lapping at the knobbled feet of unquestioning plebs. Such comfort as the poem offers the reader resides in the assurance that this old habit of going to the seaside is "still going on," even if reader and writer no longer share it. A cold comfort, as always. Larkin tries, he has said, to preserve experience both for himself and for others, but his first responsibility is to the experience.

The next big poem is the famous three-part effort that appeared in the *Observer*, "Livings." A galley-proof of it is still folded into the back of my copy of *The Less Deceived*. I think it an uncanny piece of work. The proof is read to shreds, and I can still remember the day I picked it up in the office. Larkin had the idea—preserved, in concentrated form, in one of the poems in this volume, "Posterity"—that a young American Ph.D. student called Jake Balokowsky is all set to wrap him up in an uncomprehending thesis. The first part of "Livings" is full of stuff that Balokowsky is bound to get wrong. The minor businessman who annually books himself into "the———Hotel in——ton for three days" speaks a vocabulary as well-rubbed and subtly anonymous as an old leather couch. Balokowsky will latch on well enough to the idea that the poem's narrator is a slave to habit,

> . . . wondering why
> I keep on coming. It's not worth it. Father's dead:
> He used to, but the business now is mine.
> It's time for change, in nineteen twenty-nine.

What Jake will probably miss, however, is the value placed on the innocuous local newspaper, the worn décor, the ritual chat, the non-challenging pictures and the ex-Army sheets. It's dependable, it's a living, and "living" is not a word Larkin tosses around lightly. Judging the narrator is the last thing Larkin is doing. On the contrary, he's looking for his secret. To be used to comfort is an enviable condition. Beer, whisky, cigars and silence—the privileges of the old mercantile civilization which Larkin has been quietly celebrating most of his life, a civilization in which a place like Leeds or Hull (see "Friday Night in the Royal Station Hotel") counts as a capital city. There *is* another and bigger life, but Larkin doesn't underestimate this one for a minute.

In fact he conjures it up all over again in the third part of the poem. The setting this time is Oxford, probably in the late seventeenth century. The beverage is port instead of whisky, and the talk, instead of with wages, tariffs and stock, deals with advowsons, resurrections and regicide. Proofs of God's existence lie uncontested on dusty bookshelves. "The bells discuss the hour's gradations." Once again the feeling of indoor warmth is womblike. Constellations sparkle over the roofs, matching the big sky draining down the estuary in Part I.

The central poem of the trio squirms like a cat caught between two cushions. Its narrator is conducting a lone love affair with the sea.

> Rocks writhe back to sight.
> Mussels, limpets,
> Husband their tenacity
> In the freezing slither—
> Creatures, I cherish you!

The narrator's situation is not made perfectly clear. While wanting to be just the reverse, Larkin can on occasion be a difficult poet, and here, I think, is a case of over-refinement leading to obscurity. (Elsewhere in this volume "Sympathy in White Major" is another instance, and I have never been able to understand "Dry Point" in *The Less Deceived*.) My guess—and a guess is not as good as an intelligent deduction—is that the speaker is a lighthouse keeper. The way the snow ("O loose moth world") swerves against the black water, and the line "Guarded by brilliance," seem somehow to suggest that: that, or something similar. Anyway, whoever he is, the narrator is right in among the elements, watching the exploding sea and the freezing slither from seventy feet up on a stormy night. But we see at the end that he, too, is safe indoors. On the radio he hears of elsewhere. He sets out his plate and spoon, cherishing his loneliness. In this central panel of his triptych, it seems to me, Larkin is saying that the civilizations described in the side panels—one decaying, the other soon to lose its confidence—have an essence, and that this is it. The essence can be preserved in the soul of a man on his own. This is not to suggest that there is anything consolingly positive under Larkin's well-known negativism: the only consoling thing about Larkin is the quality of his art.

"High Windows," the next stand-out poem, shows an emotional progression Larkin had already made us used to.

> When I see a couple of kids
> And guess he's fucking her and she's
> Taking pills or wearing a diaphragm,
> I know this is paradise . . .

Larkin is a master of language-levels and eminently qualified to use coarse language for shock effects. He never does, however. Strong language in Larkin is put in not to shock the reader but to define the narrator's personality. When Larkin's narrator in "A Study of Reading Habits" (in *The Whitsun Weddings*) said, "Books are a load of crap" there were critics—some of them, incredibly, among his more appreciative—who allowed themselves to believe that Larkin was expressing his own opinion. (Kingsley Amis had the same kind of trouble, perhaps from the same kind of people, when he let Jim Dixon cast aspersions on Mozart.) It should be obvious at long last, however, that the diction describes the speaker. When the speaker is close to representing Larkin himself, the diction defines which Larkin it is—what mood he is in. Larkin is no hypocrite and has expressed envy of young lovers too often to go back on it here. The word "fucking" is a conscious brutalism, a protective way of not conjuring up what's meant. However inevitable it might be that Jake Balokowsky will identify this opening sentiment as a Muggeridgean gesture of contempt, it is incumbent on us to realize that something more interesting is going on.

Everyone young is going down "the long slide" to happiness. The narrator argues that his own elders must have thought the same about him, who was granted freedom from the fear of Hellfire in the same way that the kids are granted freedom from the fear of pregnancy. But (and here comes the clincher) attaining either freedom means no more than being lifted up to a high window, through which you see

> . . . the deep blue air, that shows
> Nothing, and is nowhere, and is endless.

There is no doubt that the narrator is calling these callous sexual activities meaningless. What's open to doubt is whether the narrator believes what he is saying, or, given that he does, whether Larkin (wheels within wheels) believes the narrator. Later in the volume there is a poem called "Annus Mirabilis" which clearly contradicts the argument of "High Windows."

> Sexual intercourse began
> In nineteen sixty-three
> (Which was rather late for me)—
> Between the end of the Chatterley ban
> And the Beatles' first LP.

Evincing an unexpected sensitivity to tone, Jake could well detect an ironic detachment here. To help him out, there is a suggestion, in the third stanza, that the new liberty was merely license.

> And every life became
> A brilliant breaking of the bank,
> A quite unlosable game.

It all links up with the bleak view of "High Windows." What Jake might not spot, however, is that it contrasts more than it compares. "Annus Mirabilis" is a jealous poem—the fake-naive rhythms are there for self-protection as much as for ironic detachment. Larkin can't help believing that sex and love ought by rights to have been easier things for his generation, and far easier for him personally. The feeling of having missed out on something is one of his preoccupations. The thing Balokowsky needs to grasp is that Larkin is not criticizing modern society from a position of superiority. Over the range of his poetry, if not always in individual poems, he is very careful to allow that these pleasures might very well be thought meaningful. That he himself finds them meaningless might have something to do with himself as well as the state of the world. To the reader who has Larkin's poetry by heart, no poet seems more open. Small wonder that he finds it simply incomprehensible when critics discuss his lack of emotion. Apart from an outright yell for help, he has sent every distress signal a shy man can.

.   .   .

"The Old Fools"—even the ex-editor of the *Listener* blew his cool over that one, billing it as "marvellous" on the paper's masthead. And marvellous it is, although very scary. There is a pronounced technical weakness in the first stanza. It is all right to rhyme "remember" with "September" if you make it quite clear why September can't be July. Does it mean that the Old Fools were in the Home Guard in September 1939? It's hard to know. Apart from that one point, though, the poem is utterly and distressingly explicit. Once again, the brutalism of the opening diction is a tip-off to the narrator's state of mind, which is, this time, fearful.

> What do they think has happened, the old fools,
> To make them like this? Do they somehow suppose
> It's more grown-up when your mouth hangs open and drools . . .

Ill-suppressed anger. The crack about supposing "it's more grown-up" is a copybook example of Larkin's ability to compact his intelligibility without becoming ambiguous. Supposing something to be "more grown-up" is something children do: ergo, the Old Fools are like children—one of the poem's leading themes stated in a single locution.

> Why aren't they screaming?

Leaving the reader to answer: because they don't know what's happening to them. The narrator's real fears—soon he switches to a personal "you"—are for himself. The second stanza opens with an exultant lyrical burst: stark terror never sounded lovelier.

> At death, you break up: the bits that were you
> Start speeding away from each other for ever
> With no one to see. It's only oblivion, true:

We had it before, but then it was going to end,
And was all the time merging with a unique endeavour
To bring to bloom the million-petalled flower
Of being here.

The old, he goes on to suggest, probably live not in the here and now but "where all happened once." The idea takes some of its force from our awareness that that's largely where Larkin lives already — only his vision could lead to this death. The death is terrifying, but we would have to be like Larkin to share the terror completely. The reader tends to find himself shut out, glad that Larkin can speak so beautifully in his desperation but sorry that he should see the end in terms of his peculiar loneliness. There is always the edifying possibility, however, that Larkin is seeing the whole truth and the reader's defence mechanisms are working full blast.

.   .   .

If they are, "The Building" will quickly break them down. Here, I think, is the volume's masterpiece — an absolute chiller, which I find myself getting by heart despite a pronounced temperamental aversion. The Building is the house of death, a Dantesque hellhole — one thinks particularly of *Inferno* V — where people "at that vague age that claims/ The end of choice, the last of hope" are sent to "their appointed levels." The ambience is standard modernist humdrum: paperbacks, tea, rows of steel chairs like an airport lounge. You can look down into the yard and see red brick, lagged pipes, traffic. But the smell is frightening. In time everyone will find a nurse beckoning to him. The dead lie in white rows somewhere above. This, says Larkin with an undeflected power unique even for him, is what it all really adds up to. Life is a dream and we awake to this reality.

O world.
Your loves, your chances, are beyond the stretch
Of any hand from here! And so, unreal,
A touching dream to which we all are lulled
But wake from separately. In it, conceits
And self-protecting ignorance congeal
To carry life . . .

There is no point in disagreeing with the man if that's the way he feels, and he wouldn't write a poem like "The Building" if he didn't feel that way to the point of daemonic possession. He himself is well aware that there are happier ways of viewing life. It's just that he is incapable of sharing them, except for fleeting moments—and the fleeting moments do not accumulate, whereas the times in between them do. The narrator says that "nothing contravenes / The coming dark." It's an inherently less interesting proposition than its opposite, and a poet forced to devote his creative effort to embodying it has only a small amount of space to work in. Nor, within the space, is he free from the paradox that his poems will become part of life, not death. From that paradox, we gain. The desperation of "The Building" is like the desperation of Leopardi, disconsolate yet doomed to being beautiful. The advantage which accrues is one of purity—a hopeless affirmation is the only kind we really want to hear when we feel, as sooner or later everybody must, that life is a trap.

There is no certain way of separating Larkin's attitude to society from his conception of himself, but to the extent that you can, he seems to be in two minds about what the world has come to. He thinks, on the one hand, that it's probably all up; and on the other hand that youth still has a chance. On the theme of modern life being an unmitigated and steadily intensifying catastrophe he reads like his admired Betjeman in a murderous mood—no banana blush or cheery telly teeth, just a tight-browed disdain and a toxic line of invective. "Going, Going" is particularly instructive here. In "How Distant" we hear about

> . . . the departure of young men
> Down valleys, or watching
> The green shore past the salt-white cordage
> Rising and falling

Between the "fraying cliffs of water" (always a good sign when there's a lot of water about) the young adventurers used to sail, in the time of what we might call *genuine newness*. Larkin's objections to modern innovation are centred on its lack of invention—it's all fatally predictable. Jimmy Porter was nostalgic for the future. Larkin is anticipatory about the past. He longs for the time when youth meant the possibility of a new start.

This is being young,
Assumption of the startled century
Like new store clothes,
The huge decisions printed out by feet
Inventing where they tread,
The random windows conjuring a street.

The implication being that the time of adventure is long over. But in "Sad Steps," as the poet addresses the Moon, youth is allowed some hope.

One shivers slightly, looking up there.
The hardness and the brightness and the plain
Far-reaching singleness of that wide stare

Is a reminder of the strength and pain
Of being young; that it can't come again,
But is for others undiminished somewhere.

An elegantly cadenced admission that his own view of life might be neurotic, and excellent fuel for Jake's chapter on the dialectical element in Larkin in which it is pointed out that his poems are judiciously disposed in order to illuminate one another, Yeats-style. The Sun and Moon, like Water, bring out Larkin's expansiveness, such as it is. It's there, but you couldn't call it a bear-hug. Time is running out, as we hear in the wonderfully funny "Vers de Société":

Only the young can be alone freely.
The time is shorter now for company,
And sitting by a lamp more often brings
Not peace, but other things.

Visions of The Building, for example.

The book ends on an up-beat. Its next to last poem, "Show Saturday," is an extended, sumptuous evocation of country life ("Let it always be there") which has the effect of making the rural goings-on so enviably cosy that the reader feels almost as left out as the narrator. The final piece is an eerie lyric called "The Explosion," featuring the ghosts of miners walking from the sun towards their waiting wives. It is a superb thought superbly expressed, and Larkin almost believes in it, just as in "An Arundel Tomb" (the closing poem of *The Whitsun Weddings*) he almost believed in the survival of love. Almost believing is all right, once you've got believing out of it. But faith itself is extinct. Larkin loves and inhabits tradition as much as Betjeman does, but artistically he had already let go of it when others were only just realizing it was time to cling on. Larkin is the poet of the void. The one affirmation his work offers is the possibility that when we have lost everything the problem of beauty will still remain. It's enough.

II. SMALLER AND CLEARER

Philip Larkin once told Philip Oakes—in a *Sunday Times* magazine profile which remains one of the essential articles on its subject—how he was going to be a novelist, until the novels stopped coming. First there was *Jill* in 1946, and then there was *A Girl in Winter* in 1947, and after those there were to be several more. But they never arrived. So Philip Larkin became the leading poet who once wrote a brace of novels, just as his friend Kingsley Amis became the leading novelist who occasionally writes poems: the creative labour was divided with the customary English decorum, providing the kind of simplified career-structures with which literary history prefers to deal.

It verges on the unmannerly to raise the point, in Larkin's case, that the novels were in no sense the work of someone who had still to find his vocation. Chronology insists that they were written at a time when his verse had not yet struck its tone—*The North Ship*, Larkin's mesmerized submission to Yeats, had only recently been published, and of *The Less Deceived*, his first mature collection, barely half the constituent poems had as yet been written. But the novels had struck *their* tone straight away. It is only now, by hindsight, that they seem to point forward to the poetry. Taken in their chronology, they are impressively mature and self-sufficient. If Larkin had never written a line of verse, his place as a writer would still have been secure. It would have been a smaller place than he now occupies, but still more substantial than that of, say, Denton Welch, an equivalently precocious (though nowhere near as perceptive) writer of the same period.

The self-sufficient force of Larkin's two novels is attested to by the fact that they have never quite gone away. People serious in their admiration of Larkin's poetry have usually found themselves searching out at least one of them—most commonly *Jill*, to which Larkin prefixed, in the 1964 edition, an introduction that seductively evoked the austere but ambitious Oxford of his brilliant generation and in particular was creasingly funny about Amis. Unfortunately this preface (retained in the current paperback) implies, by its very retrospection, a status of obsolescence for the book itself. Yet the present reissue sufficiently proves that *Jill* needs no apologizing for. And *A Girl in Winter* is at least as good as *Jill* and in some departments conspicuously better. Either novel is guaranteed to jolt any reader who expects Larkin to look clumsy out of his bailiwick. There are times when Larkin *does* look that, but they usually happen when he tempts himself into offering a professional rule of thumb as an aesthetic principle—a practice which can lay him open to charges of cranky insularity. None of that here. In fact quite the other thing: the novels are at ease with a range of sympathies that the later poems, even the most magnificent ones, deal with only piecemeal, although with incomparably more telling effect.

Considering that Evelyn Waugh began a comic tradition in the modern novel which only lately seems in danger of dying out, and considering Larkin's gift for sardonic comedy—a gift which by all accounts decisively influenced his contemporaries at Oxford—it is remarkable how non-comic his novels are, how completely they do not fit into the family of talents which includes Waugh and Powell and Amis. *Jill* employs many of the same properties as an Oxford novel by the young Waugh—the obscure young hero is casually destroyed by his socially superior contemporaries—but the treatment is unrelievedly sad. Larkin's hero has none of the inner strength which Amis gave Jim Dixon. Nor is there any sign of the Atkinson figures who helped Jim through the tougher parts of the maze. Young John comes up to Oxford lost and stays lost: he is not a symbol of his social condition so much as an example of how his social condition can amplify a handicap—shy ordinariness—into tragedy. All the materials of farce are present and begging to be used, but tragedy is what Larkin aims for and what he largely achieves.

The crux of the matter is John's love for Jill—a thousand dreams and one kiss. Jill is a clear forecast of the Larkin dream girl in the poems. But if John is Larkin, he is hardly the Larkin we know to have dominated his generation at Oxford. He is someone much closer to the author's central self, the wounded personality whose deprivation has since been so clearly established in the poems. What is remarkable, however (and the same thing is remarkable about the poems, but rarely comes into question), is the way in which the hero's desolation is viewed in its entirety by the author. The author sees the whole character from without. The novel does something which very few novels by twenty-one-year-old writers have ever done. It distances autobiographical material and sets events in the global view of mature personality.

As if to prove the point, A *Girl in Winter* is a similar story of callow love, but seen from the girl's angle. The book perfectly catches the way a young woman's emotional maturity outstrips a young man's. Katherine, a young European grappling with England (an inversion of the Larkin-Amis nightmare in which the Englishman is obliged to grapple with Europe), is morally perceptive—sensitive would be the right word if it did not preclude robustness—to an unusual degree, yet Larkin is able to convince us that she is no freak. While still an adolescent she falls in love with her English pen-pal, Robin, without realizing that it is Robin's sister, Jane, who is really interested in her. Time sorts out the tangle, but just when Katherine has fallen out of love Robin shows up on the off-chance of sleeping with her. Katherine quells his importunity with a few apposite remarks likely to make any male reader sweat from the palms, although finally she sleeps with him because it's less trouble than not to. Yet Katherine is allowed small comfort in her new maturity. The book is as disconsolate as its predecessor, leaving the protagonist once again facing an unsatisfactory prime.

A contributory grace in both novels, but outstanding in A *Girl in Winter*, is the sheer quality of the writing. Larkin told Oakes that he wrote the books like poems, carefully eliminating repeated words. Fastidiousness is everywhere and flamboyance non-existent: the touch is unfaltering. Katherine "could sense his interest turning towards her, as a blind man might sense the switching on of an electric fire." Figures of speech are invariably as quiet and effective as that. The last paragraphs of A *Girl in Winter* have something of the cadenced elegance you find at the close of *The Great Gatsby*.

Why, if Larkin could write novels like these, did he stop? In hindsight the answer is easy: because he was about to become the finest poet of his generation, instead of just one of its best novelists. A more inquiring appraisal suggests that although his aesthetic effect was rich, his stock of events was thin. In a fictional texture featuring a sore tooth and a fleeting kiss as important strands Zen diaphanousness always threatened.

(What is the sound of *one* flower being arranged?) The master lyric poet, given time, will eventually reject the idea of writing any line not meant to be remembered. Larkin, while being to no extent a dandy, is nevertheless an exquisite. It is often the way with exquisites that they graduate from full-scale prentice constructions to small-scale works of entirely original intensity, having found a large expanse limiting. Chopin is not too far-fetched a parallel. Larkin's two novels are like Chopin's two concertos: good enough to promise not merely more of the same but a hitherto unheard-of distillation of their own lyrical essence.

III. Yeats vs. Hardy in Davie's Larkin

In recent months Philip Larkin, based as always in Hull, and Donald Davie, back in Europe from California, have been conducting a restrained slugging match concerning Larkin's fidelity to the *locus classicus* in modern times, as defined—or distorted, if you are of Professor Davie's persuasion—in *The Oxford Book of Twentieth-Century English Verse*. Important issues have been raised, and it will be some time before any keeper of the peace will be able to still them. The time is propitious for an assessment of Professor Davie's *Thomas Hardy and British Poetry*, which in a normal climate might be politely—and erroneously—half-praised as a well-bred squib, but for the duration of hostilities demands to be regarded as live, heavy-calibre ammunition.

Professor Davie is a poet of importance—of such importance, indeed, that his academic title can safely be set aside for the remainder of this article—and from poets of importance we want works of criticism that are less safe than strange. There is nothing safe about this volume, and a lot that is strange. *Thomas Hardy and British Poetry* is a surprisingly odd book, but it is also a considerable one. In fact, the forces ranged against each other in the current squabble can now be said to be more evenly matched than might at first appear.

A good part of the secret of what Larkin really thinks about art is distributed through the pages of *All What Jazz*, and if you want to take the weight of Larkin's aesthetic intelligence, it is to that collection (and not so much to his so-far uncollected criticisms of poetry in *Listen*, although they count) that you must go. On the Davie side, we are given, in this new book, a view of his thought which is at the very least as luminous as the one made available in *Ezra Pound: Poet as Sculptor*. When Davie talks about Hardy he sounds like Larkin talking about jazz. To put it

crudely, on their pet subjects they both talk turkey. But this doesn't mean
that either man makes himself plain. Larkin worships Bix Beiderbecke
and deplores Charlie Parker, believing that Parker destroyed with arid
intellectualism the art to which Beiderbecke contributed by lyrical
instinct. Conveying this distinction, Larkin apparently makes himself
clear; but it would be a suicidally foolish critic who thought that such a
distinction could be used unexamined as a light on Larkin's poetry. In
poetry, Larkin is Beiderbecke and Parker combined: his criticism chooses
sides among elements which are in balance within his complex creative
personality. Similarly with Davie: his critical position calls for an even
more cautious probing, since he is less aware of self-contradictions by the
exact measure that he is more receptive to Literary influence. *Thomas
Hardy and British Poetry* raises confusion to the level of criticism: it is a
testament to Britain's continuing fertility as an intellectual acreage in
which ideas will flourish at rigour's expense, the insights blooming like
orchids while the valid syllogisms wither on the vine.

Davie starts by proposing Hardy as a more important influence than
Yeats on the poetry of this century. The distinction between *is* and *ought*
is not firmly made, with the result that we spend a lot of our time wondering whether Hardy has been the big influence all along, or merely
should have been. "But for any poet who finds himself in the position of
choosing between the two masters," Davie says, "the choice cannot be
fudged; there is no room for compromise." The reason why there is no
room for compromise is not made as clear as the ordinary reader might
require. "Hardy," it is said, "has the effect of locking any poet whom he
influences into the world of historical contingency, a world of specific
places at specific times." Yeats, apparently, doesn't have this effect: he
transcends the linear unrolling of recorded time and attains, or attempts
to attain, the visionary. Davie says that the reader can delight in both
these approaches, but that the writer has to choose. It is difficult, at first,
to see why the writer can't employ the same combinative capacity as the
reader. Difficult at first, and just as difficult later.

The other important thing happening at the beginning of the book
concerns Larkin. Davie mentions Larkin's conversion from Yeats to
Hardy after *The North Ship* in 1946, thus tacitly proposing from the start
that Larkin was doing the kind of severe choosing which Davie asserts is
essential. Neither at this initial point, nor later on when Larkin is considered at length, is the possibility allowed that Yeats's influence might have
lingered on alongside, or even been compounded with, Hardy's influ-

ence. One realizes with unease that Davie has not only enjoyed the preface to the reissue of *The North Ship*, he has been utterly convinced by it:
instead of taking Larkin's autobiographical scraps as parables, he is treating them as the realities of intellectual development. Larkin conjures up
a young mind in which Hardy drives out Yeats, and Davie believes in it.

But Davie's main comments about Larkin are postponed until some
sturdy groundwork has been put in on Hardy. We are told that Hardy's
technique is really engineering, and that he is paying a formal tribute to
Victorian technology by echoing its precisioned virtuosity. A little later on
we find that Davie doesn't wholly approve of this virtuosity, and is pleased
when the unwavering succession of intricately formed, brilliantly
matched stanzas is allowed to break down—as in "The Voice," where, we
are assured, it breaks down under pressure of feeling.

A crucial general point about technique has bulkily arisen, but Davie
miraculously succeeds in failing to notice it. At one stage he is almost
leaning against it, when he says that Hardy was usually "highly skilled
indeed but disablingly modest," or even "very ambitious technically, and
unambitious every other way." For some reason it doesn't occur to Davie
that having made these admissions he is bound to qualify his definition
of technique in poetry. But not only does he not qualify it—he ups the
stakes. Contesting Yeats's insistence that Hardy lacked technical accomplishment, Davie says that "In sheer *accomplishment*, especially of
prosody, Hardy beats Yeats hands down" (his italics). Well, it's a poser.
Yeats's critical remark about Hardy doesn't matter much more than any
other of Yeats's critical remarks about anybody, but Davie's rebuttal of it
matters centrally to his own argument. He is very keen to set Yeats and
Hardy off against each other: an opposition which will come in handy
when he gets to Larkin. But keenness must have been bordering on fervour when he decided that Hardy had Yeats beaten technically in every
department except something called "craft"—which last attribute, one
can be forgiven for thinking, ought logically to take over immediately as
the main subject of the book.

Davie argues convincingly that we need to see below the intricate surface form of Hardy's poems to the organic forms beneath. But he is marvellously reluctant to take his mind off the technical aspects of the surface
form and get started on the problem of what technical aspects the organic
form might reasonably be said to have. "We must learn to look through
apparent symmetry to the real asymmetry beneath." We certainly must, and
with Hardy Davie has. But what Davie has not learnt to see is that with

Yeats the symmetry and asymmetry are the same thing—that there is no distance between the surface form and the organic form, the thing being both all art and all virtuosity at the same time. Why, we must wonder, is Davie so reluctant to see Yeats as the formal master beside whom Hardy is simply an unusually interesting craftsman? But really that is a rephrasing of the same question everybody has been asking for years: the one about what Davie actually means when he praises Ezra Pound as a prodigious technician. Is it written in the stars that Donald Davie, clever in so many other matters, will go to his grave being obtuse in this? Why can't he see that the large, argued Yeatsian strophe is a technical achievement thoroughly dwarfing not only Pound's imagism but also Hardy's tricky stanzas?

Davie is continually on the verge of finding Hardy deficient as a working artist, but circumvents the problem by calling him a marvellous workman whose work tended to come out wrong for other reasons. In "During Wind and Rain" he detects a "wonderfully fine ear," which turns out to be a better thing than "expertise in prosody"—the wonderfully fine ear being "a human skill" and not just a "technical virtuosity." It ought to follow that knowing how to get the ear working while keeping the virtuosity suppressed is of decisive importance to poetic technique. It ought to follow further that because Hardy couldn't do this—because he wasn't even aware there was a conflict—he spent a lot of his time being at odds with himself as a poet. What Davie is struggling to say is that Hardy wasn't enough of an artist to make the best of the art that was in him. But the quickness of the pen deceives the brain, and Davie manages to say everything but that.

The strictures Davie *does* put on Hardy are harsh but inscrutable. There is in Hardy a "crucial selling-short of the poetic vocation." In the last analysis, we learn, Hardy, unlike Pound and Pasternak (and here Yeats, Hopkins and Eliot also get a mention), doesn't give us a transformed reality—doesn't give us entry "into a world that is truer and more real than the world we know from statistics or scientific induction or common sense." This stricture is inscrutable for two main reasons. First, Hardy spent a lot of his time establishing a version of reality in which, for example, lovers could go on being spiritually joined together after death: nothing scientific about that. Second, even if he had not been at pains to establish such a version of reality—even if his themes had been resolutely mundane—his poetry, if successful, would have done it for him. In saying that Hardy's poetry doesn't transform statistical, scientific reality, Davie is saying that Hardy hasn't written poetry at all.

It should be obvious that Davie, while trying to praise Hardy as an artist, is actually diminishing him in that very department. Less obviously, he is also diminishing art. To look for a life-transforming theme, surely, is as self-defeating as to look for a life-enhancing one. Good poetry transforms and enhances life *whatever it says*. That is one of the reasons why we find it so special. In this case, as in so many others, one regrets the absence in English literary history of a thoroughly nihilistic poet. The Italians had Leopardi, who in hating existence could scarcely be said to have been kidding. Faced with his example, they were obliged at an early date to realize that there is poetry which can deny a purpose to life and yet still add to its point.

Larkin, Davie insists, follows Hardy and not Yeats. "Larkin has testified to that effect repeatedly," he announces, clinching the matter. Yeats's influence was "a youthful infatuation." The ground is well laid for a thoroughgoing misunderstanding of Larkin on every level, and after a few backhanded compliments ("The narrowness of range . . . might seem to suggest that he cannot hear the weight of significance that I want to put on him, as the central figure in English poetry over the past twenty years"— narrowness of range as compared with whom? With people who write worse?) Davie buckles down to the task.

Hardy, we have already learnt, was neutral about industrialism because his technique mirrored it: his skill as a constructor implicated him. With Larkin it is otherwise. Larkin can feel free to hate industrialism because he has no special sense of himself as a technician: "The stanzaic and metrical symmetries which he mostly aims at are achieved skilfully enough, but with none of that bristling expertise of Hardy which sets itself, and surmounts, intricate technical challenge."

By this stage of the book it is no longer surprising, just saddening, that Davie can't draw the appropriate inferences from his own choice of words. Being able to quell the bristle and find challenges other than the kind one sets oneself—isn't that the true skill? The awkward fact is that unless we talk about diction, and get down to the kind of elementary stylistic analysis which would show how Larkin borrowed Hardy's use of, say, hyphenated compounds, then it is pretty nearly impossible to trace Larkin's technical debt to Hardy. Not that Davie really tries. But apart from understandably not trying that, Davie clamorously doesn't try to find out about Larkin's technical debt to Yeats. And the inspiration for the big, matched stanzas of "The Whitsun Weddings" is not in Hardy's "intricacy" but in the rhetorical majesty of Yeats. In neglecting to deal with that inspiration, Davie limits his meaning of the word "technique" to something critically inapplicable. Technically, Larkin's heritage is a combination of Hardy and Yeats—it can't possibly be a substitution of the first by the second. The texture of Larkin's verse is all against any such notion.

Mistaking Larkin's way of working is a mere prelude to mistaking his manner of speaking, and some thunderous misreadings follow as a consequence. In Larkin, we are told, "there is to be no historical perspective, no measuring of present against past." Applied to the author of "An Arundel Tomb," this assertion reminds us of the old Stephen Potter ploy in which a reviewer selected the characteristic for which an author was most famous and then attacked him for not having enough of it.

According to Davie, Larkin is a Hardyesque poet mainly in the sense that he, too, "may have sold poetry short." With Larkin established as such a baleful influence, the problem becomes how to "break out of the greyly constricting world of Larkin." Davie enlists the poetry of Charles Tomlinson to help us do this, but it might have been more useful to linger awhile and ask if Larkin isn't already doing a good deal by himself to help us get clear of his dreary mire—by going on writing, that is, with the kind of intensity which lit up the gloom and made us notice him in the first place. Here again, and ruinously, Davie is dealing in every reality except the realities of art. He cannot or will not see that Larkin's grimness of spirit is not by itself the issue. The issue concerns the gratitude we feel for such a grimness of spirit producing such a beauty of utterance.

Near the end of the book, Davie draws a useful distinction between poets and prophets. The prophet is above being fair-minded: the poet is not. The poet helps to shape culture, with which the prophet is at war. Prophetic poetry is necessarily an inferior poetry.

To this last point one can think of exceptions, but generally all this is well said, and leaves the reader wondering why Davie did not then go back and find something centrally and vitally praiseworthy in the limitations of the Hardy tradition. Because it is the Hardy tradition which says that you can't be entirely confident of knowing everything that reality contains, let alone of transcending it. The Hardy tradition is one of a mortal scale. It does *not* hail the superhuman. As Larkin might put it, it isn't in the exaltation business. That is the real point which Davie has worriedly been half-making all along. In a striking way, *Thomas Hardy and British Poetry* is an eleventh-hour rejection of Davie's early gods. Somewhere in there among the dust and hubbub there is a roar of suction indicating that the air might soon be cleared.

IV. THE NORTH WINDOW

To stay, as Mr. Larkin stays, back late
Checking accessions in the Brynmor Jones
Library (the clapped date-stamp, punch-drunk, rattling,
The sea-green tinted windows turning slate,
The so-called Reading Room deserted) seems
A picnic at first blush. No Rolling Stones
Manqués or Pink Floyd simulacra battling
Their way to low-slung pass-marks head in hands:
Instead, unpeopled silence. Which demands

Reverence, and calls nightly like bad dreams
To make sure that that happens. Here he keeps
Elected frith, his thanedom undespited,
Ensconced against the mating-mandrill screams
Of this week's Students' Union Gang-Bang Sit-in,
As wet winds scour the Wolds. The Moon-cold deeps
Are cod-thronged for the trawlers now benighted,
Far North. The inland cousin to the sail-maker
Can still bestride the boundaries of the way-acre,

The barley-ground and furzle-field unwritten
Fee simple failed to guard from Marks and Spencer's
Stock depot some time back. (Ten years, was it?)
Gull, lapwing, redshank, oyster-catcher, bittern
(Yet further out: sheerwater, fulmar, gannet)
Police his mud-and-cloud-ashlared defences.
Intangible revetments! On deposit,
Chalk thick below prevents the Humber seeping
Upward to where he could be sitting sleeping,

So motionless he lowers. Screwed, the planet
Swivels towards its distant, death-dark pocket.
He opens out his notebook at a would-be
Poem, ashamed by now that he began it.
Grave-skinned with grief, such Hardy-hyphened diction,
Tight-crammed as pack ice, grates. What keys unlock it?
It's *all gone wrong*. Fame isn't as it should be—

No, nothing like. "The town's not been the same,"
He's heard slags whine, "since Mr. Larkin came."

Sir John arriving with those science-fiction
Broadcasting pricks and bitches didn't help.
And those Jap Ph.D.s, their questionnaires!
(Replying "Sod off, Slant-Eyes" led to friction.)
He conjures envied livings less like dying:
Sharp cat-house stomp and tart-toned, gate-mouthed yelp
Of Satchmo surge undulled, dispersing cares
Thought reconvenes. In that way She would kiss,
The Wanted One. But other lives than this—

Fantastic. Pages spread their blankness. Sighing,
He knuckles down to force-feed epithets.
Would Love have eased the joints of his iambs?
He can't guess, and by now it's no use trying.
A sweet ache spreads from cramp-gripped pen to limb:
The stanza next to last coheres and sets.
As rhyme and rhythm, tame tonight like lambs,
Entice him to the standard whirlwind finish,
The only cry no distances diminish

Comes hurtling soundless from Creation's rim
Earthward—the harsh *recitativo secco*
Of spaces between stars. He hears it sing,
That voice of utmost emptiness. To him.
Declaring he has always moved too late,
And hinting, its each long-lost blaze's echo
Lack-lustre as a Hell-bent angel's wing,
That what—as if he needed telling twice—
Comes next makes this lot look like Paradise.

"Wolves of Memory" from *Encounter*, June 1974

"Smaller and Clearer" from *New Statesman*, March 21, 1975

"Yeats *vs.* Hardy in Davie's Larkin" from *Times Literary Supplement*, July 13, 1973

"The North Window" from *Times Literary Supplement*, July 26, 1974

"Don Juan in Hull" later included in *At the Pillars of Hercules*, 1979

4. An Affair of Sanity

Required Writing by Philip Larkin

Every reviewer will say that *Required Writing* is required reading. To save the statement from blinding obviousness, it might be pointed out that whereas "required writing" is a bit of a pun—Larkin pretends that he wouldn't have written a word of critical prose if he hadn't been asked—there is nothing ambiguous about "required reading." No outside agency requires you to read this book. The book requires that all by itself. It's just too good to miss.

Required Writing tacitly makes the claim that it collects all of Larkin's fugitive prose, right down to the speeches he has delivered while wearing his Library Association tie. There is none of this that an admirer of his poems and novels would want to be without, and indeed at least one admirer could have stood a bit more of it. The short critical notices Larkin once wrote for the magazine *Listen* are, except for a single fragment, not here. As I remember them, they were characteristically jam-packed with judgements, observations and laconic wit.

If Larkin meant to avoid repetitiveness, he was being too modest: incapable of a stock response, he never quite repeats himself no matter how often he makes the same point. On the other hand there is at least one worrying presence. The inclusion, well warranted, of the prefaces to *Jill* and *The North Ship* can hardly mean that those books will be dropped from his list of achievements, but the inclusion of the long and marvellous introductory essay to *All What Jazz*, an essay that amounts to his most sustained attack on the modernist aesthetic, carries the depressing implication that the book itself, which never did much business, might be allowed to stay out of print. That would be a shame, because jazz is Larkin's first love and in the short notices collected in *All What Jazz* he gives his most unguarded and exultant endorsement of the kind of art he likes, along with his funniest and most irascible excoriation of the kind he doesn't.

Jazz is Larkin's first love and literature is his first duty. But even at the full stretch of his dignity he is still more likely to talk shop than to talk down, and anyway his conception of duty includes affection while going beyond it, so as well as an ample demonstration of his capacity to speak generally about writing, we are given, on every page of this collection, constant and heartening reminders that for this writer his fellow-writers, alive or dead, are human beings, not abstractions.

Human beings with all their quirks. Larkin proceeds as if he had heard of the biographical fallacy but decided to ignore it. "Poetry is an affair of sanity, of seeing things as they are." But he doesn't rule out the possibility that sanity can be hard won, from inner conflict. He has a way of bringing out the foibles of his fellow-artists while leaving their dignity at least intact and usually enhanced. To take his beloved Hardy as an example—and many other examples, from Francis Thompson to Wilfred Owen, would do as well—he convincingly traces the link between moral lassitude and poetic strength. This sympathetic knack must come from deep within Larkin's own nature, where diffidence and self-confidence reinforce each other: the personal diffidence of the stammerer whose childhood was agony, and the artistic self-confidence of the born poet who has always been able to feel his vocation as a living force.

The first principle of his critical attitude, which he applies to his own poetry even more rigorously than to anyone else's, is to trust nothing which does not spring from feeling. Auden, according to Larkin, killed his own poetry by going to America, where, having sacrificed the capacity to make art out of life, he tried to make art out of art instead.

It might be argued that if the Americanized Auden had written nothing else except "The Fall of Rome" then it would be enough to make this contention sound a trifle sweeping. It is still, however, an interesting contention, and all of a piece with Larkin's general beliefs about sticking close to home, which are only partly grounded in the old anguish of having to ask for a railway ticket by passing a note. He is not really as nervous about Abroad as all that: while forever warning us of the impossibility of mastering foreign languages, he has the right Latin and French tags ready when he needs them, and on his one and only trip to Germany, when he was picking up a prize, he favoured the locals with a suavely chosen quotation in their own tongue.

Lurking in double focus behind those thick specs is a star student who could have been scholarly over any range he chose. But what he chose was to narrow the field of vision: narrow it to deepen it. He isn't exactly telling us to Buy British, but there can be no doubt that he attaches little meaning to the idea of internationalism in the arts. All too vague, too unpindownable, too disrupting of the connections between literature and the life of the nation.

Betjeman was the young Larkin's idea of a modern poet because Betjeman, while thinking nothing of modern art, actually got in all the facts of modern life. Like all good critics Larkin quotes from a writer almost as creatively as the writer writes, and the way he quotes from *Summoned by Bells* traces Betjeman's power of evocation to its source, in memory. The Betjeman/Piper guidebooks, in which past and present were made contemporaneous through being observed by the same selectively loving eye, looked the way Larkin's poetry was later to sound—packed with clear images of a crumbling reality, a coherent framework in which England fell apart. An impulse to preserve which thrived on loss.

In *Required Writing* the Impulse to Preserve is mentioned often. Larkin the critic, like Larkin the librarian, is a keeper of English literature. Perhaps the librarian is obliged to accession more than a few modern books which the critic would be inclined to turf out, but here again duty has triumphed. As for loss, Larkin the loser is here too ("deprivation is for me what daffodils were for Wordsworth") but it becomes clearer all the time that he had the whole event won from the start.

Whether he spotted the daffodil-like properties of deprivation, and so arranged matters that he got more of it, is a complicated question, of the kind which his critical prose, however often it parades a strict simplicity, is equipped to tackle. Subtle, supple, craftily at ease, it is on a par with his poetry—which is just about as high as praise can go. *Required Writing* would be a treasure house even if every second page were printed upside down. Lacking the technology to accomplish this, the publishers have issued the book in paperback only, with no index, as if to prove that no matter how self-effacing its author might be, they can be even more so on his behalf.

Observer, November 25, 1983; later included in
Snakecharmers in Texas, 1988

P O S T S C R I P T

To track the closing stages of Larkin's career was among the delights of being a literary critic in the late twentieth century, but the pleasure was not unmixed. Larkin's poetry was, and will always remain, too self-explanatory to require much commentary. Puzzle poems like "Sympathy in White Major" were few, and on the whole his work made a point of declining in advance all offers of academic assistance. So in praising his accomplishment there was always a risk of drawing attention to the obvious. After I tentatively suggested in print that the source of illumination in the central panel of the "Livings" triptych might be a lighthouse, Craig Raine thrust his impatient face very close to mine and hairily hissed: "Of *course* it's a lighthouse!" And of course it was. It's all there in the poem, if you look hard enough: and no one else's poetry ever so invited you to look hard and look again.

There was edifying fun to be had, however, in pointing out how Larkin's incidental prose was of a piece with his verse. As a device for self-protection, Larkin was fond of proclaiming his loneliness, misery and bristling insularity, but his prose is there to prove his generous and unprejudiced response to the spontaneous joys of life. With T. S. Eliot, the essay on Marie Lloyd is a one-off: clearly he loved the music hall, but he never contemplated allowing the instinctive vigour of popular culture to climb far beyond the upper basement of his hierarchical aesthetic. Larkin never contemplated anything else. His poem about Sidney Bechet saluted the great saxophonist not just as a master, but as *his* master. For Larkin, pre-modern jazz was the measure of all things: he wanted his poetry to be as appreciable as that. His touchstone for the arts lay in what came to be called the Black Experience.

Helping to make this clear turned out to be useful work, because after his death the scolds moved in. They wanted to dismiss him as a racist, and might have carried the day if a body of sane opinion had not already been in existence. He was also execrated as a provincial, a misogynist and a pornophile. He was none of those things except by his own untrustworthy avowal, usually framed in the deliberately shocking language he deployed in his letters for the private entertainment of his unshockable friends. In his everyday behaviour he did the best a naturally diffident man can to be courteous, responsible and civilized at all times, and in his poetry he did even better than that. In no Larkin poem is there an insensitive remark that is not supplied with its necessary nuances by another poem. To believe Larkin really meant that "Books are a load of crap" you yourself have to believe that books are a load of crap. The arts pages are nowadays stiff with people who do believe that, even if they think they believe otherwise: all they really care about is the movies. There are people reviewing books, even reviewing poetry, who can read only with difficulty, and begrudge the effort. No writer, alive or dead, is any longer safe from the fumbling attentions of the semi-literate literatus.

But here again, the exponential proliferation of bad criticism can scarcely deprive the good critic of a role—quite the contrary. There has to be someone to save what ought to be obvious from the mud-slide of obfuscation, if only by asking such childishly elementary questions as: if you can't see that it took Larkin's personality to produce Larkin's poetry, what *can* you see? And if you can't accept Larkin's poetry as a self-sustaining literary achievement, what are you doing putting pen to paper?

Reliable Essays, 2001

5

POETRY'S IDEAL CRITIC:
RANDALL JARRELL

As a figure representing the Poet's Fate, Randall Jarrell bulks large in the necrology of the American heavies: the patchwork epics of both John Berryman and Robert Lowell are liberally embroidered with portentous musings on his death. Is this, one wonders, what Jarrell's name now mainly means? The thought is enough to chill the bones.

Luckily Jarrell's publishers are now doing what they can to dispel the graveyard mists. Whether his *Complete Poems* did much for his reputation is debatable: his poetry, though he would have hated to hear it said, was a bit light on those Blakean "minute particulars" he thought good poetry should have a lot of—there was a tendency to the prosaic which rigorous selection did something to disguise. He once said that even a good poet was a man who spent a lifetime standing in a storm and who could hope to be struck by lightning only half a dozen times at best. Disablingly true in his case. One would memorize a needle thrust like "The Death of the Ball Turret Gunner" and wonder why someone who could command that kind of penetration should spend so much time lapsing into a practised, resourceful, elegant but in the end faintly wearying expansiveness. He thought that writing came first and that the Age of Criticism—i.e., of writing about writing—was a bad dream from which we needed to pinch ourselves awake. A bitter truth then, that his writing was merely distinguished whereas his writing-about-writing was inspired. Jarrell is poetry's ideal critic, and the current reissue of *Poetry and the Age* couldn't be more welcome. If ever there was a necessary book, this is it.

A few more like it and there would still be a chance of saving the human-ities for humanity.

A Shaw rather than a Beerbohm, a Sickert rather than a Wyndham Lewis, Jarrell had one of those rare critical minds which are just as illu-minating in praise as in attack. We never feel, when reading him, that he is at his most concentrated when he is being most destructive. It is in the effort to draw our attention to merit that he achieves real intensity, and there are very few critics of whom that can be said. Yet there was nothing indulgent about his capacity for admiration. In his definitive essay on Frost, he grants—indeed rubs in—the poet's defects of personality with an epigrammatic disgust which would dominate the argument, were it not for his insistence that Frost's cracker-barrel Wisdom shouldn't distract us from the fact that being wise about life is nevertheless one of the things his poems do supremely well. Jarrel can see clearly that the best of Frost is the best critic of the worst, and that the Critical Task (a locution which would never have crossed his lips) is to demonstrate how good that best is—the best which we tend to reduce to the level of the unremarkable by being so knowing about the worst. Jarrell was against knowingness, and possessed the antidote: knowledge. His wide knowledge of literature impresses you at every turn. He alludes without effort, compares without strain, and makes being simple seem easy.

John Crowe Ransom and Walt Whitman are as well served as Frost. Speaking for myself, Jarrell's remarks helped give me the courage of my secret convictions about Ransom (I had thought it would be intellectual sui-cide to admit that his luxuriant diction struck me as a kind of strength); they were also instrumental in dismantling a self-designed, home-constructed apparatus of formalistic priggery that had kept me from Whitman for ten years. Better introductions to such a brace of obfuscation-ridden poets could-n't be imagined. Opening his Whitman essay, for example, Jarrell typically outlines the kind of misunderstanding he thinks needs to be eradicated:

> But something odd has happened to the living, changing part of Whit-man's reputation: nowadays it is people who are not particularly inter-ested in poetry, people who say that they read a poem for what it says, not for how it says it, who admire Whitman most. Whitman is often written about, either approvingly or disapprovingly, as if he were the Thomas Wolfe of 19th-century democracy . . .

True when it was said, and true now. That Whitman was read by people who couldn't read seemed to me to be sufficient reason for refraining from reading much of him myself. Jarrell, though, had the confidence and independence to insist that to defend your taste by such a refusal is simply to connive at philistinism and encourage the view that Whitman was an ordinary rhetorician. On the contrary, he was an extraordinary one, whose worst language was not just awful, but unusually awful ("really *ingeniously* bad"), and whose finest flights were poetry about which there could be no argument. ("If the reader thinks that all this is like Thomas Wolfe he *is* Thomas Wolfe; nothing else could explain it.") Quoting the passage from "I understand the large hearts of heroes" down to "I am the man, I suffered, I was there," Jarrell says that Whitman has reached a point at which criticism seems not only unnecessary but absurd, since the lines are so good that even admiration feels like insolence. Jarrell's use of quotations approaches the mark Walter Benjamin set for himself, of writing a critical essay consisting of nothing but. The catch—that the quality of the quotation is self-demonstrating only to the reader who doesn't need telling—was one Jarrell recognized and was worried by. Luckily he didn't let it stop him.

The essay on Wallace Stevens is as important as the others already mentioned. Written as a review of *The Auroras of Autumn*, it measures the aridity of Stevens's later work by evoking the exfoliating fruitfulness of the earlier, and gets the whole of the poet's career into proportion without even a hint of cutting him down to size. But the strictures are gripping when they come. Of *The Auroras of Autumn* Jarrell says that one sees in it

> the distinction, intelligence, and easy virtuosity of a master—but it would take more than these to bring to life so abstract, so monotonous, so overwhelmingly *characteristic* a book.

Italics his, and transfixingly placed.

With Jarrell, the urge to share a discovered excellence leads to a mastery of critical language which can only be called creative. The forms of Marianne Moore's poems, he writes,

> have the lacy, mathematical extravagance of snowflakes, seem as arbitrary as the prohibitions in fairy tales; but they work as those work—disregard them and everything goes to pieces.

Not satisfied with that, he goes on:

> Her forms, tricks and all, are like the aria of the Queen of the Night: the intricate and artificial elaboration not only does not conflict with the emotion bat is its vehicle.

If his experience had not been so rich, he could not have been so right: it takes range to achieve such a fine focus.

Scattered throughout this book are minor moments of the trouble which in a later collection of essays, A Sad Heart at the Supermarket, coalesced into a persistent anxiety. The foe of academic crassness and critical arrogance, Jarrell was obliged to rely on the good sense of those who read books for love. He knew they were in a minority but was too much of an American fully to accept the fact that this had something to do with inequality: he seemed to think that if you could just speak plainly enough you would break through. There is a distressing moment in A Sad Heart at the Supermarket when he tries to tell his popular-magazine audience that the word "intellectual" is not one to be frightened of since a mechanic or carpenter is just as much an intellectual about practical things as a poet is about literature. He chose not to notice that the two states of mind are not interchangeable, and probably never began to realize that his own critical writings, among the most readily intelligible of the century, depend for a good part of their clarity on a scope of cultural reference so broad that only the educated can take it in. Too much of a democrat to take pride in his own uniqueness, Jarrell hungered for an egalitarian society with uniformly high standards. Wishful thinking, but of a noble kind. Those sensitive to literature can be taught literature, but sensitivity to literature cannot be taught—a point which should be borne in mind by anyone who runs away with the idea that setting Poetry and the Age as a first-year text would humanize our university English schools overnight. It wouldn't, but it's a measure of Jarrell's gifts that even the most level-headed reader suddenly finds himself suspecting that it could.

New Statesman, October 26, 1973;
previously included in At the Pillars of Hercules, 1979

POSTSCRIPT

Not knowing much about him apart from his work, I wrote about an ideal Jarrell. Later on I found out that his reputation among his American contemporaries was as a vituperative reviewer of their poetry. He was repaid for this habit by attracting vituperative reviews in his turn, retaliatory hatchet-jobs which led him first to an attempted suicide and then to a successful one: if that, indeed, was what his death was. The last point is still in dispute. But there should be no dispute about his cogent force as a critic. If it had been less, his fellow poets would have cared less when he carped: they could have dismissed him, with some justification, as a would-be poet envious of his rivals, and a shameless aspirant for academic preferment.

My colleague the late Ian Hamilton had a large knowledge of American literary politics. In London, as the most admired editor of his day, he was necessarily engaged in literary politics himself, but they were of a different kind, concerned entirely with poetry and never with its attendant prestige. He regarded the American poetic world as a living museum of egomaniacs trying to write their own descriptive tickets, and he built up hilarious anecdotal dossiers on all of them. There was a clear-cut cultural difference, which Hamilton was the first to analyse. In Britain, even the most important poets, and only when they felt like it, wrote poems one at a time. Later rather than sooner they would be collected into a book, for which there would be no prize more valuable than a week's supply of cigarettes. In America, the poetic heavies were always "working on a book of poems," usually with the benefit of a large support system—a sojourn at the expense of the Corporation of Yaddo, for example—and almost invariably with the intention of winning a National Book Award at the very least. For the securing of the awards, the poet's hunger for self-promotion and the upmarket media taste for the alpha celebrity went hand in hand: they were made for each other. There were always exceptions, and the exceptions were among the best: to my mind—if not to Hamilton's, which harboured little affection for formal bravura—Richard Wilbur and Anthony Hecht have been enhanced in their achievement by their ability to stay out of the loop, a reticence that was implicit in their care for craft. But you heard less and less about Wilbur, and never enough about Hecht. They didn't make enough noise. America was a different planet, inhabited by larger, if lumbering, beings.

The fruits of Hamilton's interplanetary observation can be read in his posthumous volume *Against Oblivion*, from which Jarrell emerges as an unsettling example of ambition on the rampage. I have no doubt that Hamilton's portrait of the real man was an accurate one, but equally don't doubt that my portrait of the ideal man is finally more true. The weakness of Jarrell's poetry is that he could never disappear into it. The strength of his criticism is that he could. We can't return to the state of naivety in which all we knew of him was what he wrote. But the critic's job is to get back to that first response despite subsequent knowledge. When Jarrell wrote about other poets, with his eye on their achievement rather than on his own ambition, he was a touchstone. Admittedly he found that easier to do if they were dead. If they were still alive, he sometimes sounded as if he was trying to kill them. Harsh reviews are written in Britain and Australia too, but usually in the belief that nobody will suffer irreparable damage. In America, and especially in Jarrell's generation, that belief did not hold; and the thought that Jarrell took a razor to his wrist because of what somebody said about him in a newspaper was powerful evidence that some of the energy of the American post-war literary world came from the childishness of its practitioners. Deadly serious about being thought successful as artists, they forgot that a better guarantee of seriousness would have been to pursue their art even if they were thought to have failed. The risk run by the adepts of a spiritual activity in a materialist society became threateningly clear: when all the measures are set internally, peer-group pressure can be fatal. Lowell, Berryman, Delmore Schwartz, Sylvia Plath: to any of them, nothing mattered more than the ticker tape that carried the stock market quotation of their status. A ten-point drop could send them to the window sill: for the artist concerned with his own share price, it is always 1929. High on the short list of good things that can be said about the Beat poets is that they sought out an audience and let it decide. The mandarins would have fared better if they had done the same. As things happened, the best and the brightest had too much respect for one another's opinion. Jarrell was merely among the most prominent. He should have cared less about what the others said. They all should have.

2003

6

TWO ESSAYS ON
THEODORE ROETHKE

I. On His *Collected Poems*

When Theodore Roethke died five years ago his obituaries, very sympa-
thetically written, tended to reveal by implication that the men who
wrote them had doubts about the purity and weight of his achievement
in poetry. Now that his collected poems have come out, the reviews, on
this side of the water at least, strike the attentive reader as the same obituaries rewritten. Roethke was one of those men for whom poetic significance is claimed not only on the level of creativity but also on the level
of being: if it is objected that the poems do not seem very individual, the
objection can be headed off by saying that the man was a poet apart from
his poems, embodying all the problems of writing poetry "in our time." It
is a shaky way to argue, and praise degenerates quickly to a kind of complicity when what is being praised is really only a man's ability to hold up
against the pressures of his career. Criticism is not about careers.

   From the small amount of information which has been let out publicly, and the large amount which circulates privately, it seems probable
that Roethke had a difficult life, the difficulties being mainly of a psychic
kind that intellectuals find it easy to identify with and perhaps understand
too quickly. Roethke earned his bread by teaching in colleges and was
rarely without a job in one. It is true that combining the creative and the
academic lives sets up pressures, but really these pressures have been
exaggerated, to the point where one would think that teaching a course
in freshman English was as perilous to the creative faculties as sucking up
to titled nobodies, running errands for Roman governors, cutting purses,
grinding lenses, or getting shot at. If Roethke was in mental trouble, this

should be either brought out into the open and diagnosed as well as it can be or else abandoned as a point: it is impermissible to murmur vaguely about the problems of being a poet in our time. Being a poet has always been a problem. If the point is kept up, the uninformed, unprejudiced reader will begin to wonder if perhaps Roethke lacked steel. The widening scope and increasing hospitality of academic life in this century, particularly in the United States, has lured many people into creativity who really have small business with it, since they need too much recognition and too many meals. Plainly Roethke was several cuts above this, but the words now being written in his praise are doing much to reduce him to it.

This collection is an important document in showing that originality is not a requirement in good poetry—merely a description of it. All the longer poems in the volume and most of the short ones are ruined by Roethke's inability to disguise his influences. In the few short poems where he succeeded in shutting them out, he achieved a firm, though blurred, originality of utterance: the real Roethke collection, when it appears, will be a ruthlessly chosen and quite slim volume some two hundred pages shorter than the one we now have, but it will stand a good chance of lasting, since its voice will be unique. In this respect, history is very kind: the poet may write only a few good poems in a thousand negligible ones, but those few poems, if they are picked out and properly stored, will be remembered as characteristic. The essential scholarly task with Roethke is to make this selection and defend it. It will need to be done by a first-rate man capable of seeing that the real Roethke wrote very seldom.

Of his first book, *Open House* (1941), a few poems which are not too much reminiscent of Frost will perhaps last. Poems like "Lull" (marked "November, 1939") have little chance.

> Intricate phobias grow
> From each malignant wish
> To spoil collective life

It is not assimilating tradition to so take over the rhythms of poetry recently written by another man, especially a man as famous as Auden. It is not even constructive plagiarism, just helpless mimicry. To a greater or lesser degree, from one model to the next, Auden, Dylan Thomas, Yeats and Eliot, Roethke displayed throughout his creative life a desperate unsureness of his own gift. In his second book, *The Lost Son*, published in 1948, the influence of Eliot, an influence which dogged him to the end, shows its first signs with savage clarity.

> Where's the eye?
> The eye's in the sty.
> The ear's not here
> Beneath the hair.

There are no eyes here, in this valley of dying stars. In his five-part poem *The Shape of the Fire* he shows that he has been reading *Four Quartets*, giving the game away by his trick—again characteristic—of reproducing his subject poet's most marked syntactical effects.

> To see cyclamen veins become clearer in early sunlight,
> And mist lifting out of the brown cat-tails;
> To stare into the after-light, the glitter left on the lake's surface,
> When the sun has fallen behind a wooded island;
> To follow the drops sliding from a lifted oar,
> Held up, while the rower breathes, and the small boat drifts quietly
>   shoreward;

The content of this passage shows the pinpoint specificity of the references to nature which are everywhere in Roethke's poetry. But in nearly all cases it amounts to nature for the sake of nature: the general context meant to give all this detail spiritual force usually has an air of being thought up, and is too often just borrowed. In the volume *Praise to the End!*, which came out in 1951, a certain curly-haired Welsh voice rings loud and clear. It is easy to smile at this, but it should be remembered that a poet who can lapse into such mimicry is in the very worst kind of trouble.

> Once I fished from the banks, leaf-light and happy:
> On the rocks south of quiet, in the close regions of kissing,
> I romped, lithe as a child, down the summery streets of my veins.

In the next volume, *The Waking* (1953), his drive towards introspective significance—and a drive towards is not necessarily the same thing as possessing—tempts him into borrowing those effects of Eliot's which would be close to self-parody if it were not for the solidly intricate structuring of their context.

> I have listened close
> For the thin sound in the windy chimney,
> The fall of the last ash
> From the dying ember.

There it stands, like a stolen car hastily resprayed and dangerously retaining its original number-plates. His fascination with Yeats begins in this volume—

> Though everything's astonishment at last,

—and it, too, continues to the end. But whereas with Yeats his borrowings were mainly confined to syntactical sequences, with Eliot he took the disastrous step of appropriating major symbolism, symbolism which Eliot had himself appropriated from other centuries, other languages and other cultures. The results are distressingly weak, assertively unconvincing, and would serve just by themselves to demonstrate that a talent which has not learnt how to forget is bound to fragment.

> I remember a stone breaking the edifying current,
> Neither white nor red, in the dead middle way,
> Where impulse no longer dictates, nor the darkening shadow,
> A vulnerable place,
> Surrounded by sand, broken shells, the wreckage of water.

Roethke's good poems are mostly love poems, and of those, most are to be found in the two volumes of 1958 and 1964, *Words for the Wind* and *The Far Field*. Some of his children's poems from *I Am! Says the Lamb* are also included, and there is a section of previously uncollected poems at the very end of the book including a healthy thunderbolt of loathing aimed at critics. Roethke achieved recognition late but when it came the critics treated him pretty well. Now that his troubled life is over, it is essential that critics who care for what is good in his work should condemn the rest before the whole lot disappears under an avalanche of kindly meant, but effectively cruel, interpretative scholarship.

2. On His *Selected Letters*

Ralph J. Mills, Jr., has done a good, solid, scholarly job of selecting and editing Roethke's letters. He has picked the ones that "illustrate particularly his career as a poet": not a bad brief for an editor to give himself at this stage. When a biography appears we should get the rest of the picture, including a straight account of Roethke's psychic upsets—an account which would be welcome, after all these years of innuendo, if it were not that having it available will almost certainly complete the work of elevating Roethke to emblematic status as a casualty of the age.

If this sounds rough, perhaps it is best to get the gloves off early. I don't like much of Roethke's poetry, and the little of it I do like I don't like intensely. I like this book of letters scarcely at all. A biography that spills all the beans could well tip the balance towards active loathing. Very little of such a negative tropism would be solely Roethke's fault—when we react against a reputation, it is rarely the fault of the reputed—but likewise very little of it would be unfounded. It would be a justifiable contempt directed against a reputation in which the man has got mixed up with the work. For at the centre of Roethke's reputation is the idea that the man has an artistic status away from his poems; that the weaknesses of the poems are to be attributed to the psychic damage inflicted on him as a consequence of practising his art in a hostile society; that these weaknesses, having such symbolic value, are perhaps strengths. Even if Roethke's poetry itself were very strong there would be good reasons for attacking such a line of thought, because really it is not a line of thought at all: it is a chain of error.

As it is, Roethke's poetry is quite weak even at its best—though I do not mean to say that it didn't cost him great effort, and perhaps his sanity, and perhaps even his life. But what you have here in this amalgam of Roethke the poet and Roethke the Sick Man is an art-surrogate: what is under consideration, indeed adulation, is a Career.

It is evident from these letters that Roethke himself was prone to think in careerist terms, but that much is an accident: it's probable that Mailer and Lowell and other important Americans do too, and go much further in regarding themselves as children of their time, victims of a culture and that kind of thing. The case would not be altered if Roethke had had no such idea in his head. What matters is the critical view taken. And it should be obvious by now that the general critical view of Roethke has not a great deal to do with poetry, and everything to do with his efforts (heroic efforts, considering what he went through: but heroism is a term of accentuation, not necessarily of approval) to get established as a poet, to Make It.

Roethke proved, like the visitor to Brigadoon who wished the village into existence on a day it was not scheduled to appear, that if you want something deeply enough anything is possible. What he wanted to be was a great artist, and by the end of his career there were one or two really great artists (certainly Auden) willing to concede that Roethke was of their company. But just as often as they are right in such judgements, real artists are wrong. Like anybody else, they tend to admire sincerity, dedication, industry, openness, intellectual generosity, a sense of fun—and like anybody else they have trouble, once they know him, in getting the man who possesses these attributes separated from his work. Which is as far as I want to pontificate along this particular line, except to say that it seems probable that in Roethke's case the general critical view has followed the lead of his fellow poets, who simply liked him, just as much as it has followed the lead of industrious scholarship, which finds his work such a luxuriant paradise of exfoliating symbols. In both cases what is now needed is some healthy scepticism, even at the cost of seeming harsh. The sceptical mind cannot long be totally impressed by opinions current within the freemasonry of poets: such opinions are often things of comfort. Still less can it be impressed by the academic discovery and canonization of a perfectly representative modernist: here a sharp nose ought to smell pastiche.

A straight read through Roethke's *Collected Poems* should convince even the moderately informed reader that Roethke's incipient individuality as a voice was successively broken down by a series of strong influences—from the close of the 1930s these were, roughly in order: Auden, Eliot, Dylan Thomas, Yeats and Eliot again. Estimations of Roethke's poetry which do not confront this problem can't really be of much use, since the question of originality, if it arises at all, can never be peripheral: originality is more than a requirement in good poetry, it is a description of it. Most critics dealing with Roethke are ready to admit the question but seem to believe that his tendencies towards pastiche were momentary weaknesses, instantly corrected when a true subject came up. The more perceptive among them might go on to admit that even Roethke's most admired poems, the ones felt to be uniquely his, are stained at the edges with the tinctures of other men's gifts. Very few, however, would admit that Roethke is *saturated* with these tinctures—that a "major" Roethke poem like *The Shape of the Fire*, for example, is soaked right through with the cadences, and therefore with the sensibility, of *Four Quartets*. From *Open House* (1941) through to *The Waking* (1953) it is almost as though he responded to each new challenge as it came up—or rather that he shadow-boxed in the style of each new champion. In *Open House* it was Auden. In *The Lost Son* it was Eliot. In *Praise to the End!* it was Dylan Thomas. In *The Waking* it was Yeats (arriving late) and Eliot (who had never been away). In the last two volumes, *Words for the Wind* and *The Far Field*, though the influences of Yeats and Eliot never wholly died, he hit a nice line of regret and wrote his best love poems. But all in all it's a sad story, and one that Mr. Mills (perhaps unintentionally) makes clearer by including a few unpublished poems along with the letters. One of these, "Suburban Lament," enclosed with a letter to Stanley Kunitz in June 1940, tells you all you need to know about how hard Roethke was hit by Auden.

> Even the simple and insentient are unhappy:
> Horn-honkers find their neighbours unresponsive;
> Mechanical sheep stop bleating at the curbstone:
> Hands yank the shade before an unlighted window;
> A child bursts into tears before the hard-kneed stranger,
> The pure in heart cherish obscene ambition . . .
>
> Not enough feet have passed in this country,
> Stones are still stones, and the eye keeps nothing,
> The usurious pay in full with the coin of the gentle,
> Follies return on the heads of innocent children,
> The evil and silly remain too long in tenure,
> And the young, mimetic, fall into the old confusion.

And the not-so-young, too: when he wrote this Roethke was thirty-two years old, which is a bit late to get knocked sideways by another voice. A year later (the editor says "probably") he enclosed another sub-Auden effort in a letter to Dorothy Gordon.

> Though the geography of despair had no limits,
> To each was allotted some corner of comfort

Where, secure as a seed, he could sit out confusion.
But this is another regime: the preposterous bailiff
Beats on the door with his impossible summons
And the mad mayor holds nightly sessions of error.

In 1939 he had written to Louise Bogan: "Oh, why am I not smart like Auden?" Too much of his first volume, *Open House*, revealed his success in getting smart *exactly* like Auden. In being able to add these unpublished poems to the Auden-influenced poems in *Open House*, what we have is not an improved case—the case must be made on the evidence of the published volume alone—but a broadened field of study in which to observe something strange and rather terrible going on: something more intimately bound in with Roethke's neuroses, I suspect, than has yet been realized. Admiration, emulation and, always, aspiration, as the perpetual *doppelgänger* tries to catch up with the *zeitgeist*. A career conceived of as staying level with the leaders.

Evidently the Dylan Thomas influence was in the wind as early as 1947, although it shows to full effect only in the volume *Praise to the End!* which came out in 1951. Writing to John Sargent, his editor at Doubleday, Roethke made a few suggestions about how to flog a batch of poems to *Harper's Bazaar*.

As you say, these people are very name-conscious. If Aswell [of *Harper's Bazaar*. C.J.] got the idea that Auden, Bogan, Burke, Martha Graham, W. C. Williams, Shapiro, etc., think these are fresh and exciting, she would jump at the scheme, I think. Auden, for instance, liked this last one best; read it over four or five times, kept saying "This is extremely good," etc. The last part,—the euphoric section,—made him think of Traherne, as I remember: no "influence" but the same kind of heightened tone, I think he meant. I mention this because Aswell is currently on a Dylan Thomas jag: sees that Welshman in everything. If she trots out his name, give her the admirable Bogan's dictum. Said that eminent poet and critic: "You do what Thomas thinks he does."

This letter is crucial in several ways. First of all it shows that Roethke was aware, and wary, that an accusation of Thomas-influence might be made. Second it shows that Roethke was beginning to develop defence mechanisms; in this case the *common ancestor*, the pre-modern poet who

perhaps influenced both him and the man he could be accused of copying. A month later he was writing to John Crowe Ransom: "But I am
nobody's Dylan: I never went to school to him. If there's an ancestor, it's
Traherne (the prose)."

By 1948 the Thomas-Traherne connection is firmly installed as a
mental tic, and he writes to Babette Deutsch:

> An eminent lady poet said, "You do what Thomas thinks he does." The
> remark seems unnecessary: I do what I do; Thomas does what he does.
> My real ancestors, such as they are, are the bible, Mother Goose, and
> Traherne.

Unnecessary as it may have been to the field of critical judgement,
Bogan's remark was obviously vitally necessary to Roethke's estimation of
himself. In the letters at least there is no further sign of the common
ancestor until 1959, when a letter from Mr. Mills proposing a book on
Roethke incidentally triggers off the whole notion again. Mr. Mills regret-
tably does not include his own letter but says in a footnote that he had
mentioned to Roethke that "certain parts of 'Meditations of an Old Woman' seemed to contain parodies of Eliot; however, I did not mean to be
understood as thinking the individual poems or the group of them constituted mere parodies." Mr. Mills's footnote reads with the beautiful sincerity of a collector writing to van Meegeren and mentioning that certain
sections of the Vermeer seem to be reacting strangely to X-rays, but let
that pass. What counts is Roethke's reply.

> (I'm oversimplifying: what I want to say is that *early*, when it really mat-
> ters, I read, and really read, Emerson (prose mostly), Thoreau, Whitman,
> Blake, and Wordsworth; Vaughan and real slugs of dramatic literature—
> Jacobeans, Congreve, & W.S., of course.) My point is this: I came to
> some of Eliot's and Yeats's ancestors long before I came to them; in fact,
> for a long time, I rejected both of them. . . . So what in the looser line
> may seem in the first old lady poem to be close to Eliot may actually be
> out of Whitman, who influenced Eliot *plenty*, technically (See S. Mus-
> grove, T. S. Eliot and Walt Whitman, U. of New Zealand Press—again
> not the whole truth, but a sensible book.)—and Eliot, as far as I know,
> has never acknowledged this—oh no, he's always chi-chi as hell: only
> Dante, the French, the Jacobeans, etc. My point: for all his great gifts,

particularly of the ear, Eliot is not honest, in final terms, even about purely technical matters. It's here I guess your point about the *parody* element comes in—though I hate to call such beautiful (to my mind) poems mere parodies.

To get this interchange between novice and guru down to ground level, all we have to do is look at "Meditations of an Old Woman" (*Words for the Wind*, 1958). Here are some sample fragments, easily flaked off:

> All journeys, I think, are the same:
> The movement is forward, after a few wavers . . .

> As when silt drifts and sifts down through muddy pond-water
> Settling in small beads around weeds and sunken branches,
> And one crab, tentative, hunches himself before moving along the
>   bottom,
> Grotesque, awkward, his extended eyes looking at nothing in
>   particular . . .

> There are no pursuing forms, faces on walls:
> Only the motes of dust in the immaculate hallways,
> The darkness of falling hair, the warnings from lint and spiders,
> The vines graying to a fine powder . . .

Roethke's subject matter is nominally different from Eliot's, but the forms are the same, with the result that he is using somebody else's poetry to write with. It's in this sense that Roethke is a representative modernist—he can write in all the modern styles that matter, at the price of writing very little that matters. To be a fan of Roethke's it is necessary to have read nothing else. In the same letter to Mr. Mills Roethke goes on to say:

> I can take this god damned high style of W.B.Y. or this Whitmanesque meditative thing of T.S.E. and use it for other ends, use it as well or better. Sure, a tough assignment. But while Yeats' historical lyrics seem beyond me at the moment, I'm damned if I haven't outdone him in the more personal or love lyric. Why Snodgrass is a damned earless ass when he sees Yeats in those love-poems. . . . Teckla Bianchini, one of W. H. Auden's closest friends and a woman of unimpeachable verity, told me

on the beach at Ischia that Wystan had said that at one point he was worried that I was getting too close to Yeats, but now he no longer did
because I had outdone him, surpassed him, gone beyond him. Well, let's
say *this* is too much, in its way . . .

Somewhere between the "god damned high style" and "the Whit-
manesque meditative thing" most of Roethke's later poetry got lost.

Roethke's difficult life was full of worries about his tenure at each
and every one of his many universities, forcing him to seek and circulate
testimonials to his teaching abilities: there are enough of these in the
book to convince anyone that he must have been a remarkable teacher.
Against this must be put his applications (which Mr. Mills unwisely
includes) for Guggenheims, Fulbrights, and sojourns under the wing of
the Corporation of Yaddo. They make destructive reading. Roethke
waited a long time to be accepted as a poet, and when he had been could
never accept that it had happened: he was always waiting for the final
reassurance—a common trait in people who are uncertain of their work.
No amount of Pulitzers, or even Nobels, can satisfy a need like that. In a
way the critics who see him as a casualty of the age are right—it's only the
context that they've got wrong. He was a casualty of the American age of
the Career in the Arts, an age which has even managed to industrialize
the traditional rhetoric of the practising artist and so decorate in eternal
terms what is really a vulgar struggle for preferment.

Times Literary Supplement, 1970

POSTSCRIPT

Put together, these two pieces look now like a single dance on a lonely
grave. Certainly the vocabulary was too harsh: "condemn," "contempt,"
"loathing" are strong words springing from a weak conception of the critical task, which is not that of a vigilante—the Leavisite *odium theolog-
icum* must have got into me even when I had publicly dedicated myself
to keeping it out. But there was still good reason to question Roethke's
reputation: it had been brought into existence by his ambition, and criticism soon dies if the artistic will is taken for the deed, whereupon the art
dies too. It was care for poetry, I like to think, that made me so careless
about a poet's feelings—and just because he was dead was of course no

good reason for speaking as if he couldn't hear. If I would be more tactful now, it might be because the passion is gone. There is also the possibility that although I wanted my own poetry to go a different way, it depended on a parodic element, so I didn't want to allow an unconscious use of what I proposed to use consciously. Critics who write poetry themselves, on however diffident a scale, always shape their criticism to personal poetic ends as well as universal critical ones, though they do better with the second thing if they acknowledge the first. There is at least one glaring falsity of tone: "It will need to be done by a first-rate man" can only mean "I would do it myself but I haven't got the time," so it was not a judicious thing to say. But on the whole I would say all this the same way now. If poetry and the criticism of it had agreed standards there would be less bitchery. As things are and will probably always be, the whole field is as inherently contentious as ice-dancing: the judges can never be popular, especially when they invade the rink.

The Metropolitan Critic, 1992

7

CHARLES JOHNSTON'S
CATACOMB GRAFFITI

Poems and Journeys by Charles Johnston
Eugene Onegin by Aleksandr Pushkin,
translated by Charles Johnston

Appearing unannounced in 1977, Charles Johnston's verse rendering of *Eugene Onegin* established itself immediately as the best English translation of Pushkin's great poem there had yet been. It was an impressive performance even to those who could not read the original. To those who could, it was simply astonishing, not least from the technical angle: Johnston had cast his *Onegin* in the *Onegin* stanza, a form almost impossibly difficult in English, and had got away with it. Only an accomplished poet could think of trying such a feat. Yet as a poet Charles Johnston was scarcely known. Indeed, his profile was not all that high even as Sir Charles Johnston, career diplomat and quondam High Commissioner for Australia. All the signs pointed to gentlemanly dilettantism—all, that is, except the plain fact that anyone who can convey even a fraction of Pushkin's inventive vitality must have a profoundly schooled talent on his own account.

Now a small volume of Johnston's own creations, called *Poems and Journeys*, has quietly materialized, in the unheralded manner which is obviously characteristic of its author. It seems that most of the poems it contains previously appeared in one or other of two even smaller volumes, *Towards Mozambique* (1947) and *Estuary in Scotland* (1974), the second of which was printed privately and the first of which, though published by the Cresset Press, certainly created no lasting impression in the literary world. The poems were written at various times between the late 1930s and now. There are not very many of them. Nor does the Bodley Head seem to be acting in any more forthcoming capacity than that of jobbing printer. "Published for Charles Johnston by the Bodley Head" sounds only one degree less bashful than issuing a pamphlet under your own imprint. But this time Johnston will not find it so easy to be ignored. *Poems and Journeys* is unmistakably an important book. Leafing through it, you are struck by its assured displays of formal discipline, but really, from the translator of *Onegin*, that is not so surprising. Hard on the heels of this first impression, however, comes the further realization that through the austerely demanding formal attributes of Johnston's verse a rich interior life is being expressed. Johnston's literary personality is not just old-fashioned: it is determinedly old-fashioned. He has set up the standards of the clubbable English gentry as a bulwark against encroaching chaos. Even those of us whose sympathies are all in the other direction will find it hard not to be swayed by his laconic evocation of the secret garden. It doesn't do, we are led to assume, to go on about one's predicament. Yet somehow a stiff upper lip makes eloquence all the more arresting.

Johnston's diplomatic duties took him to Japan before the war. After Pearl Harbor he was interned for eight months. After being released in an exchange of diplomatic agents, he was sent to the Middle East. After the war there were various other appointments before he took up his post in Australia. Clearly the accent has always been on uncomplaining service. Nor do the poems in any way question the idea of dutiful sacrifice: on the contrary, they underline it. Trying to identify that strangely identifiable voice, you finally recognize it as the voice of someone who has not talked before, but who has been so amply described that you think you know him. Johnston is the sort of man who has been written about under so many names that when he writes something himself he sounds like a legend come to life. He is the faithful servant of Empire, who now emerges, unexpected but entirely familiar, as its last poet.

By an act of imagination, without dramatizing himself, Johnston has made poetry out of his own background. The same background has produced poetry before but most of it has been bad, mainly because of an ineluctable cosiness. Johnston, however, is blessed with a distancing wit. He has the intensity of gift which makes facts emblematic without having to change them. It is the classical vision, which he seems to have possessed from the start, as the first two lines of an early poem about Japan clearly show:

Over the rockbed, over the waterfall,
Tense as a brushstroke tumbles the cataract.

The visual element is so striking it is bound to seem preponderant, but there is more at work here than just an unusual capacity to see. To choose a Greek classical measure, alcaics, is an inspired response to the inherent discipline of a Japanese landscape subject: the native poets and painters have already tamed their panorama to the point that their decorum has become part of it, so to match their formality with an equivalent procedure from the poet's own cultural stock is an imaginative coup. Then there is the subtle control of sonic effects, with the word "tense" creating stillness and the word "tumbles" releasing it into motion. He sees something; he finds the appropriate form; and then he exploits technical opportunities to elaborate his perception. The classic artist identifies himself.

But everything he was saying was said from under a plumed hat. The Lake Chuzéji of his early poems was the playground of the foreign diplomats. They raced their boats on it, giving way to each other in such elaborate order of precedence that only a *chef de protocole* knew how to steer a perfect race. They committed genteel adultery around its edges. A man of Johnston's mentality, no matter how well he fitted in by breeding, must sometimes have doubted the validity of his role. He was, after all, a double agent, both loyal functionary and universal observer. But he had not yet conceived of his complicated position as his one true subject—hence a tendency, in these early efforts, towards a Georgian crepuscularity, which even affects his otherwise scrupulously alert diction. Locutions like "when day is gone" crop up with their tone unqualified: something which would not happen again once his manner was fully developed.

Internment helped develop it. The work commemorating this experience is called "Towards Mozambique" and is one of the three original long poems in the book. Datelined "Tokyo 1942–London 1946," it should now be seen, I think, as one of the outstanding poems of the war, even though it is less concerned with fighting than with just sitting around waiting. Exiles traditionally eat bitter bread, but the narrator is more concerned to reflect than to rail against fate. The poem has something of Ovid's sadness in the *Epistulae ex ponto*, except that Johnston is not being sorry just for himself. He is bent on understanding misunderstanding—the tragedy of incomprehension which has brought Japan to war against the West.

The personal element of the tragedy comes not just from the feeling of his own life being wasted (and anyway, much of the poem seems to have been written after the internment was over) but from regret for the years that were wasted before, when diplomacy was being pursued to no effect. He reflects on what led up to this. A lot did, so he chooses a form which leaves room to lay out an argument—the Spenserian stanza whose clinching alexandrine both Byron and Shelley, in their different ways, found so seductive:

> Wakening, I watched a bundle tightly packed
> That scaled with clockwork jerks a nearby staff.
> Hoist to the top, I saw it twitched and racked
> And shrugged and swigged, until the twists of chaff
> That held it to the halyard broke, and half
> Released the packet, then a sharper tease
> Tore something loose, and with its smacking laugh
> The Jack was thrashing furiously down breeze,
> Mocking the feeble stops that lately cramped its ease.

Ripping, what? (The ambiguity in the third line, incidentally, is less a grammatical error than a mark of class. Osbert Lancaster and Anthony Powell have both always let their participles dangle with abandon, and Evelyn Waugh, in the same chapter of his autobiography which tells us that only those who have studied Latin can write English, perpetrates at least one sentence whose past participle is so firmly attached to the wrong subject that there is no prising it loose. This habit has something to do, I suspect, with a confusion between the English past participle and the Latin ablative absolute.) But some of the young diplomats were not content to shelter behind Britannia's skirts. Greatly daring, they took what opportunities they could to mingle with the locals—to penetrate, as it were, the membranes of inscrutable reserve:

> Climbing with shoeless feet the polished stairs,
> Gay were the evenings in that house I'd known.
> The mats are swept, the cushions that are chairs

Surround the table like a lacquer throne.
The geisha have been booked by telephone,
The whisky brought, the raw fish on the ice,
The green tea boiled, the saké in its stone
Warmed to a turn, and seaweed, root and spice
Await their last repose, the tub of nutcrisp rice.

The scene is set, and soon a wall will slide,
And in will run, professional as hell,
Our geisha team, brisk as a soccer side,
We'll ask the ones we like, if all goes well,
To luncheon at a suitable hotel . . .

Everything in the diplomatic colony is ordered, decorous and unreal. The unreality becomes most apparent during periods of leave in Shanghai, where a phoney aristocrat rules society:

"Le tennis, ce jeu tellement middle-class,"
Drawls the duchesse, whose European start,
Whose Deauville background manages to pass
For all that's feudal in this distant part.
The locals thought she couldn't be more smart,
And prized admission to her little fêtes,
And searched through Gotha with a beating heart,
But vainly, for the names of her estates,
And for the strange device emblazoned on her plates.

But only in the enforced idleness of internment is there time to see all this in perspective. Long months of contemplation yield no grand might-have-beens or if-onlys. Nor, on the other hand, do they bring nihilistic resignation. Britain's imperial role is not repudiated. Neither is its inevitable passing particularly regretted. Instead, there is redemption in the moment:

Time passed. A tramcar screaming in the dark
Of total blackout down the Kudan hill
Strikes, out of wire, spark on cascading spark,

Lights from below the cherry swags that spill,
In all the thickness of the rich April,
Their pink festoons of flower above the street,
Creamy as paint new-slapped. I looked my fill,
Amazed to find our world was so complete.
Such moments, in the nick, are strange and sharply sweet.

A stanza MacNeice would have been proud to have written. Even in these few examples you can see how Johnston is beginning to realize the lexical freedom that strict forms offer. Up to the point where restriction cramps style, the more demanding the stanza, the greater the range of tone it can contain. Slang phrases like "professional as hell" and "in the nick" sound all the more colloquial for being pieced into a tight scheme.

The second long poem in the book, "Elegy," is written in memory of Johnston's brother Duncan, "killed leading a Royal Marine Commando raid on the Burma Coast, on the night of February 22nd 1945." This, too, ranks high among poems of the war. On its own it would be enough to class Johnston with Henry Reed, Bernard Spencer, F. T. Prince and Norman Cameron. It is a high-quality example of what can· by now be seen to be a particular school of Virgilian plangency, the poetry of the broken-hearted fields. But it is probably not one of Johnston's best things.

It loses nothing by its air of doomed gentility. The narrator could be Guy Crouchback talking: there was a seductive glamour about the squires going off to war, and a potent sorrow when they did not come home. But though Johnston can be impersonal about himself, he cannot be that way about his brother. The poem tries to find outlets for grief in several different formal schemes, including blank verse. The stiff upper lip relaxes, leaving eloquence unchastened. There is no gush, but there is too much vague suggestion towards feeling, made all the more unsatisfactory by your sense that the feeling aimed at is real, harsh and unblunted even by time. A first-hand experience has aroused a second-hand artistic response. The air is of an Owenesque regret, of the dark barge passing unto Avalon in agony, of a drawing-down of blinds. The few details given of the lost, shared childhood leave you wanting more, but the author is caught between his forte and an ambition foreign to it: he is a poet of controlled emotion who can give way to anguish only at the cost of sapping his own energy:

> Only through the hard
> Shaft-face of self-esteem parsimonious tears
> Are oozing, sour distillate from the core
> Of iron shame, the shame of private failure
> Shown up by the completeness of the dead.
> I wrote in the fierce hope of bursting loose
> From this regime, cracking its discipline . . .
> I wrote, but my intense assertion found
> No substance and no echo, and all I did
> Was raise an empty monument to grief.

"Elegy" is something better than an empty monument, but it is tentative beside its predecessor "Towards Mozambique," and scarcely begins to suggest the abundant assurance of its successor, the third long poem in the book, "In Praise of Gusto." This contains some of Johnston's best work and instantly takes its place as one of the most variously impressive long poems since Auden and MacNeice were at their peak. It is not as long as either "Letter to Lord Byron" or *Autumn Journal* but it has much of their verve and genial bravura. It embodies the quality to which it is dedicated.

"In Praise of Gusto" returns to some of the same subject matter dealt with in earlier works, but this time it is all brought fully within the purview of what can now be seen to be his natural tone, a tone which taps its power from the vivacity of experience. His dead brother is again mentioned. This time all the emphasis is on the life they enjoyed together when young. Nevertheless the effect of loss is more striking than it is in "Elegy," where death is the direct subject. One concludes, aided by hindsight, that Johnston loses nothing, and gains everything, by giving his high spirits free rein. It might have taken him a long time completely to realize the best way of being at ease with his gift, but with consciously formal artists that is often the case. The last thing they learn to do is relax.

The poem is written in two different measures, the *Onegin* stanza and the stanza which Johnston insists on referring to as *Childe Harold*, although really Spenser has the prior title. Johnston's mastery of the latter form was already proven. But by this time he could read fluent Russian and had obviously become fascinated with the breakneck measure in which *Eugene Onegin* unfolds its story. The *Onegin* stanzas of "In Praise of Gusto" give every indication that their author will one day be Pushkin's ideal translator. As well as that, they serve the author's present purpose. The *Onegin* stanza is a born entertainer. As Johnston points out in his Author's Note, "it has an inner momentum, a sort of infectious vitality of its own." It packs itself tight and then springs loose like a self-loading jack-in-the-box. Comic timing is crucial to it:

> Beauties who manage the conjunction
> Of glamour and fireside repose
> Pack what I call without compunction
> The deadliest of knockout blows.
> Japan bewitched me. Half forgotten
> Were home and faith. The really rotten
> Part of it all, which, when it came
> Back later, made me sweat with shame,
> Was that our worlds were fast dividing
> And that my fondness must ignore
> The headlong chute direct to war
> Down which Japan was quickly gliding
> With all its ravishingly queer
> Compound of sensual and austere.

The rapacious hostesses of pre-war Shanghai and wartime Alexandria now find their perfectly appropriate rhythmic setting. One of the many things that attracted Johnston to his Russian exemplar must have been the way Pushkin gives full value to the glamour of imperial court life without romanticizing its meretriciousness. Nobody who admires both will ever tire of counting the ways in which Pushkin and Mozart are like each other. Each could see all the world as it was yet neither could reshape it in any way except by making masterpieces. Even their own disasters lifted their hearts. (Pushkin said that trials and tribulations were included in his family budget.) Everything that happened belonged. Johnston has something of the same defiant exuberance:

> How Egypt's hostesses detested
> The victories in our campaign:
> "Assez de progrès," they protested,
> "Vous étiez bien à Alamein";
> And then they'd stress in full italics

The point of being close to Alex,
The races and the gay weekends
Of bathing parties with one's friends.
They saw no merit in advancing
Far from the nightclub and the beach
Out beyond invitation's reach
To worlds remote from cards and dancing
With absolutely not a face
They'd ever seen in the whole place.

But the *Onegin* stanza enforces epigrammatic terseness. As a countervailing force, Johnston employs the Spenserian stanza to luxuriate in his visual memories. Without sinning against cogency, they amply exploit this traditionally expansive form's magically self-renewing supply of pentameter—a copiousness of rhetorical space which is symbolized, as well as sealed, by the long sweep of the alexandrine at the end:

Mersa Matruh. A fathom down, the sun
Lights on the faintest ripple of the sand
And, underseas, decyphers one by one
The cursive words imprinted on the strand
In the Mediterranean's fluent hand;
For eastern waters have the graceful trick,
By way of compliment from sea to land,
Of signing their imprint, with curl and flick
Of the vernacular, in floweriest Arabic.

An extended metaphysical conceit has been matched up to a rigorous physical form: two kinds of intellectual strictness, yet the effect is of a single, uncalculated sensory celebration.

The essence of classical composition is that no department of it gets out of hand. After aberrations in artistic history the classic principle reasserts itself as a balancing of forces. In "In Praise of Gusto" Johnston uses his Spenserian stanzas to specify his remembered visions, but he uses them also to unfold an argument. The same contrast and balance of perception and rhetoric was demonstrated by Shelley—a romantic with irrepressible classic tendencies—when he used the same stanza in "Adonais." Shelley obtains some of his most gravid poetic effects by deploying what sounds like, at first hearing, a prose argument. The same applies, *mutatis mutandis*, to Johnston, when he remembers what the Western Desert looked like after the battles:

> Such scenes have potency, a strange effect,
> Contagion with an undefined disease.
> They throw a chill on all whom they infect,
> Touch them with sadness, set them ill at ease.
> The sense that friends now dead, or overseas,
> Fought here and suffered, hoped here and despaired,
> Transports us outside time and its degrees.
> Here is a new antique, already paired
> With the most classic sites that scholar's trowel has bared.

The poem begins in the *Onegin* stanza, takes a long excursion in the Spenserian and returns to the *Onegin*. Though tipping its plumed hat to a younger version of the author—a satirical youth who "shot down other people's fun"—it conveys a wholehearted acceptance of the good life, which apparently includes plenty of foie gras, champagne and personally slain partridges. If Dr. Leavis were still with us it would be hard to imagine him appreciating any of this, especially when he noted the book's dedication to Sacheverell Sitwell, familiarly addressed as Sachie. Yet the spine of the poem's argument is that prepared pleasures, though it is churlish to eschew them, are not what inspires gusto, which is

> Immediately sustained delight,
> Short-lived, unhoped for, yet conclusive,
> A sovereign power in its own right.
> It lends itself to recognition
> More aptly than to definition . . .

The reason it can't easily be defined is that it is something more all-pervading even than a view of life. It is a way of being alive. Those gifted with it, if they have artistic gifts as well, can tell the rest of us what it is like. Reviewing his own life in search of its traces, Johnston now becomes one of those who have done so. The poem ends in a clear-eyed exultation.

The fourth long poem in the book is a translation of "Onegin's Journey" which was originally designed to go between the present chapters 7 and 8 of *Eugene Onegin*. Pushkin eventually decided to leave it out, but it remains a logical subject for the translator of *Eugene Onegin* to tackle. He makes the accomplished job of it that you would expect, revelling in the inspiration engendered by the physical obstacles of the tetrameter and the rhyme that continually looms too soon. They help contain his prolific knack—so appropriate in a translator of Pushkin—for sonic effects.

Throughout his work Johnston is to be found exploiting prosodic conventions (such as eliding "the" into the initial vowel of the next word) for all they are worth. Sometimes he overcooks it, so that you have to read a line twice to pick out the rhythm. Sometimes the conversational stress and the metrical stress separate to the point where the reader must strain to put them back in touch with each other. Usually, though, Johnston maintains the old rules only in order to increase the number of ways he can speak freely. All those ways are on view in his rendition of "Onegin's Journey." But anyone wanting to acquaint himself with Pushkin would be advised to turn in the first instance to the *Eugene Onegin* translation itself, which Penguin has now brought out.

The appearance of this great translation in a popular format is made even more significant by the fact that it carries a twenty-page introduction specially written by John Bayley. The author of the most distinguished book on Pushkin in any language, Bayley here gives the essence of his thoughts on Pushkin in general and *Eugene Onegin* in particular. Bayley's book has always been the best full-length introduction to Pushkin, but until now Edmund Wilson's essay in *The Triple Thinkers* (backed up by two further pieces in *A Window on Russia*) has been the best short one. Now Bayley has captured the second title as well as the first. I recommend this essay without hesitation as the first thing to read on Pushkin.

As for the translation itself, it is what it was hailed as when it came out, and what it will go on being for the foreseeable future. Johnston knows better than I do what it lacks of the original. When, in chapter 8, he makes Tatyana tell Onegin, "Today it's turn and turn about," he is well aware that there is an element of artificiality. In the original, Tatyana says just, "Today it is my turn," and it is one of the mightiest lines in all poetry. There is endless artifice in Pushkin but no artificiality. Yet by patient craft Johnston has kept to a minimum those necessarily frequent occasions when the painfully demanding form of the stanza forces an awkward phrase. Much more often he hits off the correct blend of intricate contrivance and easily colloquial expression. He catches the spirit of the thing, and a large part of the spirit of the thing is the *formal* spirit of the thing.

To a remarkable extent, Johnston possesses, not just the same sort of temperament as his model, but the same sort of talent. We had no right to expect that any English poet who combined these attributes would make translating Pushkin the object of his life. But as *Poems and Journeys* shows, Johnston has done a few things of his own. He has recently finished a translation of Lermontov's *The Demon.* There are other Russian poems one can think of that he would be ideally fitted to give us, among them the last and most intensely organized of Pushkin's tetrametric creations, *The Bronze Horseman.* But on the strength of this volume it might also be wished that Johnston would go on to compose a long original work which would go even further than "In Praise of Gusto" towards transforming the age he has lived through into art.

One of the things art does is to civilize the recent past. In *Poems and Journeys* there are poems, both long and short, which add significantly to the small stock of works that have helped make sense of the British Empire's passing and of Britain's part in the Second World War. Johnston's voice might have been more often heard in this respect, but he chose perfection of the life rather than of the work. As Auden noted, some artists have everything required for high distinction except the desire to come forward.

If Johnston had come forward earlier and more assertively, there can be no doubt that he would have received a hearing. In some of his short pieces he makes fun of the "Trend Police" and describes the poems turned out by himself and his fellow gifted amateurs as "catacomb graffiti." In fact, the Trend Police would not have stood much chance of shouting down work done to this standard. The *locus classicus* is in no more danger of being obscured than the privileged orders are in danger of losing their privileges, although Johnston would have you think, in his more predictable moments, that the contrary was true in each case.

The best reason for Johnston to think of himself as a part-time poet was that as a full-time diplomat he was well placed to write the kind of poetry which is necessarily always in short supply—the poetry of the man who spends most of his day being fully professional at something else, the poetry for which the young Johnston so admired Marvell.

Yours to restore the wasted field
And in distress to health
To serve the Commonwealth;

Yet with a wider-sweeping eye
To range above the land, and spy
The virtue and defect
Of empires, to detect

In vanquished causes, and in kings
Dethroned, the tragedy of things,
And know what joys reside
Where the Bermudas ride.

In recent times we have grown used to the externally formless epic —
Berryman's *Dream Songs*, Lowell's *History* — and striven to convince ourselves that it possesses an internal form which makes up for its lack of
shape. But this pious belief has become harder and harder to sustain. The
virtues of the informal epic are prose virtues, not poetic ones. Only discipline can give rise to the full freedom of mature art. Charles Johnston has
given us a better idea than we had any right to hope for of what Pushkin's
epic sounds like. But his long poems suggest that he has it in him to
write an epic of his own. Even if he does not, his small but weighty output of original work, now that we have at last come to know it, enriches
the poetic legacy of his generation and helps clarify that nebulous, nearby
area of literary history where uninspired innovation creates its permanent
disturbance.

London Review of Books, 1980; later included in
From the Land of Shadows, 1982

POSTSCRIPT

To meet, Sir Charles Johnston was something out of the past, and the past
wasn't even mine. He was an empire builder, and I came out of the
empire he built. Somebody like him probably stepped ashore in Botany
Bay with Captain Cook and explained to the Aboriginal reception committee, in a very clear voice, that he could recommend a good tailor.
Upon his retirement from the diplomatic service he set about publishing,

in small volumes under his own imprint, all the poetry he had written, and writing a lot more. But he never overproduced. Every poem was the finished product, four-square and deeply polished, like a rosewood military chest neatly packed with an administrator's kit. The total effect was formal, confidently traditional, expensively turned out and unapologetically direct, and as such was duly ignored by most of the regular reviewers. But one of his little books was dedicated to his translation of *Eugene Onegin*. Much occupied with Pushkin at the time, I was able to recognize the Johnston version as a success, and am still proud of having been among the first to say so. Having tried to write in the Onegin stanza myself, I was in a position to salute Johnston's astonishingly high level of sustained technical accomplishment, and having used the original as one of my textbooks for learning Russian, I knew Pushkin's meaning well enough to spot that his translator had worked the miracle of transferring it almost intact. So it was not entirely out of naivety that I hailed Johnston's translation without reserve. Making it clear that unstinting praise was the kind he liked—he was direct in that way too—he invited me round to his flat. We were four for lunch. Johnston's wife, a Russian princess descended by not too many generations from one of the military heroes in *War and Peace*, had had a stroke by that stage which rendered her silent, but she was a keen observer. She observed me as if she had last seen someone like me on the wrong side of a barricade. The Johnstons made a majestic couple: an appropriate adjective, because their other guest, and therefore my opposite number across the tiny table, was the Queen Mother.

Conversation, except of course from the princess, was free and often funny, but there was no denying that the scene harked back to a vanished era. I wouldn't have been surprised if the lady in the hat had picked up a bottle of champagne by the neck, walked out on to the balcony and launched a battleship. I wouldn't even have wondered how the battleship had got there. I was too busy wondering how I had got there. It was an eloquent demonstration of what art can do to join worlds. Johnston's world was on its way out, my world was on its way in, and my suspicion of his must have been nothing beside his of mine. But classically ordered verse provided a common ground. Perhaps because of the phenomenon that Freud calls *Doppelgängerscheu*, our personal acquaintance didn't develop much beyond that date. Like any writer, of whatever background, he was concerned with himself above all things, and I soon felt bound to make it clear to him how in that respect, if in no other, he had met his match. In the daunting energy of his Indian summer he went on turning out his little volumes, and forthrightly indicated his belief that a further instalment of publicity from my pen would not come amiss. (He wasn't rude, he just had no notion of how the literary world is supposed to work, lacking as he did even the slightest connection with it.) Cravenly I never found the words to convey that I thought this might be a bad plan. I just made myself scarce. But his work stayed with me as an extreme example of what I have always held—presumably by instinct, considering that the contrary evidence begins with Shakespeare—to be a truth about poetry: that it can release its full force only within a framework. Frameworks don't come more framed or fully worked than they do in the verse of Charles Johnston. At first reading, his meticulous carpentry looks like his main concern. But then you notice, singing inside it, phrases that would never have been there otherwise. Build the cage well enough and it will fill itself with rare birds. It takes a rare bird to do it, but he was certainly one of those.

Reliable Essays, 2001

8

NABOKOV'S GRAND FOLLY

Eugene Onegin: A Novel in Verse by Aleksandr Pushkin,
translated with a commentary by Vladimir Nabokov

*Nabokov Translated: A Comparison of Nabokov's Russian and
English Prose* by Jane Grayson

In the week of his death, it is instructive to remember that Nabokov's translation of *Eugene Onegin* was a project dear to his heart. Expert opinions of the recent second edition were not much more favourable than they were for the first, mainly because the translator had not done enough to eliminate what were earlier judged to be eccentricities of diction, while the commentary obstinately remained unmodified in all its idiosyncrasies. There is undoubtedly a sense in which the whole enterprise is a great folly. But even those Russianists who have been most inclined to question Nabokov's success in transmitting the essence of Pushkin are usually willing to concede that this cranky monument of scholarship might at least come in useful to the beginner.

As it happens, I am in a position to test this idea, being very much a beginner with Pushkin, and therefore in dire need of a good crib. Pushkin is never wilfully complicated, but his simplicities can be highly compressed. There are times when even an advanced student of the language is certain to need help, while the stumbler is likely to bog down completely. I should say at the outset that in several respects Nabokov's Folly serves the turn. It is a work to be valued, although even the tyro is bound to find it silly as well as brilliant.

The ideal crib, of course, should merely be the servant of the original. But Nabokov was incapable of being anybody's servant, even his admired Pushkin's: in paying homage to his giant predecessor he did his best to keep his own ego in the background, but ever and anon it shouldered its way forward. Nabokov's theory of translation was based on "humble fidelity" to the original, yet try as he might to give us nothing more pretentious than a word-for-word equivalent, he still managed to make Pushkin sound like Nabokov.

Nor is the commentary free from quirks. In fact it is largely made up of them. He has set out to be more scholarly than the scholars; it is doubtful whether anybody else inside or outside Russia knows as much about Pushkin; but you don't have to know a thousandth as much to realize that Nabokov is no more *reasonable* on this subject than on any other. I switch to the present tense because it would be unfitting to talk about the author of so cantankerous a commentary as if he were not alive—he is at you all the time, continually asserting himself against those hordes of translators and academics who have either misunderstood Pushkin or, worse, understood him too quickly. But there are limits to how far insight can go without common sense to back it up.

Following Gautier, Nabokov thought the ideal translation should be an interlinear lexicon. The theory is ably expounded by Jane Grayson in her painstaking *Nabokov Translated*, a book which has the additional merit of showing that in the case of his own writings the master is tactfully flexible about putting it into practice. But where *Eugene Onegin* is concerned there can apparently be no departure from dogma. Throughout the commentary, Nabokov is forever telling you the words he *might* have used in the translation if he had set out to do anything so misguided as convey the spirit of the original. But no, he has resisted against overwhelming odds: awkwardness is not only not to be avoided, it is positively to be sought, if that happens to be the price of exactitude.

There is something in this view, although not as much as Nabokov thinks. It is true that a translator who sets out to render the "spirit" is likely to traduce the original author. But Nabokov's paroxysms of accuracy traduce Pushkin's spirit as thoroughly as any academic poetaster has ever done. He makes Pushkin sound like a Scrabble buff. Certainly there are words in Pushkin that don't now mean what they once did, and even words that would have seemed odd at the time. Hence the modern foreign reader's need for more help than an ordinary dictionary can provide. But none of this means that Pushkin wants to be puzzling. On the contrary, what impresses you about him is his unforced naturalness of tone. The sad thing about Nabokov's translation is that he is not really capable of echoing such a quality. Instead, he dithers pedantically in the very area of verbal sophistication which for Pushkin was never more than a playground.

It is well known that Nabokov keeps saying "mollitude" where either "bliss" or "languor" would have done. Sometimes you can make a better case for "bliss" than for "languor" and sometimes vice versa, but what nobody normal can doubt is that there is no case to be made for "mollitude." Yet after all the uproar which greeted his use of "mollitude" in the first edition, here it still is in the second, having the effect, every time it appears, of wrinkling the reader's brow. The idea behind using "mollitude" is evidently to convey something of the Russian word's Frenchified feeling. But "mollitude" does nothing to make the English reader think of French influence. It just makes him think about the weight of the OED.

At least he can find "morgue" in the *Concise*, defined in roughly the same way Nabokov uses it, to mean "arrogance." But arrogance is scarcely the first thing an English reader thinks of when he sees the word "morgue." He thinks of dead bodies on zinc tables. Why not just use "arrogance"? The answer, I'm afraid, is that Nabokov wants to indulge himself in the Euphuism of "I marvelled at their modeish morgue." (In the introduction we learn of Onegin and Lensky that "both are blasé, bizarre beaux." Always the virtuoso of his adopted tongue, Nabokov never quite grasped that half the trick of composing in English is *not* to write alliteratively.)

Why use "trinkleter" where "haberdasher" would have done? Why "larmoyant" for "lachrymose"? What does "debile" give you that "feeble" doesn't? Why "cornuto" for "cuckold"? Certainly the Russian word has horns which the Italian word reproduces. Unfortunately the Italian word is not in English. Nor is Nabokov correct in supposing that there is any word in *Inferno* III, 9, which might mean "forever." He quibbles so relentlessly himself that you would have to be a saint not to quibble back.

On this showing, Nabokov has no call to despise those less informed translators who have had the temerity to cast their versions in rhyme. His unrhyming version sounds at least as weird as the very worst of theirs. But as a crib it is the best available, especially in this second edition, where each line matches a line in the original — even, in many cases, to the extent of reproducing the word order. Worse than useless for the reader without Russian, for the learner Nabokov's translation would be just the ticket, if only the commentary were better balanced. But Nabokov's ambitions as a scholar are thwarted by his creativity. He starts shaping the facts before he has fully submitted himself to them. He is immensely knowing, but knowingness is not the same as knowledge.

Expending too much of his energy on being bitchy about other writers, scholars and critics, Nabokov the commentator sounds at best like. A. E. Housman waspishly editing an obscure classic. At worst he sounds like A. L. Rowse trying to carry a daft point by sheer lung-power. Calling Dostoevsky "a much over-rated, sentimental and Gothic novelist" is dull if it is meant to be funny and funny if it is meant to be serious. We are told that Balzac and Sainte-Beuve are "popular but essentially mediocre writers." I can't pretend to know much about Balzac, but I am reasonably familiar with Sainte-Beuve, and if he is mediocre then I am a monkey's uncle. Madame de Staël is thoroughly patronized ("a poor observer") without any mention being made of the fact that Pushkin himself thought highly of her. As for Tchaikovsky's version of *Eugene Onegin*, it is not a "silly opera." It is a great opera.

But most of this is casual snidery. Distortions of Pushkin's meaning are less forgivable. Commenting on the exchange of dialogue between Tatyana and her nurse, Nabokov, forgetting even to mention *Romeo and Juliet*, concentrates on discrediting the official Soviet view of the nurse as a Woman of the People. Yet that view is part of the truth. When the nurse talks about being given in marriage without regard to her own wishes, she is illuminating the condition of slavery. Tatyana might not be really listening to her, but Pushkin is listening, and so should the reader be. This acute social awareness runs right through Pushkin, building up all the time, until in the later prose he provides the model for the social consciousness of all the Russian literature to come. There is nothing naive about taking cognizance of this elementary fact. Nabokov is naive in trying to avoid it. Pushkin really *is* the Russian national poet, even if the Soviet regime says so. Above all, he is the national poet of all the people who have been persecuted by that regime in the name of an ideal of justice which Pushkin's very existence proves was once generous and merciful.

Nabokov seems determined to miss the point of what is going on even among the main characters. He tells us all about the books Tatyana has read but fails to notice her gifts of psychological penetration. He can't seem to accept that Tatyana ends by slamming the door in Onegin's face. He claims to detect in Tatyana's final speech "a confession of love that must have made Eugene's experienced heart leap with joy." Incredibly, the moral force of Tatyana's personality seems to have escaped him. Nor can he see that Onegin is arid and Lensky fruitful; that the difference between them is the same difference Pushkin saw between Salieri and

Mozart; and that the outcome is the same—envy and revenge. Presuming to avoid sentimentality, Nabokov's homage diminishes its object, limiting the reader's view of the range of emotion which Pushkin embraced. Pushkin's artistic personality was the opposite of Nabokov's. Pushkin had negative capability. Not that Pushkin can be equated with Keats, even if you think of Keats's sensibility combined with Byron's airy manner. *Eugene Onegin*'s stature is Shakespearean: you have to imagine a Shakespeare play written with the formal compactness of a poem.

On technique Nabokov gives us what we had a right to expect from the man who invented John Shade. (If only Shade, instead of Charles Kinbote, had written this translation!) There is a long disquisition on prosody which is ruined by pseudoscience. (The spondee is proved mathematically not to exist.) But when Nabokov calls Pushkin's tetrameter "an acoustical paradise," and takes time to examine the miracle of simple words producing great sonorities, he is writing criticism of the first order. He is also good on trees, houses, carriages, visitors' books, methods of travel, manners—although even here he can't resist going over the top. He finds himself saying that Pushkin was not especially sympathetic with the Russian landscape. There is a certain pathos about that, as if Nabokov were trying to insert himself into the physical reality of the old, lost Russia that will never now return. A doomed attempt and a superfluous one, since by pointing to the source of its literary tradition Nabokov has helped remind us of the Russia that really *is* undying, and in which his place is now secure.

New Statesman, 1977; later included in
From the Land of Shadows, 1982

POSTSCRIPT

Edmund Wilson was no fool, but his magisterial self-confidence could make him do foolish things, and one of the most foolish was to lay himself open to Nabokov's genius for aggressive pedantry by suggesting that Nabokov might have lost his grip on the Russian language. Wilson was merely a gifted amateur student of languages. Nabokov was a Russian, and thus well qualified to make Wilson's pontifications on the subject look ridiculous. In the subsequent outburst of hilarity, it was forgotten that Wilson had generously helped Nabokov to secure his position in the

United States. It was also forgotten that Nabokov himself was capable of the misplaced self-confidence of the autodidactic crank. For an appreciation of the resources Nabokov could bring to his prose when writing fiction, there is nothing better than Martin Amis's introduction to the Everyman reissue of *Lolita*. But I still think Kingsley Amis had a point when he took a passage of that novel apart and detected as much self-admiration as evocation. Nabokov would have to be rated as a writer of sublime talent if he had composed nothing else except *Speak, Memory*. But there is such a thing as getting so close to language that you can no longer keep your distance from what you are writing about with it, and that awkward propensity really shows up in Nabokov's version of *Eugene Onegin*.

I was careful, when reviewing it, not to claim too much knowledge of the original and thus fall into the same trap in which Wilson's corpse already lay impaled, with plenty of bamboo stakes left unoccupied for further victims. But I wouldn't have needed a word of Russian—except perhaps *nyet*—to know that something weird was going on. Nabokov had scrupulously registered the minor meanings from moment to moment but the grand meaning (or moral: there is no other word for it) he had either missed or misinterpreted. Why he should have done so remains a puzzle, but the clue might lie somewhere in the absurdity of his remarks about Tchaikovsky's opera. Among Russians familiar with both opera and poem, there are not many who would say that either makes the other trivial: in the light of historical events, they would rather count their blessings, and leave the two masterpieces in fruitful, complementary contention. Nabokov admitted that he had a tin ear for music, so why did he not disqualify himself in this instance? The answer might be elementary: he couldn't bear the competition. If he thought an area was his, he would turn his full firepower on anyone else who strayed into it. He was solipsistically proprietorial about Russia, the novel and art itself. Perhaps forced exile encourages that condition. But we can't expect every great artist to have a great soul. If more of them were like Verdi, we could read artists' biographies for uplift; but we would be so repelled by Wagner that we would forget to listen, or by Picasso that we would forget to look.

Reliable Essays, 2001

9

STEVIE SMITH: NOT DROWNING
BUT WAVING

Stevie: A Biography of Stevie Smith by Jack Barbera
and William McBrien

Some would say that Stevie Smith was as daft as a brush. Others would say that she was pretty much of a bitch. Calling her mad was always the best way to get out of admitting that she could be cruel, just as calling her naive was always the best way to get out of admitting that her poetry made almost everybody else's sound overwrought. It was an effect she intended, and was not above occasionally crowing about.

> Many of the English,
> The intelligent English,
> Of the Arts, the Professions
>   and the Upper Middle Classes,
> Are under-cover men,
> But what is under the cover
> (That was original)
> Died . . .

Few people except the Queen, who gave her a medal and asked her to tea, were brave enough to let on in public that Stevie Smith's poetry was the kind they liked best because it didn't sound like poetry at all. In private, however, she always had a following, which in her later years grew to embrace a large minority of Britain's intelligent readers, so that she became something of a living treasure. Sir John Betjeman was more widely loved—he was more lovable—but the bookish were proud of Stevie as the British sometimes are of an old concrete pillbox that is allowed to go on disfiguring an otherwise perfect cow pasture because it reminds them of a time when they felt united.

> Perhaps England our darling will
>   recover her lost thought
> We must think sensibly about our
>   victory and not be distraught,
> Perhaps America will have an idea,
>   and perhaps not.

She fitted in by not fitting in at all. Least of all did she fit into modern literary history, and that is probably why there has always been a certain amount of interest in her across the Atlantic from where she lived and wrote. Some of the brighter young American academics, hankering for a less deterministic version of their subject, would like to see it refocused on the individual talent. A more individual talent than Stevie Smith's you don't get.

This excellent biography originated in the United States. Its authors cherish Stevie in the same intense way as those American liberal-arts professors on sabbatical leave who, having booked into a different West End theatrical production every night, end up, sometimes at the expense of their judgement, more in love with London than anyone who lives there could ever be. But the tireless Messrs. Barbera and McBrien—they even sound like a pair of sleuths—have cracked the case. They have fallen all the way for Stevie's marvellous spontaneity without being seduced by that little-girl act of hers or overawed by the ostentatiously suicidal *Weltschmerz* that for most of her long adult life made it seem unlikely she would get through another day without trying to end it all under a bus. To what degree her naivety was false and her vulnerability tougher *au fond* than an old boot will remain conjectural, although nobody from now on will want to conjecture without adducing at least some of the evidence that Barbera and McBrien so meticulously provide. But there cannot now be, if there ever was, any doubt about her poetry. It was never naive and seldom out of control. Stevie Smith was an artist of the utmost sophistication, pursuing the classic course of returning to simplicity through refinement, calculating her linguistic effects with such precision that they sound as innocently commanding as a baby's cry in the night.

Nobody heard him, the dead man,
But still he lay moaning:
I was much further out than you thought
And not waving but drowning.

Stevie spent most of her almost seventy years looking after her aunt in Palmers Green, which in the course of time graduated from being near London to being well inside it but without getting any closer to the centre of the literary action. She would journey in by public transport to her stuffy job as secretary to a publisher, and, at the end of a tiresome day, journey back out again. Weekends in the country—she had Rilke's knack for securing invitations, although nothing like his punctilio as a guest—provided what little adventure she ever knew. Her pre-war *Novel on Yellow Paper* (an unforgettable work that has nevertheless needed to be rediscovered several times since the day it was first greeted, correctly, as a masterpiece) contains most of whatever had happened to her up until then, and altogether too much of what had happened to her friends, some of whom never forgave her for putting embarrassing facts unaltered into her fiction. She had been to Germany and found out something about it, although not enough to help her realize that the old-style anti-Semitism of Hilaire Belloc had irrevocably lost whatever charm it had ever had. For a while she was fashionable, but she did not live fashionably. On those smart country weekends her only function was that of spare wheel. Her sexuality was either infantile or uncommonly well hidden for someone who made a practice of saying unfortunate things. What she really knew about was books.

She read prodigiously, absorbing the whole of English poetry right down to the level of its technique. At school, she had been obliged to get poems by heart. Sayability was her criterion, even during the ten years it took her to find her own voice. After she found it, she never wrote a line that could not be read aloud by a bright child. No child, though, has ever had her range of allusion. In *Novel on Yellow Paper* the narrator—called Pompey but otherwise indistinguishable from the actual Stevie—wonders whether she has read too much. Stevie probably did read too much for her own happiness, but for her poetry the result was a well of association sunk through centuries. She also read a great deal outside English, particularly in French, and especially Racine, whose decorous example helped inspire the finely calibrated play of tone which permitted her to run wild in an ordered manner. A line of hers may look as shapeless as a holdall but it can take a long time to unpack.

> Come death, you know you must come
>   when you're called
> Although you're a god.

It is meant to be Dido speaking, but you can't, and aren't meant to, read the words "Come death" without thinking of the song "Come away, come away, death" in *Twelfth Night*. On the page opposite "Dido's Farewell to Aeneas" in the *Collected Poems* (Oxford, 1976), the first line of "Childe Rolandine" shows how the frame she constructed for her seemingly primitive pictures was, in the strict sense, a frame of reference:

> Dark was the day for Childe Rolandine the artist
> When she went to work as a secretary-typist . . .

It was a dark tower to which Shakespeare's—and, later, Browning's—Childe Roland heroically came. Stevie, unheroically rotting behind a secretarial desk, has found a way to raise her lament beyond the personal. In this borrowed poetic context, a prosaic complaint brings the reader bang up to date:

> It is the privilege of the rich
> To waste the time of the poor . . .

Throughout her work, free-verse poems alternate with more formal compositions, but the free verse always gestures towards form and the forms always wander off. She strove industriously to make it look as if she didn't quite know what she was doing. She knew exactly. Her poetry has the vivid appeal of the Douanier Rousseau's pictures or Mussorgsky's music, but where they lacked schooling she only pretended to lack it. Closer analogies would be with Picasso painting clowns or Stravinsky writing ballets. She knew everything about how poetry had sounded in the past, and could assemble echoes with the assurance of any other modern artist. Clearly, her historicism was, in her own mind, the enabling justification for plain utterance. How the two things were technically connected is more problematic. When she uses the cadences of the Bible to promote her atheism, the trick is obvious, but often the most an admiring reader can do is ruefully admit that she somehow reminds him of every poet since Chaucer while speaking so naturally that she might be just coming round from a general anaesthetic.

"Not waving but drowning" was, and remains, her most famous line. No doubt the Queen asked her about it while pouring the tea. After a long time in critical oblivion, Stevie returned to *ex cathedra* applause in the 1960s, both as a poet and as a performer. But the pundits were out-shouted by the public. Her little-girl act was a big hit on the stage, where, once again, she knew precisely what she was up to. At any poetry reading in which she participated, she was the undisputed star turn. Not drowning but waving, she took her curtain calls like Joan Sutherland. Yet there is no reason to doubt that her life was desperate to the end.

> Why do I think of Death as a friend?
> It is because he is a scatterer
> He scatters the human frame
> The nerviness and the great pain
> Throws it on the fresh fresh air
> And now it is nowhere
> Only sweet Death does this . . .

Her poems, if they were pills to purge melancholy, did not work for her. The best of them, however, work like charms for everyone else. Barbera and McBrien were right to go in search of her. It was worth the legwork and the long stake-out. Stevie Smith is a rare bird, a Maltese falcon. English literature in the modern age, crushed by the amount of official attention paid to it, needs her strangeness, the throwaway artistry that takes every trick, the technique there is no point in analysing because you would have to go on analysing it for ever. In life, she could be a pain in the neck even to those who loved her. Her selfishness was a trial. She would heist the salmon out of the sandwiches and leave the bread to be eaten by others. Even in her work, she can be so fey that the skin crawls. But when she is in form she can deconstruct literature in the only way that counts—by constructing something that feels as if it had just flown together, except you can't take it apart.

The New Yorker, September 28, 1987;
later included in *The Dreaming Swimmer*, 1992

POSTSCRIPT

If I had called Barbera and McBrien's book a portent, I would have been mistaken, because it was merely a reminder. In-depth, archive-plumbing research on British literary matters has always been a field in which Americans have figured prominently. The American universities have the money to pay for the foraging expedition, and the American publishers have the patience to wait for the fat manuscript. Readers of Louis Menand's excellent group portrait of the American nineteenth-century pragmatists *The Metaphysical Club* will find that all the prominent thinkers and academics spent time in Europe as if air travel had already been invented. To American scholars, the Atlantic has never been much more than a ditch: a narrower one, indeed, than the Rio Grande. But the privilege of local critics is to be stained by local colour. Visiting scholars tread a gangway above the mud. Taking a royal road into the learned circle, they meet too few philistines, and the cave doors of Grub Street are closed. On a rich diet of art and knowledge, they tend to miss the common food of custom and instinct. When I was an undergraduate in Cambridge I heard a visiting American professor deliver an address on the forms of ridicule in Swift. Judging by his ponderous delivery, he had somehow missed the point that the ridicule depended for its force on conversational ease, and one suspected that it was because he had never seen a roomful of London literati when they were hitting the sauce. It is not the same as a pack of dons passing the decanter around High Table.

2003

I0

GALWAY KINNELL'S GREAT POEM

The best Hitchcock film was directed by someone else. *Charade* would
not be as good as it is if Hitchcock had not developed the genre it epito-
mizes, but Hitchcock could never have created a film so meticulous,
plausible, sensitive, light-footed and funny. It took Stanley Donen to do
that: temporarily Hitchcock's student, he emerged as his master. Similarly Galway Kinnell's great poem *The Avenue Bearing the Initial of
Christ into the New World* is the long Ezra Pound poem that Pound himself could never have written. It could not have been written without
Pound's *Cantos* as a point of departure, but it is so much more human,
humane and sheerly poetic that you realize why Pound's emphasis on
technique and language, fruitful to others, was barren for himself. A
poetic gift will include those things—or anyway the capacity for them—
but finally there is an element of personality which brings them to their
full potential, and only as a means to an end. With more on his mind
than Pound and fewer bees in his bonnet, Kinnell could actually do what
Pound spent too much of his time teaching. Pound went on and on about
making you see, but the cold truth is that in the *Cantos* there are not
many moments that light up. Kinnell's poem has got them like stars in
heaven. It is almost unfair.

> Banking the same corner
> A pigeon coasts 5th Street in shadows,
> Looks for altitude, surmounts the rims of buildings,
> And turns white.

Pound *wanted* to sound like that, but found it hard. He made it hard for himself. He was always looking for his vision of history in the way he said things. Kinnell, for the stretch of his own much shorter very long poem, has a vision of history that comes from history. The *Cantos*, the twentieth-century version of Casaubon's "Key to All the Mythologies" from *Middlemarch*, ranges through all time and all space looking for a pattern, tracing specious lines of connection in which Pound progressively entangles himself, until finally he hangs mummified with only his mouth moving, unable to explain even his own era, a nut for politics whose political role was to be the kind of Fascist that real Fascists found naive. Kinnell's poem, moving only in the region of New York's Avenue C at the end of World War II, is sustained throughout by historical resonance—the very quality which Pound, yearning to achieve it, always dissipated in advance with his demented certainties.

Along and around Avenue C, in the Lower East Side, flows the whole rich experience of immigrant America and its relationship to the terrible fate of modern Europe. Blacks and Puerto Ricans and Jews and Ukrainians toil in uneasy proximity but at least they are alive and there is a law. Only the animals and the fish are massacred. An official, empty letter of condolence from a concentration camp front office to a victim's family is quoted while a Jewish fishmonger guts the catch. It is the sort of effect which Pound, exalting it with the name of juxtaposition, practised like a bad journalist. In Kinnell's poem it attains true complexity, principally because he has the negative capability—the sanity—to let his audience do the interpreting, from their common knowledge.

Pound had a theory about the Jews. Kinnell knew what theories like that led to and presumed that his readers knew too. *The Avenue Bearing the Initial of Christ into the New World* was one of the first, and remains one of the few, adequate works of art devoted to the Holocaust. The Hassidim walk Avenue C bent over with the weight of their orthodoxy, unassimilable as spacemen. Faced with their intransigence, Kinnell has no easy democratic message. He has the difficult one—the message that America, or at any rate the tip of Manhattan, has something to offer more interesting, and perhaps less threatening, than the prospect of homogeneity. An anti–*Waste Land* that sees the potential creativity in apparent chaos, his poem celebrates diversity, out of which unpredictability comes, a cultural complexity which the artist can only describe.

Helping him to describe it is a gift for evocation which makes it advisable to leave Ezra Pound out of account altogether, since he spent, presumably from preference, little time saying that one thing was like another. *The apparition of these faces in the crowd/leaves on a wet, black bough.* Pound manufactured a few examples like that and then talked about them. Kinnell's less effortful knack for the arc-light metaphor should serve to remind us that the Martian movement must have been landing its flying saucers long before they were first detected.

> We found a cowskull once; we thought it was
> From one of the asses in the Bible, for the sun
> Shone into the holes through which it had seen
> Earth as an endless belt carrying gravel . . .

All the more striking for steering clear of extravagance, that particular coup is from a poem called "Freedom, New Hampshire." Nowadays Les Murray studs his poems about country Australia with similar effects, but gets them closer together. Kinnell, in his shorter poems, spaced them out. There was too much else going on. He overstrained his verbs like Lowell, substituted the next-less-intelligible noun throughout the stanza like Wallace Stevens, piled on the archaic diction in a belated tribute to John Crowe Ransom, and above all indulged in rhapsodic apostrophes to the City which recalled Hart Crane the way that Crane had once recalled Walt Whitman.

> And thou, River of Tomorrow, flowing . . .

Like so many poets, especially American poets, who consciously attempt to forge an idiom, Kinnell synthesized the idioms of other poets, many of whom had themselves been up to the same doomed trick. Forging an idiom is forgery, even when dressed up as subservience. Almost everything Kinnell wrote was in agitated, self-conscious homage to some-one—William Carlos Williams and Robert Frost loomed like faces on Mount Rushmore—and too often the homage was technical. But Kinnell's proper rhythm and true clarity were there waiting to be brought out at the moment when a strong enough subject turned him away from ambition and towards achievement. *The Avenue Bearing the Initial of*

Christ into the New World is one coup after another, a succession of illuminations like his stunning image of the Avenue's traffic lights going green into the far dusk. Here are the vegetable stalls:

> In the pushcart market on Sunday,
> A crate of lemons discharges light like a battery.
> Icicle-shaped carrots that through black soil
> Wove away like flames in the sun.
> Onions with their shirts ripped seek sunlight
> On green skins. The sun beats
> On beets dirty as boulders in cowfields,
> On turnips pinched and gibbous
> From budging rocks, on embery sweets,
> Peanut-shaped Idahos, shore-pebble Long Islands and Maines,
> On horseradishes still growing weeds on the flat ends,
> Cabbages lying around like sea-green brains
> The skulls have been shucked from . . .

The fish market goes on for several stanzas, at the thematic centre of the poem because the deaths of millions of humans are being called up by the deaths of millions of creatures similarly dumped from one element into another. Admirers of Elizabeth Bishop's precisely observed poems about fish might find it daunting to note how Kinnell sees just as much detail before soaring up and out into extra relevance like Marianne Moore taking off on a broom.

> . . . two-tone flounders
> After the long contortion of pushing both eyes
> To the brown side that they might look up,
> Lying brown side down, like a mass laying-on of hands,
> Or the oath-taking of an army.

This is magic poetry in the sense that you can't tell how he does it and can be dissuaded from the idea that he might be a sorcerer only by the consideration that other people are billed as magicians too. What finally establishes Kinnell's *magnum opus* as a successful poem, however, is its ordinary poetry—ordinary in the sense that it does not astonish, but does persuade, and even, in the bitter end, console.

> Fishes do not die exactly, it is more
> That they go out of themselves, the visible part
> Remains the same, there is little pallor,
> Only the cataracted eyes which have not shut ever
> Must look through the mist which crazed Homer.

Compare this with Hart Crane's famous, wilfully beautiful line about the seal's wide spindrift gaze towards Paradise and you can see what Kinnell had that Crane hadn't. With no ordinary language interesting enough to fall back on, Crane was trying to sound as if he had a lot to say. Kinnell had a lot to say. All he needed was a theme to contain it. But for an intelligence whose attention is everywhere, sharp in all directions, a still point of focus is not easily found. On Avenue C he found it.

Galway Kinnell wrote his one great tragic, celebratory poem and never anything quite like it again, possibly because it is as long as a modern epic can well be even though everything that matters is included. I think that an event drove him to begin it, and a particular historic conjunction allowed him to complete it. In Europe humanity had been brought to the point where it might have lost faith in its own right to exist; and then America had saved the world. Later on things were less simple. It was the right moment; Kinnell was the right man; and a poem was written which was wonderful against all the odds — even those formidable odds posed by the very business of being a poet at all, in an age when art has become so self-aware that innocence can be found only at the end of a long search.

The Dreaming Swimmer, 1992

POSTSCRIPT

If you read Ezra Pound early on — and when I was coming of age in Australia in the late 1950s we all did — you can spend a lifetime wondering how he ever got under your skin. He was still alive when my bunch were getting started, and one of us, Richard Appleton, the black-clad glamour boy of Sydney's Downtown Push, was in regular correspondence with him. (Though the Downtown Push was more concerned with gambling than with the arts, the occasioned poet was allowed in as long as he showed clear signs of dissipation.) A correspondence with Pound was not difficult to initiate—an indication of abject worship usually worked the trick—but it was difficult to break off, because Pound had a warehouse full of Social Credit pamphlets that he was keen to send out to the qualified reader, definable as anybody who would not throw them on the fire. Along with the pamphlets, alas, came material even more corrosive: advice on poetic technique. Appleton, who was born with a formal sense that made his meticulous carpentry poetic in itself, was among the most gifted young Australian poets of his time. But his obsession with Pound was as fatal to his mind as his impression that Benzedrine was a form of food was fatal to his body. Appleton suppressed the natural coherence of his gift in order to sound like the *Cantos*, an aim in which he succeeded all too well. By the time of his premature death, his poems were not only in fragments, he was *calling* them fragments—always a bad sign. His self-induced disintegration as an artist was a *memento mori* that I never forgot, and ever since, although I have never written an article devoted solely to Pound, I have made a habit of referring to him in articles written about other poets, with the hope that the references will make some other young potential epigone think twice about worshipping at the old lunatic's altar. As time goes by, the chances diminish that anyone will think of doing so even once, which I suppose is another kind of loss. Simplified by the pitiless machinery of success, the shape of the past changes, and the disturbing aberrations pass out of history, having failed to do their work. Pound's version of the Fascist era never arrived, and indeed it was never there, even under Fascism, although Pound managed to convince himself that Mussolini had actually read his presentation volume of the *Cantos*. (Admittedly, Mussolini told him so, but Mussolini also told the Italian people that they were going to win the war.) In the long run, a poet like Galway Kinnell could do what Pound vaunted himself as doing but never could: make poetry from history. Pound staked everything on that, and was bound to fail; not because he couldn't write poetry, but because he was debarred by nature from understanding history; he thought his gift for the dogmatic epigram was a guarantee of universal scope. Having failed, he faded; gradually but beyond recovery. Even in the academy, where developmental theories of poetry are automatically favoured, his early reputation as an innovator has been swallowed up by his later reputation as a snake-oil salesman, a process aided by the sad fact that it was his second phase that he himself valued the more highly. By now the victory for forgetfulness is almost complete, and the well-funded tumulus of Poundian scholarship is eroding in the wind. But it is hard, though necessary, not to be sad, if only for all that wasted excitement, not all of which was his. Some of it was ours. There was a time when I would spread open a slim volume of the *Cantos* on a table of the Women's Union cafeteria at Sydney University and sit there reading as excited as I could be. But I was excited by a possibility. Read many years later, Kinnell's poem was the actuality, and poetry, despite appearances, is all actuality: it can depart from the real, but only in order to intensify it.

2003

II

LES MURRAY AND
HIS MASTER SPIRITS

Over the hundreds of years it has taken for the colonies of the old European empires to become nations, there have been cases—most notably, of course, the United States—where a creole literature has made an important addition to the literature of the homeland, but there has been no case quite comparable to that of Australian poetry in this century. The Spanish poetry of the Americas comes close—a history of poetry in the Spanish language that did not give Rubén Darío a crucial place would be no history at all—but even that has little to compare with the burgeoning of Australian poetry in the last hundred years. Trainee midwives on tenterhooks, Australian nationalists eager for every sign of a successful parturition from the homeland have a lot to go on. Though it remains necessary to call them unwise, it would be unwise to call them fools. What they really want is for Australia to become the new U.S.A.: the ex-colony that made it all the way to the status of world power. The more likely realization of so gullible a wish would be Australia as an extra American state—a new Alaska with a better climate, or at most a new California with a better social security system. But since it undoubtedly would also have a better literature, there is something to be said, from the cultural viewpoint, for these dreams of autarky. Barry Humphries's yodelling alter ego, Sir Les Patterson, minister for the Yartz, has never been entirely wrong on that point: it is only by missing the larger point that his view becomes ridiculous. A culture can never flourish as a hedge against the world. It isn't a bastion for nationalism, it is an international passport.

The best known internationally among his generation of Australian poets, Les Murray would count as a nationalist if there were such a thing as a purely political view. Up to and including the prospect of severing all monarchist ties with Britain he believes politically in the Australia he gave a name to: the Vernacular Republic. But as his collections of densely wrought essays prove, when it comes to culture he also believes that such a thing as purely political belief can't be had. The secret of his pre-eminence as a writer of critical prose in Australia today is his capacity not to simplify what he would like to change. Blessed with a sense of history and the gifts to articulate it, he would be an important man of letters even if he never wrote a poem, and he would be a vital shaping influence of Australia's emergent poetic tradition if only by dint of his anthologies. Murray favours what Ezra Pound used to call the active anthology: one whose poems are chosen because they are all inventions, and not just representative of their authors' reputations. Wide-ranging and generous in his choices, adept—sometimes too adept—at leaving himself out of the picture, he chooses from the creole heritage to bring out the full complexity of the relationship between the Australian poets of previous generations and the old Empire that was always on their minds even when they tried to repudiate it.

Murray's anthologies could easily have been more tendentiously selective. In his *New Oxford Book of Australian Verse* he includes a striking proportion of Aboriginal poetry: any Mexican anthology that included so much Indian poetry would be accused of pushing the *mestizo* ideal to the point of nationalist fervour. But not even his Oxford book tries to pretend that the imperial past was a state of false consciousness from which Australia had to awake before it could breathe free air. Because he has played so straight with the complexities of history, Murray has established impeccable credentials for himself as an interpreter of his country's present. As a consequence, everything he does as a man of letters takes on a growing burden of responsibility. His poetry can look after itself: none better. But he finds his merest book review being scrutinized for political resonance, and an anthology like his new, quirkily named *Fivefathers* acquires a significance beyond the literary. Speaking as a devout cultural reactionary, my own first reaction to Murray's latest survey of his literary forefathers (Fivefathers equals forefathers plus one: I just got it) is that if all the other nationalists were as judicious as he, the prospect of a republic would be a lot less daunting. To borrow Thomas Mann's classic formulation about Goethe, Murray is radical enough to understand the good.

Murray's Fivefathers were all active in what he tellingly calls the pre-Academic era, when Australian poets had to make their way without any support from the as yet undeveloped academic industry, and were not necessarily the worse off for it. First-time readers of Australian poetry in Britain, at whom this Carcanet publication must principally be aimed, should be warned that another criterion for inclusion is death. None of these five fathers is among the living or even the recently departed, which means that there are some comparable contemporary figures who are not present and should be sought elsewhere. There are fathers like A. D. Hope, mothers like Judith Wright and Gwen Harwood, and sisters, cousins and aunts who should ideally be here too. But Murray's anthologizing activities always lead you in that direction: each of them feels like the beginning of the ideal inclusive book, the one that, nothing but art, contains *all* the art. What we need to remember is that such a book can no longer be compiled: Australian poetry has become too big a subject— has become a *field*, to which we need a *guide*, and eventually quite a few more of those academic help-words of which Murray is so rightly suspicious, believing as he does that they threaten the death of personality. Like all true humanist critics an implacable enemy of literary theory, he wants us to experience his five fathers as living men, and it is permissible to suspect that he wants this with particular urgency in the case of the first father in the queue, Kenneth Slessor, from whose work Murray's selection is particularly lavish and—dare one say it?—loving. Of this father, Murray speaks as a true son.

At Sydney University in the late 1950s, most of the young poets were men but would haunt the cafeteria of the Women's Union, Manning House. The reason was simple: in Manning House you could linger over a single coffee cup for hours without getting thrown out, whereas from the Men's Union ejection followed precipitately upon the first gurgling of the dregs. With the conspicuous exception of Murray—even in those days, he stood out like Sydney Greenstreet miscast as Ginger Meggs—few of the Manning House poets had the heritage of Australian poetry much on their minds. My own *Stammtisch* would be decorated with slim Faber volumes in their original glamorous wrappers, all purchased from Tyrrel's second-hand bookshop at the Quay end of George Street: Auden, Mac-

Neice, T. S. Eliot and the occasional impressively fat black-bound fascicle of Pound's *Cantos*, which inchoate effusion I held at the time to be omniscience distilled into a crucible of obsidian. Robert Hughes wouldn't even be reading in English: if he hadn't already memorized it, he would be carrying *Mon coeur mis à nu*, muttering lines from it while he drew caricatures in the margin. Home-grown literary magazines like *Meanjin* and *Westerly* were for old lecturers in gowns who cared about Vance Palmer and were sincerely, absurdly, bent on setting up a Department of Australian Literature. For them, and for Murray.

For the rest of *les jeunes*, the very concept of an Australian literature seemed far away, yet even those of us already committed in advance to a breakaway existence knew about Slessor. Everyone owned a copy of *One Hundred Poems*. In those days books of poetry published in Australia looked and smelled like books published in the Soviet Union throughout its benighted career: i.e., they looked like tat and smelled like glue. Cherishably well-presented volumes like the Edwards and Shaw edition of A. D. Hope's *The Wandering Islands* were the very rare exceptions. Slessor's *One Hundred Poems* was an Angus and Robertson booklet bound in an uneasy combination of paper and stiff cardboard. It was pitiably unimpressive to look at. But we all knew that the stuff inside it was the best Australian poetry anybody had yet seen. Shamefully, at least one Manning House *habitué* for too long employed this awareness as an excuse to dismiss everyone else, and even in Slessor's case I had been away from Australia for twenty years before I took his full measure as an artist, memorized everything, and began the long job, which his example necessitated, of getting the national literature into perspective within my own mind.

The main point to make about Murray's relationship with Slessor is that Murray saw Slessor's pivotal importance straight away, and with a thoroughness that helped determine his own attitude to his privileges and duties as a poet in Australia, as opposed to the poets *from* Australia that most of the rest of us vaguely dreamed of ourselves as being, if not yet then some day soon. At his own table in Manning House, Murray always looked as if he was dug in to stay. A boy from the country for whom Sydney was exotic enough, he approached Slessor personally, made his admiration clear, presented his own work for criticism, and was eventually rewarded with Slessor's acknowledgement that he, Murray, had been determined by fate to pick up and carry on the torch that Slessor had dropped. In private life, when the company is suitable, Murray has been

known to recount the details of this apostolic succession. His pride is justifiable, and a nice example of the anecdotal human scale that still vesti-
gially applies to the Australian literary life even in this later age of arts-
section hype, globe-girdling travel, and the isolation that forms unbidden
around famous names. I got that story out of him over a glass of white
wine at Australia House the last time he read in London, and it was only
a few weeks ago, in Bloomsbury, at a publisher's jamboree for booksellers,
that David Malouf easily secured my agreement to the proposition that
Murray's critical prose was by far the best thing of its kind being written
in Australia now. The idea of an Australian international literary mafia is
not a very good one (principally because it is not a very good metaphor)
but if there is something to the notion of an extended family of those
devoted to literature, then in a large part it goes back to Slessor, a godfa-
ther in the best, most benign sense, even when—perhaps especially
when—he was no longer creative.

Just why Slessor has to be thought of as dropping the torch, rather
than merely setting it into an iron ring against a stone wall to burn by
itself once his arm was tired, is a subject Murray is ideally equipped to
treat one day, in an essay that should be a pleasure to read, even if tragic.
The foundations have been laid by Geoffrey Dutton's excellent biography, but we need an analysis that traces the line of destruction from the
personality into the poetry. Alcohol had something to do with it; and alcoholism in turn had something to do with Slessor's disappointment in the
culture that had grown up, or failed to grow up, around him: a disappointment which had somehow been prepared for, within his estimation
of himself, by his comparative failure as a war correspondent *vis-à-vis*
such stars as Alan Moorehead; and so on. But there can be no doubt
about the intensity with which the torch burned while he could still run
with it. In his "Five Visions of Captain Cook," when he wanted to evoke
the confidence that the junior officers of the *Endeavour* had in their captain's powers of navigation, he did it like this.

> Men who ride broomsticks with a mesmerist
> Mock the typhoon.

Just try forgetting that. Slessor favoured the extended, multi-part
poem, but he was always epigrammatic even at his most thematically
expansive. After returning to it many times over thirty or more years, I can

now see his twelve-part poem "The Old Play" as a masterly set of varied tones and dictions, but his sheer power of compressed evocation is still at the heart of it.

> In the old play-house, in the watery flare
> Of gilt and candlesticks, in a dim pit
> Furred with a powder of corroded plush,
> Paint fallen from angels floating in mid-air,
> The gods in languor sit.

Otherwise an admirer of Sickert, I have always found his theatre paintings disappointingly dark: his muddy palette is meant to call up faded glory, but only the fading shows. In Slessor's lines you can see the glory. *Furred with a powder of corroded plush* is something better than an image: it is an attitude, regret distilled into an elixir. In his most famous multi-part poem, "Five Bells," such stellar moments gravitate together and join up: the whole effort is alive with sayability, assembled from a kit whose parts are quotations.

> The naphtha-flash of lightning slit the sky,
> Knifing the dark with deathly photographs . . .

> You have no suburb, like those easier dead
> In private berths of dissolution laid —
> The tide goes over you, the waves ride over you
> And let their shadows down like shining hair . . .

I have never written or even spoken about Slessor without quoting those last two lines. Precisely registering what the surfer sees on the sand beneath him when he ducks under an incoming dumper, they were with me when I left Sydney; they were my way back to him when I later sat down to read everything he ever wrote; and perhaps, eventually, they were my way home. But Murray's extensive selection proves that such clean, clear, shapely, and striking simplicity—the speakable directness that many of us would like to feel is, or should be, the defining characteristic of Australian poetry—was hard won from a deep complexity of mind and spirit, and from an inherently tortuous connection with the whole heritage of European culture. Slessor was a learned man who knew just where and when to place his epigraphs from Heine. Natural utterance did not come naturally: it was a quiet triumph of sustained artifice. Finally our realization of the full impact of his poetry depends on *his* realization that the search for a personal voice would have to be self-conscious, if only because the demand for a national voice had taken on a political dimension. In this regard it is a pity that Murray did not have room to include more of Slessor's light verse (the term was never more of a misnomer: the merest lyric drips with melancholy) from the two collections *Darlinghurst Nights* and *Backless Betty from Bondi,* because it was those two books that most clearly pointed up the source of the discipline that sharpened his sense of form and loaded his line without blurring it—Tin Pan Alley. The impact of the American forces during World War II, both as comrades in arms and as what amounted to an occupying power, decisively shifted Australia's position in the old Empire, and Slessor not only presaged the whole event during the Depression years, he set the linguistic limits for it, outlining the tonal range in which an Australian poet, as an agent instead of a patient, could write about a wider world.

The other four of the Fivefathers wrote about the world before it widened. As a result they seem further back in time than Slessor does, even when their period of flowering was more recent. Murray puts a high value on Roland Robinson, who spent a lifetime trying to incorporate the totemic properties of traditional Aboriginal poetry into his own. The same urge, less subtly realized, inspired the Jindyworobak movement. Robinson had a wider range of tones than the Jindyworobaks, but he was still, and thus still is, limited by the assumption that a proper name from an Aboriginal language has automatic resonance. Nobody would expect to get away with this when quoting from any other foreign language: it is always a plea by a would-be anthropologist with a political programme, and it always stops a poem dead in its tracks.

> Now that the fig lets fall her single stars
> of flowers on these green waters I would be
> withdrawn as Gul-ar-dar-ark the peaceful dove . . .

Later on in the same poem, Geek-keek the honeyeater shows up, demanding the same good faith that his name is not a misprint, or a harassed black-tracker's short way of saying "Take a hike, honky" to an importunate enquirer. As was bound to happen, the subsequent recovery of actual Aboriginal poetry by specialists in the original languages—a process amply drawn upon in Murray's Oxford anthology, and which continues—pointed up the essential wilfulness of this whole premature attempt to lend native art dignity by misappropriating its detachable tokens. Even at the time, the general impression was of petty larceny masquerading as ethnology, like André Malraux swiping statuettes from pagodas. Later on, in retrospect, the sad spectacle of wasted time spread like a dry lake through a generation. Robinson was an especially poignant example because he had the talent to compose thoroughly in English without having to doll up flat language in borrowed trinkets: the Australian love poem has a sumptuous heritage, and Robinson's "The Creek" is one of the loveliest poems in it.

> I make my camp beside you, a dove-grey
> deep pool fretting its fronds and tangled
> flowers. Waratahs burn above you. You
> give me billyfuls of rainwater wine, a
> bright wing-case, a boronia petal, a white
> rose tinted tea-tree star.

All of this bush detail is easily recognizable and appreciated by any Australian and none of it would be made more poetic if it were to be substituted for by an Aboriginal word: indeed the opposite effect would be achieved, to the detriment not only of English but of the Aboriginal language as well, which would be made to sound as the Jindyworobaks invariably made it sound—like a formula for boredom. But there was nothing shameful about their doomed fight. It was part of an impulse to make a new nation conscious of the awkward fact that it had existed as a country long before its colonial history began: a fact which it was in the interests of its bourgeoisie to overlook, and of its powerful squattocracy to deny.

For all practical purposes, "squatter" was the Australian word for the creole or the sabra in his most self-confident form: the squatters inherited the earth and it would have been no surprise if whole generations of the landed families had grown up thinking of nothing except their own interests. Australia has yet another reason to bless its luck that so many of its landed gentry cultivated the arts and sciences as well as the soil. However

close their connection with "home," meaning England, they did a disproportionate amount to form the character of the country they were
born in — endowing its art galleries, enriching its universities, setting a
humane course for its cultural institutions. David Campbell, Murray's
third Fivefather, was a glistening example of a type that filled the Australian social pages only a generation ago: the MacArthur-Onslows, the
Bonythons. They are still there, but nowadays keep a lower profile.
Campbell's profile filled the sky. While at Cambridge before the war he
played rugby for England. In the RAAF he won two DFCs. He would
have made such a perfect husband for Princess Margaret that the joy his
poetry takes in his colonial background — seemingly exultant that his
background is in the foreground — acquires overtones of heroism.

> Here's to Sydney by the summer!
> Body-surfing down a comber
> Where the girls are three a gallon
> To a beach of yellow pollen . . .

For daring young men like Campbell, the arts they practised with
such confident grace seemed just another part of *noblesse oblige*, and all
the more daunting for their seeming ease. Like the black bullock's horns
mounted on the grille of the returned Mosquito pilot Kym Bonython's
white Bristol sports saloon, Campbell's poems were the bagatelles of a
dandy. But the successful throwaway gesture is fated to live, and Campbell's perfect little poem "Mothers and Daughters" is remembered today
by men who, when they were young, got no closer to the incandescent
women it describes than the social pages of *Pix* and *Women's Weekly*,
leafed through at the barber's in sullen envy.

> The cruel girls we loved
> Are over forty,
> Their subtle daughters
> Have stolen their beauty;
>
> And with a blue stare
> Of cruel surprise
> They mock their anxious mothers
> With their mother's eyes.

For the sons of the squatters, at home anywhere in the world where there were country houses, turning up breezily at Buckingham Palace to collect their gongs, Australian cultural isolation was a non-problem. To James McAuley, Fivefather number four, it was a burning issue, and he eventually reached the conclusion that there was no salvation outside the church. For McAuley in the late—some might say the sclerotic—phase of his conservatism, the Catholic Church was not just the symbol but the living presence of the international order he thought his country needed to be part of, or it would have no standards except its own. There was a paradox in his position, because the Church stood behind and above the heritage of Irish immigration that gave the Labor Party its electoral strength and provincialism its abiding force. Luckily he thrived on paradoxes. They appealed to his sense of symmetry. He had a formal gift that comes singing out of this anthology with the chamfered and inlaid neatness of a Van Eyck angel's spinet. In stanzas lusciously sonorous he evoked austerity as if thirsting for a vinegar-soaked sponge.

> Where once was a sea is now a salty sunken desert,
> A futile heart within a fair periphery;
> The people are hard-eyed, kindly, with nothing inside them,
> The men are independent but you could not call them free.

Since free was exactly what the independent men *did* call themselves, McAuley could not expect to be popular for taking this position, but he didn't care. A local Ortega relishing his role as a fastidious rebel against the mass-market future, he was fated to embrace austerity all too successfully—the later epic poetry was thought tedious even by lifelong admirers—but he never lost his unmatched capacity to conduct a prose argument through a poetic form: "Because," a lament for his parents and the love he never got from them or could give back, is one of the great modern Australian poems and would be worth acquiring this book for just on its own.

The same might be said for several of the poems in the selection from the last of the Fivefathers, Francis Webb, whose fitting task is not to fit into this book or any other except those entirely his. Even at the time, Webb was a one-off, an El Greco–style stylistic maverick: making an entirely unexpected appearance in a tradition, he could be seen to have emerged from it, but he distorted the whole thing. Webb was a clinical case, a schizophrenic who spent a lot of time in hospital and eventually disintegrated, but Murray, with typical penetration, has never fallen for the easy notion that Webb's poetry is psycho in itself. The answer to the biologist's trick question of whether there was something wrong with El Greco's eyes is no, because if there had been he would have compensated for it. Similarly Webb's poetry is the way it is because of his inner vision, not because of scrambled perceptions. If his cognitive apparatus had been muddled he would have attempted simplicities. As things were and are, his synaesthetic effects have to be compared with Baudelaire, Rimbaud and the hallucinatory extravaganzas that the British Apocalyptic poets of the 1940s aimed for without achieving. The guarantee of Webb's urge to transcendental integration was the purity of his fragments. Wherever two or three of his admirers are gathered together, you will hear these particles flying. (My own favourite hemistitch, from a poem omitted here, is "Sunset hails a rising": one day I'm going to call a book that and lay the beautiful ghost of an idea that must have come to him in one of his fevers, like a cooling drop of sweat.) In the enforced retreats of his hospitals and the injected lucidities of his drugs, there might well have been something prophetic about Webb. Certainly he guessed that the Australian poets would become a success story, and feared the consequences.

> Now yours is the grand power, great for good or evil:
> The schoolboy (poor devil!) will be told off to study you . . .

Webb was Murray's predecessor in guessing that an efflorescent culture would set the challenge of studying it without ceasing to love it. With music and painting, both of which flourish in Australia as if the molecules of the air had been redesigned specifically to nourish them, it is easy to keep passion pure: when the orchestra strikes up, the commentary must cease, and in the art gallery you can always neglect to hire the earphones. But when the academic age dawned it became chasteningly clear that poetry would be hard to separate from its parasitic buzz. One of the penalties for success was a proliferation of middle-men, and eventually, as feminism institutionalized itself, middle-women. The new *Oxford Book of Australian Women's Verse*, however, is a welcome sign that the essentials are being remembered. Unlike the notorious *Penguin Book of Australian Women Poets* of 1987, Susan Lever's anthology is unburdened by didactic jargon and makes commendably little fuss about the necessarily agonizing problem of getting everybody in without leaving too many good poems out. Fledgling feminists will receive an encouraging message about self-realization growing with time. Those of us who have always taken the importance of women poets in Australia for granted (in the 1950s we were male chauvinist pigs almost to a man, but none of us was going to argue with Gwen Harwood or Judith Wright) will be left free to detect a more edifying progression. Presumably it must apply to the men as well, although perhaps the women—careful now—were always more likely to register its effects: anyway, in this verse chronicle, as the century wears on, the poets become more, instead of less, precise about domestic detail, until nowadays, against all expectation, the housewife tradition looks unbreakably strong.

One of the great strengths of the generation that included Judith Wright and Gwen Harwood lay in the harsh fact that they had no time to be careerists: they wrote from necessity, in the exiguous spare time left over from looking after their men. You would think that the new freedoms would have led to a plunge back into time, a local re-run of the *rentier* aesthetic leisure once enjoyed by the bluestockings of Britain and America, an inexorable push towards the free bohemian status of Edna St. Vincent Millay: that the ethereal would beckon. But not on this showing. It was once uniquely Gwen Harwood's way to write about music and philosophy as if they were the bread of life she had brought home from the shops. But here is the proof that it has since become standard practice, thus helping to create, for the Australian reader, perhaps the least alienated and divisive literary culture on earth. Try this, from Susan Hampton's "Ode to a Car Radio."

> My right eye leaking blood coming home
> from Casualty, patched, pirate view, & changing gears
> past Rooms to Let $12 p.w. beside Surry Hills Smash Repairs
> & a beer gut emerging from a pub door at ten, well,
> you can picture the general scene
> & click! clear as glass, the flute opening
> to Prokofiev's *Romeo and Juliet*, cool & sweet
> as a parkful of wet trees.

Ms. Hampton was one of the hectoring editors of the aforementioned Penguin anthology but I forgive her, as long as she goes on writing like that. Prokofiev gets into the poem unquestioned, which is exactly the way things ought to be, because Australia is a place where classical music is in the air. It didn't happen by accident. Australia became a clever country because clever people, many of them refugees from harsh political experience in Europe, were wise enough not to accept unquestioned the prevalent intellectual assumptions about the necessary divorce between democracy and art. For the poets of the pre-Academic generation, art was in their lives as sustenance and salvation. Their successors have caught the habit, in the only tradition worth taking the trouble to define, the handing on of a copious view. One of my favourite poems in this book is by Vicki Raymond, whose work I will seek out from now on. Talking about static electricity in the office, she brings off a quietly tremendous coup worthy of the poet whose name she invokes.

> You can even feel it through your clothes,
> which crackle lightly like tinfoil.
> It's as though you were turning into
> something not right, but strange; your hair
> floats out like Coleridge's
> after he'd swallowed honeydew.

According to the notes, Vicki Raymond is an expatriate who has lived in London since 1981. Well, it's an Australian poem wherever it was written. The expatriates are part of all this too, but if put to the question they would have to admit that the vitality grown at home in their absence has come to form the core of the total astonishment, generating the power behind what makes a small country recognizable to the world in the only way that matters—its voice, the sound of freedom.

Times Literary Supplement, July 5, 1996;
later included in *Even As We Speak*, 2001

12

THE GREAT GENERATION OF AUSTRALIAN POETRY

First A. D. Hope and then Judith Wright, two of the most famous twentieth-century Australian poets died in the millennium year, and with them the first great phalanx of modern Australian poetry ran out of living representatives. When my generation was nursing its callow dreams of getting established, most of the future patriarchs and matriarchs were still only in their forties but they dominated the skyline: they looked more established than the Sydney Harbour Bridge, than the Melbourne Club, than the Great Dividing Range. Each commanding not just a name but a physical presence, they had first call on the available limelight. Hope, Wright, James McAuley, Douglas Stewart and Gwen Harwood were only the most prominent. David Campbell seemed keen to prove that his wartime productivity had been just the start. Francis Webb, though terminally schizophrenic in a mental hospital, kindly continued to receive visits from young hopefuls who rightly suspected that he might be more original than they were.

Kenneth Slessor, the precursor, was far gone in his latter-day cocktail-fuelled dandyism but lived long enough to meet Les Murray personally and anoint him as a future torch-bearer. Similarly, Christopher Brennan in his cups had once smiled on the young A. D. Hope. The smile was probably a bit lopsided, but Hope, though he himself grew older with more grace, remembered the moment fondly. According to his own account, written in extreme old age but with typical clarity of detail, he had tracked Brennan down to a pub toilet, where the permanently plastered polymath was pointing Percy at the porcelain — or perhaps, considering Brennan's stature as a classical scholar, he was pointing Propertius at the porphyry. Hope attracted the swaying Brennan's attention by pencilling the first half of a rude Latin inscription from Pompeii at eye level above the urinal. Brennan took the pencil, completed the inscription, noted that it was in Saturnian metre, and delivered a comprehensive lecture on accentual metres right through the period of classical verse. And *then* he buttoned his fly.

Growing old was something these legends seemed slow to do, especially if you were waiting for them to give you breathing space. R. D. Fitzgerald—born, like Slessor, at the turn of the century and for some time considered his equal—had suffered a weakening of the reputation but still bulked large: there was a mild uproar when McAuley gave Fitzgerald's *Forty Years' Poems* a bad review. McAuley died sooner than he should have—cancer took him in 1976—but when I was a student he was still to be seen in his acerbic prime, fulminating away on the far right. I can remember a tight-lipped, buttoned-up lecture he gave in Sydney University's Wallace Theatre. His nominal subject was left-wing incomprehension of the recently published *Dr. Zhivago*, but the real object of his ire seemed to be liberalism in general, starting with the invention of moveable type, or perhaps the wheel. By that stage Australia's most adamantine ultra-Catholic made the Vatican look soft on communism, but anybody who thought McAuley was through as a poet would have been making a mistake: "Because," one of his very best things, was a product of his last phase. Those of us who had panned his epic (*Captain Quiros* was essentially a lament for Australia's having missed out on being part of a Catholic empire) were obliged to admit that he went down in a blaze of lyrics.

The year of McAuley's death was the first year I could afford a trip back to Sydney, where I heard quite ordinary people quoting bits of "Because." ("Judgment is simply trying to reject/ A part of what we are because it hurts." He could put a hook right through your head.) Hearing him quoted reminded me of what literary life had been like before I left. In theory there *was* no literary life, but in practice a supposedly philistine society was already saturated with poetry through many layers.

When I was growing up, the "Argonauts" programme on ABC radio featured a delightfully pedantic character called Anthony Inkwell, played by none other than A. D. Hope. The school reader called *The Wide Brown*

Land read like a thriller. (Douglas Stewart edited one of its revisions.) Some of the home-grown comic strips had dialogue better than a play: *Wally and the Major, Ginger Meggs, Bluey and Curly.* ("When Bluey drinks, everybody drinks!" shouts Bluey. Everyone in the pub orders a beer and downs it in one. "When Bluey pays, everybody pays!" shouts Bluey, and goes down in a screaming heap.) Thus a generation was painlessly initiated into a concern with language. The nineteenth-century Australian tradition that Les Murray was later to call "newspaper poetry" had never died—one trusts it never will—and it was quite common for newly published poems to be talked about as current events.

When Gwen Harwood bailed out of the *Bulletin*, she gave its editor a poem he was proud of having published until someone pointed out that its capitalized letters at the beginning of each line formed the valedictory acrostic SO LONG BULLETIN FUCK ALL EDITORS. I was serving out my year on the *Sydney Morning Herald* at the time and I can remember the kerfuffle on the editorial floor when a copy of that issue of the *Bulletin* was brought in and crooned over by rugby scrums of delighted journos. Everyone who could push a pen laughed about it in the pubs: all were agreed that it was the wittiest outrage since the Ern Malley hoax—which, only fifteen short years before, with Hope whispering encouragement from the wings, had been cooked up by the young McAuley, along with the only slightly older Harold Stewart. Not to be confused with his namesake Douglas Stewart, Harold Stewart was one of those born fringe dwellers who depend for their income by finding money in the street. A homosexual racked by a doomed love for McAuley, decades later he ended up in Japan collecting haikus. Douglas Stewart, on the other hand, was cut out from the start for a career as a listed building. Self-exiled from New Zealand, Stewart took over the *Bulletin*'s Red Page and diligently built himself an unassailable place as mentor for the emergent poetry. (Kiwis in Australia are like Canucks in the U.S.: they try harder.) In my time Douglas Stewart was not only still around, he was at the height of his influence, magisterially fulfilling his role as editor of the Angus and Robertson pocket collections of canonical Australian poets. Many of them were his personal friends, but there was no point objecting, because canonical was what they were. They were a *pleiade*, those fiery people, and all the more so for being so individualistic. There had been no literary establishment to further their initial achievements. So they had built one. You could be impressed or not—I was only one of the young writers who petulantly tried to ignore the whole thing—but the only way to escape its looming presence was to get on a ship.

Part of the edifice they built was the critical assessment of Australia's poetic heritage. Now that they have become part of that heritage themselves, the new critical task is to assess them. They have made it easy for us: every name from that period wrote at least a handful of poems powerful enough to travel through time and space without benefit of academic apparatus. For them it was not quite so simple: the indigenous past could be claimed as a foundation, but to the surveyor's sceptical glance it was a shaky one, and the urge to firm it up with an injection of scholarship was hard to resist. In truth, their own poetry was written in the context of the modern international achievement, where Yeats and Eliot, rather than Brennan and Shaw Neilson, were the pervasive immediate ancestors. But in politics, nationalism called, with its inevitable attendant imperative to cook the books. The results were sometimes questionable, but we need to remember that the impulse must have seemed like a responsibility, or so many mavericks would not have adopted professorial robes. For Slessor and Fitzgerald, the Grand Old Men, the academy had not been available as a support system. For *les jeunes*, most of whom were born around 1920, the universities of the pre- and immediate post-war years were available as a refuge, a reservoir of scholastic back-up, and a base from which they might begin the long job of broadcasting their views about the hidden depths of the national achievement.

Sydney University, in particular, was a nerve centre. A. D. Hope, a crucial decade older than the others, had been there in the late 1920s and had covered himself with academic honours. At Oxford he went haywire and came away with a gentleman's Third. To hindsight, it looks as if fate wanted him to be back in Sydney and firmly placed at the Teachers' College so that he could offer the benefit of his poetic experience when McAuley showed up there as a trainee in the late 1930s. In fact it worked the other way: McAuley scrutinized Hope's manuscripts and not vice versa. Hope was, and would always be, a modest man. McAuley was quite the other thing. His multiple personality—intellectual by day, ragtime musician by night, seducer anytime—ideally fitted him for the university's perennial connection with a downtown bohemia. It didn't matter if you were officially enrolled or not, because the nightlife was a seminar with piano accompaniment. The atmosphere is well evoked in Cassandra

Pybus's *The Devil and James McAuley* (1999), whose early chapters amount to the best thing yet published about the poetic ferment that started in the early 1940s: she is not very profound about the poetry, but she is terrific on the ferment. It should be remembered that Sydney University was still comparatively small time in those days. The age of expansion had not yet begun, and indeed when the war was over it still hadn't. Only after the Menzies government introduced the Commonwealth Scholarship scheme did the universities become the catalytic towers for Australia's final refinement into the meritocratic society we know today. By the late 1950s, Sydney University was a bustling initial assembly point for the new artistic and media elites, which, having come up out of nowhere, nowadays inevitably tend to reminisce about their alma mater as if it were the somewhere that really counted. Peter Porter, a boy from Brisbane, has several times been heard to say that Sydney University gives its graduates a self-confidence denied to those who never went there.

Porter enjoys talking himself down: to the admiring observer, he never seemed to lack self-confidence when he set about occupying his world-ranking position. But viewed on the Australian scale, there is something to what he says. Sydney University is a hot spot. The thing to bear in mind is that in the 1940s it wasn't that yet. The upcoming literary mandarins would help to make it so, but at the time they were not joining a new power structure. They were the misfit products of an old one. The working class and the lower middle class could not afford to send their children to university. (In an otherwise markedly egalitarian society, this was one of the few limitations that made it meaningful to talk about a class structure at all.) The student body was provided mainly by the entrenched bourgeoisie and the squattocracy, social strata united in their unbending conservatism. Any student with artistic ambitions was a conscious rebel against his own background, and that went double if it was her own background.

A clear instance was Judith Wright. In the year before her death an autobiography came out. Called *Half a Lifetime*, it confirmed the impression she had always liked to give, of a daughter of the landed gentry whose upbringing had given her a disturbing insight into how white civilization stole the black man's country, and who had gone on to find her authenticity not just through her art but through a modest existence dedicated to living off the land without exploiting it any further. She had already, in the Homerically entitled *The Generations of Men* (1959), given an account of her family's history on the land: unavoidably it was a good story, as the story of a dynasty perpetuating itself always is, but she left no doubt that she regarded the whole epic as an offence against natural law. Taken together, the volumes that record her family saga and the way she left it behind add up to a vital work—rather more vital, if the truth be told, than her later poetry—but what it leaves out is the turmoil of her personal transition from chrysalis to butterfly. The official biography, *South of My Days*, published two years before her death—it is pleasing to note that the great lady made her exit to the sound of trumpets—gives us some of the facts. Its author, Veronica Brady, doesn't always seem to know what the facts signify, but her determination to leave nothing out pays off. Though an academic by profession, she is a nun by vocation, and is perhaps too pure to realize just how revolutionary her country girl turned out to be when she arrived in Sydney and opened her mind and heart to the freedoms of *la vie de Bohème*.

At the university, the young Judith radicalized her politics. As an unmatriculated student she was never in line for a degree, but her originality remains chastening even in retrospect. Twenty years later I sat listening to the same anthropology lectures she heard and it simply never occurred to me that the stuff about the Aboriginals was dynamite. Young Judith got the point from the jump. On that and every other social issue, she went left in a big way, although communism was too authoritarian to hold her: too authoritarian, and possibly too plebeian. Essentially a patrician proto-hippie, she would remain unique until the late 1960s made her look normal. But to be radical in politics was unremarkable: the Depression was not yet over. (In Australia the Depression and the war were continuous: fifteen years in a hard school.) Her really radical radicalism was in her love life.

Upstate, in the vast rural area where New South Wales has its own New England, in the territory of the grand families where the marriageability of daughters counted—it still does—she had been a hopeless case. In Sydney's Kings Cross she found her context. Along with Darlinghurst and Paddington, Kings Cross has been romanticized in retrospect as a combination of the Left Bank, Schwabing, Greenwich Village and ancient Rome on a Saturday night. Actually, there was barely a square mile where unconventional behaviour could have been observed by an invisible man. Even in my day, the area's resident succubus, Rosaleen

Norton, got into the newspapers mainly for wearing green eyeshadow and staying up past her bedtime. Pre-war, it counted as devil worship to drink red wine out of a teacup. My father and mother shared a room in Darlinghurst but they were careful to get married first: somebody might have called the police. Yet Judith Wright took lovers. In the plural! Still amazing after sixty years, this news is set down by her biographer in a neutral tone, as if it were merely a defiant gesture, and not the equivalent of throwing a bomb at the Governor General. For once it is the lack of salacious details, and not their irrelevant plenitude, that drives the reader crazy. Who were these men?

They didn't get into her poetry. Reading between the lines of her early poems, you can just about deduce that there might have been more than one Lothario on the scene, but not more than two, and they both sound the same. As the war got under way, some of her first love poems propelled their best lines into the collective memory. The opening stroke of "The Company of Lovers" rang a passing bell for an epoch:

> We meet and part now all over the world.
> We, the lost company.

But after that, the poem faded. As with any other subject, she turned passion into an abstraction. She could cantilever an extended line like nobody else: generations of schoolchildren, and not just the boys, have had good cause to remember "Your delicate dry breasts, country that built my heart." She was the mistress of the stately measure. But too much of her poetry was unpeopled, undetailed and finally unrealized. Clearly she meant to speak for all women—her first two books rank high among the Australian poetry by women that leaves the men sounding Neanderthal—but she rarely did it with the same universal applicability that Gwen Harwood achieved by speaking for herself. Even early on, there were only a few poems by Wright that yielded to being remembered entire, and later she seemed bent on defeating the possibility, as her vocabulary moved beyond the abstract into a kind of profligate inertia. Flames danced, blood pulsed and crystals hummed in an unspecific dreamtime of ectoplasmic images that never swam into focus before they dissipated. In short, she lost it. But when Les Murray hinted that this might be so, he did not get lynched: a sure sign that Wright's generation had produced,

as an incidental benefit, a critical climate in which it would be possible
to pass a limiting judgement on a totemic literary figure without seeming
to bring the whole national achievement into question.

In her life as an environmental activist, Wright was a lioness. She
took on whole conglomerates in open battle, and saved the Barrier Reef
practically single-handed. But she would never have dared to say about
Christopher Brennan what Murray said about her. Her nationalist commitment ruled that out. It would have been too true. The poets of the
1940s consolidated a national literary culture by writing to world standards. A nationalist impulse is never sufficient to do that: all it can guarantee is to produce a more self-conscious provincialism. But those same
poets also felt compelled to act as critics, scholars, editors, archivists and
anthologists, and in those roles they had to be nationalists, or else be seen
to repudiate the literary heritage of their own country. A. D. Hope was
well equipped to have done just that, had he wished. He was thoroughly
acquainted with the main body of English literature back to Chaucer and
beyond. He read easily in a dozen languages. (Late in life, when he was
translating *The Lusiads* of Camões, he did it directly from the Portuguese,
with no cribs.) His first collection of poems, *The Wandering Islands*, was
delayed for years by the threat of censorship, but when, in 1955, he finally
published it, the impact was enormous, and not just in Australia. Since it
contained scarcely a single specifically Australian reference, the book
travelled well. He could have set up shop anywhere in the English-speaking world. But he had already hung out his shingle as the curator of Australia's national literature. First at Melbourne University after the war,
and then during his long tenancy as professor of English at the Australian
National University in Canberra, he gave Australian writing the same
comprehensive attention that he gave to the rest of the world. The comprehensive attention did not include indulgence. The harsh things he
said about Gerard Manley Hopkins (he was as wrong about Hopkins as
he was right about Yeats) were a caress compared with what he did to
Patrick White, who resented Hope's assault on his early prose until the
day he died. Contemporary writers had good cause to be apprehensive
about Hope's relentless crusade against loose language. But it was notable
that when he talked about the Australian writers of the past he was reluctant to erode their reputations. Quite apart from his continuing regard for
Brennan, he was determined, for example, to go on finding the longueurs
of Joseph Furphy structurally functional: in other words, *Such Is Life* was

meant to be tedious. At least he caned Miles Franklin for saying that Furphy was better than Henry James, Proust and James Joyce. Hope's collection of critical articles *Native Companions* (1974) is full of instances where special pleading is made plausible by acumen. But as the title hints, special pleading is the purpose.

Judith Wright's equivalent volume, *Preoccupations in Australian Poetry* (1965), worked the same strategy. She was a discriminating critic, but she wasn't going to give Brennan away. Well capable of seeing that his World War I propaganda poetry was inexcusably awful, she still wanted to preserve a lyrical harbinger. It was a lie, of course: international Modernism was the harbinger, not Brennan, whose connection to his admired Mallarmé had been the same as the connection of the "Paris end" of Melbourne's Collins Street to Paris. But it was a necessary lie, one that felt as if it ought to be true. Douglas Stewart's critical collection *The Broad Stream* (1975) was in the same case. Stewart was illuminatingly enthusiastic about the balladeers. But he also managed to say approving things about Norman Lindsay's novels. *The Magic Pudding* is still read by every Australian child whose parents buy books at all, and there were few male poets of the great generation, from Slessor onwards, who were not influenced by Lindsay's unflagging labours as a sexual libertarian, a species of which pre-war Australia possessed few examples who were not in gaol. (As an artist with the female form for a stock in trade, Lindsay was surrounded by strapping models who looked as if they might like a young poet for breakfast—a dream come true.) But Lindsay was a hopelessly slapdash novelist, and for someone of Stewart's fastidious taste to have pretended otherwise can have only a political explanation.

The politics worked. By conjuring up the foundations of a nationalist edifice from the past, the poets built an ideal world—Australian literature—in which they could confidently pursue their real work, which was to get on with their poetry without feeling flattened from the start by the weight of Britain's example. And if some of the reputations they rescued from the cellar were fragile, others were well worth dusting off. The poet-critics made their best judgements when they edited active anthologies intended to show the line of succession since the days of Henry Lawson and Banjo Patterson. McAuley's *A Map of Australian Verse* (1975) was particularly good. Sweating the luminaries down to a few strong poems each, he intercalated short critical articles to analyse their strengths—and, in the vexed case of Brennan, the weaknesses. Letting go of Brennan altogether was still out of the question, but McAuley was able to say that Shaw Neilson, who knew much less about English literature and nothing at all about any other literature, was the better poet. He simply wrote better poems.

Through their widespread critical activity and their tireless anthologizing—anthologies sold well, but they were hard work—the great generation had taken a long route to a goal they had scarcely glimpsed when they started out: but, aided by the unarguable quality of the poetry they themselves had produced, they finally got there. They had made a beginning on the essential job of switching the emphasis from the poetic career to the actual poems, and done it without abandoning the past, where even the failures could now be seen to have made a contribution, if only by marking the wrong tracks with their bleached bones. Australian poetry consisted of good poems written by Australians: and that was it. The way was open for the next generation to speak in an Australian voice, which could now, at last, be defined as a voice that had no need to worry if it did not sound British. There was no other definition it needed.

The next generation was in the enviable position of spending the money daddy made. Inevitably the results were not always edifying. Where poetry had once been a life sentence for the elect, it now became a lifestyle for the ambitious. Every kookaburra thought he was a songbird. But to a gratifying extent it has been the story of a nation achieving eloquence without just talking to itself. Luckily the critical tradition has been passed on. Les Murray, for example, has proved to be a critic as finely tuned as his masters, and even better as an anthologist. His A Working Forest (1997) is the first collection of essays to read about Australian literature, and The New Oxford Book of Australian Verse (augmented edition 1991) is a wonderland of a book that would be indispensable for its Aboriginal poetry alone—in a single bold gesture he pushed back the far boundary of Australia's cultural past from 1788 all the way to the dreamtime. But a less striking boldness is the one that really counts: without fear or favour, he picked his way through the output of his predecessors as if they were contemporaries, and found the poems that live. The predecessors turned out to be mortal, and from that the contemporaries have taken courage. Now every aspirant realizes, or should realize, that it's not the career that matters: it's getting something said that will speak for itself. A measure of how the Australian poetic world has been enriched is that Murray does not dominate it, either as critic or as poet. Except for Porter,

Murray makes incomparably more impact abroad than any other Australian national, but at home, though he is *primus*, he is definitely *inter pares*. Nobody would want to be without Chris Wallace-Crabbe's critical views, which are as sharply focussed as his verse; or without the wild lyrical flights of Bruce Dawe, who was the first to remind Australia that it was the American voice, and not the British one, that threatened to drown us out. A typical Dawe poem has no more structure than an evening in the pub, but radiates a humane intelligence that makes you want to join him at the bar. When Bruce drinks, everybody drinks. We lost John Forbes too early, and his unique voice is rightly praised: but some of his uniqueness he got from Dawe. When Forbes started a poem with "Spent tracer flecks Baghdad's/bright video game sky" he was developing a tone that Dawe discovered, principally by watching the television screen, through which the world's griefs came to remind the lucky country that it had never been as isolated as it feared or fancied.

Once again, however, it is poems that matter, not reputations; and I can think of dozens of Australian poems I have read enthralled in the last few years whose authors I couldn't name to save my life. Such profligacy of achievement is the surest sign of a culture in the ascendant, but the inescapable result of an outburst of energy in the present is that the past, even the near past, begins to look different. Of the first wave, Hope looks stronger than ever for the first two thirds of his career, but some of the later work, when he lost the tension of his line, is starting to sound garrulous. McAuley gets more interesting personally and less so poetically: a bad bargain. Wright, we can now see, paid a progressively more severe penalty for her lone stand against modern industrial society: she left out too much of its detail, and her timeless language has dated, as deliberately timeless language always does. Harwood, on the other hand, gets better all the time: the poems she wrote about her randy European music teachers are like chapters of a phantom novel that you wish existed. Rosemary Dobson, a secondary figure in the 1940s, has ascended to prominence now that the foreign travels she condensed into her verse have become the common experience of everyone who can afford to fly—which means practically everyone.

Australians feel better about wanting to see the world because they know now that the world wants to see Australia. After the Sydney Olympics, Australia's long identity crisis is over at last, even for the dullards who never realized that no such thing ever really existed. (In the last year of the war, when Australia was coping with the cultural threat of American troops tipping too much for taxis, Stalin was wiping out the few aspects of Polish civilization that Hitler had missed. Poland had an identity crisis. Australia just had a problem.) No stable, liberal and prosperous democracy has the slightest need for nationalism: it's an insult to a less fortunate world. National pride, though, is a different thing. Aided by the post-war immigration that brought memories of all the world's sufferings to temper and anneal the national consciousness, Australia's cultural upsurge by now amounts to a legitimate source of pride. The poets of the great generation were in at the start of it, gave it a manner of speaking and deserve respect, although there is no need to stand to attention with one hand over the heart. After all, it's Australia we're talking about, where even the most exalted language draws its rhythm and cadence from the vernacular, and a pretty rough vernacular at that. The first memorable phrase in the colony might have been coined by a convict who was stung by a bull ant, and the resplendent modern age of Australian poetry probably started when Hope met Brennan in the used beer department.

Times Literary Supplement, January 5, 2001;

later included in *The Best Australian Essays, 2001*

POSTSCRIPT

More than forty years of self-imposed exile, though nowadays I make frequent visits home, have had the merit of keeping me out of Australian literary politics. Hence I have been able to take a detached view of developments in Australian poetry, which have been manifold, often beneficial and sometimes breathtaking, like a long, fully dressed version of the Sydney Olympics with the whole nation for an arena. As the previous two articles demonstrate, I have been unable, in recent years, to restrain myself from providing a commentary, but I had the advantage of knowing that whatever I said would do no harm. The day has passed when home thoughts from abroad could make much difference, either through encouragement or through belittlement.

There is no reason, however, to think that the literary politics I was glad to leave behind do not continue unabated. On the tom-toms I hear about hatreds between poets, feuds between editors and grisly forms of verbal assassination. But even from my distant perch, it is obvious that the

Australian literary life, especially in poetry, also continues to be blessed by the local sense of the ridiculous, which rules out any posturings as a man of destiny. The careerism that infected American poetry after World War II took a more benign form in Australia. There was much jockeying for government grants—understandably, because with such a small population few writers of any kind can live on sales alone—but the prizes were not big enough to encourage foul play, and the worst injuries were to pride. Hardly anybody committed suicide, and despite the example of the erratically inspired Francis Webb it did not even become fashionable to go mad. The tragedies, when they happened, were more real than willed.

The worst tragedy was the early death from leukaemia of Philip Hodgins, who was greatly gifted, and fulfilled more of that great gift than his brief span and failing energy might have allowed. His poetry is not much known outside Australia. There is a lot of very good Australian poetry that isn't, and what Australia must come to terms with is that this is a desirable state of affairs. When a burgeoning culture produces more wealth than it can easily export, it starts to get interesting, through sharing the condition of the mountain to which Mahomet must come, and the better mousetrap to which the world must beat a path.

2003

PART II

FICTION

AND

LITERATURE

13

D. H. LAWRENCE

IN TRANSIT

If one were to take a wax pencil and trace Lawrence's travels on a globe of the world, the result would be an enigmatic squiggle: a squiggle that started off minutely preoccupied in Europe, was reduced still further to a fat dot formed by the cramped wartime movements within England, broke out, enlarged itself to a bold transoceanic zigzag which at one wild moment streaked right around the planet, and then subsided again into more diffident, European vagaries—still restless, but listless, tailing off. The pencil should properly come to a halt at Vence, in the Alpes Maritimes, although if we substituted for it another pencil of a different colour we might legitimately add one last, sweeping leg to the journey, as Lawrence's mobility recovered in death and his ashes rode back mindlessly to New Mexico.

In a few minutes we could map the wanderings of nearly two decades. It wouldn't tell us much, apart from the obvious fact that he liked to move about. He was in search of something, no question of it. Headquarters, the fissure into the underworld—it had many names. But one is permitted to doubt whether it could ever have been found, the doubt being engendered less by the world's nature than by an assessment of Lawrence's insatiable hunger for meaning. There is a tendency, once Lawrence's odyssey has been identified as a spiritual quest, to suppose that Lawrence had a firm idea of his spiritual object: hence the notion that he was in revolt against twentieth-century society, or post-Renaissance Europe, or post-Columbian America, or whatever you care to name. Lawrence was in revolt all right, but the revolt encompassed almost everything he knew in the present and nearly all the past he ever came to know, and this ability to exhaust reality through intimacy shows up in his travels as much as in anything else he did.

It was not so much that familiarity bred contempt—and anyway, there were some familiarities of which he never quite tired—as that it bred unease. Never to find things important enough is the mark of a dreamer. Lawrence, thoroughly practical and businesslike in matters large and small, was no ordinary dreamer: nevertheless he could get no lasting peace from his surroundings, and as time went by felt bound to look upon them as an impoverished outwardness implying a symbolic centre—and this despite an unrivalled ability to reflect the fullness of physical reality undiminished onto the page. Lawrence is beyond the reach of any other modern writer writing about what can be seen, since whatever could be seen he saw instantaneously and without effort— which is probably why he could regard it as nothing but the periphery of the real. If he had lived longer, his novels might well have lost any touch at all with worldly objects: the sense of actuality which other men serve long apprenticeships to attain was for him a departure point. And again if he had lived longer, he might well have exhausted the Earth with travel. Had he not placed such an emphasis on turning inwards to the dark, fiery centre, we could by now have been tempted to imagine him turning out- wards, away from the tellurian cultures depleted by the ravenous enquiry of his imagination and towards an uncapturable infinity that actually exists—orchestrations of dark suns, unapproachable galaxies peopled by Etruscans who stayed on top, nebulae like turquoise horses, the ocean of the great desire. Quetzalcoatl's *serape*! Sun-dragon! Star-oil! Lawrence was in search of, was enraged over the loss of, a significance this world does not supply and has never supplied. For a worldling, his symbolist requirements were inordinate. As a spaceman he might have found repose. Heaven knows, he was genius enough not to be outshone by the beyond. He could have written down a supernova.

Supposing, though, that this was what his journeyings were all in aid of—home. The supposition is at least part of the truth, although by no means, I think, the largest part. If home was ever anywhere, it was at the Del Monte and Flying Heart ranches in New Mexico—whose moun- tains seemed to be the place he could stay at longest without feeling com- pelled to move on. Yet there were still times when he missed Europe, just as, in Europe, there were so many times when he missed America, and just as, on either continent, there were troubled times when he missed England. Headquarters tended to be where Lawrence was not. Places abandoned because they did not possess the secret could be fondly remembered later on—perhaps they had had the secret after all. But it never occurred to Lawrence that there *was* no secret. Out of all the thousands of pages of his incredibly productive short life, the great pathos which emerges is of this extraterrestrial unbelonging—far more frightening, in the long run, than the social challenges which by now we have absorbed, or else written off as uninformative propositions. Critical unreason often occurs in creative genius, but creative unreason rarely does: for a talent to be as big as Lawrence's and yet still be sick is a strange thing. It's easily understandable that people equipped to appreciate his magnitude as a writer should take the intellectually less taxing course, declaring Lawrence to be a paragon of prophetic sanity and the world sick instead.

Lawrence's first travels were to London, Brighton, the Isle of Wight, Bournemouth. Readers of the early letters will be rocked back on their heels to find the same descriptive power turned loose on Brighton as later reached out to seize the dawn over Sicily, the flowers in Tuscany, the Sinai desert, the spermlike lake in Mexico and the ranches after snow. Then, in 1912, the first run to Metz, which was then in Germany: Waldbröl in the Rhineland, Munich, Mayrhofen in Austria. A walk over the Tyrol. Lake Garda. Back to England in 1913, then back to Bavaria. Lerici. England again. The war confined these short European pencil strokes to a fitfully vibrating dot within England, covering Sussex, Hampstead, Cornwall; an angry return to London after being hounded from the coast and possible contact with the High Seas Fleet; Berkshire, Derbyshire.

In 1919, free to quit England, he broke straight for Italy: Turin, Lerici, Florence, Rome, Picinisco, Capri. In 1920, Taormina, in Sicily. Malta. In 1921, Sardinia, Germany, Austria, Italy, Taormina again. (Taormina is a node, like—later on—Taos, and the Villa Mirenda at Scandicci, outside Florence.)

In 1922, the emboldened pattern struck outwards to Ceylon. Australia for two months. Then America: Taos, the Del Monte ranch, the mountains. In 1923 he was in Mexico City, New York, Los Angeles, Mexico again and . . . England. In 1924 France, Germany, New York, Taos. The Flying Heart ranch, alias the Lobo, alias the Kiowa. Oaxaca, in Mexico.

The year 1925 ended the period of the big pattern. After a wrecking illness in New Mexico he returned to London. Then Baden-Baden. Spotorno. In 1926, Capri, Spotorno and the Villa Mirenda in Scandicci—his last real place to be. Germany, England, Scotland. Italy.

In 1927 he toured the Etruscan tombs. A score of names cropped up in his itinerary: Volterra, Orvieto, Tarquinia—short strokes all over Tuscany and Umbria, the Etruscan places. Then to Austria and Germany, and in 1928 to Switzerland, with the Villa Mirenda abandoned. Gsteig bei Gstaad, Baden-Baden (the Kurhaus Plättig) and the Ile de Port-Cros, Toulon. From low-lying sun-trap to *Höheluftkurort* the short strokes moved trembling. Bandol, in the south of France. He was in Paris in 1929, then Palma de Mallorca, Forte dei Marmi, Florence, Bandol again. In 1930 Vence, and death.

Even in Vence he wasn't too sick to use his amazing eyes. There isn't a place on the list that he didn't inhabit at a glance. And yet as we read on and on through the magnificence of his travel writings, a little voice keeps telling us that the man was never there. The man, the spaceman, never travelled except in dreams. Dreaming, while dying, of India and China and everything else that lay beyond the San Francisco gate. Dreaming of altogether elsewhere, of an England that was not England, of a Europe that was never Europe.

It was a great day, Frieda said, when they walked together from the Isartal into the Alps. Lawrence wrote it down, in a way that takes us straight there. But where was he? "We stayed at a Gasthaus," he wrote to Edward Garnett, "and used to have breakfast out under the horse-chestnut trees, steep above the river weir, where the timber rafts come down. The river is green glacier water." Compare this to one of the famous opening sentences of *A Farewell to Arms*—"In the bed of the river there were pebbles and boulders, dry and white in the sun, and the water was clear and swiftly moving and blue in the channels"—and we will find Lawrence's descriptive prose both more economical and less nostalgic, the effortless reportage of an infallibly observant visitor.

Still on the same descriptive trail, go south to Italy ("I love these people") and look at Lerici. "And in the morning," he wrote to Lady Cynthia Asquith, "one wakes and sees the pines all dark and mixed up with perfect rose of dawn, and all day long the olives shimmer in the sun, and fishing boats and strange sails like Corsican ships come out of nowhere on a pale blue sea, and then at evening all the sea is milky gold and scarlet with sundown." The fake-naive rhythms, suitable for consumption by titled ladies, can't mask the searing power of that simplicity. "The mountains of Carrara are white, of a soft white blue eidelweiss, in a faint pearl haze—all snowy. The sun is very warm, and the sea glitters." It still does, even though polluted with a thoroughness which even Lawrence would have hesitated to prophesy. "The Mediterranean is quite wonderful—and when the sun sets beyond the islands of Porto Venere, and all the sea is like heaving white milk with a street of fire across it, and amethyst islands away back, it is too beautiful." It's small wonder that Lawrence could talk about art having characteristics rather than rules, and even disparage the idea of art altogether. He had it to burn.

Reality offered Lawrence no resistance. Mysticism did, and it was into mysticism that he poured his conscious energy. Turning to *Twilight in Italy*, we can find something on every page to match the descriptions in the letters. Here is Lake Garda at dawn.

In the morning I often lie in bed and watch the sunrise. The lake lies dim and milky, the mountains are dark blue at the back, while over them the sky gushes and glistens with light. At a certain place on the mountain ridge the light burns gold, seems to fuse a little groove on the hill's rim. It fuses and fuses at this point, till of a sudden it comes, the intense, molten, living light. The mountains melt suddenly, the light steps down, there is a glitter, a spangle, a clutch of spangles, a great unbearable suntrack flashing across the milky lake, and the light falls on my face.

But superb as this is, it isn't what this book or any other Lawrence book is about. *Twilight in Italy* is about north and south, hill and dale— it is the tentative prototype for a great sequence of increasingly confident polarities, by which Lawrence the traveller was to go on splitting the world in two until there was nothing left of it but powder. The Bavarian highlanders, it appears, "are almost the only race with the souls of artists . . . their processions and religious festivals are profoundly impressive, solemn, and rapt." Again, they are "a race that moves on the poles of mystic sensual delight. Every gesture is a gesture from the blood, every expression a symbolic utterance." Your Bavarian highlander "accepts the fate and the mystic delight of the senses with one will, he is complete and final. His sensuous experience is supreme, a consummation of life and death at once." Whether drinking in the Gasthaus, or "hating steadily and

cruelly," or "walking in the strange, dark, subject-procession" to bless the
fields, "it is always the same, the dark, powerful mystic, sensuous experience is the whole of him, he is mindless and bound within the absolute-
ness of the issue, the unchangeability of the great icy not-being which
holds good for ever, and is supreme." Yes, it was all happening in
Bavaria—or rather, it was all to happen later on in Bavaria. But the thing
to grasp here is that word "dark." Not only (as is well known) is it the key
adjective in all of Lawrence, but Lawrence's travels can usefully be summarized as an interminable search for a noun it could firmly be attached
to.

No sooner is Lawrence in Italy than we discover that the Italians
have dark interiors too. "The Italian people are called 'Children of the
Sun.' They might better be called 'Children of the Shadow.' Their souls
are dark and nocturnal." A feature of the dark soul is unconsciousness, as
in the spinning-woman, whose mind Lawrence can apparently read. "She
glanced at me again, with her wonderful, unchanging eyes, that were like
the visible heavens, unthinking, or like the two flowers that are open in
pure clear unconsciousness. To her I was a piece of the environment.
That was all. Her world was clear and absolute, without consciousness of
self. She was not self-conscious, because she was not aware that there was
anything in the universe except *her* universe."

But the darkly unconscious haven't got it all their own way. Much
later in the book, during the fascinating passage that deals with the local
production of *Amleto*, Lawrence spies a mountain-man in the audience:
he is of the same race as the old spinning-woman. "He was fair, thin, and
clear, abstract, of the mountains. . . . He has a fierce, abstract look, wild
and untamed as a hawk, but like a hawk at its own nest, fierce with love
. . . it is the fierce spirit of the Ego come out of the primal infinite, but
detached, isolated, an aristocrat. He is not an Italian, dark-blooded. He is
fair, keen as steel, with the blood of the mountaineer in him. He is like
my old spinning woman."

To reconcile this mountain-man with the spinning-woman, we must
assume she was never dark-blooded, when a good deal of what we were
told about her when we were reading about her suggested that she was.
And indeed, looking back, we find that she *hasn't* been given a dark soul
or dark blood—she is simply "the core and centre to the world, the sun,
and the single firmament." Lawrence hasn't at this stage entirely identified the dark soul with the earth's centre, so it's still possible to combine

abstractness with being at the centre of the world, and, presumably, dark-bloodedness with *not* being at the centre of the world. What's difficult to reconcile, however, even when stretching the idea of poetic consistency until it snaps, is a Bavarian highlander's dark-bloodedness with a mountain-man's clear abstractness: if these conditions are both different from an ordinary Italian's dark-bloodedness, are they different in different ways?

The awkward truth is that Lawrence left his Bavarian highlanders behind in his opening chapter and forgot about them while writing the bulk of the book, which even without them would still be extremely difficult to puzzle out. The confusion confesses itself in the passage about Paolo and Maria. Paolo is a native of San Gaudenzio, and therefore a hill man—fair, eyes-like-ice, unalterable, inaccessible. Maria is from the plain—dark-skinned, slow-souled. "Paolo and she were the opposite sides of the universe, the light and the dark." Nothing could be clearer. "They were both by nature passionate, vehement. But the lines of their passion were opposite. Hers was the primitive, crude, violent flux of the blood, emotional and undiscriminating, but wanting to mix and mingle. His was the hard, clear, invulnerable passion of the bones, finely tempered and unchangeable." As an opponent to, or complement of, the passion of the blood, the passion of the bones was evidently judged by Lawrence to be somewhat unwieldy—it never again made such an unabashed appearance. Pretty soon, the blood's passion became the only kind of authentic passion you could have.

In *Twilight in Italy*, though the destructive mechanization of the world had already clearly been perceived, Lawrence still had something to say for abstractness, intellectuality and cognate non-dark attributes. In 1915 he wrote to Lady Ottoline Morrell from Ripley, in Derbyshire: "It is a cruel thing to go back to that which one has been. . . . Altogether the life here is so dark and violent; it all happens in the senses, powerful and rather destructive: no mind or mental consciousness, unintellectual. These men are passionate enough, sensuous, dark—God, how all my boyhood comes back—so violent, so dark, the mind always dark and without understanding, the senses violently active. It makes me sad beyond words." It's not the first time that the word "dark" is used like a comma, but it's one of the few times—all early—when Lawrence freely admitted the possibility that the dark soul could be as murderous on its own as intellect could. The emphasis was still on keeping a balance, on checking the word against the thing it was supposed to stand for. Lawrence's later history is the story of darkness being awarded a steadily more automatic virtue, the periodic calls for an equilibrium of forces degenerating into unfathomable proposals about establishing the correct relationship between the components of darkness itself.

Lawrence's "dash" (his word) to Sardinia produced a book—*Sea and Sardinia*—which clearly shows his untroubled ability to uproot all the attributes he has just so triumphantly detected in a place, move them on to the next place and then condemn the first place for either not having them in sufficient strength or never having had them. In Cagliari the men "stood about in groups, but without the intimate Italian watchfulness that never leaves a passer-by alone." Looks as if the Italians' dark blood wasn't dark enough, an impression confirmed by the menacing loins of the Sardinian peasant, "a young one with a swift eye and hard cheek and hard, dangerous thighs. . . . How fascinating it is, after the soft Italians, to see these limbs in their close knee-breeches, so definite, so manly, with the old fierceness in them still. One realizes, with horror, that the race of men is almost extinct in Europe . . ." Plainly the war period has helped sour Lawrence on Europe altogether, but even taking that convulsive time-lag into account, it's still difficult to square up *Sea and Sardinia* with *Twilight in Italy*. The real difference, it appears, is that Italy is *connu* and therefore sterile, whereas Sardinia is unknown and therefore isn't. "There are unknown, unworked lands where the salt has not lost its savour. But one must have perfected oneself in the great past first."

Whether in the vegetable market near the start of the book or at the peasants' procession near the end, Lawrence's colour sense is at its sumptuous best, and in general *Sea and Sardinia* is a remarkable piece of visualization. "When we came up, the faint shape of land appeared ahead, more transparent than thin pearl. Already Sardinia. Magic are high lands seen from the sea, when they are far, far off, and ghostly translucent like icebergs." Beautiful writing, but no lasting pledge. Lawrence was in and out of Sardinia in a hurry, and spent a good half of 1921 sitting in Taormina getting sick of Europe, which can't be said to exclude Sardinia. Just as Sardinia had it over Italy, somewhere else had it over the whole of Europe. "I would like to break out of Europe," he wrote to Mary Cannan. "It has been like a bad meal of various courses . . . and one has got indigestion from every course." He was thinking of "something more vel-

vety"—Japan, perhaps, or Siam. The south of Europe was better than the
north, but there was no denying that even the south had gone off: "I can't
get the little taste of canker out of my mouth," he told Catherine Carswell, "The people—" A few days later he was telling E. H. Brewster that
they were *canaille, canaglia, Schweinhunderei,* stinkpots. "A curse, a mur-
rain, a pox on this crawling, sniffling, spunkless brood of humanity."

   In his mind Lawrence was already embarked for Ceylon, and in
another few days Mabel Dodge—by inviting him to Taos—had made it
possible for him to project his mental journey right around the globe.
Europe was promptly pronounced to be "a dead dog which begins to
stink intolerably." England (in the same letter, written to S. S. Koteliansky) was declared "a dead dog that died of a love disease like syphilis." Bad
news for Koteliansky, who was living in it at the time. (This letter also featured the Lawrentian pearl about "one of those irritating people who have
generalized detestations. . . . So unoriginal.")

   "I feel I can't come—" Lawrence wrote to Brewster in January 1922,
"that the East is not my destiny." Later in the same month, destiny doubled back, and Lawrence decided to go via Ceylon after all. "I feel it is
my destiny," he wrote to Mabel Dodge, "to go east before coming west."
Destiny pulled another double-cross in Ceylon, where Lawrence found
the velvety Orient inane. "The East, the bit I've seen," he told Mary Cannan, "seems silly." As he frequently did when off-balance, he thought of
England, telling Robert Pratt Barlow that "the most living clue of life is
in us Englishmen in England, and the great mistake we make is in not
uniting together in the strength of this real living clue—religious in the
most vital sense—uniting together in England and so carrying the vital
spark through . . . the responsibility for England, the living England, rests
on men like you and me and Cunard—probably even the Prince of
Wales. . . ." The Prince of Wales was indirectly responsible for Lawrence's
"Elephant" poem, the most tangible result of the Singhalese sojourn
apart from a disillusioning close-up of inscrutable platoons of dark people
with dark eyes—"the vastness of the blood stream, so dark and hot and
from so far off."

   As far as the East went, darkness was a dead loss. Not that the contradiction with many things he'd said before, or with nearly everything he
said later, ever slowed him down. The task was to push his mystical system around the planet until it clicked; there was no obligation to explain
why it kept going wrong.

Australia was a country Lawrence couldn't characterize . . . "the spell of its indifference gets me." Mystical content, zero. "This is the most democratic place I have *ever* been in," he wrote to Else Jaffe, "And the more I see of democracy the more I dislike it. . . . You *never* knew anything so nothing, *nichts, nullus, niente,* as the life here." The situations in *Kangaroo* are mainly imported, and it's doubtful if Lawrence ever gave Australia much thought after the first few days. Nevertheless the settings in *Kangaroo* have small trouble in being the most acutely observed and evocative writing about Australia that there has so far been—bearing out my point that Lawrence could reproduce reality with no effort whatsoever. Trollope, Kipling, Conrad, Galsworthy and R. L. Stevenson all visited Australia at one time or another, but if any of them was capable of bringing off a piece of scene setting like the opening chapter of *Kangaroo*, he didn't feel compelled to. The moment he got to Thirroul, Lawrence despatched letters announcing his longing for Europe—the dead dog lived again. The central situation in *Kangaroo* looks to be about Italian Fascism—the Australian variety, which emerged much later, was very different. But *Kangaroo* is a bit more than a European play with an Australian set designer. It has an interesting early scene in which Lawrence makes Lovat out to be a prig, reluctant to lend Jack Callcott a book of essays in case it bores him. " 'I might rise up to it, you know,' said Jack laconically, 'if I bring all my mental weight to bear on it.' " There is a hint, here, that someone might have shaken Lawrence by urging him to lay off the intensity. It's a rare moment of self-criticism, and almost *the* moment of self-deprecating humour. Lawrence was perhaps a touch less certain about the aridity of the Australian spirit than he let on.

America. Lorenzo in Taos—it was a giant step. It rapidly became clear that the most dangerous item of local fauna was Mabel Dodge, the hostess who favoured will over feeling—a priority always guaranteed to grate on Lawrence, whose will and feeling were united in Destiny. "My heart still turns most readily to Italy," he told Mary Cannan—a strong sign of unease—and "I even begin to get a bit homesick for England . . ." A certain sign. At this stage Lawrence had decided that the Indians couldn't be copied. "And after all, if we have to go ahead," he wrote to Else Jaffe, "we must ourselves go ahead. We can go back and pick up some threads—but these Indians are up against a dead wall, even more than we are: but a different wall." And to Catherine Carswell: "*Però, son sempre Inglese.*" Even after moving to the Del Monte, putting a helpful seventeen miles between himself and the Mabel-ridden Taos, Lawrence was detecting the same *innerlich* emptiness in his surroundings as had wasted his time in Australia. Mexico, however, worked differently, and he was soon telling the much-maligned Middleton Murry that if England wanted to lead the world again she would have to pick up a lost trail, and that the end of the trial lay in—Mexico.

The Plumed Serpent is a work of uncanny poetic force which manages to keep some sort of shape despite intense distorting pressures from Lawrence's now-rampant mysticism. Kate, with her European blood and conscious understanding, is outdistanced by dark-faced silent men with their columns of dark blood and dark, fiery clouds of passionate male tenderness. In addition to the oppressive symbolic scheme, there are moments which lead you to suspect that the author might simply be cracked—as when he suggests that Bolshevists are all born near railways. Yet chapter 5, "The Lake," is one of Lawrence's supreme stretches of writing. The boatman "pulled rhythmically through the frail-rippling, sperm-like water, with a sense of peace. And for the first time Kate felt she had met the mystery of the natives, the strange and mysterious gentleness between a scylla and charybdis of violence: the small poised, perfect body of the bird that waves wings of thunder and wings of fire and night in its flight." Frail-rippling—what a writer. The transparent purity of the book's descriptions is inseparable from its symbolic structure, which is an opposition between principles that no ordinary mortal will ever be able to clarify, since Lawrence himself could only grope towards them with incantatory phrase-making.

The book's incandescent set pieces—the burning of the images, the execution of the traitors and so on—are spaced apart by impenetrable thickets of unmeaning. "But within his own heavy, dark range he had a curious power," Kate learns of Cipriano. "Almost she could *see* the black fume of power which he emitted, the dark, heavy vibration of his blood . . . she could feel the curious tingling heat of his blood, and the heavy power of the *will* that lay unemerged in his blood." What the Bavarian highlanders and plains Italians had lost, the sons of Quetzalcoatl had gained.

Lawrence learned about Indians during the hiatus between writing the tenth and eleventh chapters of *The Plumed Serpent*. His mystical conclusions are distributed between the later part of that novel (e.g., the snake in the fire at the heart of the world) and *Mornings in Mexico*, a travel book of unusual difficulty, even for Lawrence. Certainly he no longer pleads for a balance between the disparate consciousnesses of the white man and the dark man. You can't, it appears, have it both ways. The most you can hope for is to harbour a little ghost who sees in both directions. Yet ghost or no ghost, Lawrence seems to be trying hard to belong to the Indian way, to the "abdomen where the great blood-stream surges in the dark, and surges in its own generic experiences." What we seek in sleep, Lawrence says, the Indians perhaps seek actively, "the dark blood falling back from the mind, from sight and speech and knowing, back to the great central source where is rest and unspeakable renewal." Relieved by some of his most brilliant descriptive passages, the rhetoric is short of totally suffocating, but still fearsomely turgid. It takes the letters to remind us that he could write in an unfevered way during this period. "Here the grass is only just moving green out of the sere earth," he wrote to Zelia Nuttall, "and the hairy, pale mauve anemones that the Indians call owl flowers stand strange and alone among the dead pine needles, under the wintry trees. Extraordinary how the place seems *seared* with winter: almost cauterized. And so winter-cleaned, from under three feet of snow." A cold towel for the reader's forehead. Green glacier water.

Back in Europe to stay, Lawrence unpacked his mystical machine and set about applying it to the Etruscans. At the same time, and without any disabling sense of contradicting himself, he started rehabilitating Europe, even the long-forsaken north. "I am very much inclined to agree," he wrote to Rolf Gardiner in July 1926, "that one must look for real guts and self-responsibility to the Northern peoples. After a winter in Italy—and a while in France—I am a bit bored by the Latins, there is a sort of inner helplessness and lack of courage in them. . . ." Writing from Lincolnshire to E. H. Brewster, he claimed to have rediscovered "a queer, odd sort of potentiality in the people, especially the common people. . . ." The common English people, back in the running at long last! Whether or not the Prince of Wales qualified wasn't stated.

As a traveller through ordinary space, Lawrence got back on slanging terms with his repudiated Europe. Baden-Baden, for example, was a *Totentanz* out of Holbein, "old, old people tottering their cautious dance of triumph: *wir sind noch hier*. . . ." As a traveller through time and thought, he moved on a grander scale. *Etruscan Places* is a gentle book, endearingly characteristic in its handy division between Etruscan and Roman and disarmingly uncharacteristic in its emphasis on delicacy and humour: it's the book of a strong man dying. "We have lost the art of living," he writes, "and in the most important science of all, the science of daily life, the science of behaviour, we are complete ignoramuses." The Etruscans weren't like that. Their art had the "natural beauty of proportion of the phallic consciousness, contrasted with the more studied or ecstatic proportion of the mental and spiritual Consciousness we are accustomed to." The contrast, as always, is asserted with a degree of confidence which is bound to draw forth a preliminary nod of assent. It remains a fact, however, that this kind of argument has practically nothing to do with post-Renaissance art or pre-Renaissance art or any kind of art, since art is more likely to depend on those two sorts of proportion being in tension than on one getting rid of the other. Lawrence's binomial schemes were useless for thinking about art, as those of his disciples who tried to employ them went on to prove. Without them, though, we wouldn't have had *his* art.

In January 1928, Lawrence told Dorothy Brett that he still intended coming back to the ranch. "It's very lovely," he wrote to Lady Glenavy, "and I'd be well there." But his seven-league boots were worn through, and he was never to get out of Europe alive. We have only to read "Reflections on the Death of a Porcupine" or the last part of *St. Mawr* to realize that his ashes ended up on the right spot. The mountains were a cherished place. They weren't home, though. Home was at the Source, and the Source—he said it himself—is past comprehension.

D. H. Lawrence, edited by Stephen Spender, 1972

P O S T S C R I P T

Stephen Spender kindly asked me to write this piece for one of those collections of articles by many hands which are supposed to celebrate the many-sided genius of a great writer. Inevitably they end up remaindered, but the opportunity to write at some length can be beneficial for critics grown too accustomed to composing in a thousand-word breath. I thought Lawrence was a greatly gifted writer. I just didn't think he was a great writer. To put it another way, I thought he could write but didn't like what he wrote. In this piece I managed to express both halves of the antinomy with sufficient illustrative material to get beyond mere contentiousness and into the realm of reasoned argument. Since one of the principles I eventually developed as a critic was that a limiting judgement of an artist should be offered only after full submission to whatever quality made him remarkable in the first place, I count this piece as an early success. I ought to have ended it, however, with the logical conclusion that because Lawrence commanded a power of poetic evocation far beyond his capacity for prose argument, his most characteristic work should be sought amongst his poetry, where indeed it can be found: his animal poems are among the unignorable ignition points of twentieth-century literature, and no syllabus of modern poetry that leaves them out can be trusted as a guide to what it puts in.

The Metropolitan Critic, 1994

14

THE PERPETUAL PROMISE
OF JAMES AGEE

The two volumes of Agee's bye-writings called *The Collected Poems of James Agree* and *The Collected Short Prose of James Agee* don't add anything revolutionary to our picture of the author, but what they do add is good and solid. The *Collected Poems* volume reissues the whole of the long-lost "Permit Me Voyage" and tacks on about three times as much other material, thereby vastly enlarging the field in which Agee can be studied as a poet. The results of such a study are likely to be mixed, since his disabling limitations as a poet are revealed along with the continuity of his dedication and seriousness: poetry just didn't bring out the best in him. The *Collected Short Prose* volume, on the other hand, is a book which demands to be considered—some of the pieces collected in it are as weighty and as rich as scraps and shavings can well get.

"He had so many gifts," Dwight Macdonald once wrote of Agee, "including such odd ones, for intellectuals, as reverence and feeling." Very true, and what is more he had them at an early age. The early *Harvard Advocate* short stories included here are quite astonishing in their moral maturity: the emotional wisdom that other men must strive to attain seems to have been present in Agee as a gift, and it's easy to see why he impressed his contemporaries as some kind of Rimbaud of the under-standing—the range of sympathy inspires not just awe, but a certain dread. Indeed it's possible to argue, in the light of these early efforts, that to have it all is to have too much. Men whose minds and talents grow through the recognition and correction of error probably find it easier to shape their lives. Agee had a deficient practical sense, largely bungled his

career, completed only a tenth of what was in him and habitually over-
wrote—economy, for an artist with a faculty of registration as fertile as his,
didn't mean weeding the garden so much as chopping the orchids down
with a machete. Only the kind of sensitivity which develops can come up
with a novel like *The Great Gatsby*—to produce a book like that in its
maturity, it has to be capable of writing *This Side of Paradise* in its youth.
A saving obtuseness was simply never part of Agee's equipment. With his
entire creative life stretching ahead of him, he had almost nothing left to
learn.

   "Death in the Desert," from the October 1930 issue of the *Harvard
Advocate*, is the story of a young man hitch-hiking through the slump. At
first glance it's anybody's story of a college boy going on the bum to discover America, and turns on the seemingly elementary moral point that
the kind couple who pick him up won't stop for a Negro in serious trouble. But the control of the narrative, the modulations of the tone, the registration of speech patterns and the presentation of character combine to
turn the story away from neatness and towards complexity, judgement
permanently suspended. The narrator (Agee in thin disguise) has a boil
in his ear. At the beginning of the story, where he waits an eternity to be
picked up while crippled hobos get lifts with ease, the boil looks like a
comic device.

   For a while I talked with a peg-legged man of perhaps sixty; he spent his
   winters with his niece and her husband in St Louis. In the summers he
   got out of their way. His luck was always good, he said—too damned
   good. This summer he'd been through St Louis twice already. Unless he
   did something about it, he'd be there again inside of a week. Did I have
   a cigarette? Thanks. . . . All the while, as he talked, he watched the cars
   come up the road, and flicked his thumb eastward as each one
   approached. He stood always with his peg leg towards town. Before long
   a Chandler, after running a half-mile gauntlet of men, slowed down for
   him. He took another cigarette and was gone.

      For the rest of us, rides came more slowly. My ear was too sore, by now,
   to make talking a pastime. I sat down on my coat and decided that it was
   rather less than necessary on days like this. After a couple of hours, I considered the manifold advantages of being conspicuously a cripple. After
   another hour I had the idea of holding up a sign:

SORE EAR
PLEASE

The humour reminds us of one previous writer, Lardner, and of several subsequent writers, especially Salinger, whose early stories like "This Sandwich Has No Mayonnaise" echo the tone precisely (consider the way that story's platoon sergeant translates his man-management problems into movie marquee slogans like FOUR MUST GO—FROM THE TRUCK OF THE SAME NAME). But the sore ear turns out to be a lot more than just a comic device. It's because of the nagging twinges he is suffering that the narrator decides to make no protest when the driver who picks him up eventually steps on the accelerator instead of the brake and races past the desperate Negro's outstretched arms. Agee is making the subtle point that we are likely to treat ourselves as a special case when we are in pain, and defer our duties on the assumption that the Fates, or our better selves, will understand. Like the bad tooth in *Darkness at Noon*, the boil resists all attempts to make something symbolical of it—it's just a fact, leading to more facts, in a sequence of marvellously analytical probings and worryings. Agee was twenty when he wrote the story. An ounce more talent and he would have sunk into the earth.

Another *Advocate* story, "They That Sow in Sorrow Shall Reap," is similarly . . . well, precocious is the wrong word: prodigious. The young Agee character is immured in a dreadful boarding house, whose master is an ageing and barely repressed queer. They strike a silent bargain, in which the old man is allowed to adore but not to touch, beyond the occasional friendly squeeze of the shoulder. Agee introduces a young acquaintance into the boarding house. The old man tries the friendly squeeze and gets slapped in the mouth. All the tacit understandings upon which the house has previously run, and especially the relationship between the old man and his wife, promptly collapse. Agee the character is reduced to tacit agonies of self-recrimination and regret, while Agee the writer records the to-ings and fro-ings in the shattered household with customary mastery. Supposing Agee had dropped dead the following year— wouldn't we be justified, on this showing, in the conjecture that he might have been one of the great writers of the century?

The real tragedy, looking back, is not in the presence of *Let Us Now Praise Famous Men* or *A Death in the Family* or all the other part-realized things, unsatisfactory though they are, but in the absence of that sequence of novels which might have recollected his life—a sequence for the writing of which he had qualifications rivalling Proust's. Unfortunately an "autobiographical novel" (his quotes) was only one among many of the long-term Agee projects. Recollection was fundamental to the cast of his mind, but it wasn't his creative obsession. He wasn't neurotic enough. If people had hated him more he might have taken revenge; if he had hated himself sufficiently, he might have made redress; as it was, he had only love to drive him forward, and love makes poor fuel in its pure state. It's a heavy irony that through Agee the "positive" creative attitude which people like Archibald MacLeish were currently calling for could well have established its own tradition. That it failed to come about was not just MacLeish's loss but everybody's, not least those who had seen the disingenuousness of the "positive" propaganda but who would be compelled in the future to watch the American novel wave goodbye to everything Agee represented. It's been said that Agee wasn't bored by virtue—another way of saying that he could see what was interesting about normality. When he went down, he took three or four decades of ordinary American life with him, and the middlebrow salvage operations—O'Hara, Cheever and the like—got nowhere near lifting the hulk.

The two "satiric" pieces included in *The Collected Short Prose* are from later in the day and are in a familiar Agee vein of phantasmagoria: the letter from Agee to Macdonald quoted in Macdonald's "Jim Agee, A Memoir" (printed as an appendix to the excellent critical essay on Agee in *Against the American Grain*) gives a better idea of the referential lushness of his intelligence when he allowed it to run wild. There was something compulsive about the way he piled on the detail, and friends who received such letters might well have frowned through their delight—why take so much time and trouble, and to what purpose? Here are some scraps from the letter to Macdonald:

I think *The Brothers Karamazov* deserves the co-operation of all the finest talents in Hollywood and wd. richly repay all research & expenditure. A fullsized replica, complete down to the last topmizznmst, of the Mad Tsar Pierre (Charles Laughton). Papa Karamazov (Lionel Barrymore). His comic servant Grigory (Wallace Beery). Grigory's wife (Zazu Pitts). Smerdyakov (Charles Laughton). Smerdyakov's Familiar, a cat named

Tabitha (Elsa Lanchester, the bride of Frankenstein). Zossima (Henry B. Walthall) . . . Miusov (Malcolm Cowley) . . . in Alyosha's Dream: Alyosha (Fred Astaire). Puck (Wallace Beery). Titania (Ginger Rogers or James Cagney). . . . Routines by Albertina Rasch. Artificial snow by Jean Cocteau. . . . Entire production supervised by Hugh Walpole. . . . To be played on the world's first Globular Screen, opening at the Hippodrome the night before *Jumbo* closes. . . . Artificial foreskins will be handed out at the north end of the Wilhelmstrasse to anyone who is fool enough to call for them.

Stuff like this reminds us of the many reasons why Perelman was unassailable—to begin with, he was far funnier. And Perelman wrote his madcap collages as therapy: Agee at this time (1936) was not involved in Hollywood and had no frustrations to work off, except perhaps the frustration of not being part of it all. There is something cancerous about this side of his talent. It produces cells uncontrollably, and the longer satirical piece included here (called "Dedication Day," and nominally given over to goosing the scientists and politicians responsible for the first atomic bombs) runs away with itself in a fashion simultaneously boring and worrying.

As convincing demonstrations of just how sensitive Agee was, there are two small fragments—"Run Over," about a cat hit by a car, and "Give Him Air," about a human car-crash victim dying—which are strictly unbearable: you'd need nerves of steel to read them twice. At the end of the first piece Agee notes in parenthesis that "Things like this are happening somewhere on the earth every second." It's one of the peculiarities of Agee's writing that he can achieve delicacy and subtlety but never distance. He took everything right on the chin. This doesn't mean that all his material presented itself to him as having equal value, but it did present itself with equal impact. If he'd cared less, he might have been able to shape things more easily. A man who doesn't know which way to turn finds it hard to get his head down. His doomed application for a 1937 Guggenheim grant is printed here—there are forty-seven separate projects.

For the Guggenheim people it must have been like trying to estimate Leonardo da Vinci in an early period. What were they to make of "Extension in writing; ramification in suspension; Schubert 2-cello Quintet"? ("Experiments, mostly in form of the lifted and maximum-suspended

periodic sentence. Ramification [and development] through developments, repeats, semi-repeats, of evolving thought, of emotion, of associ-
ates and dissonants.") Don't ring us: we'll ring you. The awkward truth is
that the capacity for general thought which Macdonald praised in Agee
worked mainly as a drawback, blurring his creative focus. His comparatively low productivity isn't sufficiently explained by pointing to his
chaotic style of life, and it's even possible to suggest—tentatively, remembering we are strangers—that the style of life might have been in part a
reflection of a gift continually troubled by the search for the one idea that
would temporarily suppress all the others. Where can will-power come
from in a mind so short of limitations?

Travel notes and movie projects end the book. The fragments of
filmscript bear out Macdonald's acute remark that Agee's scripts were the
work of a frustrated director—details of camera angles and lighting (precisely the stuff that no film director ever wants to see in a script) are gone
into at numbing length. As it happened, Agee spent the 1930s a long way
away from the Hollywood salt mines, toiling naked in a salt mine of
another type—the Luce magazines. The long (fifty-seven-page) and
praiseworthy introduction to the *Collected Short Prose* book is by Robert
Fitzgerald, a friend of Agee's, and valuably complicates the story of Agee's
connections with *Time, Life* and *Fortune* (or *Dime, Spy* and *Destiny* as
Philip Barry called them) which Macdonald recounts with forbidding
plangency in his memoir. (As demonstrated most notably by his embalm-
ing job on Hemingway, Macdonald has a tendency to wrap up a dead
body and throw away the key to the sarcophagus: all done in the name of
preservation, but a touch too slick.) "Under a reasonable dispensation,"
Mr. Fitzgerald writes,

> a man who had proved himself a born writer before he left the university
> could go ahead in that profession, but this did not seem to be the case in
> the United States in 1932. Neither in Boston nor New York nor else-
> where did there appear any livelihood appropriate for a brilliant Presi-
> dent of *The Harvard Advocate*, nor any mode of life resembling that free-
> dom of research that I have sketched as ours at Harvard. In the shrunken
> market the services of an original artist were not in demand. Hart Crane
> and Vachel Lindsay took their lives that spring. Great gifts always set their
> possessors apart, but not necessarily apart from any chance to exercise

them; this gift at that time pretty well did. . . . Agree thankfully took the first job he could get and joined the staff of *Fortune* a month after graduation.

Which settles the question of why Agee joined Luce in the first place. Nevertheless, Macdonald is surely right in arguing that the Luce ambience did Agee crippling damage by offering him the illusion of being able to do serious work. The years clocked up and words went down the drain in thousands—nothing to be much ashamed of, but nothing to be proud of either. It was the state, familiar to all young writers in harness, of doing well without doing anything properly. Perhaps Hollywood would have been better, but he was without bargaining power and without that you stood an excellent chance of getting yourself killed. It took prestige like Faulkner's to be able to use Hollywood: failing that, Hollywood used you. As it was, Agee became the supreme critic of the period's films, and began to participate only after the industry had embarked on its long and agonizing modification of the studio system.

Even then, results were not robust. Apart from the charming *The Bride Comes to Yellow Sky*, there is nothing substantial except the largely unknown and fiercely underrated *The Night of the Hunter*, one of the key works in the whole Agee canon. The one and only film directed by Charles Laughton (who in his last years was reprising Captain Bligh opposite Abbott and Costello and who stands with Peter Lorre as an example of what the Hollywood mill could do to the European intellectual), it incarnates Agee's conception of the struggle between love and hate—Robert Mitchum, as the homicidal preacher, has the letters of these two short words inscribed on his knuckles, and stages a wrestling match between his two hands to mesmerize his victims.

It is a unique film, a taste of what Agee might have done. But he spent too much of his time and hopes involved with John Huston, a semi-artist of overwhelming personal charm who launched Agee's career as a script-writer by getting him to "lick the book" of *The African Queen*, which as a Bogart-Hepburn vehicle won its Oscars but did not add up to very much. Reputedly it was an early morning, killer-diller tennis match with Huston that first put a strain on Agee's heart. Certainly it would be neat symbolism: Agee was not equipped to stay in the running with men like Huston, whose lives were geared to turning out work just above (never too far above) the Hollywood norm and who put their real creativity into the lifestyle that stuns and the pace that kills. Creatively, Agee had no gear except top—he could never have worked Faulkner's trick of giving them nothing but a refined and characteristic version of what they wanted. Sometimes they were right, too. In a film like *The Big Sleep*, some of the most memorable Chandler dialogue isn't Chandler's but Faulkner's written with his left hand: of Bogart's famous line "She tried to sit in my lap while I was standing up," the first half is Chandler and the second half—which precisely fits the lightened, racy tone Hawks gives the film visually—is Faulkner. Faulkner, who took the money and ran, got more out of Hollywood and put more back than Chandler, who gave it everything he had as a writer, saw little on the screen to show for it and was well-nigh consumed by bitterness.

In a cooperative enterprise you play percentages or lose all. The difference between the two men (a temperamental difference in the ability to see what was likely and possible) is worth drawing, since Agee was a larger and more complete example of Chandler's type—all artist and nothing but an artist. Hollywood ate men like that for breakfast. It's remarkable, given Agee's psychology, that he got as much done out there as he did.

Closing these two books with that mixture of gratitude and regret which any writing by Agee seems invariably to call from us, we can vary Tolstoy's question and ask—how much talent does a man need? "He could get magic into his writing the hardest way, by precise description," says Macdonald, and quotes this passage from A *Death in the Family*:

First an insane noise of violence in the nozzle, then the still irregular sound of adjustment, then the smoothing into steadiness and a pitch as accurately tuned to the size and style of stream as any violin . . . the short still arch of the separate big drops, silent as a held breath, and the only noise the flattering noise on leaves and the slapped grass at the fall of each big drop. That, and the intense hiss with the intense stream; that, and that same intensity not growing less but growing more quiet and delicate with the turn of the nozzle, up to that extreme tender whisper when the water was just a wide bell of film.

He could write, all right. But Macdonald didn't draw attention to the underlying pathos of paragraphs—stanzas?—like this. "Words cannot embody," Agee wrote in *Let Us Now Praise Famous Men*, "they can only describe." Yet he poured torrents of energy into making them embody. He was beyond words. Everything he wrote, and not just the scripts, was the work of a frustrated director: the page was a wrap-around screen with four-track stereophonic sound. Fundamentally anti-economical, it was the approach of a putter-in rather than a leaver-out, and all too frequently his prose had a coronary occlusion right there in front of you. It's the reason why even his famous essay on the silent comedians is somehow debilitating, and by extension the reason why his film criticism as a whole was finally less influential than Parker Tyler's (who couldn't write half so well): too much of his effort went into making the prose re-create, point for point, what he had seen.

Agee's inability to be narrowly professional was part of his humanity. He was versatile in an age that doesn't understand versatility. Yet it's possible to imagine him getting more things finished—or would be possible, if it weren't for the suspicion that something was wrong from the start. Half the reward of being an artist is becoming one. Agee missed out on that.

Times Literary Supplement, 1972

POSTSCRIPT

Agee was one of my heroes as a critic. At Cambridge, Sonny Mehta had Agee's collected film criticism in his unique private library. I borrowed the book, practically memorized it, and added Agee to the long list of modern American critical journalists—it started with James Gibbons Huneker, although further in the background there was always Mark Twain—whose colloquial verve gave me support for writing about serious art in a conversational manner, and about unserious art as if it counted. So I was already an admirer of Agee before I read his short fiction. I had no warrant for calling O'Hara and Cheever "middlebrow"—a word I would never countenance now, because it is good for nothing except to define the sort of person who would use it. At the time I was still in the process of being bowled over by Dwight Macdonald, and especially by his collection of pieces *Against the American Grain*: the word "middlebrow," if not actually coined by him, was wielded by him to some effect, although in the long run it left him in too splendid an isolation.

On the evidence of Agee's short stories, it is now plain, he could have found a way ahead by writing very short novels, or linked novellas, in the manner later exemplified by Andre Dubus and Raymond Carver. The lure of the big novel led him astray, and eventually to nowhere. But in any case of unfulfilled promise there are usually personal factors operating to make nonsense of critical analysis. For example, Agee drank as heavily as Faulkner, but without Faulkner's canny knack of husbanding his strength. I was taking a chance, by the way, when I ascribed that line in the movie of *The Big Sleep* to Faulkner: one of Hawks's hack cronies might have supplied it during a poker game. There are no prizes for spotting that I had myself in mind when I said Agee was versatile in an age that doesn't understand versatility. What I neglected to add was that no age ever has. Leonardo had people telling him that he was spreading himself thin.

The Metropolitan Critic, 1994

POSTSCRIPT (II)

Has anyone noticed how the lawn-watering scene from *A Death in the Family* sounds like Nicholson Baker? The same droplets fall on the same lawn in *The Fermata*. Smart critics looking for antecedents of Baker's miraculously micrometric registration might care to take a look. It won't change anything, but it is always salutary to have further evidence that even the most extreme originality is usually an inherited event.

Agee, if he had known how to work in solitude like Baker, might have left us a longer shelf of fully realized books. But Agee needed a context. The Luce magazines merely wasted his time, but Hollywood would probably have ruined him even had he been more in demand. Later on, Terry Southern, a comparably innovative writer, was led to destruction after cracking Hollywood at top level. Living up to his new income even after it disappeared, he slaved on a succession of doomed projects, assiduously dissipating the lustre of his gift as he worked his way towards oblivion. In that respect, he and Agee can be mentioned in the same breath, but we should be slow to interpret their inability to work the system as an exalted dedication to their calling. It wasn't as if they didn't know they were being tempted. They just weren't canny enough when they succumbed. Today, a writer as individual as David Mamet can survive and flourish in the context of the movies, and do much to raise their standard:

but it takes a nose for business on a level with his ear for dialogue. Thus equipped, he can express everything that's in him. Taken together, Agee and Southern expressed only a fraction of what was in either: a bad way for artists to be joined in kinship. Both of them, however, resist being patronized. They did enough to show us what they could do. Hence our disappointment that they didn't do more of it. Let us now praise famous men: it's a harder exhortation to obey when they waste their gifts, but praise is still what they are owed, for having expressed the gift to the extent that we became aware of it at all.

2003

15

THE SHERLOCKOLOGISTS

Sir Arthur Conan Doyle wrote little about Sherlock Holmes compared with what has been written by other people since. Sherlock has always been popular, on a scale never less than worldwide, but the subsidiary literature which has steadily heaped up around him can't be accounted for merely by referring to his universal appeal. Sherlockology—the adepts call it that, with typical whimsy—is a sort of cult, which has lately become a craze. The temptation to speculate about why this should be is one I don't propose to resist, but first there is the task of sorting the weighty from the witless in the cairn of Sherlockiana—they say that, too—currently available. What follows is a preliminary classification, done with no claims to vocational, or even avocational, expertise. Most decidedly not: this is a field in which all credentials, and especially impeccable ones, are suspect. To give your life, or any significant part of it, to the study of Sherlock Holmes is to defy reason.

.   .   .

It is also to disparage Doyle, as John Fowles pointed out in his introduction to *The Hound of the Baskervilles*, one of the four Sherlock Holmes novels handsomely reissued in Britain early last year, each as a single volume. This is an expensive way of doing things, but the books are so good-looking it is hard to quarrel, although the childhood memory of reading all the Sherlock Holmes "long stories" in one volume (and all the short stories in another volume), well printed on thin but opaque paper, dies hard. Still, the new books look splendid all lined up, and the introductions are very interesting. Apart from Fowles, the men on the case are Hugh Greene (A *Study in Scarlet*), his brother Graham Greene (*The Sign of Four*) and Len Deighton (*The Valley of Fear*). What each man has to say is well worth hearing, even if not always strictly relevant to the novel it introduces. When you add to this four-volume set of the novels the five-volume reissue of the short story collections, it certainly provides a dazzling display.

To follow the order in which Doyle gave them to the world, the short story collections are *The Adventures of Sherlock Holmes* (introduced by Eric Ambler), *The Memoirs of Sherlock Holmes* (Kingsley Amis), *The Return of Sherlock Holmes* (Angus Wilson), *His Last Bow* (Julian Symons) and *The Case-Book of Sherlock Holmes* (C. P. Snow). The dust-wrappers of all nine volumes are carried out in black and gold, a colour combination which in Britain is supposed to put you in mind of John Player Specials, a ritzy line in cigarettes. Doing it this way, it will set you back £21.20 in English money to read the saga through.

A less crippling alternative would be to purchase the Doubleday omnibus introduced by the old-time (in fact, late) Sherlockian Christopher Morley, which reproduces the whole corpus—four novels and fifty-six short stories—on goodish paper for slightly under nine bucks, the contents being as nourishing as in the nine-volume version. The question of just how nourishing that *is* is one that begs to be shirked, but honour demands I should stretch my neck across the block and confess that Holmes doesn't seem quite so fascinating to me now as he once did. Perhaps only an adolescent can get the full thrill, and the price of wanting to go on getting it is to remain an adolescent always. This would explain a lot about the Sherlockologists.

.   .   .

The best single book on Doyle is *Sir Arthur Conan Doyle, l'homme et l'oeuvre*, a thoroughgoing monograph by Pierre Nordon which came out in its original language in 1964 and was translated into English as *Conan Doyle* a couple of years later. By no coincidence, it is also the best thing on Sherlock. In his chapter on "Sherlock Holmes and the Reading Public" Nordon says most of what requires to be said about the basis of Sherlock's contemporary appeal. On the sociological side our nine introducers can't do much more than amplify Nordon's points, but since all of them are working writers of fiction (with the exception of Hugh Greene, who has, however, a profound knowledge of the period's genre literature) they usually have something of technical moment to add—and disinterested technical analysis is exactly what the Sherlock saga has for so long lacked. The Sherlockologists can't supply it, partly because most of them are nuts, but mainly because the deficiencies of Doyle's stories are what they thrive on: lacunae are what they are in business to fill, and they see Doyle's every awkwardness as a fruitful ambiguity, an irrevocable licence for speculation. The professional scribes, even when they think highly of Doyle, aren't like that. They haven't the time.

Hugh Greene reminds us that the Sherlock stories were head and shoulders above the yellowback norm. This is still an essential point to put: Doyle was the man who made cheap fiction a field for creative work. Greene also says that A Study in Scarlet is broken-backed, which it is. Graham Greene calls one of Doyle's (brief, as always) descriptive scenes "real writing from which we can all draw a lesson" but doesn't forget to insist that the subplot of The Sign of Four is far too like The Moonstone for comfort. (He also calls the meeting of Holmes and Watson in A Study in Scarlet unmemorable, an accurate perception denied to the Sherlockians who gravely installed a plaque in St. Bartholomew's hospital to commemorate it.)

Of The Hound of the Baskervilles, the only successful Sherlock novel, John Fowles gives an unsparing critical analysis, on the sound assumption that anything less would be patronizing. He sees that Doyle's great technical feat was to resolve "the natural incompatibility of dialogue and narration" but isn't afraid to call Doyle's inaccuracy inaccuracy. (He is surely wrong, however, to say that if Doyle had really wanted to kill Holmes he would have thrown Watson off the Reichenbach Falls. It is true that Sherlock couldn't exist without Watson, but there is no possible question that Doyle was keen to rub Holmes out.)

Len Deighton, a dedicated amateur of technology, assures us that Doyle really did forecast many of the police methods to come—the business with the typewriter in "A Case of Identity," for example, was years ahead of its time. Since Nordon, eager as always to demystify Sherlock, rather down-rates him on this point, it is useful to have the balance redressed. Unfortunately Deighton says almost nothing pertaining to The Valley of Fear, the novel which he is introducing. It seems likely that there was no editor to ask him to.

So it goes with the introduction to the short story collections. All of them are informative, but some of them tell you the same things, and only one or two illuminate the actual book. Kingsley Amis, as he did with Jane Austen and Thomas Love Peacock, gets down to fundamentals and admits that the Sherlock stories, for all their innovations in space and compression, are seldom "classical" in the sense of playing fair with the reader. Eric Ambler talks charmingly about Doyle's erudition; Angus Wilson pertinently about the plush Nineties (1895–1898, the years of *The Return*, were Sherlock's times of triumph); Julian Symons penetratingly about how Doyle shared out his own personality between Holmes and Watson; and C. P. Snow—well, he, of all the nine, it seems to me, is the one who cracks the case.

His personality helps. Lord Snow not only sees but admits the attractions of the high position in society to which Sherlock's qualities eventually brought him, with Watson striding alongside. It might have been Sherlock's bohemianism that pulled in the crowds, but it was his conservatism that glued them to the bleachers. This was Pierre Nordon's salient observation on the sleuth's original appeal, but Lord Snow has outsoared Nordon by realizing that the same come-on is still operating with undiminished force. Sherlock was an eccentrically toothed but essential cog in a society which actually functioned.

The life led by Holmes and Watson in their rooms at 221B Baker Street is a dream of unconventionality, like Act I of *La Bohème*. (A Sherlockologist would step in here to point out that Henri Murger's *Scènes de la Vie de Bohème*, the book on which the opera was later based, is perused by Watson in *A Study in Scarlet*.) Although Len Deighton is quite right to say that the busy Sherlock is really running the kind of successful medical consultancy which Doyle never enjoyed, it is equally true to say that Holmes and Watson are living as a pair of Oxbridge undergraduates were popularly thought to—and indeed did—live. Holmes is a maverick scientist who treats science as an art, thereby conflating the glamour of both fields while avoiding the drudgery of either. He is free of all ties; he does what he wants; he is afraid of nothing. He is above the law and dispenses his own justice. As with Baudelaire, boredom is his only enemy. If he can't escape it through an intellectual challenge, he takes refuge in drugs.

Sherlock in *The Sign of Four* was fixing cocaine three times a day for three months: if he'd tried to snort it in those quantities, his aquiline septum would have been in considerable danger of dropping off. Morphine gets a mention somewhere too—perhaps he was also shooting speedballs. Certainly he was a natural dope fiend: witness how he makes a cocktail of yesterday's cigarette roaches in "The Speckled Band." In *The Valley of Fear* he is "callous from overstimulation." All the signs of an oil-burning habit. Did he quit cold turkey, or did Watson ease him down? Rich pickings for the ex-Woodstock Sherlockologists of the future. All of this must have been heady wine for the contemporary reader endowed by the Education Act of 1870 with just enough literacy to read the *Strand* magazine, helped out by a Sidney Paget illustration on every page.

.   .   .

George Orwell thought Britain needed a boys' weekly which questioned society, but Sherlock, for all his nonconformity, set no precedent. He fitted in far more than he dropped out. Sherlock was the house hippie. His latter-day chummings-up with crowned heads (including the private sessions with Queen Victoria which drive card-carrying Sherlockologists to paroxysms of conjecture) were merely the confirmation of a love for royalty which was manifest as early as "A Scandal in Bohemia." "Your Majesty had not spoken," announces Holmes, "before I was aware that I was addressing Wilhelm Gottsreich Sigismond von Ormstein, Grand Duke of Cassel-Felstein, and Hereditary King of Bohemia." The language, as so often in the Holmes stories, is part-way a put-on, but the relationship is genuine: Sherlock is as eager to serve as any of his cultural descendants. From Sanders of the River and Bulldog Drummond down to Pimpernel Smith and James Bond, all those gifted amateur soldiers can trace their ancestry to Sherlock's bump of reverence. Physically a virgin, spiritually he spawned children numberless as the dust.

At least 30 per cent of London's population lived below the poverty line in Sherlock's heyday, but not very many of them found their way into the stories. Doyle's criminals come almost exclusively from the income-earning classes. They are clinically, not socially, motivated. There is seldom any suggestion that crime could be a symptom of anything more general than a personal disorder. Doyle's mind was original but politically blinkered, a condition which his hero reflects. When Watson says (in "A Scandal in Bohemia") that Holmes loathes "every form of society with his whole Bohemian soul," it turns out that Watson means socializing. Society itself Holmes never queries. Even when he acts above the law, it is in the law's spirit that he acts. Nordon is quite right to insist that Sherlock's London, for all its wide social panorama and multiplicity of nooks and crannies, shouldn't be allowed to get mixed up with the real London. (He is quite wrong, though, to suppose that Orwell—of all people—mixed them up. Orwell said that Doyle did, but Nordon has taken Orwell's paraphrase of Doyle's view for Orwell's own opinion. He was helped to the error by a misleading French translation. Pan-culturalism has its dangers.)

. . .

Holmes was a nonconformist in a conformist age, yet still won all the conformist rewards. It was a double whammy, and for many people probably works the same magic today. I suspect that such reassurance is at the centre of the cosy satisfaction still to be obtained from reading about Sherlock, but of course there are several things it doesn't explain. The first of these is the incessant activity of the hard-core Sherlockologists, the freaks who are on the Baker Street beat pretty well full time. Most of them seem to be less interested in getting things out of the Sherlock canon than in putting things in. Archness is the keynote: coyly pedantic about imponderables, they write the frolicsome prose of the incorrigibly humourless. The opportunity for recondite tedium knows no limit. This playful racket has been going on without let-up since well before Doyle died. The output of just the last few months is depressing enough to glance through. Multiply it by decades and the mind quails.

Here is *Sherlock Holmes Detected*, by Ian McQueen. It is composed of hundreds of such pseudo-scholarly points as the contention that "A Case of Identity" might very well be set in September, even though Holmes and Watson are described as sitting on either side of the fire— because their landlady Mrs. Hudson is known to have been conscientious, and would have laid the fire ready for use even before winter. And anyway, Mr. McQueen postulates cunningly, Holmes and Watson would probably sit on either side of the fire *even if it were not lit*. Apparently this subtle argument puts paid to other Sherlockologists who hold the view that "A Case of Identity" can't possibly be set in September. Where that view originated is lost in the mists of fatuity: these drainingly inconsequential debates were originally got up by Ronald Knox and Sydney Roberts and formalized as an Oxford *vs.* Cambridge contest in deadpan whimsy, which has gradually come to include the less calculated ponderosity of interloping enthusiasts who don't even realize they are supposed to be joking. Mr. McQueen's book sounds to me exactly the same as Vincent Starrett's *The Private Life of Sherlock Holmes*, which came out in 1933 and seems to have set the pace in this particular branch of the industry.

Two other volumes in the same Snark-hunting vein are *The London of Sherlock Holmes* and *In the Footsteps of Sherlock Holmes*: both written by Michael Harrison, both published recently, and both consisting of roughly the same information and photographs. Both bear the imprint of the same publishing house, which must have an editor whose blindness matches the blurb-writer's illiteracy. Mr. Harrison goes in for the same brand of bogus precision as Mr. McQueen. We hear a lot about what "must have" happened. We are shown a photograph of the steps which Sherlock's brother Mycroft "must have used" when going to his job at the Foreign Office. This music hall "must have been visited" by Sherlock. There is the usual interminable speculation about the whereabouts of 221B, coupled with the usual reluctance to consider that Doyle himself obviously didn't give a damn for the plausibility of its location. The only authentic problem Mr. Harrison raises is the question of which of his two books is the sillier.

·   ·   ·

Messrs. McQueen and Harrison are toddling in the giant footsteps of W. S. Baring-Gould, who compiled *The Annotated Sherlock Holmes*, which went into such scholastic minutiae with the determination of mania. Baring-Gould was also the father of yet another branch of the business—fake biographies. In his *Sherlock Holmes: A Biography of the World's First Consulting Detective* (1962) Baring-Gould sent Sherlock to Oxford. In her contribution to H. W. Bell's *Baker Street Studies* thirty years earlier, Dorothy Sayers sent him to Cambridge. Doyle sent him to neither.

Current biographical efforts are in the same footling tradition. Here is an untiringly industrious novel by John Gardner called *The Return of Moriarty*, in which the Greatest Schemer of All Time returns alive from the Reichenbach. It doesn't daunt Mr. Gardner that he is transparently ten times more interested in Moriarty than Doyle ever was. In "The Final Problem" Sherlock tells Watson that the silent struggle to get the goods on Moriarty could be the greatest story of all, but Doyle never wrote it. The reason, as Angus Wilson divines, is that Moriarty was a less employable villain than his sidekick, Moran. Moriarty was merely the Napoleon of Crime, whereas Moran was the "best heavy game shot that our Eastern Empire has ever produced"—which at least *sounded* less vague.

But the vagueness in Doyle is what the speculators like. And here is *The Seven-Per-Cent Solution*, pretending to be "a reprint from the reminiscences of John H. Watson, M.D., as edited by Nicholas Meyer." This time Sherlock and Mycroft turn out to be repressing a shameful, nameless secret. In books like this, speculation is supposed to be veering towards the humorous. The transgression would be funny, if only it made you laugh. Mr. Meyer's comic invention, however, is thin. But at least he is *trying* to be silly.

.   .   .

The most foolish book of the bunch, and quite frankly the loopiest stretch of exegesis since John Allegro dug up the sacred mushroom, is *Naked Is the Best Disguise*, by Samuel Rosenberg, which has been welcomed in the United States with reviews I find inexplicable. Mr. Rosenberg's thesis, briefly, is that Moriarty is Nietzsche and that Doyle is acting out a psycho-drama in which Sherlock is his superego suppressing his polymorphous perversity. Even if it had been reached by a convincing show of reasoning, this conclusion would still be far-fetched: fetched, in fact, from halfway across the galaxy. But it has been reached by no kind of reasoning except casuistry. Mr. Rosenberg argues in one place that if a Sherlock Holmes adventure is set in a house with two storeys, that means there are two *stories*—i.e., two levels of meaning. His arguing is of the same standard in every other place.

It seems that Mr. Rosenberg used to work as a legal eagle for a film studio, protecting it from plagiarism suits by finding a common literary ancestor who might have influenced both the plaintiff's script and the script the studio had in the works. He must have been well worth his salary, because he can see similarities in anything. (His standards of accuracy spring from the same gift: he spells A. J. Ayer's name wrongly on seven occasions.) It would be overpraising the book to call it negligible, yet both *Time* and the *New York Times*, among others, seem to have found it a meaty effort.

Though *Naked Is the Best Disguise* considers itself to be high scholarship, it reveals itself instantly as Sherlockology by worrying over the importance of minor detail in stories whose major action their author could scarcely be bothered to keep believable. The chronology of the Holmes saga is indefinitely debatable because Doyle didn't care about establishing it. Early on, Sherlock was ignorant of the arts and didn't know the earth went around the sun: later, he quoted poetry in several languages and had wide scientific knowledge. Sherlock was a minor occupation for Doyle and he was either content to leave such inconsistencies as they were or else he plain forgot about them. Mysteries arising from them are consequently unresolvable, which is doubtless their attraction. Programmes for explicating Sherlock are like Casaubon's Key to All Mythologies, which George Eliot said was as endless as a scheme for joining the stars.

.   .   .

Uniquely among recent Sherlockiana, *The Sherlock Holmes Scrapbook*, edited by Peter Haining, is actually enjoyable. It reproduces playbills, cartoons, production stills, and—most important—some of the magazine and newspaper articles which set Sherlockology rolling. (One of them is a piece of jokey speculation by Doyle himself—a bad mistake. If he wanted to trivialize his incubus, he couldn't have chosen a worse tactic.) Basil Rathbone easily emerges as the most likely looking movie incarnation of Holmes. Sidney Paget's drawings are better than anything else then or since. (What we need is a good two-volume complete *Sherlock Holmes* with all of Paget and none of Baring-Gould.) The whole scrapbook is a great help in seeing how the legend grew, not least because it shows us that legends are of circumscribed interest: too many supernumeraries—belletrist hacks and doodling amateurs with time to burn—contribute to them. As you leaf through these chronologically ordered pages you can see the dingbats swarming aboard the bandwagon.

Doyle's brainchild could scarcely survive this kind of admiration if it did not possess archetypal attributes. Sherlockology is bastardized academicism, but academicism is one of the forces which Doyle instinctively set out to fight, and Sherlock, his Sunday punch, is not yet drained of strength. Sherlock was the first example of the art Dürrenmatt later dreamed of—the art which would weigh nothing in the scales of respectability. Doyle knew that Sherlock was cheap. What he didn't guess before it was too late to change his mind was that the cheapness would last. The only coherence in the Holmes saga is a coherence of intensity. The language is disproportionate and therefore vivid. "He was, I take it, the most perfect reasoning and observing machine that the world has seen." The images are unshaded and therefore flagrant. "I took a step forward: in an instant his strange headgear began to move, and there reared itself from among his hair the squat diamond-shaped head and puffed neck of a loathsome serpent."

But Sherlock's world was all fragments, and no real world could or can be inferred from it. In *The Valley of Fear* the Scourers work mischief to no conceivable political purpose. Moriarty machinates to no ascertainable end. The Sherlockologists would like to believe that this abstract universe is concrete, and that large questions of good and evil are being worked out. But the concreteness is only in the detail; beyond the detail there is nothing; and the large questions must always lack answers.

Doyle asked and tried to answer the large questions elsewhere, in the spiritualist faith which occupied his full mental effort. Eventually his seriousness went out of date, while his frivolity established itself as an institution. But since his mind at play could scarcely have played so well if it had not been so earnest a mind, there is no joke.

New York Review of Books, February 20, 1975;
later included in *At the Pillars of Hercules*, 1979

POSTSCRIPT

Genre fiction presents the critic with an insoluble problem, because he is the last person it was written for. Writers of science fiction and crime novels, though they have always craved respectability, could once count on being smothered with learned commentary only in the fanzines. In the post-modern era, respectability for the genre writers has arrived with a rush: *Hannibal* got as much attention in the culture pages on one weekend as Kafka did in a lifetime. Things were probably better the way they were. In the genres, inventiveness counts most and writing counts least, which is lucky, because hardly anyone who can invent can write. The few who can do both (with Simenon as the outstanding example) are worthy of celebration, but those literary critics who celebrate too hard betray themselves as finding literature dull. When young I read and re-read almost everything by Arthur Conan Doyle except the historical romances. I can still remember the excitement of trekking back up to Kogarah's house-sized public library to renew my take-out of *The Complete Professor Challenger Stories*, a chubby volume whose heft is imprinted so exactly in my brain that fifty years later I am reminded of it when I pick up something of the same weight. I was born in a small private hospital just around the corner, and in retrospect my trips to the library seem part of the same process.

Youthful passion is the right kind of attention to give genre fiction. Mature consideration, especially if it has never been preceded by the youthful passion, is the wrong kind. I still think Doyle was some kind of great man. But to place him among the literary artists is bound to shrink the vocabulary we should have available for acknowledging those who really are. If we have to go back to the radiant books of our youth, it is better to go back as a comedian than a critic. What we will rediscover is the way we used to daydream, and our superseded daydreams of glamour, sex, bravery and deductive brilliance are always funny when they are not shameful. The best-ever traveller *à la recherche du trash perdu* was S. J. Perelman in *Listen to the Mocking Bird*. Paying his belated respects to *The Sheik*, *Graustark*, *Black Oxen* and *Three Weeks*, he hit a rich seam of comic stimuli. But not even he could mine it for long, because he soon ran out of bad books that he had once truly loved. Bad books that you merely liked won't do. The present equipoise doesn't work without the past madness.

Reliable Essays, 2001

16

RAYMOND CHANDLER

"In the long run," Raymond Chandler writes in *Raymond Chandler Speaking*, "however little you talk or even think about it, the most durable thing in writing is style, and style is the most valuable investment a writer can make with his time." At a time when literary values inflate and dissipate almost as fast as the currency, it still looks as if Chandler invested wisely. His style has lasted. A case could be made for saying that nothing else about his books has, but even the most irascible critic or most disillusioned fan (they are often the same person) would have to admit that Chandler at his most characteristic is just that—characteristic and not just quirky. Auden was right in wanting him to be regarded as an artist. In fact Auden's tribute might well have been that of one poet to another. If style is the only thing about Chandler's novels that can't be forgotten, it could be because his style was poetic, rather than prosaic. Even at its most explicit, what he wrote was full of implication. He used to say that he wanted to give a feeling of the country behind the hill.

Since Chandler was already well into middle age when he began publishing, it isn't surprising that he found his style quickly. Most of the effects that were to mark *The Big Sleep* in 1939 were already present, if only fleetingly, in an early story like "Killer in the Rain," published in *Black Mask* magazine in 1935. In fact some of the very same sentences are already there. This from "Killer in the Rain":

The rain splashed knee-high off the sidewalks, filled the gutters, and big cops in slickers that shone like gun barrels had a lot of fun carrying little girls in silk stockings and cute little rubber boots across the bad places, with a lot of squeezing.

Compare this from *The Big Sleep*:

Rain filled the gutters and splashed knee-high off the pavement. Big cops in slickers that shone like gun barrels had a lot of fun carrying giggling girls across the bad places. The rain drummed hard on the roof of the car and the burbank top began to leak. A pool of water formed on the floorboards for me to keep my feet in.

So there is not much point in talking about how Chandler's style developed. As soon as he was free of the short-paragraph restrictions imposed by the cheaper pulps, his way of writing quickly found its outer limits: all he needed to do was refine it. The main refining instrument was Marlowe's personality. The difference between the two cited passages is really the difference between John Dalmas and Philip Marlowe. Marlowe's name was not all that more convincing than Dalmas's, but he was a more probable, or at any rate less improbable, visionary. In *The Big Sleep* and all the novels that followed, the secret of plausibility lies in the style, and the secret of the style lies in Marlowe's personality. Chandler once said that he thought of Marlowe as the American mind. As revealed in Chandler's *Notebooks* (edited by Frank McShane and published by the Ecco Press, New York), one of Chandler's many projected titles was *The Man Who Loved the Rain*. Marlowe loved the rain.

Flaubert liked tinsel better than silver because tinsel possessed all silver's attributes plus one in addition—pathos. For whatever reason, Chandler was fascinated by the cheapness of LA. When he said that it had as much personality as a paper cup, he was saying what he liked about it. When he said that he could leave it without a pang, he was saying why he felt at home there. In a city where the rich were as vulgar as the poor, all the streets were mean. In a democracy of trash, Marlowe was the only aristocrat. Working for twenty-five dollars a day plus expenses (Jim Rockford in the TV series *The Rockford Files* now works for ten times that and has to live in a trailer), Marlowe was as free from materialistic constraint as any hermit. He saw essences. Chandler's particular triumph was to find a style for matching Marlowe to the world. Vivid language was the decisive element, which meant that how not to make Marlowe sound like too good a *writer* was the continuing problem. The solution was a kind of undercutting wit, a style in which Marlowe mocked his own fine phrases. A comic style, always on the edge of self-parody—and, of course, sometimes over the edge—but at its best combining the exultant and the sad in an inseparable mixture.

For a writer who is not trying all that hard to be funny, it is remarkable how often Chandler can make you smile. His conciseness can strike you as a kind of wit in itself. The scene with General Sternwood in the hothouse, the set piece forming chapter 2 of *The Big Sleep*, is done with more economy than you can remember: there are remarkably few words on the page to generate such a lasting impression of warm fog in the reader's brain. "The air was thick, wet, steamy and larded with the cloying smell of tropical orchids in bloom." It's the rogue word "larded" which transmits most of the force. Elsewhere, a single simile gives you the idea of General Sternwood's aridity. "A few locks of dry white hair clung to his scalp, like wild flowers fighting for life on a bare rock." The fact that he stays dry in the wet air is the measure of General Sternwood's nearness to death. The bare rock is the measure of his dryness. At their best, Chandler's similes click into place with this perfect appositeness. He can make you laugh, he gets it so right—which perhaps means that he gets it too right. What we recognize as wit is always a self-conscious performance.

But since wit that works at all is rare enough, Chandler should be respected for it. And anyway, he didn't always fall into the trap of making his characters too eloquent. Most of Marlowe's best one-liners are internal. In the film of *The Big Sleep*, when Marlowe tells General Sternwood that he has already met Carmen in the hall, he says: "She tried to sit in my lap while I was standing up." Bogart gets a big laugh with that line, but only half of the line is Chandler's. All that Chandler's Marlowe says is: "Then she tried to sit in my lap." The film version of Marlowe got the rest of the gag from somewhere else—either from William Faulkner, who wrote the movie, or from Howard Hawks, who directed it, or perhaps from both. On the page, Marlowe's gags are private and subdued. About Carmen, he concludes that "thinking was always going to be a bother to her." He notices—as no camera could notice, unless the casting director flung his net very wide—that her thumb is like a finger, with no curve in its first joint. He compares the shocking whiteness of her teeth to fresh orange pith. He gets you scared stiff of her in a few sentences.

Carmen is the first in a long line of little witches that runs right through the novels, just as her big sister, Vivian, is the first in a long line of rich bitches who find that Marlowe is the only thing money can't buy. The little witches are among the most haunting of Chandler's obsessions and the rich bitches are among the least. Whether little witch or rich bitch, both kinds of woman signal their availability to Marlowe by crossing their legs shortly after sitting down and regaling him with tongue-in-the-lung French kisses a few seconds after making physical contact.

All the standard Chandler character ingredients were there in the first novel, locked in a pattern of action so complicated that not even the author was subsequently able to puzzle it out. *The Big Sleep* was merely the first serving of the mixture as before. But the language was fresh and remains so. When Chandler wrote casually of "a service station glaring with wasted light" he was striking a note that Dashiell Hammett had never dreamed of. Even the book's title rang a bell. Chandler thought that there were only two types of slang which were any good: slang that had established itself in the language, and slang that you made up yourself. As a term for death, "the big sleep" was such a successful creation that Eugene O'Neill must have thought it had been around for years, since he used it in *The Iceman Cometh* (1946) as an established piece of low-life tough talk. But there is no reason for disbelieving Chandler's claim to have invented it.

Chandler's knack for slang would have been just as commendable even if he had never thought of a thing. As the *Notebooks* reveal, he made lists of slang terms that he had read or heard. The few he kept and used were distinguished from the many he threw away by their metaphorical exactness. He had an ear for depth—he could detect incipient permanence in what sounded superficially like ephemera. A term like "under glass," meaning to be in prison, attracted him by its semantic compression. In a letter collected in *Raymond Chandler Speaking*, he regards it as self-evident that an American term like "milk run" is superior to the equivalent British term "piece of cake". The superiority being in the range of evocation. As it happened, Chandler *was* inventive, not only in slang but in more ambitiously suggestive figures of speech. He was spontaneous as well as accurate. His second novel, *Farewell, My Lovely* (1940)—which he was always to regard as his finest—teems with show-stopping metaphors, many of them dedicated to conjuring up the gargantuan figure of Moose Malloy.

In fact some of them stop the show too thoroughly. When Chandler describes Malloy as standing out from his surroundings like "a tarantula on a slice of angel food" he is getting things backwards, since the surroundings have already been established as very sordid indeed. Malloy ought to be standing out from them like a slice of angel food on a tarantula. Chandler at one time confessed to Alfred A. Knopf that in *The Big Sleep* he had run his metaphors into the ground, the implication being that he cured himself of the habit later on. But the truth is that he was always prone to overcooking a simile. As Perelman demonstrated in *Farewell, My Lovely Appetizer* (a spoof which Chandler admired), this is one of the areas in which Chandler is most easily parodied, although it should be remembered that it takes a Perelman to do the parodying.

"It was a blonde," says Marlowe, looking at Helen Grayle's photograph. "A blonde to make a bishop kick a hole in a stained-glass window." I still laugh when I read that, but you can imagine Chandler jotting down such brainwaves *à propos* of nothing and storing them up against a rainy day. They leap off the page so high that they never again settle back into place, thereby adding to the permanent difficulty of remembering what happens to whom where in which novel. The true wit, in *Farewell, My Lovely* as in all the other books, lies in effects which marry themselves less obtrusively to character, action and setting. Jessie Florian's bathrobe, for example. "It was just something around her body." A sentence like that seems hardly to be trying, but it tells you all you need to know. Marlowe's realization that Jessie has been killed—"The corner post of the bed was smeared darkly with something the flies liked"—is trying harder for understatement, but in those circumstances Marlowe *would* understate the case, so the sentence fits. Poor Jessie Florian. "She was as cute as a washtub."

And some of the lines simply have the humour of information conveyed at a blow, like the one about the butler at the Grayle house. As always when Chandler is dealing with Millionaires' Row, the place is described with a cataloguing eye for ritzy detail, as if F. Scott Fitzgerald had written a contribution to *Architectural Digest*. (The Murdock house in *The High Window* bears a particularly close resemblance to Gatsby's mansion: *vide* the lawn flowing "like a cool green tide around a rock.") Chandler enjoyed conjuring up the grand houses into which Marlowe came as an interloper and out of which he always went with a sigh of relief, having hauled the family skeletons out of the walk-in cupboards and left the beautiful, wild elder daughter sick with longing for his uncorruptible countenance. But in several telling pages about the Grayle residence, the sentence that really counts is the one about the butler. "A man in a striped vest and gilt buttons opened the door, bowed, took my hat and was through for the day."

In the early books and novels, before he moved to Laurel Canyon, when he still lived at 615 Cahuenga Building on Hollywood Boulevard, near Ivar, telephone Glenview 7537, Marlowe was fond of Los Angeles. All the bad things happened in Bay City. In Bay City there were crooked cops, prostitution, drugs, but after you came to (Marlowe was always coming to in Bay City, usually a long time after he had been sapped, because in Bay City they always hit him very hard) you could drive home. Later on the evil had spread everywhere and Marlowe learned to hate what LA had become. The set-piece descriptions of his stamping ground got more and more sour. But the descriptions were always there—one of the strongest threads running through the novels from first to last. And even at their most acridly poisonous they still kept something of the wide-eyed lyricism of that beautiful line in *Farewell, My Lovely* about a dark night in the canyons—the night Marlowe drove Lindsay Marriott to meet his death. "A yellow window hung here and there by itself, like the last orange."

There is the usual ration of overcooked metaphors in *The High Window* (1942). Lois Morny gives forth with "a silvery ripple of laughter that held the unspoiled naturalness of a bubble dance." (By the time you have worked out that this means her silvery ripple of laughter held no unspoiled naturalness, the notion has gone dead.) We learn that Morny's club in Idle Valley looks like a high-budget musical. "A lot of light and glitter, a lot of scenery, a lot of clothes, a lot of sound, an all-star cast, and a plot with all the originality and drive of a split fingernail." Tracing the club through the musical down to the fingernail, your attention loses focus. It's a better sentence than any of Chandler's imitators ever managed, but it was the kind of sentence they felt able to imitate—lying loose and begging to be picked up.

As always, the quiet effects worked better. The backyard of the Morny house is an instant Hockney. "Beyond was a walled-in garden containing flower-beds crammed with showy annuals, a badminton court, a nice stretch of greensward, and a small tiled pool glittering angrily in the sun." The rogue adverb "angrily" is the word that registers the sun's brightness. It's a long step, taken in a few words, to night-time in Idle Valley. "The wind was quiet out here and the valley moonlight was so sharp that the black shadows looked as if they had been cut with an engraving tool." Saying how unreal the real looks makes it realer.

"Bunker Hill is old town, lost town, shabby town, crook town." *The High Window* has many such examples of Chandler widening his rhythmic scope. Yet the best and the worst sentences are unusually far apart. On several occasions Chandler is extraordinarily clumsy. "He was a tall man with glasses and a high-domed bald head that made his ears look as if they had slipped down his head." This sentence is literally effortless: the clumsy repetition of "head" is made possible only because he isn't trying. Here is a useful reminder of the kind of concentration required to achieve a seeming ease. And here is another: "From the lay of the land a light in the living room . . ." Even a writer who doesn't, as Chandler usually did, clean as he goes, would normally liquidate so languorous an alliterative lullaby long before the final draft.

But in between the high points and the low, the general tone of *The High Window* had an assured touch. The narrator's interior monologue is full of the sort of poetry Laforgue liked—*comme ils sont beaux, les trains manqués.* Marlowe's office hasn't changed, nor will it ever. "The same stuff I had had last year, and the year before that. Not beautiful, not gay, but better than a tent on the beach." Marlowe accuses the two cops, Breeze and Spangler, of talking dialogue in which every line is a punchline. Criticism is not disarmed: in Chandler, everybody talks that kind of dialogue most of the time. But the talk that matters most is the talk going on inside Marlowe's head, and Chandler was making it more subtle with each book.

Chandler's descriptive powers are at their highest in *The Lady in the Lake* (1943). It takes Marlowe a page and a half of thoroughly catalogued natural detail to drive from San Bernardino to Little Fawn Lake, but when he gets there he sees the whole thing in a sentence. "Beyond the gate the road wound for a couple of hundred yards through trees and then suddenly below me was a small oval lake deep in trees and rocks and wild grass, like a drop of dew caught in a curled leaf." Hemingway could do bigger things, but small moments like those were Chandler's own. (Nevertheless Hemingway got on Chandler's nerves: Dolores Gonzales in *The Little*

Sister is to be heard saying "I was pretty good in there, no?" and the name-less girl who vamps Marlowe at Roger Wade's party in *The Long Goodbye* spoofs the same line. It should be remembered, however, that Chandler admired Hemingway to the end, forbearing to pour scorn even on *Across the River and into the Trees*. The digs at Papa in Chandler's novels can mainly be put down to self-defence.)

The Little Sister (1949), Chandler's first post-war novel, opens with Marlowe stalking a bluebottle fly around his office. "He didn't want to sit down. He just wanted to do wing-overs and sing the prologue to *Pagli-acci*." Ten years before, in *Trouble Is My Business*, John Dalmas felt like singing the same thing after being sapped in Harriet Huntress's apart-ment. Chandler was always ready to bring an idea back for a second air-ing. A Ph.D. thesis could be written about the interest John Dalmas and Philip Marlowe take in bugs and flies. There is another thesis in the ten-dency of Chandler's classier dames to show a startling line of white scalp in the parting of their hair: Dolores Gonzales, who throughout *The Little Sister* propels herself at Marlowe like Lupe Velez seducing Errol Flynn, is only one of the several high-toned vamps possessing this tonsorial fea-ture. "She made a couple of drinks in a couple of glasses you could almost have stood umbrellas in." A pity about that "almost"—it ruins a good hyperbole. Moss Spink's extravagance is better conveyed: "He waved a generous hand on which a canary-yellow diamond looked like an amber traffic light."

But as usual the would-be startling images are more often unsuc-cessful than successful. The better work is done lower down the scale of excitability. Joseph P. Toad, for example. "The neck of his canary-yellow shirt was open wide, which it had to be if his neck was going to get out." Wit like that lasts longer than hyped-up similes. And some of the dia-logue, though as stylized as ever, would be a gift to actors: less super-charged than usual, it shows some of the natural balance which marked the lines Chandler has been writing for the movies. Here is Marlowe sparring with Sheridan Ballou.

"Did she suggest how to go about shutting my mouth?"
"I got the impression she was in favour of doing it with some kind of heavy blunt instrument."

Such an exchange is as playable as anything in *Double Indemnity* or *The Blue Dahlia*. And imagine what Laird Cregar would have done with Toad's line "You could call me a guy what wants to help out a guy that don't want to make trouble for a guy." Much as he would have hated the imputation, Chandler's toil in the salt mines under the Paramount mountain had done things for him. On the other hand, the best material in *The Little Sister* is inextricably bound up with the style of Marlowe's perception, which in turn depends on Chandler's conception of himself. There could be no complete screen rendition of the scene with Jules Oppenheimer in the studio patio. With peeing dogs instead of hothouse steam, it's exactly the same layout as Marlowe's encounter with General Sternwood in *The Big Sleep*, but then there was no filming *that* either. The mood of neurotic intensity—Marlowe as the soldier-son, Sternwood/Oppenheimer as the father-figure at death's door—would be otiose in a film script, which requires that all action be relevant. In the novels, such passages are less about Marlowe than about Chandler working out his obsessions through Marlowe, and nobody ever wanted to make a film about Chandler.

In *The Long Goodbye* (1953) Marlowe moves to a house on Yucca Avenue in Laurel Canyon and witnesses the disintegration of Terry Lennox. Lennox can't control his drinking. Marlowe, master of his own thirst, looks sadly on. As we now know, Chandler in real life was more Lennox than Marlowe. In the long dialogues between these two characters he is really talking to himself. There is no need to be afraid of the biographical fallacy: even if we knew nothing about Chandler's life, it would still be evident that a fantasy is being worked out. Worked out but not admitted—as so often happens in good-bad books, the author's obsessions are being catered to, not examined. Chandler, who at least worked for a living, had reason for thinking himself more like Marlowe than like Lennox. (Roger Wade, the other of the book's big drinkers, is, being a writer, a bit closer to home.) Nevertheless Marlowe is a daydream—more and more of a daydream as Chandler gets better and better at making him believable. By this time it's Marlowe *vs.* the Rest of the World. Of all Chandler's nasty cops, Captain Gregorius is the nastiest. "His big nose was a network of burst capillaries." But even in the face of the ultimate nightmare Marlowe keeps his nerve. Nor is he taken in by Eileen Wade, superficially the dreamiest of all Chandler's dream girls.

It was a near-run thing, however. Chandler mocked romantic writers who always used three adjectives but Marlowe fell into the same habit when contemplating Eileen Wade. "She looked exhausted now, and frail, and very beautiful." Perhaps he was tipped off when Eileen suddenly caught the same disease and started referring to "the wild, mysterious, improbable kind of love that never comes but once." In the end she turns out to be a killer, a dream girl gone sour like Helen Grayle in *Farewell, My Lovely*, whose motherly clutch ("smooth and soft and warm and comforting") was that of a strangler. *The Long Goodbye* is the book of Marlowe's irretrievable disillusion.

> I was as hollow and empty as the spaces between the stars. When I got home I mixed a stiff one and stood by the open window in the living-room and sipped it and listened to the ground swell of the traffic on Laurel Canyon Boulevard and looked at the glare of the big, angry city hanging over the shoulder of the hills through which the boulevard had been cut. Far off the banshee wail of police or fire sirens rose and fell, never for very long completely silent. Twenty-four hours a day somebody is running, somebody else is trying to catch him.

Even Marlowe got caught. Linda Loring nailed him. "The tip of her tongue touched mine." His vestal virginity was at long last ravished away. But naturally there was no Love, at least not yet.

Having broken the ice, Marlowe was to be laid again, most notably by the *chic*, leg-crossing Miss Vermilyea in Chandler's next novel, *Playback* (1958). It is only towards the end of that novel that we realize how thoroughly Marlowe is being haunted by Linda Loring's memory. Presumably this is the reason why Marlowe's affair with Miss Vermilyea is allowed to last only one night. (" 'I hate you,' she said with her mouth against mine. 'Not for this, but because perfection never comes twice and with us it came too soon. And I'll never see you again and I don't want to. It would have to be for ever or not at all.' ") We presume that Miss Vermilyea wasn't just being tactful.

Anyway, Linda Loring takes the prize, but not before Marlowe has raced through all his usual situations, albeit in compressed form. Once again, for example, he gets hit on the head. "I went zooming out over a dark sea and exploded in a sheet of flame." For terseness this compares favourably with an equivalent moment in *Bay City Blues*, written twenty years before.

Then a naval gun went off in my ear and my head was a large pink fire-
work exploding into the vault of the sky and scattering and falling slow
and pale, and then dark, into the waves. Blackness ate me up.

Chandler's prose had attained respectability, but by now he had less
to say with it—perhaps because time had exposed his daydreams to the
extent that even he could see them for what they were. The belief was
gone. In *The Poodle Springs Story*, his last, unfinished novel, Marlowe has
only one fight left to fight, the war against the rich. Married now to Linda,
he slugs it out with her toe to toe. It is hard to see why he bothers to keep
up the struggle. Even heroes get tired and not even the immortal stay
young forever. Defeat was bound to come some time and although it is
undoubtedly true that the rich are corrupt at least Linda knows how corruption ought to be done: the classiest of Chandler's classy dames, the
richest bitch of all, she will bring Marlowe to a noble downfall. There is
nothing vulgar about Linda. (If that Hammond organ-*cum*-cocktail-bar in
their honeymoon house disturbs you, don't forget that the place is only
rented.)

So Marlowe comes to an absurd end, and indeed it could be said
that he was always absurd. Chandler was always dreaming. He dreamed
of being more attractive than he was, taller than he was, less trammelled
than he was, braver than he was. But so do most men. We dream about
our ideal selves, and it is at least arguable that we would be even less ideal
if we didn't. Marlowe's standards of conduct would be our standards if we
had his courage. We can rationalize the discrepancy by convincing ourselves that if we haven't got his courage he hasn't got our mortgage, but
the fact remains that his principles are real.

Marlowe can be hired, but he can't be bought. As a consequence, he
is alone. Hence his lasting appeal. Not that he is without his repellent
aspects. His race prejudice would amount to outright fascism if it were
not so evident that he would never be able to bring himself to join a
movement. His sexual imagination is deeply suspect and he gets hit on
the skull far too often for someone who works largely with his head. His
taste in socks is oddly vile for one who quotes so easily from Browning
("the poet, not the automatic"). But finally you recognize his tone of
voice.

It is your own, daydreaming of being tough, of giving the rich bitch
the kiss-off, of saying smart things, of defending the innocent, of being the

hero. It is a silly daydream because anyone who could really do such splendid things would probably not share it, but without it the rest of us would be even more lost than we are. Chandler incarnated this necessary fantasy by finding a style for it. His novels are exactly as good as they should be. In worse books, the heroes are too little like us: in better books, too much.

1977; later included in *At the Pillars of Hercules*, 1979

POSTSCRIPT

The most terrible thing that ever happened to Raymond Chandler was not his failed suicide attempt but what was said by one of the cops who were called to the scene. The cop said that Chandler dramatized himself. One is sure he did, although he never admitted it in print. He wanted to appear hardbitten; the turmoil in his own soul was off limits; and his determination to keep it that way was the chief reason why he remained a writer of genre fiction despite the talent which always promised something else. Whether something else would necessarily have been something better is another question. Examining his own thought processes would have given him more to take in, but by temperament he was not particularly exploratory even when it came to the outside world, a less dangerous place: he was essentially one of those housebound writers who take their ivory tower with them wherever they go, even into the underworld. A few months on the fringes of the low life gave him the atmospheric details for a whole career, as we can tell by the way they steadily go out of date when we read him through. In Hollywood he barely left the bungalow: he was right in the middle of the richest single subject America could present, but the thought of writing about it either never occurred to him or posed too great a challenge to his protective self-regard. Instead, sadly for both him and us, he wrote *for* Hollywood, fulfilling the requirements.

He did the same for his genre, except that he overfulfilled them. The thrill of his books was that they were so much better written than they needed to be. The thrill remains. I still go back to him: not for his stories, which despite their wilful complexity seem thinner all the time, but for the rightness of the metaphor, the balance of the sentence, the drive of the paragraph. If I had not already grown out of genre fiction when I started to read him, he would have helped me to. He was right about style—which is, after all, the only thing we take away from that warehouse of expendable fables we absorbed when we were young. The style *was* the substance. From all those hundreds of jobbing writers who give us their candy-flavoured fantasies, we synthesize an ideal of resonant narrative, and look for it again in the artists who give us reality. There could be a worse way in. Think what it would be like to be brought up on literature: neat gin through a rubber teat, and rump steak for pabulum.

Reliable Essays, 2001

17

BITTER SEEDS:
SOLZHENITSYN

I wonder if, despite the critical success of *The Gulag Archipelago*, Solzhenitsyn's reputation is quite as high as it was when *August 1914* had not yet seen the light, when its author was still in Russia and when the KGB were obviously looking for some plausible means of stopping his mouth. Even at that arcadian stage, however, I can well remember arousing the scorn of some of my brighter contemporaries by calling Solzhenitsyn a great imaginative writer. This was put down to my customary hyperbole, to my romanticism, to my bad taste, or to all three. Yet it seemed to me a sober judgement, and still seems so. I think Solzhenitsyn is a creative artist of the very first order.

What tends to disguise this is an historical accident—the accident that most of his imaginative energy has had to be expended on the business of reconstructing reality. He has been trying to remember what a whole country has been conspiring, for various reasons, to forget. In such a case it is a creative act simply to find a way of telling some of the truth, as many people realized instinctively when they greeted Nadezhda Mandelstam's first volume of memoirs as the poetic work it is. But to tell as much of the truth as Solzhenitsyn has already told—and all of this truth must be *recovered*, from sources whose interests commonly lie in yielding none of it up—is a creative act of such magnitude that it is hard to recognize as a work of the imagination at all. On the whole, it seems, we would rather think of Solzhenitsyn as an impersonal instrument, a camera photographing the surface of another, airless planet. Hence the common complaint that he is a bit short on human warmth, the general agreement that there is something eerily mechanical about him. Even before *August 1914* (whose characters tended to be described by reviewers as having keys sticking out of their backs) there was talk of how *Cancer Ward* and *The First Circle* proved that Solzhenitsyn was not Tolstoy.

I can recall this last point being made in an argument I had with one of the more gifted members of what I must, I suppose, with chagrin, get used to thinking of as the next generation. He hadn't yet got round to reading *War and Peace* or *Anna Karenina* or *Resurrection*, but in the intervals of urging upon me the merits of Northrop Frye he nevertheless conveyed that he thought he had a pretty fair idea of what Tolstoy had been all about, and that Solzhenitsyn's novels weren't in the same league.

Not only did I concede the truth of such a judgement, I insisted on it. Solzhenitsyn's novels are not Tolstoy's, and never could have been. Tolstoy's novels are about the planet Earth and Solzhenitsyn's are about Pluto. Tolstoy is writing about a society and Solzhenitsyn is writing about the lack of one. My argument might have a touch of sophistry (perhaps one is merely rationalizing Solzhenitsyn's limitations), but surely there is something wilfully unhistorical about being disappointed that Pierre Bezhukov or Andrey Bolkonsky or Natasha Rostov find no equivalents in *Cancer Ward*. Characterization in such wealthy detail has become, in Solzhenitsyn's Russia, a thing of the past, and to expect it is like expecting the fur-lined brocades and gold-threaded silks of the Florentine Renaissance to crop up in Goya's visions of the horrors of war. Solzhenitsyn's contemporary novels—I mean the novels set in the Soviet Union—are not really concerned with society. They are concerned with what happens after society has been destroyed. And *August 1914*, an historical novel in the usual sense, looks to be the beginning of a long work which will show the transition from one state to the other. It is already fairly clear that Solzhenitsyn plans to carry the novel forward until he ends up telling the story of the 1917 Revolution itself, as well as, if he is granted time enough, of the Civil War afterwards. Here one should remember his talks with Susi in the "eagle's perch" of the Lubyanka, in *The Gulag Archipelago*, Part I, chapter 5. While recollecting them he writes: "From childhood on, I had somehow known that my objective was the history of the Russian Revolution and that nothing else concerned me.

Solzhenitsyn is explicit about his belief that he is linked to Tolstoy in some sort of historical mission. His detractors have made much of the meeting between Tanya and Tolstoy in chapter 2 of *August 1914*. But

Solzhenitsyn, even though he is a proud man (and it is a wonder that his pride isn't positively messianic, considering what he has been through and the size of the task which circumstances have posed him), isn't, it seems to me, an especially conceited one. He doesn't see his connection with Tolstoy as one of rivalry. What he sees is an apostolic succession. He knows all about Tolstoy's superiority. But when Tanya fails to get Tolstoy to admit that love might not be the cure for everything, Solzhenitsyn is showing us (by a trick of retroactive prophecy, or clairvoyance through hindsight) that Tolstoy's superiority will be a limitation in the age to come. What will count above everything else for the writer in the Russian future is *memory*. In the prison state, you should own only what you can carry with you and let your memory be your travel bag. "It is those bitter seeds alone which might sprout and grow someday" (*The Gulag Archipelago*, Part II, chapter 1). The lesson is Tolstoyan, but the context is not. Solzhenitsyn's argument has nothing to do with the perfecting of one's soul. All he is saying—in a tone unifying realism and irony—is that if you try to keep anything tangible the prison-camp thieves will break what is left of your heart when they take it. (An instructive exercise here is to read some of, say, *Resurrection* just after having absorbed a chapter or two of *The Gulag Archipelago*. The unthinkable has occurred: Tolstoy seems to have become irrelevant to Russia.)

There can't be much doubt that *August 1914* did damage to Solzhenitsyn's stature in the short run. But in the long run it will probably be the better for him to be liberated from the burden of fashionable approval, and anyway it is far too early to judge *August 1914* as a novel. Most of the reviewers who found it wanting in comparison with *War and Peace* had probably not read *War and Peace* recently or at all: certainly those who talked of its shape or construction had never read it, since *War and Peace* is a deliberately sprawling affair which takes ages to get started. *August 1914* reads like a piece of scene setting, a slow introduction to something prodigious. I would like to see a lot more of the project before deciding that Solzhenitsyn has failed as a novelist. But it is possible to concede already that he might have failed as a nineteenth-century novelist.

It can be argued that because the setting of *August 1914* is pre-Revolutionary the characters and situations ought therefore to be more earthily lifelike than they are—more Tolstoyan, in a word. I suppose there is something to this. Tolstoy was a transfigurative genius and probably

Solzhenitsyn is not; probably he just doesn't possess Tolstoy's charm of evocative utterance. But the loss in afflatus is surely a small thing compared to what we gain from Solzhenitsyn's panoramic realism. In clarifying the history of the Soviet Union (and Solzhenitsyn is already, by force of circumstance, the pre-eminent modern Russian historian) he is making a large stretch of recent time his personal province. He has been writing a bible, and consequently must find it hard to avoid the occasional God-like attribute accruing to him: omniscience, for example. It must be a constant temptation to suggest more than he knows. Yet when dealing with events taking place in the course of his own lifetime he never seems to, and I would be surprised if he ever did much to break that rule when writing about the pre-Revolutionary period. The use of documents in *August 1914* has been called a weakness. The inspiration for this technique is supposed to come from John Dos Passos, and the purported result is that *August 1914* is as flawed as *U.S.A.* Well, for any novel to rank with *U.S.A.* would not be all that bad a fate, and anyway critics who take this line are underestimating the importance to Solzhenitsyn of documentation of all kinds. He goes in for this sort of thing not because he lacks imagination but because that is imagination—to suppose that the facts of the Russian past can be recovered, to suppose that evidence can still *matter*, is an imaginative act. But to assess the boldness of that act, we must first begin to understand what has happened to the truth in the Soviet Union. And it's Solzhenitsyn who more than anyone else has been helping us to understand.

In writing about World War I, Solzhenitsyn can't help having the benefit of his peculiar hindsight. Everything in *August 1914* and its succeeding volumes is bound to be illuminated by what we know of his writings about the Soviet Union. There is no way he can escape this condition and it is childish, I think, to wish that he could. It could well be that the war novel will be artistically less than fully successful because we will have to keep thinking of its author as the author of *The Gulag Archipelago* or else miss out on its full force. But we had better accept such a possibility and learn to be grateful that at least the novel is being written. Because nobody else—certainly not Sholokhov—could have written it: Solzhenitsyn's war novel is based on the idea that the truth is indivisible.

At a guess, I would say that Solzhenitsyn's lack of the Tolstoyan virtues will turn out to be an artistic strength as well as a philosophical one. Until recently the key Russian novel about World War I, the Revolution and the Civil War was *Dr. Zhivago*. The book was overrated on publication and is underrated now, but it will always be an instructive text for the attentive reader. One defends Pasternak's right, argued through the leading character, to live and create without taking sides. One can see the importance of the principle which Pasternak is eager to incarnate in Zhivago and Lara. Lara is, if you like, the Natasha that Solzhenitsyn seems doomed never to create. Lara and Yuri are Natasha and Andrey, lovers surrounded by chaos, a private love in the middle of public breakdown. But Pasternak can't seem to avoid an effect of Tolstoy-and-water. Really the time for all this is past, and the rest of his book helps to tell us so. The point about the Civil War lies with the millions who are *not* surviving it—Pasternak, in focussing on these blessed two, is luxuriating despite himself.

However reluctantly and fragmentarily, *Dr. Zhivago* affirms that Life Goes On: Pasternak is old-world. Solzhenitsyn, one of the "twins of October" (his term for Russians who were born in the first years of the Revolution and came of age just in time to witness the 1937–38 purges, fight in World War II and be imprisoned by Stalin), doesn't believe that life went on at all. He thinks that it stopped, and that death started. In his World War I novel we can expect to hear portents of the future strangeness. But the predominant tone—and this we can already hear—will almost certainly be one of scrupulous political realism. Not *realpolitik*, but the truth about politics. This is what Pasternak was in no position to treat and what the great common ancestor, Tolstoy, simply got wrong. Tolstoy's early appearance in *August 1914* is undoubtedly strategic: he is the innocent, dreaming genius who just has no idea whatsoever of the new world to come.

Two representative moments serve to show how the force of *August 1914* is potentiated by acquaintance with Solzhenitsyn's later work, especially with *The Gulag Archipelago*. In chapter 6 we are told that Roman thinks of himself as superior and imagines that his superiority lies in his brutal frankness. But the truly illustrative detail, presented without comment, is Roman's admiration for Maxim Gorky. (Solzhenitsyn's contempt for Gorky is touched on in *The First Circle* and expressed at length in *The Gulag Archipelago*.) And in chapter 61, when the two engineers Obodovsky and Arkhangorodsky meet in amity, their friendly optimism is a mere hint of the intense, regretful passage in *The Gulag Archipelago* 1, 5, where

Solzhenitsyn laments the destruction of the engineers in the 1920s as the blasting of Russia's best hope. In the *August 1914* passage we read:

> Although there was no similarity or even contact between the lives, experience and specialised interest of the two men, they shared a common engineering spirit which like some powerful, invisible wing lifted them, bore them onwards and made them kin.

In the *Gulag Archipelago* passage the same emotion is multiplied, in the kind of paragraph which led several critics to comment (approvingly, let it be admitted) on the book's supposed lack of sobriety:

> An engineer? I had grown up among engineers, and I could remember the engineers of the twenties very well indeed: their open, shining intellects, their free and gentle humour, their agility and breadth of thought, the ease with which they shifted from one engineering field to another, and, for that matter, from technology to social concerns and art. Then, too, they personified good manners and delicacy of taste; well-bred speech that flowed evenly and was free of uncultured words; one of them might play a musical instrument, another dabble in painting; and their faces always bore a spiritual imprint.

It is evident that the optimism of the two friends about the new Russia to come is being treated ironically, but unless we know about Solzhenitsyn's feelings concerning what happened subsequently to the engineers (whose show trials in 1928 are treated at length in Robert Conquest's *The Great Terror*, but without, of course, the epigrammatic power Solzhenitsyn unleashes on the subject in *The Gulag Archipelago*) we are unlikely to realize just how bitterly ironical he is being. Whether this is a weakness of the novel isn't easily decided. My own view is that Solzhenitsyn has done the right thing in neutralizing his viewpoint. We have to provide a context from our own knowledge—knowledge which Solzhenitsyn is busy supplying us with in other books. The most pressing reason he writes history is to make the truth public. But a subsidiary reason, and one that will perhaps become increasingly important, is to make his own fiction intelligible. He writes history in order that his historical novel might be understood.

Because Solzhenitsyn deals with modern events over which there is not merely dispute as to their interpretation, but doubt as to whether they even happened, he is obliged to expend a great deal of effort in saying what things were like. The task is compounded in difficulty by the consideration that what they were like is almost unimaginable. To recover the feeling of such things is an immense creative achievement. In Coleridge's sense, it takes imagination to see things as they are, and Solzhenitsyn possesses that imagination to such a degree that one can be excused for thinking of him as a freak. He is a witness for the population of twentieth-century shadows, the anonymous dead: all the riders on what Mandelstam in his poem called the Lilac Sleigh. Solzhenitsyn can imagine what pain is like when it happens to strangers. Even more remarkably, he is not disabled by imagining what pain is like when it happens to a *million* strangers—he can think about individuals even when the subject is the obliteration of masses, which makes his the exact reverse of the ideological mentality, which can think only about masses even when the subject is the obliteration of individuals. Camus said it was a peculiarity of our age that the innocent are called upon to justify themselves. Nowhere has this been more true than in Soviet Russia, where the best the condemned innocent have been able to hope for is rehabilitation. But Solzhenitsyn has already managed, at least in part, to bring them back in their rightful role—as prosecutors.

Of the ideological mentality Solzhenitsyn is the complete enemy, dedicated and implacable. Here, perhaps, lies the chief reason for the growing uneasiness about the general drift of his work. Nobody in the left intelligentsia, not even the Marxists, much minds him suggesting that in the Soviet Union the Revolution went sour. But almost everybody, and not always covertly, seems to mind his insistence that the Revolution should never have happened, and that Russia was better off under the Romanovs. In *Dr. Zhivago* Pasternak showed himself awed by the magnitude of historical forces: reviewers sympathized, since being awed by historical forces is a way of saying that what happened should have happened, even though the cost was frightful. Nobody wants to think of horror as sheer waste. Solzhenitsyn says that the Soviet horror was, from the very beginning, sheer waste. Politically this attitude is something of a gift to the Right, since it practically aligns Solzhenitsyn with Winston Churchill. It is no great surprise, then, that on the liberal Left admiration is gradually becoming tinctured with the suspicion that so absolute a fellow might be a bit of a crank.

In *The Great Terror* Robert Conquest valuably widened the field of attention from the purges of 1937–38 to include the trials of the late 1920s—a reorientation which meant that the age of destruction overlapped the golden era of the Soviet Union instead of merely succeeding it, and also meant that while Stalin still got the blame for the Terror, Lenin got the blame for Stalin. But in *The Gulag Archipelago* Solzhenitsyn does a more thorough job even than Conquest of tracing the Terror back to the Revolution itself: he says that the whole court procedure of the typical Soviet show trial was already in existence in 1922, and that the activities of the Cheka from the very beginning provided a comprehensive model for everything the "organs," under their various acronyms, were to perpetrate in the decades to come. He has no respect for the Revolution even in its most pristine state—in fact he says it never was in a pristine state, since pre-Revolutionary Russia was totally unsuited for any form of socialism whatsoever and no organization which attempted to impose it could escape pollution. It is the overwhelming tendency of Solzhenitsyn's work to suggest that the Russian Revolution should never have happened. He can summon respect for ordinary people who were swept up by their belief in it, but for the revolutionary intelligentsia in all its departments his contempt is absolute. The hopeful young artists of the golden era (see the paragraph beginning "Oh ye bards of the twenties," *The Gulag Archipelago* I, 9) were, in his view, as culpable as the detested Gorky: Solzhenitsyn's critique of the Soviet Union is a radical critique, not a revisionist one. In condemning him as a class enemy, the regime is scarcely obliged to lie.

(Nevertheless it lies anyway—or perhaps the citizens invent the lies all by themselves. Not much is known of these matters inside the Soviet Union and Solzhenitsyn is generally just a name. One sometimes forgets that *One Day in the Life of Ivan Denisovich* is the only book of his which has ever been published there. A friend of mine just back from Russia tells me that he got into an argument with the director of a metalworkers' sanatorium on the Black Sea. This man was in his early fifties and had fought in World War II. He declared that Solzhenitsyn not only *is* a traitor, but *was* a traitor during the war—that he had been a Vlasov man. Now Solzhenitsyn's understanding of Vlasov is an important element of *The Gulag Archipelago*. But Solzhenitsyn was a Red Army artillery officer who fought *against* Germany, not with it. In view of how this elementary truth can be turned on its head, it's probably wise of Solzhenitsyn to harbour as he does the doubt that the facts, once rediscovered, will spread, like certain brands of margarine, straight from the fridge. There is nothing automatic about the propagation of the truth. As he often points out, not even experience can teach it. The prison camps and execution cells were full of people who were convinced that their own innocence didn't stop all these others being guilty.)

Solzhenitsyn finds it no mystery that the Old Bolsheviks condemned themselves. He resolves the apparent conflict between Koestler's famous thesis in *Darkness at Noon* (Koestler said they cooperated because the Party required their deaths and they had no spiritual resources for disobeying the Party) and Khrushchev's much later but equally famous insistence that they were tortured until they gave up ("Beat, beat, beat . . ."). According to Solzhenitsyn, the Old Bolsheviks were devoid of individuality in the first place, and simply had no private convictions to cling to: certainly they weren't made of the same moral stuff as the engineers they had connived at destroying ten years before, many of whom had preferred to be tortured to death rather than implicate the innocent. In the second place, the Old Bolsheviks had never been as marinated in suffering as they liked to pretend. Koestler was wrong in supposing that torture alone could not have cracked them, and Khrushchev was apparently also wrong in supposing that they needed to be tortured all that hard. Czarist imprisonment was the only kind the Old Bolsheviks had ever known and it was a picnic compared to the kind they themselves had become accustomed to dishing out. Solzhenitsyn sees no tragedy in the Old Bolsheviks. He doesn't talk of them with the unbridled hatred he reserves for the prosecutors Krylenko and Vyshinsky, but there is still no trace of sympathy in his regard. Here again is an example of his disturbing absolutism. He shows inexhaustible understanding of how ordinary people could be terrified into compliance. But for the ideologues trapped in their own system his standards are unwavering—they ought to have chosen death rather than dishonour themselves and their country further. He pays tribute to the Old Bolsheviks who suicided before they could be arrested (Skrypnik, Tomsky, Gamarnik) and to the half dozen who died ("silently but at least not shamefully"—*The Gulag Archipelago* I, 10) under interrogation. He condemns the rest for having wanted to live. They should have been beyond that.

Solzhenitsyn takes a lot upon himself when he says that it was shameful for men not to die. Yet one doesn't feel that his confidence is presumptuous—although if one could, he would be less frightening. I remember that when I first read *The First Circle* the portrait of Stalin seemed inadequate, a caricature. My dissatisfaction, I have since decided—and Solzhenitsyn's writings have helped me decide—was a hangover from the romantic conviction that large events have large men at the centre of them. Tolstoy really did sell Napoleon short in *War and Peace*: Napoleon was a lot more interesting than that. But Stalin in *The First Circle* must surely be close to the reality. The only thing about Stalin on the grand scale was his pettiness—his mediocrity was infinite. Solzhenitsyn convinces us of the truth of this picture by reporting his own travels through Stalin's mind: the Archipelago is the expression of Stalin's personality, endlessly vindictive, murderously boring. Time and again in his major books, Solzhenitsyn makes a sudden investigative jab at Stalin, seemingly still hopeful of finding a flicker of nobility in that homicidal dullard. It never happens. That it could produce Stalin is apparently sufficient reason in itself for condemning the Revolution.

With Solzhenitsyn judgement is not in abeyance. He doesn't say that all of this happened in aid of some inscrutable purpose. He says it happened to no purpose. There is little solace to be taken and not much uplift to be had in the occasional story of noble defiance. First of all, the defiant usually died in darkness, in the way that Philip II denied Holland its martyrs by drowning them in secret. And when Solzhenitsyn somehow manages to find out who they were, he doesn't expect their example to light any torches. There are no eternal acts of faith or undying loves. (The typical love in Solzhenitsyn is between the Love Girl and the Innocent, or that unsatisfactory non-affair at the end of *Cancer Ward*—just a brushing of dazed minds, two strangers sliding past each other. No parts there for Omar Sharif and Julie Christie.) Everything is changed: there is no connection with the way things were.

It should be an elementary point that Solzhenitsyn is a critic of the Soviet Union, not of Russia. Yet even intelligent people seemed to think that there may have been "something in" his expulsion—that he had it coming. (It was edifying to notice how the construction "kicked out" came to be used even by those nominally on his side.) This sentiment has, I think, been intensified by Solzhenitsyn's argument with Sakharov. It has become increasingly common to hint that Solzhenitsyn has perhaps got above himself, that in telling the world's largest country what it ought to do next he is suffering from delusions of grandeur. Yet it seems to me perfectly in order for Solzhenitsyn to feel morally superior to the whole of the Soviet political machine. Its human integrity is not just compromised but fantastic, and he has lived the proof. He has good cause to believe himself Russia personified, and I am more surprised by his humility in this role than by his pride. To the suggestion that he is a mediocre artist with great subject matter, the answer should be: to see that such stuff *is* your subject matter, and then to go on and prove yourself adequate to its treatment—these are in themselves sufficient qualifications for greatness. Solzhenitsyn's forthcoming books (apparently there are to be at least two more volumes of *The Gulag Archipelago*) will, I am convinced, eventually put the matter beyond doubt. But for the present we should be careful not to understand the man too quickly. Above all we need to guard against that belittling tone which wants to call him a reactionary because he has lost faith in dreams.

The New Review, October 1974; later included in
At the Pillars of Hercules, 1979

POSTSCRIPT

For its time, the embattled tone of the above piece was not completely inappropriate. Though Stalinism had never got much of a grip on the British intelligentsia, there was still a widespread refusal on the Left to believe that Lenin was a prototypical Stalinist in all but name. Later on the refusal modulated to a mere reluctance, but it is not yet a readiness even now; and thirty years ago you could still buy a fight by wondering aloud if the Cheka had really made a contribution to human progress. I can well remember the young Christopher Hitchens defending the Bolshevik takeover's necessary historical role, while the no longer young Robert Conquest quietly (very quietly: he had a maddening tendency to whisper even then) pointed out that there was nothing historically necessary about a hijack.

In those days I had the luxury of hearing both of them at the same lunch table every week, although they spent more time entertaining the assembled *convivio* than going for each other's throats. Once again, London's sense of community between writers forbade the worst excesses of ideological conviction. But even in the atmosphere of amused tolerance, there was a reputation for frivolity to be earned by anyone daring to suggest that the great social experiments in the East had been lethal from their inception. I'm pleased to say that I earned it. Nowadays, I would like to think, the frivolity looks like simple realism. But here again, London is lucky. In Paris, the battles within the cultivated world left even New York looking like Arcadia. In the works of François Furet and Jean-François Revel, especially of the latter, we can see how hard the few liberal intellectuals had to fight if they were not to be shouted down by the many diehards. *The Gulag Archipelago* consists almost entirely of verifiable facts. In France it was reviewed by the *gauchiste* press as if it were a work of fiction, like *The Protocols of the Elders of Zion*. When *Le Livre Noir du Communisme* came out in 1997, it received similar treatment. Three decades have made little difference, and bad blood makes it hard for the intellectuals to sit down together. To a lesser but still marked extent, the same applies in New York.

In London, ideology has never mattered that much. It could be said that this is only because ideas have never mattered much at all, but it would not be quite true. The truth, and the saving grace, is that nobody thinks them glamorous. You can't be a star for what you say, only for the way you say it. Far from being driven apart by differing opinions, Hitchens and Conquest were drawn together by their common love of language. The long consequence of their encounters in those years can be enjoyed in the opening pages of Hitchens's little book *Orwell's Victory* (2002), where its author is to be found conceding that Conquest might have had a point about the Bolsheviks all along. But those who never doubted that he did can't expect credit for having been right. What we can expect is to be dismissed for having been *on* the Right. To be a liberal democrat was considered reactionary then, and to have been so then is to be considered reactionary now. People who have abandoned erroneous opinions would be giving up too much if they ceased to regard people who never held them as naive. As Revel pointed out, the Left demands a monopoly of rectification.

As for Solzhenitsyn's subsequent reputation, it would be foolish to leave the implication floating that he might have come good on his gigantic novel. He didn't. It was great only in size. As an essayist and historian, he weakened his own position by assailing the West for its inability to achieve spiritual unity—as if liberty and spiritual unity did not rule each other out. He became, alas, a bit of a crank. But it was edifying to note how many pundits took their opportunity to diminish his importance retroactively, as if he had never done much except emphasize the obvious. It had never been obvious: not to them, at any rate.

2003

18

GO BACK TO THE COLD!

The Honourable Schoolboy by John le Carré

John le Carré's new novel is about twice as long as it should be. It falls with a dull thud into the second category of his books—those which are greeted as being something more than merely entertaining. Their increasingly obvious lack of mere entertainment is certainly strong evidence that le Carré is out to produce a more respectable breed of novel than those which fell into the first category, the ones which were merely entertaining. But in fact it was the merely entertaining books that had the more intense life.

The books in the first category—and le Carré might still produce more of them, if he can only bring himself to distrust the kind of praise he has grown used to receiving—were written in the early and middle 1960s. They came out at the disreputably brisk rate of one a year. *Call for the Dead* (1961), *A Murder of Quality* (1962), *The Spy Who Came in from the Cold* (1963) and *The Looking Glass War* (1965) were all tightly controlled efforts whose style, characterization and atmospherics were subordinate to the plot, which was the true hero. Above all, they were brief: *The Spy Who Came in from the Cold* is not even half the length of the ponderous whopper currently under review.

Elephantiasis, of ambition as well as reputation, set in during the late 1960s, when *A Small Town in Germany* (1968) inaugurated the second category. Not only was it more than merely entertaining, but it was, according to the *New Statesman*'s reviewer, "at least a masterpiece." After an unpopular but instantly forgiven attempt at a straight novel (*The Naive and Sentimental Lover*), the all-conquering onward march of the more than merely entertaining spy story was resumed with *Tinker, Tailor, Soldier, Spy* (1974) which was routinely hailed as the best thriller le Carré had written up to that time.

The Honourable Schoolboy brings the second sequence to a heavy apotheosis. A few brave reviewers have expressed doubts about whether some of the elements which supposedly enrich le Carré's later manner might not really be a kind of impoverishment, but generally the book has been covered with praise—a response not entirely to be despised, since *The Honourable Schoolboy* is so big that it takes real effort to cover it with anything. At one stage I tried to cover it with a pillow, but there it was, still half visible, insisting, against all the odds posed by its coagulated style, on being read to the last sentence.

The last sentence comes 530 pages after the first, whose tone of myth-making portent is remorselessly adhered to throughout. "Afterwards, in the dusty little corners where London's secret servants drink together, there was argument about where the Dolphin case history should really begin." The Dolphin case history, it emerges with stupefying gradualness, is concerned with the Circus (i.e., the British Secret Service) getting back on its feet after the catastrophic effect of its betrayal by Bill Haydon, the Kim Philby figure whose depredations were the subject of *Tinker, Tailor, Soldier, Spy*. The recovery is masterminded by George Smiley, nondescript hero and cuckold genius. From his desk in London, Smiley sets in motion a tirelessly labyrinthine scheme which results in the capture of the Soviet Union's top agent in China. Hong Kong is merely the scene of the action. The repercussions are worldwide. Smiley's success restores the Circus's fortunes and discomfits the KGB. But could it be that the Cousins (i.e., the CIA) are the real winners after all? It is hard to tell. What is easy to tell is that at the end of the story, a man lies dead. Jerry Westerby, the Honourable Schoolboy of the title, has let his passions rule his sense of duty, and has paid the price. He lies face down and lifeless, like someone who has been reading a very tedious novel.

This novel didn't *have* to be tedious. The wily schemes of the Circus have been just as intricate before today. In fact the machinations outlined in *The Spy Who Came in from the Cold* and *The Looking Glass War* far outstrip in subtlety anything Smiley gets up to here. Which is part of the trouble. In those books character and incident attended upon narrative, and were all the more vivid for their subservience. In this book, when you strip away the grandiloquence, the plot is shown to be perfunctory. There is not much of a *story*. Such a lack is one of the defining characteristics of le Carré's more recent work. It comes all the more unpalatably from a writer who gave us, in *The Spy Who Came in from the Cold*, a narrative so remarkable for symmetrical economy that it could be turned into an opera.

Like the Oscar Wilde character who doesn't need the necessary because he has the superfluous, le Carré's later manner is beyond dealing in essentials. The general effect is of inflation. To start with, the prose style is overblown. Incompatible metaphors fight for living space in the same sentence. "Now at first Smiley tested the water with Sam—and Sam, who liked a poker hand himself, tested the water with Smiley." Are they playing cards in the bath? Such would-be taciturnity is just garrulousness run short of breath. On the other hand, the would-be eloquence is verbosity run riot. Whole pages are devoted to inventories of what can be found by way of flora and fauna in Hong Kong, Cambodia, Vietnam and other sectors of the mysterious East. There is no possible question that le Carré has been out there and done his fieldwork. Unfortunately he has brought it all home.

But the really strength-sapping feature of the prose style is its legend-building tone. Half the time le Carré sounds like Tolkien. You get visions of Hobbits sitting around the fire telling tales of Middle Earth.

Need Jerry have ever gone to Ricardo in the first place? Would the outcome, for himself, have been different if he had not? Or did Jerry, as Smiley's defenders to this day insist, by his pass at Ricardo, supply the last crucial heave which shook the tree and caused the coveted fruit to fall?

Forever asking questions where he ought to be answering them, the narrator is presumably bent on seasoning mythomania with Jamesian ambiguity: *The Lord of the Rings* meets *The Golden Bowl*. Working on the principle that there can be no legends without lacunae, the otherwise omniscient author, threatened by encroaching comprehensibility, takes refuge in a black cloud of question marks. The ultimate secrets are lost in the mists of time and/or the dusty filing cabinets of the Circus.

Was there really a conspiracy against Smiley, of the scale that Guillam supposed? If so, how was it affected by Westerby's own maverick intervention? No information is available and even those who trust each other well are not disposed to discuss the question. Certainly there was a secret understanding between Enderby and Martello. . . .

And after a paragraph like that, you get another paragraph like that.

And did Smiley *know* of the conspiracy, deep down? Was he aware of it, and did he secretly even welcome the solution? Peter Guillam, who has since had two good years in exile in Brixton to consider his opinion, insists that the answer to both questions is a firm *yes*. . . .

Fatally, the myth-mongering extends to the characterization. The book opens with an interminable scene starring the legendary journalists of Hong Kong. Most legendary of them all is an Australian called Craw. In a foreword le Carré makes it clear that Craw is based on Dick Hughes, legendary Australian journalist. As it happens, Australian journalists of Hughes's stature often *are* the stuff of legend. In the dusty little corners where London's journalists do their drinking, there is often talk of what some Australian journalist has been up to. They cultivate their reputations. After the Six Day War one of them brought a jeep back to London on expenses. But the fact that many Australian journalists are determined to attain the status of legend does not necessarily stop them being the stuff of it. Indeed Hughes has been used as a model before, most notably by Ian Fleming in *You Only Live Twice*. What is notable about le Carré's version, however, is its singular failure to come alive. Craw is meant to be a fountain of humorous invective, but the cumulative effect is tiresome in the extreme.

"Your Graces," said old Craw, with a sigh. "Pray silence for my son. I fear he would have parley with us. Brother Luke, you have committed several acts of war today and one more will meet with our severe disfavour. Speak clearly and concisely omitting no detail, however slight, and thereafter hold your water, sir."

Known to be an expert mimic in real life, le Carré for some reason has an anti-talent for comic dialogue. Craw's putatively mirth-provoking highfalutin is as funny as a copy of *The Honourable Schoolboy* falling on your foot. Nor does Craw do much to justify the build-up le Carré gives

him as a master spy. The best you can say for him is that he is more
believable than one of his drinking companions, Superintendent
"Rocker" Rockhurst, the legendary Hong Kong policeman. "Rocker"
Rockhurst? There used to be a British comic-strip character called Rock-
fist Rogan. Perhaps that was the derivation. Anyway, it is "Rocker" Rockhurst's main task to preserve order among the legendary Hong Kong journalists, who are given to drinking legendary amounts, preparatory to
engaging in legendary fistfights. Everything that is most wearisome about
journalism is solemnly presented as the occupation of heroes. No wonder, then, that espionage is presented as the occupation of gods.

Le Carré used to be famous for showing us the bleak, tawdry reality
of the spy's career. He still provides plenty of bleak tawdriness, but romanticism comes shining through. Jerry Westerby, it emerges, has that
"watchfulness" which "the instinct" of "the very discerning" perceives as
"professional." You would think that if Westerby really gave off these
vibrations it would make him useless as a spy. But le Carré does not seem
to notice that he is indulging himself in the same kind of transparently
silly detail which Mark Twain found so abundant in Fenimore Cooper.

It would not matter so much if the myth-mongering were confined
to the minor characters. But in this novel George Smiley completes his
rise to legendary status. Smiley has been present, on the sidelines or at the
centre, but more often at the centre, in most of le Carré's novels since the
very beginning. In Britain he has been called the most representative
character in modern fiction. In the sense that he has been inflating
almost as fast as the currency, perhaps he is. His latest appearance should
make it clear to all but the most dewy-eyed that Smiley is essentially a
dream.

It could be, of course, that he is a useful dream. Awkward, scruffy
and impotent on the outside, he is graceful, elegant and powerful within.
An impoverished country could be forgiven for thinking that such a man
embodies its true condition. But to be a useful dream Smiley needs to be
credible. In previous novels le Carré has kept his hero's legendary omniscience within bounds, but here it springs loose. "Then Smiley disappeared for three days." Sherlock Holmes, it will be recalled, was always
making similarly unexplained disappearances, to the awed consternation
of Watson. Smiley's interest in the minor German poets recalls some of
Holmes's enthusiasms. But at least the interest in the minor German
poets was there from the start (*vide* "A Brief History of George Smiley" in

Call for the Dead) and was not tacked on later *à la* Conan Doyle, who constantly supplied Holmes with hitherto unhinted-at areas of erudition. Conan Doyle wasn't bothered that the net effect of such lily-gilding was to make his hero more vaporous instead of less. Le Carré, though, ought to be bothered. When Smiley, in his latest incarnation, suddenly turns out, at the opportune moment, to be an expert on Chinese naval engineering, his subordinates might be wide-eyed in worship, but the reader is unable to resist blowing a discreet raspberry.

It was Smiley, we now learn, who buried Control, his spiritual father. (And Control, we now learn, had two marriages going at once. It is a moot point whether or not learning more about the master plotter of *The Spy Who Came in from the Cold* leaves us caring less.) We get the sense, and I fear are meant to get the sense, of Camelot, with the king dead but the quest continuing. Unfortunately the pace is more like Bresson than like Malory.

Smiley's fitting opponent is Karla, the KGB's chief of operations. Smiley has Karla's photograph hanging in his office, just as Montgomery had Rommel's photograph hanging in his caravan. Karla, who made a fleeting physical appearance in the previous novel, is kept offstage in this one — a sound move, since like Moriarty he is too abstract a figure to survive examination. But the tone of voice in which le Carré talks about the epic mental battle between Smiley and Karla is too sublime to be anything but ridiculous. "For nobody, not even Martello, quite dared to challenge Smiley's authority." In just such a way T. E. Lawrence used to write about himself. As he entered the tent, sheiks fell silent, stunned by his charisma.

There was a day when Smiley generated less of a nimbus. But that was a day when le Carré was more concerned with stripping down the mystique of his subject than with building it up. In his early novels le Carré told the truth about Britain's declining influence. In the later novels, the influence having declined even further, his impulse has altered. The slide into destitution has become a planned retreat, with Smiley masterfully in charge. On le Carré's own admission, Smiley has always been the author's fantasy about himself — a Billy Batson who never has to say "Shazam!" because inside he never stops being Captain Marvel. But lately Smiley has also become the author's fantasy about his beleaguered homeland.

The Honourable Schoolboy makes a great show of being realistic about Britain's plight and the consequently restricted scope of Circus activities. Hong Kong, the one remaining colony, is the only forward base of operations left. There is no money to spend. Nevertheless the Circus can hope to make up in cunning—Smiley's cunning—for what it lacks in physical resources. A comforting thought, but probably deceptive.

In the previous novel the Philby affair was portrayed as a battle of wits between the KGB and the Circus. It was the Great Game: Mrs. Philby's little boy Kim had obvious affinities with Kipling's child prodigy. But the facts of the matter, as far as we know them, suggest that whatever the degree of Philby's wit, it was the Secret Service's witlessness which allowed him to last so long. Similarly, in the latest book, the reader is bound to be wryly amused by the marathon scenes in which the legendary code-breaker Connie (back to bore us again) works wonders of deduction among her dusty filing cabinets. It has only been a few months since it was revealed that the real-life Secret Service, faced with the problem of sorting out two different political figures who happened to share the same name, busily compiled an enormous dossier on the wrong one.

There is always the possibility that in those of its activities which do not come to light the Secret Service functions with devilish efficiency. But those activities which do come to light seem usually on a par with the CIA's schemes to assassinate Castro by poisoning his cap or setting fire to his beard. *Our Man in Havana* was probably the book which came closest to the truth.

This novel still displays enough of le Carré's earlier virtues to remind us that he is not summarily to be written off. There is an absorbing meeting in a soundproof room, with Smiley plausibly outwitting the civil servants and politicians. Such internecine warfare, to which most of the energy of any secret organization must necessarily be devoted, is le Carré's best subject: he is as good at it as Nigel Balchin, whose own early books—especially *The Small Back Room* and *Darkness Falls from the Air*—so precisely adumbrated the disillusioned analytical skill of le Carré's best efforts.

But lately disillusion has given way to illusion. Outwardly aspiring to the status of literature, le Carré's novels have inwardly declined to the level of pulp romance. He is praised for sacrificing action to character, but ought to be dispraised, since by concentrating on personalities he succeeds only in overdrawing them, while eroding the context which used to give them their desperate authenticity. Raising le Carré to the plane of literature has helped rob him of his more enviable role as a popular writer who could take you unawares. Already working under an assumed name, le Carré ought to assume another one, sink out of sight and run for the border of his reputation. There might still be time to get away.

New York Review of Books, 1977; later included in
From the Land of Shadows, 1982

POSTSCRIPT

The Soviet Union still looked like lasting forever, so there was no reason to believe that George Smiley would not stay in business for as long as his inventor could keep churning out the manuscripts. If he churned them out more slowly, it was only because they were getting bigger. He was probably in the middle of one when the Berlin Wall came down. Since then, many of us have been waiting for the book about how Smiley played a small but crucial role in bringing Moscow Central to its knees. The book has not yet emerged, perhaps because *A Perfect Spy*—much more concerned with its creator than with his most famous creation— insisted on emerging instead. Nor has there been any sign of Smiley's realigning himself against the new menace. Le Carré never numbered a knowledge of Arabic among Smiley's attainments, but surely the omniscient slyboots must have been conversant with that language all along, as with Chinese naval engineering.

One suspects, however, that Smiley's real problem has been with Jack Ryan. Under the previous dispensation, the British could punch above their weight in Secret Intelligence because it had more to do with ordinary intelligence than with techno know-how. Tom Clancy can't write with anything like le Carré's air of literary distinction, but he knows where the mainframe computers are buried, no smart bomb can outsmart him and he can find his way around a graving dock for nuclear submarines. The last submarine le Carré was on board had coal bunkers. The commercial success of Tom Clancy has the clear merit that nobody of any taste will confuse his fantasies with art. Le Carré's commercial success partly depended on that very confusion, because readers who credited themselves with a literary bent bought his books along with those who hit the beach with one blockbuster per year. It was a pity, though, that le Carré let the changed world sap his motivation. More concerned with the all-too-real Carlos than with Karla, *The Little Drummer Girl* proved that le Carré could transfer his tested schemata to the field of free-lance terrorism, and he might yet transfer them all the way to September 11. Perhaps he has, and another big Smiley saga is on the way: one in which his mastery of Koranic scholarship will prove instrumental. If Smiley comes back, he will be getting old, but Captain W. E. Johns kept Biggles flying into the jet age, and Biggles was only a man of action. Wise old birds can never be old enough. "Help me, Obi-Wan Kenobe, you're my only hope." Alec Guinness played Smiley on television in exactly the same way that he later played the Jedi knight emeritus for the big screen: with heavy, condescending eyelids as he imparted wisdom to the next generation. The wish is powerfully basic, and we all want it fulfilled: we want to believe that by the time we are ready for the rest home, time will have distilled our accumulated experience into profundity, and the young might even come to visit, just to hear us pronounce.

2003

19

A BLIZZARD OF TINY KISSES

Princess Daisy by Judith Krantz

To be a really lousy writer takes energy. The average novelist remains unread not because he is bad but because he is flat. On the evidence of *Princess Daisy*, Judith Krantz deserves her high place in the best-seller lists. This is the second time she has been up there. The first time was for a book called *Scruples*, which I will probably never get around to reading. But I don't begrudge the time I have put into reading *Princess Daisy*. As a work of art it has the same status as a long conversation between two not very bright drunks, but as best-sellers go it argues for a reassuringly robust connection between fiction and the reading public. If cheap dreams get no worse than this, there will not be much for the cultural analyst to complain about. *Princess Daisy* is a terrible book only in the sense that it is almost totally inept. Frightening it isn't.

In fact, it wouldn't even be particularly boring if only Mrs. Krantz could quell her artistic urge. "Above all," said Conrad, "to make you see." Mrs. Krantz strains every nerve to make you see. She pops her valves in the unrelenting effort to bring it all alive. Unfortunately she has the opposite of a pictorial talent. The more detail she piles on, the less clear things become. Take the meeting of Stash and Francesca. Mrs. Krantz defines Prince Alexander Vassilivitch Valensky, alias Stash, as "the great war hero and incomparable polo-player." Stash is Daisy's father. Francesca Vernon, the film star, is her mother. Francesca possesses "a combination of tranquillity and pure sensuality in the composition of the essential triangle of eyes and mouth." Not just essential but well-nigh indispensable, one would have thought. Or perhaps that's what she means.

This, however, is to quibble, because before Stash and Francesca can generate Daisy they first have to meet, and theirs is a meeting of transfigurative force, as of Apollo catching up with Daphne. The scene is Deauville, 1952. Francesca the film star, she of the pure sensuality, is a reluctant spectator at a polo game—reluctant, that is, until she claps eyes on Stash. Here is a description of her eyes, together with the remaining component of the essential triangle, namely her mouth. "Her black eyes were long and widely spaced, her mouth, even in repose, was made meaningful by the grace of its shape: the gentle arc of her upper lip dipped in the centre to meet the lovely pillow of her lower lip in a line that had the power of an embrace."

And this is Stash, the great war hero and incomparable polo-player: "Valensky had the physical presence of a great athlete who has punished his body without pity throughout his life and the watchful, fighting eyes of a natural predator. His glance was bold and his thick brows were many shades darker than his blonde hair, cropped short and as coarse as the coat of a hastily brushed dog. . . . His nose, broken many times, gave him the air of a roughneck. . . . Not only did Valensky never employ unnecessary force on the bit and reins but he had been born, as some men are, with an instinct for establishing a communication between himself and his pony which made it seem as if the animal was merely an extension of his mind, rather than a beast with a will of its own."

Dog-haired, horse-brained and with a bashed conk, Stash is too much for Francesca's equilibrium. Her hat flies off.

"Oh no!" she exclaimed in dismay, but as she spoke, Stash Valensky leaned down from his pony and scooped her up in one arm. Holding her easily, across his chest, he urged his mount after the wayward hat. It had come to rest two hundred yards away, and Valensky, leaving Francesca mounted, jumped down from his saddle, picked the hat up by its ribbons and carefully replaced it on her head. The stands rang with laughter and applause.

Francesca heard nothing of the noise the spectators made. Time, as she knew it, had stopped. By instinct, she remained silent and waiting, passive against Stash's soaking-wet polo shirt. She could smell his sweat and it confounded her with desire. Her mouth filled with saliva. She wanted to sink her teeth into his tan neck, to bite him until she could taste his blood, to lick up the rivulets of sweat which ran down to his open collar.

She wanted him to fall to the ground with her in his arms, just as he was, flushed, steaming, still breathing heavily from the game, and grind himself into her.

But this is the first of many points at which Mrs. Krantz's minus capability for evocation leaves you puzzled. How did Stash get the hat back on Francesca's head? Did he remount, or is he just very tall? If he did remount, couldn't that have been specified? Mrs. Krantz gives you all the details you don't need to form a mental picture, while carefully withholding those you do. Half the trick of pictorial writing is to give only the indispensable points and let the reader's imagination do the rest. Writers who not only give the indispensable points but supply all the concrete details as well can leave you feeling bored with their brilliance—Wyndham Lewis is an outstanding example. But a writer who supplies the concrete details and leaves out the indispensable points can only exhaust you. Mrs. Krantz is right to pride herself on the accuracy of her research into every department of the high life. What she says is rarely inaccurate, as far as I can tell. It is, however, almost invariably irrelevant.

Anyway, the book starts with a picture of Daisy ("Her dark eyes, not quite black, but the colour of the innermost heart of a giant purple pansy, caught the late afternoon light and held it fast. . . .") and then goes on to describe the meeting of her parents. It then goes on to tell you a lot about what her parents got up to before they met. Then it goes on to tell you about *their* parents. The book is continually going backward instead of forward, a canny insurance against the reader's impulse to skip. At one stage I tried skipping a chapter and missed out on about a century. From the Upper West Side of New York I was suddenly in the Russian Revolution. That's where Stash gets his fiery temperament from—Russia.

"At Chez Mahu they found that they were able only to talk of unimportant things. Stash tried to explain polo to Francesca but she scarcely listened, mesmerized as she was with the abrupt movements of his tanned hands on which light blonde hair grew, the hands of a great male animal." A bison? Typically, Mrs. Krantz has failed to be specific at the exact moment when specificity would be a virtue. Perhaps Stash is like a horse not just in brain but in body. This would account for his tendency to view Francesca as a creature of equine provenance. "Francesca listened to Valensky's low voice, which had traces of an English accent, a brutal man's voice which seemed to vibrate with an underlying tenderness, as if he were talking to a newborn foal. . . ."

There is a lot more about Stash and Francesca before the reader can get to Daisy. Indeed, the writer herself might never have got to Daisy if she (i.e., Mrs. Krantz) had not first wiped out Stash and Francesca. But before they can be killed, Mrs. Krantz must expend about a hundred and fifty pages on various desperate attempts to bring them alive. In World War II the incomparable polo-player becomes the great war hero. Those keen to see Stash crash, however, are doomed to disappointment, since before Stash can win medals in his Hurricane we must hear about his first love affair. Stash is fourteen years old and the Marquise Clair de Champery is a sexpot of a certain age. "She felt the congestion of blood rushing between her primly pressed together thighs, proof positive that she had been right to provoke the boy." Stash, meanwhile, shows his customary tendency to metamorphose into an indeterminate life-form. "He took her hand and put it on his penis. The hot sticky organ was already beginning to rise and fill. It moved under her touch like an animal." A field mouse? A boa constrictor?

Receiving the benefit of Stash's extensive sexual education, Francesca conceives twins. One of the twins turns out to be Daisy and the other her retarded sister, Danielle. But first Stash has to get to the clinic. "As soon as the doctor telephoned, Stash raced to the clinic at 95 miles an hour." Miserly as always with the essentials, Mrs. Krantz trusts the reader to supply the information that Stash is attaining this speed by some form of motorized transport.

Stash rejects Danielle, Francesca flees with Danielle and Daisy. Stash consoles himself with his collection of jet aircraft. Mrs. Krantz has done a lot of research in this area but it is transparently research, which is not the same thing as knowledge. Calling a Junkers 88 a Junker 88 might be a misprint, but her rhapsody about Stash's prize purchase of 1953 is a dead giveaway. "He tracked down and bought the most recent model available of the Lockheed XP-80, known as the Shooting Star, a jet which for many years could out-manoeuvre and outperform almost every other aircraft in the world." USAF fighter aircraft carried "X" numbers only before being accepted for service. By 1953 the Shooting Star was known as the F-80, had been in service for years and was practically the slowest thing of its type in the sky. But Mrs. Krantz is too fascinated by that "X" to let it go. She deserves marks, however, for her determination to catch up on the arcane nomenclature of boys' toys.

Stash finally buys a farm during a flying display in 1967. An old Spitfire packs up on him. "The undercarriage of the 27-year-old plane stuck and the landing gear could not be released." Undercarriage and landing gear are the same thing—her vocabularies have collided over the Atlantic. Also an airworthy 27-year-old Spitfire in 1967 would have been a very rare bird indeed: no wonder the undercarriage got in the road of the landing gear. But Mrs. Krantz goes some way towards capturing the excitement of machines and should not be mocked for her efforts. Francesca, incidentally, dies in a car crash, with the make of car unspecified.

One trusts that Mrs. Krantz's documentation of less particularly masculine activities is as meticulous as it is undoubtedly exhaustive, although even in such straightforward matters as food and drink she can sometimes be caught making the elementary mistake of piling on the fatal few details too many. Before Stash gets killed he takes Daisy to lunch every Sunday at the Connaught. After he gets killed he is forced to give up this practice, although there is no real reason why he should not have continued, since he is no more animated before his prang than after. Mrs. Krantz has researched the Connaught so heavily that she must have made herself part of the furniture. It is duly noted that the menu has a brown and gold border. It is unduly noted that the menu has the date printed at the bottom. Admittedly such a thing would not happen at the nearest branch of the Golden Egg, but it is not necessarily the mark of a great restaurant. Mrs. Krantz would probably hate to hear it said, but she gives the impression of having been included late amongst the exclusiveness she so admires. There is nothing wrong with gusto, but when easy familiarity is what you are trying to convey, gush is to be avoided.

Full of grand meals served and consumed at chapter length, *Princess Daisy* reads like *Buddenbrooks* without the talent. Food is important to Mrs. Krantz: so important that her characters keep turning into it, when they are not turning into animals. Daisy has a half-brother called Ram, who rapes her, arouses her sexually, beats her up, rapes her again and does his best to wreck her life because she rejects his love. His passion is understandable, when you consider Daisy's high nutritional value. "He gave up the struggle and devoured her lips with his own, kissing her as if he were dying of thirst and her mouth were a moist fruit." A mango? Daisy fears Ram but goes for what he dishes out. "Deep within her something sounded, as if the string of a great cello had been plucked, a note of remote, mysterious but unmistakable warning." Boing.

Daisy heeds the warning and lights out for the U.S.A., where she becomes a producer of television commercials in order to pay Danielle's hospital bills. She pals up with a patrician girl called Kiki, whose breasts quiver in indignation — the first breasts to have done that for a long, long time. At such moments one is reminded of Mrs. Krantz's true literary ancestry, which stretches all the way back to Elinor Glyn, E. M. Hull and Gertrude Atherton. She is wasting a lot of her time and too much of ours trying to be John O'Hara. At the slightest surge of congested blood between her primly pressed together thighs, all Mrs. Krantz's carefully garnered social detail gives way to eyes like twin dark stars, mouths like moist fruit and breasts quivering with indignation.

There is also the warm curve of Daisy's neck where the jaw joins the throat. Inheriting this topographical feature from her mother, Daisy carries it around throughout the novel waiting for the right man to kiss it *tutto tremante*. Ram will definitely not do. A disconsolate rapist, he searches hopelessly among the eligible young English ladies — Jane Bonham-Carter and Sabrina Guinness are both considered — before choosing the almost inconceivably well-connected Sarah Fane. Having violated Sarah in his by now standard manner, Ram is left with nothing to do except blow Daisy's secret and commit suicide. As Ram bites the dust, the world learns that the famous Princess Daisy, star of a multi-million-dollar perfume promotion, has a retarded sister. Will this put the kibosh on the promotion, not to mention Daisy's love for the man in charge, the wheeler-dealer head of Supracorp, Pat Shannon ("larky bandit," "freebooter," etc.)?

Daisy's libido, dimmed at first by Ram's rape, has already been reawakened by the director of her commercials, a ruthless but prodigiously creative character referred to as North. Yet North finally lacks what it takes to reach the warm curve of Daisy's neck. Success in that area is reserved for Shannon. He it is who undoes all the damage and fully arouses her hot blood. "It seemed a long time before Shannon began to imprint a blizzard of tiny kisses at the point where Daisy's jaw joined her throat, that particularly warm curve, spendthrift with beauty, that he had not allowed himself to realise had haunted him for weeks. Daisy felt fragile and warm to Shannon, as if he'd trapped a young unicorn [horses again — C.J.], some strange, mythological creature. Her hair was the most intense source of light in the room, since it reflected the moonlight creeping through the windows, and by its light he saw her eyes, open, rapt and glowing; twin dark stars."

Shannon might think he's got hold of some kind of horse, but as far as Daisy's concerned she's a species of cetacean. "It was she who guided his hands down the length of her body, she who touched him wherever she could reach, as playfully as a dolphin, until he realised that her fragility was strength, and that she wanted him without reserve."

Daisy is so moved by this belated but shatteringly complete experience that she can be forgiven for what she does next. "Afterward, as they lay together, half asleep, but unwilling to drift apart into unconsciousness, Daisy farted, in a tiny series of absolutely irrepressible little pops that seemed to her to go on for a minute." It takes bad art to teach us how good art gets done. Knowing that the dithyrambs have gone on long enough, Mrs. Krantz has tried to undercut them with something earthy. Her tone goes wrong, but her intention is worthy of respect. It is like one of those clumsy attempts at naturalism in a late-medieval painting—less pathetic than portentous, since it adumbrates the great age to come. Mrs. Krantz will never be much of an artist but she has more than a touch of the artist's ambition.

Princess Daisy is not to be despised. Nor should it be deplored for its concern with aristocracy, glamour, status, success and things like that. On the evidence of her prose, Mrs. Krantz has not enough humour to write tongue-in-cheek, but other people are perfectly capable of reading that way. People don't get their morality from their reading matter: they bring their morality to it. The assumption that ordinary people's lives could be controlled and limited by what entertained them was always too condescending to be anything but fatuous.

Mrs. Krantz, having dined at Mark's Club, insists that it is exclusive. There would not have been much point to her dining there if she did not think that. An even bigger snob than she is might point out that the best reason for not dining at Mark's Club is the chance of finding Mrs. Krantz there. It takes only common sense, though, to tell you that on those terms exclusiveness is not just chimerical but plain tedious. You would keep better company eating Kentucky Fried Chicken in a launderette. But if some of this book's readers find themselves daydreaming of the high life, let us be grateful that Mrs. Krantz exists to help give their vague aspirations a local habitation and a name. They would dream anyway, and without Mrs. Krantz they would dream unaided.

To pour abuse on a book like this makes no more sense than to kick a powder puff. *Princess Daisy* is not even reprehensible for the three million dollars its author was paid for it in advance. It would probably have made most of the money back without a dime spent on publicity. The only bad thing is the effect on Mrs. Krantz's personality. Until lately she was a nice Jewish lady harbouring the usual bourgeois fancies about the aristocracy. But now she gives interviews extolling her own hard head. "Like so many of us," she told the *Daily Mail* on 28 April, "I happen to believe that being young, beautiful and rich is more desirable than being old, ugly and destitute." Mrs. Krantz is fifty years old, but to judge from the photograph on the back of the book she is engaged in a series of hard-fought delaying actions against time. This, I believe, is one dream that intelligent people ought not to connive at, since the inevitable result of any attempt to prolong youth is a graceless old age.

London Review of Books, 1980; later included in
From the Land of Shadows, 1982

POSTSCRIPT

John Gross did me the honour of reprinting this piece in the closing pages of his *Oxford Book of Essays*. Some of the reviewers of that excellent anthology thought that it tailed off pretty sharply when it got to me, not so much because my prose was ill-behaved as because my subject was inherently trivial. But there were ample precedents. A good proportion of the most pertinent criticism in the language has been written in the form of book reviews that attack a supposed success in defence of a value. My only shame is that in all such cases, the destructive piece was made constructive because something had been taken too seriously, and needed to be demoted. Nobody except her investment bankers had ever taken Judith Krantz seriously. But there had still been a false estimation that needed to be opposed: a false estimation not about her book's place in culture—which was transparently the same as the place of a garbage scow in a yacht club—but about culture itself. *Princess Daisy*'s gargantuan commercial success had been condemned as meretricious. I thought we had more important cultural distortions to worry about than that. I also thought—why not admit it?—that Judith Krantz had turned out a masterpiece of unintentional humour, and that there were possibilities for intentional humour in analysing how she did it. The challenge was to be as funny when I tried as she was without trying at all. But if there had not been a serious point to be made, it wouldn't have been worth the effort.

2003

20

—

A DEATH IN LIFE

The Fatal Shore by Robert Hughes

For the longest part of its short history, Australia preferred to forget that it began as a penal colony. Australian historians born under the British Empire would accentuate the positive. When, in recent years, a new stamp of historians, usually harbouring no great love for Australia's constitutional ties with Britain, began to tell the real story of what the formative years of the white man's Australia had been like, it became apparent why forgetfulness had been so nearly complete. The story was horrible. Luckily, few of them were able to tell it with more than a modicum of evocative power, or the result would have been hard to bear. Now, in *The Fatal Shore*, Robert Hughes, an Australian-born critical writer of pronounced literary gifts, has summed up all previous efforts, exceeded them in force of expression and brought the whole deadly business back to life. The result *is* hard to bear—or would be, if it were not so clearly one of those rare achievements in the writing of history by which the unimaginably inhumane is brought to book without making us give up on humanity. Such redemptive work can't be done without artistry: there are degrees of anguish which only style can make us contemplate, since merely to recount them would leave us cold.

Hughes might have attempted this book in his youth, and got the story out of proportion, even if he had not skimped it. Fortunately, he has made *The Fatal Shore* the *magnum opus* of his maturity. By now his sense of historical scale is sound, as for this task it needed to be. It would have been easy to call the Australian system of penal settlements a Gulag Archipelago before the fact. The term "concentration camp," in its full modern sense, would not have been out of place: at least one of the system's satellites, Norfolk Island, was, if not an out-and-out extermination camp, certainly designed to make its victims long for death, like Dachau in those awful years before the war when the idea was not so much to kill people as to see how much they could suffer and still want to stay alive. And, indeed, Hughes draws these parallels. The analogies are inescapable. But he doesn't let them do his thinking for him. He is able to bring out the full dimensions of the tragedy while keeping it in perspective. The penal colony surely prefigured the modern totalitarian catastrophe. Equally surely it did not. It was a unique event, with unique consequences: the chief consequence being Australia itself, which has come a long way in 200 years—a point sufficiently proved by its ability to produce a book like this. The literature of the totalitarian dystopias emerged in spite of them, and could reach only one conclusion. Australia is a more difficult subject, however damning the raw evidence.

To the penal colony, the cat-o'-nine-tails was a tool more basic than the hoe. On Norfolk Island, where the camp was commanded by a succession of sadists, there were other forms of torture as well, some of them as vile as could be conceived before the age of electricity. But flogging provided the steady rhythm of torment. What made the whipping on Norfolk Island unique was that it so often got out of hand. At Port Arthur, in Van Diemen's Land—now called Tasmania—there was less chance of the flagellator's ecstasy releasing his victim to a premature death. The idea was to impress the subject with the mechanical inexorability of his fate, even when he was being punished for nothing except the dementia or paralysis induced by previous punishment. Norfolk Island was the personal expression of whichever maniac was running the place. Port Arthur was impersonal, a research establishment where the machine that ruined you was run by technicians whose only concern was for its perfection: Kafka's penal colony, so often thought of as a harbinger, now turns out to have harked back.

But there are echoes of these things throughout history, in which the only reliable constant is the form taken by extreme cruelty when it is given absolute licence. Hughes, while aware of the general considerations, declines to lose himself among them. He keeps it specific. Enough to say that Norfolk Island and Port Arthur were there to inspire terror even in those convicts who were so recalcitrant that they were not terrified already by everyday life in the penal colony proper. The outlying camps were dumps for those who were held to be unassimilable elements in the main camp, where the city of Sydney now stands. But the main camp was itself a dump. Every convict sent there was held to be unassimilable in England. Whether he had stolen a thimble or forged £1,000 was immaterial. There was no notion that poverty might have created thieves: only that thieves might create revolution. They had to go. The colony was a way of getting rid of them without hanging them. It is a nice question whether transportation was intended as an alternative more humane than hanging, or less. Everyone knew what hanging looked like. But Australia was an unknown terror. So far away that no solid news ever came out of it, it was a black hole for facts. Dreadful stories percolated back to England of what went on out there, and there was always pressure from home to ensure that what went on remained so unattractive that any potential miscreant in the British Isles would fear it more than the rope and the hulks, and think twice before breaking the law, lest the law be obliged to break him, or her. There was thus a constant dispute between the liberal persuasion, which wanted Australia to rehabilitate criminals, and the illiberal persuasion, which wanted it to scare them. The first persuasion eventually won out, but not before the second had done its worst.

There was no need to give the place a bad name. It did that well enough by itself. Female convicts were forced into concubinage on the voyage out. Their sluttishness having been thus established, on arrival they were sorted like cattle, with officers taking the first pick. There were never enough women, so sodomy was rife among the men. Boys were initiated by rape, but to become an adult convict's punk at least ensured some protection against the others. Nothing except unquestioning docility could protect anyone against the lash. Male convicts on the chain gangs, flogged perpetually as they did one-tenth of the work they might have done willingly for a pittance, could have been excused for wondering if Norfolk Island could be worse. It was, because there the work was entirely pointless. Around Port Jackson and the country opening up westward towards the Blue Mountains, the road cutting and stump grubbing had some purpose, no matter how inefficiently it was done. Despite itself, the slave-labour camp grew into something better than that. Most of the convicts were put out to assigned labour, with the prospect of working their way to rehabilitation; the chance of freedom proved to be a carrot more powerful than the stick.

One of Hughes's best gifts is his ability to analyse the way a social order arose out of a disciplinary regime. It wasn't much of a social order to start with, because even the free settlers were not the most imaginative of people, and the convicts, far from being instinctive exemplars of the democratic spirit, were mostly so ignorant of where Australia was that they thought China was next door; escapees would set out to walk there, and eat each other on the way. Students of the American Revolution, accustomed to the mental capacities of the nascent superpower's founding citizens, will search Australia's early history in vain for a comparable group of visionaries. The Rum Corps, a cabal within the garrison, deposed the governor only because they wanted the free exercise of their monopoly in booze; it was scarcely the Boston Tea Party. Hughes is well aware that the resemblance ends almost as soon as it starts. Nevertheless, a nation emerged, and did so partly because men like Governor Macquarie—no Thomas Jefferson but no fool, either—were determined that it should.

Hughes is careful not to romanticize the convicts. The thief who stole a loaf of bread didn't always steal it from someone who had a hundred loaves. He might have stolen it from someone who had one loaf. To have grown up in the prisons and the hulks was no education for anything except crime. The few literate convicts—counterfeiters, and, later on, Chartists and Irish separatists—were cut off from home by their sentence and cut off from each other by the system. Isolated, they lost heart. Yet, on the whole, the convicts represented a lot of energy going to waste, and it was necessary only to release that energy in order for them to turn their new country, which none of them had ever wanted to come to, into a place from which most of them did not want to go home. The gold rush in the middle of the nineteenth century brought the transportation system to an end, because no incipient felon could be made to fear a place that so many free men were booking their own passage to reach, often selling all they had. The bad dream was already over—for the white man, at least.

For the black man, the disaster was unmitigated. Here again there is a parallel, but it is more with South Africa than with the United States, unless we try to keep Wounded Knee in mind and forget Harpers Ferry. The Australian Aborigines were never a *casus belli* between white men, not even as a pretext. Instead, the white men united against them. The revisionist who would like to pin another mass atrocity on the occupying power, however, will get no quick help from Hughes. In Van Diemen's

Land, the soldiers might have driven the Aborigines like game, but on the mainland it was the convicts who posed the greater threat to the native population. The brutalized convicts had to feel superior to someone, and the Aborigines were ideal casting. They toiled not, and were hated for it. When the Aborigines helped the troopers track escapees, the convicts hated them even more. The troopers could offer their black collaborators no reward that did not corrode their tribal ways and make them less fit to survive. What the Aborigines needed was their land, untouched. They would have had to fight for it, and for that they would have needed solidarity. But on the day in 1788 when the First Fleet arrived in Sydney Harbour the tribe on the north shore spoke a language that the tribe on the south could not understand. The Aborigines were not one people. It is racism to suppose they were. There was not, and could not have been, an Aboriginal general. They would have needed an Eisenhower, and couldn't produce even a Crazy Horse. There had never been any need to, until we got there.

By "we" I mean Australians. All of us now feel the force of the plural personal pronoun. Some of us feel it so strongly that we move national self-consciousness to the forefront of the political agenda, often with tiresome results. Touchiness, however, is inevitable. Australian writers, painters, singers, actors, film directors, scientists, sportsmen and tycoons make a disproportionate bang in the world. The outsider could be forgiven for thinking that everything must be for export. But in all these fields there is quite a lot going on at home as well. The Australian can get a bit impatient when he hears his country judged according to what its expatriates are up to, even when the judgement is praise; and when the expatriates do the judging, especially if it is dispraise, he is likely to become inflamed.

But, with due notice that the case is being put broadly, what has happened is this. Up until the late 1960s, Australia undervalued itself as a country, or anyway its intelligentsia thought it did, giving this alleged Cinderella complex the unlovely journalistic title "the cultural cringe." But the vogue for self-discovery, felt in those years throughout the Western world, was a passion by the time it reached Australia, rather as the Depression in the 1930s struck harder and stayed longer there than it did anywhere else. With the advent of Gough Whitlam's government, in the 1970s, Australia had begun to esteem itself at what its social commentators—an increasingly numerous and vociferous class—thought was a just valuation. Diffidence had turned to self-assertion. The change was welcome, but there was an obvious danger of hyped-up expectations, to which some of the country's more stentorian promoters duly succumbed. The cringe became a snarl. Tub-thumping was heard in areas where a reasoned tone might have been more suitable. Hughes's excellent book on Australian painting, *The Art of Australia*, adumbrated this new confidence but proved to be atypical in its tact. While analysing, appraising and ordering the Australian painters with an authority that no indigenous critic had achieved before, Hughes was careful not to tear his country's heritage loose from its world context, and made it clear that it was only because he *had* a world view, gained during his travels, that he was able to come home and see clearly what the Australian painters had achieved.

Australian defensiveness about the success of its expatriates was not to be allayed, and probably won't be by *The Fatal Shore*, either. Here again, political zeal inevitably distorts the picture. Ardent republicans would like Australia to be self-sufficient in the arts the way that it is in minerals. The idea that any one country can be culturally self-sufficient is inherently fallacious, but in the forward rush of Australian confidence during Gough Whitlam's period of government, when grants were handed out to anybody with enough creative imagination to ask for one, reason was thrown into the backseat. For the last fifteen years, Australian artists in all fields, supposedly free at last from the imposition of being judged by alien—i.e., British—standards, have been judged by their own standards, and almost invariably found to be the authors of significant works. The glut of self-approval has been most evident in literature, which in normal circumstances customarily produces a strong critical movement to accompany any period of sustained creativity but in Australia's case has largely failed to do so. The undoubted fact that some very good things have been written can't stave off the consideration that many less good things have been given the same welcome.

A consideration is all it is. Creativity can get along without criticism. When Pushkin—who was in the position of having to think what form a national culture might take—called for a dispassionate criticism, he wasn't calling for help in writing poems, which he could do by himself. He was merely stating his wish to write them in a civilized atmosphere, whose absence was reducing him to isolation, and thereby damaging his individuality. The individual needs a community. In Australia, while literature is rapidly becoming a cash crop, a literary community has been slower to emerge. Criticism is too often, in the strict sense, tendentious. Scale is duly hailed, ambition lauded, but the direction of the book— does it point the way? does it give us purpose?—is usually the basis of assessment. There are not many critics detached enough to quibble over detail, and ask why so many great writers have produced so little good writing.

This is where Hughes's book will come in handy. It will be thoroughly read in the schools, whereas many of the new masterpieces are skimmed dreamily at the beach. When workaday books are well written, a culture starts to pick up: the best of the spoken language is fed back into itself, by way of writers whose ear for speech informs the content of their prose, and whose mastery of composition makes them selective. In this respect, Hughes is hard to fault. The Australian landscape has been captured like this by few painters and by no other writers at all, because anyone as vivid also gushed, and anyone as elegant was dull. Here is the entrance to Port Arthur:

> Both capes are of towering basalt pipes, flutes and rods, bound like faces into the living rock. Their crests are spired and crenellated. Seabirds wheel, thinly crying, across the black walls and the blacker shadows. The breaking swells throw up their veils.

In the late 1950s, as an architecture student at Sydney University, Hughes was the artiest young man on the scene. His blond hair growing naturally in a thick layer cut, his lanky form Englishly decked out in lamb's wool, suede and corduroy, he sloped forward on long-toed desert boots while aiming at you a cigarette whose startling length suggested that he was about to launch a poisoned dart. Instead, he drew you. He drew anything that caught his eye, which was almost everything; and he drew it with uncanny speed and accuracy. Eventually, he decided that his graphic work was derivative, and gave it up. Although it is true that he absorbed other people's styles one after the other, he might have arrived at this renunciation too early. When there was no one else left to absorb, the real Hughes might have emerged, as happened in his prose. In those years, you could always tell what he had been reading the day before. Even today, he is a magpie for vocables: no shimmering word he spots in any of the languages he understands, and in several more that he doesn't, is safe from being plucked loose and flown back to his nest. Omnivorous rather than eclectic, that type of curiosity is the slowest to find coherence. But his fluency was always his own, and by persistence he has arrived at a solidity to match it: a disciplined style that controls without crippling all that early virtuosity, and blessedly also contains his keen glance, getting the whole picture into a phrase the way he once got his fellow-students' faces into a single racing line. It is exactly right, as well as funny, to call a merino sheep "a pompous ambling peruke." Scores of such felicities could be picked out, but only on the understanding that they are not the book's decoration. They are its architecture.

There are several benefits that accrue to the Australian writer who turns himself into an expatriate. The first advantage of going away is obvious: it is the wider view he brings with him if he comes home. Hughes, a member of one of the grandest Australian Catholic families, was not very provincial even before he left, but in London in the early 1960s he was in no danger of shivering rejected in an Earl's Court bedsit. While some of his contemporaries were doing exactly that, he had rooms in Albany, the exclusive address for gentlefolk just off Piccadilly. Hughes found his true fame later on, in America, but he would not be able to say plausibly that Britain turned down what he had to offer. Before the immigration laws toughened up in the 1970s, Australian overachievers found Britain hospitable, sometimes absurdly so. The British class system, hidebound within itself, was easily penetrated by the colonial whose accent it could not place accurately in the social scale. In London, the Australian expatriates breathed dirtier air than at home but found life more interesting. The experience did not stop some of the short-stay visitors going home as convinced republicans. But for a long voyager like Hughes it became that much harder to cast Britain as the villain, either currently or in retrospect. One of the hard issues he is prepared to face in *The Fatal Shore* is that the growth of the penal colony into a living society can't be interpreted as merely a liberal refutation of the mother country at her most repressive. England was also present at the spontaneous creation that grew out of the planned destruction. The ties with "home" were real. The past is not to be argued away for the sake of a political programme.

The second advantage enjoyed by the expatriate Australian literary practitioner is just as obvious. Travel not only broadens the view; it sharpens the gaze. Hughes might have remained comparatively blind to the uniqueness of his native topography if he had never left it. Coming back to it, he sees it without any intervening veil of familiarity. Laudably intent on looking at what happened where it happened, he has travelled widely within his own country, to places most of his compatriots have never seen but will see now through his eyes:

> As you approach it [Macquarie Harbour, in Tasmania], sea and land curve away to port in a dazzle of white light, diffused through the haze of the incessantly beating ocean. All is sandbank and shallow; the beach that stretches to the northern horizon is dotted with wreckage, the impartial boneyard of ships and whales.

A third advantage is less talked about but ought to become more evident, now that *The Fatal Shore* has given us such a conspicuous example. The Australian expatriate, the stay-away writer, loots the world for cultural references. If he can write like Hughes, he may combine these into a macaronic, coruscating prose that would be as precious as a cento or an Anacreontic odelette if it were not so robust, vivid and clearly concerned with defining the subject, rather than just displaying his erudition:

> The Norfolk Island birds had forgotten man had ever been there; one could pick them out of the bushes, like fruit. Even today, a walk along the cliffs—where the green meadow runs to the very brink of the drop and the bushes are distorted by the eternal Pacific wind into humps and clawings that resemble Hokusai's *Great Wave* copied by a topiarist—is a fine cure for human adhesiveness. One sees nothing but elements: air, water, rock and the patterns wrought by their immense friction. The mornings are by Turner; the evenings, by Caspar David Friedrich, calm and beneficent, the light sifting angelically down towards the solemn horizon.

Nothing home-grown in Australia sounds quite like that, yet it is essentially Australian writing—the product of an innocent abroad who has consciously enjoyed every stage of his growing sophistication without allowing his original barbaric gusto to be diminished. Here the vexed question of what place the expatriate has in Australia's cultural history is answered in terms of intensity, as critical questions always must be. The best comparison is with that period of American prose when literary jour-

nalists were enjoying both the American idiom and the privilege of load-
ing it with a cosmopolitan culture. The comparison should not be forced:
American writers mostly had their Europe all around them at home,
whereas Australians had to sail in search of it, or thought they did. (Even
as early as the 1950s, the post-war immigration of European refugees had
changed Australian culture profoundly, from the kitchen upwards, but
those native Australians who sailed in the opposite direction were following a surer instinct than has subsequently been made out: they might
have eaten baklava in Melbourne, but the Parthenon was still in Athens.)

Yet the similarity is striking. That feeling transmitted by the sheer
scope of James Gibbons Huneker, which rises to a fever in the style of
George Jean Nathan, is the feeling you get from the Australian expatriate
writers at their most exuberant: that the world is theirs, and that they are
trying to pack it all in, possessing it through the naming of its names.
Barry Humphries, Australia's unchallenged genius of cabaret and intimate revue, not only wields a vast culture himself but incongruously
lends it to his characters, so that his most famous creation, the housewife
superstar and arch-philistine Dame Edna Everage—who by now has
taken on such an independent life that she hosts talk shows in both Australia and Britain—turns out to know more than seems plausible about,
say, German Expressionism. The poetry of the London-based expatriate
Peter Porter, often thought of by even the most favourable British critics
as being a showcase for his learning, sins less through calculation in that
regard than through the lack of it. Porter just loves the adventure of creativity—anybody's creativity. The message of his work, far from being
"Look how much I've read," is "Look how much there is to read." There
are lines by Porter that might be sentences by Hughes, and vice versa. Not
that one suggests anything so organized as a school. (The present
reviewer was at the table in the Groucho Club in London, last December, when Hughes and Porter met for the first time, Hughes having wandered the world for twenty-five years, and Porter for ten years longer than
that.) But the very fact that this is not a school might be what makes it a
movement: an expatriate movement in Australian writing which comple-
ments the achievement at home—without, of course, presuming to
replace it.

In fact, some of the more spectacular of the Australian cultural stay-
aways don't seem very concerned about what happens where they come

from. Germaine Greer (whose polemics are at their most effective when uttered with the kind of zest I am talking about, and at their weakest when she affects to be weary of the world) turns up in Australia mainly to stun the local talk-show hosts and harangue the feminists for so slavishly clinging to ideas she gave them in the first place. Then she takes off again. The almost dementedly clever Oxford academic Peter Conrad is nowadays ready to turn aside and sum up Australian literature—having already, in his *Everyman History of English Literature*, dealt with the old country's written heritage—but there is no doubt that his chief concern is with the world entire: his prose, like Greer's, pops and fizzes with the strain of fitting in a self-assured opinion about absolutely everything. Australia's itinerant literati, like its media entrepreneurs, are world-eaters. Perhaps it is revenge for isolation: the Empire (among Australian expatriates the joke is old by now) strikes back.

In many respects the most damaging counterblow yet, *The Fatal Shore* is nevertheless open to criticism from several points of view. The book is dedicated to Hughes's godson, the son of a barrister who recently had the pleasure of making one of Britain's leading civil servants look ridiculous in an Australian court. The poor man had been sent out there in a misguided attempt to secure the Australian government's cooperation in repressing a book about MI5; the Australian judiciary, only lately set free from the constitutional tie by which its highest court of appeal sat in Britain, made its independence felt. But republicans pleased by the dedication might not find the book that follows wholly to their liking. If they use it to condemn the past, they will have to condemn themselves along with it, Hughes having shown how serious Sartre was when he made his apparently frivolous remark about not being able to quarrel with history, because it led up to him. Still, if the trend towards republicanism proves inexorable, Hughes will at least have helped to make the transition more intelligent, by raising the level of debate.

Professional historians will no doubt cavil about the unacademic eclecticism of Hughes's research techniques, although if they do so they will be paying him that tacit compliment of accepting him among their number, and anyway it is hard to see how his use of correspondence, in particular, could be more fastidious. If letters by convicts have been quoted from before, the job has never been done with such sympathy, so keen an ear for the telling phrase. Geoffrey Blainey's *The Tyranny of Dis-*

tance must retain the title of the most startlingly original book of Australian history, but *The Fatal Shore* runs it close, and is less like a thesis.

A more serious criticism could be made through the area in which the book most obviously excels. As a literary work, it rather tails off, as if its author had got tired of it. If Hughes plans another volume, telling the story up to Federation, at the turn of the century, it will be very welcome, though the period has already been well covered by historians. But, on the evidence of his text, his interest flags after Australia has ceased to be a paradox—a birth in death—and he interprets the approach of relative normality as a signal to pack up.

Even so, a more roundly conclusive final chapter would have been gratifying. Earlier chapters amply prove that Hughes would have been capable of it. He has that rarest ability among pictorially talented writers, of making a plain prose statement that covers the case. His television series *The Shock of the New* was good to look at but even better to hear. Giving us his view of the stack of bricks that the Tate Gallery had purchased and displayed as a work of art, Hughes made his point so simply that it didn't sound like an epigram: "Anyone *except* a child can make such things." (Cocteau's famous remark about the poetic prodigy Minou Drouet—"Every child is a genius except Minou Drouet"—is funnier, but not so true.) As the art critic of *Time*, since 1970, Hughes has had the obligation of covering the world art beat in readily accessible prose most weeks of the year. Bigger stories, such as the Rothko-legacy scam, he has been able to treat at length in the *New York Review of Books*. While the typical homebound Australian literary genius veers between undisciplined newspaper articles and fictional masterpieces that grow extra chapters of self-justification if challenged, Hughes has had to perfect himself in the good journalistic practice of seeing the point and keeping to it.

For his discovery of the diligent man inside his own bohemianism ("Live like a bourgeois," said Flaubert, "think like a demigod") New York has rewarded Hughes well, not least with much free time. This book is what he did with it. He went home and rediscovered his country, with an eidetic intensity that recalls Sidney Nolan doing the same thing, and in a prose that adds something to Patrick White's vision of the Australian landscape—clarity, straightforwardness, a sparkling simplicity without distortion. Finally, the best thing about *The Fatal Shore* is just that: going about other business, it doesn't *try* to be a work of art. Even on a subject like this, and at such length, Hughes has managed to speak with the arresting verve that Australians of today, fancying themselves, not without reason, as natural democrats, would like to think of as their peculiar tone of voice—the breath of sanity.

The New Yorker, March 23, 1987; later included in
Snakecharmers in Texas, 1988

POSTSCRIPT

Did Robert Hughes benefit by making his base in New York instead of London? Obviously so. As an art critic, it put him in the centre of the action, and in his amplified task as a general cultural commentator it has given him the best of two worlds, because his books arrive in Britain with all the impetus of American success behind them. The latter aspect is too seldom mentioned. For all the British literary world's justifiable pride in its self-sufficiency, American prestige works the same trick with the British media as the PX of a U.S. Air Force base used to work with British teenage girls. And Hughes's television programmes, merely well regarded on the minority outlets of the U.S., are hailed as major events when transferred to British mainstream channels, especially now that British public service broadcasting has largely given up on initiating any projects of similar scope and depth. Both tactically and strategically, Hughes could hardly have handled his exile better. The only drawback was slow to emerge, but it was edifying when it did.

When it came to the 1999 referendum on whether Australia should break its constitutional ties with Britain and become a republic, Hughes was a star performer of the unfortunately named Republican Movement. (Movement? *Bewegung?* Bad idea.) Unfazed by the long flight home across the Pacific, he could outwrite and outspeak anybody on his own side, and he left everybody on the other side sounding inarticulate. But his Americanized glamour helped to intensify the suspicion that the prominent republicans might be a bunch of silvertails with their own aims. For the Australian people, the "silvertail" is the person who has quite enough privileges already. The result of the referendum set the Republican Movement back on its heels. Like several others among the disappointed leadership, Hughes showed a tendency to blame the popu-

lation for missing its historic opportunity. Catching him out of countenance, the press, itself overwhelmingly pro-republican, nevertheless took
delight in calling him a carpetbagger. Like many another successful Australian expatriate, Hughes has proved by the trajectory of his career that
the climb into orbit is the easy part: it's the re-entry that's hard.

2003

21

PRIMO LEVI'S
LAST WILL AND TESTAMENT

The Drowned and the Saved by Primo Levi,
translated by Raymond Rosenthal

Primo Levi's last book, *The Drowned and the Saved*—published in Italy before he committed suicide—is the condensed, poised summation of all his written work, which includes novels, memoirs, poems, short stories and critical articles. All his books deal more or less directly with the disastrous historical earthquake of which the great crimes of Nazi Germany constitute the epicentre, and on whose shifting ground we who are alive still stand. None of the books is less than substantial and some of them are masterpieces, but they could all, at a pinch, be replaced by this one, which compresses what they evoke into a prose argument of unprecedented cogency and force. If the unending tragedy of the Holocaust can ever be said to make sense, then it does so in these pages. The book has not been as well translated as one could wish—Levi's supreme mastery of prose is reduced to something merely impressive—but its status as an indispensable guidebook to the infernal cellars of the age we live in is beyond doubt from the first chapter.

That we need guidance is one of the things Levi was always insistent about. He insisted quietly, but on that point he never let up. In a tough joke on himself, he acknowledged his kinship with the Ancient Mariner—the epigraph of this book is from Coleridge's poem—but he didn't apologize for telling his ghastly tale. The mind will reject this kind of knowledge if it can. Such ignorance doesn't even have to be willed. It is a protective mechanism. Levi was in no doubt that this mechanism needs to be overridden. Not knowing about what didn't suit them was how people let the whole thing happen in the first place.

A powerful aid to not knowing was the scale of the horror, hard to imagine even if you were there. The SS taunted the doomed with the assurance that after it was all over, nobody left alive would be able to credit what had happened to the dead, so there would be nothing to mark their passing—not even a memory. Levi's argument, already a summary, is difficult to summarize further, but if a central tenet can be extracted it would have to do with exactly that—memory. Beyond the evidence, which is by now so mountainous that it can be challenged only by the insane, there is the interpretation of the evidence. To interpret it correctly, even we who are sane have to grasp what things were really like. Levi is trying to make us see something that didn't happen to us as if we remembered it. There are good reasons, I think, for believing that not even Levi could fully succeed in this task. We can't live with his memories, and in the long run it turned out that not even he could. But if he has failed he has done so only to the extent of having been unable to concoct a magic potion, and in the process he has written a classic essay.

In Auschwitz, most of Levi's fellow Italian Jews died quickly. If they spoke no German and were without special skills, nothing could save them from the gas chambers and the ovens. Like most of the deportees from all the other parts of Nazi-occupied Europe, they arrived with small idea of where they were, and died before they could find out. Levi's training as a chemist made him exploitable. The few German words he had picked up in his studies were just enough to convey this fact to the exploiters. In the special camp for useful workers—it is fully described in his first and richest book, *Survival in Auschwitz*—Levi was never far from death, but he survived to write his testimony, in the same way that Solzhenitsyn survived the Gulag, and for the same reason: privilege. If Solzhenitsyn had not been a mathematician, we would probably never have heard of him as a writer. But if Levi had not been a chemist we would certainly never have heard of him as a writer. In the Soviet labour camp, death, however plentiful, was a by-product. The Nazi extermination camp was dedicated exclusively to its manufacture. Luck wasn't enough to bring you through. You had to have an edge on all the others. The proposition sounds pitiless until Levi explains it: "We, the survivors, are not the true witnesses." The typical prisoner did not get out alive. Those at the heart of the story had no story.

Shame, according to Levi, is thus the ineluctable legacy of all who lived. Reduced to a bare ego, the victim was under remorseless pressure to ignore the fate of everyone except himself. If he had friends, he and his friends were against the others, at least to the extent of not sharing with them the extra piece of bread that could make the difference between life and death within the conspiratorial circle but if shared outside would not be even a gesture, because everyone would die. During a heatwave, Levi found a few extra mouthfuls of water in a rusty pipe. He shared the bounty only with a close friend. He might have told others about this elixir of life, but he did not. Luckily, his self-reproach, though patently bitter, helps rather than hinders his effort to re-create for us the stricken landscape in which feelings of complicity were inescapable.

One of Levi's several triumphs as a moralist—for once, the word can be used with unmixed approval—is that he has analysed these deep and complicated feelings of inexpungible shame without lapsing into the relativism that would make everyone guilty. If everyone was guilty, then everyone was innocent, and Levi is very certain that his persecutors were not innocent. The Nazis were as guilty as the Hell they built. The good citizens who decided not to know were less guilty but still guilty. There were many degrees of guilt among those who were not doing the suffering. Some of them were as innocent as you can be while still being party to a crime. But parties to a crime they all were. The victims of the crime had nothing at all in common with those who planned it or went along with it. The victims who survived, and who were ashamed because they did, were not responsible for their shame, because they were driven to it. Even if they did reprehensible things—in the area of behaviour that Levi calls the Grey Zone—they could reasonably contend that they would never have contemplated such conduct in normal circumstances, from which they had been displaced through no fault of their own.

Levi has no harsh words even for those most terribly contaminated of survivors, the *Sonderkommando* veterans. The few still alive decline to speak. Levi believes that the right to silence of these men, who chose to live at the price of cooperating with the killers, should be respected. He is able to imagine—able, momentarily, to make *us* imagine—that the chance of postponing one's own death was hard to turn down, even at the cost of having to attend closely upon the unspeakable deaths of countless others. Levi manages to sympathize even with the Kapos, not all of whom were sadists, and all of whom wanted to live. Levi has no sympathy for the persecutors, but he is ready to understand them, as long as he is not asked to exonerate them. His patience runs out only when it comes to those who parade their compassion without realizing that they are trampling on the memory of the innocent dead. As a writer, Levi always keeps his anger in check, the better to distribute its intensity, but occasionally you sense that he is on the verge of an outburst. One such moment is when he reproves the film director Liliana Cavani, who has offered the opinion "We are all victims or murderers, and we accept these roles voluntarily." Faced with this brand of self-indulgent vaporizing, Levi expresses just enough contempt to give us an inkling of what his fury would have been like if he had ever let rip. To confuse the murderers with their victims, he says, "is a moral disease or an aesthetic affectation or a sinister sign of complicity; above all, it is precious service rendered (intentionally or not) to the negators of truth."

Levi might have written like that all the time if he had wished. But his sense of proportion never let him down. The offence was too great for individual anger to be appropriate. Emerging from his discussion of the Grey Zone of behaviour, in which the survivors, pushed to the edge of the pit, were excusably reduced to base actions that they would not have dreamed of in real life, he goes on to discuss the inexcusably base actions of those engineers of cruelty who made sure that even the millions of victims murdered immediately on arrival would have an education in despair before they died. In a chapter called "Useless Violence," Levi reminds us that we should not set too much store by the idea that the Nazi extermination programme was, within its demented limits, carried out rationally. Much of the cruelty had no rational explanation whatsoever. No matter how long it took the train to reach the camp, the boxcars were never provided with so much as a bucket. It wasn't that the SS were saving themselves trouble: since the boxcars had to be sent back in reasonable shape to be used again, it would actually have been *less* trouble to provide them with some sort of facility, however crude. There was no reason not to do so except to cause agony. Old people who were already dying in their homes were thrown onto the trains lest they miss out on the death the Nazis had decided was due them, the death with humiliation as a prelude.

You would expect Levi's voice to crack when he writes of such things, but instead it grows calmer. He doesn't profess to fully comprehend what went on in the minds of people who could relish doing such things to their fellow human beings. His tone of voice embodies his reticence. He is not reticent, however, about any commentator who *does* profess to fully understand, without having understood the most elementary facts of the matter. After the protracted and uncertain journey recorded in *The Reawakening*, Levi at last returned to Italy, and there was told that his survival must surely have been the work of Providence: fate had preserved him, a friend said, so that he might testify. In this book Levi characterizes that idea as "monstrous": a big word for him—almost as big as any word he ever uses about the events themselves.

He is firm on the point, but this firmness is only a subdued echo of how he made the same point at the end of the "October 1944" chapter of *Survival in Auschwitz*, where the prisoner Kuhn, after the terrifying process of selection for the gas chambers has once again passed him by, loudly and personally thanks God. In the earlier book Levi was scornful of Kuhn's selfishness in believing that the Providence that had ignored so many should be concerned to preserve him. ("If I was God, I would spit at Kuhn's prayer.") In this book, the same argument is put no less decisively, but more in sorrow than in anger, as if such folly were ineradicable, a part of being human. Though Levi was never a fatalist, at the end of his life he seems to have been readier to accept that human beings are frail and would prefer to misunderstand these things if given the opportunity. Wonderfully, however, he remained determined not to give them the opportunity. At the very time when he feared that the memory and its meaning might slip from the collective human intelligence and go back into the historic past that we only pretend concerns us, Levi's trust in human reason was at its most profound. Transparent even in its passion, level-headed at the rim of the abyss, the style of his last book is an act of faith.

From the translation, however, you can't always tell. Raymond Rosenthal has mainly done a workmanlike job where something more accomplished was called for, and sometimes he is not even workmanlike. *The Drowned and the Saved* ranks with Nadezhda Mandelstam's *Hope Against Hope* as a testament of the age, but Nadezhda Mandelstam's translator was Max Hayward, whose English was on a par with her Russian. One doesn't want to berate Mr. Rosenthal, who has toiled hard, but one might be forgiven for wishing that his editors had noticed when he needed help. If they weren't aware that a paragraph by Levi always flows smoothly as a single rhythmic unit, they should at least have guessed that a sentence by Levi is never nonsense—and when it comes down to detail the translation all too often obscures what Levi took pains to make clear, dulls the impact of his most precisely calculated effects, and puts chaos back into the order he achieved at such cost.

There doesn't seem to have been much editorial control at all. Punctuation is arbitrary and spellings have been left unchecked. In the original Italian text, Levi left a handful of German words—part of the uniquely ugly vocabulary of Naziism—untranslated, so that they would stand out with suitable incongruity. In this Englished version they are treated the same way, but some of them are misspelled, which might mean either that Mr. Rosenthal does not read German or that he does not read proofs, but certainly means that the editors were careless. A *Geheimnisträger* is a bearer of secrets. If *Geheimnisfräger* means anything, it would mean an asker of secrets, which is the opposite of what Levi intended. This kind of literal misprint can happen to anyone at any time and is especially likely to be introduced at the last moment while other errors are being corrected, but another piece of weird German seems to have originated with the translator himself. "There is an unwritten but iron law, *Zurüchschlagen*: answering blows with blows is an intolerable transgression that can only occur to the mind of a 'newcomer,' and anyone who commits it must be made an example." The word should be *zurückschlagen*, with a lower case "z" because it is not a noun, and a "k" instead of the first "h." Worse, and probably because the word has not been understood, the first comma and the colon have been transposed, thereby neatly reversing the sense. What Levi is saying is that it was against the law to strike back. The English text says that this law was called: to strike back. An important point has been rendered incomprehensible.

The translator's Italian is good enough to make sure that he usually doesn't, when construing from that language, get things backward, but he can get them sidewise with daunting ease, and on several occasions he puts far too much trust in his ear. To render *promiscuità* as "promiscuity," as he does twice, is, in the context, a howler. Levi didn't mean that people forced to live in a ghetto were tormented by promiscuity. He meant that they were tormented by propinquity. The unintentional suggestion that they were worn out by indiscriminate lovemaking is, in the circumstances, a bad joke. Similarly, the Italian word *evidentemente*, when it means "obviously," can't be translated as "evidently," which always implies an element of doubt; that is, means virtually the opposite. "Also in the certainly much vaster field of the victim one observes a drifting of memory, but here, evidently, fraud is not involved." Thus a point about which Levi is morally certain is made tentative. Again, the word *compor-tamenti* is good plain Italian, but "behaviours" is sociologese: the transla-tor has left room for the reader to suspect that Levi was prone to jargon, when in fact he eschewed it rigorously, out of moral conviction.

Sometimes neglect attains the level of neologism. When Levi says that the daily life of the Third Reich was profoundly *compenetrato* by the Lager system, the word *compenetrato* is hard to translate; "penetrated" isn't comprehensive enough, but you certainly can't render it as "com-pentrated," which looks like a misprint anyway and, even if it had an "e" between the "n" and the "t," would still send you straight to the diction-ary—and it would have to be a big one. Such a verbal grotesquerie, how-ever, at least has the merit of being easy to spot. More insidious are trans-positions of meaning which sound plausible. There are sentences that have, under a troubled surface, an even more troubled depth. "But it is doubtless that this torment of body and spirit, mythical and Dantesque, was excogitated to prevent the formation of self-defence and active resist-ance nuclei: the Lager SS were obtuse brutes, not subtle demons." Here *nuclei di autodifesa o di resistenza attiva*, which could have been trans-lated in the same word order and sounded like good English, has been pointlessly inverted to sound like sociologese; and *escogitato* has been taken straight when it needed, for naturalness, to be turned into some simpler word, such as "planned" or "devised." But you could make these repairs and still leave the deeper damage undisturbed. The word "doubt-less" should be "doubtful." Retroactively this becomes clear. The rest of the paragraph eventually tells you that its first sentence is nonsensical. There is the satisfaction of solving a brain-teaser. It is an inappropriate pleasure; Levi was not writing *Alice's Adventures in Wonderland*. Having actually been through the looking-glass into the realm of perverted logic, he came back with an urgent commitment to lucidity. Watching his helpers frustrate him in this aim is not pleasant.

Most of these glitches are at the level of vocabulary and grammar. Another inadequacy, though it matters less for the purpose of initial com-prehension, has the eventual effect of denying us knowledge of Levi's intimacy with the literary tradition to which he contributed and by which he was sustained. As his book of essays *Other People's Trades* explicitly reveals, Levi was cultivated in the literatures of several languages. But the literature of his own language had cultivated him. He was *compenetrato* with the poetry and prose of his national heritage. In this book he acknowledges quotations from Manzoni and Leopardi, but, like most Italian writers, he assumes that allusions to Dante need not be flagged. It was foolishly confident of the editors of this English edition to assume the same thing.

Levi often echoes Dante. All too frequently, the translator fails to alert us that this is happening. To leave the allusions unexplained is to weaken the central meaning, because they are always functional. A typical instance is in the passage about those Nazis who for ideological reasons had ended up among the prisoners: "They were disliked by everyone." The word *spiacenti*, which would not occur in everyday language, is a reference to *Inferno* III, 63, where it describes those who have been rejected by both God and God's enemies. By the translator's simply rendering what is said, without explaining what is meant, a powerful use of literary allusion has been turned into patty-cake. Still, the sense survives, and there are worse faults in a translator than to be occasionally clueless. It is worse to be careless. Levi may have literally said that he was "intimately satisfied by the symbolic, incomplete, tendentious, sacred representation in Nuremberg," but *sacra rappresentazione* means a medieval morality play and can't be used here in its literal form without making Levi sound mystical at the very moment when he is making a point of sounding hard-headed.

In Italy, the school editions of Levi's books are thoroughly annotated—in several cases, by Levi himself. It would have been better if his English-language publishers had waited for the school editions to come out and then had them translated, notes and all. Unfortunately, the world of publishing has its own momentum. One can't complain about there having been so much eagerness to get Levi's books translated, but a side effect of the haste has been that his achievement, so coherent in his own language, looks fragmented in ours. He has had several translators, of varying competence. His carefully chosen titles have sometimes been mangled in translation—especially by his publishers in the United States, who have on the whole been less sensitive than his publishers in Britain to his delicate touch. *Se Questo È un Uomo*, called *If This Is a Man* in Britain, in the current United States edition is called *Survival in Auschwitz*—a journalistic come-on that no doubt has its merits as an attention-getter but can't be said to prepare the way for a narrative that dedicates itself to avoiding stock responses. In the UK, the title of *La Tregua* is translated as *The Truce*, which is accurate, but in the United States it appears as *The Reawakening*, which is inaccurate, because the whole point of the book is that Levi's long voyage home was merely a pause between two periods of struggle—one to survive physically and the other to cope mentally. As for his important novel *La Chiave a Stella*, it can only be regretted that his publishers across the Atlantic tried so hard to help him. A *chiave a stella* is indeed a kind of wrench, but it is not a monkey wrench. "The Monkey Wrench," however, would not have been as awkward a title as the one that the book was given, *The Monkey's Wrench*. To translate "La Chiave a Stella" literally as "The Star-Shaped Key" might have been too poetic for Levi—who is always too truly poetic to be enigmatic—but a momentary puzzle would have been better than a lasting blur. Levi's exactitude, after all, is not incidental to him. It's him.

Books have their fortunes. If the transmission of Levi's body of work into our language might have gone better, it could also have gone worse. Clearly, all concerned tried their best. It is impossible to imagine that anyone involved—whether translator, editor, designer or executive—thought lightly of the task. Presumably, Levi's approval was sought and obtained for those clumsy titles: he could read English, and in the last years of his life he attended evening classes, so that he might learn to speak it more fluently. He was vitally interested in guarding the safe passage of his books to a wider world. Yet the results of the transference—in our language, at any rate—are less than wholly satisfactory. Thus we are given yet further evidence that the declension that Levi said he most feared—the way the truth "slides fatally toward simplification and stereotype, a trend against which I would like here to erect a dike"—is very hard to stem.

How worried should we be about this tendency? Obviously, we should be very worried. But in what *way* should we be worried? The answer to that, I think, is not so readily forthcoming. Most of us choose our friends according to whether or not they understand these matters—or, at any rate, we decline to keep any friends who don't. We are already worried, and might even protest, if pushed to it, that we are worried enough—that if we were any more worried we would get nothing done, and civilization would collapse anyway. What we are really worried about is all those people who *aren't* worried, especially the young. We assume, along with Santayana, that those who cannot remember the past are condemned to repeat it. Anything written or filmed about the Holocaust—any essay, play, novel, film documentary or television drama, from this brilliant book by Levi all the way down to the poor, stumbling and execrated miniseries *Holocaust* itself—is informed by that assumption. Critical reaction to any such treatment of the Holocaust is governed by that same assumption. When it is argued that a rendition of the experience must be faithful to the experience, and that the effectiveness of the rendition will be proportionate to the fidelity, the argument is based on that same assumption. An assumption, however, is all it is. Hardbitten on the face of it, on closer examination it looks like wishful thinking.

It is undoubtedly true that some people who cannot remember the past are condemned to repeat it. But some people who can't remember the past aren't. More disturbingly, many of those who can remember the past are condemned to repeat it anyway. Plenty of people who remembered the past were sent to die in the extermination camps. Their knowledge availed them nothing, because events were out of their control. One of the unfortunate side effects of studying German culture up to 1933, and the even richer Austrian culture up to 1938, is the depression induced by the gradual discovery of just how cultivated the two main German-speaking countries were. It didn't help a bit. The idea that the widespread study of history among its intellectual elite will make a nation-state behave better is a pious wish. Whether in the household or in the school playground, ethics are transmitted at a far more basic level than that of learning, which must be pursued for its own sake: learning is not utilitarian, even when—especially when—we most fervently want it to be.

We should face the possibility that written learning, even in the unusually affecting form of an essay like *The Drowned and the Saved*, can be transmitted intact only between members of an intelligentsia already in possession of the salient facts. Clearly, the quality of written speculative discussion will influence the quality of artistic treatments of the subject, in whatever form they may be expressed. Here again, however, we should face the possibility that it might not necessarily be the artistic work of highest quality which influences the public. From Alain Resnais's breathtaking short film *Nuit et Brouillard*, of 1956, to the recent documentary *Shoah*, most of the screen treatments of the fate of the European Jews have been considered by those who know something about the subject to have spread at least a modicum of enlightenment, if only in the form of a useful myth. The exception was the aforementioned American miniseries *Holocaust,* which, although it won a few prizes, also received a worldwide pasting—especially from those critics who saw it in the United States, where it was punctuated by commercials. Even in Britain, where I saw it, any critic who found merit in it was likely to be told that he was insensitive to the subject. But whether those of us who had a good word to say for *Holocaust* were being as crass as it was crude is beside the point here. The point is that it was *Holocaust,* out of all these productions, that had the direct, verifiable historic effect. Just before the miniseries was screened in West Germany, a statute of limitations on Nazi crimes was about to come into effect. After the miniseries was screened, the statute was rescinded. Public opinion had been decisive. It could be said that this was a very late stage for the German people to get wise. It could even be said that if it took a melodrama like *Holocaust* to wake them up, then they were best left sleeping. But it couldn't be denied that a clumsy story had broken through barriers of unawareness that more sophisticated assaults had not penetrated.

Not just of Germany but of all other countries it was, of course, true that the wider public hadn't seen the more sophisticated efforts, so there was no comparison. But this merely proved that if the wider public is to be reached the message has to be popularized. Whether popularized necessarily means vulgarized is the obvious question, to which the answer, however reluctantly given, surely has to be yes. If the *mobile vulgus* is what you want to reach, then there is no virtue in constructing something too oblique for its members to be attracted by, or, if they are attracted, to understand. The more you insist that the event's implications are endless, and the more you pronounce yourself worried that the event's implications somehow haven't been taken in by the general run of humanity, the more you must be committed to some process of reduction. The trick is to popularize without traducing, to simplify without distorting—to vulgarize without violating. At its best, this process will be a distillation, but it is hard to see how dilution can be avoided for long. And, indeed, there are good reasons for supposing that any effort, even the best, to convey the importance of this subject is bound to render it less than it was. Arthur Miller's television film *Playing for Time* was rightly praised. The performances of Jane Alexander and Vanessa Redgrave were on a par with Meryl Streep's in *Holocaust,* with the difference that Miss Alexander and Miss Redgrave were working with a screenplay that was content to evoke by suggestion what it could not show without cosmeticizing. Nothing was shirked except one thing. Though the story about the two brave lovers who escaped was a true one, it was not true that after recapture they died facing each other with one last look of love. The two recaptured runaways are given a private shared moment on the point of death, as if, though their fate was sealed, they could to some extent choose the manner of it. It is a brilliantly dramatic scene. But it is dramatic licence. In reality, there was no choice. In *The Drowned and the Saved* Levi tells what really happened to the two who fled. The Nazis did not allow them any last beautiful moment. Only a work of art can arrange that—and, of course, we want it to, we demand it. It is hard to see how, against this demand to give the meaningless meaning, the full facts, in all their dreadful emptiness, can prevail. We will always look for consolation, and will always need to be talked out of it.

Levi tried to talk us out of it. There is no reason to believe he gave up on the task, because there is no reason to believe he thought that it could ever be fully accomplished in the first place. If we think he died of disappointment, we mistake him, and underestimate the frightfulness he was telling us about. Writing about Tamburlaine, Burckhardt said there were some episodes of history so evil that they weren't even of any use in defining the good: they were simply a dead loss. For all his tough-mindedness about erstwhile horrors, Burckhardt had no inkling that there were more to come. When they came, they were worse. For Burckhardt, the slaughterhouse happened in history: he was able to look back on it with a steady gaze. For Levi, it was life itself. The shock was never over, the suffering was never alleviated. The reason for his suicide, so bewildering at the time, is now, in retrospect, not so hard to guess. In the first chapter of this book he quotes his friend Jean Améry, who was tortured by the Gestapo and committed suicide more than thirty years later: "Anyone who has been tortured remains tortured." Levi's admirable sanity might have been produced in part by his dreadful memories, but it was maintained in spite of them. A fit of depression induced by some minor surgery was enough to open the way out which only a continuous act of will had enabled him to keep closed. His style to the end—and, on the evidence of this last book, even more at the end than at the beginning— had the mighty imperturbability of Tacitus, who wrote the truth as though it were worth telling even if there was nobody to listen and no prospect of liberty's being restored. But if Schopenhauer was right to call style the physiognomy of the soul, nevertheless the soul's face has a body, and in Levi's case the body had been injured. Once again, the urge for consolation can lead us astray. We would like to think that in time any pain can be absorbed, rationalized, given a place. But gratuitous violence is not like childbirth; it serves no purpose, and refuses to be forgotten.

Levi's admirers can be excused if they find it more comforting to be appalled by his demise than to admit how they had been lulled by the example of his sweet reason—lulled into believing that what he had been through helped to make him a great writer, and that the catastrophe therefore had that much to be said for it, if no more. But part of his greatness as a writer was to warn us against drawing up a phoney balance sheet. The idea that it takes extreme experience to produce great literature should never be left unexamined. The great literature that arises from extreme experience covers a very narrow band, and does so at the cost of bleaching out almost the whole of life—the everyday world that enjoys, in Nadezhda Mandelstam's great phrase, "the privilege of ordinary heartbreaks." Catastrophes like the Holocaust—and if it is argued that there have been no catastrophes quite like the Holocaust it can't usefully be argued that there won't be—have no redeeming features. Any good that comes out of them belongs not to them but to the world they try to wreck. Our only legitimate consolation is that, although they loom large in the long perspectives of history, history would have no long perspectives if human beings were not, in the aggregate, more creative than destructive. But the mass slaughter of the innocent is not a civics lesson. It involves us all, except that some of us were lucky enough not to be there. The best reason for trying to lead a fruitful life is that we are living on borrowed time, and the best reason to admire Primo Levi's magnificent last book is that he makes this so clear.

The New Yorker, May 23, 1988; later included in
The Dreaming Swimmer, 1992

POSTSCRIPT

Why did Primo Levi kill himself? Answers abound, but the best of them still seems to me to be the counterquestion I incorporated into my review: why didn't he do so earlier? Knowing what he knew, he must have found life hard to bear. Survivalism, an early form of Holocaust denial, was already in the air while he was undertaking his last great works. His reaction to Liliana Cavani's reckless bromides on the subject could have equally arisen from a hundred other stimuli. The suggestion that he was tipped over the edge by an uncomprehending book review is better than plausible, although it can't rule out the possibility that his weakened physical condition was enough to do the trick. (I was wrong, incidentally, to say that the surgery was "minor": it was massive, and the after-effects would have been more than enough to induce terminal depression in a man who had seen nothing worse than Disneyland on a wet day.) Finally the argument about his demise is worse than useless, because it displaces the attention that should be focussed on what he achieved when he was alive: a written temple to the necessity of recollection.

As to that, I don't see why the discussion should ever stop. New forms of Holocaust denial crop up all the time. Trying to prove that Hitler never gave the order is one of them. Trying to postpone retroactively the starting date of the *Endlösung* is another. The latest, at the time of writing, is the idea that we have all heard too much on the subject. A quick answer would be that they obviously haven't heard too much in Austria. A slower answer would take in the possibility that the Nazi assault on human values was a disease of such virulence that all its antibodies are dangerous too: we will never feel well again. The best we can hope to feel is a bit more intelligent. By that measure, a sign of intelligence would be to give up looking for consolation in an area where it is not to be had: whatever illuminates Virgil's *lugetes campos*, the weeping fields, it can never be the light of the sun. It was good news that in the last days of the millennium a book by a Jew, Marcel Reich-Ranicki, was at the top of the best-seller list in Germany, and that its central subject was what happened in the Warsaw ghetto. To the hungry eye, it looked like a closing of the ring, a squaring of accounts, a reassurance that the matter was in hand. But at the same moment the David Irving libel trial was getting under way in London, and the news from there could not have been worse, because whatever the outcome the innocent dead would be defiled all over again, as arguments were heard that millions of them had never died at all, and had therefore never even lived.

I was wrong about Burckhardt: he *did* guess that something awful was on the way. He just didn't realize how big it would be. Nobody did: not even the perpetrators. Just because they only gradually woke up to the dizzy magnitude of what they could get away with, we should not fool ourselves that they were slow to have the intention. As Victor Klemperer's monumental diaries (*I Shall Bear Witness* and *To the Bitter End*) sadly prove, the Holocaust was under way from the moment the Nazis came to Power. The only reason we failed to spot it is that the first victims died by their own hand.

Reliable Essays, 2001

22

PRIMO LEVI AND
THE PAINTED VEIL

What do we need to be told about Primo Levi that he doesn't tell us himself? In his middle twenties he spent a year in Auschwitz. Later on he wrote a book about it, the book we know as *If This Is a Man*: one of the great books of the twentieth century, and possibly the greatest among its sad category of great books we wish had never needed to be written at all. The book is beyond anybody else's power to summarize, since it is already a summary. The same might be said of his other writings, which were published intermittently during the remainder of his life and cumulatively suggested that one of the best reasons to continue living, after one had seen the world at its worst, was to get things written that would establish a place for the introspective self even in a context of overwhelmingly destructive historic forces.

But a commercial exploitation of his personal history was the last thing on his mind. Slow to commit himself as a full-time professional writer even after he was famous, he went on earning a salary as an industrial chemist. Though his waxing fortunes would have permitted a move up, he never left the flat in Turin where he had spent his whole life except for those fateful two years away when he was young: one year in Milan, the other in Poland. Everyone who knew him knew that his home life was hard. Having assigned to his wife the duty of looking after his ailing mother, and having thus made sure that they would spend a claustrophobic day with each other before he came home to them in the evening, he had created conditions for himself that might have been considered too obvious a stress-inducing mechanism even by Goldoni. And it all went on for years, whereas a Goldoni play only seems to.

But Levi never complained in public. Though Turin is a tight-lipped town, there were friends of friends who said that he complained to certain women, some of whom in turn complained that he was never allowed out for long. It seemed a fair inference that his reasons to stay were better than his reasons to leave, always granted that his wife was not herself struggling with the question of whether to keep him or kick him out. In his creative work there were hints at personal unhappiness, but the obliquity served only to bolster the impression that to preserve a decent reticence was a condition for creating at all. He must have struck some kind of workable balance, because he never stopped writing for long. In Italy, where there is a Booker committee around every corner, literary prizes count. He won them all. In the wider world, he was on his way to the Nobel Prize. It was only a matter of time. His life was a testament to the virtues of getting the past in proportion. All over the world, his admirers took solace from his true success, which was to grow old gracefully in spite of everything: think of what had happened to Primo Levi, and yet he still wanted to create, to live a life of order, to stick with it to the end.

Thus it was doubly, shockingly unexpected when, at the age of sixty-seven, at the apartment block in Turin, he killed himself by throwing himself down the stairwell. Though the possibility should not too soon be ruled out that he told us quite a lot about this before he did it, there is certainly no denying that he couldn't tell us much about it afterwards. Previously, he had left little room for other commentators to be more profound about his life than he could. Now they had space to operate. They also had what looked like an open invitation. There was a mystery to be investigated. Why, exactly, did he kill himself? Auschwitz had been ages ago. Could it have something to do with that other mystery, the mystery of his private life? For modern biographers, who increasingly feel less inhibited about writing to a journalistic brief, the prospect was hard to turn down. Two of them moved into the Turin area and got on the case. We must try to be grateful that they proved so diligent. They interviewed everybody except each other. The diligence, however, has produced two books which, arriving at the same moment, weigh on the spirit almost as much as they do on the muscles. You can just about hold one of them in each hand, but not for long.

Called simply *Primo Levi*, Ian Thomson's effort is already heavier than a house-brick. More mysteriously entitled *The Double Bond*, Carole Angier's is heavier than Ian Thomson's, partly owing to the abundance of material yielded by her talents as a mind-reader. To increasingly comic effect, women pining for the allegedly maladroit Levi ("like a child in matters of the heart," even though—perhaps because?—"a Colossus of thought") show up under sobriquets to protest that nothing will make them speak, little knowing that Angier has access to their brainwaves by telepathy. Unvoiced appetencies, normally resistant to verbal notation, are transcribed at length. Even on the level of ascertainable fact, rarely can she make a point in less than a page. She turns subtlety into a blunt instrument. She refuses, for example, to be fooled by the seemingly obvious connection between Primo Levi's direct experience of Auschwitz and his suicide forty years later. She is confident on the subject. "Not Auschwitz, but his own private depression, killed him in the end." If she means that the memory of Auschwitz might not have been enough to kill him without his private depression, there could be some sense to what she says, and thus reason for the confidence. But if she means that the private depression would have killed him even without Auschwitz, she is being confident about what she can't possibly know. She could be in a position of certainty only if Levi had killed himself before he got to Auschwitz. But he killed himself afterwards. It was long afterwards, and in the interim he had accumulated plenty more experience to be depressed about; but to assert that his most terrible memory played no crucial part in the decision that sent him over the balustrade is to make a far larger claim to knowledge about the way his mind worked than he ever did.

Ian Thomson is less given to speculation, which is the main reason that his book is considerably shorter than Carole Angier's. Since life, too, is short, and time reading about Primo Levi will probably be time taken away from reading Primo Levi unless the reader is devoted to no other subject, it should logically follow that if either book is to be recommended, Thomson's should be the one. Apart from his harder head, another reason for Thomson's comparative conciseness is that he simply writes with more snap than his rival can command, although like many another in the new generation of serious literati he somehow dodged the remedial English course on the way to his honours degree. At school Levi had a friend called Giorgio. "Phlegmatic, lazy, sensitive and generous,

Levi called him 'Giorgione.' . . ." Surrounding evidence suggests that all those adjectives apply to Giorgio, not Levi, but the word order suggests the opposite. "To brutalize" does not mean to treat like a brute; "exult" does not mean "exalt"; "refute" does not mean "rebut"; "contend" does not mean "oppose"; and participles, if they are meant to dangle occasionally, ought not to dangle so far that they confuse the sense. Of Natalia Ginzburg: "Born to an exemplary anti-Fascist family, her father was arrested in Turin in 1934 . . ." But unless there were exemplary anti-Fascist families before the advent of Fascism, it was she, and not her father, who was born to the exemplary anti-Fascist family. These blemishes in written English would be less striking if Levi himself had not been a fastidious master of Italian prose, which he learned to write at a time when a mistake was a mistake and not a sign of free expression.

Luckily Thomson's brio and sense of relevance are proof against his solecisms. Into his smaller space he packs with reasonable neatness most of the pertinent facts adduced by Angier, plus a few more that she somehow missed, perhaps because she was busy dreaming up code-names for the ever-increasing crowd of women whose lips were sealed. She didn't find out, for example, that in 1939 Levi's parents enrolled him for English lessons with a woman called Gladys Melrose, a Londoner scratching an existence in Turin as a teacher for Berlitz. Gladys Melrose ignited Levi's admiration for Aldous Huxley: an admiration which was to have large consequences later, when Levi formed the Huxleyan aim of studying the extermination camp as a laboratory of behaviour. Thomson also notes, as Angier does not, Levi's fondness for Louis Armstrong. A taste for good-time jazz is not necessarily a sure sign of a sunny nature (Mussolini's passion for Fats Waller was of no help to the Ethiopians) but it does suggest at least the capacity for lightness of spirit. It's the kind of detail that adds to our picture of Levi's character by making room for a quality he must have had but which is not often enough mentioned: a charming openness, on the mental level at any rate, to those easy pleasures from which, he was inclined to believe, his nature had shut him out. Did he snap his fingers as he listened to "Sugar Foot Stomp"? Did he hum along with "Savoy Blues"? Nobody ever asked, and at this rate nobody ever will, because not even Ian Thomson seems to realize that those little concrete details outrank any amount of abstract speculation.

His publisher, alas, shares the same obtuseness. Louis Armstrong, though present on page 118 of Thomson's book, is missing from its index.

So are Fred Astaire and Ginger Rogers. They are in the text, but they don't make it to the status of a fact that a scholar might want to look up later on. Yet there is a danger of depopulating Levi's imagination if we automatically assume that his principal mental symbols for two lovers swept away by passion were Paolo and Francesca from Canto V of the *Inferno*. The Fascist regime had banned Hollywood movies by 1941, but in Milan there were bootleg screenings. At one of those screenings, Levi marvelled at Fred and Ginger dancing in *Top Hat*. It was one of the last things he did before he went off and joined the doomed little group of young *resistenti* who behaved as if they had been trained for nothing else except to get arrested. He fell in love with one of them. Her name was Vanda. What did he see in his mind's eye, in the last hour they ever spent together? Was it Paolo and Francesca riding on the storm, or was it Fred and Ginger floating a magic millimetre above a white floor, touching each other with the lyrical chasteness that reduces the soul of a shy young man to a sob of longing? Because Levi is a classic, there is a bad tendency to think that he was raised on a strictly classic diet. But he took everything in: probably the main reason why he was able to take in even Auschwitz. Dreadful grist, but a brilliant mill.

You know you are getting old when the biographers scramble the most elementary facts about World War II, as if it all happened before their time: which, of course, it did. Thomson gives us a picture of Levi, in the Lager infirmary, finding out from German and Polish newspapers that the Allies were "moving towards Normandy." No newspaper of any nationality could possibly have carried such information. The newspapers might have said that the Allies were moving further into Normandy, or else were moving out of it as they expanded their bridgehead south and east; but if the newspapers had said that the Allies were moving *towards* Normandy they would have been privy to the biggest Allied secret of the war. On the other hand, Thomson has a sure sense of what Jewish bourgeois society was like in Turin before Mussolini made the unforced error of copying the Nuremberg laws.

Thomson paints a picture of assimilation rather than persecution. In Germany and Austria, it was the very success of the assimilation that got the anti-Semitic intellectuals so excited, with disastrous consequences: but for Italy this had never been true. Anti-Semitic theorizing had never been powerful enough to infect even the Church, whose rank and file were later to behave very well during the Nazi round-up, with the result that the Italian branch of the Final Solution was a relative flop. The theory being lacking, there had never been much practice. Thomson's version of young Primo is bullied because he is a shrimp, not because he is a Jew: is bullied, in fact, even by other Jews. Angier can't resist wheeling the anti-Semites on early, as if Fascism had always been bound to bring them to power. But not even the Fascists, some of whom were Jews, had harboured any such expectation until Mussolini fell prey to the brainstorm that did as much as anything else to demoralize the country. (Most of the more intelligent Fascist hierarchs realized that their dream was on its way downhill from the moment that Mussolini issued the Manifesto of Racial Scientists in 1938, but they were counting on the usual gap being maintained between rhetoric and actuality.) In Angier's book, the Holocaust is practically waiting to grab Levi in the school playground. Levi told his Italian biographer, Fiora Vincenti, a story about his being given a hard time at school by a pair of athletic boys. Making it clear that a more powerfully equipped biographer is now on the scene, Angier goes on interpreting the story until the athletic boys end up as Jew-baiters. The interpretation is longer than the story; and anyway, if that was what Levi meant, why wouldn't he have said it? She puts herself continually in the untenable position of knowing more than he does about the one subject he knew more about than anybody, and of wanting to get more said when saying everything he could was his principal object.

Admittedly, "everything he could" did not always mean everything he knew. There is such a thing as a decorum that goes out of date. As Thomson notes, Levi held back from evoking the pitiable scene at Fossoli when the SS gleefully photographed the prisoners as they squatted defecating in the railway siding before the train departed. Typically, the SS got a particular charge out of photographing the women. Luciana Nissim, who was there, recorded the moment in her *Memoir from the House of the Dead*, which was published before Levi had finished writing *If This Is a Man*. Thomson plausibly conjectures that Levi was held back by "some strange puritan stringency," but to a man of his generation—and, indeed, of mine—it is the word "strange" that would seem strange. Why add insult to injury by speaking of the unspeakable? That the SS could visit such barbarism on women was the proof that the devil was loose. For all his determination to tell the whole truth, Levi thought he could not do it unless the devil within himself was kept on a short leash: vengeance and hatred were his enemies, not his friends. And decorum: well, that *was* his friend. Look what had happened when it had been outlawed, in that militarized bedlam where anything went and only luck could save you.

"Only luck could save you" was a favourite admonition of Nadezhda Mandelstam to anyone cherishing the illusion that in Stalinist times there might have been a strategy for dodging fate. Solzhenitsyn knew that it was only the accident of his being a mathematician that saved his life. Levi knew that it was his qualification in chemistry that kept him in the work camp and out of the gas chamber. But a lot of other lucky breaks were necessary as well. He had a few words of German; he fluked a double soup ration; and, at the end, the scarlet fever he almost died of saved him from the forced march on which he would have died for certain. One of the many great things about him was that he never attributed all these strokes of fortune to a benevolent fate. When, after the war, someone in Italy said that Providence had intervened so that Levi might bear witness, Levi got uncontrollably angry for one of the few times in his life. Here lies the full meaning of the "Kuhn's prayer" sequence in *If This Is a Man*: a full meaning which Angier goes on worrying at in an unnecessary attempt to make it fuller still.

Kuhn thanked God for sparing him. When Levi said that if he had been God he would have spat at Kuhn's prayer, Levi was saying that there was no such thing as divine intercession for an individual case. The point isn't really all that hard to understand. Levi, after all, devoted the best of his magnificent literary powers to driving it home. Levi also made the uncomfortable point that when it came to surviving the initial selections, high qualities of character were more likely to be a drawback than an advantage. Angier, when praising the "bold" personality of one of Levi's female contemporaries, does so by imagining her being caught up in the Holocaust: "I think she might have survived." But Levi spent a good part of his last book, *The Drowned and the Saved*, pointing out that the Lager system punished any signs of fighting back with certain death. So unless her boldness had been accompanied by a prophetic capacity to keep it concealed, Levi's friend wouldn't have lasted five minutes. Angier's intuitive grasp of survival potential is the very kind of sophisticated incomprehension of his message which added to Levi's despair in the later part of his life.

The question remains of how desperate he was already. It will always remain, because it is unanswerable. For all we know, suicide is the mandatory escape route for anyone with clear sight, and the rest of us get to die in bed only because we have the gift of regrowing our cataracts from day to day. Seen steadily and seen whole, life is hard to bear even in conditions of civilized normality. In Levi's case, there was the Holocaust. Later on there were all the forms of its denial: forms that he tirelessly analysed, but with a growing sense that he was trying to mop up the incoming tide. It could be argued that these later disappointments would have been enough to tip him over the edge even if he had never had direct experience of the Holocaust in the first place. But since he did have such experience, it seems perverse to subtract it from the equation, especially when Levi himself made a famous statement on the subject as long after the event as 1978, the year in which his fellow survivor Jean Améry drank poison. Levi had always been impressed by Améry's contention that the man who has been tortured once stays tortured. Writing about Améry's suicide, he returned to the same idea. Thomson quotes what Levi said.

Suicides are generally mysterious: Améry's was not. Faced by the hopeless clarity of his mind, faced by his death, I have felt how fortunate I have been, not only in recovering my family and my country, but also in succeeding to weave around me a "painted veil" made of family affections, friendships, travel, writing and even chemistry.

Carole Angier is very bold to leave this crucial passage out, although one can see that it might have interfered with the main thrust of her original research, in which it is established, to her satisfaction at any rate, that Levi, if he recovered his family, certainly did not succeed in weaving around himself any kind of veil, whether painted or otherwise, when it came to family affections. Not only was the young Primo Levi "pathologically shy" (not just shy) but the older, post-Auschwitz Primo Levi stayed that way, torn between the wife he was unable to leave and the women he could not allow himself to love. There is no notion that Levi might have been honouring his wife for her loyalty, love and sacrifice, and that the other women, in declining to twist his arm, might have been honouring him through respecting his real wishes. Early or late, he was the victim of a sex problem—a view Angier sticks to even while, on her own evidence, the ageing hero looks to be grappling with the same sex problem as Warren Beatty. The child was the father of the man, and the man was a child in matters of the heart. Why? Because he was depressed all his life. What depressed him? Depression. Thus Angier reduces a moral genius to a helpless plaything of his own childhood and adolescence, a message we might find comforting. But we should watch out for that kind of reassurance. In the democratic component of liberal democracy, there is a sore point called egalitarianism, and the craze for biography might be one of its products. The craze for biography puts the reader on a level with superior people. Part of the effect of Thomson's book, and the whole effect of Angier's, is to suggest that Primo Levi was a bit like us; which is only a step away from suggesting that we are a bit like him. *Magari*, as the Italians say: if only it were true.

Times Literary Supplement, June 21, 2002

·

POSTSCRIPT

In a book review there is room to say only so much, but perhaps I should have found room to say that Levi himself didn't approve of the term "Holocaust." Unfortunately, to open a question of terminology would have imposed the obligation of following it up, and in this case to no clear end, because a preferable term has been slow to present itself. When we tell people that they don't know enough about the Holocaust, at least they have some idea of what it is we are saying they don't know enough about. If we tell them that they don't know enough about the Shoah, they aren't even aware of what subject it is that we suppose them to be ignorant of.

On this point it is important to remember that Levi, while never less than scrupulous in his personal use of language, was generously prepared to accept that other people could feel keenly even if they spoke clumsily. As I noted in my review of *The Drowned and the Saved*, the American TV miniseries *Holocaust* was much derided by experts when it was first screened, but it was not derided by Levi. He thought its heart was in the right place.

As he grew older, Levi found out the hard way that the precious truth he was trying to guard had more to fear from misplaced fastidiousness than from vulgarity. Were there such a thing as life after death, he would have found out from his biographies that the truth itself can be put to inhuman use, and not only by tabloid journalists. Reputable scholars can persuade themselves that duty requires a full disclosure of any truffle unearthed. Very few among even the more serious reviewers of these two books raised the question of what Levi would have thought about the prospect of the women in his life having their privacy intruded upon while they still breathed. Until the day he died, he did his best to protect all concerned from the consequences of having loved him. The day after, all bets were off. It is offensive to pretend that we have a right to behave this way because Levi was a great man who gave us our best account of what it was like to share the fate of the anonymous millions, and who, therefore, is a proper object of study in all details, no matter how embarrassing they might happen to be for his family and intimate friends. Now that his protesting voice is supposedly silent (and how truly vulgar his biographers are to suppose that), his dearest wish — to restore and preserve the concept of a private life — is trampled upon simply and solely because he was famous. His loved ones are maltreated because he shared the fate of Elvis Presley.

None of this is to say that a decent, proportionate biography of a literary figure can't be useful, if only to cancel myths and correct false assumptions. When I reviewed *The Drowned and the Saved* I assumed that the foreign language Levi was trying to perfect on the eve of his death was English. From the biographies I learned that it was German. Levi never got as far with English as one was inclined to hope. In the world of fulfilled wishes, Levi would have acquired an exact ear for English, realized that the American titles of some of his books were worse than useless, and done something to set things straight. Alas, there was no time, and we would probably have remained stuck with the titles anyway: for legal reasons, they are set in stone. For a long time to come, the most important single book about the inexorable terrors of state-sponsored mass murder will go on billing itself as a guide to getting by in tough conditions: *Survival in Auschwitz*.

2003

23

THE ALL OF ORWELL

Who wrote this? "Political language—and with variations this is true of all political parties, from Conservatives to Anarchists—is designed to make lies sound truthful and murder respectable, and to give an appearance of solidity to pure wind." But you guessed straight away: George Orwell. The subject stated up front, the sudden acceleration from the scope-widening parenthesis into the piercing argument that follows, the way the obvious opposition between "lies" and "truthful" leads into the shockingly abrupt coupling of "murder" and "respectable," the elegant, reverse-written coda clinched with a dirt-common epithet, the whole easy-seeming poise and compact drive of it, a world view compressed to the size of a motto from a fortune cookie, demanding to be read out and sayable in a single breath—it's the Orwell style. But you can't call it Orwellian, because that means Big Brother, Newspeak, the Ministry of Love, Room 101, the Lubyanka, Vorkuta, the NKVD, the MVD, the KGB, KZ Dachau, KZ Buchenwald, the *Reichsschrifttumskammer*, Gestapo HQ in the Prinz-Albrecht-Strasse, *Arbeit macht frei*, *Giovinezza*, *Je suis partout*, the compound at Drancy, the Kempei Tai, Let a Hundred Flowers Bloom, *The Red Detachment of Women*, the Stasi, the Securitate, Cro-Magnon Latino death squad goons decked out in Ray-Bans after dark, that Khmer Rouge torture factory whose inmates were forbidden to scream, Idi Amin's Committee of Instant Happiness or whatever his secret police were called, and any other totalitarian obscenity that has ever reared its head or ever will.

The word "Orwellian" is a daunting example of the fate that a distinguished writer can suffer at the hands of journalists. When, as almost invariably happens, a totalitarian set-up, whether in fact or in fantasy—in Brazil or in *Brazil*—is called Orwellian, it is as if George Orwell had conceived the nightmare instead of analysed it, helped to create it instead of helping to dispel its euphemistic thrall. (Similarly Kafka, through the word "Kafkaesque," gets the dubious credit for having somehow wished into existence the same sort of bureaucratic labyrinth that convulsed him to the heart.) Such distortions would be enough to make us give up on journalism altogether if we happened to forget that Orwell himself was a journalist. Here, to help us remember, are the twenty volumes of the new complete edition, cared for with awe-inspiring industry, dedication and judgement by Peter Davison, a scholar based in Leicester, who has spent the last two decades chasing down every single piece of paper his subject ever wrote on and then battling with publishers to persuade them that the accumulated result would supply a demand. The All of Orwell arrives in a cardboard box the size of a piece of check-in luggage: a man in a suitcase. As I write, the books are stacked on my desk, on a chair, on a side table, on the floor. A full, fat eleven of the twenty volumes consist largely of his collected journalism, reproduced in strict chronology along with his broadcasts, letters, memos, diaries, jottings, *et* exhaustively and fascinatingly *al*. The nine other volumes, over there near the stereo, were issued previously, in 1986–87, and comprise the individual works he published during his lifetime, including at least two books that directly and undeniably affected history. But, lest we run away with the idea that *Animal Farm* and *Nineteen Eighty-Four* are the core of his achievement, here, finally, is all the incidental writing, to remind us that they were only the outer layer, and could not have existed without what lay inside. Those famous, world-changing novels are just the bark. The journalism is the tree.

A four-volume edition of the journalism, essays and letters, which was published in 1968 (co-edited by Ian Angus and Orwell's widow, Sonia), had already given us a good idea of how the tree grew, but now we get an even better chance to watch its roots suck up the nutrients of contemporary political experience and— But it's time to abandon that metaphor. Orwell never liked it when the writing drove the meaning. One of his precepts for composition was "Let the meaning choose the word, and not the other way around." For him prose style was a matter in which the ethics determined the aesthetics. As a writer, he was his own close reader. Reading others, he was open to persuasion, but he would not be lulled, least of all by mellifluous rhetoric. Anyone's prose style, even his, sets out to seduce. Orwell's, superficially the plainest of the plain, was of a rhythm and a shapeliness to seduce the angels. Even at this distance, he needs watching, and would have been the first to admit it.

.   .   .

Orwell was born into the impoverished upper class—traditionally, for its brighter children, a potent incubator of awareness about how the social system works. Either they acquire an acute hunger to climb back up the system—often taking the backstairs route through the arts, *à la* John Betjeman—or they go the other way, seeking an exit from the whole fandango and wishing it to damnation. Orwell, by his own later accounts, went the other way from his school days onwards. In one of his last great essays, "Such, Such Were the Joys," he painted his years at prep school (where he nicknamed the headmaster's gorgon of a wife Flip) as a set of panels by Hieronymus Bosch:

> "Here is a little boy," said Flip, indicating me to the strange lady, "who wets his bed every night. Do you know what I am going to do if you wet your bed again?" she added, turning to me. "I am going to get the Sixth Form to beat you."

Orwell had a better time at Eton—it sounds as if he would have had a better time in Siberia—but twenty years later, after he left it, reviewing his friend Cyril Connolly's partly autobiographical *Enemies of Promise*, he poured scorn on Connolly's fond recollections of the place. When Connolly proclaimed himself fearful that after his climactic years of glory at Eton nothing in the rest of his life could ever be so intense, Orwell reacted as if Flip had just threatened to deliver him to the Sixth Form all over again: " 'Cultured' middle-class life has reached a depth of softness at which a public-school education—five years in a luke-warm bath of snobbery—can actually be looked back upon as an eventful period."

Orwell often reviewed his friends like that. With his enemies, he got tough. But it should be said at the outset that even with his enemies he rarely took an inhuman tone. Even Hitler and Stalin he treated as men rather than as machines, and his famous characterization of the dogma-driven hack as "the gramophone mind" would have lost half its force if he had not believed that there was always a human being within the fanatic. His comprehension, though, did not incline him to be forgiving: quite the reverse. Society might have made the powerful what they were as surely as it had made the powerless what they were, but the mere fact that the powerful were free to express whatever individuality they possessed was all the more reason to hold them personally responsible for crushing the freedom of others. When they beat you, you can join them or you can join the fight on behalf of those they beat. It seems a fair guess that Orwell had already made his choice by the time Flip threatened him with a visit from the Sixth Form.

.   .   .

In the early part of his adult life, he was a man of action. He wrote journalism when he could—for him it was more natural than breathing, which, thanks to a lurking tubercular condition, eventually became a strain—but he wanted to be where the action was. Already questioning his own privileged, if penny-pinching, upbringing and education, he went out to Burma at the age of nineteen and for the next five years served as a colonial policeman—an experience from which he reached the conclusion (incorporated later into his novel *Burmese Days* and his essays "Shooting an Elephant" and "A Hanging") that the British Empire was a capitalist mechanism to exploit the subjugated poor. Back in Europe, he found out what it was like to be a proletarian by becoming one himself—*Down and Out in Paris and London, The Road to Wigan Pier*—and expanded his belief about the exploitative nature of the Empire to embrace the whole of capitalist society, anywhere. He volunteered for service in Spain in the fight against Franco, and the selfless comradeship of ordinary Spaniards risking their lives to get justice—*Homage to Catalonia*—confirmed his belief that an egalitarian socialist society was the only fair and decent alternative to the capitalist boondoggle, of which Franco's Fascism, like Hitler's and Mussolini's, was merely the brute expression.

So here, already formed, were two of his three main political beliefs—about the awfulness of capitalism and the need for an egalitarian alternative. There was nothing uncommon about them except their intensity: plenty of intellectuals from his middle-class background had reached the same conclusions, although few of them as a result of direct experience. The third belief was the original one. It was more than a belief, it was an insight. Again, he was not the only one to have it, or at any rate part of it: though such illustrious invitees to the Soviet Union as Bernard Shaw, H. G. Wells and the Webbs had been fooled into admiration by the standard tricks of Potemkin Village set-dressing, Bertrand Russell, André Gide, E. E. Cummings, Malcolm Muggeridge and several other visiting commentators had already spotted that the vaunted socialist utopia was a put-up job, and in 1938 the Italian-born Croatian ex-Communist Anton Ciliga, in his book *Au Pays du Grande Mensonge* (In the Land of the Big Lie), gave a detailed account of the Gulag system, which he knew from the inside. But nobody ever expressed his revulsion better or more lastingly than Orwell, who got it right without ever having to go there.

He went somewhere else instead. Discovering in Spain, from the behaviour of the Russian representatives and their Communist adherents, that the Soviet Union was as implacable an enemy of his egalitarian aspirations as Nazi Germany or Fascist Italy, he developed the idea that it wasn't enough to be against Mussolini and Hitler: you had to be against Stalin as well, because the enemy was totalitarianism itself. That was as far as he got before his career as a man of action came to an end. Shot in the throat by a sniper, he recuperated, but if he had stayed in Spain any longer he would have almost certainly been murdered. The anarchist group in whose ranks he had fought, the POUM, was being liquidated on Soviet orders, and his name was on the list. (The evidence is all here, in Volume XI, and it is enough to bring on a cold sweat: losing Orwell to the NKVD would have had the same devastating effect on our intellectual patrimony that the loss of the historian Marc Bloch and the literary critic Jean Prévost to the Gestapo had on the French.)

Back in England with his three main beliefs—capitalism was a disease, socialism was the cure and communism would kill the patient—the erstwhile man of action carried on his cause as a man of letters. For part of the Second World War, he was a member of the Home Guard, and for a further part he was with the BBC, preparing broadcasts for India, but as far as the main action went he was an onlooker. No onlooker ever looked on more acutely. The journalism he wrote at the close of the 1930s and in the 1940s would have been more than enough by itself to establish him as having fulfilled his life's purpose, which he made explicit in his last years: "What I have most wanted to do is to make political writing into an art." The whole heavy atmosphere of the prelude to the war, the exhausting war itself, and its baleful aftermath: it's all there, reported with a vividness that eschews the consciously poetic but never lapses from the truly dramatic, because he had the talent and the humility to assess even a V-1 in terms of its effect on his own character, using his soliloquy to explain the play:

> Every weapon seems unfair until you have adopted it yourself. But I would not deny that the pilotless plane, flying bomb, or whatever its correct name may be, is an exceptionally unpleasant thing, because, unlike most other projectiles, it gives you time to think. What is your first reaction when you hear that droning, zooming noise? Inevitably, it is a hope that the noise *won't stop*. You want to hear the bomb pass safely overhead and die away into the distance before the engine cuts out. In other words, you are hoping that it will fall on somebody else.

Along with the exterior drama, however, an interior drama is now, at long last, fully revealed. Tracking his mind from note to memo, from letter to book review, from article to essay, we can see what happened to those early beliefs—which two of them were modified, and which one of them was elaborated into a social, political, ethical and even philosophical concept whose incorporation into *Animal Farm* and *Nineteen Eighty-Four* would make him into a man of action all over again, a writer whose books helped to bring down an empire, even if it wasn't the same empire he originally had in mind.

First, though, with the Spanish war over and the full European war not yet begun, he had another battle on his hands, bloodless this time but almost as noisy: the battle against Britain's left-wing intellectuals. He realized that they had wilfully declined to get the point about Spain: they still saw communism as the only bulwark against Fascism. Worse, they thought that the Moscow trials were justified or otherwise to be condoned—a price worth paying to Build Socialism. Orwell's conviction that no socialism worth having could be built that way set him at odds with the progressive illuminati of his generation, and that altercation was made sharper by how much he and they had in common. He, too, had had the generosity to declare his own privileges meaningless if they were bought at the expense of the downtrodden. He, too, believed that the civilization that had given birth to him was a confidence trick. And, although he had already concluded that free speech was the one liberal institution no putative future society could abolish if it was to remain just, he still thought that the plutocratic oligarchy allowed liberal institutions to continue only as part of the charade that favoured the exploitation of the poor. (In the 1960s, the same notion lived again, as "repressive tolerance.") Fascism, he proclaimed, was just bourgeois democracy without the lip service to liberal values, the iron fist without the velvet glove. In 1937, he twice ventured the opinion that democracy and Fascism "are Tweedledum and Tweedledee." In the same year, he warned that "the moneyed classes" might trick Britain into "another imperialist war" with Germany: language hard to distinguish from Party-line boilerplate.

Orwell could always see the self-serving fallacy of pacifism, but he had a soft spot for Bertrand Russell's version of it, which should have been detectable as pure wind even at the time, when Hitler had already spent more than five years abundantly demonstrating that the chances of the non-violent to temper his activities by their moral example were exactly zero. But Orwell gave the philosopher's well-intended homilies a sympathetic review. Orwell was thus in line with the Labour Party, which, from the opposition benches, railed against the threat of Fascism but simultaneously condemned as warmongering any moves towards rearmament. It was the despised reactionaries, with Chamberlain at the head of the Conservative government and Churchill growling encouragement from the back benches, who actively prepared for war against Hitler. Distancing himself from the Communists and their fellow-travellers in his attitude to the USSR, Orwell was dangerously close to them in supposing bourgeois democracy to be teetering on the rim of history's dustbin, into which more realistic forces would combine to shove it beyond retrieval. In Germany, the same aloof attitude on the part of the social democrat intellectuals had fatally led them to high-hat the Weimar Republic while the Communists and the Nazis combined to strangle it, but Orwell had not yet fully learned the lesson. On the Continent, or already fleeing from it, there were plenty of veteran political commentators who had learned it all too well at the hands of one or the other of the two extremist movements and sometimes both, but apart from Franz Borkenau, Arthur Koestler and perhaps Boris Souvarine it is remarkable how few of them influenced Orwell's views. By international standards he was a late developer.

Pre-war, Orwell was in a false position, and his journalistic output during the war is largely the story of how he came to admit it. But before he started getting round to that, he had one more, even more glaring, false position still to go. When the war began he said that Britain was bound to be defeated unless it had a social revolution, which might even require an armed uprising. Possibly he had been carried away by the rifles issued to the Home Guard, and had visions of an English POUM taking pot shots at the oppressor. (Orwell rose to the rank of sergeant in the Home Guard, but Davison should have found room to say, in a footnote, that his hero was notoriously more enthusiastic than competent: a Court of Inquiry was conducted after he supervised a mortar drill that almost resulted in the decapitation of one of his men.) Even in 1941, well after the Battle of Britain demonstrated that this bourgeois democracy might well hope to withstand Hitler, we can still hear Orwell promising that "England is on the road to revolution" and that to bring the revolution about a "real English socialist movement" would be "perfectly willing to use violence if necessary."

But if a pious wish helped to sustain him, the facts were simultaneously hard at work on a mind whose salient virtue was its willingness to let them in. He had noticed that Poland, whatever the condition of its liberal institutions under the pre-war regime, was immeasurably worse off now that the Nazis and the Soviets (following the letter of the Molotov-Ribbentrop Pact's secret protocols, although he had no means of knowing that yet beyond guesswork) had combined to expunge all traces of its civilization, including as many of its intelligentsia as they could round up. There were steadily accumulating written indications that he was becoming more and more impressed by the one fact about his country he had never been able to argue away. A state against which he could say out loud that he "was perfectly willing to use violence if necessary" might have something to be said for it—something central, and not just peripheral—if it was not perfectly willing to use violence against him.

Probably armed more by his ability to interpret news than by solid reading of social theorists, Orwell can be seen elaborating his own theory of society towards the point where he would begin to abandon some of its postulates, which had come from classical Marxism and its dubious historiographic heritage. Reviewing, in that same year, 1941, a book of essays about the English Revolution of 1640 edited by the Marxist historian Christopher Hill, Orwell pinpointed "the main weakness of Marxism," its inflexible determination to attribute to "the superstructure" (his quotation marks as well as mine) even the most powerful human motives, such as patriotism. Orwell asked the Marxist contributors an awkward question: "If no man is ever motivated by anything except class interests, why does every man constantly pretend that he is motivated by something else?"

Orwell had spent a lot of time before the war saying that class interests were indeed predominant—especially the interest of the ruling class in sacrificing the interests of every other class in order to stay on top—but now he had discovered his own patriotism, and typically he followed up on the climbdown. Even before the war, he had been impressed by how the English people in general had managed to preserve and develop civilized values despite the cynicism of their rulers. Now he became less inclined to argue that all those things had happened merely because the sweated labour of colonial coolies had paid for them, and were invalidated as a result. He was even capable, from time to time, of giving some of the cynical rulers a nod of respect: Orwell's praise of Churchill was never better than grudging, but nobody else's was ever more moving, because nobody else would have so much preferred to damn Churchill and all his works. From the early war years until the end of his life, Orwell wrote more and more about British civilization. He wrote less and less about the irredeemable obsolescence of bourgeois democracy. He had come to suspect that the democratic part might depend on the bourgeois part.

Most of the left-wing intellectuals hadn't. After Hitler clamorously repudiated his non-aggression pact with Stalin by launching Operation Barbarossa, they were once again able to laud the virtues of the Soviet Union at the tops of their voices. Even on the Right, keeping Uncle Joe sweet was regarded as mandatory. In this matter, Orwell showed what can only be described as intellectual heroism. Though his unpalatable opinions restricted his access to mainstream publications—most of his commentaries were written for *Tribune*, an influential but small-circulation weekly newspaper backed by the Labour Party's star heavyweight, Aneurin Bevan—Orwell went on insisting that the Soviet regime was a tyranny, even as the Red Army battled the Panzers to a standstill on the outskirts of Moscow. At this distance, it is hard to imagine what a lonely line this was to take. But when it came to a principle Orwell was the sort of man who would rather shiver in solitude than hold his tongue.

Solitude fitted his character. Though he was sociable, and even amorous, in his everyday life, he didn't look it: he looked as gauntly ascetic as John Carradine, and in his mental life he was a natural loner. Collectivist theories could appeal to his temperament for only so long, and in this strictly chronological arrangement of his writings we can watch him gradually deconstructing his own ideology in deference to a set of principles. Even with this degree of documentation, it is not easy to see quite when he shifted aside a neat notion in order to let an awkward fact take over, because for a crucial period of the war he metaphorically went off the air. Literally, he had gone on it. For a two-year slog, from 1941 to late 1943, he expended most of his time and energy broadcasting to India for the BBC. Belated market research on the BBC's part revealed that not many Indians were listening (you guessed it: no radios), but the few who did manage to tune in heard some remarkable stuff from a man who had expended so much ink on insisting that the British would have to quit India. Orwell told them the truth: that they had a better chance with the British than with the Japanese. He also scripted weekly summaries of the war's progress. Writing on January 10, 1942, he remarked on a tonal shift in Germany's official pronouncements:

Until a week or two ago, the German military spokesmen were explaining that the attack on Moscow would have to be postponed until the spring, but that the German armies could quite easily remain on the line they now occupied. Already, however, they are admitting that a further retreat—or, as they prefer to call it, a rectification of the line—will be necessary. . . . Before the end of February, the Germans may well be faced with the alternative of abandoning nearly all their conquests in the northern part of the Russian front, or of seeing hundreds of thousands of soldiers freeze to death.

It was an optimistic forecast for 1942, but it all came true in 1943, and it showed two of Orwell's best attributes operating at once: he had a global grasp, and he was able to guess the truth by the way the other side told lies. The broadcasts make such good reading today that you almost feel sorry he ever stopped. From these indirect sources, you can surmise something of what was going on deep within his mind, and when he started writing journalism again he retroactively filled in some of the gaps. From the realization that the violent socialist revolution would not take place, he was apparently moving towards the conclusion that it should not. Reviewing a collection of Thomas Mann's essays published in English translation in 1943, he praised Mann in terms that would have been impossible for him before the war: "He never pretends to be other than he is, a middle-class Liberal, a believer in the freedom of the intellect, in human brotherhood; above all, in the existence of objective truth." While careful to point out that Mann was pro-socialist, and even excessively trustful of the USSR, Orwell went on to note, approvingly, that "he never budges from his 'bourgeois' contention that the individual is important, that freedom is worth having, that European culture is worth preserving, and that truth is not the exclusive possession of one race or class." For Orwell, who had once preached that bourgeois democracy existed solely in order to bamboozle the proletariat into accepting its ineluctable servitude, this was quite a switch.

At no time did Orwell come quite clean about having rearranged the playing field. Near the end of 1943 he conceded that he had been "grossly wrong" about the necessity of a revolution in order to stave off defeat. But to concede that he had been "grossly wrong" about his view of society was beyond even him, and no wonder. It would have been to give away too much. By now he was always careful to say that he wanted a *democratic* socialism, and was even ready to contemplate that reconciling a command economy with individual liberty might be a problem: but he still clung tenaciously to the socialist part of his vision, in his view the only chance of decent treatment for everyone. Piece by piece, however, he was giving up on any notion that his socialist vision could be brought about by coercion, since that would yield liberty for no one. If he had lived long enough, his fundamental honesty might have given us an autobiography which would have described what must have been a mighty conflict in his soul. As things are, we have to infer it.

His socialist beliefs fought a long rearguard action. In that same year, 1943, he gave *The Road to Serfdom* a review tolerant of Hayek's warnings about collectivism, but there was no sign of Orwell's endorsing the desirability of free market economics. Orwell was still for the centralized, planned economy. He never did quite give up on that one, and indeed, at the time, there must have seemed no necessity to. To stave off defeat, Britain had mobilized its industry under state control—had done so, it turned out, rather more thoroughly than the Nazis—and, with the war won and the country broke, even the Royal Family carried ration books without protest. So a measure of justice had been achieved.

In hindsight, the post-war British society that began with the foundation of the National Health Service *was* the socialist revolution—or, to put it less dramatically, the social-democratic reformation which Orwell had gradually come to accept as the only workable formula that would further justice without destroying liberty. The Welfare State began with shortages of almost everything, but at least the deprivations were shared, and for all its faults, British society, ever since World War II, has continuously been one of the more interesting experiments in the attempt to reconcile social justice with personal freedom. (The Scandinavian societies might be more successful experiments, but not even they find themselves interesting.) If Orwell had lived to a full span, he would have been able, if not necessarily delighted, to deal with the increasing likelihood that his dreams were coming true. Even as things were, with only a few years of life left to him, he might have given a far more positive account, in his post-war journalism, of how the British of all classes, including the dreaded ruling class, were at long last combining to bring about, at least in some measure, the more decent society that had haunted his imagination since childhood. But he was distracted by a prior requirement. His own war wasn't over. It had begun all over again. There was still one prominent social group who had learned nothing: the left-wing intellectuals.

The last and most acrimonious phase of Orwell's battle with the left-wing intelligentsia began not long after D-Day. As the Allied forces fought their way out of Normandy, a piece by Orwell landed on a desk in America. *Partisan Review* would publish a London Letter in which Orwell complained about the Western Russophile intellectuals who refused to accept the truth about Stalinist terror. Clearly, what frightened him was that, even if they did accept it, Soviet prestige would lose little of its allure for them. For Orwell, the Cold War was already on, with the progressive intellectuals in the front rank of the foe. Orwell was the first to use the term "cold war," in an essay published in October 1945 about the atomic bomb—the very device that would ensure, in the long run, that the Cold War never became a hot one. At the time, however, he saw no cause for complacency.

But unreconstructed *gauchiste* pundits who would still like to dismiss Orwell as a "classic" Cold Warrior can find out here that he didn't fit the frame. For one thing, Orwell remained all too willing to accuse the West of structural deficiencies that were really much more contingent than he made out. When he argued, in the pages of *Tribune*, that the mass-circulation newspapers forced slop on their readership, he preferred to ignore the advice from a correspondent that it was really a case of the readership forcing slop on the newspapers. He should have given far more attention to such criticisms, because they allowed for the possibility—as his own assumptions did not—that if ordinary people were freed from exploitation they would demand more frivolity, not less.

To the end, Orwell's tendency was to overestimate the potential of the people he supposed to be in the grip of the capitalist system, while simultaneously underestimating the individuality they were showing already. In his remarks on the moral turpitude of the scientists who had cravenly not "refused" to work on the atomic bomb—clearly he thought they should have all turned the job down—there was no mention (perhaps because he didn't yet know, although he might have guessed) of the fact that many of them were European refugees from totalitarianism and had worked on the bomb not just willingly but with anxious fervour, convinced, with excellent reasons, that Hitler might get there first.

On the other hand, he was still inclined to regard Stalin's regime as a perversion of the Bolshevik Revolution instead of as its essence: as late as 1946, it took the eminent émigré Russian scholar Gleb Struve (the future editor of Mandelstam and Akhmatova) to tell him that Zamyatin's We, written in 1920 but never published in Russia, might well have been, as Orwell thought, a projection of a possible totalitarian future, but had drawn much of its inspiration from the Leninist present. If Orwell took this admonition in, he made little use of it. (He made great use of We, however: if the English translation of Zamyatin's little classic had been as good as the French one, a lot more of Nineteen Eighty-Four's reviewers might have spotted that Orwell's phantasmagoria was a bit less sui generis than it seemed.) Already in 1941, reviewing Russia under Soviet Rule by the émigré liberal de Basily, Orwell had taken on board the possibility that Lenin's callous behaviour made Stalin inevitable—after all, Lenin had actually said that the Party should rule by terror—but neither then nor later did Orwell push this point very hard. It flickers in the background of his anti-Soviet polemics and can be thought of as the informing assumption of Animal Farm and Nineteen Eighty-Four, but in his journalism he was always slow to concede that the Bolshevik Revolution itself might have been the culprit. Perhaps he thought he had enough trouble on his hands already, just trying to convince his starry-eyed Stalinist contemporaries that they had placed their faith in a cynic who left their own cynicism for dead, and would do the same to them if he got the chance. "The direct, conscious attack on intellectual decency comes from the intellectuals themselves."

.   .   .

As a journalist, Orwell had laboured long and hard for small financial reward, and overwork had never been good for his delicate health. Life was pinched, not to say deprived, especially after his wife and faithful helpmeet Eileen (he was an unfaithful spouse and she may have been as well, but they depended on each other) died as a result of a medical blunder. The success of *Animal Farm*, in 1945, could have bought him a reprieve. He upped stakes to a small farmhouse on the island of Jura, in the Hebrides, and cultivated his garden. Though he overestimated the strength he still had available for the hard life he lived there—he could grow vegetables to supplement his ration, but it took hard work in tough soil—the place was a welcome break from the treadmill of London. Mentally, however, he found no peace. A heightened anguish can be traced right through his last journalism until he gave it up to work on *Nineteen Eighty-Four*. The left-wing intellectuals, already promoting the revisionism that continues into our own day, not only were giving Stalin the sole credit for having won the war but were contriving not to notice that he had rescinded the few liberties he had been forced to concede in order to fight it; that his rule by terror had resumed; and that in the Eastern European countries supposedly liberated by the Red Army any vestige of liberty left by the Nazis was being stamped flat. Once again, crimes on a colossal scale were being camouflaged with perverted language, and once again the intellectuals, whose professional instinct should have been to sick it up, were happily swallowing the lot. It took a great deal to persuade him that reasoned argument wasn't enough. But it wasn't, so he wrote *Nineteen Eighty-Four*.

There are still diehards who would like to think that *Nineteen Eighty-Four* is not about the Soviet Union at all. Their argument runs: *Animal Farm* is a satire about what happened in Russia once upon a time, but *Nineteen Eighty-Four* is a minatory fantasy about something far bigger—the prospect of a world divided up into a few huge centres of absolute power, of which a Soviet-style hegemony would be only one, and the United States, of course, would be another. It is just possible that Orwell thought the Marshall Plan was meant to have the same imperialist effect in Europe as the Red Army's tanks. He never actually said so, but people as intelligent as Gore Vidal believe much the same thing today. The late Anthony Burgess sincerely believed that *Nineteen Eighty-Four*, because the Ministry of Truth bore such a strong resemblance to the BBC canteen, had been inspired by the condition of post-war Britain under rationing. As Orwell said so resonantly in his essay "Notes on Nationalism," "One has to belong to the intelligentsia to believe things like that: no ordinary man could be such a fool."

He didn't mean that all intellectuals are *ipso facto* fools—he himself was an intellectual if anybody was—but he did mean that verbal cleverness, unless its limitations are clearly and continuously seen by its possessor, is an unbeatable way of blurring reality until nothing can be seen at all. The main drive of all Orwell's writings since Spain had been to point out that the Soviet Union, nominally the hope of mankind, had systematically perverted language in order to cover up the wholesale destruction of human values, and that the Western left-wing intellectuals had gone along with this by perverting their own language in its turn. To go on denying that *Nineteen Eighty-Four* was the culmination of this large part of Orwell's effort is to defy reason. At the time, denying it was still not a wholly unreasonable reaction. After all, the democracies couldn't have won the war without the Soviet Union, and the book was so bleak and hopeless. Maybe it was about something else.

If they didn't get it in the West, they got it in the East. From the day of the book's publication until far into the Thaw, it meant big trouble for any Soviet citizen who had a copy in his possession. In the years to come, now that the Soviet archives are opening up, there will be a fruitful area of study in trying to decide which were the Western cultural influences that did most to help the Evil Empire melt down. For all we know, the jokes were always right, and it was the Beatles albums and the bootleg blue jeans that did the trick. But it is a fair guess that of all the imported artefacts it was the books that sapped the repressive will of the people who ran the empire or who were next in line to do so. Robert Conquest's *The Great Terror* might well turn out to be the key factor in the unprecedented turnaround by which those state organizations with a solid track record of pre-emptive slaughter somehow began to spare the very lives they would previously have been careful to snuff out: it is said that even the KGB read it, perhaps as the quickest way of finding out what their predecessors had been up to. (There is no doubt at all, by the way, that they eventually read *Nineteen Eighty-Four*. When head of the KGB, Andropov had a special edition printed and circulated.)

But for all we know they might have been just as much subverted by *samizdat* translations of *The Carpetbaggers* and *Valley of the Dolls*. Nor, of course, can the effect of the dissident literature, whether written in exile or home-grown, be dismissed as merely unsettling, although for the books written at home there will always be the consideration of whether they could have even been conceived of if the set-up were not already crumbling in the first place. What we are talking about is a contrary weather-system of opinion that eventually took over a whole climate, and to trace its course will be like following the dust of Ariadne's crumbled thread back into a ruined labyrinth. But it will be a big surprise if *Nineteen Eighty-Four*, even more than *The Gulag Archipelago*, does not turn out to be the book that did most, weight for weight, to clear thousands of living brains of the miasma sent up through the soil by millions upon millions of dead bodies. It was a portable little slab of spiritual *plastique*, a mind-blower.

But if the part played by Orwell's dystopian novels in the dismantling of the Sovietized monolith will always be hard to assess, there is less difficulty about measuring the effect of his last period of journalism on his own country. Self-immured on Jura, he was a Prospero running on the reserve tank of his magic. Orwell was only forty-two, but he had little physical strength left, and although many friends and colleagues sent him letters and books, and presents of rice and chocolate, and some even made the slow and tricky journey to visit him, he was short of love. A widower of some fame and no longer without means, he offered his affections to a succession of young women and found himself in the humiliating position of being respected and refused. When it emerged recently that he handed a list of fellow-travellers to a government propaganda unit, suggestions that he had conspired in a witch-hunt carried little force. McCarthyism was a non-starter in Britain, and most of those named on the list were already glad to have it known that they had aligned their prayer mats in the direction of the Kremlin. But if he lapsed from his own standards by tittle-tattling in school the most likely reason was that his Foreign Office contact was a noted beauty. He was sending her a bouquet.

The young woman who finally accepted him, Sonia Brownell (renowned in literary London as the Venus of Euston Road), married him practically on his deathbed: cold comfort. He kept a diary of what was happening in his garden—small things growing as the great man withered. For us, the only consolation is that he could speak so clearly even as the walls of his lungs were giving way against the tide of blood.

"Britain has lost an empire but has not found a role," said Dean Acheson. Raymond Aron said something better: "*L'Angleterre a perdu son empire, sans perdre sa civilization morale.*" In helping Britain to maintain and extend its moral civilization, Orwell's voice was surely crucial. The succession of magnificent essays he wrote as the harsh war wound down into an austere peace add up to a political event in themselves, the culmination of his journalism as a textbook example of how a sufficiently informed commentary on events can feed back into history and help to shape its course.

It takes nothing from Davison's achievement to say that these last essays are probably best encountered in the *Collected Essays*, or even in a single small volume, such as *Inside the Whale*, where they will be found to have the effect of poems, as the paragraphs succeed one another with the inevitability of perfectly wrought stanzas, with every sentence in the right place yet begging to be remembered on its own, like a line from a magisterial elegy. "Notes on Nationalism," "The Prevention of Literature," "Politics and the English Language," "Why I Write," "Politics vs. Literature: An Examination of 'Gulliver's Travels' "—read for and by themselves, they tell you all you need to know about Orwell except the one fact so poignantly revealed here: that they were the work of a man who was not only dying but dying young. Very few writers about politics have said much in their forties that is lastingly true; and even Orwell undoubtedly would have continued to deepen, enrich, modulate and modify his opinions.

But he had come a long way, and, by coming as far as the great last essays, he left a precious heritage to the country that he loved in spite of itself. Though the appeal to a totalitarian model of a just society (and the corresponding contempt for piecemeal solutions) was to remain possible in the academy, it became much more difficult in everyday political journalism, simply because Orwell had discredited the idea in a plain style that nobody could forget and everybody felt obliged to echo. The theoretical work that disenfranchised all total transformations was done by others, such as Karl Popper, Raymond Aron, Leszek Kolokowski and Isaiah Berlin. Orwell never got around to figuring all that out in detail. But he felt it, and the language of his last essays is the language of feeling made as clear and bright as it can ever get.

.   .   .

How clear is that? Finally, it comes down to a question of language, which is only appropriate, because, finally, Orwell was a literary man. Politics inspired Orwell the way the arts had always inspired the great critics, which gives us the clue to where he got the plainly passionate style that we are so ready to call unique. It is unique, in its flexibility of speech rhythms and its irresistible force of assertion, but he didn't invent it; he invented its use. George Saintsbury had something of Orwell's schooled knack for speaking right out of the page, and Shaw had almost all of it: Orwell isn't often outright funny, but Shaw, in his six volumes of critical writings about music and theatre, deployed the full range of Orwell's debunking weapons with a generous humour to drive them home. Orwell called Shaw a windbag, but had obviously taken in every word the old man wrote. And there are many other critics who could be named, all the way up to the young F. R. Leavis, whom Orwell read with interest, if not without a certain distaste for his joyless zeal.

Orwell was a superb literary critic himself: he is the first person to read on Swift, on Dickens, and on Gissing, and if he had lived to finish his essay on Evelyn Waugh it would have been the best thing on the subject, the essay that really opens up Waugh's corrosively snobbish view of life without violating his creative achievement. Had Orwell lived to a full term, he might well have gone on to become the greatest modern literary critic in the language. But he lived more than long enough to make writing about politics a branch of the humanities, setting a standard of civilized response to the intractably complex texture of life. No previous political writer had brought so much of life's lesser detail into the frame, and other countries were unlucky not to have him as a model. Sartre, for example, would have been incapable of an essay about the contents of a junk shop, or about how to make the ideal cup of tea—the very reason he was incapable of talking real sense about politics.

In one of the very last, and best, of his essays, "Lear, Tolstoy, and the Fool," Orwell paid his tribute to Shakespeare. He was too modest to say that he was paying a debt as well, but he was:

Shakespeare was not a philosopher or a scientist, but he did have curiosity: he loved the surface of the earth and the process of life—which, it should be repeated, is *not* the same thing as wanting to have a good time and stay alive as long as possible. Of course, it is not because of the quality of his thought that Shakespeare has survived, and he might not even be remembered as a dramatist if he had not also been a poet. His main hold on us is through language.

A writer has to know a lot about the rhythms of natural speech before he can stretch them over the distance covered by those first two sentences. Each of them is perfectly balanced in itself, and the second is perfectly balanced against the first—the first turning back on itself with a strict qualification, and the second running away in relaxed enjoyment of its own fluency. They could stand on their own, but it turns out that both of them are there to pile their combined weight behind the third sentence—the short one—and propel it into your memory. It hits home with the force of an axiom.

And it isn't true—or, anyway, it isn't true enough. Elsewhere in the essay, Orwell shows signs of being aware that the relationship of Shakespeare's language to the quality of his thought can never be fully resolved in favour of either term. But not even Orwell could resist a resonant statement that fudged the facts—a clarity that is really an opacity. Yes, Orwell did write like an angel, and that's the very reason we have to watch him like a hawk. Luckily for us, he was pretty good at watching himself. He was blessed with a way of putting things that made anything he said seem so, but that was only a gift. His intellectual honesty was a virtue.

Orwell's standards of plain speaking always were and still are a mile too high for politicians. What finally counts with politicians is what they do, not how they say it. But for journalists how they say it counts for everything. Orwell's style shows us why a style is worth working at: not just because it gets us a byline and makes a splash but because it compresses and refines thought and feeling without ceasing to sound like speech—which is to say, without ceasing to sound human. At a time when ideological politics still exercised such an appeal that hundreds of purportedly civilized voices *had* ceased to sound human, Orwell's style stood out. The remarkable thing is that it still does. Ideologues are thin on the ground nowadays, while any substantial publication has a would-be George Orwell rippling the keys in every second cubicle, but the daddy of modern truth-tellers still sounds fresh. So it wasn't just the amount of truth he told but the way he told it, in prose transmuted to poetry by the pressure of his dedication. This great edition, by revealing fully for the first time what that dedication was like, makes his easy-seeming written speech more impressive than ever, and even harder to emulate. To write like him, you need a life like his, but times have changed, and he changed them.

The New Yorker, January 18, 1999

POSTSCRIPT

Even if our intention is the most abject homage, we can't write in praise of heroes without taking their limitations into account, because unless we had noticed their limitations we wouldn't be writing at all: they would have silenced us. While you are reading them, the great stylists make you want to give up, and in the case of Orwell, the stylist with the anti-style, the effect can last a long time after you have finished reading. I was in bed with a convenient nervous breakdown when I read the four volumes of his collected journalism that came out in 1969. I already knew the standard essays quite well, but the accumulated impact of reading them again, along with all the other material which had become generally available for the first time, would have kept me away from the typewriter for years if I hadn't noticed something fundamentally wrong amongst everything that he got right.

He was wrong about the British Empire. He never gave up on the idea that it was a fraud, designed with no other end in view except to stave off rebellion at home by eking out the miseries of capitalism with the exploited fruits of coolie labour in the colonies. Born under the Empire myself, with few coolies in sight, I knew it to be a more equivocal thing. Orwell's Procrustean notions on the subject might have served as a useful reservoir of polemical force, but their heritage was all too obvious. In 1902, G. A. Hobson's book *Imperialism* promoted the idea that colonial possessions were critical for advanced, or "finance," capitalism. In 1916 Lenin took the idea over for his *Imperialism, the Highest State of Capitalism,* and after the Revolution it became a standard item of Comintern dogma, working its worldwide influence even on those left-inclined intellectuals who refused to swallow the party programme hook, line and sinker. They spat out the line and sinker, but they stayed hooked.

I was thus being as kind as I could to suggest, in my *laudatio*, that Orwell inherited some of his theoretical precepts from classic Marxism. He got at least one of them, and perhaps the most misleading one, from classic Leninism — a still more dubious patrimony. Even in Orwell's own time, it should have been evident that the idea was a misconception. The mere existence of Sweden, for example, was enough to refute it. Sweden had a capitalist system, advanced social welfare and no imperial dreams that had not died with Gustavus Adolphus. After Orwell's death, when the last of the British Empire was given up and the final accounts came in, it became easy to question whether colonialism had ever yielded a dividend, let alone supported Britain as a capitalist economy. But Orwell, who justly prided himself on his capacity to puncture received notions, should have questioned the assumption when questioning was hard. Had he done so, however, it might have made him a less effective speaker for the independent Left. It might have sapped the confidence that energized his style. Any successful style is a spell whose first victim is the wizard. Unless he is alert to the trickery of his own magic, he will project an air of Delphic infallibility that can do a lot of damage before the inevitable collapse into abracadabra. The obvious example is Shaw, but no master stylist has ever been exempt from the danger. It follows that there is always something useful to say, even about the man who appears to say everything. Orwell said what mattered, and will always matter, about totalitarianism. But he never got far with saying what mattered about democracy. He thought it was a capitalist trick. It's a lot trickier than that.

Even As We Speak, 2001

24

MARK TWAIN,
JOURNALIST

Two volumes of the Library of America containing all that matters of Mark Twain's journalism—*Tales, Sketches, Speeches, and Essays* is the title—came out last autumn, and have kept at least one reader going ever since, with the occasional pause to consult the two volumes of Twain's major writings which were published in the same format a decade or so ago. There is an almost audible clicking into place: this covetable quartet of books gangs up like gauge blocks, those machine-shop measures that don't need anything except their trueness to keep them together. At least two more Twain volumes are yet to come, but for now it's hard to imagine a set more satisfactory than this—four volumes just as neat as all the others in the Library of America, and even more solid, energetic, genial and creative: it makes a good gift suggestion for the new administration. If President Clinton is a better speechmaker than President Bush, it is mainly because he steals better stuff. He should steal from the best: Mark Twain, who could rock the room for an hour while talking nothing except sense, and would have staved off Arsenio Hall without needing a saxophone.

For some years, it has been becoming clearer that the Library of America is the symbol for itself that the United States has long been in search of. Colonial Williamsburg is too Disneyfied to stand for tradition, Disneyland too childish to stand for innovation, Mt. Rushmore too big to stand in your living room. You can line up the Library of America on a few shelves. Of course, the French could do the same sort of thing earlier. The Pléiade was the library that Edmund Wilson had in mind when he caned the Modern Language Association for burying the country's intellectual heritage while pretending to preserve it, sponsoring volumes that owed too much to pedantry, not enough to readability, weighed a ton and looked like hell. Wilson kept up the campaign for a long time but seemed to stand no better chance of winning it than of beating his income-tax rap. Then the Library of America made Wilson's dream happen. From its first few volumes it was obvious that the Library of America had struck the ideal balance between authority and portability. Its volumes begged irresistibly to be picked up, like brilliant children.

Remarkably, they didn't lose this unthreatening quality even as they multiplied. If you own more than about thirty of the sixty-five volumes so far, monumentality becomes a present danger: the massed black jackets loom like midnight, and it starts to look as if the Pléiade had chosen better—first, to wear white, and then, when that started looking like a cliff of snow, to let the horizontally striped gold-blocked spines show through a transparent jacket, like scaling ladders to a Fabergé Bastille of imprisoned wisdom. But you can always alleviate the pangs of gazing at a wall of uniformity by taking one of the Library of America volumes down and letting it fall open in the hand. If this is dignity, it is user-friendly. And with these two volumes of Twain's minor writings here is the original, unashamed vitality that lies at the heart of the whole enterprise. You could just about convince yourself that *Huckleberry Finn* was a work of literature in the Old World style, aimed at a refined public—after all, it certainly has the rank, if not the manner. But Twain's journalism is a daunting reminder that he was ready to lavish everything he had on everybody, every time. He was democratic all the way down to his metabolism. For Twain, there was no division between democracy and creativity. They were versions of the same thing: exuberance.

Twain's fugitive pieces have been collected before; but now we have, with just the right amount of critical apparatus, the authoritative texts, and all arranged chronologically, so that we can watch him grow. He grew like bamboo in the rain. His first hit was a newspaper sketch called "Jim Smiley and His Jumping Frog." Twain wasn't the first American journalist to write tall tales under a pen name; Petroleum V. Nasby, whom Twain knew and admired, was one of several practitioners already in the field. Nor was Twain the first to combine the high style with the low, squandering highfalutin resources on a shaggy-dog story. What was new, attention-getting and instantly popular was the quality of the evocation when he worked the switch out of mandarin diction into the concrete vernacular.

The story of the Jumping Frog is told to Twain by a yarn-spinner—"good-natured, garrulous old Simon Wheeler"—who isn't afraid to be boring: "Simon Wheeler backed me into a corner and blockaded me there with his chair—and then sat down and reeled off the monotonous narrative which follows this paragraph." Twain is true to his word: Wheeler is what the British would call a crasher. His story of Jim Smiley and the Jumping Frog goes on for pages before it even gets to the frog. Much more of it would put the reader to sleep, even though Twain the narrator makes it clear that the verbosity belongs to his interlocutor, not to him. But Wheeler's drone goes on just long enough to ensure that we are given the set-up for the story without suspecting how funny it's going to get. We hear that Jim Smiley, who owns the champion jumping frog, suckers himself into a bet with a hustler who appears to know nothing about frogs. But while Smiley is out of the room (Twain rather muffs this bit: we don't find out Smiley has left the room until *after* we are told about how the stranger works his trick) the stranger fills Jim's precious frog with a meal of lead shot. At just the moment when the champion frog gets the cue to unleash its usual stunning jump, Wheeler's long-winded vocabulary snaps into focus. The champion frog "give a heave, and hysted up his shoulders—so—like a Frenchman, but it wasn't no use—he couldn't budge; he was planted as solid as a anvil." The anvil is good, but Twain's mentor, Artemus Ward, might have done it. The Frenchman's shrug is what makes it Twain. You can see it happening.

The Jumping Frog story was reprinted in periodicals all over the United States following its publication in 1865, and two years later it was the keynote piece of Twain's first collection, *The Celebrated Jumping Frog of Calaveras County, and Other Sketches*. Twain was disappointed with the way the book's publication was handled, and was further miffed to find that it didn't sell very well, but the Jumping Frog had already done its job in the periodicals. The young Mark Twain was made, and so was a tradition. It was a comic tradition, but now more than ever that shouldn't be taken to mean that it was merely humorous. Every subsequent American humour writer writes in the range of tones established by Twain. When Thurber says of his fellow economics student the football player Bolenciecwcz that "while he was not dumber than an ox he was not any smarter," he is in touch with Twain. Even so cosmopolitan a *pas-*

ticheur as S. J. Perelman, whose macaronic vocabulary seems bent on superseding provincialism as its first impulse, sounds, when he has a picture to evoke, like Twain talking. There is a Perelman story that begins with the narrator waiting for his date to show up. The story goes off somewhere else, and long after we have forgotten about the date she finally appears, "sobbing drunk with a Marine on either arm."

That instant of clarity, with all the baroque vocabulary suddenly forgotten, wouldn't have been the same if Twain hadn't first written such pieces as his tour-de-force diatribe of 1882, "The McWilliamses and the Burglar Alarm," in which the new burglar-alarm system makes the house so attractive to burglars that they come to live there, until there is "not a spare bed in the house; all occupied by burglars." The burglars take the alarm system, along with everything else. You could be watching the characters accumulate in the New Old Lompoc House, W. C. Fields's favoured hostel in *The Bank Dick*, or—to go beyond America, as Twain's influence almost immediately did—you could be listening to Stephen Leacock talking about his first bank account, or Henry Lawson telling his story about the Loaded Dog, the dog that got its teeth fastened into a bomb and terrorized a mining camp. Leacock was active in Canada and Lawson was an Australian determined to free the natural speech of his countrymen from the thralldom of literary preciosity. Twain's style had reached both of them, and in America it was all-pervasive almost from the start.

Unfortunately, American humour, like every other American product, has long since paid the inevitable penalty attached to any consumable in a society of abundance. There are so many choices that they all seem the same. It isn't really like that—nobody sane has to watch the comedy channel all the time it's on the air—but it seems like that. There is a humour glut, as if being funny were an escape from reality. Twain never thought so. For him, humour was a way—and just one of the ways—to escape from unreality. He wanted to get the whole of life into his most casual work. He was a comic writer in the classic sense: Dante's divinely inspired cosmos was a comedy because it mixed low speech with high, the profane with the sacred. In that sense, even Shakespeare's tragedies were comedies. Twain was in the recognizable position of the storyteller who emerges during the formative history of his country and helps to provide its characteristic voice, thereby incidentally reinforcing the general rule that genius arrives early. Twain and Dickens, in their public position so similar—best-selling authors who electrified audiences when they read aloud—were different in this: Dickens was only metaphorically creating a world, whereas Twain was literally creating a nation.

. . .

Perhaps re-creating would be a better word. Like Shakespeare arriving after Bloody Mary left, Twain was lucky in his timing. The new nation looked as if it had just finished destroying itself, in the Civil War. The young Twain had managed to stay out of the war's way. In "The Private History of a Campaign That Failed," a piece written in 1885, he looks back twenty-five years to the young man he was when history suddenly boiled up all around him. As slave-owners went, Twain's family had been liberal and even enlightened, but when the war started Twain didn't hesitate to join a small volunteer group of Confederate riders hiding out in the woods. He just hesitated about what to do next. So did they all. One night, a strange rider materialized from the direction of the Union camp. Twain had a sixth share in shooting him down—or, anyway, he remembered it that way. That was enough for him. He faded away to the West. If President Clinton gets this set of books as a birthday gift from his wife, he will find consolation here, because if Twain didn't know what to do about a war that split the nation's heart he did know what to do about healing the wound. When that war was over and he started to publish in earnest, he treated the two sides as if they belonged together. Not that he spread any soft soap. He was fierce on the liberal issues. Mrs. Clinton will find her spirit here, too: perhaps the President should give her the gift.

Twain's journalism is full of contempt for racism in all its forms. Like Swift, he had a low opinion of the human race in general, reserving his admiration for individuals. He was not much given to admiring ethnic authenticity, but he condescended on a cultural basis rather than a racial one. For any creed or colour that was being persecuted he was a vocal champion. Chinese immigrants given a bad time by the locals could count on one kind voice, at least. His initial sympathy for America's Cuba adventure was based on his contempt for Spain's horrific colonial record, which was almost as bad as its domestic record. When the United States began to show Spanish tendencies in the Philippines, Twain soon started condemning American colonialism, too. As with the Spanish, so with any other European nation: he was always ready to point out that the Old

World had dirty hands. Belgium's depredations in the Congo survived the invective of Roger Casement, but King Leopold II's reputation was settled forever by Twain's "King Leopold's Soliloquy," which had Leopold performing absurd mental gymnastics to disown the atrocities committed in his name.

Twain knew that the brute facts of imperialism undid all pretensions to civilization on the part of the old countries. But he never lost sight of the great crime at home. In view of recent suggestions, inspired by the dubious spirit of political correctness, that *Huckleberry Finn* and other major works of Twain should be swept from the library shelves because of the picture they paint of black people, it is useful to read through Twain's journalism and see just how much time and effort he put into fighting Jim Crow. When the first lynchings occurred in Missouri, he wept for his home state in a plangent threnody called "The United States of Lyncherdom." It is all written in one long sob: "And so Missouri has fallen, that great state! Certain of her children have joined the lynchers, and the smirch is upon the rest of us." In another essay, Twain reminded the evangelists that their fathers had thumped the same Bibles while perpetrating the same blasphemy, "closing their doors against the hunted slave."

There is enough said outright in the journalism to remind us, if we needed reminding, that Twain speaking in story form was and remains the great post-bellum writer about the condition of whites and blacks in the America they share. Only his vocabulary can blur the point, and it is a nice question whether the fault is his rather than ours. In the fictional South inhabited by Tom Sawyer and Huck Finn and Pudd'nhead Wilson, even the blacks call blacks niggers. It was the way things were. But if you can see past what you hear, the great message of those books is about human equality, and how racism violates it, reducing everyone to servitude, and no one more than the supposed master. The emotional centre of *Huckleberry Finn* is Jim's story of how he escaped. Huck listens silently, as well he might, because it is only by grace that Jim is not including him in the vast system rigged against a slave's bid for freedom—the whole white civilization.

In *Pudd'nhead Wilson*, the sixteenth-black Roxy is an invention that Toni Morrison might have been proud of: indeed, it is hard to read *Beloved* without wondering whether Roxy might have been one of the models for its heroine. Roxy has a boy baby—only a thirty-second black, but that's enough. Twain shirks the probability, which the modern reader instantly suspects, that Roxy's owner must have been the father, but he doesn't shirk anything else. Roxy's boy, black even though he doesn't look it, is doomed to be a chattel. So she swaps him for the owner's all-white baby of the same age. What happens to the changelings gives no comfort to the sentimental, for whom a more satisfactory story would have centred on the white boy turned into a black, in the way that Kipling's *Captains Courageous* made the rich boy poor, and so revealed the actual world to him. Twain concentrates on the black boy turned into a white. He grows up as a wastrel, thief, liar and cheat. We are at liberty to suppose that he got the seeds of these characteristics from his white father, but we would have to ignore what Twain spells out: Twain is saying that a slave-owning household is a bad one to grow up in—even worse for the personality than the shack where the slaves live, with the fear of being sold down the river.

Reading *Pudd'nhead Wilson*, we would like to rewrite it so that the slave boy's natural goodness reforms the whole system by example. But one of Twain's points—and the point that, apart from his vocabulary, is most likely to irritate the politically correct—is that natural goodness doesn't come any more easily to the oppressed than it does to the oppressor. The only person of noble character in the book is Roxy, and she is no genius: she can't tell that the bank she puts her hard-earned money into will fold; she doesn't know how to avoid being whipped until her back looks "like a washboard." (Toni Morrison's terrifying descriptions of Sethe's wounds from whipping in *Beloved* deserve their high reputation, but as a climactic passage in a horror story they can't hope to have the unexpected impact of Twain's quiet phrase slipped into a light narrative, like a bite in a kiss.)

Twain thought that the Negro question was the biggest issue facing America both past and present, and he gave it his best efforts, in his private life as in his public work. His personal conduct on the issue was impeccable. It is well known that Twain helped finance the education of Helen Keller. Less well known is that he supported one of the first black students to attend Yale all the way through college without meeting him more than once. Twain thought that to do such a thing was a white man's plain duty and shouldn't depend on the personal qualities of the beneficiary. Twain thought that the white man's debt was endless. He didn't come out on the side of the Union just because it won. The Southern cause had depended on repressing a minority, and that made the cause irredeemable.

Twain had the same sympathy for all oppressed minorities, including (this would have got him into trouble if he had lived later) the workers. Harbouring no illusions about the benevolence of unrestrained capital or the innate wisdom of the free market, Twain guessed that there would have to be an organized union movement to secure elementary rights for those who had to sweat. But he allowed no crude prejudice against those who made money from them. Accepting human villainy to be even more fundamental than human decency, Twain didn't believe you needed a conspiracy theory to explain piracy. He deplored anti-Semitism, and pointed out that the Jews were good at making money because so many of them were honest. He was one of the most vocal Dreyfusards after Zola.

Twain's sympathy for American Indians might not be apparent in an early piece like "The Noble Red Man," of 1870, which would not please Marlon Brando, but really Twain was just mocking the idea that the Noble Red Man had lived in a civil order that made modern American civilization look barbaric by comparison. Twain didn't believe that you could set about dealing with the deficiencies of modern America unless you first stopped dreaming of Arcadia. He was as optimistic as one could be about modern life without seeing it through pink glasses.

Twain's sympathy for women might similarly seem questionable by modern standards—on the whole, he preferred to joke about the issue of women's suffrage rather than face it—but he was a long way ahead of his time. His work is full of flirtation that now seems like condescension. "There may be prettier women in Europe, but I doubt it," he writes about the women of Genoa in *The Innocents Abroad*. "The population of Genoa is 120,000; two-thirds of these are women, I think, and at least two-thirds of the women are beautiful. They are as dressy, and as tasteful and as graceful as they could possibly be without being angels," etc. Andrea Dworkin probably wouldn't like that much. Twain suffered from gallantry, chivalry and all the other virtues that we have since been instructed are vices in disguise. But he always spoke against the exploitation of women as servants and married chattels, regretted the conditions that doomed them to do less than they could and never doubted that they could do anything. His article reflecting on Joan of Arc's trial is a clarion call that could fill an issue of *Ms*. In private, he was famously tender to his sick daughters and lived in a state of controlled despair about his invalid wife: he was so devoted to her that he was thought saintly by powerful men of his acquaintance, some of whom weren't saintly at all and had been, by implication, flayed in his regular philippics against the great crime of seduction. (When it turned out that Maxim Gorky, during his tour of America, was sharing his hotel suite with a mistress, Twain ceased to call on him, not because he had broken the law but because he had violated custom.)

In fact, Twain was so blameless that he is likely to make us uncomfortable. Nowadays, the press—the cultural press, which is no less implacable than the doorstep reporters, only a bit slower—would try to get something on him. In his last years, he compensated for the loss of his dearest daughter by cultivating the friendship of preteen young ladies he called "angelfish." Shades of Lewis Carroll and Ernest Dowson, not to neglect Roman Polanski and the Mia Farrow version of Woody Allen! A promising field of inquiry. On second thoughts, it seems more likely that as he neared the end of his great long life the prospect of new life became incandescent to him. Inviting his young friends to tea, corresponding with them as they grew up, he was passing on his love of the world, which he loved even more than his country, although he could see the world's faults more clearly than anyone else. But he didn't despair about correcting them. Having despaired of the human race in the first instance, he was free to cheer any of its achievements, and he thought America among the greatest. His journalism shows, in a more readily detected form than his books, that he cherished and relished America's entire creativity in a way far beyond the literary—or, at any rate, in a literary way that didn't leave out the political but brought his country's every institution and custom under scrutiny, whether to be celebrated or castigated. William Dean Howells was right to call him the Abraham Lincoln of American literature.

Howells was one of the few American men of letters and cultural figures who saw Twain's literary stature from the beginning. Most of them, even when they revelled in his work, missed the point initially. In a country nominally dedicated to a new start and equal rights, there was still a nervous tendency to keep high art and popular entertainment rigidly separate: the urge to build a first-rate culture came to the aid of snobbery. In the European countries, high culture was self-assured enough to acknowledge the possibility of art up from nowhere. Twain the entertainer won his first celebrity at home, but the first solid admiration for Twain the great artist happened elsewhere. The Jumping Frog made him famous all over America. *The Innocents Abroad* made him famous all over the world, and, paradoxically, it was in the old countries, to which America was supposed to be the democratic alternative, that the artist found himself at home. His first internationally famous book was a product of his tentative initiation into foreign travel, and after that he was almost always on the move, clocking up thousands of miles like a modern frequent flier, but with one big difference: he was never blasé about it. The thrill of discovery that he transmitted made him irresistible even to those inhabitants of exotic lands who might otherwise have felt patronized by being discovered.

The Innocents Abroad is a weak book by Twain's later standards. Even his gift for parody, one of the basic weapons in his comic armoury, was a blunt instrument before he learned that if it was to stay sharp it would have to spend most of the time in its scabbard. In *Huckleberry Finn*, the duke's all-purpose Hamlet soliloquy is the paradigm case of all bardic spoofs. In *The Innocents Abroad*, the parodic instant history of Abelard and Héloïse could have been the product of Twain's first pseudonym, W. Epaminondas Adrastus Perkins: "She lived with her uncle Fulbert, a canon of the cathedral of Paris. I do not know what a canon of a cathedral is, but that is what he was. He was nothing more than a sort of a mountain howitzer, likely, because they had no heavy artillery in those days. Suffice it, then, that Heloise lived with her uncle the howitzer, and was happy." And so on.

But if Twain's comic fantasy had a long way to go before it would be infallibly funny, his gusto for the reality in front of him was fully developed right from the start. He saw everything, relished everything, and without playing the yokel as much as you might think. Re-reading the book now, you can see what he had that all of us have lost. He was first in on the new mobility—the first great writer to be a traveller without having had to be an explorer. He is discovering the world as a world citizen: a true *Weltbürger* is speaking to the people he is travelling among just as much as to those at home—to them and for them.

They loved him for it. In the twentieth century, foreign nations that have been defeated by American power—or, even harder to forgive, saved by it—have comforted themselves with the reassuring caricature of the know-nothing American traveller, who might as well not have left home. In the nineteenth century, Twain was the know-everything traveller, who made his homeland seem doubly attractive by so engagingly representing its energy and creativity. His natural ear for the melody of his own language applied to other languages, too. He could read French well enough to make a good job of pretending to misunderstand it. Late in his life, spending a lot of time in Italy, he acquired enough of its language to write a wildly inventive piece concerning a story in an Italian newspaper about some fatal imbroglio. His German was good enough to enable him to read easily.

He was no scholar in any language but an easily nourished dabbler in anything he took up. The mistake is to mark him low for being unsystematic. He was, but genius often is. His opinions on literature were pragmatic, not to say erratic. He could praise Cervantes's romanticism and not say a word for Jane Austen's realism, although her keen appreciation of the power of money in human affairs lies far closer to his cast of mind than any amount of tilting at windmills. But really Twain was not interested in literature as such. He was interested in it as a part of everything else. When pointing out what he didn't know about art, one is always wise to remember what he did know about, say, science. His was a wide-ranging mind. He was American global expansionism before the fact.

In England, he was lionized by royalty, the literary establishment, the whole flattering system. Oxford gave him an honorary degree. (Saint-Saëns and Rodin got their degrees at the same ceremony as Twain: cue music and fade up the sound of chisel on marble.) Shaw was only one of the big names who called him a great master of the English language. More remarkably, his magic survived translation—indirect proof that it was his point of view that drove his style, and not vice versa. His work was translated into all the major languages. The Kaiser requested an audience. Nor was the encounter one of those ill-advised diplomatic gestures called for on a whim and arranged by equerries, of the type in which Irving Berlin was called into the presence of Winston Churchill, where he was surprised to find that the conversation had little to do with popular music, a puzzle later resolved when it turned out that Churchill had thought he was consulting Isaiah Berlin on matters of diplomacy. The Kaiser had read Twain's books and thought *Life on the Mississippi* to be the best. (The porter at Twain's hotel in Vienna held the same opinion.) At least when Twain was abroad, he didn't suffer from being unappreciated. He could have easily suffered from the opposite.

At home, he became accustomed to a high standard of living: even during his recurrent periods of financial embarrassment, there was usually a millionaire friend to provide a private railroad car or a trip on a yacht. But that was nothing to how he lived it up in less democratic lands. The grand hotels of the European spas routinely offered him a reduced tariff, or no tariff at all, just to have his fame on the premises. In Tuscany, he lived in a villa, like Bernard Berenson. He could make himself at home no matter how high the ceiling and exalted the company. Countesses plumed like birds of paradise ate out of his hand. Yet he was never corrupted. The Innocent Abroad stayed innocent. How was that?

Surely the main reason was America itself. He had a pride in his country all the more robust for his loathing of patriotism, which he thought the enemy of common brotherhood. It follows that he thought America was its friend—a contention he could propound without sounding naive, because he never blinked his country's follies while praising its virtues. The Henry James option—to go abroad and set up shop where artists were more coddled—had no appeal for Twain. For one thing, he was much loved in his homeland, even when he wasn't fully understood. For another, and more important, he would have regarded exile as patronizing, a betrayal of the enterprise that was his burgeoning nation, a flight from adventure into safety, and a craven endorsement of those who looked down from what they imagined were the heights of civilization on a land that he refused to believe was anything less than history's great opportunity for human fulfilment.

This explains the touch of anger that creeps in when he dismantles Matthew Arnold's snooty observations on Grant's use of the English language. There is no evidence that Twain disliked Arnold personally. When they met they seem to have got on like two sets of facial hair on fire. But in print Twain took obvious glee, masquerading as regret, in picking Arnold's prose style apart to show that it wasn't as classical, or even as grammatical, as its perpetrator thought. Arnold, according to Twain, had no call to speak *de haut en bas*: the *haut* just wasn't all that high. As a corollary, and without having to say so, Twain demonstrated that the *bas* wasn't all that low: his homespun demotic was more economical than Arnold's solemn rodomontade, and in prose the economical *is* the classical.

Twain's celebrated demolition of James Fenimore Cooper is based on the conviction that American English is a classical style that has to be protected against the impurities of posturing humbug. Twain traced Cooper's exfoliating verbiage to its roots in the besetting sin of inaccurate observation. "Fenimore Cooper's Literary Offenses" and "Fenimore Cooper's Further Literary Offenses," both collected here, are killingly funny—funnier, even, than Macaulay's pitiless inspection of the poetry of Robert Montgomery. Poor Montgomery was celebrated at the time, but obviously, to anyone with literary taste, doomed to oblivion, a destination to which Macaulay could only help him along. Cooper is still with us, but Twain did his best to make sure that Cooper's mystery-mongering flimflam wouldn't be allowed to pass itself off as a model of American prose style. By implication, his own prose style got the job.

What he did to Cooper was only a closer-to-home version of the treatment he habitually handed out to foreign critics of the Arnoldian stamp. The guardian of clear speech at home, Twain didn't have to bend the knee when pundits abroad curled their lip. Arnold's idea of a high culture increasingly and necessarily out of reach of a brutalized populace—an idea destined to generate a whole library of its own in the age to come—got its most penetrating answer from an American. Arnold should have stayed on his own turf, where pity for the emerging proletariat was a more plausible attitude. "Wragg is in custody," a four-word sentence in a newspaper, inspired Arnold to a long lament on the predestined cultural impoverishment of the workers—a feat of prescience based mainly on Arnold's confident assumption that Wragg was inherently a more wretched surname than, say, Arnold. Such sensitivity, however commendable, entailed presuppositions about civilization which Twain, speaking as an American, wasn't inclined to buy. He just didn't think that civilization had been all that civilized. "Hard," he called it, "and glittering, and bloodless, and unattainable."

Twain provided the same enlightening information for the French pundit Paul Bourget, and for any other Old World panjandrum who tried to high-hat the new nation. He went at them as if they were imperialists, which, in a way, they were: cultural imperialists. What he couldn't guess was that he was himself one of the pioneers of a cultural imperialism fated to have a large share in determining the history of the twentieth century.

He couldn't guess it because he was a nineteenth-century figure—the hardest thing to remember when you are caught up in reading him. He seems so close in time that you wouldn't be surprised to look up from the book and see him talking to Larry King on television. But he can seem so familiar only because the America we like best sounds like him, not because he sounds like it. He was there first. Even his personal weaknesses presaged the America we have come to know and like from its infinitely exportable popular culture. Twain had a weakness for profitable schemes. The first of them did make a profit: when Twain personally published Grant's memoirs, the deal worked out so well that he thought he had revolutionized the publishing industry. "The prosperity of the venture," as Howells pointed out, "was the beginning of Clemens' adversity, for it led to excesses of enterprise which were forms of dissipation." Twain's further ventures into private enterprise oscillated between a waste of time and a waste of money, not always his own. The typesetting machine he thought would revolutionize printing eventually did so, but not his version of it. He went broke in a big way. Like Sir Walter Scott, he heroically wrote himself out of debt, but as soon as enough money accumulated he was back into another scheme. For years, he maintained his faith in a much-publicized energy food, which in his time performed the same function as the vitamin pills that the British bodice-ripper author Barbara Cartland so enthusiastically favours now—that of helping naturally energetic people convince themselves that they are medically savvy beyond the ken of doctors.

Yet Twain, for all his susceptibility to plausible wheezes, was no crank. He was crazy about know-how. He was a can-do merchant, a prototype for Gyro Gearloose and all those nutty inventors who go on building weird machines in the backyard sheds of American popular culture, even in the space age. And after all, some of the machines work. Twain's typesetting machine almost did. Twain was in tune with the mechanical efflorescence of the new nation. For him, there was no separation between machinery and poetry. You couldn't even call him a proto-Futurist, because for him art and machinery had never grown apart to the point of needing to be reunited. He had been brought up to the practical. The printing house was his high school and the river-boat his university. He could make things work. It was one of the qualities that the women of Paris loved about the liberating American troops of 1944—all those Tom Sawyers and Huck Finns who rode six to a jeep. It wasn't just that they could get you chocolate and sheer stockings: when they had finished kissing you, they could fix your bicycle.

.   .   .

If that sounds like sentimentality now, it is only because of the devastating effect on America's image, and especially its self-image, wrought by the Vietnam War. Since then, instead of a jeep full of smiling boys with girls jumping in to join them we think first of scowling men tumbling out of a helicopter to torch a village. We think of some fat-bottomed sergeant checking crates of ice-cream-making equipment off a C-130 at Cam Ranh Bay while the local girls are being sold into prostitution outside the wire, of the CIA supervising torture sessions in which the questions and the answers are both in a language they don't understand except for the screams. America cast itself as the villain and agreed when the rest of the world hissed. Actually, there was reason even at the time to believe that the average grunt was more remarkable for his kindness than for his insensitivity to an alien culture. Later on, even the Italian journalist Oriana Fallaci—whose articles (especially her interview with Kissinger, the granting of which he subsequently called the most stupid mistake he ever made) did so much to put America in the bad light that many Americans conceded was deserved—changed her tune. Interviewed in her turn by the Italian magazine *King*, she said that her abiding memory of Vietnam was of how well-mannered the American boys had been, even when they didn't have the slightest idea of where they were or what they were supposed to be doing there.

Vietnam was only part of a post-war pattern in which the United States, whether by accident or design, propped up the kind of authoritarian regimes whose sinister luminaries wore dark glasses indoors. All too often, especially in Latin America, it was by design. *Realpolitik* was held to be mandatory. But the real trouble with *realpolitik* was that it wasn't real. In foreign policy, ruthlessness undid the best thing America had going for it: benevolence. In the Western countries, it handed the Marxist intellectuals an opportunity—ultimately fatal to them, since it encouraged them to stay Marxist long after their opposite numbers in the East had given up—to misinterpret twentieth-century history. It became temptingly easy to argue that the machinations of American foreign policy were what had stopped the Western European countries from going fully socialist after the Second World War. But American Machiavellianism wasn't what did that. What did it was American generosity: the Marshall Plan. The same applied to the occupation of Japan. The Japanese economic superstate that we are now all so concerned about was made possible by America. If that was Machiavellianism, it was of a strangely self-defeating kind.

Diehard opponents of the American Empire—on this subject Gore

Vidal remains determined to be only half as clever as he is—insist that America rebuilt the defeated nations only to secure markets, and so forth. This seductive notion first took off along with the economies of the rebuilt nations. Quite often, it was noised abroad in newspapers and magazines that owed their editorial freedom to guarantees insisted upon by the victorious Allies, with America in the forefront. Suspicion of American power became harder to quell as American power went on increasing. Perhaps that was a good thing: about power, suspicious is the way we should always be. But to focus on America's misuse of its economic and military strength was to abdicate the obligation, and the opportunity, to talk about the aspect of American power that actually worked—its cultural influence, the thing that made America irresistibly attractive even after it had just finished dropping bombs on you.

The Japanese had been told that the American GIs would rape their women. The threat was easy to believe, since the right to rape civilians was an unofficial but commonly granted reward for conquest in the Imperial Japanese Army. But in the American Army of Occupation the penalty for rape was imprisonment or death. When the GIs handed out gum instead, the Japanese got the point in the first five minutes. The Germans had got the point while the war was still on. German civilians threatened with liberation by the Russians headed in the opposite direction. Surrendering to the Americans became the rule in the *Wehrmacht* when the SS or the military police weren't watching. Any defeated nation had something with which to compare America—itself as it had previously been. America's allied nations, their gratitude either tinged by jealousy or annulled by it, were less inclined to admire but just as bound to compare: America was their measure, whether as a challenge or as a threat. America's problem was that it had no standard of comparison except its own ideal of itself.

The problem got worse, and by now it is acute. This is where America's congenital insulation from the less fortunate contemporary world, and its isolation from the needy past brought about by abundance in the present, has played the Devil. Both from the Right and from the Left, America attacks itself for lapsing from its supposedly normal condition as the ideal state. But the ideal state is a platonic concept destined to be even more frustrating than platonic love. For the Right, modern America is a disappointing lapse from godliness, purity and order. For the Left, modern America is a disappointing lapse from social justice. Increasingly, the argument between them is about language and its legalistic interpretation, with the Constitution as the unquestioned yet ineffable ur-document, as if God's will were literally a will, leaving everything he ever owned to America, but on certain conditions, all of which conflict.

In sober moments, we know that the Constitution of the United States would mean nothing without the laws that grow out of it and back it up. Without them, the rights it promulgates would be no better guaranteed than those enshrined in the old Soviet Constitution, a document that, as the dissident sociologist Alexander Zinoviev suggested, was published only in order to find out who agreed with it, so that they could be dealt with.

Americans, however, are less inclined to realize that the laws would mean nothing without the spirit that gave rise to them, and that this spirit was first made manifest in the country's classic literature. To see the problem, it helps to be outside America looking in. Angst at falling short of its dreams for itself has sapped the country's initial confidence that it could alter circumstances in its own favour: the lure of the ideal has stymied the practical. It is a dream to imagine that even the most comprehensive laundering of language would expunge racism from human consciousness. The realistic alternative is to deny racist consciousness practical expression. It won't be easy, but to disarm the population would be a good start. A start can't be made, though, because the gun lobby has too much power. On this point, as on so many others, left-wing idealists and right-wing idealists work in a fearful synergy to undo the possibility of practical government. Seemingly conflicting interests have combined to erode an institution.

.   .   .

As a more recent institution, one that is actually still growing rather than falling apart, the Library of America provides a heartening example of what can be done. Perhaps it will give courage to people who would like to see public television properly funded. In the United States, public-service institutions, unless they are operating in a field where private enterprise has no urge to compete, are in the position of a heresy against an orthodoxy. But in matters of the mind they are essential to the nation's health. Twain was in no doubt on the point. In 1898, having grown old in the new country, he warned against the consequences of a free-market culture. Thirty years before, he said, Edwin Booth had played Hamlet a hundred nights in New York. Now Hamlet was lucky to get a look-in.

Comparing the Burg Theatre, in Vienna, with Broadway, he thought Broadway was nowhere. "You are eating too much mental sugar; you will bring on Bright's disease of the intellect."

As we now know, Broadway was to be the *fons et origo* of twentieth-century popular culture in its most sophisticated form: the musical show. But Twain still had a right to speak, because the popular culture that was on its way wouldn't have been the same without him. What he couldn't guess—because he was only a genius, not a clairvoyant—was that it would go so far, that entertainment would become, on such a scale, mere entertainment. Modern America is a society of abundance in almost every aspect, even when it comes to quality. The visitor who prides himself on his sophistication is first startled, then benumbed, to find that everything he thought treasurable where he came from is present in America, only more so. If he is interested in the Books of Hours of the early Renaissance, he will find the world's greatest collection in the Pierpont Morgan Library. He can be a world expert on Ming vases and still not survive the shock of turning a corner on Melrose Avenue in Los Angeles to find a glass-fronted warehouse chock-full of them. There are classical-music lovers in London who pay for a return plane trip from New York with what they save buying a suitcaseful of CDs at American prices. A few years ago, in a music shop on Broadway, I reached into a discount bin and fished out a boxed set of cassettes of the Mahler First and Second Symphonies in the touchstone performances conducted by Bruno Walter. Five bucks. It made me annoyed that I had previously paid so much, and then afraid that I was not paying enough. The precious was practically free. It was value without price.

But that doesn't offset the menace of price without value. The abundance isn't intelligently distributed, and never could be by a free market, whose famous invisible hand is incurably short of a brain. Unless public-service institutions are made robust, the art will go to the elite that knows what it wants, while those who might have wanted it but never found out about it are stuck with the junk. Twain was an elitist: when he punished Cooper for supposing that "more preferable" was a more impressive way to say "preferable" he was saying that literary expression isn't just self-expression. But he would have been appalled to be told in advance that the enlightenment of the American people was going to be a matter of niche marketing. He would have regarded that, surely correctly, as a boondoggle.

Though beset by remorse for his own failings, Twain had a sure sense of his rank, but he didn't imagine that he had attained it by his own unaided efforts. He had an institution to help him—the world literary heritage, which he regarded as belonging to America by right, because America was the world's country. Twain's own contribution, daring in every way, was most daring in its dedication to the principle that the institution belonged to the people, and not to its adepts. He was a man so superior he needed no support from self-esteem. One wonders whether the Kaiser, for once in his life face to face with a real aristocrat, realized the implications.

They weren't revolutionary—not politically, anyway. Though a devout republican at home, Twain abroad had a soft spot for monarchs. But culturally he was a bigger revolutionary than Karl Marx, and, in the long run, more successful, because what Marx started went backward in the end, while the popular culture to which Twain gave such a boost has gone on expanding. Doing that, it has necessarily left him behind. The precocious modernity that makes him seem so close to us can only obscure, not obviate, the dependence of his inspiration on a more immediate world than any we know—or anyone will ever know again, unless the industrialized world dismantles itself. The young Twain rode on stagecoaches and talked to strangers. He saw people murdered. Death and disease struck his family at a time when such things didn't happen just to other people; they happened to everybody. Life has improved, but in improving it has grown less real, and there is no going back except through a disaster.

Huckleberry Finn may survive the misguided clean-up of the library shelves. Unless I lost count, there are forty-two instances of the word "nigger" in the first fifteen chapters of the book, but its heart is so obviously in the right place that it may weather the intentions of the politically correct, whose salient folly is to arouse false expectations of the past. Even if Huck makes it, however, he won't ever again be read by everybody. Professional admiration for the book will remain intense. (In *Green Hills of Africa*, when Hemingway names *Huckleberry Finn* as the book that made American literature, for a moment the campfire fabulist is speaking the truth.) Amateur enjoyment must remain restricted to those who actually read books instead of just hearing about them or watching the video of the movie. Twain was marginalized by the popular culture he helped to create. It had to happen.

Where these four beautiful books will have their effect, along with the Library of America as a whole, is in the academy. With a few exceptions (which have been punished ferociously by qualified reviewers who realize that this project, above all others, is too important to permit lapses from its own standards) every volume in the collection is a model of scholarship in service to literature. By now the damage reports are in and we know that a whole generation of students have had literature killed for them by the way they have been obliged to study it. Instead of the books, they have had to study theories about the books, always on the assumption that the theorists are wiser than the authors. And finally scholasticism, as always, has reduced itself to absurdity, with the discovery by the theorists that there were no authors. There weren't even any books, only texts, and there wasn't any history for the texts to emerge from, because history was just a set of signs, too.

Well, here are the books, with not a text in sight except as a reasoned agreement on what the author actually wrote. Every volume in the Library has a chronology to help you follow the life of the author (who actually existed), with pertinent notes to place him in the context of history (which exists, too). Armed with this subsidiary information, the student will be able to give a book the only "reading" that counts—the one by which the book brings something to him, without his bringing a load of hastily acquired pseudoscience to it. The authors will emerge as the living human beings who made the larger Constitution, the one behind the document. And one author will emerge as even more alive than the rest, stricken by tragedy but unquenchable in his delight, shaking his head as if he had seen everything—even the future that is our frightening present—and not given up.

The New Yorker, June 14, 1993; later included
in *Even As We Speak*, 2001

POSTSCRIPT

My reference to the temptation *Huckleberry Finn* might offer to the politically correct text-cleansers was made at a time when it still looked possible that gentle ridicule would stave off the menace. Alas, the New York State Board of Regents went on to prove itself in deadly earnest, applying their principles of selection to the school library bookshelves with the same intractable enthusiasm as the thought police of an ideological power. How this totalitarian residue should have come to flourish in a nominally liberal democratic state is a nice question. Part of the answer, I suspect, is that the democratic component of liberal democracy contains an ideological breeding ground, commonly known as egalitarianism. An indeterminate abstract concept masquerading as an ideal, it encourages any amount of censorship to be imposed in its name. There could be no more important specific task for the humanities than to oppose it by protecting the integrity of the classic books, as part of the broad, general and increasingly urgent task of liberalizing liberal democracy before it democratizes itself out of existence. For encouragement, we can daydream with delight of how a New York Regents examination paper might be answered by Mark Twain come back to life.

Considering his disapproval of prominent men who allowed their lust to interfere with the accepted forms, Twain might also have been pretty scathing about my warm invocations of Bill Clinton. But at the beginning of Clinton's presidency the picture looked bright for any observer who thought that the Difference Principle of John Rawls was the truest guide to what an American government should do: benefit the poor. In the long run, that was roughly what Clinton's administration did, although he finally blotted even that part of his record by benefiting some of the rich with absurd pardons cynically bestowed as he made his exit. But it was the record of his private behaviour that determined the general opinion of him, and would probably, alas, have determined Twain's opinion of him too. Twain's implacable conventionality on the subject of sexual conduct was an example of the way America was not like Europe.

A century later, the media uproar over the Monica Lewinsky affair proved that the difference had scarcely changed. As the consequences of Clinton's private folly drove him all the way to a public impeachment, mighty decathletes of the boudoir like François Mitterrand and Jacques Chirac must have been astonished. Each had been able to spend decades exercising the *droit de seigneur* with no thought of recrimination from the press, the surrounding culture or even, apparently, from their wives. No doubt that was what was wrong with both of them. There is unquestionably something self-serving about the European reluctance to identify the private and the public life, just as there is unquestionably something admirable about the American assumption that they should form a unity. Unfortunately there is also something dogmatic about the "should."

Compelled by such a concretized ideal, the real unity is between conventionality and legalism. If only love can lead to marriage, any new love must lead to divorce. Innocent people start to disappear, and at the level of intellect and sensitivity as well as at the level of kitsch and glitz, Saul Bellow's wives join Elizabeth Taylor's husbands among the legions of the discarded, to the long-term profit of nobody except lawyers. Despite the almost universal opinion that they should join in this grotesque process, the Clintons have so far failed to do so—a reluctance on their part that is surely worth consideration, if not endorsement.

Very few American journalists have been reckless enough to suggest that the fated couple might be held together by passion; or that his attractiveness to women might be one of the things she finds exciting about him; or that a part of the attractiveness might reside in a gallantry as irrepressible as his libido. On that last point, it is still considered naive, in American company, to even hint at the possibility that the President, when he told his first lies about Monica Lewinsky, might have been just as concerned to protect her future as to protect his job. It was said at the time, and is still said, that she meant nothing to him except as an available intern. There is certainly a sense in which charm is the capacity to lavish intimacy on strangers. But Clinton's charm might well be of the order in which a casually met woman is led to deduce very quickly that she is not a stranger at all: that he cares for her fate. (The deduction might not even be erroneous, at the time.) To say that Clinton had no concern for his young admirer was to demonize him, and to demonize him was to call her an idiot: something which many of those who claimed to be repelled by his contempt for women were quick to do, thus ruling out the possibility that the same charm which seduced her might have seduced them. But they should have ruled it in. Anybody can see through a man like that from a distance. The trick is to see through him from close up.

Clinton was a guest speaker at the Hay-on-Wye Literary Festival in 2001. The media stampede from London towards Wales was not to be believed. British female journalists who had been under the impression that they despised him learned otherwise when they came within range of his aftershave. A high proportion of them, by American standards, subsequently went into print with the opinion that the way he was alleged to behave around women might have been at least partly determined by the way women behaved around him. High office was no doubt a factor, but a similarly seismic effect was never recorded in the case of Jimmy Carter, who was confined to committing adultery in his heart, and got into quite enough trouble just for that. Mark Twain the great liberator also contributed to the building of a prison, whose inmates are under the continual obligation to prove that they have clean hands, in accordance with the principle that if you have done nothing wrong, you have nothing to fear—except from the principle itself, which has a way of expanding to include thought in the realm of action.

2003

25

CASANOVA COMES AGAIN

Casanova, outed long ago as a flagrant heterosexual, is out again. This time he's out in paperback—the whole of his memoirs, in six hefty double volumes. What a pity he couldn't be here for a launch party at, say, the Algonquin. He always said that his literary career was the one that really mattered. In his small talk for the assembled *prominenti* he would have said it again, even as he put the moves on the younger and more personable females at the thrash: the editors, the journalists, the PR flacks, the bimboid wannabes toting the canapés. Feeling his age but galvanized by the attention, he would have taken on the biggest challenge in the room: the drenchingly beautiful, impeccably refined junior editor on the point of marrying the tortoise-necked publishing tycoon jealously quavering in the background. As the lights dim for a screened montage of his big moments on film, Casanova talks his target out the double doors, down the stairs and into a cab. Most weekends, like the modest, well-brought-up girl she is, she takes the jitney home to East Hampton, but when Cas explains that he gambled away the last of his *per diem* stash the previous night she immediately offers to cover the cab fare with her spare change. Step on it! The publisher's heavies are already on the sidewalk and scoping the street through their dark glasses. Back upstairs, the indignant publisher has personally lifted the phone to consign the entire print run of Casanova's great book to a garbage scow, but our hero's authorial ambitions never did stand a chance against his primal urge.

Lesser writings aside, *History of My Life* is Casanova's main claim to the literary importance that he always dreamed of in the intervals—sometimes lasting for days on end—between chasing skirt. The claim has to be called successful, if with some reluctance. When the first instalment of the hardback edition came out, in 1966, bigwigs of the literary world united to rain hosannas on its editor and translator, Willard R. Trask, for restoring a masterpiece to just pre-eminence after its long history of being bowdlerized, rewritten by interfering hacks, truncated, mistranslated and attacked from the air. (A Second World War bomb through the roof of the Brockhaus office, in Leipzig, almost did to the manuscript what the bomb through the roof of the Eremitani church in Padua did to Mantegna's frescoes.) Since then, there has been time to think, and wonder whether many of the mandarins who heaped Casanova's *capolavoro* with praise ever read it again, or even read in it. For one thing, it isn't a book for a literal-minded age in which the authenticity of a quotation has to be guaranteed by marking supplied words with square brackets. What about all that dialogue, remembered in detail over the stretch of decades? Did he carry a tape recorder? A limiting judgement would have plenty to go on.

But that's just it: plenty is what the book has—plenty of everything, even without the sex. There are swindles and scandals, pretensions and inventions, clerics, lyrics and bubbling alembics, sword fights at midnight and complots at the palace, bugs in the bed and bedlam in the tavern, masked balls, balls-ups and shinnying up drainpipes, flummery, mummery and summary executions. All that, as the journalists say, plus a pullulating plankton field of biddable, beddable broads, through which Casanova moves with the single-minded hunger of a straining whale, yet somehow brings the whole populated ocean of eighteenth-century society to phosphorescent life. The book teems. It flows. It does everything but end. Written in his old age, the memoirs, recounting his picaresque manoeuvres almost day by day, could get only so far before he croaked, leaving uncovered his most fascinating and possibly most edifying years— the declining years, when the old magic had finally and forever ceased to work. But the memoirs got far enough to establish a pattern that becomes as predictable to the reader as a flimflam man's tent show on tour. Casanova checks into the inn, checks out the upmarket talent, screws the pick of the bunch, screws up a business deal and moves on. Roaming the whole of Europe, he penetrates the local high society in each new place, penetrates all the attractive females up to and including the nobility, works some scam to raise funds, blows it and blows town. (The two previous sentences say the same thing with the words changed. Casanova's prose works the same effect for thousands of pages, the miracle being that it isn't worked to death.)

To call Casanova's *chef d'oeuvre* repetitive is like calling Saint-Simon snobbish or de Sade sadistic. Repetition is what he lived for, especially with beautiful women. Variety had to be serial, or it wasn't variety. After he had done all the different things with the same woman, he wanted to do all the same things with different women. He could never get enough of them, and there were more of them than even he could envision. Think of it: there was one born every minute! Every second! But the eternal problem with which he faces us is that he didn't feel like that at the time. He dealt wholesale but he thought retail. Each love affair was the only one that counted for as long as it lasted. Sometimes it lasted only a matter of minutes, but the liaison got the whole of his attention, even if the Inquisition was waiting for him down on the street. He never had one eye on the clock. He had both eyes on his beloved's face, utterly caught up in the moment when her crisis of ecstasy made her soul his. Anxiety that such a revelation might never come again, as it were, conferred the precious gift of delay. He writes, "I have all my life been dominated by the fear that my steed would flinch from beginning another race; and I never found this restraint painful, for the visible pleasure which I gave always made up four fifths of mine." Four-fifths is 80 per cent whichever way you slice it: a lot to give away. But then it was by giving that he took. Even in—especially in—bed, he could convince them that it wasn't about him, it was about them. This was, and remains, a winning formula.

.   .   .

There were serving maids whom he routinely leaped on just because he bumped into them on the stairs, and there was the occasional faded *grande dame* he more or less had to satisfy because it was easier than talking his way out of it, but on the whole he never got it on with a woman who he didn't think, while she lay in his arms, was the woman of his dreams, the one designed to appeal to his imagination by the qualities of her mind and soul as well as the beauty of her body. Women knew that about him just by the way he looked at them. He was a great lover because they knew in advance that he would love them greatly—that he cherished each one's unique individuality even though he adored them holus-bolus, as a sex, as a race, as an angelic species. The question remains whether Casanova's infinitely replicated experience of once-in-a-lifetime love has anything to do with love at all. If you believe it hasn't, he and his book are easily dismissed: they have the same significance as JFK jumping a secretary in the White House elevator and telling a crony a few minutes afterwards that he got into the blonde. If you believe it has, then Casanova is still here, now more than ever haunting the civilized world's collective consciousness, and the book of his life, for all its mephitic undertow, has the reverberating ring of an awkward truth: this man is the man you would be if you were free to act.

One of the things you would have to be free from, of course, is sexual morality. But to call Casanova free from sexual morality invites a rejoinder: sexual morality was the only kind of morality he had. About sex, he had at least a few principles, which are best examined after one notes the thoroughness with which he lacked them in all other departments. Living always beyond his means and forever running to escape the consequences, in his life as an adventurer, even more than in his loves, he was ready for anything. He made it up as he went along, and it all came true. Even his name was a fabrication: he really was Giacomo Girolamo Casanova, but his title, Chevalier de Seingalt, was one he gave himself. He was born in 1725, into a theatrical family in Venice, and on the social scale of the time show folk ranked not far above grave-diggers. Casanova's self-election to noble status was in itself a theatrical coup, and his career is best regarded as a succession of vaudeville numbers with nothing to link them except a rapidly falling and rising curtain.

As a boy, he bled easily and was thought mentally backward, but his father was astute enough to secure the patronage of the Grimani family, who staked Casanova to a course at the University of Padua, the idea being that he would have a career in the Church. Casanova graduated— one of the few examples of his properly finishing anything he began—but his entry into Holy Orders was occluded by his entry into the sister of the priest who was giving him instruction. Back in Venice and into bed with two sisters, he started attracting patrons on his own account—a talent that remained with him until the end, although the even more useful talent of keeping his patrons sweet was one he sadly lacked. Offered an ecclesiastical post in the Calabrian province of Martorano, Casanova took one look at the place and called off the deal. He knew he was meant for higher things. In Rome, he met the Pope—big game. Unfortunately, there was some fuss over a woman, and he had to skip town. After a spell in Constantinople brought him nothing but more women, he moved on to Corfu and there added to his handicaps by acquiring a taste for gambling unmatched by any concomitant ability: as a general rule, applicable to his entire lifetime, he could quit gambling only when he was in debt, and dealt with the debt by blowing the scene.

In Venice once more, he scraped a living with a violin, mastered at high speed so that he could join a theatre orchestra. A new patron was so impressed by Casanova's knowledge of the occult sciences that he considered legally adopting the prodigy into his noble family. Since Casanova's knowledge of the occult sciences was largely imaginary, there was no reason he could not have gone on expanding it until the deal was clinched, but once again scandal intervened. The tribunal in charge of religion and morals wanted to question him about possible offences in both fields. Even worse, Casanova had reason to believe that the Inquisition wanted to hear about those occult sciences. Time to take a powder.

It was 1749, Casanova was twenty-four, and he was on his way, which is to say on the run, seemingly forever. In Lyons, he was a Freemason; in Paris, he wrote plays; in Vienna, he met intolerance of his amatory success. Back to Venice yet again, where he was charged with sorcery and imprisoned in the notorious Leads. His daring escape was the basis of a subsequent book, which earned him some measure of the authorial prestige he always craved. Returning to Paris, he founded a lottery, the proceeds of which he neglected to abscond with—a rare lapse. He later established a silk manufactory there with hopes of success, which his success at getting a titled mistress pregnant soon translated into failure. In Geneva, he met Voltaire. In London, he was presented at court, presented a false bill of exchange, got busted and left with little to show for his stay except a fourth dose of the clap. In Berlin, Frederick the Great thought highly of him, and offered him a post as tutor to the Pomeranian Cadet Corps, but, typically, he aimed higher still, and headed for St. Petersburg and fortune. Catherine the Great offered him nothing.

In Warsaw, he fought a duel. An accusation—it was false, but it jibed with his billing—that he had embezzled the Paris lottery funds caught up with him there. Banished from Poland, he moved on to be expelled from Vienna, mainly because Maria Theresa had heard that he had been expelled from Poland. So on to Paris, in order to be expelled from France. It was as if his mug shot had been put out by Interpol. During a stretch in a Spanish slammer, he wrote a three-volume opus about Venice, probably designed as a sop to the Venetian State Inquisition. If that was his idea, it worked: in 1774, at the age of forty-nine, he got a pardon. The Inquisition got him all the same—not as a victim but as a fink. In this role, as a paid informer, he had regular employment at last. How could he screw it up? He wrote a satire that satirized the wrong patrician, and was banished all over again.

In Vienna, he finally got lucky by ingratiating himself with Count Waldstein, who, in 1785, appointed him librarian of his castle in Bohemia. There, growing old and bored, Casanova began writing his memoirs in 1789, the year of the French Revolution—an event whose significance almost entirely escaped him. He had never been that kind of revolutionary, and by now he wasn't even a rebel: he had gone legit at long last. But even while he lived out his days in provincial isolation he always dreamed of Venice, where, had he ever returned, he would undoubtedly have accomplished his own ruin all over again. In his last summer alive, two years before the century ended, the Inquisition pardoned him, but it was too late.

It was always too late, or too early, or too something. In a life of opportunism, he took every opportunity to make a shambles of anything he had managed to achieve. Confusion was a compulsion, as if everything had to be tested to the point of destruction, to prove that it wasn't real. And, in fact, nothing *was* real, except women. Women were something he could grasp, however briefly, and if you seek the rhythm of Casanova's mind working—instead of just his feet running away from trouble—it is to what he says about women that you must turn. And one of the first things he says, in the preface to his *magnum opus*, is proved by the rest of it to be true: "Feeling that I was born for the sex opposite to mine, I have always loved it and done all that I could to make myself loved by it." Feminists should not seize too quickly on the generalized term "the sex opposite to mine." The operative words are "to make myself loved." That's what he really wanted to do, and that's what he really did. Women really existed for him. Everything else was a fantasy, even his literary ambitions—except in the case of this one great book, whose greatness, for all the sordid detail of unwashed linen and down-at-heel shoes, depends on making reality fantastic, a dream world like *The Thousand and One Nights.*

.   .   .

In the last act of *Don Giovanni*, Mozart consigns the great lover to Hell. Even today—in fact, today more than ever—this is a conclusion morally satisfactory for the audience, even though some of its members will be committing adultery that very night, and a few of them may have committed it during the intermission. But all of them respect the conventions. The rat had it coming to him. That's the way we are supposed to feel about the Don and all his confrères in libertinage, with Casanova as the arch exemplar: that for their crime of callously pillaging the emotional life of their helpless victims they deserve punishment, and might even have been visited with it ahead of time, through their never having properly lived. But Lorenzo Da Ponte was not the sole author of the opera's libretto. His collaborator-*cum*-technical-adviser was Casanova himself, who knew better—or, at any rate, knew that that's not all we feel. We also feel envy. When Woody Allen said that he wanted to be reincarnated as Warren Beatty's fingertips, he was articulating a longing widely felt among men. The moral consensus of today would like to pretend that a Lothario's deadly charm is no less reprehensible than a paedophile's sack of candy. But nobody except a pervert envies a pervert. There are few men, no matter how virtuous, who do not envy the seducer.

If the seducer really were a rapist in disguise, he would be easier to condemn. But all too obviously his success depends at least as much on co-operation as on coercion. The virtuous man's envy is made worse by the consideration that if the virtuous woman takes a holiday from the straight and narrow the seducer is the very man she is likely to choose as an accomplice, just because he is irresponsible, passing through, and won't be coming back. Among the recently bereaved, the faithful but bored and the businesswomen whose poetry has been insufficiently appreciated, the seducer cruises for his easiest prey: the woman of substance who wants an amorous encounter that doesn't mean anything. Later on, she can tell us that it didn't mean anything. But we know very well that at the time it meant everything. The louse got the best of her; he gets the best of all of them.

By the standards of the great lovers in our own century, Casanova didn't run up all that big a total. (Richard Burton scored at the rate of a *Luftwaffe* fighter pilot on the Russian front.) But today's dedicated stick man has the advantage of modern communications. For Casanova, the hunting grounds were days apart by slow coach. Factor that in and you have to marvel at what he achieved. A statistical check of the complete book turns up a figure of a hundred and thirty-two full-scale conquests. The breakdown by nationality reveals him as sowing the seed of a united Europe. Forty-seven Italian women said *si*. Nineteen French women said *oui*. Ten Swiss women said *si, oui* or *ja*. There were eight German, five English, and ten women from sundry other countries. The total has to be reduced somewhat if you count the twelve sets of doubles as single victories, but doubtless it could be restored and even extended by the tussles that he thought weren't worth a mention, having taken place too low on the social scale. Nevertheless, twenty-four servant girls are registered as having succumbed, along with, at the top of the range, eighteen gentlewomen and fifteen members of royalty. There were only two nuns, which must have meant that the convents were hard to crack, because nothing inflamed him like spiritual refinement. Nor was he put off by brains ("The older I grew," he writes in Volume XI, "the more what attached me to women was intelligence"), although he endorsed the assumption, standard in his time, that men were naturally smarter than women and therefore he would never have to face the difficulty of dealing with a woman who mentally outstripped him. Even the divine Henriette, the greatest love of his life, he admired for her accomplishments without ever considering that they might shame him into inferiority. Though disarmingly ready to admit his occasional foolishness, he was confident about his superior mind. In that respect, his mind was commonplace, a point seized on by Arthur Schnitzler in the most interesting work ever inspired by Casanova, the novella *Casanovas Heimfahrt* (*Casanova's Homecoming*).

In Schnitzler's novella, Casanova, over the hill and under the weather, is heading home to Venice for one last crack at straightening out his business affairs, getting himself off the hook with the authorities, etc.—the usual unfounded hopes exacerbating the same old permanent imbroglio, but by now the energy that made it all into an adventure is almost gone. Nevertheless, this time he is determined that nothing can halt him on his homeward path—except, of course, one thing. An old friend, now enviably well set up in life, tells him about his house guest, a girl of unusual intelligence and grace. Casanova, stopping off just to clap eyes on this paragon, resolves to stay and win her. So far, so blah: but Schnitzler gives the story a twist that makes it unlike anything in Casanova's memoirs. This time, the girl really is Casanova's mental superior. She has a gift for mathematics that shows up his vaunted capacity in that field as a cabalistic mishmash. To top off that humiliation, she is, *mirabile dictu*, not attracted to him physically. He is too old for her, and she has a young lover. To nail her, Casanova must resort to a trick. The brilliance of Schnitzler's story lies in what kind of trick it is. Casanova has to pretend to be the young lover. In the darkness, she doesn't realize that the man making great love to her is the great lover himself. Casanova's identity counts for nothing. For treating her as an object whose emotions do not count, he is treated as an object in his turn: the rapist is raped.

As a hanging judge, Schnitzler was sitting behind a shaky bench. He himself pursued brilliant young females more ardently the older he became, and his series of wonderful, untranslatable plays concerning that very subject of intergenerational affections was based on a private life that would get him pilloried today. But before saying that Schnitzler was unwarrantedly tough on Casanova, one must admit that there is plenty to be tough about. Casanova did indeed rape at least one servant girl. ("I resolved to have her by using a little violence.") And he was indeed a cradle snatcher, on a career basis: Roman Polanski was threatened with a stretch in Chino for a lot less. Of Casanova's registered victories, twenty-two were between eleven and fifteen years of age, twenty-nine between sixteen and twenty, only five were over thirty, and only one was over fifty. That he loved women for their individuality should not be doubted — his sketchy prose condenses into lyricism when evoking a woman's character — but the point needs to be qualified by the consideration that he preferred their individuality to be in its formative stage, so that he could, as it were, get in on it. He had an automatic, full-throttle response to anything, seen from any angle, that might conceivably turn out to be a beautiful young woman — a shadow in the alley, a light footstep on the stairs. His incandescent love affair with Henriette began when he had seen nothing of her except a bump under the coverlet. But, with all that admitted, when we read what he has to say about his love for, and with, Henriette it is hard to remain suitably censorious. When, to cap the effect on him of her beauty and her gift for philosophy, she unexpectedly reveals her prowess on the violin, he is not just further delighted with her, he is delighted for her — a crucial plus.

> She did not thank the company for having applauded her; but turning to the professor she told him, with an air of gracious and noble courtesy, that she had never played a better instrument. After thus complimenting him,

she smilingly told the audience that they must forgive the vanity which had induced her to increase the length of the concert by half an hour.

This compliment having put the finishing touch to my astonishment, I vanished to go and weep in the garden, where no one could see me. Who can this Henriette be? What is this treasure whose master I have become? I thought it impossible that I should be the fortunate mortal who possessed her.

In moments like this—and his enormous book is abundantly peppered with them—Casanova's prose is energized by the sort of spiritual generosity made possible to a man only through the recognition that the woman he adores has a life separate from his, and can be "possessed" only in the metaphorical sense. Casanova, cuckolding honest husbands right and left, never more than one step ahead of the law and continually dogged by inopportune doses of the clap, might seem an unlikely candidate to be a moralist. But, given the times, he was. He had scruples about passing the clap on, and not just because it would have got him into trouble. For reasons too complicated to repeat here but fully recorded in convincing detail, he nobly refrained from seducing a desperate young beauty who had escaped from her troubles by flinging herself into his practised arms:

> To restore her courage and to give her blood a chance to flow freely, I persuaded her to undress and get under the covers. Since she had not the strength, I had to undress her and carry her to the bed myself. In so doing, I performed a new experiment on myself. It was a discovery. I resisted the sight of all her charms without any difficulty. She went to sleep, and so did I, lying beside her, but fully dressed. A quarter of an hour before dawn I woke her and, finding her strength restored, she did not need me to help her dress.

He also admitted, in cold print, if with a hot flush, to sixteen separate instances of having his attentions rejected. Since no mere rake ever admits to anything except progress, this statistic alone should be enough to prove that Casanova was something other and better than a heartless monster. For the rake, the woman is not really alive. For Casanova, nothing could be more alive: that was his problem, and it lies at the heart of the problem he presents us with today. His success as a philanderer was dependent in part on his acuity as a psychologist. Conventional behaviour, without which civilization cannot exist, closes out possibilities. The faithful, while no doubt attaining satisfactions that the faithless can never know, must doom themselves to realizing some of our most haunting dreams only as fantasies. Casanova, by living those fantasies, knew their force.

What are these dreams of unbridled bliss doing in our poor minds? Casanova didn't know, either, but he did know that they are as intense for women as for men. In that regard, he was a kind of genius, and his book remains a ground-breaking work of modern psychology. Freud was a back number beside him. Freud thought that the fine women of Vienna who didn't want to sleep with their husbands were mentally disturbed. Casanova would have solved their problems in an hour on the couch.

Casanova's pretensions to morality are absurd not because his moral sense doesn't exist but because it is based on his desires. As if life were art, he deduced his rules of conduct from the pursuit of beauty. What made him irresistible, apart from his looks and his charm, was the poetic power of his *visione amorosa*; his women thought, correctly, that they were his inspiration. What made him reprehensible was his conviction that love could justify any and all conduct. But no less reprehensible is it for us, today, to deny that desire, with an awkward frequency, can be felt with all the force of love, and with enough of love's poetry to convince the person feeling it that he is in a state of grace—which is always a flying start towards convincing the person at whom he directs it that she might as well join him. Giving in to desire is not the only, or even the best, method of dealing with it, but failing to admit its power and all-pervasiveness is a sure formula for being swept away by it when it floods its banks, as sooner or later it always does. Casanova, by contriving, against all the odds posed by his chaotic personality, to transfer his awareness of that perennial conundrum from life to print, attained his literary ambitions after all, and lives on in his magnificently ridiculous book as some kind of great man— the most awkward kind, the man we call a force of nature because he reminds us of nature's force.

The New Yorker, August 25 and September 1, 1997;
later included in *Even As We Speak*, 2001

The glaring fault in the above piece is that I didn't mention the equally glaring fault in Schnitzler's story about Casanova's journey home. If I had had the extra space, I would have asked the question that brings the narrative crashing down in answer. How could the girl have mistaken the old roué for her young lover, even in the dark? His teeth were in ruins. He would have had to kiss her with his mouth closed. Also he was gone in the hams, and in every other muscle except, presumably, one. (Actually, considering his well-attested prostate problem, he might have been in trouble there, too.) She would have been holding a bag of loose bones. Schnitzler was an experienced amatory operator who must have recognized the absurdity, but perhaps he was depending on a decorous readership who wouldn't.

2003

26

HAMLET IN PERSPECTIVE

Fifteen years ago I was an undergraduate at Cambridge and then later on I stuck around for a while as a postgraduate. I hope I was too weather-beaten to fall for the mystique that these old dens of privilege supposedly generate, but I can't deny that I've got the sort of affection for Cambridge that anybody feels for a place where he read a lot and thought a lot and wasted a lot of time. Hamlet feels the same way about his university— Wittenberg.

Hamlet has to act out his destiny on the sleet-spattered battlements of Elsinore, while Horatio makes regular trips back to Wittenberg for the port and walnuts and the relative safety of academic intrigue. Many a time in Fleet Street, as I've sat there sucking my typewriter and waiting desperately for inspiration, I've envied those of my contemporaries who stayed on to become academics—the Horatios. In other words, I identify with Hamlet. In my mind's eye, he even looks a bit like me. Perhaps a couple of stone lighter, with blond hair and more of it: one of those rare Aussies who happen to fence quite well and stand first in line of succes-sion to the throne of Denmark.

I don't think this is mad conceit because I think all men and most women who've ever read or seen the play feel that its hero is a reflection of themselves. What's more, I think Shakespeare felt the same way. All his characters in all his plays—men or women, heroes or villains—are aspects of himself because his was a universal self and he knew it inside out. Shakespeare was everybody. But Hamlet is probably the character who comes closest to reflecting Shakespeare's whole self. When I think of what Shakespeare was like, I think of Hamlet. Shakespeare probably didn't behave like that, and he almost certainly didn't talk like that. Hamlet talks a great deal and Shakespeare probably spent most of his time listening. At the end of the night's revelry in the tavern, he was probably the only one sober and the only one silent. Nor was Shakespeare famous for being indecisive. From what little we know of him, he was a practical man of affairs. But he was a practical man of affairs in the theatre, which gave unlimited scope to his imagination. He was an art prince, like Michelangelo. If he'd been the other kind of prince, his imagination would have become his enemy, the enemy of action.

In Shakespeare's time, the biggest question of the day was how the Prince should rule. When *Hamlet* was being written, as the sixteenth century turned into the seventeenth, the stable reign of Queen Elizabeth, amid universal trepidation, was drawing to its end. The Earl of Essex, "the glass of fashion, and the mould of form, the observed of all observers," had dished himself through not knowing how to do what when. Essex died on the block somewhere about the time that Hamlet was being born on the page. Shakespeare was a keen student of these weighty matters. He was a keen student of everything. Not that *he* ever went to university. His university was the theatre. The same has held true for a lot of our best playwrights, right down to the present day. Osborne, Pinter, Stoppard— they were all educated in the university of life. Shakespeare was a gigantic natural intellect who had no more need of a university than Einstein had, who didn't go to one either. But Shakespeare did have a contemplative mentality. We know that much for certain because we've heard so little about him. Only in the theatre did Shakespeare create experience; in the outside world he was content to reflect upon it.

Shakespeare knew that he was a man of outstanding gifts. Talent of that magnitude is never modest, although it is almost always humble. He knew that he could dream up a whole kingdom and breathe so much life into it that it would live in men's minds, perhaps for ever. But he also knew that he didn't have what it took to rule a real kingdom for a week. He lacked the limitations. He wasn't simple enough, and it was out of that realization that he created Hamlet, who is really a changeling. Hamlet is what would happen if a great poet grew up to be a prince. He might speak great speeches, but the native hue of resolution would be "sicklied o'er with the pale cast of thought."

"To be, or not to be"—I wish I'd said that. By now that speech has been translated into every major language on earth and most of the minor ones, and it is remarkable how the first line always seems to come out sounding the same. *"Sein, oder nicht sein,"* runs the German version, *"das ist die Frage,"* which perhaps lacks the fresh charm of the English subtitle in the recent Hindi film version — "Shall I live, or do myself in? I do not know." Today, Hamlet belongs to the world. He's come a long way from Elsinore. And there's no reason why not. After all, Shakespeare not only didn't go to university, he didn't go to Denmark, either.

The plot he inherited. A Scandinavian scholar called Saxo Grammaticus wrote an early version. Hamlet was called Amleth and his wicked uncle Claudius was called Feng, who sounds like the leading heavy in *Flash Gordon Conquers Denmark*. Saxo's story was the basis for a later English stage version by Kyd, of *Spanish Tragedy* fame. Shakespeare took over the property and transformed it out of all comparison, although not out of recognition; that old warhorse of a plot is still there inside it. Shakespeare civilized it. He moved it inside the mind and inside the house. He updated *Hamlet* into the Elizabethan age.

One of the things that makes Shakespeare a great man of the theatre is that he knew the real thing when he saw it. He knew that power couldn't be wished out of the world. If power were used wisely and firmly, then everyone might thrive. If it were mismanaged, corruption ensued as surely as rats brought plague, and the whole State went rotten. Shakespeare believed in order and degree. He believed in justice, too, but he didn't think there was any hope of getting it unless the civil fabric was maintained. The idea of social breakdown was abhorrent to him. He knew that he was a kind of prince himself, but he had no illusions about how long his own kingdom would last if the real one fell into disarray. To Shakespeare, Hamlet's tragedy was not just personal but political. Like Prince Hal in an earlier play and like Mark Antony in a later one, or even King Lear, Hamlet has responsibilities. And because Hamlet can't meet those responsibilities he gets a lot of good people killed for nothing and loses his kingdom to the simple but determined Fortinbras.

Nowadays we tend to see Hamlet's blond head surrounded by the flattering nimbus of nineteenth-century Romanticism, which held that Hamlet was a sensitive plant with a soul too fine for the concerns of this world. But Shakespeare was too realistic to be merely romantic. And, of course, he was too poetic to be merely realistic. He knew that there was more in this world than the mere exercise of power. He could feel it within himself—imagination, the supreme power. But even that had its place. In the wrong place it could have tragic consequences. The first reason Hamlet hesitates is dramatic. If Fortinbras were the play's hero, it would be all over in five minutes instead of five acts, with Fortinbras heading for the throne by the direct route—over Claudius's twitching corpse. But the second reason Hamlet hesitates is that he has puzzled his own will by thinking too precisely on the event.

Throughout history, the thoughtful onlooker has been astonished at the man of action's empty head. Napoleon and Hitler, to take extreme examples, did the unthinkable because they lacked the imagination to realize that it couldn't be done. With Hamlet, it's the opposite. More than 300 years before Freud, Montaigne, a great student of the human soul, whose essays Shakespeare knew intimately, identified the imagination as the cause of impotence. Because Hamlet can't stop thinking, he can't start moving. Hence his melancholy. Happiness has been defined as a very small, very cheap cigar named after him, but really Hamlet is as sad as a man can be. He's doubly sad because of his capacity for merriment. Clowns don't want to play Hamlet half as much as Hamlet wants to play the clown, but always the laughter trails off. He loses his mirth and the whole world with it. He does this with such marvellous words that he stuns us into admiration. No actor can resist turning Hamlet's defeat into a victory.

From the moment the part was there to be played, every important actor has looked on his own interpretation of Hamlet as defining him not just as a talent but as a human being. And every Hamlet has studied the Hamlet before him in an almost unbroken succession from that day to this. Burbage, the original Hamlet, gave way to Joseph Taylor; Taylor gave way to Betterton. Pepys saw Betterton play Hamlet in Lincoln's Inn Fields, in 1661, and said that Betterton played the Prince's part beyond imagination, "the best part, I believe, that ever man played." Pepys spent a whole afternoon learning "To be, or not to be" by heart. And as the seventeenth century became the eighteenth, Betterton was still playing Hamlet in his seventieth year, when Steele saw him and said that, for action, he was perfection. Hamlet was at centre stage all over the world. In London he was at Covent Garden, he was in the Haymarket, but, above all, he was at Drury Lane, where great actor after great actor strove to convince the audience that to play Hamlet stood as far above ordinary acting as Hamlet in the play stands above the Players.

In the early eighteenth century, the great tragedian Wilks played Hamlet at Drury Lane. According to contemporary accounts, when the Ghost came on, Wilks climbed the scenery. When he climbed back down again, some time later, he used his sword not to fend off his companions who were trying to keep him from the Ghost but to attack the Ghost. And he did this while wearing a complete tragedian's outfit—full-bottomed wig, plumes and a cape. The outfit was the only complete thing about his performance because, like most of his successors, he cut the text drastically. When Garrick came on, he came on in elevator shoes and stole one of the Ghost's best lines. "O, horrible! O, horrible! most horrible!" Dr. Johnson thought Garrick was over the top, but most of the playgoing public concurred in the opinion that Garrick was unbeatable in the role.

As the eighteenth century gave way to the nineteenth, Kemble arrived and the romantic interpretation of Hamlet began to arrive with him. Hazlitt didn't think much of Kemble in the role. He thought he played it with a fixed and sullen gloom, but I think we recognize that gloom as the beginning of the romantic interpretation of Hamlet which has persisted almost down to our own day. Hazlitt didn't think much of Kean, either. He thought his performance was a succession of grand moments, but had no real human shape. Everybody else thought Kean was marvellously natural, especially in his appearance, and he *looked* like the Hamlet we know today—short hair, black clothes, white lace collar. And on they came—Macready, Barry Sullivan, Edwin Booth, whom some people thought was the ideal Hamlet but who had his thunder stolen by Irving—and the total effect of the nineteenth-century actor-managers was to establish Hamlet as the romantic, alienated outcast, the poet who perhaps couldn't write poetry but could certainly speak it, the man who was just too good for this world.

As the nineteenth century gave way to the twentieth, a truly revolutionary actor-manager arrived on the scene—Johnston Forbes-Robertson—revolutionary because he widened the focus of attention from the central character to the whole play, and never again was it possible to argue plausibly that the play was anything less than the miraculous sum of its parts. Nowadays we never think of any interpretation of the central character, no matter how brilliant—Gielgud's vividly mental, Olivier's vividly physical—as anything more than a contribution to the total character, just as we never think of any cut version, no matter how consistent within itself, as anything more than a contribution to the total play.

The world could go on changing unimaginably and Hamlet would still have everything to say to us. Whenever we hear of some new atrocity and wonder impotently what life is for, we always find that he got there ahead of us. Hamlet poses the eternal question of whether life is worth living. The answer that he appears to arrive at is that it isn't, but the way he says so makes us realize that it is. Hamlet has been given the creative vitality of Shakespeare himself. Even though robbed of will, he's still the embodiment of individuality. Hamlet is what it means to be alive. So all those actors were right, after all. Hamlet's tragedy really is a triumph. A prince of the imagination, he inherits his kingdom in eternity, even if Fortinbras inherits it on earth.

Boris Pasternak, who translated *Hamlet* into Russian, also wrote a famous poem in which Hamlet faces something even worse than his own doubts—a world in which his doubts are not permitted.

> Yet the order of the acts is planned,
> And there is no way back from the end.
> I am alone.

Pasternak wasn't the first, and probably won't be the last, to see Hamlet as the supreme symbol of liberty. As the doomed Prince of Denmark, Hamlet must act out his tragic fate, but as a mind he remains free. He fails in the outer world only because his inner world is so rich. Scorning necessity, he reflects upon his own existence—"In my mind's eye, Horatio." Hamlet is the human intelligence made universal, so he belongs to all of us. "For which of us," wrote Anatole France, addressing Hamlet, "does not resemble you in some way?" We're all like him because we all think, and it's because, on top of all its other qualities, its hero incarnates the dignity of human consciousness, that *Hamlet* is the greatest play by the greatest writer who ever lived.

The Listener, May 29, 1980; later included in
Even As We Speak, 2001

POSTSCRIPT

The above piece started life as a television script. I went on to write scores of them, and some of them, especially the voice-overs for my *Postcard* travel programmes, I count among my most careful writing. But as I got better at it, there was steadily less warrant for trying to boil the words out of their hard-won amalgam with the pictures. As experience accumulated, I learned to avoid delivering pieces to camera during the shoot, because that required a script too soon finalized. I preferred to write the whole commentary in the editing room, as a voice-over in which some of the most eloquent moments would consist of silence, because the pictures were doing the work. In the programme about *Hamlet*, the pictures hardly mattered. I stood in front of castles of the type that Shakespeare "must have" known about, and to illustrate the concept of Hamlet's university education I walked significantly around Cambridge. What I said sounds a lot less awkward on the page. I eventually reprinted the commentary as a delayed response to numerous written requests. People who had seen the programme wanted a copy of the script. Its flattered author was a long time realizing that their requests added up to damning proof that the visual aspects of the programme had been a waste of time. If they hadn't been, the requests would have been for a tape.

2003

CULTURE

AND

CRITICISM

27

F. R. LEAVIS IN AMERICA

With 150 pages of text devoted to only four pieces, *Lectures in America* by F. R. Leavis and Q. D. Leavis is far from being a collection of writings by-the-way. In spite of the ambling tone, perhaps too faithfully retained from its original lecture form, each piece is a distillation, rather than a dilution, of complexities of thought brought into being by one or the other of these two highly original minds and worked over for a long time: the book would take about four hours to read out, and took about four decades to think up. The first three pieces are general ones on the unity of culture, on Eliot and on Yeats: all these are by F. R. Leavis himself. The fourth and last piece, a fusion of two lectures, deals closely with *Wuthering Heights*, has four appendixes, and is composed by Q. D. Leavis. Reading from the back of the book to the front (there is no reason why you should, but it is revealing), you will proceed from criticism that opens and looks hard at a single book to criticism that closes books and gazes above and across them at the contemporary scene. The gaze is unfriendly. It is a brave, not a weak unfriendliness, but it is most unsettling. *Lectures in America* is a disturbing book, difficult to sum up and easy to distort, and it has mostly been reviewed favourably rather than well.

It is not that F. R. Leavis ranges beyond his reviewers' competence as literati, but that he ranges beyond their preparedness to discuss cultural issues as matters of life and death—of what life should be like, of what furthers it, what cheapens it and what defeats it. Although he has always made a point of disclaiming philosophical rigour (most specifically in the fine essay "Literary Criticism and Philosophy" in *The Common Pursuit*), he is a philosopher in the true sense, and has been recognized as such by all who have read him since he first began to work, in the intensity of their acceptances and rejections if not in their vocabulary. In Britain in this century Croce's old rule about the philosophical spirit has been obeyed: if it can find no home in the philosophy schools, it will descend to, and take up residence in, the nearest activity in which men are committing their whole understanding. As anyone capable of grasping the issues is well aware, in Britain the mental battles that matter, the battles which involve the intellectual passions, have for a long time now been fought out in the field of "literary criticism" in the first instance, with the result that literary criticism has constantly seemed, to those intent on providing it with habitable professional limits, to be getting above itself. The descent of scholarship to data processing they can just live with—jokes can be made, and there's no denying those machines are impressive. The ascent of criticism to philosophy, however, looks more damaging—and *is* more damaging, since diffidence is denied its due respect.

F. R. Leavis's objection to practising criticism in what he conceived to be a philosophical way was that criticism could not afford to be preoccupied with method. He could equally have said that *philosophy* could not afford to be preoccupied with method. As things have turned out, he has been far more free than professional philosophers to speak on issues. He has been able to identify the issues as they come up and go on to get them right, get them wrong or get them confused. This is the work that philosophy is bound to do or else pay the penalty of falling back upon the investigation of its own ways and means. When F. R. Leavis says that the English school should be the centre of the university (he says it again here, in the first lecture "Luddites? or There Is Only One Culture," a piece in which many often-heard themes return as in the last minutes of a *Ring* cycle rather scrappily conducted), the assertion sounds at first absurdly pretentious. But rephrase it in terms of his own intellectual commitment, say that the first concern of the university should be to create philosophers, and it makes, on a traditional view, more sense—while being even more subversive of the modern order as he characterizes that state, or tendency, of affairs. He might accept the victory of "the blind enlightened menace" (magnificent phrase) as inevitable, but he refuses to accept the inevitable as the good. The bravery of this stand remains to be admired even if one does not agree with his diagnosis of the present, his interpretation of the past or his premonition of the future.

The reinstatement of a truly embracing concept of culture; a reversal of the "alienating" tendency of industrialism and a restoration of the unity of work and purpose; the dismissal of the debilitating "leisure" concept—it probably can't be done. F. R. Leavis admits it probably can't be done but doesn't cease to press for it, to point to the danger even as the danger becomes an unstoppable reality. His enormously complicated (and always knottily expressed) view of historical change has been strong in so far as it has enabled him to give a clear account of the changing conditions of creativity, and weak in so far as it has slid towards pessimism—towards an impression, implicit in even his finest work, that the conditions of life are working now towards the utter defeat of the creative spirit. Britain's political continuity has perhaps saved him from a more thorough pessimism (that and his own temperament): like his equal in America, Edmund Wilson (for whom he seems to have had little time), he has benefited from an early disinclination to identify the coherence of culture with the political integrity of Europe, and his continuing rage is not to be equated with the resigned despair of the European panoptic scholars who compared the ruined present with the supposed unity of the past and forgivably reached the conclusion that the thread was at last broken. As he is once again at pains to avow, he is not to be saddled with the advocacy of a return to the past:

> We [he and Denys Thompson in *Culture and Environment*] didn't recall this organic kind of relation of work to life in any nostalgic spirit, as something to be restored or to take a melancholy pleasure in lamenting; but by way of emphasizing that it was *gone*, with the organic community it belonged to, not to be restored in any foreseeable future.

And as well as not being nostalgic about the wheelwright's shop, he is of course even more emphatically not misty-eyed about the disappearance of a supposedly integrated Christendom. As a consequence, F. R. Leavis is not vulnerable to an attack on his bases in the past. Nevertheless he has a view of the flow of history in recent times which is open to attack. He sees the tide of mediocrity, of second-rate work and inhuman charity, rising ever higher. He consistently underestimates the capacity of the productive spirit, both creative and critical, to survive and flourish, and faced with the spectacle of a swarm of seaside trippers listening to pop on transistor radios he reacts in the very tones of Malcolm Muggeridge, his phrases differing only in their cost per word. Beethoven's name coming up, F. R. Leavis does not suggest that these people would have listened to his music once upon a time, but he does suggest that some kind of conspiracy, some inexorable rigging of the circumstances, is getting in the road of their doing so now. Well of course it is, but what are the factors? This is where we have only the famous tone of voice, and not the much more important clarity of statement, to answer us. Whether nostalgically or not, the past is vaguely invoked—an organic unity then that is not an organic unity now. Standards. Life. For life. But suppose that culture were one factor in a plurality, had always been and must always be one factor in a plurality, ranged then, now and for always *against forces that are ranged against it*. Suppose that, and you will quickly see that when we ask a man of F. R. Leavis's stature to beware of pessimism, we are not asking him to embrace optimism. The choice is not between pessimism and optimism, but between both these things and truth.

It is no more polite but a lot less trivial to attribute to a calculated pessimism, rather than to a quirk of temperament, those recurring themes in his work which do most to cheapen the level of discussion and whose wholesale adoption infallibly marks the more boneheaded of his disciples. The dread "modish literary world" is with us again in this book, once again working in far-flung, intricately connected conspiracies across modish literary London for the downfall of standards and against life. Well, there's something in it, but you'd be amazed to know how often the singleness of utterance among mediocrities is to be explained not by their clubbing up but by their being mediocrities. F. R. Leavis is unable to give a clear account of the second-rate or to show that he has any idea of how culture needs to be staffed and run by differing orders of intellect in proper relationship to one another. Pessimistically, he is always assuming that the gangs are increasing their grip, buying their way to power with cocktails and flattery or fingering the independent operator for a quick, lethal dose of "misrepresentation." Even more nebulous and rapidly fatal than the modish literary world is the much-feared social world. "Eliot's intelligence doesn't show to advantage in the social world. . . . I don't think I need spend time over shades and transitions of meaning." Of course you don't. Your audience is already rippling with knowing laughter and nodding agreement, just as it did at Eliot. Or perhaps you do.

This shying away from detail, while at the same time giving a tremendous air of having the social realities well weighed up, leaves the problem signposted but invisible, like a whale between death and destruction. In fact it is not possible for life, in the past, the present or the future, to offer us the example of great men moving in a milieu which is equal to them: if it were, it would not be a milieu, and the men would not be great. It's sad but necessary to say that F. R. Leavis's view of society (if something so subtle can be designated by that term) is very seriously hurt by pessimism, to the point that his feeling for language deserts him and actual bromides—not just characteristic turns of phrase—turn up in a prose otherwise free of dead talk.

But as for the actual working-class people who *can* be regarded as characteristic, it's not anything in the nature of moral indignation one feels towards *them*, but shame, concern and apprehension at the way our civilization has let them down—left them to enjoy a "high standard of living" in a vacuum of disinheritance.

Well, our civilization can only have "let them down" if it was at some time possible for our civilization to have seen and wilfully neglected to pursue a better course. But for "our civilization" or anybody else's such a choice never reveals itself as a choice at the crucial time. Also (and this is a cliché, but the point being made here is that in this passage he let himself in for it) those ideas of disinheritance are handed down from above. In reality (and reality includes *all* the passions that drive society) the transition from that condition of "inheritance" (it probably means "organic kind of relation of work to life") to the "high standard of living" is a neutral one. As a neutral transition, it can be analysed infinitely, or at any rate down to the level of the individuals concerned. But once judged pessimistically, it ceases to yield information about the present *or* the past. History acquires a downward curve. It becomes possible to write a sentence beginning, "The problem is to reestablish an effective educated public . . ." Just "establish" would have done.

The essay on Eliot is called "Eliot's Classical Standing" and leaves nothing to be desired except a few pages on *The Waste Land*, which was bypassed to save time but which might very well be treated in future editions of what really is a superb essay—no, lecture; one forgets. Not many lectures, and few enough essays, go so far towards tracing the main course of a creative life while never ceasing to emphasize the impossibility of simplifying it. When speaking of Eliot's poetry, F. R. Leavis isolates his concept of significance by marking the difference between the "sincere" and the "social" Eliot—the "social" being whatever force it was that induced him to infiltrate superstition into *The Cocktail Party*. He sees Eliot's creative career as "a sustained, heroic and indefatigably resourceful quest of a profound sincerity of the most difficult kind," a quest which finds realization in "one astonishing major work" (*Four Quartets*). In fine, all Eliot's poetry can be read as one longish poem getting, aberrations aside, progressively better. This is not a startling conclusion to reach—the quotable judgements in the lecture sound quite ordinary—but the way of reaching it is wholly original and will have to be contended with from now on. The measure of the "sincerity" is daringly made dependent on subtly implied estimates of the poet's personality, the poet in his creative manhood having been regarded by the lecturer as a polar intellect over a period of decades.

Whether or not in discussing that necessity of fully human life which is wanting—discussing as Eliot evokes it that which might meet human spiritual need—one finds oneself dealing in Christian theology depends on who one is. I myself think I am paying a high tribute to the genius of the poet when I express my conviction that as literary critic one had better not find oneself doing that—and that it needs literary criticism to do justice to Eliot.

By thus leaving a theological approach out of the question he makes room for judgements upon Eliot's *personal* truth to the spiritual needs and lacks he presumes to deduce from a long contemporaneous study of the work in its development. It would be interesting to see how steadily these judgements would hold if all the major work, and not just a few selected passages, were to come under close discussion. But even in this restricted space, the approach makes possible some revolutionary statements, as when he abruptly decides to "risk saying crudely that in relation to his own quest, Eliot over-valued what Dante had to offer him." The inference is that Shakespeare would have been better than Dante at helping Eliot in what "should" have been of importance: to deal with "the creative relation between the sexes in all its significance." To come to grips with the implications of this short but heavily scored line of argument it is not only necessary to know exactly what you think of Eliot, it is necessary to know exactly what you think of Dante.

"Yeats: The Problem and the Challenge" isn't up to the Eliot piece for several reasons. To begin with, it is too restrictive: "Sailing to Byzantium," "Byzantium" and "Among School Children" are the only qualifiers for the title of "fully achieved thing." This *has* to be wrong. In outflanking the dreaded "fully equipped commentators" F. R. Leavis is concerned with identifying and isolating the major poems (not just the many Yeats poems "worth having") which do not require "that one should bring up any special knowledge or instructions from outside." But here one of his most valuable strains of thought, the one which has always been able to evaluate academic pressures and characterize rampant scholarship as a cultural threat, has been mightily over-asserted. Yeats's poems explain each other where they do not explain themselves, and it is possible to go a long way towards a full understanding of his work without ever once opening any ancillary volume by him or anybody else: his intention of writing a magic book of the arts was fulfilled.

F. R. Leavis's whole argument—it is intricately developed—about the extra-poetical in Yeats could as well be detached from that poet and attached to, say, Eliot—in relation to whom, it seems plain, some *very* extra-poetical considerations are gone into in the lecture next door. Looking at the two essays in conjunction, it seems likely that such considerations are rationalized when admiration is total and developed into a limiting commentary when it is not.

> It is characteristic of Yeats to have had no centre of unity, and to have been unable to find one. The lack is apparent in his solemn proundings about the Mask and the Anti-self, and in the related schematic elaborations.

Not the same, apparently, as being solemn about the Etruscans.

Throughout this piece on Yeats, the appreciation of the few poems does not link up with the limiting of the many: the appreciation and the limiting do not spring from the one impulse, despite the vigour with which singleness of viewpoint is asserted. It can be added, perhaps impertinently, that this lecture, like the others, contains several endearingly familiar turns of speech and all on its own offers us one of the master's most memorable put-downs.

I remember vividly the impact of *The Tower*, of which I have a first edition, acquired in the way in which I have acquired such first editions as I have had—I bought it when it first came out.

What a burn! Yet here again you see what he is driving at; rejecting the fashionable, recalling the essential.

I don't believe in any "literary values," and you won't find me talking about them; the judgements the literary critic is concerned with are judgements about life.

When a man offers "the friction, the sense of pregnant arrest, which goes with active realizing thought and the taking of a real charged meaning," he is not offering something he will be honoured for in any conventional way. But as a living force in the plurality of society his recognition is assured, and his name becomes a known quality. *Lectures in America* helps to define that quality even more closely.

Times Literary Supplement, 1969

POSTSCRIPT

Trying to get Queenie Leavis out of the road in one line was the biggest single *bêtise* I committed in that period. It was worse than a crime: it was a mistake, because the old lady boiled over and went for me. She wanted to know why someone so obviously unqualified had been sent to judge her work. She was right about that, although not completely. I had indeed not read much of the recent scholarship on the subject of her lecture, "Wuthering Heights"; but I had read *Wuthering Heights* recently enough to wonder if she had ever read it at all, in the sense that ordinary mortals do. The apparent premise of her lecture was that nobody had ever understood *Wuthering Heights* before she picked it up. I thought she was crazy. I was just reluctant to say so. To venture a few strictures about her husband's share of *Lectures in America* had already taken all the courage I could muster.

Though a few chips had appeared in his plinth by that stage, F. R. Leavis's prestige was still mighty, so it was quite standard procedure to screw up the tone of awe a notch or two when going against him. Also I retained, as I still retain, a high regard for some of his early work. But I had never thought him much of a judge of poetry. To my mind his praise of T. S. Eliot was decisively undermined by his often-stated conviction that Ronald Bottrall was Eliot's successor, and I couldn't see the point of his insistence that Shelley was not Shakespeare: it wasn't as if anybody had asserted the contrary. On top of these particular misjudgements there was his pervasive indulgence in the language of calumny. Special venom was reserved for fellow critics who had arrived at his conclusions before he did. When he finally decided that Dickens was a great writer, he took particular care to vilify any other critics who had ever said so: they hadn't been right in the right way. He treated D. H. Lawrence the way the scholiasts had once treated Virgil, as a voodoo talisman. I already thought that there were totalitarian tendencies in all this but had not yet found the nerve to say so: hence the strained tone, of respect trying to conceal repulsion. When I called his view of history "enormously complicated," the "enormously" was the tip-off. I not only didn't really believe it, I thought his view of history was the opposite of complicated—i.e., actively simplistic and misleading. But I didn't yet dare to say what I thought, partly because not enough people seemed to be thinking it. Later on, with the back-up provided by having absorbed the life's work of real historians such as Pieter Geyl and Golo Mann, I found the moxie to declare, instead of just hint, that Leavis's historiographic rigmarole was a religious dogma in disguise.

The Metropolitan Critic, 1994

28

A WHOLE GANG OF NOISE:
SUSAN SONTAG

Despite the relative civility with which *Against Interpretation* was greeted, Susan Sontag's reputation in this country has never really recovered from her first disastrous appearance with Jonathan Miller in an episode of *Monitor* which could have been called "Captain Eclectic and Thinkwoman Meet Public Ridicule." The medium was the massacre: scarcely anybody came out of the programme with prestige intact and Miss Sontag was immediately incorporated into the British intelligentsia's typology of dreadful examples. Her appearances in print—a less damaging medium revealing neither her self-assurance rivalling Ethel Merman's nor her nonstop ponderosity which rendered even Miller unable to get a word in edgeways—have by now done something to correct this bad impression. In fact some of the home guard one might normally expect to be more careful when handling imported brainpower have started to overcorrect. "She has all the qualities of an excellent critic," avers A. Alvarez in an unwise statement which the publishers are now employing on the jacket of *Styles of Radical Will*: "she is intelligent, perceptive, and impressively well informed." Can't agree. She certainly possesses the qualities named, but conspicuously lacks the one quality every critic must have and an excellent critic must have in abundance: the capacity not to be carried away by a big idea.

Except for the two political essays in the book, one of them being the truly superlative "Trip to Hanoi," her work is customarily marked by the use of a half-argued, hugely magnetic central notion which attracts examples to its surface so quickly and in such quantity that its outlines are immediately obscured. Sainte-Beuve once said that Montaigne sounds like one continuous epigram but Miss Sontag, like Harold Rosenberg most of the time and Hugh Kenner all the time, sounds like one continuous aphorism. The opportunity to stop the flow and ponder is rarely offered. When it is, usually by an overglib employment of a "thus" or a "nothing less," the results yielded by a good hard think are seldom happy. Her long essay on pornography, for example, is an impressive against-interpretation job of getting facts in and prejudices out, but even in this field, where she seems to have read absolutely everything, the urge to generalize blocks the way of ordinary observation: you need only have read Restif de la Bretonne, let alone the modern pornographers, to realize that her statements about the use of speech in pornography are wide of the mark. Similarly in her essay on Godard it's the little things that bring on the big objections and the eventual wondering whether the thesis really is a thesis. She briefly notes that Godard's handling of torture scenes is pretty sketchy. Card-carrying Godard fans have long since realized that they must defend him at this point or lose all: *they* say that the master's imagination is so exquisite he can't sully it by trying to represent (or *redeem*, to employ the dusty vocabulary of Kracauer which Miss Sontag puts herself on record as admiring) reality in such things. But Miss Sontag doesn't feel bound to defend him since what she is postponing is not interpretation but judgement.

Wherein lies the fallacy and this lady's besetting intellectual vice — because judgement is not some higher brain function you turn on after a set period of omnivorous data-gathering, it's a process which should be continuously operative and in the critic *is* continuously operative. Thus (there, now I'm doing it) her contention that Godard needs to be regarded in the totality of his films is easily countered by the contention that you will gain no wisdom from a fool's utterance by cancelling the rest of your appointments and listening to him all day.

Miss Sontag attempts to break free of the historical burden and ready herself for the new but her attempt, fulsomely documented and exhaustingly fluent, doesn't alter the fact that the historical burden is only burdensome *historically*: aesthetically the giants of the past are our contemporaries and must be competed with as if they were still around — we've changed, but we haven't changed as much as we *haven't* changed, and Miss Sontag unconsciously concedes this point by being vague about when Modern Man actually got started — i.e., stopped being the old kind.

There is great play here with Hegel as the last of the religious philosophers: it appears that his materialistic component got picked up and carried forward but his spiritual component got neglected, which only goes
to show that Miss Sontag hasn't made much headway with Italian idealism. None of her broad arguments about modern trends and currents of
thought is very trustworthy and there is a tendency to identify the unholy
American mess with a crisis in Western civilization, a notion which ought
to be resisted. The best and only solid part of the book is "Trip to Hanoi"
but it should quickly be added that you only have to write one thing as
good as that to earn a name. Here for once her prose has grace, her argument clarity and her whole literary personality a human presence.

The Listener, 1969

POSTSCRIPT

Susan Sontag deserved rather better than this: after all, it was she who
wrote "Trip to Hanoi," not I. But the really reprehensible thing I did then
that I wouldn't have done later was to go along with the bad press she had
received after her notorious *Monitor* appearance. It certainly was a deli-
ciously absurd moment in television history when Ms. Sontag, or Miss
Sontag as she then would have been called, turned up at Andy Warhol's
celebrated Factory to interview him and spent half an hour of precious
screen-time examining the aesthetic implications of his failure to keep
the appointment. She might have discussed the moral implications with
some profit—he had been vilely rude, and we all might have benefited
from having had that pointed out. Jonathan Miller no doubt regretted
later on, in less indulgent times, that he had helped his protégée to drop
herself in it. The publicity that accrued stuck to her for years. But since
all publicity is binding publicity, and television publicity is intensely so,
the task of the critic is to help sort out the real person from the image that
has trapped him, or in this case her.

The real Sontag was, and is, a very clever woman—and a brave one,
as I found out much later when I met her in New York and heard her on
the subject of Sarajevo, where she had taken considerable risks to stage
Waiting for Godot in circumstances that even Samuel Beckett might have
found too appropriately eschatological. If she was carried away by big
ideas, at least she had the courage to speculate over a wide cultural range,

and often to original effect. An enthusiasm for the collected cinematic works of Jean-Luc Godard looked less ludicrous at the time, when the later films had not yet arrived to sow irreversible suspicion even in his most unquestioning fans that the earlier films might have been trivial all along. The sceptical Alvarez wrote a Fontana Modern Masters booklet about Godard, and it was far less corrosive than Jonathan Miller's companion volume on Marshall McLuhan. "Can't agree" was an over-colloquial, and hence under-spontaneous, way of saying "I can't agree." Wouldn't do it now. Sontag's empirical acuteness would have shone more brightly for being less veiled in whirling conceptual fluff. She wrote the way Salome danced, but the head she wanted was yours. Her relentless intellectualism asked to be appreciated uncritically for its aesthetic impact, with the inevitable corollary that if you couldn't take it you left it alone. She had, however, more staying power than her impatient young critics gave her credit for, and when the time came her proclivity for treating any subject as grist to her mill made her an indispensable commentator on the disease that struck her but found it so hard to strike her down. Nowadays, when I re-read her early work, I can see that strength in embryo, waiting to be born and flourish. It is a commonplace that books have their histories. It is less commonly noticed that the people who write them have their histories too, so that you can't quite know why they are like that at the start until you see what they do later.

The Metropolitan Critic, 1994

29

GERMAINE GREER:
GETTING MARRIED LATER

Germaine Greer's first and very considerable book *The Female Eunuch* drops into the intelligentsia's radar accompanied by scores of off-putting decoy noise-sources: a panicky response is virtually guaranteed. Granada Publishing (the command group for MacGibbon and Kee) have done an impressive job with the highbrow press, and weeks before publication date Dr. Greer was already well known.

If this makes it seem that the reviewer is too concerned with media reactions and media values, let it be made clear that there is little chance of any other kind of reactions and values operating in the present instance. Germaine Greer is a storm of images; has already been promoted variously as Germaine de Staël, Fleur Fenton Cowles, Rosa Luxemburg and Beatrice Lillie; and at the time of writing needs only a few more weeks' exposure in order to reoccupy the corporeally vacant outlines of Lou Andreas-Salomé, George Sand, Marie von Thurn und Taxis-Hohenlohe and Marjorie Jackson (the Lithgow Flash). Media-hype is never sadder than when something decent is at the centre of the fuss. These forebodings might be wrong, and there could just be a slim chance that *The Female Eunuch* will be appreciated on its merits. But I wouldn't count on it.

The book's merits are of a high order. It possesses a fine, continuous flow of angry power which both engenders and does much to govern the speed-wobble of its logical progression; it sets out an adventurous analysis of social detail which does much to offset the triteness of its theoretical assumptions; and all in all it survives its flaws of style, falsities of assessment and excesses of sentimentality to present an argument of terrific polemical force. "Now as before, women must refuse to be meek and guileful, for truth cannot be served by dissimulation. Women who fancy that they manipulate the world by pussy power and gentle cajolery are fools. It is time for the demolition to begin." It's a revolutionary position from first to last, and a lot of people, many of them ladies, are going to be interested in taking the sting out of it, principally by institutionalizing the authoress. A six-foot knock-out freak don with three degrees and half a dozen languages who can sing, dance, act, write and turn men to stone with an epigram—what a target for the full media treatment!

Meanwhile the book's content demands summary and analysis, neither of which is easy to give. *The Female Eunuch* begins with a lushly overwritten dedication to various female companions in the struggle and ends with twenty pages of dauntingly erudite notes. In between are four main sections of argument and one minor section: "Body," "Soul," "Love," "Hate" and (the minor one) "Revolution," which last I found to be mainly rhetoric. Of the main sections, the first one, "Body," is the most ill-considered, so it's rather a pity that it sets the terms of the book as well as the tone. She argues very well in the "Soul" section that the supposedly ineluctable differences of emotional and intellectual make-up between the sexes are imposed by stereotype and are consequently alterable, if not eliminable and indeed reversible. There was not the slightest need to peg this argument back to the "Body" section and there pronounce that the differences of physical shape between men and women are likewise metaphysically determined. It makes for a poor start and surely a false one. The anthropological, ethnological, biological and chromosomal evidence adduced is scarcely convincing, and the notes given for this section are relatively thin—relative, that is, to the mass of reading which has been drawn upon to substantiate the arguments of the subsequent sections. The import of this opening section really amounts to the notion that women and men are more similar than they are different, which is unarguable, like its converse: like its converse it is merely a chosen emphasis, providing a preliminary to argument. It is one thing to say that "the 'normal' sex roles that we learn to play from our infancy are no more natural than the antics of a transvestite," since that deals with the psychology of the business. It is another thing to say that in order "to approximate those shapes and attitudes which are considered normal and desirable, both sexes deform themselves, justifying the process by referring to the primary, genetic difference between the sexes." (Shapes? The *whole* shape? Everybody? All the time?) And it is a hell of a thing to say both those things in two succeeding sentences.

"But of 48 chromosomes only one is different: on this difference we base a complete separation of male and female, pretending as it were that all 48 are different." Only if we are clowns. What we actually do is something far more insidious: realizing that differences based on physique are not seriously worth considering, we keep everything on a mental plane, and attribute to women intellectual virtues we do not possess, in order to palm off a mass of responsibilities we don't propose to handle. The same trick works in reverse: women flatter men in much the same way. The result, until recently, has been a workable (I don't say just) division of labour. A good deal of the woman's share (I don't say a fair share) of the labour centres on the fact that she has the babies—which is where the physical difference really does come in, or did. After Miss Greer has cleaned up the question of subsidiary physical differences (it appears that women wouldn't have so much subcutaneous fat if they didn't leave so much skin exposed on things like, for example, legs) and gets on to the social forms and structures which are governed by this one remaining, glaring physical difference, the book picks up. Because she instantly realizes that if women are to be free, the reproduction of the race is the rap they have to beat.

All the ensuing major sections of *The Female Eunuch* really amount to a brilliant attack on marriage and the psychological preparation for it, and on the nuclear family which is the result of it. This attack traces all the correct connections, from Barbara Cartland's powdered cleavage to the aspirin industry that thrives on frustration, from the doomed cosmetic ritual to the furtive adultery, and from the mother who sacrifices everything to the son who is grateful for nothing. The case has seldom been so well argued. One misses the wit that Dr. Greer wields in conversation, but the headlong rush of mordant disenchantment is all there. The book would be worth the price merely to read her anatomizing of the advice columns in the women's magazines—an effort comparable in approach (and, one hopes, in effect) to Gabriella Parca's masterly *Le Italiane si confessano*.

Passages of sympathetic fury like this constitute the book's solid worth: there are enough of them to establish Dr. Greer as an individual voice in popular social debate for some time to come. But suppose we take her condemnation of the received relationship between the sexes for granted—what alternatives does she offer? On this point, the book runs into trouble.

On a practical level—the level of *likelihoods*, of what might conceivably be brought about—Dr. Greer recommends little that you will not find equally well put (and put equally passionately) in the prefaces to *Man and Superman* and *Getting Married*. If the ideas of female freedom, liberation from the "feminine" stereotype and the economic key to sexual equality strike the new semi-intelligentsia as revolutionary, it will only be because of the thoroughness with which touch has been lost with the old radical tradition. Here as elsewhere in the wide spectrum of the currently fashionable revolutionary spirit, it's the theoretical atavism of the practical recommendations which strikes the concerned reader as extraordinary. One gets the sense, after a while, that living philosophical insights curve away from history to re-enter it later on as psychodrama, posturings and myth. Perhaps Pareto's diagrams on this subject were correct after all, and something like this has to happen before ideas take the form of action: but it is very eerie to be an onlooker. When Dr. Greer conjures up a loose-knit, "organic" family, with several footloose fathers for the organic kids, and sets the imagined scene in Italy, we smile for two reasons. Not just because of the ill-judged setting (the courtyard would be stiff with the khaki Alfas of the *carabinieri di pronto intervento* before you could get the toys unpacked), but because the idea itself has already been and gone—the grass grew over it long ago in some abandoned Owenite phalanx, the kids grew up, moved out and went square.

But just because ideas like this have been and gone, it doesn't mean that the wished-for condition couldn't come again, and this time to stay. The question is: for how many? So far, only for a few. And for how long? Up to now, usually not long. The problem of substituting individual initiative for received social forms can be solved, but only at the cost of an extraordinary application of energy, and usually only in conditions of privilege.

The coming generations are obviously going to get many of the privileges that the old socialists fought for, prepared the ground for, but saw distorted, half-realized and even abandoned. This is one of the reasons why the old radical hands are intolerant of the new bloods: the new bloods lack the intellectual preparation, the realization of continuous difficulty. The main message of the preface to *Getting Married* was that no matter how much she needed to be free, a woman needed to marry in order to protect herself socio-economically. Shaw had no illusions about what most marriages were. But equally he had no illusions about the currently feasible alternatives. The main message of *The Female Eunuch* is that the nuclear family is a menace, that the feminine role is a poisonous sham and that the farce ought to be wound up. If this position now looks tenable, it's not because Dr. Greer has a capacity for analysis superior to Shaw's, but because the socio-economics of the matter have changed. The opportunities for making a claim to individuality have vastly increased. But one can recognize this fact without being seduced by it—without forgetting that the benefits of living a liberated life are probably not to be measured on the scale of happiness. To do Dr. Greer credit in this regard, it is not an easier life she is asking for, but a more difficult, more honourable one.

She does not gloss over the fact that the alternatives will take a lot of guts. In my view, though, she seriously overrates the reserves of creative initiative that people have to draw upon. There is a sound assessment of their personal likelihoods behind the instinct of most people to settle for a quiet, unadventurous life. It's unusual for even highly gifted people to be original, to express a "unique" self, in more than just a few areas. Dr. Greer argues that the female state of mind is enforced by the stereotype. She doesn't consider that the stereotype might have grown out of the state of mind—doesn't consider, that is, that the state of mind might be logically prior, historically evolved out of a steadily reinforced realization that most women, like most men, are not heroic.

Like most of the recent revolutionary ideologists, Dr. Greer glibly assumes that it is desirable for everybody to be not only fully aware of their condition, but fully politicized. This is to overrate the amount of originality a civilization can sustain, while simultaneously underrating the mass of people in it, whose ordinary affairs should rightly be regarded as consumingly complex and self-justifying, rather than as a poor substitute for the life of adventure which the genuine originals supposedly enjoy. Dr. Greer brilliantly uncovers the hoaxes governing ordinary feminine subservience, but always with the air that the millennium will arrive once these poor dumb ladies realize they are being conned. What just might happen, though, if the polemic message of her book gets through to a wide range of women, is something better: a further measure of equality. Getting a square shake is not as exciting to look at as blazing your way to immortality, but it counts.

The Female Eunuch states the case for altering all the conditions that leave women less free than men. In doing this, it creates several kinds of confusion about the amount and nature of the freedom conceivably available to either. But perhaps the case needs to be wrongly stated in order to take effect, to convince the next lot of guileless women seemingly predestined for a life of frustration and cheap dreams that there's no need to go through with it—you can just walk away from it, and hang loose. Getting married later, rather than sooner, would be a good start.

The Observer, 1970

POSTSCRIPT (I)

Considering the provocation, which included the unsettling spectacle of a contemporary becoming world famous overnight, this piece could have been worse. I still think it encapsulates the only possible balanced view both of what Germaine Greer was pronouncing to be necessary and of what she could reasonably hope to play a part in bringing about—two things that needed to be seen in strict relationship to each other. The reference to the Italian feminist Gabriella Parca was no mere window-dressing: in Italy, women's rights were a serious and sometimes deadly matter to those wives who could not hope to divorce even the most violent husbands. I would still write the last sentence the same way but nowadays would be careful to add that nature doesn't agree, and that feminism's reluctance to admit its absolute dependence on advanced technology was, and remains, its single greatest weakness. There is no natural order worth going back to. A just society is well worth working for, but any suggestion that it won't be a version of the modern industrial society we already have can only be moonshine.

The Metropolitan Critic, 1994

POSTSCRIPT (II)

In June 1946, the distinguished Argentinian woman of letters Victoria Ocampo visited the Nuremberg tribunal and took meticulous notes of what she saw in the auditorium. What she didn't see was any women. The absence of women among the accused Nazi hierarchs, she concluded, was all the more reason why there should have been some among the judges. It is a measure of the symbolic status deservedly attained by Germaine Greer that you can't read such a pregnant statement without thinking of her. Outside Latin America, few among even the most literate people have heard of Victoria Ocampo. In the whole world, few among even the least literate have not heard of Germaine Greer. At this distance it is hard to imagine what she must have been like before she was famous. I was there before it happened, and can only say that it was no surprise when it did. Her powers of expression were always bound to require the biggest stage on offer. In full flight of conversation she commanded a spontaneity of outrageous image that left any listening male writer ready to give up his pen—the Freudian implications are fully appropriate—so it was a foregone conclusion that if she ever wrote the same way she spoke she would stun the world. That was the key to her: her fearless, vaulting fluency was the embodiment of the energetic originality that she generously believed was ready to break out in all women, if only they could storm the walls society had put up to keep it in. Other women's liberationists merely had views, which they expressed more or less well. Germaine Greer expressed a capacity for life. As a consequence, time spent on analysing her equally startling capacity to contradict herself was time wasted. Another false trail was to look for the source of her inspiration in the rock culture of the 1960s. It might seem fustian to say so now, but the truth about the rock culture was that it was male chauvinist to the core: if anything, she reacted against it, a Janis Joplin without the heroin habit and with every talent except for being a victim.

Australia's very own Queen Christina had precursors among males who despised bourgeois conformity from the haughty viewpoint of the aristocratic aesthete. There was a whole tradition of them: men like de Tocqueville and Ortega were merely the most illustrious. But the man who counted was Byron, with whom she had a love affair that defied death. When you consider the position, ambition and achievement of gifted women in the Romantic era, you are getting close. The emergent Germaine Greer was neither of her time nor ahead of it: she was a hundred and fifty years too late. She was, and is, a Romantic visionary whose dream of universal female liberation can never come true, because the dream of universal male liberation can never come true either. For most people, conformity is a blessing, conferred by a society which has been centuries in the making, and to which the alternative is a slaughterhouse. Most people are not artists, and to imagine that they might be is the only consistent failure of her remarkable imagination.

Reliable Essays, 2001

30

THE METROPOLITAN CRITIC

Edmund Wilson writes in the 1957 chapter of *Upstate*:

> Looking out from my window on the third floor, I saw the change made
> here by autumn in the landscape and the atmosphere: they become dis-
> tinctly more serious, Nature begins to warn us, reassuming her august
> authority; the luxury of summer is being withdrawn.

In context, this passage carries many times the weight of any ordinary
nature-notes: the book is already half over, a splitting head of steam has
been built up and the reader is by now in no doubt that the luxury of
summer is being withdrawn from the writer himself, from the historical
district in which he writes, from all the artists he has ever personally
known and from the America which he has for so long chronicled and
which he is now ceasing even to distrust—*Upstate* shivers with the portent of an advancing ice-cap. Wilson's monumental curiosity and zest of
mind have not grown less, but by now they are like Montaigne's, exiled
within their own country and awaiting, without real hope, a better age
which will know how to value them. Self-confidence remains, but confidence in one's function ebbs; one's books do not seem to have been
much use; the public weal has proved itself an illusion and private life is
running out of time. "C'est icy un livre de bonne foy, lecteur," wrote
Montaigne, dampening the reader's ardour.

Il t'advertit dez l'entree, que ie ne m'y suis proposé aulcune fin, que domestique et privee: ie n'y ay eu nulle consideration de ton service, ny de ma gloire; mes forces ne sont pas capables d'un tel dessein.

Just so long as we understand each other.

Wilson's tone is similarly self-sufficient. "The knowledge that death is not so far away," he writes in 1963,

that my mind and emotions and vitality will soon disappear like a puff of smoke, has the effect of making earthly affairs seem unimportant and human beings more and more ignoble. It is harder to take human life seriously, including one's own efforts and achievements and passions.

That was the year in which he was writing *The Cold War and the Income Tax*—a profound growl of dissatisfaction about owing the United States government a swathe of back taxes which it would only have wasted on building and dropping bombs if he had handed it over. Dealings with the revenue men were prolonged and wearying, making a general disappointment with life understandable. In 1966 things were going better, but his view of existence didn't much lighten. To go with his Kennedy Freedom Medal he was given a $1,000 award by the American Academy of Arts and Sciences and a $5,000 National Book Award, but he found himself feeling let down rather than puffed up. "They make me feel that I am now perhaps finished, stamped with some sort of approval and filed away. . . ." He is hard on himself, and no softer on humanity as a whole. "Reading the newspapers, and even the world's literature, I find that I more and more feel a boredom with and even scorn for the human race." In such ways his darkening mood is overtly stated, but what gives it power—and makes *Upstate* such an elegiac and at times unmanning book—is the way in which the selectivity of his impressions presents picture after picture of decay, confusion and loss. Talcottville, N.Y., is presented as a last vestige of the old, hopeful America, and Wilson—not hiding or even sheltering, just waiting—takes up residence there each summer to find that the new and vengeful America has always moved a bit closer. Not that it matters much any more.

By the end of the book we're a long way from the mood in which Wilson first evoked Talcottville, in his "The Old Stone House" essay of

1933, later collected in *The American Earthquake*. In the first place, that essay recalled the hopes of the New Englanders who had grown sick of narrowness and were all for pushing on into the realm of unlimited opportunity:

> I can feel the relief myself of coming away from Boston to these first uplands of the Adirondacks, where discarding the New England religion but still speaking the language of New England, the settlers found limitless space. They were a part of the new America, now forever for a century on the move.

The thrill of the great American experiment is still there in the writing, and even though this old essay was just as disenchanted as the new book is, the disenchantment worked in reverse: Talcottville was the opposite of a refuge, representing a past that needed to be escaped from, not returned to.

Thirty years or so later, in *Upstate*, he is cricking his neck to get back to it, but it is too late. Material progress has already made its giant strides. Juvenile delinquents and uproarious bikers maraud and destroy. The John Birch Society slaps up flagrant stickers. Treasured windows on which poet friends have inscribed verses with a diamond pen are shattered in his absence. The Sunday *New York Times* is too heavy for him to carry. There is a spider in the bathtub of a motel. An old acquaintance, Albert Grubel, keeps him abreast of the ever-escalating car-crash statistics. His daughter Helena grows up and starts having car-crashes of her own. In 1963 he finds out that he has for all this time been living virtually on top of a SAC air base, and is therefore slap in the middle of a prime target area. By the end of the book there is a distinct possibility that a four-lane highway will be constructed a few inches from his front door.

The detail is piled on relentlessly, and if there were nothing else working against it, then *Upstate* would be a dark book indeed. But several things stop it being disabling. First, there are revelations of the Wilsonian character, as when he faces the bikers and asks them why they can't ride on the highway instead of around his house, or when he argues about iambic pentameters with Nabokov (who insists that Lear's "Never, never, never, never never" is iambic), or when he tells Mike Nichols that Thurber is not alone in lacking self-assurance and that he, Wilson, often gets up at four o'clock in the morning to read old reviews of his books. In bits and pieces like these there is enough singularity and sheer quirkiness to keep things humming.

Second, there is evidence of the Wilsonian curiosity, as when he deepens his knowledge of the county's history, or when he becomes interested in the founding and the subsequent fate of the old Oneida community. Wilson can't stop learning things, and it's worth remembering at this point that the curious information which crops up in the book is only the topmost molecule of the outermost tip of the iceberg. In the period covered by *Upstate* (1950–1970), Wilson was producing exhaustively prepared books like *The Shock of Recognition* and *Patriotic Gore*, breaking into new cultures with books like *The Scrolls from the Dead Sea*, *Apologies to the Iroquois* and *O Canada*, turning out important investigatory pamphlets like *The Cold War and the Income Tax* and *The Fruits of the MLA* (a crucially important attack on boondoggling academicism which has yet to be published in Britain) and editing *A Prelude* and the second and third in his series of literary chronicles, *The Shores of Light* and *The Bit Between My Teeth*—the first, *Classics and Commercials*, having appeared in 1950.

Only the European panoptic scholars come near matching Wilson for learning, and for sheer range of critical occupation there is no modern man to match him, not even Croce. If *Upstate* tends to give the impression that his wonted energy now only faintly flickers, the reader needs to remind himself sharply that the mental power in question is still of an order sufficient to illuminate the average city. Seemingly without effort, Wilson dropped *A Piece of My Mind* (1957) somewhere into the middle of all this hustle and bustle, and in the chapter entitled "The Author at Sixty" announced:

> I have lately been coming to feel that, as an American, I am more or less in the eighteenth century—or, at any rate, not much later than the early nineteenth. . . . I do not want any more to be bothered with the kind of contemporary conflicts that I used to go out to explore. I make no attempt to keep up with the younger American writers; and I only hope to have the time to get through some of the classics I have never read. Old fogeyism is comfortably closing in.

Taking him at his word on this last point, most critics and reviewers were relieved, which was very foolish of them.

But on the first point, about feeling himself to be an eighteenth-century or nineteenth-century figure, Wilson was making a just estimate, even if he meant only that he didn't drive a car and couldn't bear to pronounce the word "movies." As Alfred Kazin argued in his review of *The American Earthquake* (collected in his fine book *Contemporaries*), the men to compare Wilson with are the literary artists driven by historical imaginations—men like Carlyle.

The third thing which lightens the darkness of *Upstate* is the author's gradually revealed—and revealed only gradually even to himself—interest in a local young woman striving to better herself. Perhaps without really willing it, Wilson is telling a subtle story here: flashes and fragments are all we get. But by the time the book is over, we are convinced that her story is the story of the book, and that the story has gone against the mood. Kazin suggested that Wilson's secret was to gaze at America with a cold eye without being cold on America. *The American Earthquake* inexorably recorded the shattering effects of industrialism and the spiritual confusion of the New Deal, but it was not a hopeless book—it responded to the period's vitalities, even (while castigating it) the vitality of Henry Ford. *Upstate* very nearly *is* a hopeless book, and for a long while we suspect that Wilson *has* gone cold on America. But finally we see that he hasn't, quite: as the girl Mary works to establish herself in a way that her European origins would probably not have allowed, the American adventure haltingly begins all over again, at the eleventh hour and in the fifty-ninth minute.

Against the Stygian background of the book's accumulated imagery it is not much hope to offer, but it is not nothing, and Wilson was never in the consolation business anyway. Which leaves us—as we shelve *Upstate* beside *A Prelude* and prudently leave room for the books dealing with the thirty uncovered years between them—with the question of what business Wilson *has* been in.

What does Wilson's effort amount to? Is there an atom of truth in his dispirited suggestion that his books have dated? Supposing—as seems likely—that Wilson belongs with the great, copious critical minds like Saintsbury, Sainte-Beuve, Croce, Taine: is he doomed to survive like them only as an emblem of the qualities a mind can have, Saintsbury for gusto, Sainte-Beuve for diligence, Croce for rigour, Taine for drama? Wilson makes Van Wyck Brooks's output look normal, Eliot's look slim, Empson's, Trilling's and Leavis's look famished. Just how is all this avoirdupois to be moved forward? We need to decide whether critical work which has plainly done so much to influence its time vanishes with its time or continues. To continue, it must have done something beyond maintaining standards or correcting taste, important as those functions are: it must have embodied, not just recommended, a permanent literary value. And we do not have to re-read much of Wilson's criticism— although it would be a year of perfect pleasure to re-read all of it—to see that it does embody a value, and embodies it in a way and to a degree that no other corpus of twentieth-century work has approached. But this value, so easily sensed, is very difficult to define, since it must perforce reside in whatever is left after opposing high estimations of Wilson have cancelled each other out. Lionel Trilling (in "Edmund Wilson: A Background Glance," collected in A *Gathering of Fugitives*) says that an interest in ideas is the very essence of Wilson's criticism. Alfred Kazin, on the other hand, says that ideas are things Wilson is not at home with. If both these men admire the same thing in Wilson, what is it?

The answer is that Wilson has a mental style—a mental style which reveals itself in the way he writes. He is proof by nature against metaphysics of any kind (sometimes to the damaging extent that he cannot grasp why men should bother to hold to them), and this characteristic gives his work great clarity. He never has to strive towards perspicuity, since he is never tempted even momentarily to abandon it. And in more than fifty years of activity he has put up such a consistent show of knowing what he means—and of writing it down so that it may be readily understood—that he has invited underestimation. The most difficult escape Houdini ever made was from a wet sheet, but since he was in the business of doing difficult-looking things he had to abandon this trick, because to the public it seemed easy. What Wilson was doing was never easy, but he had the good manners to make it look that way. If he could only have managed to dream up an objective correlative, or a few types of ambiguity, or if he had found it opportune to start lamenting the loss of an organic society, he would be much more fashionable now than he is. But we can search his work from end to end without finding any such conversation-piece. What we do find is a closely argued dramatic narrative in which good judgement and misjudgement both stand out plainly. The dangerous excitement of a tentatively formulated concept is absent from his work, and for most of us this is an excitement that is hard to forgo: the twentieth century has given us a palate for such pepper.

But there is another, more durable excitement which Wilson's entire body of work serves to define. There is a clue to it in *Upstate*, in the passage where Wilson discusses the different courses taken by Eliot and Van Wyck Brooks:

> They were at Harvard at the same time, Brooks of the class of 1908, Eliot of 1910, and both, as was natural then, went, after college, to England. Eliot took root there, but Brooks said that, during the months he spent in England, he found himself preoccupied with American subjects. This difference marks the watershed in the early nineteen hundreds in American literary life. Eliot stays in England, which is for him still the motherland of literature in English, and becomes a European; Brooks returns to the United States and devotes himself to American writing, at the expense of what has been written in Europe. Eliot represents the growth of an American internationalism: Brooks, as a spokesman of the twenties, the beginnings of the sometimes all too conscious American literary self-glorification which is part of our American imperialism

As it happened, Wilson was to go on to cover American subjects with all Brooks's thoroughness and more; and to parallel Eliot's internationalism while yet holding to the tacit belief that the American achievement could well be crucial in the continuity of that internationalism; and to combine these two elements with a total authority of preparation and statement. For that preparation, he had the brilliant education available in pre-war Princeton to a young man ready to grasp it. For that statement, he was obliged to evolve a style which would make his comprehensive seriousness unmistakable in every line. Out of these two things came the solid achievement of judgements based on unarguable knowledge ably supplied to meet an historical demand. From the beginning, Wilson was a *necessary* writer, a chosen man. And it is this feeling of watching a man proving himself equal to an incontestably important task — explaining the world to America and explaining America to itself — which provides the constant excitement of Wilson's work.

Commanding this kind of excitement his prose needed no other. Wilson grew out of the great show-off period of American style. He could not have proceeded without the trail-blasting first performed by Mencken and Nathan, but he was fundamentally different from them in not feeling bound to overwrite.

Wilson's style adopted the Mencken-Nathan toughness but eschewed the belligerence—throwing no punches, it simply put its points and waited for intelligent men to agree. It assumed that intelligence could be a uniting factor rather than a divisive one. In the following passage (from "The Critic Who Does Not Exist," written in 1928 and later collected in *The Shores of Light*) this point is made explicitly:

What we lack, then, in the United States, is not writers or even literary parties, but simply serious literary criticism (the school of critics I have mentioned last, ie, Brooks, Mumford and Joseph Wood Krutch, though they set forth their own ideas, do not occupy themselves much with the art or ideas of the writers with whom they deal). Each of these groups does produce, to be sure, a certain amount of criticism to justify or explain what it is doing, but it may, I believe, be said in general that they do not communicate with one another; their opinions do not really circulate. It is astonishing to observe, in America, in spite of our floods of literary journalism, to what extent literary atmosphere is a non-conductor of criticism. What actually happens, in our literary world, is that each leader or group of leaders is allowed to intimidate his disciples, either ignoring all the other leaders or taking cognizance of their existence only by distant and contemptuous sneers. H. L. Mencken and T. S. Eliot present themselves, as I have said, from the critical point of view, as the most formidable figures on the scene; yet Mencken's discussion of his principal rival has, so far as my memory goes, been confined to an inclusion of the latter's works among the items of one of those lists of idiotic current crazes in which the *Mercury* usually includes also the recall of judges and paper-bag cookery. And Eliot, established in London, does not, of course, consider himself under the necessity of dealing with Mencken at all . . . Van Wyck Brooks, in spite of considerable baiting, has never been induced to defend his position (though Krutch has recently taken up some challenges). And the romantics have been belaboured by the spokesmen of several different camps without making any attempt to strike back. It, furthermore, seems unfortunate that some of our most important writers—Sherwood Anderson and Eugene O'Neill, for example—should work, as they apparently do, in almost complete intellectual isolation, receiving from the outside but little intelligent criticism and developing, in their solitary labours, little capacity for supplying it themselves.

Wilson's innovation was to treat the American intelligentsia as if it were a European one, speaking a common language. "For there is one language," he wrote in the same essay, "which all French writers, no matter how divergent their aims, always possess in common: the language of criticism." That was the ideal, and by behaving as if it had already come about, he did a great deal to bring it into existence. The neutral, dignified tone of his prose was crucial here: it implied that there was no need for an overdose of personality, since writer and reader were on a level and understood one another. As Lionel Trilling has convincingly argued, Wilson's years in an editorial chair for *The New Republic* were a big help in getting this tone right—he was in action continuously (more than two-thirds of the pieces in *The Shores of Light* first appeared in *The New Republic*) before a self-defining audience of intelligent men, all of whom were capable of appreciating that opinions should circulate.

The literary chronicles, especially *The Shores of Light*, are commonly valued above Wilson's more integrated books, and although it seems likely that the people doing the valuing have not correctly judged the importance of the latter, the evaluation nevertheless seems just at first glance. As has often been pointed out, there is nothing in criticism to beat the thrill of hearing Wilson produce the first descriptions and definitions of the strong new American literature that was coming up in the 1920s— the first essays on Fitzgerald and Hemingway will always stand as the perfect objects for any literary journalist's envy and respect. But here again we must remember to avoid trying to nourish ourselves with condiments alone. What needs to be appreciated, throughout the literary chronicles, is the steady work of reporting, judging, sorting out, encouraging, reproving and re-estimating. The three literary chronicles are, among other things, shattering reminders that many of the men we distinguish with the name of critic have never judged a piece of writing in their lives—just elaborated on judgements already formed by other men.

A certain demonstration of Wilson's integrity in this regard is his ability to assess minor and ancillary literature about which no general opinion has previously been built up: *The Shock of Recognition* and *Patriotic Gore* are natural culminations of Wilson's early drive towards mining and assaying in territory nobody else had even staked out. Wilson is a memory; he never at any stage believed that the historic process by which writings are forgotten should go unexamined or be declared irreversible. Remembering is one of the many duties the literary chronicles perform:

not so spectacular a duty as discovering, but equally important. For Wilson's self-imposed task of circulating opinions within an intelligent community (a community which depends on such a process for its whole existence), all these duties needed to be scrupulously carried out, and it is the triumph of the literary chronicles that they were carried out in so adventurous a way.

Unless all these things are held in mind, the true stature of the literary chronicles cannot be seen, even by those who value them above the rest of Wilson's work. In *The Shores of Light* it is necessary to appreciate not just "F. Scott Fitzgerald" and "Emergence of Ernest Hemingway" but also pieces like "The Literary Consequences of the Crash," "Talking United States," and "Prize-Winning Blank Verse." In *Classics and Commercials* we need to cherish not only the stand-out hatchet-jobs like "Who Cares Who Killed Roger Ackroyd?" and "Tales of the Marvellous and the Ridiculous" but also the assiduous labour of weighing up—never impatient, even when repelled—which went into essays like "Glenway Wescott's War Work" and "Van Wyck Brooks on the Civil War Period." And unless we can get rid of the notion that picking winners was Wilson's only true calling in life, we will have no hope at all of reaching a true estimation of *The Bit Between My Teeth*—a book disparaged as tired and thin by reviewers who in the full vigour of youth could not have matched the solidity of the least piece in it. "The Pre-Presidential T.R." and "The Holmes-Laski Correspondence" are masterly examples of what Wilson can accomplish by bringing a literary viewpoint to historical documents; and "The Vogue of the Marquis de Sade" got the whole Sade revival into focus and incisively set the limits for its expansion.

The literary chronicles would have been more than enough by themselves to establish Wilson's pre-eminence: to a high degree they have that sense of the drama of creativity which Taine had been able to capture and exploit. If people are going to read only some of Wilson instead of all of him, then the chronicles are what they should read. But it is one thing to say this, and another to accept the assumption—distressingly widespread in recent years—that *Axel's Castle* and *The Wound and the Bow* and *The Triple Thinkers* have in some way done the work they had to do and may be discarded, like used-up boosters. There is not much doubt about how such an idea gained currency, books of long essays being so much harder to read than books of short ones. But there is no reason for anyone who has actually read and understood a book like

Axel's Castle to go along with such a slovenly notion. When, in the Yeats chapter of that book, Wilson compared the Yeats of 1931 to the Dante who was able "to sustain a grand manner through sheer intensity without rhetorical heightening," he was writing permanent criticism, criticism which can't be superseded, certainly not by pundits who are boning up their Dante from a parallel text instead of learning it the hard way from a teacher like Christian Gauss. It is barbarism of a peculiarly academic kind to suppose that truths of this order—not insights, explications, or glosses, but truths—can be appropriated to a databank or dismissed as obsolete. A Dantesque "epigrammatic bitterness" is *precisely* the quality to see in the mature Yeats, and in 1931, before the last poems were written, it was virtually prescient to be able to see it, since that quality had not yet reached its full concentration.

Wilson paid heavy penalties for being plain—or rather we paid heavy penalties for not seeing the force of his plainness. In the Eliot chapter of *Axel's Castle* he said something about Eliot that forty years of theses and learned articles have done their best to bury, something which we are only now capable of seeing as criticism rather than conversation, the intervening hubbub of academic industry having revealed itself as conversation rather than criticism:

> We are always being dismayed, in our general reading, to discover that lines among those which we had believed to represent Eliot's residuum of original invention had been taken over or adapted from other writers. . . . One would be inclined *a priori* to assume that all this load of erudition and literature would be enough to sink any writer, and that such a production as "The Waste Land" must be a work of second-hand inspiration. And it is true that, in reading Eliot and Pound, we are sometimes visited by uneasy recollections of Ausonius, in the fourth century, composing Greek-and-Latin macaronics and piecing together poetic mosaics out of verses from Virgil. Yet Eliot manages to be most effective precisely—in "The Waste Land"—where he might be expected to be least original—he succeeds in conveying his meaning, in communicating his emotion, in spite of all his learned or mysterious allusions, and whether we understand them or not.
>
> In this respect, there is a curious contrast between Eliot and Ezra Pound.

With Pound, Wilson was like Tallulah Bankhead faced with a tricksy production of Maeterlinck: he wasn't afraid to announce, "There's less in this than meets the eye." With Eliot, he was bold enough to say that things were simpler than they appeared at first blush. Both these judgements were backed up by a deep learning which had nothing to fear from either man, by a sense of quality which knew how to rely on itself, and by a seriousness which was not concerned with putting up a front.

There is no need to go on with this part of the argument. It's more merciful simply to state that Wilson's entire critical corpus will go on being read so long as men are prepared to read widely and well. His strategy of using magazines—first *The New Republic*, later *The New Yorker*—as shipyards in which to assemble books was triumphantly successful. He is the ideal of the metropolitan critic, who understood from the beginning that the intelligence of the metropolis is in a certain relation to the intelligence of the academy, and went on understanding this even when the intelligence of the academy ceased to understand its relation to the intelligence of the metropolis. When Wilson called the Modern Language Association to order, he performed the most important academic act of the post-war years—he reminded the scholars that their duty was to literature.

For Wilson literature has always been an international community, with a comprehensible politics of its own. He learned languages not just out of passionate curiosity but out of quasi-political purpose, becoming acquainted with whole literatures in the same way that a man who carries an international passport proves himself a part of the main. As late as the mid-1950s Wilson was apologizing for not having done enough in this line: he has always been a trifle guilty about failing to get interested in Portuguese and Spanish. But to a chastening extent he had already made himself the universal literatus, and in the later decades of his life we find him becoming increasingly conscious that this is his major role—if he has any significance in the realm of action, then this is it. Modesty has never been among Wilson's characteristics, but a certain diffidence does creep in, of which the quietism and resignation of *Upstate* are the logical culmination. The central paradox of Wilson remains unresolved: he has put himself above the battle, inhabiting an empyrean of knowledge by now fundamentally divorced from an unworkable world. The paradox was vicious from the beginning, becoming more and more so as modern history unfolded in front of him. Wilson was a born internationalist in literature and a born isolationist in politics, and there is a constant tension between the achieved serenity of his literary judgement and the threatening complexity of his self-consciousness as an American.

A patrician individualist by nature, Wilson was automatically debarred from running with the pack. His radicalism in the 1920s and 1930s had a decisive qualitative difference from any Marxist analyses currently available: it was elitist, harking back to the informed democracy of the American past, and therefore on a richer historical base than the hastily imported European doctrines which bemused his contemporaries. Wilson's reports on Detroit are as devastating as Marx on the working day, but the intensity is the only connexion. Wilson was revolted by industrialism's depredations—if the ecological lobby ever wants to put a bible together, there are sections of *The American Earthquake* which could go straight into Revelations—but the revulsion was just as much on behalf of what America had previously been as on behalf of what it might become. Marxism is future-directed metaphysics: Wilson's thought was bent towards the literary recovery of the estimable past.

Making no commitment to communism, Wilson was never compelled to scramble away from it, and he maintained his dignity throughout the 1930s. By 1940 he had completed his analysis of the revolutionary tradition in Europe and published it as *To the Finland Station*. In the final paragraph of that book, he declared it unlikely that the Marxist creeds would be able to bring about

a society in which the superior development of some is not paid for by the exploitation, that is, by the deliberate degradation of others—a society which will be homogeneous and cooperative as our commercial society is not, and directed, to the best of their ability, by the conscious creative minds of its members.

America went to war again, and again Wilson was isolationist: as with the First World War, so with the Second, he saw no point in America becoming involved. He was still explaining such phenomena by market pressures and the devious conniving of Big Business—it was a Fabian position, never much altered since he first picked it up from Leonard Woolf.

Wilson has difficulty in understanding how irrational forces can be so potent. In *Europe Without Baedeker* and *A Piece of My Mind* he came close to holding the Europeans collectively responsible for pulling their own houses down in ruins about their heads. It was the high point of his isolationism, further reinforced by a commitment to the American past amounting to visionary fervour. In his admiration for Lincoln we find Wilson getting very near the mysticism he spent a lifetime scrupulously avoiding. Finally he found an historical base solid-seeming enough to justify the relieved rediscovery of a Platonic Guardian class. "To simplify," he wrote in *A Piece of My Mind* (1957),

> one can say that, on the one hand, you find in the United States the people who are constantly aware . . . that, beyond their opportunities for money-making, they have a stake in the success of our system, that they share the responsibility to carry on its institutions, to find expression for its new point of view, to give it dignity, to make it work; and, on the other hand, the people who are merely concerned with making a living or a fortune, with practising some profession or mastering some technical skill, as they would in any other country, and who lack, or do not possess to quite the same degree, the sense of America's role.

That was as far as he got: the Republic he loved began to be overwhelmed by the Democracy he had never been sure about, and in the new reality of the 1960s he found himself taxed but unrepresented.

In *Upstate* Wilson is faced with the ruins of the American Dream, and appears to be forgetting what we are bound to remember: that the fragments can be built with and that this fact is in some measure due to him. The intellectual community which is now fighting for the Republic against its own debilitating tumours was to a considerable extent his personal creation. That Americans of goodwill, in the midst of wearying political confusion, can yet be so confident of their nation's creativity is again in a large part due to him. As Christian Gauss was to Wilson — master to pupil — Wilson is to nobody: nobody he can see. He now doubts the continuity he helped to define. But, beyond the range of vision now limiting itself to Cape Cod and Talcottville, there will always be young men coming up who will find his achievement a clear light. He is one of the great men of letters in our century.

Times Literary Supplement, 1972

POSTSCRIPT

Contributions to the *TLS* were still published anonymously, so I can claim the foregoing essay as a labour of love. Though Arthur Crook was editor at the time, the review was commissioned by his literary editor Ian Hamilton, who sensibly demanded some cuts: the typescript was at least another thousand words longer than this. I wish I could say that among the material excised was a more thorough discussion of Wilson's politics. While I had no sympathy with Marxism myself, I still felt that Wilson had a right to his. This allowance, however, had I made it more explicit, would have been impossible to square with the assertion that he was "proof against metaphysics of any kind." Marxism is metaphysics, and it was precisely its most metaphysical aspect that Wilson clung to longer than he should have done—the idea that capitalism depended on the degradation of the working class. It was an historicist view, and since historicism is inimical to a sense of history, it meant that Wilson went on undermining one of his own salient virtues until the end of his life.

But I can congratulate myself on getting the main point across: Wilson's scope came from a real appreciation for the whole of human achievement, and not just from the urge to further his career. An academic reviewer later poured scorn on my approving citation of the "European panoptic scholars." He wanted to know why they had to be dragged in. Since he himself, however, had failed to realize that the musicologist Alfred Einstein was not the same man as the physicist Albert, I was able to retain my conviction that a panoptic scholar was a useful thing to be. At least they knew things like that. There was always the possibility, however, that I had chosen the wrong words for the right idea: "wide-ranging scholars" might have been better, or perhaps even "scholars who knew a lot." About the category itself, whatever it was called, I was never in doubt, and with the years I grew ever more convinced that deep reading over a wide range is an absolute good, dwarfing any amount of theoretical flimflam. Wilson was the national critic of America because he had read a large part of what was worth reading not just in America but in the world entire. Nowadays the same voracious proclivity makes Marcel Reich-Ranicki the national critic of Germany.

There were several other vulnerabilities on points of style, but in those days either the literary world was more civilized or else I had fewer people out to get me. If a quotation in French was appropriate, it could be got into any of the leading magazines. Today if I even mentioned Montaigne, let alone quoted him, it would go into the clippings file as *prima facie* evidence of pretension. But there are errors of tone I shouldn't have made even at the time. It strained for effect, while retreating from the consequences, to write that Wilson's mind generated enough power "to illuminate the average city." It should have been "to illuminate a city" or else nothing: the rule with a metaphor is to focus it or drop it, but never soften it. For "intelligent men" I would now, of course, put "intelligent people." I don't think that my use of the old form made me a male chauvinist, any more than my current use of the sanitized form proves that my male chauvinism has been conquered: but unless they make grammatical nonsense such changes pay off in the belligerence they avoid, and might even do some good. To the suggestion that I should have figured all this out in advance I can only concede that I lacked the conscience, or at any rate the consciousness—which luckily the upcoming phalanx of latter-day feminists would successfully make it their task to arouse.

The reader will be relieved to hear that the later afterthoughts in this reissue [of the book named after this essay—C. J.] won't be as expansive as this one. This was the essay, however, that set the tone not only for a book, but for a career—a career that some of my mentors regretted I did not pursue further, and some of my detractors still condemn me for abandoning at the temptation of fame and filthy lucre. My best answer was, and is, that although I admired Wilson's performance I saw no reason for other people wilfully to repeat it, always supposing that they had the means: these things have to be done from the seat of the pants, not from calculation. Among Wilson's many great instinctive virtues was his capacity for bringing the same intensity of imaginative engagement to the vaudeville stage as to grand literature, so when I came to take the reviewing of television as a serious commitment I had his example to back my case. I would have gone ahead anyway, because I was *in* vaudeville. For me, the heavy stuff was the side issue. I was just glad that Wilson was good at it. He made literary achievement approachable even as the gathering force of academic industry threatened to drive it irretrievably far away— an antisocial mechanism which he was the first to isolate, analyse and warn against. Like most men who grow up without fathers I have had my heroes. Wilson is just one of them but he has never faded. I have everything written by and about him on a shelf six feet long. If his diaries had been published at the time, the original manuscript of this piece might have been twice as long and even more elegiac. The reader will scarcely need telling that it sounds like an obituary. It was, but I managed to get it done while the great man was still alive to read it. I just didn't want to let him get away with feeling unfulfilled at the end of his life, as if his example had meant nothing, when for so many of us it had been an inspiration.

The Metropolitan Critic, 1994

31

IT IS OF A WINDINESS: LILLIAN HELLMAN

Much praised in the United States, *Pentimento* deals mainly with people other than its author, but there is still a good deal of Lillian Hellman in it—possibly more than she intended—and it's hard not to think of the book as finishing off *An Unfinished Woman*, a memoir which was inundated with laurels but left at least one reader doubting its widely proclaimed first-rateness. Meaty details about Dorothy Parker, Hemingway, Scott Fitzgerald and Dashiell Hammett were not quite compensation enough for a garrulous pseudotaciturnity—distinction of style, it seemed to me, was precisely the quality *An Unfinished Woman* had not a particle of. The very first time Hammett's drinking was referred to as "the drinking" you knew you were in for a solid course of bastardized Hemingwayese. The drinking got at least a score more mentions. There were also pronounced tendencies towards that brand of aggressive humility, or claimed innocence, which finds itself helpless to explain the world at the very moment when the reader is well justified in requiring that a writer should give an apprehensible outline of what he deems to be going on. Miss Hellman was with the Russian forces when Majdanek was liberated. It struck me, as I read, that her account of her feelings, though graphic, was oddly circumscribed. She had vomited, but in recounting the fact had apparently failed to realize that no physical reaction, however violent, is quite adequate to such a stimulus. What we needed to hear about was what she *thought*, and it appeared that what she thought was, as usual, a sophisticated version, decked out with Hem-Dash dialogue, of "I don't understand these things."

On a larger scale, the same applied—and I think still applies—to her reasoning on the subject of Soviet Russia. She comes over in these two books—implicitly, since her political views have mainly to be pieced together from more or less revealing hints—as an unreconstructed and unrepentant Stalinist. There is no gainsaying her consistency and strength in such matters, even if those qualities are founded in some primal injury to the imaginative faculty. She was brave during the McCarthy era and has a right to be proud of never having turned her coat. Nevertheless it is impossible to grant much more than a token admiration to a professional clerical who can go on being "realistic" about Russia in the sense (by now, surely, utterly discredited) of believing that the Terror was simply an aberration disturbing an otherwise constructive historical movement. The "I don't understand these things" syndrome came in depressingly handy whenever she wandered on to the scene of an event about which she might have been obliged to say something analytical if she had. She was well regarded in Russia, was even there during the war, and met a lot of people. Her reporting of character and incident couldn't help but be interesting. Nevertheless, one felt, she missed out on the fundamentals. On the day she was due to meet Stalin, she was told he was busy. Shortly after which, she recorded, Warsaw fell. The implication being that Warsaw was what he was busy with. But for some reason it just doesn't cross her mind to give an opinion on the fundamental question—which remains a contentious issue to this day—of whether Stalin was busy liberating it or *not* liberating it: whether, that is, his first aim was to liberate the city or else to delay liberation until the insurrectionists of the ideologically unacceptable Uprising had been wiped out by the Germans.

Lillian Hellman was an early and impressive example of the independent woman, but she never completely forsakes feather-headed femininity as a ploy, and her continuing ability not to comprehend what was going on in Russia is a glaring demonstration. In a section of *An Unfinished Woman* dealing with a later trip to Russia, she finds herself tongue-tied in the presence of a Russian friend. We are asked to believe that her own feelings about the McCarthy period were welling up to block her speech, just as the Russian friend's experience of the recent past had blocked hers. The two communed in silence. That this equation was presented as a profundity seemed to me at the time to prove that Lillian Hellman, whatever her stature in the theatre, possessed, as an essayist, an atti-

tudinizing mind of which her mannered prose was the logically consequent expression. One doesn't underrate the virulence of McCarthyism
for a minute, and it may well be that such goonery is as fundamental to
America's history as terror is to Russia's. But the two things are so different in nature, and so disparate in scale, that a mind which equates them
loses the ability to describe either. For all its Proustian pernicketiness of
recollected detail, *An Unfinished Woman* was a very vague book.

Still, it shimmered with stars. Parker and Hammett, especially,
shone brightly in its pages. There are some additional facts about them
scattered through *Pentimento* (Hammett's name is omnipresent, as you
might expect) and in a section on the theatre and related performing arts
we hear about Edmund Wilson, Theodore Roethke, Tyrone Guthrie,
Samuel Goldwyn and Tallulah Bankhead. Just as she was good on
Parker's decline, she is good on Bankhead's: Hellman's *grandes dames* go
down to defeat in a flurry of misapplied talcum. Roethke features as the
falling-down drunk he undoubtedly was most of the time. Lowell gets a
mention. It's all good gossip, and all helps.

The bulk of the volume, however, is devoted to memoirs of non-
famous characters from Miss Hellman's past. The transatlantic reviewers
seem to have convinced themselves that this material is pretty quintes-
sential stuff. We learn from Richard Poirier, quoted on the blurb, that it
"provides one of those rare instances when the moral value of a book is
wholly inextricable from its immense literary worth, where the excitations, the pacing, and the intensifications offered by the style manage to
create in us perceptions about human character that have all but disappeared from contemporary writing." I certainly agree that the perceptive-
ness, such as it is, is closely linked to the style. What I can't see for a
moment is how trained literati can imagine that the style is anything less
than frantically mannered and anything more than painfully derivative.

"The drinking" has not reappeared, but "the joking" is there to make
up for it. We hear of an historical period called "the time of Hitler." "It is
of a windiness," says someone in a German train, and although this might
just conjecturably sound like half-translated German, what it can't *help*
sounding like is Hemingway's half-translated Spanish. Out-takes from
The Old Man and the Sea abound:

You are good in boats not alone from knowledge, but because water is a
part of you, you are easy on it, fear it and like it in such equal parts that

you work well in a boat without thinking about it and may be even safer because you don't need to think too much. That is what we mean by instinct and there is no way to explain an instinct for the theatre, although those who have it recognize each other and a bond is formed between them.

Such passages read like E. B. White's classic parody *Across the Street and into the Grill*, in which White established once and for all that Hemingway's diction could not be copied, not even by Hemingway. Nor are these echoes mere lapses: her whole approach to moral-drawing is Hemingway's—the excitations, the pacing and the intensifications, if I may borrow Richard Poirier's terminology.

That is what I thought about Aunt Lily until I made the turn and the turn was as sharp as only the young can make when they realize their values have been shoddy.

Or try this:

There are many ways of falling in love and one seldom is more interesting or valid than another unless, of course, one of them lasts so long that it becomes something else, like your arm or leg about which you neither judge nor protest.

Her approach to anecdote is Hemingway's as well. Not just in the dialogue, which is American Vernacular to the last degree ("You are fine ladies," I said after a while, "the best"), but in the withholding of information—the tip-of-the-iceberg effect. On occasions this works. She is good at showing how children get hold of the wrong end of the stick, giving their loyalties passionately to the wrong people. The first chapter, set in her childhood New Orleans and dealing with a girl called Bethe, shows us the young Lillian failing to understand that Bethe is a hoodlum's girlfriend. We are supplied with this information so grudgingly ourselves that it is easy to identify with the young Lillian's confusion. In other chapters, dealing with characters who entered her life much later on, we are already equipped with knowledge of our own about the relevant period and tend to find the by now less young Lillian's slowness to comprehend a bit of a strain, especially when the period in question is the Time of Hitler.

For action, the chapter about a girl called Julia is the best thing in the book. A childhood friend who went back to Europe, Julia was in the Karl Marx Hof in Vienna when the Austrian government troops (abetted by the local Nazis) bombarded it. She lost a leg, but kept on with the fight against Fascism. Apparently Miss Hellman, passing through Germany on her way to Russia, smuggled 50,000 dollars to Julia in her hat. The money was used to spring 500 prisoners. Miss Hellman was in no small danger when engaged on this enterprise and the results unquestionably constituted a more impressive political effectiveness than most of us ever accomplish. She still revels in the nitty-grittiness of it all: she liked 1930s radicalism a lot better than twenties "rebellion"—the twenties were all style and she is properly contemptuous of style in that vitiated sense.

But with all that said, we are still left with key questions unanswered. Miss Hellman says that she has changed Julia's name because she is "not sure that even now the Germans like their premature anti-Nazis." Since they like them well enough to have made one of them Chancellor of West Germany, it's permissible to assume that Miss Hellman means something more interesting, and that Julia was a member of the Communist Party. If she was, it's difficult to see why Miss Hellman can't come straight out and say so. If she fears that we might think the less of the young Julia for it, she surely overestimates the long-term impact of McCarthyism on her readership. Or is she just *compelled* to be vague?

For the truth is that the Julia chapter, like all the others, happens in a dream. Despite the meticulously recollected minutiae, the story reads like a spy-sketch by Nichols and May, even down to the bewilderingly complicated instructions ("You have two hours, but we haven't that long together because you have to be followed to the station and the ones who follow you must have time to find the man who will be with you on the train until Warsaw in the morning") Julia breathes to Lillian under the noses of the lurking Gestapo.

To have been there, to have seen it, and yet still be able to write it down so that it rings false—it takes a special kind of talent. But there are stretches of her writing which somehow manage to sound true, even through the blanket of her supposedly transparent prose. She liked Samuel Goldwyn and has the guts to say so. Whether or not it took bravery to like him, it still takes bravery to admit it. She is, of course, perfectly right to admire Goldwyn above Irving Thalberg. Here again her suspicion of Style led her to the truth. Scott Fitzgerald, infinitely more sensitive but overendowed with reverence, fell for Thalberg full length.

Less prominent this time but still compulsively invoked, the true hero of *Pentimento* is Dashiell Hammett. Theirs, I think, will be remembered as a great love. The only thing that could possibly delay the legend would be Miss Hellman's indefatigable determination to feed its flames. In this volume the Nick-and-Nora-Charles dialogue reads as much like a screenplay as it did in the previous one.

> I phoned the Beverly Hills house from the restaurant. I said to Hammett, "I'm in New Orleans. I'm not coming back to Hollywood for a while and I didn't want you to worry."
>
> "How are you?" he said.
>
> "O.K. and you?"
>
> "I'm O.K. I miss you."
>
> "I miss you, too. Is there a lady in my bedroom?"
>
> He laughed. "I don't think so, but they come and go. Except you. You just go."
>
> "I had good reason," I said.
>
> "Yes," he said, "you did."

I like it now and my mother liked it then, when William Powell and Myrna Loy rattled it off to each other in the thirties. The *Thin Man* movies, with their unquestioned assumption that man and wife were equal partners, played a vital part in raising the expectations of women everywhere. Such are the unappraised impulses of modern history— when the fuss dies down it turns out that turns of speech and tones of voice mattered just as much as battles.

On Broadway Lillian Hellman took her chances among the men, a pioneer women's liberationist. Her plays were bold efforts, indicative social documents which are unlikely to be neglected by students, although as pieces for the theatre they will probably date: they are problem plays whose problems are no longer secrets, for which in some measure we have her to thank. She is a tough woman who has almost certainly not been relishing the patronizing critical practice—more common in America than here, and let's keep it that way—of belatedly indicating gratitude for strong early work by shouting unbridled hosannas for pale, late stuff that has a certain documentary value but not much more. She says at one point in *Pentimento* that in her time on Broadway she was always denied the benefits of the kind of criticism which would take her properly to task.

The New Review, May 1974;
later included in *At the Pillars of Hercules*, 1979

POSTSCRIPT

Later on it became commonplace to treat Lillian Hellman as a fantasist, but it was a subversive thing to suggest at the time, and if I had tried it in a more established publication the lawyers would have been called in. Luckily *The New Review* was as blissfully impractical in legal matters as in all others, so I got the chance to be early with the news. I had no personal knowledge. I just guessed from her prose style that she couldn't lie straight in bed, as we say in Australia. Right to the end, she never gave up on the pretence that she had been a martyr in the defence of liberty. Certainly there was nothing nice about McCarthyism, but in the long view of history it was a love bite compared to the crimes she had endorsed, first by her approbation and later by her silence. Glamour, which knows no politics, eventually wrapped her in a mink coat, as one of the "legends" in an advertising campaign. I would have liked to have been wearing that coat when I finally met her socially, at a dinner party in London towards the end of her life. She gave me the shivers. Like Winifred Wagner, who looked back on Hitler with the same fond understanding Hellman bestowed on Stalin, Hellman spoke as if the pre-war past had been her personal fiefdom, and unless you had been there you couldn't know the ins and outs. She had been there all right, but had missed the point completely: a gift that can masquerade as integrity if it survives long enough to attain legendary status, whereupon small furry animals are slain in its honour, and their pelts are sewn together at the edges to keep it warm.

2003

32

MAILER'S *MARILYN*

"She was a fruitcake," Tony Curtis once told an interviewer on BBC television, and there can't be much doubt that she was. Apart from conceding that the camera was desperately in love with her, professional judgements of Marilyn Monroe's attributes rarely go much further. It would be strange if they did: there's work to be done, and a girl blessed with equivalent magic might happen along any time—might even not be a fruitcake. Amateur judgements, on the other hand, are free to flourish. Norman Mailer's new book, *Marilyn*, is just such a one.

Even if its narrative were not so blatantly, and self-admittedly, cobbled together from facts already available in other biographies, the Mailer *Marilyn* would still be an amateur piece of work. Its considerable strength lies in that limitation. As far as talent goes, Marilyn Monroe was so minimally gifted as to be almost unemployable, and anyone who holds to the opinion that she was a great natural comic identifies himself immediately as a dunce. For purposes best known to his creative demon, Mailer planes forward on the myth of her enormous talent like a drunken surfer. Not for the first time, he gets further by going with the flow than he ever could have done by cavilling. Thinking of her as a genius, he can call her drawbacks virtues, and so deal—unimpeded by scepticism—with the vital mystery of her presence.

Mailer's adoration is as amateurish as an autograph hunter's. But because of it we are once again, and this time ideally, reminded of his extraordinary receptivity. That the book should be an embarrassing and embarrassed rush-job is somehow suitable. The author being who he is, the book might as well be conceived in the most chaotic possible circumstances. The subject is, after all, one of the best possible focal points for his chaotic view of life. There is nothing detached or calculating about that view. It is hot-eyed, errant, unhinged. Writhing along past a gallery of yummy photographs, the text reads as the loopiest message yet from the Mailer who scared Sonny Liston with thought waves, made the medical breakthrough which identified cancer as the thwarted psyche's revenge and first rumbled birth control as the hidden cause of pregnancy. And yet *Marilyn* is one of Mailer's most interesting things. Easy to punish, it is hard to admire—like its subject. But admire it we must—like its subject. The childishness of the whole project succeeds in emitting a power that temporarily calls adulthood into question: The Big Book of the Mad Girl. Consuming it at a long gulp, the reader ponders over and over again Mailer's copiously fruitful aptitude for submission. Mailer is right to trust his own foolishness, wherever it leads: even if the resulting analysis of contemporary America impresses us as less diagnostic than symptomatic.

Not solely for the purpose of disarming criticism, Mailer calls his *Marilyn* a biography in novel form. The parent novel, we quickly guess, is *The Deer Park*, and we aren't seventy-five pages into this new book before we find Charles Francis Eitel and Elena Esposito being referred to as if they were people living in our minds—which, of course, they are. The permanent party of *The Deer Park* ("if desires were deeds, the history of the night would end in history") is still running, and the atom bomb that lit the desert's rim for Sergius O'Shaugnessy and Lulu Meyers flames just as bright. But by now Sergius is out from under cover: he's Norman Mailer. And his beloved film star has been given a real name too: Marilyn Monroe. Which doesn't necessarily make her any the less fictional. By claiming the right to launch vigorous imaginative patrols from a factual base, Mailer gives himself an easy out from the strictures of verisimilitude, especially when the facts are discovered to be contradictory. But Mailer's fantasizing goes beyond expediency. Maurice Zolotow, poor pained scrivener, can sue Mailer all he likes, but neither he nor the quiescent Fred Lawrence Guiles will ever get his Marilyn back. Mailer's Marilyn soars above the known data, an apocalyptic love-object no mundane pen-pusher could dream of reaching. Dante and Petrarch barely knew Beatrice and Laura. It didn't slow them down. Mailer never met Marilyn at all. It gives him the inside track.

Critical fashion would have it that since *The Deer Park* reality has been busy turning itself into a novel. As Philip Roth said it must, the extremism of real events has ended up by leaving the creative imagination looking like an also-ran. A heroine in a 1950s novel, Lulu was really a girl of the 1940s—she had some measure of control over her life. Mailer now sees that the young Marilyn was the true fifties heroine—she had no control over her life whatsoever. In the declension from Lulu as Mailer then saw her to Marilyn as he sees her now, we can clearly observe what is involved in dispensing with the classical, shaping imagination and submitting one's talent (well, Mailer's talent) to the erratic forces of events. Marilyn, says Mailer, was every man's love affair with America. He chooses to forget now that Sergius was in love with something altogether sharper, just as he chooses to forget that for many men Marilyn in fact represented most of the things that were to be feared about America. Worshipping a doll was an activity that often came into question at the time. Later on, it became a clever critical point to insist that the doll was gifted: she walks, she talks, she plays Anna Christie at the Actors' Studio. Later still, the doll was canonized. By the time we get to this book, it is as though there had never been any doubt: the sickness of the 1950s lay, not in overvaluing Marilyn Monroe, but in undervaluing her.

Marilyn, says Mailer, suggested sex might be as easy as ice cream. He chooses to forget that for many men at the time she suggested sex might have about the same nutritional value. The early photographs by André de Dienes—taken before her teeth were fixed but compensating by showing an invigorating flash of panty above the waistline of her denims—enshrine the essence of her snuggle-pie sexuality, which in the ensuing years was regularized, but never intensified, by successive applications of oomph and class. Adorable, dumb tomato, she was the best of the worst. As the imitators, and imitators of the imitators, were put into the field behind her, she attained the uniqueness of the paradigm, but that was the sum total of her originality as a sex bomb. Any man in his right mind would have loved to have her. Mailer spends a good deal of the book trying to drum up what mystical significance he can out of that fact, without even once facing the possibility of that fact representing the *limitation* of her sexuality—the criticism of it, and the true centre of her tragedy. Her screen presence, the Factor X she possessed in the same quantity as

Garbo, served mainly to potentiate the sweetness. The sweetness of the girl bride, the unwomanly woman, the *femme* absolutely not *fatale*.

In her ambition, so Faustian, and in her ignorance of culture's dimensions, in her liberation and her tyrannical desires, her noble democratic longings intimately contradicted by the widening pool of her narcissism (where every friend and slave must bathe), we can see the magnified mirror of ourselves, our exaggerated and now all but defeated generation, yes, she ran a reconnaissance through the 50s. . . .

Apart from increasing one's suspicions that the English sentence is being executed in America, such a passage of rhetorical foolery raises the question of whether the person Mailer is trying to fool with it might not conceivably be himself. If "magnified mirror of ourselves" means anything, it must include Mailer. Is Mailer ignorant of culture's dimensions? The answer, one fears, being not that he is, but that he would like to be—so that he could write more books like *Marilyn*. As Mailer nuzzles up beside the shade of this poor kitten to whom so much happened but who could cause so little to happen, you can hear the purr of sheer abandon. He himself would like very much to be the man without values, expending his interpretative powers on whatever the world declared to be important. Exceptional people, Mailer says (these words are almost exactly his, only the grammar having been altered, to unveil the epigram), have a way of living with opposites in themselves that can be called schizophrenia only when it fails. The opposite in Mailer is the hick who actually falls for all that guff about screen queens, voodoo prizefighters and wonder-boy presidents. But his way of living with it hasn't yet quite failed. And somehow, it must be admitted, he seems to get further, see deeper, than those writers who haven't got it to live with.

In tracing Marilyn's narcissism back to her fatherless childhood, our author is at his strongest. His propensity for scaling the mystical ramparts notwithstanding, Mailer in his Aquarius/Prisoner role is a lay psychologist of formidable prowess. The self-love and the unassuageable need to have it confirmed—any fatherless child is bound to recognize the pattern, and be astonished at how the writing generates the authentic air of continuous panic. But good as this analysis is, it still doesn't make Marilyn's narcissism ours. There is narcissism and there is narcissism, and to a depressing degree Marilyn's was the sadly recognizable version of the actress who could read a part but could never be bothered reading a complete script. Mailer knows what it took Marilyn to get to the top: everything from betraying friends to lying down under geriatric strangers. Given the system, Marilyn was the kind of monster equipped to climb through it. What's debilitating is that Mailer seems to have given up imagining other systems. He is right to involve himself in the dynamics of Hollywood; he does better by enthusiastically replaying its vanished games than by standing aloof; but for a man of his brains he doesn't *despise* the place enough. His early gift for submitting himself to the grotesqueness of reality is softening with the years into a disinclination to argue with it. In politics he still fights on, although with what effect on his allies one hesitates to think. But in questions of culture—including, damagingly, the cultural aspects of politics—he has by now come within an ace of accepting whatever is as right. His determination to place on Marilyn the same valuation conferred by any sentimentalist is a sure token.

.   .   .

On the point of Marilyn's putative talents, Mailer wants it both ways. He wants her to be an important natural screen presence, which she certainly was; and he wants her to be an important natural actress, which she certainly wasn't. So long as he wants it the first way, he gets it: *Marilyn* is an outstandingly sympathetic analysis of what makes somebody look special on screen, and reads all the better for its periodic eruptions into incoherent lyricism. But so long as he wants it the second way, he gets nowhere. He is quite right to talk of *Some Like It Hot* as her best film, but drastically overestimates her strength in it. Mailer knows all about the hundreds of takes and the thousands of fluffs, and faithfully records the paroxysms of anguish she caused Billy Wilder and Tony Curtis. But he seems to assume that once a given scene was in the can it became established as a miracle of assurance. And the plain fact is that her salient weakness—the inability to read a line—was ineradicable. Every phrase came out as if it had just been memorized. *Just* been memorized. And that film was the high point of the short-winded, monotonous attack she had developed for getting lines across. In earlier films, all the way back to the beginning, we are assailed with varying degrees of the irrepressible panic which infected a voice that couldn't tell where to place emphasis. As a natural silent comedian Marilyn might possibly have qualified, with the proviso that she was not to be depended upon to invent anything. But as a natural comedian in sound she had the conclusive disadvantage of not being able to speak. She was limited ineluctably to characters who rented language but could never possess it, and all her best roles fell into that category. She was good at being inarticulately abstracted for the same reason that midgets are good at being short.

To hear Mailer overpraising Marilyn's performance in *Gentlemen Prefer Blondes* is to wonder if he has any sense of humour at all. Leaving out of account an aberration like *Man's Favourite Sport* (in which Paula Prentiss, a comedienne who actually knows something about being funny, was entirely wasted), *Gentlemen Prefer Blondes* is the least entertaining comedy Howard Hawks ever made. With its manic exaggeration of Hawks's already heavy emphasis on male aggressiveness transplanted to the female, the film later became a touchstone for the Hawksian cinéastes (who also lacked a sense of humour, and tended to talk ponderously about the role-reversals in *Bringing Up Baby* before passing with relief to the supposed wonders of *Hatari*), but the awkward truth is that with this project Hawks landed himself with the kind of challenge he was least likely to find liberating—dealing with dumb sex instead of the bright kind. Hawks supplied a robust professional framework for Marilyn's accomplishments, such as they were. Where I lived, at any rate, her performance in the film was generally regarded as mildly winning in spite of her obvious, fundamental inadequacies—the *in spite of* being regarded as the secret of any uniqueness her appeal might have. Mailer tells it differently:

> In the best years with DiMaggio, her physical coordination is never more vigorous and athletically quick; she dances with all the grace she is ever going to need when doing *Gentlemen Prefer Blondes*, all the grace and all the bazazz—she is a musical comedy star with panache! Diamonds Are a Girl's Best Friend! What a surprise! And sings so well Zanuck will first believe her voice was dubbed. . . .

This is the language of critical self-deception, fine judgement suppressed in the name of a broader cause. What does it mean to dance with all the grace you are ever going to need? It doesn't sound the same as being good at dancing. The fact was that she could handle a number like the "Running Wild" routine in the train corridor in *Some Like It Hot* (Wilder covered it with the marvellous cutaways of Lemmon slapping the back of the bull fiddle and Curtis making Ping-Pong-ball eyes while blowing sax), but anything harder than that was pure pack-drill. And if Zanuck really believed that her voice was dubbed, then for once in his life he must have made an intuitive leap, because to say that her singing voice didn't sound as if it belonged to her was to characterize it with perfect accuracy. Like her speaking voice, it was full of panic.

It took more than sympathy for her horrible death and nostalgia for her atavistic cuddlesomeness to blur these judgements, which at one time all intelligent people shared. The thing that tipped the balance towards adulation was Camp—Camp's yen for the vulnerable in women, which is just as inexorable as its hunger for the strident. When Mailer talks about Marilyn's vulnerability, he means the inadequacy of her sense of self. Camp, however, knew that the vulnerability which mattered was centred in the inadequacy of her talent. She just wasn't very good, and was thus eligible for membership in the ever-increasing squad of Camp heroines who make their gender seem less threatening by being so patently unaware of how they're going over. On the strident wing of the team, Judy Garland is a perennial favourite for the same reason. If common sense weren't enough to do it, the Camp enthusiasm for Monroe should have told Mailer—Mailer of all people—that the sexuality he was getting set to rave about was the kind that leaves the viewer uncommitted.

Mailer longs to talk of Monroe as a symbolic figure, node of a death wish and foretaste of the fog. Embroiled in such higher criticism, he doesn't much concern himself with the twin questions of what shape Hollywood took in the 1950s and of how resonantly apposite a representative Marilyn turned out to be of the old studio system's last gasp. As the third-string blonde at Fox (behind Betty Grable and June Haver) Marilyn was not—as Mailer would have it—in all that unpromising a spot. She was in luck, like Kim Novak at Columbia, who was groomed by Harry Cohn to follow Rita Hayworth in the characteristic 1950s transposition which substituted apprehensiveness for ability. For girls like them, the roles would eventually be there—mainly crummy roles in mainly crummy movies, but they were the movies the studios were banking on. For the real actresses, times were tougher, and didn't ease for more than a decade. Anne Bancroft, for example, also started out at Fox, but couldn't get the ghost of a break. Mailer isn't careful enough about pointing out that Fox's record as a starmaker was hopeless in all departments: Marilyn was by no means a unique case of neglect, and in comparison with Bancroft got a smooth ride. Marilyn was just another item in the endless catalogue of Zanuck's imperviousness to box-office potential. James Robert Parish, in his useful history, *The Fox Girls*, sums up the vicissitudes of Marilyn's career at Fox with admirable brevity and good sense, and if the reader would like to make up his own mind about the facts, it's to that book he should turn.

Right across Hollywood, as the films got worse, the dummies and the sex bombs came into their own, while the actresses dropped deeper into limbo. Considering the magnitude of the luminary he is celebrating, it might seem funny to Mailer if one were to mention the names of people like, say, Patricia Neal, or (even more obscure) Lola Albright. Soon only the most fanatic of students will be aware that such actresses were available but could not be used. It's not that history has been rewritten. Just that the studio-handout version of history has been unexpectedly confirmed—by Norman Mailer, the very stamp of writer who ought to know better. The studios created a climate for new talent that went on stifling the best of it until recent times. How, for example, does Mailer think Marilyn stacks up against an artist like Tuesday Weld? By the criteria of approval manifested in *Marilyn*, it would be impossible for Mailer to find Weld even mildly interesting. To that extent, the senescent dream-factories succeeded in imposing their view: first of all on the masses, which was no surprise, but now on the elite, which is.

.   .   .

Mailer is ready to detect all manner of bad vibes in the 1950s, but unaccountably fails to include in his read-out of portents the one omen pertinent to his immediate subject. The way that Hollywood divested itself of *intelligence* in that decade frightened the civilized world. And far into the 1960s this potato-blight of the intellect went on. The screen was crawling with cosmeticized androids. Not content with gnawing her knuckles through the long days of being married to a test pilot or the long nights of being married to a bandleader, June Allyson sang and danced. Betty Hutton, the ultimate in projected insecurity, handed over to Doris Day, a yelping freckle. The last Tracy-Hepburn comedies gurgled nostalgically in the straw like the lees of a soda. The new Hepburn, Audrey, was a Givenchy clothes horse who piped her lines in a style composed entirely of mannerisms. And *she* was supposed to be class. Comedy of the 1930s and 1940s, the chief glory of the American sound cinema, was gone as if it had never been. For those who had seen and heard the great Hollywood high-speed talkers (Carole Lombard, Irene Dunne, Rosalind Russell, Katharine Hepburn, Jean Arthur) strut their brainy stuff, the let-down was unbelievable. Comic writing was pretty nearly wiped out, and indeed has never fully recovered as a genre. In a context of unprecedented mindlessness, Marilyn Monroe rose indefatigably to success. She just wasn't clever enough to fail.

Marilyn came in on the 1950s tide of vulgarity, and stayed to take an exemplary part in the Kennedy era's uproar of cultural pretension. Mailer follows her commitment to the Actors' Studio with a credulousness that is pure New Frontier. The cruelty with which he satirizes Arthur Miller's ponderous aspirations to greatness is transmuted instantly to mush when he deals with Mrs. Miller's efforts to explore the possibilities hitherto dormant within her gift. That such possibilities existed was by no means taken as gospel at the time of her first forays into New York, but with the advent of the Kennedy era the quality of scepticism seemed to drain out of American cultural life. *Marilyn* is a latter-day Kennedy-era text, whose prose, acrid with the tang of free-floating charisma, could have been written a few weeks after Robert Kennedy's death rounded out the period of the family's power. Mailer's facility for confusing the intention with the deed fits that epoch's trust in façades to perfection. He is delicately tender when evoking the pathos of Marilyn's anxious quest for self-fulfilment, but never doubts that the treasure of buried ability was there to be uncovered, if only she could have found the way. The true pathos—that she was simply not fitted for the kind of art she had been led to admire—eludes him. Just as he gets over the problem of Marilyn's intellectual limitations by suggesting that a mind can be occupied with more interesting things than thoughts, so he gets over the problem of her circumscribed accomplishments by suggesting that true talent is founded not on ability but on a state of being. Nobody denies that the snorts of derision which first greeted the glamour queen's strivings towards seriousness were inhuman, visionless. In rebuttal, it was correctly insisted that her self-exploration was the exercise of an undeniable right. But the next, fatal step was to assume that her self-exploration was an artistic activity in itself, and had a right to results.

.   .   .

Scattered throughout the book are hints that Mailer is aware that his loved one had limited abilities. But he doesn't let it matter, preferring to

insist that her talent—a different thing—was boundless. Having overcome so much deprivation in order to see that certain kinds of achievement were desirable, she had an automatic entitlement to them. That, at
any rate, seems to be his line of reasoning. A line of reasoning which is
really an act of faith. The profundity of his belief in the significance of
what went on during those secret sessions at the Actors' Studio is
unplumbable. She possessed, he vows, the talent to play Cordelia. One
examines this statement from front-on, from both sides, through a mirror
and with rubber gloves. Is there a hint of a put-on? There is not. Doesn't
he really mean something like: she possessed enough nerve and critical
awareness to see the point of trying to extend her range by playing a few
fragments of a Shakespearean role out of the public eye? He does not. He
means what he says, that Marilyn Monroe possessed the talent to play
Cordelia. Who, let it be remembered, is required, in the first scene of the
play, to deliver a speech like this:

> Good my lord,
> You have begot me, bred me, lov'd me: I
> Return those duties back as are right fit,
> Obey you, love you, and most honour you.
> Why have my sisters husbands, if they say
> They love you all? Haply, when I shall wed,
> That lord whose hand must take my plight shall carry
> Half my love with him, half my care and duty:
> Sure I shall never marry like my sisters,
> To love my father all.

Leave aside the matter of how she would have managed such stuff on
stage; it is doubtful she could have handled a single minute of it even on
film: not with all the dialogue coaches in the world, not even if they had
shot and edited in the way Joshua Logan is reputed to have put together
her performance in some of the key scenes of *Bus Stop*—word by word,
frame by frame. The capacity to apprehend and reproduce the rhythm of
written language just wasn't there. And even if we were to suppose that
such an indispensable capacity could be dispensed with, there would still
be the further question of whether the much-touted complexity of her
character actually contained a material resembling Cordelia's moral
steel: it is not just sweetness that raises Cordelia above her sisters. We are

bound to conclude (if only to preserve from reactionary scorn the qualities Marilyn really *did* have) that she was debarred from the wider range of classical acting not only by a paucity of ability but by a narrowness of those emotional resources Mailer would have us believe were somehow a substitute for it. Devoid of invention, she could only draw on her stock of feeling. The stock was thin. Claiming for her a fruitful complexity, Mailer has trouble conjuring it up: punctuated by occasional outbreaks of adoration for animals and men, her usual state of mind seems to have been an acute but generalized fear, unreliably counterbalanced by sedation.

Mailer finds it temptingly easy to insinuate that Marilyn's madness knew things sanity wots not of, and he tries to make capital out of the tussle she had with Laurence Olivier in *The Prince and the Showgirl.* Olivier, we are asked to believe, was the icy technician working from the outside in, who through lack of sympathy muffed the chance to elicit from his leading lady miracles of warm intuition. It's a virtuoso passage from Mailer, almost convincing us that an actor like Olivier is a prisoner of rationality forever barred from the inner mysteries of his profession. You have to be nuts, whispers Mailer from the depths of his subtext, to be a *real* actor. The derivation from Laing's psychology is obvious.

The author does a noble, loyal, zealous job of tracing his heroine's career as an artist, but we end by suspecting that he is less interested in her professional achievement than in her fame. The story of Norma Jean becoming Somebody is the true spine of the book, and the book is Mailer's most concise statement to date of what he thinks being Somebody has come to mean in present-day America. On this theme, *Marilyn* goes beyond being merely wrong-headed and becomes quite frightening.

As evidence of the leverage Marilyn's fame could exert, Mailer recounts a story of her impressing some friends by taking them without a reservation to the Copacabana, where Sinatra was packing the joint to the rafters every night. Marilyn being Monroe, Sinatra ordered a special table put in at his feet, and while lesser mortals were presumably being asphyxiated at the back, he sang for his unexpected guest and her friends, personally. Only for the lonely. Mailer tells such stories without adornment, but his excitement in them is ungovernable: it infects the style, giving it the tone we have come to recognize from all his previous excursions into status, charisma, psychic victory and the whole witchcraft of personal ascendancy. *Marilyn* seems to bring this theme in his work to a crisis.

In many ways *The Naked and the Dead* was the last classic novel to be written in America. The separately treated levels of the military hierarchy mirrored the American class structure, such as it was, and paralleled the class structure of the classic European novel, such as it had always been. With *The Deer Park* the American classes were already in a state of flux, but the society of Hollywood maintained cohesion by being aware of what conditions dictated the mutability of its hierarchy: Sergius the warrior slept with Lulu the love queen, both of them qualifying, while fortune allowed, as members of the only class, below which was the ruck—the unlovely, the unknown, the out. *The Deer Park* was Mailer's last attempt to embody American society in fictional form: *An American Dream* could find room only for its hero. Increasingly with the years, the broad sweep of Mailer's creativity has gone into the interpretation of reality as it stands, or rather flows, and he has by now become adept at raising fact to the level of fiction. Meanwhile society has become even more fluid, to the extent that the upper class—the class of celebrities—has become as unstable in its composition as the hubbub below. Transformation and displacement now operate endlessly, and the observer (heady prospect) changes the thing observed. Mailer's tendency to enrol himself in even the most exalted action is based on the perception, not entirely crazed, that the relative positions in the star-cluster of status are his to define: reality is a novel that he is writing.

On her way to being divorced from Arthur Miller, Marilyn stopped off in Dallas. In Dallas! Mailer can hardly contain himself. "The most electric of the nations," he writes, "must naturally provide the boldest circuits of coincidence." Full play is made with the rumours that Marilyn might have had affairs with either or both of the two doomed Kennedy brothers, and there is beetle-browed speculation about the possibility of her death having placed a curse on the family—and hence, of course, on the whole era. Mailer himself calls this last brainwave "endlessly facile," thereby once again demonstrating his unfaltering dexterity at having his cake and eating it. But this wearying attempt to establish Marilyn as the muse of the artist-politicians is at one with the book's whole tendency to weight her down with a load of meaning she is too frail to bear. Pepys could be floored by Lady Castlemaine's beauty without ascribing to her qualities she did not possess. The Paris intellectuals quickly learned that Pompadour's passion for china flowers and polite theatre was no indication that artistic genius was in favour at Versailles—quite the reverse.

Where hierarchies were unquestioned, realism meant the ability to see what was really what. Where the hierarchy is created from day to day in the mind of one man interpreting it, realism is likely to be found a hindrance.

Mailer doesn't want famous people to mean as little as the sceptical tongue says they do. To some extent he is right. There *is* an excitement in someone like Marilyn Monroe coming out of nowhere to find herself conquering America, and there is a benediction in the happiness she could sometimes project from the middle of her anguish. Without Mailer's receptivity we would not have been given the full impact of these things; just as if he had listened to the liberal line on the space programme we would not have been given those enthralling moments in *A Fire on the Moon* when the launch vehicle pulls free of its bolts, or when the mission passes from the grip of the Earth into the embrace of its target—moments as absorbing as our first toys. Mailer's shamelessness says that there are people and events which mean more than we in our dignity are ready to allow. He has nearly always been right. But when he starts saying that in that case they might as well mean what he wants them to mean, the fictionalist has overstepped the mark, since the patterning that strengthens fiction weakens fact.

· · ·

Mailer's Marilyn is a usurper, a democratic monarch reigning by dint of the allegiance of an intellectual aristocrat, the power of whose regency has gone to his head. Mailer has forgotten that Marilyn was the people's choice before she was his, and that in echoing the people he is sacrificing his individuality on the altar of perversity. Sergius already had the sickness:

> Then I could feel her as something I had conquered, could listen to her wounded breathing, and believe that no matter how she acted other times, these moments were Lulu, as if her flesh murmured words more real than her lips. To the pride of having so beautiful a girl was added the bigger pride of knowing that I took her with the cheers of millions behind me. Poor millions with their low roar!

At the end of *The Deer Park* the dying Eitel tells Sergius by telepathy that the world we may create is more real to us than the mummery of what happens, passes and is gone. Whichever way Sergius decided, Mailer seems finally to have concluded that the two are the same thing. More than any of his essays so far, *Marilyn* tries to give the mummery of what happens the majestic gravity of a created world. And as he has so often done before, he makes even the most self-assured of us wonder if we have felt deeply enough, looked long enough, lived hard enough. He comes close to making us doubt our conviction that in a morass of pettiness no great issues are being decided. We benefit from the doubt. But the price he pays for being able to induce it is savage, and Nietzsche's admonition is beginning to apply. He has gazed too long into the abyss, and now the abyss is gazing into him. Bereft of judgement, detachment or even a tinge of irony, *Marilyn* is an opulent but slavish expression of an empty consensus. The low roar of the poor millions is in every page.

Commentary, October 1973; later included in
At the Pillars of Hercules, 1979

POSTSCRIPT

Years later, when I finally met Norman Mailer in the back of a limousine in New York, he generously neglected to punch me out for a review he must have thought unfair. He certainly could have decked me had he wished, and in the limo I would not have had far to fall. I never saw a more threatening neck on a writer: his ears sat on top of it like bookends on a mantelpiece. But on this occasion he was civility itself. Perhaps he remembered that I had studded my diatribe with tributes to his gift. In retrospect I only wish that there had been more of them. Opportunities to register gratitude should never be neglected, and gratitude is what I have always felt for Mailer, over and above—or should it be under and below?—the inevitable exasperation. *A Fire on the Moon* (called *Of a Fire on the Moon* in the United States: a striding title crippled by an extra word) was to remain one of my models for how prose can reflect the adventure of high technology without lapsing into a hi-fi buff's nerdish fervour, and later he restored himself triumphantly as a writer of fiction with the remarkable *Harlot's Ghost*. But I still think he got it all wrong about Marilyn Monroe. He was right to think that film stardom hasn't got much to do with acting talent. He was just wrong about the talent. In conversation it might have been edifying, if dangerous, to pursue the point, but as I remember it he raised the subject of Iris Murdoch. Since there were about half a dozen other people in the car better qualified to pursue that topic than I, my colloquy with the patriarch was soon suspended, along with any chance of a fist fight.

It was a pity Mailer ever saddled himself with a reputation as a brawler, because in the New York literary context fisticuffs rate as a hopelessly anachronistic weapons system. At the kind invitation of Norman Podhoretz of *Commentary*, my review of Mailer's *Marilyn* was the first big piece I published in the United States. Not long afterwards, Robert Silvers asked me to write for the *New York Review of Books*, whose personnel felt about the *Commentary* crowd the way Iraq later felt about Iran. It was an ideological battlefield, and the free-floating contributor was very likely to get zapped in the contending force-fields of influence. Later on I moved to *The New Yorker* and fancied that I had got above the battle, but I never moved to New York. Fed Ex, fax and then e-mail made it steadily more easy to maintain a safely detached participation in a literary scene that resembled a John Carpenter movie with better dialogue. (Exercise: armed with a video of *Escape from New York* and a list of prominent Manhattan *culturati*, recast the roles of the Duke, Brains, Cabbie and that babe with the big maracas. Keep the Kurt Russell part for yourself.) It helps to know one's weaknesses, and the hypertrophied celebrity culture in New York appeals too much to my sweet tooth. In London I find it hard enough to preserve my rule not to be quoted on anything that I am not prepared to write about. In New York, where not to be quoted is to be considered dead, pressure from publishers would soon make it compulsory to succumb. Mailer himself is a case in point. After the criminal Jack Abbott, for whose release Mailer had campaigned, celebrated his freedom by murdering a waiter who looked at him sideways, Mailer was caught saying that Abbott's action might have had some redeeming use as a "challenge to the suburbs." But he would never have been caught *writing* something so callously foolish. Writers should stay off the air unless they can keep their equilibrium, and the media in the United States devote a lot of money and effort to making sure you can't keep that.

Reliable Essays, 2001

33

FROM LOG CABIN
TO LOG CABIN

RN: The Memoirs of Richard Nixon

Largely deservedly, Richard Nixon is in such low repute that it is hard to give him credit for anything without sounding capricious. Yet it must be said, in the teeth of all expectation, that his *Memoirs* constitute a readable book of no small literary merit and considerable human dignity. Doubtless there are ghostwriters in the picture somewhere; in the acknowledgements a large number of secretaries and editors receive thanks; but if a committee wrote this book, it was one of those rare committees which, setting out to design a horse, actually succeed in designing a horse instead of a camel.

Nixon has done many reprehensible things in his career and in a way this book is just one more of them. By internal contradictions alone, quite apart from evidence that can be brought up from outside, it is a book patently full of half-truths and false conclusions. But it is not a mean book. Nixon's faults are all on view, but so is the fact that they are faults in something substantial. His claims to a place in history are shown to be not all that absurd. He will be harder to mock from now on, although perhaps even easier to distrust.

Such a judgement should emerge naturally from any fair reading of the text. A fair reading, however, might well be prejudiced by an initial glance at the copious photographs. Featuring a hero described in the captions as RN, these tend to show Nixon at his most bogusly histrionic. During the Hiss case he profiles like a concave Dick Tracy while examining the "pumpkin papers" through a magnifying glass. His dog Checkers helps him read the newspaper on a bench in Central Park. There is a supposedly eloquent photograph of construction-union leaders' safety-helmets arranged on a White House table as an endorsement for Nixon's Cambodian adventure, with nothing in the caption to tell you that the union leaders would probably have reacted the same way if he had atom-bombed the Eskimos. Finally there are pictures commemorating his long hamming contest with Brezhnev. The most startling of these shows Brezhnev apparently sticking his tongue in Nixon's right ear. If you get no further than the photographs, your estimate of the book is bound to be wide of the mark.

The text proper is more than a thousand pages long. Most people who tackle it at all will probably start near the end, to find out what the author (for practical reasons I shall assume this to be Nixon himself) says about Watergate. But there are good reasons for beginning at the beginning and reading the whole way through. For one thing, it's a good story. Nixon's anabasis was the classic journey from log cabin to White House, and the early stages of the trip are made no less absorbing by the consideration that he was later obliged to retrace a portion of the itinerary from White House to log cabin.

Nixon's poor-but-honest Quaker background in Depression-era California is celebrated with all-American pride. The scene setting is like watered-down Steinbeck, but there is a certain gusto in the way the clichés are deployed, and the prose is grammatical. (As, indeed, it is throughout the book: apart from a solitary use of "credence" for "credibility" there are no solecisms.) Nixon's father is portrayed as a strong-willed populist, his mother as an exemplar of "inner peace." There are deaths in the family. There is no money. But deprivation is material not spiritual. At Whittier High School Nixon plays Aeneas in a production marking the two-thousandth anniversary of Virgil's death. Working his way through Whittier College, in his junior year he reads Tolstoy. Winning a place at Duke University Law School in North Carolina, he strengthens his mind with the unyielding facts of case law.

The emphasis is always on self-help. The boy Nixon professed liberalism with a populist tinge, but in effect he was already a conservative. He was always for a free economy as opposed to a managed one. He was thus a Republican from the outset. His political beliefs are the most honest things about him and it is doubtful if they ever varied. Since they were hard won, in circumstances which favoured the opposite case—if any family stood to gain from the Democratic Party, the New Deal and the welfare mentality, it was the Nixons—he should be given credit for his independence of mind.

Even when young, Nixon can never have been a charming figure, but he has every right to be proud of his upbringing. Later in life, especially after his defeat by Kennedy, it became an article of liberal belief that Nixon was embittered by resentment of the Eastern establishment and its fancy Ivy League ways. In particular he was supposed to be eaten up by envy of the Kennedys. If any of this was ever true, he has done a thorough job of covering it up in his memoirs. But there is good cause to suppose that Nixon's undoubted vindictiveness was more against liberalism as a philosophy than against the Eastern establishment as an institution. Nixon felt that liberals were fashion-conscious, changeable and unscrupulous. He felt that they would get him if he did not get them. In the end his obsession with this point led to his downfall. But we will fail to understand the strength of Nixon's mind, and the breadth of his political appeal, if we suppose that his fixations were energized by nothing except spite.

It is better to be a poor boy who makes good than a rich man's son. This general truth becomes particularly true when you compare Nixon and Kennedy according to criteria more telling than mere points of style. Nixon knew American society and politics from the ground up. Kennedy had the shallowness of the man who starts at the top. Nixon has his gaucheries, but they have always been part of the whole man. The Kennedy clan thought that Nixon lacked class. It was never strictly true, but even if it had been, there are worse things to lack. In the long view corn looks better than chic. Kennedy pretended to admire Casals. Nixon honestly thought that Richard Rodgers's score for *Victory at Sea* was great music. Nixon was the one who could actually play the piano. Nixon's homely enthusiasms were in fact part of his strength.

Unfortunately for himself, America and the world, Nixon could never see his strength for what it was. He was forever augmenting it with unnecessary cunning. If he had been less clever he might have lasted longer. But he always felt that he needed an edge—he had to get the bulge on the other guy. He claims to have joined the House Committee on Un-American Activities with "considerable reluctance." You would think from his account of the Hiss case that he had conducted the prosecution in a temperate manner. He is careful to dissociate himself from McCarthy, whose own juggernaut was soon to get rolling. But on any objective view, Nixon behaved like a demagogue throughout the hearings. Whether Hiss was guilty or not is a separate issue. Nixon tries to make Hiss's guilt a matter of historic importance, but in fact the historic importance has all to do with the way Nixon used the Fifth Amendment to undermine the spirit of the First Amendment. Nixon pioneered the McCarthyite technique of establishing silence as an admission of guilt. It was Nixon who gave McCarthy the courage to be born.

The House Committee was a Star Chamber. Nixon still professes to assume that Hiss invited suspicion by being mistrustful of the Committee. But only a fool would have expected to be tried fairly by such methods. The point recurs awkwardly a thousand pages later, when the author can be heard protesting that his own trial by Senate Judiciary Committee is a travesty of justice. If Nixon objects to the methods by which his Presidency was destroyed, then he should repudiate the methods by which he destroyed Hiss. They were the same methods. He claims that Sam Ervin and the other Watergate committee members were publicity seekers. But what, on his own admission, did the Hiss case bring him? It brought him "publicity on a scale that most congressmen only dream of achieving."

And so he was off and running—running for President. He pretends, characteristically, that such thoughts were not yet in his mind. Quoting Harry Truman's observation that the Vice-Presidency is about as useful as a fifth teat on a cow, he makes out that it was his very innocence of high ambitions which enabled him to take on the job of playing second fiddle to Eisenhower. After all, it was a thankless task. The media applied their double standards, forgiving Adlai Stevenson everything and Nixon nothing. Because Ike was too big to touch, the liberals ganged up on Nixon. Or so Nixon tells it. Certainly the attack over his supposed misuse of campaign funds must have hurt: his first response was the horribly maladroit "Checkers" speech, and the long-term result was an unquenchable hatred of the press. But he usually forgets to say how indiscriminate he himself was accustomed to being when dishing out abuse. The furthest he will go is to say that he had no choice. "Some of the rhetoric I used during the campaign was very rough. Perhaps I was unconsciously overreacting to the attacks made against me." Someone else was always unscrupulous first. Nixon, says Nixon, would have played clean if they had let him.

During Ike's 1956 campaign Nixon tries to fight high-mindedly, but he can feel that people are disappointed. They *want* him to be tough against the ruthless Stevenson. This is Nixon's message throughout: the liberal-dominated media might be against him, but the pulse from the grass roots is the country's true heartbeat. Nixon could already hear the low roar of the silent majority long before he gave it a name. Its good wishes sustained him in adversity, which arrived in 1960, when he lost the Presidential race to Kennedy. In an act of heroic self-sacrifice, Nixon talked Ike *out* of appearing on his behalf, lest Ike's heart should give way. Nevertheless he came within a whisker of not losing. He might have won on a recount, but patriotism stopped him asking for one.

As everywhere else in the book, Nixon has only good to say of JFK. But he is scornful of the Kennedy machine. "From this point on I had the wisdom and the wariness of someone who has been burned by the Kennedys and their money and by the licence they were given by the media." He certainly learned the wariness. One doubts if he learned the wisdom: anger probably exacerbated his natural vindictiveness. It must have been galling for Nixon to see Joe Kennedy's family being indulged by the press while he himself was hounded, right up to the end, for transgressions which often did not even exist. But sympathy should not mislead, although Nixon would like it to: the whole tendency of the book is to suggest that extraordinary persecution justified extraordinary retaliation.

Honourable defeat in the 1960 Presidential race was followed by ignominious disaster in the 1962 California gubernatorial contest and a duly embittered retirement to the wilderness, where the Internal Revenue Service, egged on by the White House, harassed him about his tax returns. (What he did unto others was done unto him first.) Will he run again? On Key Biscayne, Billy Graham and Bebe Rebozo help him decide. Bebe Rebozo is half of a comedy duo, Bebe Rebozo and Bob Abplanalp. It is nowadays fashionable to deride these two as shady characters, although it seems likely that they are just a pair of routinely dreary millionaires. Billy Graham is harder to explain away. Here again we see the real difference between Kennedy and Nixon. Kennedy paid lip service to the Pope. Nixon really believed in Billy Graham. Kennedy was a high-flying cynic. Nixon was low-rent sincere.

Back from nowhere, Nixon runs and wins. He has the grace to concede that his victory over Humphrey was no more convincing than his loss to Kennedy. But that's war, and here, thrown open, is the White House with all its wonders, including a refrigerator well stocked with but-ter-brickle ice cream, left by the Johnson girls so that Tricia and Julie shall not starve. Bliss!

Vietnam spoiled it all in the short term, and Watergate ruined it in the long, but before turning to those issues we ought to concede that Nixon had a lot going for him as President. Without dressing the set too much, he is able to show us in these pages that he could handle the work. Just the way he offers us proof of his political intelligence is proof of his political intelligence. The picture he paints is of a man on top of the job. With Haldeman keeping the side issues at bay, Nixon deals with the essentials. Whether in the Oval Office, at Camp David, at San Clemente or on Key Biscayne he is at the hub of America. Whether in America, Europe, China or the Soviet Union he is at the spindle of the world.

He obviously revelled in the task and doesn't fail to convey the excitement. He gives you a better idea than anybody else has of why someone should want to take the job on. He even transmits a sense of mission. You can see how he might have thought of himself, without megalomania, as ideal casting for the role. Pat was just right too. She wasn't as flash as Jackie, but she was solid: less up-to-the-minute, but more in tune with the past. She might not have known Andy Warhol person-ally, but she arranged an exhibition in the White House for Andrew Wyeth. The Nixons were proud to be square. At their best, they showed why squareness is better than sham.

It could have been an idyll. But America was at war, both in South-East Asia and in Nixon's soul. Attaining the Presidency made him feel more victimized than ever. The Democrats had bequeathed him the mess in Vietnam. Now they would attack him however he handled it. They would stop at nothing. "Therefore I decided that we must begin immediately keeping track of everything the leading Democrats did. Information would be our first line of defence." He says this on page 357. The thought is supposed to be going through his head in 1968, when he was already looking forward to the 1972 elections. A harmless enough looking statement, until you realize that he is attempting to justify, in advance, the private espionage activities carried out by the slapstick team later to become famous as the Plumbers.

Nixon makes the best possible case for himself. He was certainly in a fix about Vietnam. If he had been the cynic he is often supposed to be, he could have blamed American involvement on Kennedy and Johnson and brought the troops home. We can see now that it would have been the right thing to do, since the North Vietnamese won anyway. Even at the time it was clear to every responsible authority except the Pentagon that Vietnam was a bottomless pit. By staying to fight it out, Nixon was contravening his own idea of a sensible foreign policy. The Nixon Doctrine advocated aiding only independently viable governments and confining the assistance to hardware—roughly the same policy Carter is pursuing now.

Nixon might have got out of Vietnam straight away if he had thought it was the difficult thing to do. But the liberal opposition to the war convinced him that quitting was the easy thing to do, and he made a fetish of doing the difficult thing instead of the easy one. If the whole world begged Nixon to do the easy thing he would do the difficult one, every time. But it would be a mistake to underestimate the strength of Nixon's convictions. He thought he was saving the world from communism. He was probably right to believe that for Communists peace is never an end, only a means. He was certainly right to be untrusting. But he never understood that there was such a thing as handing the moral advantage to the other side. He thought that the other side was too immoral for that to be possible.

Kissinger thought the same way. As Nixon's National Security Adviser Kissinger was the man in charge of strategic brainwaves. It would be easy now for Nixon to blame Kissinger. More damagingly for them both, he approves of everything Kissinger did. There are successes to record: détente was probably the right move, which Nixon carried through patiently, without weakness. The Middle East policy was realistic in an area of competing unrealities. But Nixon still seems to think that the toppling of Allende was some kind of triumph, by which the Red Sandwich was undermined. The Red Sandwich was the device by which communism, squeezing inwards from Cuba and Chile, would capture the whole of South America. The Red Sandwich had to be foiled. Innocent Chileans have gone through the torments of the damned because Nixon and Kissinger thought that a sandwich had to be stopped from closing in on a continent.

It would have been better for everyone, capitalists included, if Nixon had burdened Allende with help. The best that can be said for such cat-astrophic initiatives is that they did not originate with Nixon. Eisenhower turned down Castro's requests for aid. The same sort of mistake goes all the way back to the repudiation of the Dixie Mission. Nixon's proudest boast is that he reopened the doors to China. He forgets to say that he started out as a fervent advocate of the policy which closed them.

So in foreign affairs Nixon didn't show quite the clear vision that he thinks he did. He still seems to think that the invasion of Cambodia was a "complete success." Right up to the final debacle, he and Kissinger understood everything about the war in Vietnam except what mattered. "As Kissinger saw the situation, we were up against a paradoxical situation in which North Vietnam, which had in effect lost the war, was acting as if it had won; while South Vietnam, which had effectively won the war, was acting as if it had lost." If that was indeed how Kissinger saw things, then he was seeing them backward. (Apart from a few such local out-breaks, incidentally, the word "situation" is kept under tight control.)

Meanwhile, as Nixon tells it, the liberals and radicals were wrecking the country. On page 471 he argues that the depredations of the Weath-ermen were sufficient reason for stepping up the activities of the intelli-gence agencies. Reference is made to the FBI's long history of black-bag jobs in defence of liberty. The reasoning is specious, since Nixon is really out to justify the existence of the Plumbers, who were not a government agency but a private army. On page 496 he is to be found "keeping the pressure on the people around me . . . to get information about what the other side was doing," the other side being the Democrats. He admits that he overstepped the mark, but blurs the importance of the mark he over-stepped. He was in fact subverting the Constitution of the United States, which is framed not so much for democracy as against the tyrant, and declares that a Presidential party shall not be formed. "At least, unlike previous administrations," he says on page 781, "we hadn't used the FBI." But at least the FBI is to some extent accountable for its actions. Nixon's personal fact-gathering unit was accountable to nobody—not even, apparently, to Nixon.

Nixon persuasively argues that he knew nothing about the black-bag jobs in detail. There is no good reason to suppose that he did—what use is power if you can't leave the dirty work to subordinates? But plausibility evaporates when he tries to suggest that his ignorance was genuine rather than wilful. The first unmistakable evasion comes on page 514, when he addresses himself to the matter of the raid on Ellsberg's psychiatrist's office. "I do not believe I was told about the break-in at the time." Why isn't he certain? How could he forget?

Credibility slips further on page 638, which records the day— June 18, 1972—when Nixon, at ease on Key Biscayne, first hears about the Watergate caper. Haldeman tells Nixon that the FBI will have to go further than Miami if it wishes to trace the cash found on the burglars. Nixon tells us nothing of how he reacted to what Haldeman said. An eloquent silence, because what Haldeman was really saying was that the cash was laundered. Why would Nixon accept that information without question, unless he knew that the White House was bankrolling intelligence operations with funds meant to be untraceable even by government agencies?

For the rest of the book, Nixon gives a convincing impersonation of a man standing on a landslide. As his world collapses, his prose attains the authentic poise of deep grief. But the remorse is all about the cover-up, not the crime. Just as Nixon always did the difficult thing instead of the easy thing, so he always accepted the responsibility but refused the blame. He takes the responsibility for the cover-up: his subordinates started it, but in order to protect them he allowed it to go on. He doesn't take the blame. Still less, then, does he take the blame for the crime itself. To the end of the line, the most he will admit to is an error of judgement. His aides sinned through an excess of zeal. His own sin was to let them do it.

"If I had indeed been the knowing Watergate conspirator that I was charged as being," he says on page 902, "I would have recognized in 1973 that the tapes contained conversations that would be fatally damaging." It ought to be a strong point. Unfortunately Nixon has by this time already made it clear that the main reason he considered himself guiltless was that circumstances had made extraordinary measures legitimate. He had done what he thought necessary with such self-righteousness that the possibility of ever being called to account hadn't entered his head.

Nixon's book is one long act of self-justification. To a remarkable degree the attempt succeeds. At the end his enemies are plausibly made to sound hysterical victims of what he calls "liberal chic." The House Judiciary Committee produced 7,000 pages of evidence against Nixon, but most people now would have trouble being precise about what he did wrong. The media caught Watergate fever. Rumours that he had lined his pockets assumed the status of common knowledge. He almost certainly didn't. He would never have risked losing the Presidency for the sake of personal enrichment. He lost it because he went on feeling hunted even after he was home and dry.

A House Committee created him and a Senate Committee destroyed him. Under a different system Nixon's talents might have flourished and his drawbacks been nullified. Men just as devious warm the front benches on either side of the House of Commons. The strangest thing is that none of it was necessary. He could have pulled out of the war straight away. Failing that, he could have resisted the liberal opposition by constitutional means. But to a fatal extent he was still the man he had always been. "The Presidency is not a finishing school," he says memorably on page 1,078. "It is a magnifying glass." Judging by his own case, he is only half right. The job did in fact bring out the best in him. But it also magnified the worst. Even as their President, he still felt that the liberals and intellectuals had an unfair advantage. So he tried to preserve his power by extreme means, and if he had not first resigned he would surely have been impeached for it.

The book is well enough done to establish Nixon as a tragic figure and turn the tide of sympathy. It might even put him on the comeback trail. But we ought to keep our heads. The real tragic figures are all in Chile, Vietnam and Cambodia. It is ridiculous to class Nixon with the great villains of modern history, but not so ridiculous to be more angry with him than with them. He should have known better. Nobody sane expects Russia or China to be bound by scruple. The Russians and Chinese, says Nixon—as if their endorsement supported his case—couldn't understand what the Watergate fuss was all about. Of course they couldn't. They have forgotten what freedom feels like. A state in which power does not perpetuate itself has become unimaginable to them.

In certain crucial respects Nixon forgot what America is supposed to mean. Yet the virtues of this book prove that in other respects he didn't. Even now that he has lost everything, he has difficulty seeing himself from the outside. But whatever havoc he might have played with his country's institutions, in these pages he does not betray its free spirit. The book is like a soap opera, yet the central character emerges as a human being. They were right to throw him down. Here is proof that they were not entirely wrong to raise him up in the first place.

New Statesman, 1978; later included in
From the Land of Shadows, 1982

POSTSCRIPT

Time and the archives can make a monkey out of the amateur political commentator. Hiss was guilty. It was a fact written down in Moscow, but until it came to light there was a terrific urge among the liberal-minded all over the world to believe him innocent, simply because his prosecutor had been Nixon. Never an object of love, Nixon's name, by the time this piece was written, was mud: deep mud, poisoned mud, the mud of the Mekong Delta. As the quondam witch-finder burned in the same fire he himself had once helped to light, the smoke got in the eyes of the spectators. It was a kind of aerosol myopia. Not only must Nixon be guilty of any crime he had ever been accused of, he must be guilty of any crime Caligula had been accused of as well. But for those capable of retaining an historic memory, Stalin's rap sheet remained all his own. More by instinct than judgement, I left room for the remote possibility that Nixon might have been right about Hiss all along, and that what had been reprehensible about the prosecution had been its methods. They were in transparent violation of the Constitution. People were always ready to think that about anything Nixon had ever done. It was a safe assumption. But they couldn't have it both ways. If it was Nixon who subverted the American system of justice, then the American system of justice must be worthy of esteem, and, by extension, so must America itself. At a time when the Vietnam disaster was still fresh in the minds of all, it was unfashionable to hold the view that a nation which could get rid of its chief executive on a point of principle might have something fundamentally admirable about it when compared with nations in which the chief executive could get rid of large sections of the population at the stroke of a pen. (The victorious Ho Chi Minh was already engaged in that very activity.) In pursuit of the point, I should have noted that the Supreme Court, though Nixon had done his best to stack it, handed down the decision that finally dished him—the decision that ruled his tapes into evidence. When Gerald Ford said, "Our Constitution works," he was talking something better than hot air.

And Nixon's book was something better than casuist apologetics. It gave me a taste for American political memoirs, biographies and professional commentaries that I have pursued ever since: a vast subsidiary literature that can make it very easy to feel like an outsider. I went through all the collected commentaries of Elizabeth Drew as if they were episodes of *The West Wing* on DVD, and never ceased to marvel at how a journalist could be on such a sure footing with the elected politicians. But once again, the insider pays a penalty. Inexorably infected by glamour and power, the American political pundit is apt to persuade himself that he is part of the government. Walter Lippmann practically was. In 1918 he drafted most of Woodrow Wilson's Fourteen Points, and as America's next war approached he personally invented the destroyers-for-bases deal that opened the way for Lend-Lease and Britain's salvation from Hitler. In Britain there have always been knowledgeable political journalists, but only on the understanding that they could never wield such influence. If they could, they would lose their reputations as writers. (Lippmann's reputation as a stylist was undeserved, but he was certainly thought of as some kind of writer: the resolute drabness of his prose was taken for distinction.) It's a different way of thinking about power and reputation, although one must sometimes strive to remind oneself that it is a preferable one. There are many reasons to envy Bob Woodward. His prose style isn't among them, but it must be a confidence booster to know that your books, before they are even published, are read with nervous attention in the White House, on the Hill, in Foggy Bottom and at Langley. To have attained such a position must help Woodward to bury the nagging awareness of the fluke of fate that sent him to court on the very day the Watergate burglars were drawn up on parade like the Beagle Boys in the Scrooge McDuck comic books. Woodward was just an ordinary reporter, but in America there are few limits set to personal destiny, and eventually, on the way up, he would pass the President on his way down. The piquancy of their intersecting trajectories is lessened if we deny Nixon his status as a man of substance. While he remained alive, that status was still hard to assert. I count myself lucky to have found the nerve, or perhaps retained the naivety, to assert it.

34

HARD-CORE GORE

Matters of Fact and of Fiction:
Essays 1973–1976 by Gore Vidal

Nobody dissents from marking Gore Vidal high as an essayist, not even those—especially not those—who would like to mark him low as a novelist. His *Collected Essays 1952–1972* was rightly greeted with all the superlatives going. Since one doesn't have to read far in this new volume before realizing that the old volume has been fully lived up to and in some respects even surpassed, it becomes necessary either to wheel out the previous superlatives all over again or else to think up some new ones. Rejecting both courses, this reviewer intends to pick nits and make gratuitous observations on the author's character, in the hope of maintaining some measure of critical independence. Gore Vidal is so dauntingly good at the literary essay that he is likely to arouse in other practitioners an inclination to take up a different line of work. That, however, would be an excessive reaction. He isn't omniscient, infallible or effortlessly stylish—he just knows a lot, possesses an unusual amount of common sense and writes scrupulously lucid prose. There is no need to deify the man just because he can string a few thoughts together. As I shall now reveal, he has toenails of clay.

Always courageous about unfolding himself, Vidal sometimes overcooks it. He is without false modesty but not beyond poor-mouthing himself to improve a point. "The bad movies we made twenty years ago are now regarded in altogether too many circles as important aspects of . . ." But wait a minute. It might remain a necessary task to point out that the nuttier film buffs are no more than licensed illiterates: the ability to carry out a semiotic analysis of a Nicholas Ray movie is undoubtedly no compensation for being incapable of parsing a simple sentence. But some of those bad movies were, after all, quite good. Vidal himself had his name writ large on both *The Left-Handed Gun* and *The Best Man*, neither of which is likely to be forgotten. It suits his purposes, however, to pretend that he was a dedicated candy-butcher. He wants to be thought of as part of the hardbitten Hollywood that produced the adage: "Shit has its own integrity."

As a Matter of Fact, Vidal rarely set out to write rubbish: he just got mixed up with a few pretentious projects that went sour. Summarizing, in the first of these essays, the Top Ten Best-Sellers, Vidal makes trash hilarious. But there is no need for him to pretend that he knows trash from the inside. He was always an outsider in that regard: the point he ought to make about himself is that he never had what it took to be a Hollywood hack. It was belief, not cynicism, that lured him to write screenplays. Even quite recently he was enthusiastically involved in a mammoth project called *Gore Vidal's Caligula*, once again delivering himself into the hands of those commercial forces which would ensure that the script ended up being written by Caligula's Gore Vidal.

Yet you can see what he is getting at. Invention, however fumbling, must always be preferred over aridity, however high-flown. In all the essays dealing with Matters of Fiction, Vidal is constantly to be seen paying unfeigned attention to the stories second-rate writers are trying to tell. His contempt is reserved for the would-be first-raters obsessed with technique. For the less exalted scribes honestly setting about their grinding chores, his sympathy is deep even if his wit is irrepressible. Quoting a passage from Herman Wouk, he adds: "This is not at all bad, except as prose." Taken out of context, this might seem a destructive crack, but when you read it in its proper place there is no reason to think that the first half of the sentence has been written for the sole purpose of making the second half funny.

If this were not a nit-picking exercise we would be bound to take notice of Vidal's exemplary industry. He has actually sat down and read, from front to back, the gigantic novels by John Barth and Thomas Pynchon for which the young professors make such claims. Having done so, he is in a position to give a specific voice to the general suspicion which the academic neo-theologians have aroused in the common reader's mind. Against their religious belief in The Novel, Vidal insists that there is no such thing—there are only novels. In this department, as in several others, Vidal is the natural heir of Edmund Wilson, whose *The Fruits of the MLA* was the opening salvo in the long campaign, which we will probably never see the end of, to rescue literature from its institutionalized interpreters.

But Wilson is not Vidal's only ancestor. Several cutting references to Dwight Macdonald are a poor reward for the man whose devastating essay "By Cozzens Possessed" (collected in *Against the American Grain*) was the immediate forerunner of everything Vidal has done in this particular field. It would be a good thing if Vidal, normally so forthcoming about his personal history, could be frank about where he considers himself to stand in relation to other American critical writers. In his introductory note to this book there is mention of Sainte-Beuve; in a recent interview given to the *New York Times* there was talk about Montaigne; but among recent essayists, now that Wilson is gone, Vidal seems to find the true critical temperament only among "a few elderly Englishmen." Yet you have only to think of people like Macdonald or Mary McCarthy or Elizabeth Hardwick to see that if Vidal is *primus* it is only *inter pares*: there is an American critical tradition, going back to Mencken and beyond, which he is foolish to imagine can be disowned. This is the only respect in which Vidal seems shy of being an American, and by no coincidence it is the only respect in which he ever sounds provincial.

Otherwise his faults, like his virtues, are on a world scale. In the Matters of Fact, which occupy the second part of the book, the emphasis is on the corrupting influence of power and money. Born into the American ruling class, Vidal is as well placed as Louis Auchincloss (about whom he writes appreciatively) to criticize its behaviour. He is angrily amusing about West Point, Robert Moses, ITT, the Adams dynasty and the grand families in general. Indeed it is only about Tennessee Williams and Lord Longford that he is *un*angrily funny—for the most part his humour about Matters of Fact is sulphuric. There is no question of Vidal's sincerity in loathing what he calls the Property Party. On the other hand he is a trifle disingenuous in allowing us to suppose that all connections have been severed between himself and the ruling class. Certainly he remains on good terms with the ruling class of Britain—unless Princess Margaret has become as much of an intellectual exile from the British aristocracy as he has from the American.

As a Matter of Fact, Gore Vidal is a Beautiful Person who chooses his drawing rooms with care. He hobnobs with the rich and powerful. He hobnobs also with the talented, but they tend to be those among the talented who hobnob with the rich and powerful. He likes the rich and powerful as a class. He hates some of them as individuals and attacks them with an invective made all the more lacerating by inside knowledge. For that we can be grateful. But we can also wish that his honesty about his own interior workings might extend to his thirst for glamour. Speaking about Hollywood, he is an outsider who delights to pose as an insider. Speaking about the ruling class, he is an insider who delights to pose as an outsider. In reality he is just as active a social butterfly as his archenemy Truman Capote. But in Vidal's case the sin is venial, not mortal, since his writings remain comparatively unruffled by the social whirl, whereas Capote has become a sort of court dwarf, peddling a brand of thinly fictionalized tittle-tattle which is really sycophancy in disguise. Vidal reserves that sort of thing for after hours.

Yet even with these nits picked, it must still be said that Vidal is an outstanding writer on political issues. "The State of the Union," the last essay in the book, is so clear an account of what has been happening in America that it sounds commonplace, until you realize that every judgement in it has been hard won from personal experience. Only one of its assumptions rings false, and even there you can see his reasons. Vidal still assumes that any heterosexual man is a culturally repressed bisexual. This idea makes a good basis for polemical assault on sexual intolerance, but as a Matter of Fact it is Fiction. As it happens, I have met Gore Vidal in the flesh. The flesh looked immaculately preserved. In a room well supplied with beautiful and brilliant women, he was as beautiful as most and more brilliant than any. I was not impervious to his charm. But I examined myself in vain for any sign of physical excitement. He might say that I was repressing my true nature but the real reason was simpler. It was just that he was not a female.

Not even Gore Vidal is entirely without self-delusion. On the whole, though, he is among the most acute truth-tellers we possess. Certainly he is the most entertaining. The entertainment arises naturally from his style—that perfectly disciplined, perfectly liberated English which constitutes all by itself a decisive answer to the Hacks of Academe. Calling them "the unlearned learned teachers of English" and "the new barbarians, serenely restoring the Dark Ages," he has only to quote their prose against his and the case is proved. A pity, then, that on page 260 there is a flagrant (well, all right: barely noticeable) grammatical error. "Journal-

ists who know quite as much or more than I about American politics . . ."
is not good grammar. There is an "as" missing. But the other 281 scintillating pages of error-free text go some way towards making up for its loss.

New Statesman, 1977; later included in
From the Land of Shadows, 1982

POSTSCRIPT

A quarter of a century has gone by but I would not now write any less
enthusiastically about the virtues of Gore Vidal's easy-seeming fluency.
Indeed there is one stricture that I would take back, or at least tone down.
It was true that he had a thirst for glamour, but it was also true that he did
his best to make sure it would not sap his strength. His self-exile in Rav-
ello got him away from a too-constant presence in New York, Los Angeles and London. When he was in those places, he dined in grand company several nights a week. It was on just such a night that I first met him,
and you couldn't count the countesses. Of the men, those he did not
insult hung on his words, and those he did wanted to hang themselves
afterwards. He was in demand like Talleyrand. Had he not banished himself for long periods of solitary concentration, he would have dined at the
same altitude every night of the year. His powers of self-discipline were
proved by both the volume of his work and its meticulous quality, and I
was dense to allow otherwise. Had I been prescient, however, I could
have suggested that a proclivity already noticeable might grow to a distortion. An off-shore base gave him the advantage of an outside view, but
he valued his birthright as a scion of the American East Coast political
elite too highly to let it go. In his later days this tenacious quirk has led to
destructive effects: never on his style, but often on his message.

He is as sure as John Foster Dulles ever was that American power is
decisive anywhere in the world. He warns us against it, but he takes it as
a fact. In 2001 he wrote in the *Times Literary Supplement* to expound his
conviction that the United States had tricked Japan into World War II.
With great reluctance I opposed this view in the letters column of the
same paper, and incurred his wrath by doing so. The sorcerer did not like
to see the apprentice concocting spells of his own. But the apprentice had
good reason. Born on the eve of the Pacific War, and in a country which
might well have shared the fate of Nanking, I had cause to remember the

devastation which was initiated by Imperial Japan for its own purposes, and with a strength that was all its own. The Japanese right wing is still a force, and likes nothing better than to hear illustrious figures from abroad promoting the seductive theory that the U.S. was entirely responsible for the whole event. With an eye to the future as much as to the past, the first duty of any Australian capable of getting his views on the subject published is to buttress liberal opinion in Japan, where the most elementary truths about Japan's Imperial adventure are still struggling to get into the school textbooks.

Admirably alert to the discrepancy between entrenched financial interest and democratic ideals, Vidal has always seen it as his first duty to warn America against itself, and hence the world against America. But the "hence" is suspect. There are things of this world that are decided without America's say-so—the September 11 attack was only the most spectacular—and to argue otherwise is to exemplify the very imperialism that he condemns. How well he condemns it, though. He sounds like an oracle even when he is wrong: the drawback of oracles.

2003

35

EVELYN WAUGH'S LAST STAND

The Letters of Evelyn Waugh, **edited by Mark Amory**

Unless the telephone is uninvented, this will probably be the last collection of letters by a great writer to be also a great collection of letters. It could be argued that the book should have been either much shorter, so as to be easily assimilable, or else much larger, so as to take in all of the vast number of letters Waugh wrote, but even at this awkward length it is a wonderfully entertaining volume—even more so, in fact, than the *Diaries*. Here is yet one more reason to thank Evelyn Waugh for his hatred of the modern world. If he had not loathed the telephone, he might have talked all this away.

"Would you say I was a very ill-tempered and self-infatuated man?" he asked Nancy Mitford in 1947, and added, answering his own question: "It hurts." Waugh was unhappy about himself, and on this evidence he had every right to be. People who want to emphasize his repellent aspects will find plenty to help them here. For one thing, he revelled in his contempt for Jews. In his correspondence he usually spelled the word "Jew" with a small "j" unless he was being polite to one of them for some professional reason. In a 1946 letter to Robert Henriques he asks for information about the Wandering Jew to help him in writing *Helena*. "Please forgive me for pestering you in this way. You are the only religious Jew of my acquaintance." In the letter to Nancy Mitford printed immediately afterwards, the Jews are back in lower case. "I have just read an essay by a jew [Arthur Koestler] which explains the Mitford sobriety and other very peculiar manifestations of the family." If there was ever anything playfully outrageous about this behaviour the charm has long since fled.

But when your stomach has finished turning over it is worth considering that Waugh was equally nasty about any other social, racial, or ethnic group except what he considered to be pure-bred, strait-laced, upper-class Catholic English. In addition to yids, the book is stiff with frogs, dagoes, Huns, coons, chinks, niggers, and buggers. Of necessity Waugh numbered not a few homosexuals among his acquaintances, but it should also be remembered that he knew some Jews too, and that they, like the homosexuals, seem to have been willing enough to put up with his jibes. In other words they drew a line between the essential Evelyn Waugh and the Evelyn Waugh who was a hotbed of prejudice. It wouldn't hurt us to do the same. Waugh was far too conservative to be an anti-Semite of the Nazi stamp. When he carried on as if the Holocaust had never happened, he wasn't ignoring its significance, he was ignoring it altogether. He wasn't about to modify his opinions just because the Huns had wiped out a few yids.

At the end of the *Sword of Honour* trilogy anti-Semitism is specifically identified as a scourge. The whole closing scene of the third book can confidently be recommended for perusal by anyone who doubts Waugh's emotional range. Anti-Semitism is also one of the things that Gilbert Pinfold finds poisonous about his own mind. Waugh was perfectly capable of seeing that to go on indulging himself in anti-Semitism even after World War II was tantamount to endorsing a ruinously irrational historical force. But Waugh, with a sort of cantankerous heroism, refused to let the modern era define him. He retained his creative right to interpret events in terms of past principles nobody else considered relevant. When the facts refused to sit, they were simply ignored. (It is remarkable, however, how many of them *did* sit. Re-reading his work, one is continually struck by how much he got right. He guessed well in advance, for example, that the Jews would not necessarily be much better liked by the Communists than they had been by the Nazis.)

Behaving as if recent history wasn't actually happening was one of Waugh's abiding characteristics. It is the main reason why his books always seem so fresh. Since he never fell for any transient political belief, he never dates. In the 1930s, far from not having been a Communist, he wasn't even a democrat. He believed in a stratified social order and a universal Church, the one nourishing the other. The stratified social order was already crumbling before he was born and the universal Church had disappeared during the reign of Henry VIII. His ideal was largely a fantasy. But it was a rich fantasy, traditionally based. Sustained by it, he could see modern life not just sharply but in perspective. When people say that Waugh was more than just a satirist, they really mean that his satire was coherent. It takes detachment to be so comprehensive.

Waugh seems to have been born with his world view already intact. Even for an English public school boy he sounds unusually mature. The social side of his personality was all set to go. What he had to do was make the facts fit it, since he was neither well off nor particularly well born. In view of these circumstances it is remarkable that he rarely sounds like a parvenu—just like someone waiting to come into his inheritance. If he had not been a writer he might never have made it, but there was no doubt about that side of his personality either. While still at school he was interested in the technicalities of writing and already capable of the first-class practical criticism which he lavished free of charge on his friends' manuscripts throughout his life. At Oxford he was awarded a gentleman's Third but this should not be taken to mean that he was a bad student. He was merely an original one, who absorbed a wide knowledge of history, literature and the fine arts without appearing to try. As he told Nancy Mitford a long time later, it takes a knowledge of anatomy to draw a clothed figure. Waugh's mind was well stocked.

"I liked the rich people parts less than the poor," he wrote to Henry Yorke ("Henry Green") about Yorke's early novel *Living*. This was probably a comment about accuracy, or the lack of it. Waugh's preference for the upper classes did not preclude his noting how the lower orders behaved and spoke. Falling for the Plunket Greenes and the Lygon sisters, Waugh was soon able to satisfy his craving for smart company. It would be easy to paint him as an *arriviste*, but really the success he enjoyed at one level of society seems to have sharpened his response to all the other levels. He didn't shut himself off. One of the enduringly daunting things about Waugh's early satirical novels is the completeness with which they reproduce the social setting. Those rural types at the end of *Scoop*, for example, are not caricatures. Waugh took a lot in. His pop eyes missed nothing. He narrowed his mind in order to widen his gaze.

The misery he was plunged into when his first wife left him still comes through. In the pit of despair he finished writing *Vile Bodies*, which remains one of the funniest books in the world. The connection between work and life is not to be glibly analysed in the case of any artist and least of all in Waugh's. "It has been infinitely difficult," he told Henry

Yorke, "and is certainly the last time I shall try to make a book about sophisticated people." This is a salutary reminder that he didn't necessarily *like* the Bright Young Things—he just found them interesting.

Asking whether Evelyn Waugh was a snob is like asking whether Genghis Khan was an authoritarian. The question turns on what kind of snob, and the first answer is—open and dedicated. During the war he was horrified to find himself sharing the mess with officers of plebeian background, "like young corporals." (In the *Sword of Honour* trilogy Guy Crouchback puts up stoically with such affronts. In real life Waugh was probably less patient.) He was under the impression that no Australian, however well educated, would be able to tell a real Tudor building from a false one. (Lack of background.) He doubted whether Proust ("Very poor stuff. I think he was mentally defective") ever really penetrated to the inner circles of French society: as a Jew, or jew, all Proust could have met was "the looser aristocracy."

In a 1952 letter to Nancy Mitford, Waugh is to be heard complaining about the unsmart company he had been forced to keep at dinner the previous evening. The guests had included Sir Laurence Olivier (as he then was) and Sir Frederick Ashton (as he later became). Apparently Waugh had complained to his hostess that "the upper classes had all left London." Ashton was referred to as "a most unarmigerous dancer called Ashton." Waugh had started off being pretty unarmigerous himself, but by dint of genealogical research had managed to come up with a few quarterings—a feat which he was untypically bashful enough to dismiss as having been performed "for the children." Unlike Ashton's, Waugh's own knighthood was destined never to come through, probably because he turned down the CBE. In Britain, if you want high honours, it is wise to accept the low ones when they are offered.

Such a blunder helps to demonstrate that Waugh, if he calculated, did not calculate very well. In this he differed from the true climber, whose whole ability is never to put a foot wrong. Waugh put a foot wrong every day of the week. Quite often he put the foot in his mouth. He was always offending his high-class acquaintances by being more royalist than the King. The best of them forgave him because they thought he was an important artist and because they liked him better than he liked himself. Most of them belonged to that looser aristocracy which Waugh mistakenly believed Proust had been confined to. In Britain, those aristocrats with genuine artistic interests form a very particular stratum. Waugh idealized the philistine landed gentry but his friends, many of whom came from just such a background, did not make the same mistake. In a 1945 letter quoted here in a footnote, Lady Pansy Lamb told Waugh that *Brideshead Revisited* was a fantasy. "You see English Society of the 20s as something baroque and magnificent on its last legs . . . I fled from it because it seemed prosperous, bourgeois and practical and I believe it still is. . . ."

But for Waugh it was a necessary fantasy. He thought that with no social order there could be no moral order. People had to know their place before they could see their duty. In both life and art he needed a coherent social system. His version of *noblesse oblige* was positively chivalric. Because Sir Cosmo and Lady Duff-Gordon escaped from the *Titanic* in an underloaded boat, Waugh was still jeering at them a quarter of a century later. In *Sword of Honour* the fact that Ivor has behaved badly on Crete is one of the longest and strongest moral threads in the story. Mrs. Stitch is brought back from the early novels for the specific purpose of taking pity on him in his shame.

Waugh himself had a disappointing time in the army. The head of the special force in which he hoped to distinguish himself in battle regarded him as unemployable and left him behind. In *Sword of Honour* Waugh presents himself, through Guy Crouchback, as a man misunderstood. Ford Madox Ford performed the same service for himself through Christopher Tietjens in *Parade's End*. In fact Waugh, like Ford, had probably been understood. He was simply too fantastic to have around. But the code of conduct which he so intractably expressed in real life lives on in his books as a permanently illuminating ethical vision. There is something to it, after all.

Snobbery was also Waugh's way of being humble about his art. His paragons were Mrs. Stitch and Lady Circumference, both of whom could do the right thing through sheer breeding. Lady Circumference's unswerving philistinism he explicitly regarded as a virtue rather than a vice. He thought more of aristocrats than of artists. This viewpoint had its limitations but at least it saved him from the folly of imagining that behaviour could be much influenced by intellectual fashions and left him free to spot the inevitable gap between people's characters and their political beliefs.

His Catholicism was another thing that kept him humble: saints, he pointed out, attach no importance to art. Not that he ever took a utilitar-

ian view of his faith. Waugh believed that Sir John Betjeman's Anglican-
ism was essentially self-serving and took frequent opportunities to tell him
so, with the result that their friendship was almost ruined. For Waugh,
Catholicism's uncompromising theology was an enticement. Just as he
was more royalist than the King, he was more Catholic than the Pope. He
was a convert who berated born Catholics for their moral lapses. When
Clarissa Churchill married Sir Anthony Eden, Waugh abused her for her
apostasy—Eden was a divorced man. The Church's eternal strictness was
Waugh's comfort. On the Church's behalf he welcomed new converts
among his friends with the promise of a bed turned down and a place at
the eternal table. Even more than the English social hierarchy, which in
his heart of hearts he knew was a shifting structure, the Church was his
bulwark against the modern world. Hence his unfeigned despair at the
introduction of a vernacular liturgy. "The Vatican Council," he wrote to
Lady Mosley in 1966, a month before his death, "has knocked the guts
out of me."

In real life Waugh's fight to hold back the present had the same
chance as Canute's to hold back the sea. In his books his lone last stand
seems more inspired than absurd. The progressive voices are mainly forgotten. Waugh, the arch reactionary, still sounds contemporary. As an
artist he was not moulded by his times and hence neither failed to see
them clearly nor vanished with them when they were over. As an ordinary
man he was no doubt impossibly rude but there were a lot of intelligent
people who forgave him for it, as this book proves.

Mark Amory has edited these letters with a fine touch, occasionally
calling in an independent witness when Waugh's delightful capacity for
wild exaggeration threatens to distort the historical record. It is hard on
the late S. J. Simon that the books he wrote in collaboration with Caryl
Brahms, which Waugh enjoyed, should be ascribed only to Caryl Brahms,
but apart from that I can't see many important slips, although John Kenneth Galbraith, giving this book an appropriately laudatory review in the
Washington Post, has pointed out that Father Feeny was an unfrocked
priest, not "the Chaplain at Harvard." What counts is Mr. Amory's sensitivity to the nuances of the English class system. For finding his way
around in that self-renewing maze he has the same kind of antennae as
Waugh had, with the difference that they are attached to a cooler head.
The result is an unobtrusively knowledgeable job of editing.

High-handedly rebuking his wife for writing dull letters, Waugh told her that a good correspondence should be like a conversation. He most easily met his own standard when writing to Nancy Mitford but really there was nobody he short-changed. Even the shortest note to the most obscure correspondent is vibrant with both his irascible temperament and his penetrating stare. Above all he was funny—the first thing to say about him. Writing to his wife in May 1942, he described what happened when a company of commandos set out to blow up a tree stump on the estate of Lord Glasgow. The account can be found on page 161 of this book. Anyone who has never read Evelyn Waugh could begin with that page and become immediately enthralled.

But by this time there is no argument about his stature. While academic studies have gone on being preoccupied with the relative and absolute merits of Joyce and Lawrence, Waugh's characters have inexorably established themselves among the enduring fictions to which his countrymen traditionally refer as if they were living beings. In this respect Waugh is in a direct line with Shakespeare and Dickens. Since he was public property from the beginning, a critical consensus, when it arrives, can only endorse popular opinion. The consensus has been delayed because many critics were rightly proud of the Welfare State and regarded Waugh's hatred of it as mean-minded. He was paid out for his rancour by his own unhappiness. For the happiness he can still give us it is difficult to know how to reward him, beyond saying that he has helped make tolerable the modern age he so abominated.

New York Review of Books, 1980; later included in
From the Land of Shadows, 1982

POSTSCRIPT

Merely to enjoy the novels of Evelyn Waugh, let alone to praise him as a great writer, it helps to have been born and raised in Australia. As a student at Sydney University in the late 1950s I employed his early novels as one of my most effective displacement activities to console me for my neurotic neglect of the set books. I read *Decline and Fall* and *Vile Bodies* over and over, as if they were poems. The class-conscious background of the books was no mystery to me, or to any other Australian of my generation: most of us had been brought up on *Tip-Top*, *Wizard*, *Rover* or their girlish equivalents. We knew what a public school was, even though we had never been to one, except in the sense that our public schools really *were* public. The only misapprehension I laboured under was that Waugh, because he satirized the English social structure to such effect, must have stood outside it. Later on, in England, I read everything else he had written, plus a lot that had been written about him, and realized that he had stood right in it. He turned out to have been more snobbish than any snob in his books, but it was no skin off my nose. It was clear to me that Brideshead, like King's Thursday before it, was a house built in the imagination. In real life he might have dreamed of being the master of Castle Howard, but in his creative life he had better ambitions.

For a visitor like myself it was easy to separate the petty, spiteful and intermittently demented would-be gentleman from the majestically generous artist who had given us his fantastic England. But for the reader born and raised in the actual England this necessary distinction was not so easy to make. Orwell could do it, despite the deep repugnance he felt for everything Waugh stood for both socially and politically. But Orwell had been a long time dead and his indigenous successors in the critical tradition showed few signs of having grasped his point. Forced to explain Orwell's enthusiasm for Waugh, they might well have said that it was no surprise, because both men had the same background. Even today, and to an alarming degree, background remains a factor in any Englishman's perception of the arts, because it is such a factor in his perception of society—to the extent that even the most aesthetically sensitive critic finds it hard to purge himself of the supposition that the arts serve social ends.

Cleverness is no safeguard against this peculiar obtuseness, of which F. R. Leavis, still volcanically active during my time at Cambridge, was merely the most flagrant example. There is no cleverer critic working in Britain today than Professor Carey. (The consideration that I might think this because he gave me the best review I ever got can perhaps be offset by the fact that he also gave me the worst.) Professor Carey is an adventurous reader who makes his judgements according to his enjoyment. He enjoyed *Decline and Fall* enough to hail it as a comic triumph, but judging from the general trend of his social commentary he would have liked the book even better if it had come out of nowhere. He avowedly loathes the whole ambience of the landed gentry and reserves a special hatred for the arty social climbers who danced attendance. To find, decades after the whole *galère* paddled itself out of sight, a sophisticated intelligence wasting its fine anger in this way would be comic if it were not so unsettling. What *is* it with the Poms? one asks one's shaving mirror helplessly. Evelyn Waugh was a snorting prig. He was also a great writer. Perhaps the ability to hold two such contrary facts in the mind without their clouding each other and the mind as well is the bonus for having been born elsewhere and having arrived in England just in time to see its social coherence fall apart—which no doubt it deserved to do, but to deny the fruitfulness of its last gasp looks like perversity. Although here again, where did the perversity come from, except as a lingering, recriminatory and very understandable reaction to the old iniquities?

After forty years in residence, I think I know something of the country's social tensions, but it's still a relief to be able to say that it's not my fight. We who are exempt from the local vendettas should be slow, however, to erect a relative advantage into an absolute virtue. It's always possible that we have missed the nub of the matter, and that an artist like Waugh committed, as a man, sins we have no right to gloss over. There are bright, well-read people in Argentina who will tell you that the capacity of Borges to say so little about life under the military dictatorship irredeemably weakens everything he had to say about life in general. There are veterans of the old Czechoslovakia who can't hear the name of Milan Kundera without remarking bitterly on the unbearable lightness of his not being there when it counted. I still think it a privilege of the *Weltbürger*, the man without a country, to be genuinely above such battles. But he should make it his business to know what the battle is about, because some of the people he meets might have been wounded in it, even if they look well.

Reliable Essays, 2001

36

AS A MATTER OF TACT

Responses: Prose Pieces 1953-1976 by Richard Wilbur

There is nothing surprising in the fact that the most intelligent, fastidious and refined of contemporary American poets should produce intelligent, fastidious and refined prose, but it does no harm to have the likelihood confirmed. This collection of Richard Wilbur's critical writings is an immediate pleasure to read. Beyond that, the book provides an absorbing tour of Wilbur's preoccupations, which admirers of his poetry had already guessed to be of high interest. Beyond that again, there is the harsh matter, steadily becoming more urgent, of whether or not the study of literature is killing literature.

In America, the place where crises burst first, it has long been apparent that the output of critical works from the universities, most of them uttered by intellectually mediocre student teachers, has reached the proportions of an ecological disaster. Yet here is one book, written by a Professor of English at Wesleyan University, which would have to be saved from the holocaust if President Carter were to take the sensible step of rationalizing his energy programme by ordering all academic writings on the subject of English literature to be fed directly to the flames, thereby ensuring that useless books, inflated from only slightly less useless doctoral theses, would find at least a semblance of creative life by providing enough electric power to light a pigsty, if only for a few seconds.

But then Wilbur is no ordinary professor. His university career has really been a kind of monastic hideaway, where he has been able to hole up and contemplate his principal early experience, which was the Second World War in Europe. Military service was Wilbur's first university.

If for ever afterwards he was a writer in residence, at least he was writing about something that he had seen in the outside world. In the deceptively elegant symmetries of Wilbur's early poetry could be detected a pressure of awareness which amply warranted his retreat to the cloisters.

While his contemporaries held the mirror up to chaos, Wilbur took the opposite line: the more extreme the thing contained, the more finely wrought the container had to be. Berryman and Lowell went in for stringy hair, open-necked shirts, non-rhyming sonnets that multiplied like bacilli, and nervous breakdowns. Wilbur, on the other hand, looked like an advertisement for Ivy League tailoring and turned out poems built like Fabergé toy trains. I think there is a case for arguing that by the time the 1960s rolled around Wilbur had cherished his early experience too long for the good of his work, which in his later volumes is simply indecisive. But earlier on he was not indecisive at all—just indirect, which is a different thing. The poems in *The Beautiful Changes*, *Ceremony* and *Things of This World* sound better and better as time goes on. Where his coevals once looked fecund, they now look slovenly; where he once seemed merely exquisite, he now seems a model of judicious strength; as was bound to happen, it was the artful contrivance which retained its spontaneity and the avowedly spontaneous which ended up looking contrived. There is no reason to be ashamed at feeling charmed by Wilbur's poetry. The sanity of his level voice is a hard-won triumph of the contemplative intelligence.

Selected from twenty years of occasional prose, the essays and addresses collected in *Responses* combine conciseness with resonance, each of them wrapping up its nominal subject while simultaneously raising all the relevant general issues—the best kind of criticism for a student to read. A lecture like "Round about a Poem of Housman's" could be put into a beginner's hands with some confidence that it would leave him wiser than before, instead of merely cockier. Previously available only in that useful anthology *The Moment of Poetry*, the piece gains from being set among others from the same pen. It is an excellent instance of close reading wedded to hard thinking. The general statements are as tightly focussed as the specific observations, which from so sensitive a reader are very specific indeed. By attending patiently to Housman's delicately judged tones of voice in "Epitaph on an Army of Mercenaries," Wilbur is able to show that the contempt superficially evinced for the hired soldiers is meant to imply an underlying respect. The casual reader might miss this not just through being deaf to poetry, but through being deaf to meaning in general. "A tactful person is one who understands not merely what is said, but also what is meant." But meaning is not confined to statements: in fact the sure way to miss the point of Housman's poem is to do a practical criticism that confines itself to paraphrase. A song like "It's Only a Paper Moon" and a poem like "Dover Beach" can be paraphrased in exactly the same way. (This seemingly offhand illustration is typical of Wilbur's knack for the perfect example.) It follows that meaning embraces not just statement but sound, pacing, diction. Thus the subject expands to include questions of why poetry is written the way it is. How much can the poet legitimately expect the reader to take in?

Yeats, for example, overdoes his allusions in "King and No King." It is one thing for Milton to expect you to spot the reference to the *Aeneid* when Satan wakes in Hell, but another for Yeats to expect you to know a bad play by Beaumont and Fletcher. For one thing, you can see what Milton means even if you have never read Virgil, whereas Yeats's point seems not to be particularly well made even when you have Beaumont and Fletcher at your fingertips—in fact pride at being in possession of such information is likely to colour your judgement. (Says Wilbur, who *did* possess such information, and whose judgement *was* coloured.)

It is worth pausing at this juncture to say that in a few paragraphs Wilbur has not only raised, but to a large extent settled, theoretical points which more famous critical savants have pursued to the extent of whole essays. In *Lectures in America* Dr. Leavis argues, with crushing intransigence, that Yeats's poetry needs too much ancillary apparatus to explain it, so that when you get right down to it there are only three poems in Yeats's entire *oeuvre* which earn the status of a "fully achieved thing." Wilbur takes the same point exactly as far as it should be taken, which is nowhere near as far. Possessing tact himself, he can see Yeats's lack of it, but correctly supposes this to be a local fault, not a typical one. If Dr. Leavis is unable to consider such a possibility, perhaps it might be of interest to Professor Donoghue, who in a recent issue of the *New York Review of Books* was to be heard complaining about Yeats's limitations at some length. It is a bit steep when an academic who devotes half his life to a dead poet starts doubting the poet's merits instead of questioning the effects of his own bookishness.

As for Wilbur's reference to Milton, well, it is very relevant to some of the positions adopted by Dr. Steiner, whose important gift of transmitting his enthusiasm for the culture of the past seriously overstepped itself in Milton's case. Perhaps goaded by the misplaced self-confidence of a student generation who not only knew nothing about the history of civilization but had erected their doltishness into an ideology, Dr. Steiner declared that you couldn't tell what was going on in *Paradise Lost* unless you were intimate with the classical literature to which Milton was alluding. Wilbur's fleeting look at this very topic helps remind us that Dr. Steiner got it wrong two ways at once. If you *did* have to know about those things, then Milton would not deserve his reputation. But you *don't* have to know, since the allusions merely reinforce what Milton is tactful enough to make plain.

Such matters are important to criticism and crucial to pedagogy. For all Dr. Steiner's good intentions, it is easy to imagine students being scared off if they are told that they can't hope to read an English poet without first mastering classical literature. Wilbur's approach, while being no less concerned about the universality of culture, at least offers the ignoramus some hope. Anyway, Wilbur simply happens to be right: poets allude to the past (his essay "Poetry's Debt to Poetry" shows that all revolutions in art are palace revolutions) but if they are original at all then they will make their first appeal on a level which demands of the reader no more than an ability to understand the language. Which nowadays is demanding a lot, but let that pass.

"Poetry and Happiness" is another richly suggestive piece of work. Wilbur talks of a primitive desire that is radical to poetry, "the desire to lay claim to as much of the world as possible through uttering the names of things." Employing the same gift for metaphysical precision which he demonstrates elsewhere in his essay on Emily Dickinson, Wilbur is able to show what forms this desire usually takes and how it affects the poet's proverbial necessity to "find himself." I don't think it is too facetious to suggest that this might be a particularly touchy subject for Wilbur. Complaining about the lack of unity in American culture, he seems really to be talking about his own difficulties in writing about the American present with the same unforced originality—finding yourself—which marked his earlier poems about Europe.

In the following essay, a fascinating piece (indispensable for the student of his poems) called "On My Own Work," he rephrases the complaint as a challenge. "Yet the incoherence of America need not enforce a stance of alienation on the poet: rather, it may be seen as placing on him a peculiar imaginative burden." It is a nice point whether Wilbur has ever really taken that burden up. I am inclined to think that he has not, and that the too typical quietness of his later work ("characteristic," in the sense Randall Jarrell meant when he decided that Wallace Stevens had fallen to copying himself) represents a great loss to all of us. But we ought to learn to be appropriately grateful for what we have been given, before we start complaining about what has been taken away.

"It is one mark of the good critic," Wilbur observes, "that he abstains from busywork." Except for the essays on Poe, which tend to be repetitive, this whole collection has scarcely a superfluous sentence. When Wilbur's critical sense lapses, it is usually through kindness. He makes as good a case as can be made for Theodore Roethke's openness to influence, calling admirable what he should see to be crippling. But even full-time critics can be excused for an occasional disinclination to tell the cruel truth, and on the whole this is a better book of criticism than we can logically expect a poet to come up with. If there is a gulf between English and American literature in modern times, at least there are some interesting bridges over it. The critical writings produced by some of the best American poets form one of those bridges. Tate, Berryman, Jarrell, John Peale Bishop, Edmund Wilson—those among them who were primarily critics were still considerable poets, and those among them who were primarily poets have yet managed to produce some of the most humane criticism we possess. With this superlative book, Richard Wilbur takes a leading place among their number.

New Statesman, 1977; later included in
From the Land of Shadows, 1982

POSTSCRIPT

It was no surprise that the kamikaze aspect of the American poetic career as exemplified by Lowell, Berryman and Sylvia Plath should make a journalistic splash in Britain. More worrying was that an established literary figure like A. Alvarez—who as poetry editor of the *Observer* wielded almost American powers of dispensation—should write critical articles reinforcing the notion that a near-suicidal commitment was a guarantee of seriousness. In the introduction to his influential Penguin anthology *The New Poetry*, Alvarez marked Lowell high at Larkin's expense, on the assumption that Larkin, who made fewer explicit mentions of the modern world's horrors, had found no artistic response to them. I thought that this was a false critical emphasis even when applied solely to the American picture.

I had already learned to admire Wilbur, and later on, with the encouragement of Frank Kermode, I finally got around to reading Anthony Hecht, and felt the same admiration all over again. Here were the quiet Americans who had put everything into creation, with nothing left over for self-destruction. Perhaps it was just another sign of America's world-girdling cultural hegemony that even its atypical products should have such range and influence, but it seemed only good manners to be thankful.

Wilbur, in particular, was a blessing. The right man at the right time, he was a reminder that the Americans who had been flung abroad by World War II could bring back the world into their work, absorbing it without lowering its value. Wilbur, in the best poems of *Things of This World* and *The Beautiful Changes*, absorbed Europe the way Hecht absorbed Japan in his masterful lyric "Japan." In each case, the artistic representative of the victorious power brought to a defeated, occupied country the sensitivity that would honour its real heritage. Each poet was a virtuoso of the intricate, self-invented stanza that replicated itself exactly for the length of the poem, magically refilling itself with meaning each time, like the goblet of Fortunatus. The evidence already suggests that in the long run what will count, for its international effect, is more likely to be that kind of elegant control than Lowell's "raw meat hooked from the living steer."

Looking back earlier into the twentieth century, we find that it was by no means a rare thing for American poets to match European formality at its own game. There are several poems by Elinor Wylie (try "Wild Peaches" just for a start) in which you can already hear Wilbur. But it was Wilbur, I am sure, who, in that period of concussion after World War II when a stunned planet waited upon America, spread to the whole of the English-speaking world this uniquely American manner of incorporating and re-energizing the tradition of the well-made poem.

As of this writing, I have just discovered the poetry of Stephen Edgar, who has spent decades in Hobart writing poems that have hardly made him famous even in Melbourne. In the best sense, his work is too polyphonic in its own right to betray a primary influence, but I doubt if it would have its bewitchingly exact joinery if the post-war American formal masters had not taught the lessons by example. The lessons go back through the entire tradition of those English lyrics that compound their emotional, observational and intellectual force with the enchantment of their construction. At least as old as Marvell's dew-drop or the rare birth of his love, the effect is of a dexterity of technique that offers solace without declining into an emollient.

Anthony Burgess once suggested, in *Nothing Like the Sun*, that Shakespeare found the inspiration for the enchanted language of *A Midsummer Night's Dream* by watching a slow execution at Tyburn. The devastation in Europe drove Wilbur to write "First Snow in Alsace" and "A Baroque Wall-Fountain in the Villa Sciarra." Poems like that still seem to me the best way of dealing with the poisonous memories left to us by the Nazis. Another possible poetic response to the knowledge that millions of people have been gassed is to gas yourself, but whether a poet offers proof of sincerity by doing so is a question that Wilbur's post-war lyrics ask penetratingly by their mere existence.

2003

37

THESE STAGGERING
QUESTIONS

Critical Understanding: The Powers and Limits
of Pluralism by Wayne Booth

Previous books by Wayne C. Booth, especially *The Rhetoric of Fiction*, have been well received in the academic world. Since it first made its appearance in the early 1960s, *The Rhetoric of Fiction* has gone on to establish itself as a standard work—a touchstone of sanity. Probably the same thing will happen to the book under review. *Critical Understanding* is such a civilized treatise that I felt guilty about being bored stiff by it.

I had better say at the outset that I didn't find *The Rhetoric of Fiction* too thrilling either. A prodigious range of learning is expressed in hearteningly straightforward prose, but the effect is to leave you wondering what special use there is in presenting the student with yet another codified list of rhetorical devices. Separated from the works of fiction in which Professor Booth has so ably detected them, these devices are lifeless except as things to be memorized for the passing of examinations. There is also a strong chance that any student who spends much time studying rhetorical devices will not read the works of fiction, or will read them with his attention unnaturally focussed on technical concerns.

Worrying about what students might do is the kind of activity which such books—even when they are as well done as Professor Booth's—inevitably arouse. But any student who could get seriously interested in *Critical Understanding* would have to be potty or else old before his time. You can't help wondering why it is thought to be good that the study of literature should so tax the patience. After all, literature doesn't. Boring you rigid is just what literature sets out not to do.

It could be said that abstract speculation about literature is an activity impossible to stop, so that we should give thanks to see a few pertinent books cropping up among the impertinent ones. It could be said, to the contrary, that the whole business should be allowed to sink under its own weight. By now the latter argument looks the more attractive, if for no other reason than that life is very short. But for the moment let us assume that good books like this are justified in their existence by the corrective they offer to bad books like this. Let us be grateful for Booth's civilized manner and powers of assimilation. The question then arises about whether his argument makes any sense in its own terms.

Critical Understanding purports to help us think coherently about "the immensely confusing world of contemporary literary criticism." There is nothing immensely, or even mildly, confusing about the world of contemporary literary criticism. The world of contemporary literary criticism does not exist. There is only criticism—an activity which goes on. It goes on in various ways; ways which it suits Professor Booth's book to call "modes"; "modes" which he thinks are hard to reconcile with one another, so that a world of confusion is generated, to which we need a guide. He is a very patient guide, but in the long run it is usually not wise to thank someone for offering to clarify an obfuscation which he is in fact helping to create.

Critical "modes" have no independent existence worth bothering about. They are not like the various branches of science—an analogy Professor Booth seems always to be making in some form or other, even while strenuously claiming to eschew it. The various branches of science are impersonal in the sense that anybody qualified can pursue them. But a critical "mode" is never anything except an emphasis, usually a false one. It is an expression of the critic's personality. The critical personality is the irreducible entity in criticism just as the artistic personality is the irreducible entity in art. Critical "modes" can be reconciled with one another only by taking the personality out of them. Since there is no way of doing this without depriving them of content, they remain irreconcilable. You can call it confusion if you like, but to worry about it is a waste of time.

Professor Booth has all the time in the world. There is not room in this article or indeed in the whole paper to demonstrate by quotation his strolling expansiveness of argument. To summarize his line of thought is like trying to scoop air into a heap. But as far as I understand *Critical Understanding*, it offers pluralism as the solution to the alleged problem of reconciling the various critical "modes." Three versions of pluralism are examined, belonging respectively to Ronald S. Crane, Kenneth Burke and M. H. Abrams. Professor Booth does his best, at terrific length, to reconcile these three different pluralisms with each other, but finally they don't seem able to settle down together except within the even bigger and better pluralism which is Professor Booth's own.

In Professor Booth's amiably loquacious style of discourse very little goes without saying, but if anything were to, it would be that pluralism is better than monism. Professor Booth defines his terms with both rigour and subtlety. Trying to convey his definitions in a sentence or two, one is bound to play fast and loose. But as far as I can tell, a monist believes in his own "mode" and can't see the point of anybody else's. The pluralist might favour a "mode" of his own but he is able to admit that the other fellow's "mode" might have something in it. I keep putting quotation marks around "mode," not just because of my uncertainty as to what a "mode" is, but because of strong doubts about whether there is any such thing. I suspect a critical "mode" is a critical method. If it is, then it is necessary to insist once again that there is really no such thing. There is just criticism, an activity to which various critics contribute. It is neither monism nor pluralism to say this: it is just realism. A critic's method might help him to find things out but we don't wait for his method to collapse before deciding that he is talking rubbish. Nor is it our method that detects faults in his method. We reason about his reasoning, and that's it.

Professor Booth's pluralism has a plural nature of its own, alas. When he means by pluralism that there is a multiplicity of valid critical modes or methods and that some of these might be irreconcilable, I am afraid he does not mean much. When he means by pluralism that the only real critical mode or method, criticism, is pursued in different ways and areas by various critics, he means something, even if not a lot. The latter interpretation of the word, however, would not yield up a long book, or even a long article. The first interpretation has the advantage of providing limitless opportunities to burble on. It offers all the dangerous excitement of the Uncertainty Principle.

Professor Booth is an accredited pundit and I am not, so he knows at least as well as I do that the theory of Relativity in physics lends no support to the concept of relativism in metaphysics. No relativist could have come up with Relativity. Einsteinian physics are no excuse for treating reality as a piece of elastic. Nor is the Uncertainty Principle any excuse for thinking that a proposition can hover between true and false. Einstein didn't like the Uncertainty Principle very much, believing that the Old One does not play dice. Unable to arrive at a Unified Field theory which would reconcile his own theories with other theories which seemed equally powerful, he was constrained to see his own proofs within a pluralist frame. For Professor Booth, this fact is too tempting to resist. Try as he might, he can't help suggesting that Einstein found certain lines of inquiry inconsistent with one another. He wishes his own pluralism on Einstein.

But Einstein's pluralism, in so far as it existed, had nothing to do with finding certain lines of inquiry irreconcilable with one another. He never gave up on the possibility of a Unified Field. He just gave up on his own chances of finding it. Einstein believed that there was only one mode or method of scientific enquiry—scientific enquiry.

Different things which had been uncovered by scientific enquiry might be hard to match up with each other—hard even for him—but there was no reason to think that scientific enquiry would not be able to match them up eventually, although probably part of the result would be to open fresh gaps. That was the extent of Einstein's pluralism. It was the humble admission, by a supremely realistic thinker, that not everything could be done at once by one person. It had nothing to do with superficially exciting notions about the irreconcilability of modes. Einstein thought too concretely to get interested in stuff like that.

Lesser minds are perhaps more susceptible. Pluralism might be on the verge of becoming a fad, like ecology or macrobiotic diet. Beyond that, it could easily become a cult, like Scientology. It would be a pity to see Einstein posthumously co-opted into the role of L. Ron Hubbard. The same thing could happen to Sir Isaiah Berlin, who has been getting praise in the reviews for his alleged pluralism. To a certain extent he has brought this on himself, for appearing to be impressed by Machiavelli's discovery of incompatible moralities. Machiavelli thought, among other things, that the Prince needed to be cruel in order to be kind—in other words, that ends justified means. When it comes to practice, the evidence in favour of this proposition is not noticeably better than the evidence against it, especially if Italy is your field of study. Anyway for the decent politician there is no choice: he tries to do the liberal thing in small matters as in large, just as Sir Isaiah himself would, if he was put in charge of a state.

Sir Isaiah's cast of mind is better represented by his admiration for Herzen, who distrusted the idea that good ends could be brought about by bad means. Sir Isaiah's pluralism is really just the ability to get interested in a lot of different fields. What makes him a distinguished thinker is the way he combines vitality with range and penetration. It would be sad if his sympathy for Machiavelli reinforced the notion that there is some sort of philosophical endorsement to be had for living your life to a double standard. Sir Isaiah, or any other considerable thinker who finds himself saddled with the description "pluralist," should do his best to buck it off. On those terms, pluralism can make any feather-brain a philosopher.

Professor Booth is a solid enough thinker, but he is far too apt to proclaim himself stymied when faced with the huge task of bringing order out of chaos. It would be better for his own morale, although it would lead to much shorter books, if he realized that the chaos is a mirage and that the order he brings out of it is largely uninformative. He pronounces himself daunted by the challenge of reconciling all the differently valid ways of critically responding to a poem. The luckless poem chosen for purposes of demonstration is Auden's "Surgical Ward." Auden would probably have some short, sharp things to say if he were to rise from the dead and join the discussion. He might as well: he can't be getting much peace down there, when you consider how much he is being talked about up here.

Scrupulous in his pluralism, Professor Booth offers us his educated guess at how each of his three paradigm thinkers would approach this poem. We have to take it for granted that he is faithful to their respective modes, although an independent observer might point out that the modes can't be up to much if somebody else can take them over so easily. Be that as it may, it turns out that the three modes scarcely even begin to jibe, whereupon the awed Professor Booth gives forth plangent threnodies, of which the following is merely a sample: "Regardless of whether Ronald Crane finds any one sonnet or an entire sequence to be a beautiful construct, or whether Kenneth Burke finds Auden grappling effectively with the task of curing his or the reader's ills, the 'Abrams test' remains: Does an intelligent, sensitive and informed historian find the sonnets responding to years of inquiry and to his effort to write a major history of the poem-as-moment? It is in the nature of the case that we shall quite probably never know the answer to that question."

Clearly Professor Booth envisages a discussion that can never end. The reader might have difficulty in seeing how it can even start, if it has to be conducted using terms like "a major history of the poem-as-moment" or (from elsewhere in the book) "the need for overstanding." But for the moment-as-moment we can grant that Professor Booth has brought us face to face with the unknown, perhaps even the unknowable. After all, a poem is much more complicated than a cone in space. Professor Booth makes much of this cone. If an observer sees the cone from end on, he thinks it is a circle. If the observer sees the cone from the side, he thinks it is a triangle. How can the observer be sure what he is seeing?

The answer is that he has to go on looking from different points of view, but not necessarily indefinitely. If *we* found out that the thing was a cone, why shouldn't he? Eventually he will either find out what we know or will just act on less-than-complete information. But there is no great mystery. Here as elsewhere with Professor Booth's examples, it is necessary to point out that the matter he has raised is a mare's nest. When the observer sees the base of the cone and calls the object a circle, it makes just as much sense to say that he has got things right as that he has got things wrong. He has *begun* to get things right, and within a reasonable time could well arrive at a proper identification of the object. That might open additional questions—such as what the cone is made of, or who put it there—but to say that a discussion never ends doesn't mean that we don't reach conclusions. Indeed if we didn't reach conclusions along the way there could be no discussion.

A poem is certainly a much more complicated thing than a cone in space, but there is less, rather than more, reason for carrying on as if it presented a challenge to the "inadequacy" of our modes or methods. Unless the ordinary reader is mentally defective he starts getting the poem right straight away. He might not be very sure of what it is, but he can immediately start being reasonably sure of what it isn't. After a glance at "Surgical Ward" you can see that there are a number of things it might be about. But that number is small compared with the large number of things it is manifestly not about. It is not about the fall of Rome, for example. Auden wrote a poem about that subject, but this one is not it.

So the reader, though he might be puzzled, is not completely in the dark. He can see roughly what area of experience is being talked about, and will probably concede that the reason he can't see more clearly is that what is being talked about is something oblique, which is doubtless why

Auden has expressed it in the form of a poem. He will give Auden credit for knowing what he is trying to get at, and will be slow to cross the line into that speculative territory where it is possible to suggest that Auden doesn't know what he is up to and that the poem's deepest and truest meaning is something the author had no knowledge of. The ordinary reader's ordinary reading is already a very decisive business.

Indeed it is not all that easy to see the inferiority of what the ordinary reader does by reading intelligently to what the professional critic does by applying his mode or method. A critic would have to be pretty conceited to imagine that he does a better job than the ordinary reader of deciding what the poem is about. For one thing, the ordinary reader might be more responsive than the critic.

A public, however small, is what establishes a poem, or any other work of art, as worthwhile. This public might be so small as to consist entirely of critics, but such is rarely the case. Criticism might guide the public's attention to the work of art, but unless the public responds then the work of art is a dead duck. To the public's response there is always something that informed criticism can add, but it is never as much or as important as what the public has decided on its own account. Sensibility comes first and most, formal intellect last and least. An extreme case is that of Mallarmé, who was derided as nonsensical even by fellow writers. But there was always a public who stuck by him, out of faith that anything which sounded so lovely must mean something. The meaning of some of Mallarmé's poems will never be entirely clear. This represents, if you like, a genuinely endless challenge to criticism. But it would be a very trivial critic who believed that the real work of appreciation had not already been done, long ago and by nameless amateurs.

A good critic is always an ordinary reader in the first instance. A bad critic, not being that, is usually obliged to come up with an angle in order to stay in business. If he contented himself with saying what he found to be true, he would sound platitudinous to everybody else, like that guileless American professor of drama who discovered Jimmy Porter's monologue to be composed of both long and short sentences. So he relies on his mode or method to produce impressive results on his behalf. Structuralism, in this regard, is the greatest invention since pig Latin. It can make any idiot sound unfathomable.

"When a man talks of system," said Byron, "his case is hopeless." To the extent that they are systems, critical modes or methods are aberrations. They are usually ways for mediocrities to make themselves sound interesting. Occasionally a first-rate critic is to be found promoting a mode or method but the mode or method has little value in itself except as a change of tack. The critical responses occasioned by the mode or method will be of value only to the extent that they express the critic's individuality, always supposing that he possesses such a thing. Valéry (whose *Introduction à la poétique* Professor Booth might care to re-read, in order to study the virtues of a short book) believed that a writer's artistic personality was a different thing from his personality in everyday life. He was preceded in this belief by Croce, for whom the separateness of the real-life personality and the artistic one was fundamental to his aesthetic system. It was, and continues to be, a good principle, but in practice Croce didn't hesitate to blame Verlaine's artistic inadequacies on the immorality of the poet's private life. Croce sabotaged his own system because he had something he couldn't resist saying. He thought that the test of aesthetics lay in the ability to write criticism. In fact, however, his criticism does not always square up with his aesthetics. If it did, it would not be live criticism, which finds its consistency in its own vitality, and not in relation to a supposedly logical framework.

Professor Booth's three exemplary thinkers all seem to possess individual critical minds. Hence it is no mystery that their separate lines of approach are hard to match up. The mystery would be if the opposite were the case. Nevertheless Professor Booth agonizes about "these staggering questions" over many pages assigned to each thinker and many more pages assigned to the supposed conundrum that what they have to say as individuals is hard to reduce to a single order of collective sense. Crane's pluralism, it emerges, has mainly to do with approaching poetry in terms of poetics. He is a "splitter," meaning that he makes precise discriminations. Burke's pluralism takes more heed of something called "dramatism." He is a "lumper," making large claims about what the poem "does for" the writer and the reader. Abrams takes a more historicist approach. But they are all three pluralists about modes and methods within their respective spheres, and since Professor Booth finds himself bound to be pluralist about *them*, he ends up worried about whether he has involved himself in an infinite regress, although he has apparently failed to notice the further possibility that somebody else might come along and start being pluralist about *him*.

Perhaps he is trying to thrill himself about the chance of being sucked down a black hole. For those of us with less time on our hands his dilemma looks to be no big deal. From his summaries of them, the three thinkers seem fairly human. Crane, indeed, sounds too finely discriminating to be summarized at all. As I remember his work from my student days, he commands the rare power of straightforward critical argument. The reason why Crane would not be capable of Burke's perfectly recognizable brand of hoopla has nothing to do with modes or methods. Crane has got his head screwed on. Apparently Burke has never abandoned his belief that his invented line "Body is turd, turd body" says something penetrating about Keats.

"How can we choose among criticism," asks the blurb anxiously, "if we reject the scepticism that would cancel them all?" But these are false alternatives. It is not scepticism that would cancel all "criticisms," it is simple realism that denies independent existence to any such entities. Criticism is not a science. Scientific truths would still be true if there were no humans. Critical truths are by and about minds. In order to pursue critical enquiry, humans sometimes produce systems of thought. These systems of thought may yield a certain amount of truth, from which in turn we may assimilate as much truth as we are capable of apprehending. But to set about reconciling the systems themselves is like drawing up plans for a centralized world laundry.

Criticism is simply a talent, like any other talent. Some people can tell chalk from cheese just by looking at them. Others can't tell the difference even when they taste them. But to say that criticism is simply a talent doesn't mean that a talent is something simple. A talent, both to those who possess it and to those who appreciate it, feels as rich and various as life itself. The question of whether or not critical talent is an allotrope of creative talent is beyond me. The fact that the two talents are so often present in the one head leads me to suspect that they are the same thing in different forms. Perhaps the gift of scientific investigation is yet another form. But I don't need to wait for these suspicions to be confirmed or denied before suggesting that criticism and art have a certain relationship to one another which can't be reaffirmed too often, since it is in the interests of mediocre practitioners in both fields to mix up what ought to be kept separate.

Criticism is not indispensable to art. It is indispensable to civilization—a more inclusive thing. When Pushkin lamented the absence of criticism in Russia, he wasn't begging for assistance in writing poems. He wanted to write them in a civilized country. Literary criticism fulfils its responsibility by contributing to civilization, whose dependence on criticism in all its forms is amply demonstrated by what happens when critical enquiry is forbidden. Being indispensable to civilization should be a big enough ambition for any critic. Unfortunately some critics, not always the less gifted, want to be indispensable to art. In Great Britain the extreme case of this aberration was F. R. Leavis, who behaved as if creativity had passed out of the world with D. H. Lawrence and could only be brought back by the grace and favour of his own writings. A powerful critical talent who destroyed his own sense of proportion, Leavis was our brush with totalitarianism: we caught it as a mild fever instead of the full attack of meningitis. His career was the clearest possible proof that the course the arts take is not under the control of criticism, which must either pursue its own ends or else turn silly.

Professor Booth is too humble to be a dictator. He knows his place. The worst thing you can say about him is that his place sounds so comfortable. As George M. Pullman Distinguished Service Professor of English at the University of Chicago he is obviously doing all right. Most young academics, I fear, would like to be him. It was almost better when they wanted to be F. R. Leavis. At least what they got up to in those days could not be mistaken for anything useful, mainly because anybody who could submit himself to such absolutism had to be self-selectingly obsequious. But nowadays you can build an impregnable career out of polite waffle. If Professor Booth wants to be worried about something, he should worry about that. He should turn his attention to the sociology of academicism.

Nobody objects to proper scholarship. The literary community would be sunk without it. As a denizen of Grub Street I become more and more aware that a thick fog would soon descend if scholarship and learned commentary were not kept up in the universities. Grub Street and the university make a bad marriage but a worse divorce. One can be glad that the universities continue to produce a steady output of solid work. One can even be glad that the livelier academic wits continue to moonlight in Grub Street, even though some of them—especially the ones based in Oxford—seem bent on staying precocious until the grave. But what makes the heart quail is the exponentially increasing amount of abstract speculation in book form, most of it emanating from proponents of one mode or another. There have been important books of speculation about literature, but they have usually been written by such men as Erich Auerbach and Ernst Robert Curtius—mature, greatly learned critical minds who affirmed the permanent values of civilization by their response to the historical forces which threatened it with annihilation. Those who spent their lives in universities did so as real scholars, not as arid metaphysicians in opportunistic search of a marketable subject.

The Ph.D. system continues to breed thousands of young academics who have no intention of ever setting foot outside the university for the rest of their lives. Not many of them could write an essay you would want to read. Knowing this—or, even worse, not knowing it—they write whole books that aren't even meant to be read. In both America and Britain it has become standard practice to publish Ph.D. theses as books. A great many of these publications are abstract metaphysical speculation of no value whatsoever. Some comfort can be taken from the fact that nothing is directly threatened except the forests that must be felled to make so much paper. Graduates in English show no sign as yet of emulating those Italian sociology students who would sooner blow your kneecaps off than argue the point. But in the long run it can't be good that boys and girls are being encouraged to pontificate at book length on topics about which wise men and women would consider it presumptuous to venture an aphorism.

Also there is the likelihood—some would say it is already an actuality—that the sheer volume of interpretation on offer will become a demand creating its own supply. The best route to success for a dull artist might be to create a work that needs interpretation. On the other hand, the bright artist might go out of his way to avoid the attentions of the waiting owls. The result could be a seriously split literary culture, with the dummies pretending to be clever and the clever people masquerading as oafs. We have seen something like this already in the determination of Kingsley Amis and Philip Larkin—both of them deeply cultivated—to sound like philistines rather than cooperate with the kind of academic industrialism which separates the work of art from the common people. Dürrenmatt forecast just such a schism when he made his resonant comment about the necessity to create works of art which would weigh nothing in the scales of respectability. Dodging respectability can be quite fun but with the onset of middle age it tends to get wearing.

Critical Understanding is about as good a book as you can get of its type, yet there is nothing in it which could not have been said in a compressed, allusive article a few thousand words long. In my copy pages 347–78 were missing but I can't say I was sorry. There were still nearly four hundred pages left, scarcely one of them without its suavely muted cry of anguish about the problem of being pluralistic without being eclectic. There is no such problem. To be pluralistic without being eclectic all you have to be is consistent. But really you don't have to worry even about that. Consistency comes with the ability, and vanishes with the lack of it, to see things as they are.

London Review of Books, 1980; later included in
From the Land of Shadows, 1982

POSTSCRIPT

Why did I bother? I suppose it was because I had guessed that the barbarians were at the gates, and that the sophisticates like Professor Booth would let them in. It will be noted that the structuralists were already on the scene. The spear points of the semioticists were glittering meaningfully on the horizon. As the armies of *folie raisonnante* closed in on the universities, Grub Street, I felt, was the last ditch: if it couldn't defend itself, the very idea of a jargon-free critical prose would be irretrievably lost. By now we can see that it almost was, and would have been altogether if literary theory had not had its own destruction built into it: there was no way of remembering any of it after the examination paper had been answered.

But literature would have survived anyway, like the Church in Poland under the Warsaw Pact. It was literature, not humanist criticism, that made literary theory ridiculous. Consider a single point in a single novel: the relationship between Fascination Fledgeby and Riah in *Our Mutual Friend*. Dickens has made the goy the financial exploiter, and the Jew the victim. He has turned an expectation upside down. But to know that he has, you have to know what that expectation was, and how it operated since at least the time of *The Merchant of Venice*. And where did Dickens's liberal view come from? From a realistic analysis of Victorian capitalism, or merely from his great heart?

It takes years to read the history, literature and moral philosophy leading to that single point; and there are thousands of equally significant points in that single work of art; and there are thousands of works of art. There was simply no time to read literary theory: a fact it tacitly admitted by making itself unreadable. But while it ruled the universities, a generation of teachers impervious to literature passed on their impudence to a generation of students who would have been better left idle.

2003

38

HOW MONTALE EARNED
HIS LIVING

*The Second Life of Art: Selected Essays of Eugenio
Montale,* edited and translated by Jonathan Galassi
Prime alla Scala by Eugenio Montale

If Eugenio Montale had never written a line of verse he would still have
deserved his high honours merely on the basis of his critical prose. The
product of a long life spent clearing the way for his poetry, it is critical
prose of the best type: highly intelligent without making mysteries, wide-
ranging without lapses into eclecticism or displays of pointless erudition,
hardbitten yet receptive, colloquial yet compressed. The only drawback is
that it constitutes a difficult body of work to epitomize without falsifying.

For a long time Montale's English translators added to the difficulty
by not being able to read much Italian or, sometimes and, not being able
to write much English. Then a few competent, if restricted, selections
emerged. But the problem remained of transmitting Montale's critical
achievement in its full, rich and all too easily misrepresented subtlety.
Now Jonathan Galassi has arrived to save the day. His style does not
always catch Montale's easy rhythm, but much of the time he comes
close, and the explanatory notes on their own would be enough to tell you
that he has mastered all the necessary background information. One of
the most active of Montale's previous translators was under the impression that Dante employed the word *libello* to mean "libel" instead of "little book." A dedicated and knowledgeable student of the tradition from
which he emerged, Montale was a stickler for detail, so Mr. Galassi's
wide competence comes as a particular refreshment. In all his phases as
a poet, from the early, almost Imagist toughness to the later anecdotal
relaxation, Montale started with the specific detail and let the general significance emerge. His prose kept to the same order of priority, so it is

important that the details be got right. Galassi had several volumes of prose to consider, all published late in the poet's life. *Sulla Poesia* of 1976 is the principal collection of literary criticism as such, and indeed one of the most interesting single collections of literary essays in modern times, but the earlier *Auto da Fé* of 1966 (Montale must have been unaware that Elias Canetti had given the English version of *Die Blendung* that same title) is its necessary complement, being concerned with the question of mass culture—a question made more vexing for Montale by the fact that, although he didn't like mass culture, he did like popular culture and thought that elite culture would kill itself by losing touch with it.

There are also some important discursive writings on literature in *Fuori di Casa* (1969), the book about being away from home, and the *Carteggio Svevo/Montale* (1976), which chronicles Montale's early involvement with the novelist whose merits he was among the first to recognize, and whose concern with the artistic registration of the inner life helped encourage Montale in the belief—crucial to his subsequent development—that what mattered about modern art was not its Modernism but the way it allowed private communication between individuals, the sharing of deep secrets in a time of shallow rhetoric. In addition, there is the abundant music criticism, but most of that, at the time this book was being prepared, was not yet available in book form, so Mr. Galassi largely confined himself to the general articles on music scattered through the volumes mentioned above.

Even with so considerable a restriction, however, there was a lot to choose from. The *richesse* must have been made doubly embarrassing by Montale's habit of returning to the same point in essay after essay in order to elaborate it further, so that there is a real danger, if you settle on a single essay in order to demonstrate how he has aired a given topic, of getting the idea that he glosses over difficulties in passing, whereas in fact one of his salient virtues was to stay on the case, sometimes for decades on end, until he had it cracked. To sample him is thus almost always to belittle him: it is misleading, for example, to have him speaking as an anti-academic unless you also have him speaking as an appreciator of solid scholarship, and no representation of Montale as the hermeticist young poet can be anything but a travesty unless he is also allowed to speak as the reasonable man who didn't just end up as the advocate of appreciability, but who actually started out that way. One of the big compliments Mr. Galassi should be paid is that, given this very real problem, he has selected well. All the books are fairly represented, most of the main different emphases in Montale's stable but manifold critical position are touched upon if not covered, and the quiet giant comes alive before us, as a personality and a mind.

To an extraordinary extent the two things were coextensive. Like one of those periods in Chinese history when Confucian self-discipline and Taoist impulsiveness nourished each other, Montale's inner life was both naively fruitful and sophisticatedly self-aware. It makes him great fun to read, as if the smartest man in the world were a friend of the family, one of those good uncles who aren't avuncular. In Italian the title essay of the book was called "Tornare nella Strada" ("Back into the Street"), but the term "second life" recurs throughout the piece and comes right from the centre of Montale's essentially generous artistic nature. No poet could be more learned about the cultural heritage of his own country and his learning about the cultural heritage of other countries is impressive too, but he says, and obviously believes, that it is not the appeal of art to adepts that interests him most. It is not the first life that matters, but the second life, when a theme from an opera gets whistled in the street, or a phrase from a poet is quoted in conversation. This view might sound crudely populist or even philistine when excerpted, but as argued in a long essay, and fully considered during a long career, it proves to be a highly developed exposition of the elementary precept that art must be appreciable, even if only by the happy few. It doesn't have to be immediately appreciable, and indeed in modern times any attempt to make it so is likely to be just a coldly intellectualized programme of a different kind, but if it rejects the possibility of being appreciated then it disqualifies itself as art. "The piece goes on and on," he says regretfully of Schoenberg's *Ode to Napoleon*, "but it does not live during the performance, nor can it hope to do so afterward, for it does not affect anything that is truly alive in us."

Montale realized quite early that to propose such a line would involve a perpetual obligation to dissociate himself from unwanted allies who would mock any kind of difficulty, even when it was legitimate. That there could be such a thing as legitimate difficulty Montale did not doubt, since he himself embodied it as a poet. But he also didn't doubt that Modernist enthusiasms would open the way for illegitimate difficultly in large quantities, and that the enemies of art would therefore have a lot at which to point the finger while they made their strident calls for a responsible culture. Mussolini liked quotable quotes, and Palmiro

Togliatti's idea of art was of something which people could sing or recite while they were lining up to join the Communist Party. If you don't much like Expressionism, the way you say so is bound to be modified by the fact that Hitler didn't like it either. Montale's lifelong apoliticism was very political in this sense—that he spoke for the autonomy of culture at a time when political forces were trying to co-opt it. Art should be responsible only to itself. But responsible it should be. "Mastery," he said in twenty different ways, "consists of knowing how to limit yourself." It was the necessary corollary of his other famous proposition, the one about how it isn't the man who wants to who continues the tradition, but the man who can.

The man who can is the man with inspiration. But the inspiration has to come from life. This was where Montale parted company from the Modern movement as a whole. For Montale, art which had nothing except its own technique for subject matter could only be a monster. "An art which destroys form while claiming to refine it denies itself its second and longer life: the life of memory and everyday circulation." It would be a conventional enough conclusion for any artist to reach in old age but all the evidence suggests that Montale started out with it. Even back in the 1920s, when he was the unfathomable, linguistically revolutionary young poet of *Ossi di Seppia*, he had that social humility to go with his fierce artistic pride. Maturity was part of his gift.

"Style," he wrote in 1925, the year of the first publication of *Ossi di Seppia*, "perhaps will come to us from the sensible and shrewd disenchanted, who are conscious of the limits of their art and prefer loving it in humility to reforming humanity." The idea had been made very relevant by the events of the 1920s. The international avant-garde had already projected, and was bringing into being, an art without limits. Fascism was bringing into being a reformed humanity, or supposed it was. To this latter end, the mobilization of art was alleged to be essential. In the event, Italian artists and intellectuals were slow to provide Mussolini with the accreditation he would have liked. He gave them medals but, as Montale points out, even when they accepted the medals they did not give much in return.

Montale accepted no medals and gave nothing—not to the state, anyway. What he gave, he gave to his country. As a poet he continued and deepened his original course of writing a new, compressed poetry which, from the puffy and sugared *cappuccino* that the Italian lyric had become, was a direct and vertiginous return to the Dantesque *espresso basso*. Later on, when his early manner relaxed into the luminous transparency of the love poetry and the slippered reminiscence of the verse diaries, that initial rigour was still there underneath, keeping everything in terse proportion. In the most rhetorical age of Italian history, his poetry was always as unrhetorical as could be. His prose kept the same rule, to the end of his long life—a *serietà scherzevole*, a joking seriousness, a humane ease whose steady claim on your attention reminds you that he is the opposite of dispassionate. He is a passionate man in control of himself, having seen, or guessed in advance, what self-indulgence leads to.

Montale's defence of art against utilitarian pretensions, whether from the state or on behalf of the mass audience, has general relevance for the modern world, but the specific conditions of recent Italian history brought it into being. Faced with the stentorian claims of bogus novelty, it was inevitable that he would appeal to tradition. Yet it was a tradition from which he personally was trying to fight free. Certainly his unusual capacity to speak generally about the arts without declining into abstraction springs partly from a detailed engagement with his European literary predecessors. But that much he had been born to. Eliot, with whose name Montale's was often linked, got into the European tradition from outside. Montale, born inside, had to get out from under its crushing weight. He talked his way out. Mr. Galassi's selection from Montale's many essays on Italian writers shows the poet humanizing the past, pointing out what is permanently current. The great figures rise from their tombs of scholarship and speak as contemporaries, even the grandiose and torrentially eloquent D'Annunzio, the poet who was everything Montale strove not to be. In fact, the essay on D'Annunzio leaves you thirsty for more. If it were as long as the one on Svevo, you would feel that D'Annunzio was at arm's reach, instead of still soaring around above you with goggles preposterously flashing, pursuing those "flights of omnivorous fancy which does not always turn what it touches into gold, but which will never cease to amaze us."

Montale's admiration for D'Annunzio was real, but a long way within bounds. For Svevo it was a profound sympathy. D'Annunzio wanted to conquer the world—an uninteresting prospect. Svevo's universe was in his own soul, and that interested Montale very much. Montale's young enthusiasm helped the diffident Triestine businessman to the recognition he deserved as Italy's most important modern novelist. But here again it is necessary to emphasize that Montale was much less concerned with Svevo's technical advance into Modernism than with his thematic return to a solid, communicable, everyday subject—which just happened to be the one subject everybody could recognize: namely, the failed adventures in the soul. At a time of heated bombast, Svevo offered concreteness and the slow maturity of considered awareness. "Removed from contact with the world of letters, Svevo developed in solitude." Montale was also talking about himself. He was not removed from the world of letters, which was never likely to leave him alone, but he always cultivated his solitude in a way which Svevo had helped show him was the key to being a modern artist. The life had to be private before it could be public. The other way round was just publicity.

The essay on Svevo would be enough by itself to demonstrate that Montale, if he was ever anti-academic, was not so for lack of scholarly instinct. He had respect for scholarship but was early aware that it would tend to put the past beyond reach, if only by providing "too much light." He had a knack for making then seem as close as now—the obverse of another knack, equally valuable, for sensing what was eternal about the present. The section on foreign artists has essays about Valéry, Auden and Stravinsky which bring out their full dignity. A keen student of English, he enjoyed Auden's verbal playfulness in a way which would have horrified F. R. Leavis, who admired Montale and therefore assumed that he took a stern line against frivolity. But Montale was always willing to forgive intellectual sleight-of-hand if something unexpectedly lyrical should come out of it. His admiration for Stravinsky was withdrawn only when neo-classicism, which at least allowed the possibility of spontaneous feeling, gave way to serialism, which didn't. Apart from a few sour words about Brancusi, who was a bad host, Montale never belittles a real artist, no matter how variable his work or questionable his personal odyssey, believing that "true poetry is in the nature of a gift, and therefore presupposes the dignity of the recipient." But he isn't dewy-eyed either: the false positions that creative people can get themselves into, especially politically, fascinate and appal him.

Foreign students who own the monumental, fully annotated Contini/Bettarini L'Opera in Versi of 1980 are likely to remain deprived for a long time yet of an equivalent edition of the prose. They will find Galassi's book a useful tool even if they don't need the translation. Experts might sniff at being told who Svevo was, but it doesn't hurt to be told that Federico Frezzi was a poet of Foligno who wrote a long poem in imitation of Dante, thus, apparently, earning himself immediate and lasting oblivion. Montale would have approved of a footnote that gave Federico Frezzi of Foligno the dignity he had coming. Even a very minor artist was a good thing to be.

I can't see that Mr. Galassi has fudged much in the way of information. Where Montale speaks of genius as a long patience, I think he expects us to know that Flaubert said it to Maupassant, although lately I have seen the remark attributed to Balzac. Here it is attributed to no one but Montale, who was good enough at aphorisms of his own not to need other people's wished on him. Also when the humiliated and offended are mentioned at one point, and the humiliated and afflicted at another, these are indeed accurate translations from two different essays, but Montale is almost certainly referring to the title of the same novel by Dostoevsky in both cases.

But this is nit-picking. Montale's range of literary reference is so wide that even the most alert editor is bound to let a few allusions get through unannotated. More serious is Mr. Galassi's seeming determination, despite his evident familiarity with Benedetto Croce's basic works, to remain unaware that you must be very careful not to translate the word *fantasia* as "fantasy," when it should be "imagination." In English, thanks to Coleridge, "imagination" is the categorically superior term. In Italian, after Croce, *fantasia* is categorically superior to *immaginazione*. Imprecision on this point is made galling by the fact that for Montale, as for every other Italian writing in the twentieth century, it was Croce who made precise discussion of the subject possible.

More serious still, the translation is often glutinous. Montale's enviably colloquial flow can't be reproduced unless you are sometimes content to write several sentences where he wrote one. The arbitrary genders of Italian enable a *prosatore* of Montale's gifts to construct long sentences in which you don't lose track. It's impossible to transpose them intact, as Mr. Galassi proves on several occasions by producing a construction so labyrinthine that Ariadne's thread would run out halfway.

This prevalent fault of lumpishness—so unfaithful to Montale's conversational urbanity—is exacerbated by a light peppering of strange English usages, or misusages. On page 57, to take one example, "the game is up" should be "the game's afoot" or possibly "the game is on," but as it stands it means the exact opposite of what Montale wrote. "Poetry is the art that is technically available to everyone: all it takes is a piece of paper and a pencil and the game is up." On page 134, "gild the pill" literally translates the Italian expression (*indorare la pillola*) but in English sounds like an unhappy conflation of "gild the lily" and "sugar the pill," which mean something separately but not a lot together.

The Second Life of Art, of the books in English by or concerned with Montale, is easily the most important to date. Of the books in Italian, *Prime alla Scala* has been long awaited. From 1954 to 1967 Montale wrote regular opera notices for the *Corriere d'Informazione*. It was always clear that when the pieces were collected the resulting volume would be one of the strongest on his short shelf. But the complete work, which he did not live to see published, is beyond expectation. It shows him at his best: in love with the subject and full of things to say.

Montale attended most of the La Scala first nights in the great period when much of the conducting was being done by his ideal maestro, Gianandrea Gavazzeni. The *bel canto* operas were being rediscovered, mainly because of Callas. Early and middle Verdi was being honoured for the first time as the full equivalent of the later operas and not just as the preparation for them. Meanwhile it was becoming ever clearer that the tradition could be added to only by reassessing the past. The new composers, with the qualified exceptions of Stravinsky and Britten, lacked the secret.

Montale's criticism, underpinned by his early training as a singer, was part of all this. The book abounds with solid detail. ("Her diction was clear and precisely articulated," he says of Callas, "even if her almost Venetian Italian rendered difficult the doubling of consonants.") Beyond that, in his usual way, he draws conclusions about art in general. The crisis in music is traced as it happens, by someone who was there, in 1916, at the first performance of one of Leoncavallo's last operas and lived to hear the endlessly repeated notes of a new work by Nono bore the audience starry-eyed in the name of social awareness. Yet Montale's own repeated note is one of endurance, a refusal to be crushed under the weight of justifiable pessimism: the new composers might have lost touch with any possible public except themselves, but Bellini lives again, Verdi is reborn in full glory, the past enthralls the present and reminds it of what art is. In the modern era there is no way for music *not* to be self-conscious. Being that, it has small chance of being spontaneous. But Montale, remembering how he himself found a way of being both, always talks as if other people might somehow manage it too.

These are necessary books about the arts, in a troubled period when one of the threats facing the arts is that there are too many books about them. Montale said he thought of journalism as his *secondo mestiere*, the day-job whose demands relegated his real calling, poetry, to evenings and spare time. But the fact that he was obliged to spend so much time thus earning a living is a good reason for liking the age we live in—a liking that he shared, despite everything. He was the kind of pessimist who makes you feel optimistic, even when he can't do the same for himself.

London Review of Books, February–March 1983;
later included in *Snakecharmers in Texas*, 1988

POSTSCRIPT

Sadly, the first thing I feel bound to say about this essay on Montale is that I still believe he was a great artist. It shouldn't need saying. But all too soon after his death his copybook was retroactively blotted in a big way. It emerged that a good few, and perhaps most, of his reviews of books in the English language had been written by someone else. Montale had made a practice of handing the book to a subaltern, specifying the word length, publishing the results under his own name, and splitting the payment. If it had been discovered that Vermeer had known van Meegeren person- ally, and actually supplied him with paint, the scandal could not have been more rancid. It could be said in Montale's defence that in Italy there has long been a tradition by which prominent painters whistle in the apprentices of their *bottega* to help fill the less challenging stretches of a canvas. It could also be said that in Italy there is a long tradition of outright corruption in all walks of life. At the time when Montale was posthumously rumbled, about half of Italy's politicians were facing a stretch in gaol, and nobody was surprised except them, because when *everyone* is on the take the moral outrage is confined to those who get pinched. But Montale should have been above all that.

Most of the time he was. Take away the stuff he farmed out and there is still a large amount of steady, responsible, thoughtful and generous reviewing—criticism in its most nourishing form. Take all *that* away, and there is still the poetry, which remains near the apex of European achievement in modern times. It should subtract nothing from a quiet tri- umph to find out that its author was a bit more complicated than we thought. I wouldn't go as far as to say that I was pleased when the man I revered as the epitome of selfless literary endeavour turned out to share a few characteristics with the man who fixed the World Series. But I wasn't displeased either; just even more fascinated. The way to avoid that kind of fascination is to concern yourself entirely with art and learn nothing about artists: an impossible ideal and probably a hollow one. There are still a few major compositions by Stravinsky that I haven't sat down to listen to properly. I could have devoted some of the time to them that I spent reading the first volume of Stephen Walsh's biography. It reveals Stravinsky to have been a nasty piece of work in several respects. But I don't, on that account, love the music I already know any the less, and might even feel inspired to search through the rest of it with reinvigorated concentration, having found out that the demigod really was a human being all along. There was something perfect about Montale, and now there isn't, but somehow the bones of the cuttlefish are picked cleaner than ever, now that the soul which chose them for an emblem of purity turns out to have dealt the occasional card from the bottom of the deck.

Reliable Essays, 2001

39

N. V. RAMPANT MEETS
MARTIN AMIS

"This is the big one," I told myself nervously. "The Martin Amis interview. This is the one that could make you or break you." As I neared his front door my heart was in my mouth.

No doubt he would have said it more cleverly. He would have said his heart was palpitating with trepidation like a poodle in heat in a monastery of mastiffs. Oh yes, he had the long words, Martin Amis. And he knew how to use them. He not only had the metaphors, he knew exactly what words like "metaphor" meant. He knew what "trepidation" meant. They had told him at Oxford. He had the education. He wasn't going to let you forget it. I asked myself: Why not cut your losses and get out now? But no, I told myself: because you've got something to offer too. Otherwise why would the oh-so-famous Amis be available at all?

"Come in," said a familiar voice when I knocked with trepidation. (Yes, I knew what the word meant. It was only fooling back there when I pretended I didn't.) "The door's open. Just push it." Yeah, *pushing it*, I couldn't help thinking. Maybe that's what you've been doing, Martin, old son. Or Mart, as your friends call you. Your very powerful friends who can make or break a reputation with a flick of the telephone.

On the hallway occasional table was a copy of the collected works of Shakespeare, left oh-so-carelessly lying around so as to impress the less well-read. Well, I had heard of Shakespeare, so no luck there, Martin. But where *was* Martin?

Then I saw him lurking behind the volume of Shakespeare. Martin

Amis, the oh-so-lauded so-called giant of his literary generation, was only four inches high.

"Glad you could make it. Glad in more ways than one," said Martin in his self-consciously deep voice. "Usually I drop down to the floor on a thread of cotton at about this time and start for the kitchen in the hope of getting a drink by dusk. But I've lost the thread."

Lost the thread in more ways than one, I thought, Martin, old son. Especially in this new book of yours, *Money*. But I didn't say so. I couldn't risk the notorious scorn, the laserlike contempt of his brilliantly educated mind. And I hated myself because I didn't say so. And I hated him. But not as much as I hated his book. "Congratulations on a masterpiece," I said non-committally. "I laughed continuously for two weeks and finally had to be operated on so that I could eat." It was a tactful way of saying that I hadn't been as bowled over as he might fondly imagine.

"Thanks," said the oh-so-blasé so-called genius, taking it as his due. "Do you think you could give me a lift?"

He stepped into my open hand and I carried him into the study, where I put him down on his desk beside his typewriter. I could see now that I had been wrong about his being four inches high. He was three inches high. To depress the typewriter keys he must have to jump on them individually, and altering the tab-set would need a mountain-climbing expedition. I began to pity him. I could see now why he had chosen literary success.

But I could also see why I had not chosen it. So I was grateful to him. Grateful to Martin Amis, the post-punk Petronius. Yes, Mart. I've heard of Petronius. You didn't get *all* the education. There was some left over for the rest of us, right?

Through the ostentatiously open door of the bathroom I had noticed that the bidet was full of signed first editions of books by Julian Barnes, Ian McEwan and other members of the most powerful literary mafia to hit London since old Dr. Ben Johnson ruled the roost. When I carried Martin through into the kitchen for that so-long-delayed welcoming drink, the refrigerator was full of French Impressionist lithographs piled up ostentatiously so that the casual visitor couldn't help seeing them. "Antonia gave me those," said the would-be neo-Swift oh-so-self-deprecatingly. "She said after *Money* I should write a book about Monet or Manet." He chuckled, pleased with his ostentatious modesty. Pleased with the secret language he shares only with his friends. With his friends and the beautiful Antonia Phillips, who just happens to control the *Times Literary Supplement*.

All of Martin's friends control something but this is the first time he has married one. Perhaps he will marry them all. I began to wonder who would marry me. Suddenly I noticed that Martin Amis was now only two inches high.

"Look," said Martin. "I feel I'm sort of disappearing. Do you think we could cut this short?" I was only too glad.

For finally I couldn't see what it was all meant to prove. Yes, he had published a novel every two months for ten years, was talked of in the same breath as balls-aching old Balzac, and had won the hand of one of the leading beauties of the day. But so what? He had never written a profile for the *Sunday Times Magazine*. He had spent too much time locked away reading all those books to know what was really going on in the London he was oh-so-celebrated for allegedly knowing intimately. Had he read any of *my* books, for instance? So far they existed only in manuscript, but they had enjoyed a pretty wide circulation among those not too proud—not too *old*, let's face it—to pick up a *samizdat* without using rubber gloves. Had he read *The Sandra Documents*? Had he read *Offed Infants* and *Tonto People*? Would he even bother to hear about my soon-to-be-forthcoming *The Aimed Sock*?

I should never have taken this assignment. He was afraid of me. Afraid of what I represented. Afraid of someone who was better at what he had always been best at—being young. Being unknown. Once *he* had been unknown. That had been what he had been famous for. But now he was not, and it was killing him.

When we shook hands in farewell at his front door, Martin Amis was barely one inch high. There was an empty milk bottle on the doorstep. I started to put him down carefully beside it. Then I changed my mind and put him down carefully inside it. Halfway down the street I looked back. No bigger than a bacillus with delusions of grandeur, he was drumming with microscopic fists as he slid down inside the curved wall where the side of the bottle met its base. His thin voice cried: "I need you! I need you!"

I had him where I wanted him at last.

London Review of Books, October 18–31, 1984;
later included in *Snakecharmers in Texas*, 1988

POSTSCRIPT

The many models for this parody barely needed to be goosed. All I had to do was echo their tone: a new and deadly combination of admiration and hatred. When Martin Amis came to his early prominence, the journalists who wrote about him, if they were the same age or younger, invariably discovered within themselves not only his ambitions, but his capacities. Today, young journalists who get fifteen minutes with George Clooney are unlikely to blame him for the slow progress of their film careers. Martin Amis met one undiscovered novelist after another, and in every case was led to deduce, from what they wrote about him, that he was the *reason* they were undiscovered. It was a new twist in culture-section journalism that I followed with fascination: talent as an object of blame.

More recently, Martin Amis's position as an object of fame and blame has led to unfortunate distortions in these areas of discussion on which he chooses to impinge as a commentator. A conspicuous example is provided by the publicity surrounding his book on Stalinism, *Koba the Dread*. Reviewing it, some of the historians pointed out, quite accurately, that its facts were not new. In Britain, a swarm of journalists took the opportunity to say that the information in the book was old hat. In this mini-consensus of the minimally gifted, there were two flagrant lies. One was the lie involved in overlooking the fact that a whole new generation would hear about the subject merely because Martin Amis had taken immense trouble to collate the relevant literature and express the necessary conclusions in a style brilliantly adapted to a general audience. The other lie, however, was the harsher: the quiet suggestion that they themselves, the journalists, had already been in possession of the historical truth. I can think of precisely one journalist for whom that might have been so. All the rest were bluffing.

2003

40

HITLER'S UNWITTING

EXCULPATOR

Hitler's Willing Executioners by Daniel Jonah Goldhagen

There was a hair-raising catchphrase going around in Germany just before the Nazis came to power. *Besser ein Ende mit Schrecken als ein Schrecken ohne Ende.* Better an end with terror than terror without end. Along with Nazi sympathizers who had been backing Hitler's chances for years, ordinary citizens with no taste for ideological politics had reached the point of insecurity where they were ready to let the Nazis in. The Nazis had caused such havoc in the streets that it was thought that only they could put a stop to it. They did, but the order they restored was theirs. When it was over, after twelve short years of the promised thousand, the memory lingered, a long nightmare about what once was real. It lingers still, causing night sweats. A cool head is hard to keep. Proof of that is Daniel Jonah Goldhagen's new book *Hitler's Willing Executioners*, provocatively subtitled "Ordinary Germans and the Holocaust." Hailed in the publisher's preliminary hype by no less an authority than the redoubtable Simon Schama as "the fruit of phenomenal scholarship and absolute integrity," it is a book to be welcomed, but hard to welcome warmly. It advances knowledge while subtracting from wisdom, and whether the one step forward is worth the two steps back is a nice question. Does pinning the Holocaust on what amounts to a German "national character" make sense? I don't think it does, and in the light of the disturbingly favourable press endorsement that Goldhagen has already been getting, it becomes a matter of some urgency to say why.

The phenomenal scholarship can be safely conceded: Schama and comparable authorities are unlikely to be wrong about that. Tunnelling long and deep into hitherto only loosely disturbed archives, Goldhagen has surfaced with persuasive evidence that the Holocaust, far from being, as we have been encouraged to think, characteristically the work of cold-blooded technocrats dispassionately organizing mass disappearance on an industrial basis, was on the contrary the enthusiastically pursued contact sport of otherwise ordinary citizens, drawn from all walks of life, who were united in the unflagging enjoyment with which they inflicted every possible form of suffering on their powerless victims. In a constellation of more than ten thousand camps, the typical camp was not an impersonally efficient death factory: it was a torture garden, with its administrative personnel delightedly indulging themselves in a holiday packaged by Hieronymous Bosch. Our post–Hannah Arendt imaginations are haunted by the wrong figure: for every owl-eyed, mild-mannered pen-pusher clinically shuffling the euphemistic paperwork of oblivion, there were a hundred noisily dedicated louts revelling in the bloodbath. The gas chambers, our enduring shared symbol of the catastrophe, were in fact anomalous: most of those annihilated did not die suddenly and surprised as the result of a deception, but only after protracted humiliations and torments to whose devising their persecutors devoted inexhaustible creative zeal. Far from needing to have their scruples overcome by distancing mechanisms that would alienate them from their task, the killers were happily married to the job from the first day to the last. The more grotesque the cruelty, the more they liked it. They couldn't get enough of it. Right up until the last lights went out on the Third Reich, long after the destruction made any sense at all even by their demented standards, they went on having the time of their lives through dispensing hideous deaths to the helpless.

The book concludes, in short, that there is no point making a mystery of how a few Germans were talked into it when there were so many of them who could scarcely be talked out of it. Since we have undoubtedly spent too much time wrestling with the supposedly complex metaphysics of how an industrious drone like Eichmann could be induced to despatch millions to their deaths sight unseen, and not half enough time figuring out how thousands of otherwise healthy men and women were mad keen to work extra hours hands-on just for the pleasure of hounding their fellow human beings beyond the point of despair, this conclusion, though it is nowhere near as new and revolutionary as Goldhagen and his supporters think it is, is undoubtedly a useful one to reach.

Unfortunately Goldhagen reaches it in a style disfigured by rampant sociologese and with a retributive impetus that carries him far beyond his proper objective. It would have been enough to prove that what he calls "eliminationist anti-Semitism" was far more widespread among the German people than it has suited their heirs, or us, to believe. But he wants to blame the whole population, and not just for prejudice but for their participation, actual or potential, in mass murder. He is ready to concede that there were exceptions, but doesn't think they count. He thinks it would be more informative, and more just, to stop fooling ourselves by holding the Nazis responsible for the slaughter, and simply call the perpetrators "the Germans." Didn't we call the soldiers who fought in Vietnam "the Americans"?

Well, yes—but we didn't blame "the Americans" for the atrocities committed there, or, if we did, we knew that we were talking shorthand, and that the reality was more complicated. No doubt many of the soldiers involved had a ready-to-go prejudice against the Vietnamese, but without the ill-judged, and even criminal, initiatives of their government it would have remained a prejudice. What needed examining was not simply the soldiers' contempt for alien life-forms but the government policies that had put the troops in a position which allowed their contempt to express itself as mass murder. Much of the examining was done by Americans at the time, sometimes in the face of persecution by their own government, but never without the hope of getting a hearing from the American people. So it would make little sense, except as an *ad hoc* rhetorical device, to say that it was the natural outcome of the American cultural heritage to burn down peasant huts in Vietnam. Putting up Pizza Huts would have been just as natural. And it makes no sense whatsoever to call the perpetrators of the Holocaust "the Germans" if by that is meant that the German victims of Naziism—including many Jews who went on regarding themselves as Germans to the end of the line—somehow weren't Germans at all. That's what the Nazis thought, and to echo their harebrained typology is to concede them their victory. Nothing, of course, could be further from Goldhagen's intention, but his loose language has led him into it.

The Nazis didn't just allow a lethal expression of vengeful fantasy; they rewarded it. They deprived a readily identifiable minority of German citizens of their citizenship, declared open season on them, honoured anyone who attacked them, punished anyone who helped them, and educated a generation to believe that its long-harboured family prejudices had the status of a sacred mission. To puzzle over the extent of the cruelty that was thus unleashed is essentially naive. To marvel at it, however, is inevitable, and pity help us if we ever become blasé about the diabolical landscape whose contours not even Goldhagen's prose can obscure, for all his unintentional mastery of verbal camouflage. In a passage like the following—by no means atypical—it would be nice to think that anger had deflected him from a natural style, but all the evidence suggests that this *is* his natural style.

> Because there were other peoples who did not treat Jews as Germans did and because, as I have shown, it is clear that the actions of the German perpetrators cannot be explained by non-cognitive structural features, when investigating different (national) groups of perpetrators, it is necessary to eschew explanations that in a reductionist fashion attribute complex and highly variable actions to structural factors or allegedly universalistic social psychological processes; the task, then, is to specify what combination of cognitive and situational factors brought the perpetrators, whatever their identities were, to contribute to the Holocaust in all the ways that they did.

A sentence like that can just about be unscrambled in the context of the author's attention-losing terminology, but the context is no picnic to be caught up in for 500-plus pages, and the general effect is to make a vital does of medicine almost impossible to swallow. This book has all the signs of having begun as a dissertation and it makes you wonder what America's brighter young historians are reading in a general way about their subject before they are issued with their miner's lamps and lowered into the archives. Clearly they aren't reading much in high school, but isn't there some spare time on campus to get acquainted with the works of, say, Lewis Namier and find out what an English sentence is supposed to do? If only jargon were Goldhagen's sole affliction, things would not be so bad, because what he must mean can quite often be arrived at by Sanforizing the verbiage. A "cognitive model of ontology" is probably your view of the world, or what you believe to be true; an "ideational formation" is almost certainly an idea; when people "conceptualize" we can guess he means that they think; when they "enunciate" we can guess he means that they say; and if something "was immanent in the structure of cognition" we can guess it was something that everybody thought.

But along with the jargon come the solecisms, and some of those leave guesswork limping. Goldhagen employs the verb "brutalize" many times, and gets it wrong every time except once. Until recently, when the wrong meaning took over, no respectable writer employed that verb to mean anything else except to turn someone into a brute. Nobody except the semi-literate supposed that it meant to be brutal to someone. Our author does suppose that on all occasions, except when, to show that he is aware the word is being used incorrectly, he employs quotation marks on the only occasion when he uses it correctly. But a modern historian can possibly get away with inadvertently suggesting that he has never read a book written by a historian with a classical education. It is harder to get away with providing evidence that he has never read a book of history emanating from, or merely written about, the classical world. Throughout his treatise, Goldhagen copies the increasingly popular misuse of the verb "decimate" to mean kill nearly everybody. Julius Caesar was not the only author in ancient times to make it clear that the word means kill one in ten. When Goldhagen repeatedly talks about some group of Jews being decimated, all the reader can think is: if only the death toll had been as small as that.

Still, we know what he must mean, and no disapproval of Goldhagen's style can stave off discussion of the story he has to tell with it. In the long run he mines his own narrative for implications that are not always warranted and are sometimes tendentious, but there is no way round some of his initial propositions. From the archives he brings back three main narrative strands that will make anyone think again who ever thought that the men in the black uniforms did all the dirty work and that any culpability accruing to anyone else was through not wanting to know. The mobile police battalions who conducted so many of the mass shootings in the East were drawn from run-of-the-pavement *Ordnungspolizei* (Order Police) and many of them were not even Nazi Party members, just ordinary Joes who had been drafted into the police because they didn't meet the physical requirements for the army, let alone the SS elite formations. So far we have tended, in the always sketchy mental pictures we make of these things, to put most of the mass shootings down to the *Einsatzgruppen*, SS outfits detailed by Himmler specifically for the task of pursuing Hitler's cherished new type of war, the war of biological extermination. Goldhagen is right to insist that this common misapprehension badly needs to be modified. (Here, as elsewhere, he could have gone further with his own case: the *Einsatzgruppen* themselves were a fairly motley crew, as Gitta Sereny, in her recent biography of Albert Speer, has incidentally pointed out while pursuing the subject of just how one of the best-informed men in Germany managed to maintain his vaunted ignorance for so long: if, indeed, he did.) The police battalions tortured and killed with an enthusiasm outstripping even the *Einsatzgruppen*, whose leaders reported many instances of nervous breakdown and alcoholism in the ranks, whereas the police seem to have thrived physically and mentally on the whole business, sometimes even bringing their wives in by train to share the sport. The few that did request to be relieved of their duties were granted a dispensation without penalty. Goldhagen draws the fair inference that all who stayed on the job were effectively volunteers. Very few among the innocent people they shot into mass graves were spared the most vile imaginable preliminary tortures. The standard scenario in a mass shooting was to assemble the victims first in the town centre, keep them there for a long time, terrorize them with beatings and arbitrarily selective individual deaths, and thus make sure the survivors were already half dead with thirst and fear before flogging them all the way to the disposal site, where they often had to dig their own pit before being shot into it. It was thought normal to kill children in front of their desperate mothers before granting the mothers the release of a bullet. The cruelty knew no limits but it didn't put new recruits off. If anything, it turned them on: granted, which the author does not grant, that they needed any turning on in the first place.

Had these operations been truly mechanical, there would have been none of this perverted creativity. If Goldhagen's limitations as a writer mercifully ensure that he can't evoke the wilful cruelty in its full vividness, he is right to emphasize it, although wrong to suppose that it has not been emphasized before. The cruelties are everywhere described in the best book yet written on the subject, Martin Gilbert's *The Holocaust*, which strangely is nowhere referred to or even mentioned in Goldhagen's effort. Raul Hilberg's monumental *The Destruction of the European Jews* is elbowed out of the way with the assurance that though it deals well with the victims it says little about the perpetrators, but Gilbert, who says a lot about the perpetrators, doesn't get a look in even as an unacknowledged crib, as far as I can tell. (For a work of this importance, the absence of a bibliography is a truly sensational publishing development. What next: an index on request?) It is a lot to ask of a young historian who has spent a good proportion of his reading life submerged in the primary sources that he should keep up with the secondary sources too, but Gilbert's book, with its wealth of personal accounts, *is* a primary source, quite apart from doing a lot to presage Goldhagen's boldly declared intention of showing that the detached modern industrial mentality had little to do with the matter, and that most of those who died were killed in a frenzy. But Goldhagen's well backed-up insistence that a good number of the perpetrators were not Nazi ideologues but common or garden German citizens is a genuine contribution, although whether it leads to a genuine historical insight is the question that lingers.

The second main story is about the "work" that the Jews who were not granted the mercy of a comparatively quick death were forced to do until they succumbed to its rigours. It is Goldhagen who puts the quotes around the word "work" and this time he is right, because it was the wrong word. Real work produces something. "Work" produced little except death in agony. Non-Jewish slave labourers from the occupied countries were all held in varying degrees of deprivation but at least they had some chance of survival. For the Jewish slaves, "work" really meant murder, slow but sure. Here is further confirmation, if it were needed (he overestimates the need, because the sad fact is already well established throughout the literature of the subject), that the Nazi policy on the exploitation of Jewish labour was too irrational even to be ruthless. A ruthless policy would have employed the Jews for their talents and quali-fications, concentrated their assigned tasks on the war effort, kept them healthy while they laboured, and killed them afterwards. Nazi policy was to starve, beat and torture them up to and including the point of death even in those comparatively few cases when the job they had been assigned to might have helped win the war, or anyway stave off defeat for a little longer. The Krupp armaments factories in Essen were typical in that the Jewish workers were given hell (Alfried Krupp, who might have faced the rope if he had ever admitted knowledge of the workers tortured in the basement of his own office block, lived to be measured for a new Porsche every year) but atypical in that the Jews were actually employed in doing something useful. The more usual scenario involved lifting something heavy, carrying it somewhere else, putting it down, and carry-ing back something just like it, with beatings all the way if you dropped it. What the something was was immaterial: a big rock would do fine. These were Sisyphean tasks, except that not even Sisyphus had to run the gauntlet. Tracing well the long-standing strain in German anti-Semitism which held that Jews were parasites and had never done any labour, Goldhagen argues persuasively that this form of punishment was meant to remind them of this supposed fact before they died: to make them die of the realization. Here is a hint of what his book might have been—he is really getting somewhere when he traces this kind of self-defeating irrationality on the Nazis' part to an ideal: perhaps their only ideal. It was a mad ideal, but its sincerity was proved by the price they paid for it. At all costs, even at the cost of their losing the war, they pursued their self-imposed "task" of massacring people who had not only done them no harm but might well have done them some good—of wasting them.

Many of the top Nazis were opportunists. In the end, Goering would probably have forgotten all about the Jews if he could have done a deal; Himmler did try to do a deal on that very basis; and Goebbels, though he was a raving anti-Semite until the very end, was nothing like that at the beginning. During his student career he respected his Jewish professors, and seems to have taken up anti-Semitism with an eye to the main chance. He got into it the way Himmler and Goering were ready to get out of it, because even his fanatacism was a power play. But for Hitler it was not so. According to him, Jews had never done anything useful for Germany and never could. It was a belief bound to result in his eventual military defeat, even if he had conquered all Europe and Britain with it; because in the long run he would have come up against the atomic bomb, developed in America mainly by the very scientists he had driven out of Europe. On the vital part played in German science by Jews he could never listen to reason. Max Planck protested in 1933 about what the new exclusion laws would do to the universities. In view of his great prestige he was granted an audience with the Führer. Planck hardly got a chance to open his mouth. Hitler regaled him with a three-quarters-of-an-hour lecture about mathematics, which Planck later called one of the stupidest things he had ever heard in his life. The pure uselessness of all Jews, the expiation they owed for their parasitism, was at the centre of Hitler's purposes until the last hour, and the same was true of all who shared his lethal convictions.

This bleak truth is brought out sharply by the third and main strand in Goldhagen's book, which deals with the death marches in the closing stage of the war, when the camps in the East were threatened with being overrun. The war was all but lost, yet the Nazis went on diverting scarce resources into tormenting helpless civilians. The survivors were already starving when they set out from the Eastern camps, and as they were herded on foot towards camps in the Third Reich their guards, who might conceivably have gained credit after the imminent capitulation by behaving mercifully, behaved worse than ever. They starved their charges until they could hardly walk and then tortured them for not walking faster. This behaviour seems beyond comprehension, and, indeed, it is—but it does make a horrible sort of sense if we accept that for the Nazis the war against the Jews was the one that really mattered.

Goldhagen's account of the death marches gives too much weight to the fact that these horrors continued even after Himmler issued instructions that the Jews should be kept alive. ("Perhaps it's time," he famously said to a Jewish representative in 1945, "for us Germans and you Jews to bury the hatchet.") Goldhagen doesn't consider that the guards, both men and women, were facing a return to powerlessness and were thus unlikely to relinquish their shred of omnipotence while they still had it. He prefers to contend that the killings went on because the people in general were in the grip of a force more powerful than Nazi orders: eliminationist anti-Semitism. To him, nothing but a theory in the perpetrator's mind—in this case, the Germans' view that the Jews were subhuman and thus beyond compassion—can explain gratuitous cruelty. But recent history has shown that people can become addicted to torturing their fellow human beings while feeling no sense of racial superiority to them, or even while feeling that no particular purpose is being served by the torture. In some of the Latin American dictatorships, torturers who had quickly extracted all the relevant information often went on with the treatment, simply to see what the victim could be reduced to, especially if the victim was a woman. To construct a political theory that explains such behaviour is tempting, but finally you are faced with the possibility that the capacity to do these things has no necessary connection with politics—and the truly dreadful possibility that it might have some connection with sexual desire, in which case we had better hope that we are talking about nurture rather than nature. A genetic propensity would put us all in it: Original Sin with a vengeance.

The price for holding to the conviction about the all-pervasiveness of murderous anti-Semitism among the Germans is the obligation to account for every instance of those who showed mercy. In his discussion of *Kristallnacht*, Goldhagen quotes a Gestapo report (obviously composed by a factotum not yet fully in synch with the Führer's vision) as saying that by far the greater part of the German population "does not understand the senseless individual acts of violence and terror." Why shouldn't the people have understood, if their anti-Semitism was as eliminationist as Goldhagen says it was? Later, talking about one of Police Battalion 309's operations in Bialystok, he mentions a "German army officer appalled by the licentious killing of unarmed civilians," and he dismisses a conscience-stricken Major Trapp, who, having been ordered to carry out a mass killing, was heard to exclaim, "My God! Why must I do this?" Were these men eliminationist anti-Semites, too? We could afford to consider their cases without any danger of lapsing into the by now discredited notion that the *Wehrmacht* was not implicated. Finally, during a reflection on the Helmbrechts death march, Goldhagen mentions that some of the guards behaved with a touch of humanity. He doesn't make enough of his own observation that they were the older guards—"Germans . . . old enough to have been bred not only on Nazi culture."

For Goldhagen, prejudice is the sole enemy. Other scholars, such as Raul Hilberg in his *Perpetrators, Victims, Bystanders*, have tried to show how Germans overcame their inhibitions to kill Jews. Goldhagen's monolithic thesis is that there were no inhibitions in the first place. But we need to make a distinction between Germany's undeniably noxious anti-Semitic inheritance—an age-old dream of purity, prurient as all such dreams—and the way the Nazi government, using every means of bribery, propaganda, social pressure and violent coercion in its power, turned that dream into a living nightmare. Goldhagen slides past the point, and the result is a crippling injury to the otherwise considerable worth of his book. He could, in fact, have gone further in establishing how early the Final Solution got rolling. Gilbert does a better job of showing that it was, in effect, under way after the invasion of Poland, where thousands of Jews were murdered and the rest herded into the ghettos. Goldhagen quotes some of Heydrich's September 21, 1939, order about forming the ghettos but omits the most revealing clause, in which Heydrich ordered that the ghettos be established near railheads. That can have meant only one thing. In May of 1941, Goering sent a memo from the Central Office of Emigration in Berlin ordering that no more Jews be allowed to leave the occupied territories. That, too, can have meant only one thing. Hannah Arendt was not wrong when she said about Nazi Germany in its early stages that only a madman could guess what would happen next. In 1936, Heinrich Mann (Thomas's older brother) published an essay predicting the whole event, simply on the basis of the Nuremberg laws and what had already happened in the first concentration camps. But his was a very rare case, perhaps made possible by artistic insight. It needed sympathy with the Devil to take the Nazis at their word; good people rarely know that much about evil. But well in advance of the Holocaust's official starting date there were plenty of bad people who didn't need to be told about mass extermination before they got the picture.

Here Goldhagen, in his unquenchable ire, provides a useful corrective to those commentators who persist in extending the benefit of the doubt to opportunists like Albert Speer. Gitta Sereny's book is a masterpiece of wide-ranging sympathy, but she wanders too near naivety when she worries at the non-subject of when Speer knew about what his terrible friends had in mind and whether he had actually read *Mein Kampf*. In 1936, a popular album about Hitler carried an article under Speer's name which quoted *Mein Kampf* by the chunk: of course Speer had read it, and of course he knew about the Final Solution from the hour it got under way. The top Nazis didn't conceal these things from one another. They did, however, conceal these things from the German people. Why was that? There is something to Goldhagen's contention that the people found out anyway—that eventually everyone knew at least something. But why, if they were so receptive to the idea, weren't the people immediately told everything? Surely the answer is that Hitler shared the Gestapo's suspicion about the ability of the people to think "correctly" on the subject.

He certainly had his doubts before he came to power. In the election of 1930, which won the Nazis their entrée into the political system, the Jewish issue was scarcely mentioned. And later, when the Third Reich began its expansion into other countries, in all too many cases a significant part of the local populations could be relied on to do the very thing that Goldhagen accuses the Germans of—to start translating their anti-Semitism into a round-up the moment the whistle blew. In the Baltic countries, in the Ukraine, and in Romania and Yugoslavia, the results were horrendous from the outset. A more civilized-sounding but even more sinister case was France, where the Vichy regime exceeded the SS's requirements for lists of Jewish men, and handed over lists of women and children as well—the preliminary to the mass deportations from Drancy, which proceeded with no opposition to speak of. Why weren't the Germans themselves seen by the Nazis as being thoroughly biddable from the start?

Goldhagen leaves the question untouched because he has no answer. He is so certain of the entire German population's active collaboration—or, at the very least, its approving compliance—in the Holocaust that he underplays the Nazi state's powers of coercion through violence, something that no previous authority on the subject has managed to do. He overemphasizes the idea that the German people weren't completely powerless to shape Nazi policies; he cites, for example, the widespread public condemnation of the policy that resulted in the euthanizing of physically and mentally handicapped Germans. The practice was stopped, but in that case people were protesting the treatment of their own loved ones, and the Jews were not their loved ones. There could easily have been more protests on behalf of the Jews if the penalty for protesting had not been severe and well known.

Goldhagen qualifies the bravery of the Protestant minister and Nazi opponent Martin Niemöller by pointing out—correctly, alas—that he was an anti-Semite. But he doesn't mention the case of a Swabian pastor who after *Kristallnacht* told his congregation that the Nazi assault on the Jews would bring divine punishment. The Nazis beat him to a pulp, threw him onto the roof of a shed, smashed up his vicarage and sent him to prison. And what about the Catholic priest Bernhard Lichtenberg, who, after the burning of the synagogues, closed each of his evening services with a prayer for the Jews? When he protested the deportations, he was put on a train himself—to Dachau. These men were made examples of to discourage others. They were made to pay for their crime.

Because it *was* a crime—the biggest one a non-Jewish German could commit. In Berlin (always the city whose population Hitler most distrusted), some non-Jewish German wives managed to call a temporary halt to the round-up of their Jewish husbands, but that scarcely proves that a mass protest would have been successful, or even, in the long run, tolerated without reprisal. The penalties for helping Jews got worse in direct proportion to the sanctions imposed against them, and everyone knew what the supreme penalty was: forms of capital punishment under the Nazis included the axe and the guillotine. (The axe was brought back from the museum *because* it was medieval.) Both the Protestant and the Catholic Church knuckled under to the Nazis with a suspicious alacrity in which rampant anti-Semitism was undoubtedly a factor, but the general failure of rank-and-file priests and ministers to bear individual witness has to be put down at least partly to the risks they would have run if they had done so. (Later on, when the Germans occupied Italy after the Badoglio government signed an armistice with the Allies, and the extreme anti-Jewish measures that Mussolini had stopped short of were put into effect, the round-up was a comparative failure, partly because the priests and nuns behaved so well. But they had not spent years with the threat of the concentration camp and the axe hanging over them.) In Germany, everyone knew that hiding or helping Jews was an unpardonable crime, which would be punished as severely as an attack on Hitler's life—because it *was* an attack on Hitler's life. Why, Goldhagen asks, did the population not rise up? The answer is obvious: because you had to be a hero to do so.

·　　·　　·

Eventually, of course, a small but significant segment of the German people did rise up, because they *were* heroes. About the various resistance groups of the pre-war years Goldhagen has little to say, and about the participants in the attempt on Hitler's life of July 20, 1944, he concludes that they were mostly anti-Semitic and that their rebellion against the Nazi regime was not motivated chiefly by its treatment of the Jews. But from Joachim Fest's 1994 *Staatsstreich* (Coup d'État) we know that Axel von dem Bussche-Streithorst, who was twenty-four at the time of the plot, turned against Hitler after witnessing a mass shooting of thousands of Jews at the Dubno airfield, in the Ukraine, and that Ulrich-Wilhelm Graf Schwerin von Schwanenfeld was turned towards resistance after seeing what the *Einsatzgruppen* were up to in Poland. There are further such examples in the *Lexikon des Widerstandes 1933–1945*, an honour roll of those who rebelled, and in a 1986 collection of essays by various historians entitled *Der Widerstand Gegen den Nationalsozialismus* (The Resistance Against National Socialism). The latter volume includes a list of the twenty July plotters who, after the plot failed, told the Gestapo during their interrogation that the reason for their rebellion was the treatment of the Jews. There are several names you would expect: Julius Leber, Dietrich Bonhöffer, Adolf Reichwein and Carl Goerdeler—men who had been scheming to get rid of Hitler even during the years of his success. But then there are names that smack of the *Almanach de Gotha*: Alexander and Berthold Graf Schenk von Stauffenberg, Hans von Dohnanyi,

Heinrich Graf von Lehndorff, Helmuth James Graf von Moltke. . . . There is no reason to think that these *Hochadel* sons were necessarily liberal. Some of them came from arch-conservative families, and no doubt a good number had grown up with anti-Semitism hanging around the house like heavy curtains. Most of them were career officers who had relished the chance to rebuild the German Army; some even nursed the hopelessly romantic idea that after Hitler was killed *Grossdeutschland* might remain intact to go on fighting beside the Western Allies against the Soviet Union. But about the sincerity of their disgust at what happened to the Jews there can be no doubt. Though it could scarcely have made things easier for them, they told the Gestapo about it, thereby testifying to the sacrificial element in an enterprise that may have failed as a plot but succeeded as a ceremony—the ceremony of innocence which the Nazis had always been so keen to drown.

The plot was already a ceremony before it was launched. The experienced Henning von Tresckow, who had been in on several attempts before, was well aware that it might fail but told his fellow conspirators that it should go ahead anyway, *coute que coute.* Claus Graf von Stauffenberg's famous last words *Es lebe das geheime Deutschland* have turned out to be not quite so romantically foolish as they sounded at the time. If there never was a secret Germany, the July plotters at least provided a sacred moment, and the Germans of today are right to cherish it. As for the aristocracy, though even the bravery of its flower could not offset the way that it helped to sabotage the Weimar Republic, at least it regained its honour, in preparation for its retirement from the political stage. Since then the aristocracy has served Germany well in all walks of life—the Gräfin Dornhoff, active proprietress of *Die Zeit*, one of the great newspapers of the world, would be an asset to any nation—but it has paid democracy the belated compliment of a decent reticence. Churchill, the instinctive opponent of Hitler and all his works, always thought that Prussia was the nerve centre of German bestiality. He was wrong about that. Hans Frank, outstanding even among Gauleiters for his epic savagery, was closer to the truth. Many of the July plotters had a background in the famously snobbish Prussian Ninth Infantry regiment, of which Frank himself was a reservist. Just before his own hanging at Nuremberg, Frank said that the Ninth's officers had never understood *Antisemitismus der spezifisches Nazi-Art* (anti-Semitism of the specific Nazi type). They had been unsound on the Jewish question.

How many of the German population were unsound on the Jewish question we can never now know. Probably there were fewer than we would like to think, but almost certainly there were more than Goldhagen allows. However many there were, there was not a lot they could do if they didn't want to get hurt. After the Nazis finally came to absolute power, the build-up to the annihilation of the Jews moved stage by stage, always with the occasional lull that allowed people to think the madness might be over. Certainly there were a lot of Jews who wanted to think that, and who can blame them? Seizing the chance to emigrate meant leaving behind everything they had. Some of them—especially the baptized and those who no longer practised their faith—never stopped thinking of themselves as Germans, believing, correctly, that the regime which criminalized them was a criminal regime. They thought Germany would get its senses back. They would scarcely have done so if they had thought that there were no non-Jewish Germans who thought the same.

From the year the Nazis took power right up until *Kristallnacht* in November 1938, the legal deprivations and persecutions looked selective, as if there might be some viable limit beyond which they would not go. After *Kristallnacht*, it became clearer that an all-inclusive, no-holds-barred pogrom was under way, but by then it was too late. It was too late for everyone, non-Jewish Germans included. But really it had always been too late, ever since the Nazis rewrote the laws so that their full apparatus of terror could be legally directed against anyone who disagreed with them. Is it any wonder that so many of those who retained their citizenship turned their backs on the pariahs from whom it had been stripped? When one Communist shot a storm trooper, eleven Communists were immediately decapitated in reprisal. Everyone knew things like that. Those were the first things that every German in the Nazi era ever knew—a fact worth remembering when we confidently assume that they all must have known about the last thing, the Holocaust. It can be remarkable what you don't find out when you are afraid for just yourself, let alone for your family. All you have to do is look away. And the Nazis made very sure, even when Hitler was tumultuously popular in the flush of his diplomatic and military successes, that failure to join in the exultant unanimity would not pass unnoticed. Even if you lay low, you still had to stick your right hand in the air. Max Weber defined the state as that organization holding the monopoly of legalized violence. The Nazi state overfulfilled his definition by finding new forms of violence to make legal. Probably Goldhagen realizes all that. But he doesn't say much about it, because he has a bigger, better idea that leaves the Nazis looking like last-minute walk-ons in the closing scene of *Götterdämmerung*: spear carriers in Valhalla.

Here we have to turn to his account of the growth of German anti-Semitism, which means that we have to turn back to the beginning of the book. His thesis would have gone better at the end, as a speculative afterthought, but he puts it at the front because it contains the premise that for him explains everything. Since most of it is written in the brain-curdling jargon which he later partly lets drop when he gets to the Holocaust itself, this glutinous treatise would make for a slow start even if it were consistent. But the reader is continually stymied by what is left out or glossed over. An artist in the firm grip of his own brush, Goldhagen slap-happily paints a picture of anti-Semitism pervading all levels of society, without explaining how it failed to pervade the members of the political class who contrived to grant citizenship to the Jews. Beginning early in the nineteenth century, the process of emancipation moved through the German States, culminating, in 1869, with citizenship for every Jew in the North German Confederation. (The laws were carried over into the *Kaiserreich* after German unification, in 1871.) Even in the tolerant Austria-Hungary of Emperor Franz Josef, citizenship for Jews had some strings attached, whereas in Germany civil rights for Jews remained on the books until the Nazis rewrote them. Not even in the reign of Kaiser Wilhelm II, a choleric anti-Semite by the end, were people of Jewish background deprived of their rights. They undoubtedly had trouble exercising them—prejudice was indeed everywhere, in varying degrees—but that doesn't alter the fact that they were granted them.

Perhaps those nineteenth-century politicians were thorough anti-Semites, and merely stopped short of trying to put their prejudice into law. President Truman freely used the word "nigger" among his Southern friends, but when some returning black GIs were beaten up he made the first move in the chain of legislation that eventually led (under President Johnson, who was not without prejudice, either) to voter registration by blacks in the South. There have always been people with prejudice who have nevertheless served justice, whether out of a supervening idealism, out of expediency or out of a simple wish not to be thought provincial by more sophisticated peers. In other words, there is prejudice and there is prejudice. But Goldhagen wants all the grades of anti-Semitism, from the enthusiasm of nutty pamphleteers down to the stultifying, self-protective distaste of the *Kleinbürgertum* at their pokey dinner tables, to add up to just one thing: the eliminationist fervour that led to extermination as soon as it got its chance.

Until recent times, one of Germany's recurring troubles was that it was more integrated culturally than it was politically. A case can be made for the Jews not having been integrated at all into the political structure, although you would have to eliminate a towering figure like Walther Rathenau—which is exactly what some of the Nazi Party's forerunners did. But from the time of Goethe up until the Anschluss the Jews were, at least in part, integrated into the culture; they made a contribution whose like had not been seen in Europe since Alfonso IX founded the University of Salamanca. Though they often aroused envy and spite among non-Jewish rivals, they aroused admiration in at least equal measure. Kant said that if the Muse of Philosophy could choose an ideal language, it would choose the language of Moses Mendelssohn. Goethe said that the Jewish contribution was vital. Nietzsche ranked the Jew Heine as the most important German poet after Goethe. The novelist Theodor Fontane, who started out as an anti-Semite, gave up on the idea when he realized that the Jewish bourgeoisie was a more cultivated audience than the aristocracy, which he had tried in vain to enlighten. Even the dreadful Wagner was ambivalent on the subject: when Thomas Mann's Jewish father-in-law left Germany after the Nazis came to power, all he took with him were Wagner's letters of thanks for his having helped to build the *Festspielhaus* in Bayreuth.

Which brings us to Thomas Mann. Here one is forced to wonder if whoever gave Goldhagen high marks for his thesis ever showed it to a literary colleague. As evidence of the all-pervading nature of eliminationist anti-Semitism, Goldhagen has the audacity to rope in, without qualification or explanation, a remark by Thomas Mann. Well, there is a grain of truth in it. In 1933, when Mann had already begun his long exile, he did indeed confide to his diary that it was a pity the new regime should include him along with some of the undesirable Jewish elements it was dealing with. But against this grain of truth there is a whole silo of contrary evidence. Thomas Mann had always disliked what he saw as the rootless Jewish cosmopolitanism (shades of his beloved Wagner there) that criticized because it couldn't create, and thus gave rise to a bugbear like Alfred Kerr. Mann, the Nobel Prize–winning eminence, the new

Goethe, the walking cultural icon, had a bad tendency, quite normal among writers even at their most successful, to take praise as his due and anything less as sabotage. He thought, with some justification, that the annoyingly clever Kerr was on his case. But for Jews who, in his opinion, *did* create, Mann had nothing but admiration. He had it in the first years of the century, when his conservatism was still as hidebound as the snobbery he was never to overcome: his two early encomiums for Arthur Schnitzler are models of generosity. He had scores of friendships among the Jewish cultural figures of the emigration and maintained them throughout the Nazi era, often at the expense of his time, effort and exchequer. For Bruno Walter, it was always open house *chez* Mann, because Mann honoured Walter as the incarnation of the Germany that mattered, just as he despised Hitler as its exterminating angel. Even to allow the possibility of our inferring that Mann might have thought otherwise is to perpetrate a truly stunning libel, and one can only hope that the excuse for it is ignorance.

Nowadays it has become fashionable to mock Mann's supposed equivocation *vis-à-vis* the Nazi regime in its first years, because of the time that passed before he publicly condemned it. At the time, his own children were angry with him for the same reason. We have to remember that his prestige, worldly goods and most appreciative reading public were all locked up in Germany; that he was deeply rooted in its complex society; and that at his age he did not fancy leading the very kind of rootless cosmopolitan life for which he had condemned men like Kerr. But his 1933–34 diaries (which one can safely recommend Goldhagen to read whole so that he will not in future run the risk of quoting a misleading fragment from a secondary source) reveal unmistakably, and over and over, that he loathed the bestiality of the new regime from its first hour. All Mann's *Tagebüche* through the 1930s and the war years—and hurry the day when the whole fascinating corpus is properly translated—show that he never wavered in his utter disgust at what the Nazis had done to his country. As for his opinion of what they were doing to the most defenceless people in it, he went public about that in his 1936 essay on anti-Semitism, in which he definitively penetrated, and devastatingly parodied, the unconscious logic of the Nazi mentality: "I might be nothing, but at least I'm not a Jew."

.   .   .

Historical research has by now established beyond question that the Nazi Party was principally financed not by the great capitalists of Brecht's imagination but by the *Kleinleute*—the little people. Reduced to despair by inflation and by the Depression, they assigned their hopes and their few spare pennies to the cause of the man they thought might rescue them from nothingness. He did, too—so triumphantly that they didn't suspect until the eleventh hour that he was leading them into a nothingness even more complete than the one they had come from. The Holocaust would have been unimaginable without the Nazi Party; the Nazi Party would have been unimaginable without Hitler; and Hitler's rise to power would have been unimaginable without the unique circumstances that brought the Weimar Republic to ruin. To hear Goldhagen tell it, mass murder was all set to go: a century-long build-up of eliminationist anti-Semitism simply had to express itself. But the moment when a historian says that something had to happen is the moment when he stops writing history and starts predicting the past.

After the Second World War, the British historian A. J. P. Taylor began publishing a series of books and articles which added up to the contention that Hitler's regime was the inevitable consequence of Germany's border problem, and that his depredations in the East were just a harsh version of what any German in his position would have been obliged to do anyway. Hitler's war, Taylor argued, brought Europe back to "reality," out of its liberal illusions. Then, in 1951, the German historian Golo Mann—one of Thomas Mann's three sons—made a survey of Taylor's historical writings, and took them apart. He accused Taylor of predicting the past. The Weimar Republic, Mann pointed out, had been no liberal illusion and might have survived if extraordinary circumstances hadn't conspired to undermine it. German nationalism was not a demon that always strode armed through the land—it was in the minds of men, and could have stayed there. This confrontation between the frivolously clever Taylor and the deeply engaged Golo Mann was a portent of the intellectual conflict that blew up in Germany more than thirty years later, when the learned historian Ernst Nolte foolishly went to print with an opinion that sounded like one of Taylor's brainwaves cast in more turgid prose: he stated that Nazi Germany, by attacking Russia, had simply got into the Cold War early, and that Nazi extermination camps had been the inevitable consequence of tangling with an enemy who was up to the same sort of thing. This time there were plenty of German historians and commentators ready to oppose such views, because by now the perverse urge to marginalize the Nazis had penetrated the academic world, and had been identified as a trend that needed to be stopped. Younger historians who had looked up to Nolte hastened to distance themselves from him; the glamorous Michael Stürmer, in his virtuoso summary of modern German history *Die Grenzen der Macht* (The Limits of Power), consigned Nolte's theory to a dismissive passing reference. Stürmer also wrote a sentence about Hitler that is unfortunately likely to remain all too true: "Even today, the history of Hitler is largely the history of how he has been underestimated."

Why is this so? Strangely, anti-Semitism has probably played a part. We tend to think of him as an idiot because the central tenet of his ideology was idiotic—and idiotic, of course, it transparently is. Anti-Semitism is a world view through a pinhole: as scientists say about a bad theory, it is not even wrong. Nietzsche tried to tell Wagner that it was beneath contempt. Sartre was right for once when he said that through anti-Semitism any halfwit could become a member of an elite. But, as the case of Wagner proves, a man can have this poisonous bee in his bonnet and still be a creative genius. Hitler was a destructive genius, whose evil gifts not only beggar description but invite denial, because we find it more comfortable to believe that their consequences were produced by historical forces than to believe that he *was* a historical force. Or perhaps we just lack the vocabulary. Not many of us, in a secular age, are willing to concede that, in the form of Hitler, Satan visited the Earth, recruited an army of sinners, and fought and won a battle against God. We would rather talk the language of pseudoscience, which at least seems to bring such cataclysmic events to order. But all that such language can do is shift the focus of attention down to the broad mass of the German people, which is what Goldhagen has done, in a way that, at least in part, lets Hitler off the hook—and unintentionally reinforces his central belief that it was the destiny of the Jewish race to be expelled from the *Volk* as an inimical presence.

Hannah Arendt, in her long, courageous, and much-misunderstood career, had her weak moments. In her popular *Eichmann in Jerusalem* (first published serially in *The New Yorker*) she undoubtedly pushed her useful notion of the detached desk worker too far. But she was resoundingly right when she refused to grant the Nazis the power of their *fait accompli*. She declined to suppose, as Hitler had supposed, that there really was some international collectivity called the Jews. Echoing the fourth count of the Nuremberg indictment, she called the Holocaust a crime against humanity.

The Jews were the overwhelming majority among Hitler's victims, but he also killed all the Gypsies and homosexuals he could find. He let two and a half million Russian POWs perish, most of them from the gradually applied technique of deprivation. The novelist Joseph Roth, drinking himself to death in Paris before the war, said that Hitler probably had the Christians in his sights, too. We can never now trace the source of Hitler's passion for revenge, but we can be reasonably certain that there would have been no satisfying it had he lived. Sooner or later, he would have got around to everybody. Hitler was the culprit who gave all the other culprits their chance. To concentrate exclusively on the prejudice called anti-Semitism—to concentrate even on *his* anti-Semitism—is another way of underestimating him.

.   .   .

At the end of this bloodstained century, which has topped by ten times Tamburlaine's wall of skulls, lime and living men, the last thing we want to believe is that it all happened on a whim. In the Soviet Union, the liquidation of bourgeois elements began under Lenin. By the time Stalin took power, there were no bourgeois elements left. He went on finding them. He found them even within the Communist Party. They didn't exist. They never had existed. He killed them anyway. Eventually, he killed more people than Hitler, and it was all for nothing. Far from building socialism, he ensured its ruin. His onslaught had nothing to do with social analysis, about which he knew no more than he did about biology. Unless you believe in Original Sin, there is almost no meaning that can be attached to his behaviour, except to say that he was working out his personal problems.

In China, Mao Zedong went to war against the evil landlords and the imperialist spies. Neither group actually existed. The death toll of his countrymen exceeded the totals achieved by Hitler and Stalin combined. They all died for nothing. Dying innocent, they have their eternal dignity, but there are no profundities to be plumbed in their collective extinction except the adamantine fact of human evil. In Cambodia, Pol Pot encouraged the persecution, torture and murder of everyone who wore glasses— but enough. A country, no matter how cultured, either respects the rights of all its citizens or is not civilized. The answer to the nagging conundrum of how a civilized country like Germany could produce the Holocaust is that Germany ceased to be civilized from the moment Hitler came to power. It had been before, and it has been since—a fact that might secure for Goldhagen's book, when it is published there, a considered reception, despite its contents. I look forward to reading the German critical press, especially if one of the reviewers is Marcel Reich-Ranicki. Of Jewish background (his book about his upbringing in the Warsaw ghetto is a minor masterpiece), Reich-Ranicki is one of the most brilliant critical writers in the world. I know just where I want to read his piece: in my favorite café on the Oranienburger Strasse, just along from the meticulously restored synagogue, whose golden dome is a landmark for the district. Two armed guards stand at the door, but this time in its defence— a reminder of what Germany once did not only to others but to itself, and need not have done if democracy had held together.

A shorter version first appeared in *The New Yorker*, April 22, 1996; later included in *Even As We Speak*, 2001

P O S T S C R I P T

The preceding review is reprinted in a form substantially different from the way it first appeared in *The New Yorker*. The way it looks here is much closer to the way I first wrote it. Goldhagen's book was big news at the time, so Tina Brown very properly decided that my notice should be promoted from the "back of the book" reviews department to "Critic at Large" status in the middle of the magazine. This unlooked-for elevation, however, proved to be a mixed blessing, because in a position of such prominence the *soi-disant* Critic at Large often finds himself not as at large as he would like. Suddenly he is held to be speaking for the magazine as much as for himself, and inevitably it is decided that his personal quirks should be suppressed, in the interests of objectivity. My animadversions on Goldhagen's prose style were held to be a potentially embarrassing irrelevance: to dispute his interpretation of factual events was going to be contentious enough, without getting into the subjective area of how he wrote his interpretation down. I didn't think that it was a subjective area; I thought the callow overconfidence of his jargon-ridden style was a clear index of how he had been simply bound to get his pretended overview of the subject out of shape from the start; but I knuckled under or we would have all been stymied.

It wasn't, after all, as if the editors wanted to change the main thrust of the piece. There is a fine line between being asked to say something differently and being required to say something different, but it is a clear one. When they do want you to say something different, of course, it's time to take the kill fee and quit. But this piece was guaranteed to give me trouble whatever the circumstances. Goldhagen's book aspires to be wide-ranging over both the political and cultural background to the Holocaust, and if you hope to show that his reach exceeds his grasp, you have to be pretty wide-ranging yourself, over a literature that it takes half a lifetime to absorb. It was probably as much a blessing as a curse that I had to write the piece against a deadline, and that I had to do much of the work on it while I was filming in Mexico City, away from my own library and any other library that held the relevant books. To a great extent I had to rely on what was in my memory. In retrospect, the restriction feels like a lucky break. Otherwise I would have ended up writing a review longer than the book, and it would have had footnotes hanging off it in festoons.

There is something to be said for being forced into ellipsis. Skimpiness, however, is inevitably part of the result. You wouldn't know, from Goldhagen's book, that the question of the Jewish contribution to German-speaking culture was far more complicated than he makes out. Unfortunately you wouldn't know from my review just how complicated it was. It was elementary work to rebut his line with a few simple examples. The editing process reduced them to even fewer, but the obvious point was made. It was also fudged. Goldhagen is clamorously wrong on that particular topic, but the evidence by which he might think himself right is stronger than I had the time, the room or—less forgivable—the inclination to make out. As my admired Marcel Reich-Ranicki explains in his *Der Doppelte Boden* (augmented edition, Fischer, 1992), some of the Jewish writers, though they enjoyed huge public acclaim, had ample motive for feeling rejected. The novelist Jakob Wassermann, for all his success as a best-seller, despaired of social acceptance. Among Jewish artists in Germany after World War I that state of mind was not rare, and in Austria it was common. Its epicentre had been registered by Arthur Schnitzler at the turn of the century, in a key passage of his great novel *Der Weg ins Freie* (The Path into the Clear), where a leading character spells out the impossibility of true assimilation with a mordant clarity not very different from the polemical Zionism of Theodor Herzl. There can be no doubt that Schnitzler was speaking from the heart.

The question abides, however, of whether he was speaking from a whole heart or only a part of it. Though insecurity was ever-present and outright abuse always a threat, the Jewish artists and thinkers, if assimilation to the German-speaking culture was what they wanted, had good reasons to think it was being achieved in those last years before 1933. Their influence, even their dominance, in the various fields of culture was widely acknowledged. On playbills, in concert programmes and on publishers' lists there were Jewish names that attracted an audience totalling millions. The career of Stefan Zweig, alone, would be enough to make Goldhagen's cultural theory look fantastic. Zweig's books were customarily translated into about thirty languages but his sales in the German-speaking countries would have been enough on their own to make him wealthy. It shouldn't need pointing out that his sales couldn't have been that big if they had been confined to an audience of Jewish background, a qualification which applied to only 300,000 people in the whole of Germany. Zweig was part of the German literary landscape, together with the liberal values he professed. Hans Scholl, the master spirit of the White Rose resistance group in Munich, had already turned against his Hitler Youth upbringing, but his trajectory towards outright subversion was accelerated after one of Zweig's books was taken away from him by a Nazi official. Scholl thought that if the Nazis were against *that*, they were against the Germany he cared about. (Goldhagen's failure to so much as mention the White Rose, incidentally, is the kind of omission that makes a mockery of his scientific vocabulary. In science, the fact that doesn't fit the theory eliminates the theory, not the other way about. Hans and Sophie Scholl were gentiles born into a household formed by liberal German culture, were well aware that Jews had helped to form that culture, and were ready to die for it rather than betray it. If Goldhagen wants to go on asking why the German population did not rise up, he might consider the manner in which those two brave young people perished. The guillotine is a big price to pay for a conviction.)

A necessary conclusion, about the large and well-informed German-speaking audience for the arts, would be that if they were all eliminationist anti-Semites, they must have been strangely ready to sideline their otherwise overmastering prejudice when it came to matters of aesthetic enjoyment. It's not a conclusion that Goldhagen feels bound to draw, because he doesn't even consider the matter. Nor does he consider that the abuse heaped on Jewish artists by the Nazi propaganda machine before the *Machtergreifung* was a measure of the success they had achieved in becoming a part of the landscape. Finally and fatally, he doesn't consider that the massive and irreversible damage done to German-speaking culture by the repression, expulsion and murder of the Jews was the full, exact and tragic measure of how they had been vital to it. Once again it is an awful thing to find oneself saying, but it has to be said: the *Reichskulturkämmer*, if they were still in business, couldn't have done a better job of treating the Jewish contributors to German culture as if they had been an irrelevance, simply begging to be swept away.

But a young historian can be forgiven for lacking the kind of cultural information that would bring such questions to the forefront. The richness of what the German-speaking Jews achieved before the Nazi era takes time to assess. Harder to understand is Goldhagen's apparent supposition that nothing much has happened in Germany *since* the Nazi era when it comes to his own field—history. You would never know, from his book, that whole teams of German historians, in the full knowledge that they are trying to make bricks from rubble, have dedicated themselves to the study of the catastrophe that distorted their intellectual inheritance. As in any other country at any time, there have been a few historians who have devoted prodigious resources to missing the point. Of the star revisionists mixed up in the *Historikerstreit*, Ernst Nolte and Andreas Hillgruber at least had the merit of being too blatant to be plausible: they pretty well blamed the Holocaust on the Soviet Union. Klaus Hildebrand and Michael Stürmer were more insidious because there was nothing wrong with their facts: after the Red Army crossed the German border, the retreating *Wehrmacht* really *was* fighting heroically for its country's heritage. Unfortunately their suggestion that post-war German patriotism might thus claim a solid base was hopelessly compromised by the consideration that part of the heritage was the Holocaust. In his various essays and open letters about the *Historikerstreit*, Jürgen Habermas (who, it is only fair to concede, admires Goldhagen's book) was marvellous on the equivocations and the delusions of the revisionists, but on the main point he didn't need to be marvellous: it was too obviously true. The revisionist historian can't reasonably hope to have a Germany that is not obsessed with the past. There can be no putting off shame to achieve maturity. The shame *is* the maturity.

Most of the German historians are well aware of this. The revisionists did not prevail, and the work entailed in rebutting them had already become part of the accumulated glory of Germany's indigenous historical studies as the terrible twentieth century neared its end. But if German culture really had been nourished at its root by eliminationist anti-Semitism, as Goldhagen argues, it is hard to see why so many of today's German historians should now be so concerned about the Holocaust. Very few of them are Jews, for sadly obvious reasons. Surely they, too, are "the Germans," as Goldhagen would like to put it. It can only follow that their culture has other continuities apart from the one that Goldhagen picks out. Their urge to comprehend, their respect for the facts—these things could not have started up all by themselves, out of nowhere.

There are plenty of Germans, naturally enough, who would like to think that their country as they know it today *has* started up out of nowhere. For those who would like to throw off the burden of history and move on, Goldhagen's book has been a welcome gift. Purporting to bring the past home to the unsuspecting present, he has had the opposite effect. If he has not yet asked himself why his book has received such an enthusiastic reception in Germany, he might ponder why "the Germans" should be so glad to be supplied with the argument that their parents and grandparents were all equally to blame because they inhabited a culture blameworthy in itself: we're different now. But nobody is that different now, because nobody was that different then. It will always suit the current generation of any country to blame the turpitude of their ancestors on the culture then prevailing, as if people had no choice how to act. It saves us from the anguish of asking ourselves how we might have acted had we been there, at a time when plenty of people knew there was a choice, but couldn't face the consequences of making it, and when those who did choose virtue were volunteers for torture and death.

No wonder Goldhagen is so popular. On top of leaving out the large numbers of German citizens who declined to vote for the Nazis even when there was almost no other party remaining with credible means to stop the chaos in the streets, he doesn't even mention the Germans who were so suicidally brave as to defy the Nazis after they came to power. Sacrificial witnesses to human decency, they died at the rate of about twenty-five people per day for every day that the Third Reich was in existence. They might seem to add up to a drop in the bucket, and it was terribly true that they had no real hope of having any effect, but Goldhagen is keeping questionable company when he treats a handful of powerless lives as if their deaths meant nothing in the eye of history. Some of the questionable company he is keeping is alive now. We would all find life a lot easier if we didn't have to ask ourselves how we would have measured up to the same test. Hence the temptation to suppose that nobody ever did. The challenge to one's compassion is tough enough, without compounding it by the challenge to one's conscience.

In our time and privileged surroundings there has been no such examination to pass or fail, but what makes the difference is political circumstances. The new Germany is a democracy. So was the old Germany, or it tried to be: but then the Nazis got in, and Hell broke loose. It can break loose anywhere, in any people: all people have hellish propensities. When Daniel Goldhagen has lived long enough to value democracy for what it prevents, he will be less ready to be astonished by what his fellow human beings are capable of when they are allowed. And the Germans really are his fellow human beings. To assert otherwise is to further the kind of argument which the Nazis, thereby achieving their sole lasting value, contrived to discredit beyond redemption.

Reliable Essays, 2001

41

HE THAT PLAYED THE FOOL

The Life of Kenneth Tynan by Kathleen Tynan

Kenneth Tynan had it to burn, so he burned it. The greatest critical talent since Shaw threw it all away. That, at any rate, is the generally accepted idea, which Kathleen Tynan's biography, well written though it is, and even though it tries to do the opposite, can only reinforce. It's the wrong idea, but it can't lose. To explain the man makes him less dazzling. It helps cut his intensity down to size. Put out the light, and then put out the light.

Some such process of diminishment would have been inevitable, even if its subject had not appeared so enthusiastically to cooperate. Tynan wrote too well to be easily put up with by other cultural journalists. Even when they praised him they were looking for a weakness. In his early days, a weakness was hard to find. In his very early days he was even better than that.

For Tynan at Oxford and just after, the term "genius" seems not out of place. Certainly there is no precocity to match his in the whole of English prose. You would have to go to the novels of Radiguet or the plays of Büchner to find a parallel. His first collection, *He That Plays the King*— everything in it composed before he even got to Fleet Street—is a classic book which, were it to be republished now in its slim entirety, might give the new generation of journalists in the cultural field a salutary fright.

In places, Tynan's astonishing first book is as precious as "The Unquiet Grave." There are passages that out-posture Palinurus. But you can put that down to his age (twenty-three), exacerbated by *the* age—that period of post-war austerity which produced, as a reaction, *Brideshead*

Revisited and the verse plays of Christopher Fry. What makes the collection timeless is Tynan's wit, and there is seldom anything precious about that. Tynan could make his prose speak right out of the page: he had the essential button-holing gift of the star critic.

Tynan's ostensible business, in those early days, was with heroic acting, of which, indeed, he was a peerless anatomist. But while in search of what he admired he had to see much which he did not, and about that he had the valuable gift of being amusing. "Joyce Redman tried unwisely to make novel use of her buxom build and strident voice by playing a strong, commanding Cordelia. Her best time came after she was dead." This is tough but not cruel, because it leaves the actress the possibility of being good in other parts, or in the same part played a different way. About Eileen Herlie, playing Medea at the 1948 Edinburgh Festival, he *was* cruel. "I admit that in repose she is gracious: but she lunges rather than moves, and she has common hands." Tynan was lucky to wake up next morning without finding his victim's hands fastened around his neck. In pursuit of his passion, he had forgotten her feelings, or anyway, forgotten that they mattered.

His passion was for theatre. This is what so sharply distinguishes Tynan's wit from that of previous critics whose writings are generally attributed with that quality, but who were in fact not theatre critics at all. Dorothy Parker, for example, funny though she could be, knew nothing about the theatre and had no judgement of it. She was using it as an opportunity to make wisecracks. Tynan's imperative was the very opposite. He was enslaved to the theatre. You can tell by the way he praised the great moments of his heroic actors: Olivier, Gielgud, Richardson, Wolfit, Guinness. If they tended to remember how he dispraised their weak moments, even the most bitter among them were obliged to concede that he was merciless only out of a sense of duty to high ideals. Tynan had theatre instead of religion.

He also had it instead of politics. Later on, when he got interested in politics, he treated them as theatre, which is perhaps the clue to his later diffuseness. Orson Welles, in the preface which he contributed to *He That Plays the King* (the young author, whom Welles did not know, pressed the manuscript on him unsolicited, and Welles, in one of history's few recorded cases of genius recognizing genius first off, coughed up a free plug), spotted a tendency which Tynan spent the rest of his life trying to deal with—"a confusion between high glamour and tragic truth."

The words are Welles's but the trouble was Tynan's. In everything from how he dressed to what he worshipped, Tynan behaved as if purity could be attained just by screwing theatricality up to a high enough pitch. Somewhere in that assumption was an irreconcilable contradiction. He was under no obligation to reconcile it. Merely to have identified it and discussed it would have kept him going for a fruitful lifetime into a wise old age. But the drama within himself was the only one he could not review.

Kathleen Tynan, made well aware of this fact by the sad end it led to, tries hard and honourably to find reasons. It is not the first honour she has done him. She honoured him by putting up with him when he proved, like so many writers, to be no better fitted for married life than for self-propelled flight; and now she has honoured him by writing a book brave enough to take him seriously at the level where he came, in later years, to think himself most serious—as an assault pioneer of the sexual-political revolution. There can be no doubt that he would have thanked her for taking such a dare, so it would be niggardly of the onlooker not to thank her as well. One wonders, though, whether she has really uncovered much by revealing all. It is possible to lay a false trail with discarded veils.

Let no-one doubt her bravery. Her husband, on this evidence, was a psychological disaster area. His own explanation for his kinky sexuality was an identity crisis dating from his illegitimate childhood. On the other hand, he came to regard his kinky sexuality as a form of expression, with a right to be heard. He started off with the worthy aim of wanting to abolish the Lord Chamberlain and ended up with the less endearing determination to dress up as Louise Brooks. It was the usual story of a man being caught up with by the era he helped instigate, and making a guy of himself by trying to outrun it. But it meant harrowing times for his biographer, who can be forgiven for painting a picture of that sensitive face, skull-like from the beginning, being eaten up by the anguish within.

Such turmoil would explain anyone's decline. Perhaps, however, it explains itself. Tynan's penchant for transsexual dressing and the milder forms of flagellation did not cramp his prose style in the first place, so why should it have done so later on? When the marvellous boy hit Fleet Street, he went as far as his gift could take him—all the way to immortality.

Readers of the *Observer* could turn to his column and find sentences good enough to leave their breakfast cold. "His tragedy," Tynan said of

Uncle Vanya, "is that he is capable only of comedy." Shaw himself is no comparison: you have to go back to Coleridge to find so much character analysis in such a short space.

Tynan became a force for good in the theatre. He helped raise its intelligence by the way he criticized it. And, as Kathleen Tynan points out, he was equally forceful when he took on the post of *dramaturg* for the National Theatre in what has proved, in retrospect, to be its formative period, before it got its own building.

Olivier, the man in charge, emerges from this book like the giant he was and is, but it is to Tynan's lasting credit that when the man was matched with his hour, he, Tynan, was a match for the man. In service of Olivier, all of Tynan's knowledge, judgement and love of the theatre were put to good use.

So where was the vice? It was in the virtue. He loved theatre so much that he thought life should be like that. It was not his trendiness that caught up with him in the 1960s, it was his seriousness. His late-flowering admiration for Brecht might not have been fatal if he had abetted it by some capacity for political analysis. But he tried to learn politics *from* Brecht. Tynan's evocations of the Berliner Ensemble productions (to be found in his collection *Curtains*) are alive in all respects except the intellect. He didn't think to ask why Brecht's company had never been invited to tour the Soviet Union, or why Brecht himself had never written a single line, let alone a complete play, in direct criticism of any aspect of the East German regime. He could be so foolish only because he had failed to take history in. It was too dull for him.

Tynan had read every play in the world but very few serious books. There was no time. He dined in smart company almost every night. He lived the high life and could not bear to be away from it. He could have conquered his emphysema if he had kept to the desert air, but it would have wasted his sweetness. He had to be near the action—not because he was a snob, but because it was theatrical. The entrance on to the stage of Olivier as Othello was succeeded by the entrance into the dining room of Princess Margaret. For Ken Tynan, these events were comparable.

If Kathleen Tynan seems to think the same, the sin is more venial in her than it was in her husband. She has some innocent pleasure coming, after the pain he caused her, her worst pain arising from the requirement that she should witness his. No wonder she looks for a profound cause of why he fell to pieces. Without making light of the bewilderment he brought to his women and children, however, it should be possible to conjecture that he disintegrated for the same reason that a meteor does, which consumes itself in order to be brilliant, and presumably wouldn't, if consulted, choose another course. To want an unfallen Kenneth Tynan would be to want the moon.

Observer, September 27, 1987;
later included in *The Dreaming Swimmer*, 1992

POSTSCRIPT

Generously hoping to illuminate the legend by showing us the man, Kathleen Tynan's biography of her husband inadvertently helped bring his reputation down to earth, but it had a lot further to sink. Fifteen years later his diaries were published. We already knew that his sexual imagination was like a Japanese comic book for adolescent males, but here were the pages that had previously been glued together. Faced with the shocking-pink evidence of flagellation and buggery, even some of his remaining admirers bailed out. If this had been the real man, what was the reputation ever worth? But in the age of biography the critic's duty, even when writing about another critic, is to go on plugging away at the elementary truth that the only real man is in his published writings. Armed with the biographical details, the journeymen conspire to haul him down to their level. Jobbing columnists would like to believe that Tynan wrote a version of what they write: a trifle snazzier, perhaps, but of the same order. Not a chance. Ordinary expository prose, no matter how workmanlike, has only a formal connection with the style that electrifies. The difference is in the concentration of dramatic effect. Supernumeraries sometimes stray into the spotlight if they are lucky. Tynan never strayed out.

2003

42

BERTRAND RUSSELL STRUGGLES AFTER HEAVEN

Two twentieth-century philosophers whose names are inseparable, Ludwig Wittgenstein and Bertrand Russell, were such a great double act that there simply has to be a buddy movie sooner or later. At last, the material is all set to be licked into a script. Ray Monk has now matched his justly lauded biography of Wittgenstein with a fat and equally enthralling first volume wrapping up the earlier half of Bertrand Russell's long life— *Bertrand Russell: The Spirit of Solitude 1872–1921*—and is sitting on the hottest Hollywood prospect since Paul Newman and Robert Redford signed on for *Butch Cassidy and the Sundance Kid*. Every A-list male star will want to play Wittgenstein—the philosopher who blew away all the other philosophers, including Russell—so, although Lyle Lovett looks the part and Arnie has the accent, Tom Cruise will probably get the job, armed with a Tatlin-tower lopsided bouffant coiffure personally teased out by the great José. ("Mmm! You look like *beeg theenker* now!") Nobody bankable—not even Steve Martin, a philosophy wonk who can actually explicate *Principia Mathematica* while wearing a plastic arrow through his head—will want to play the physically unappealing Russell, so the way should be clear for the perfect choice: Gene Wilder. Fluctuating uncontrollably between idealism and disillusion, forever persuaded that sexual fulfilment is at hand in the form of a luscious girl in a red dress, Wilder's persona, like his appearance, exactly fits a part that should revive his career. The only strike against Wilder is that even he has a bit too much gravitas for the role. On the evidence of Monk's book, Russell, for all his clipped speech and pipe-sucking air of cerebral precision, was a zany, a pantaloon, a fourth Stooge. Monk does his best to lend Russell dignity and stature, but that's the way it comes out, like a fanfare from a whoopee cushion.

It took Russell a long time to get to here. While he was alive, he was a sage. Even in his last phase, when he recklessly allowed himself to be set up as the star turn in various World Peace tent shows that had little to do with any known world and nothing to do with peace, he was regarded as, at worst, a super-mind whose bonnet had been unaccountably penetrated by fashionable bees. In his early life, he was universally assumed to be a genius. For all most of us know, he was. Most of us, when we give our opinion on such subjects as analytical philosophy and symbolic logic, are only grazing, the way we are with relativity theory, quantum mechanics and how a mobile telephone works: the best we can hope to do is talk a good game, backed by the consensus of those who really know. Ray Monk, who really knows, says that the young Bertrand Russell's brilliantly original thinking in mathematics and symbolic logic laid the foundations of analytical philosophy and helped open up the field of theory which made our modern computerized world possible. Glad to take all this on trust, I will add it to the store of dinner-table science talk by which I contrive to maintain some kind of communication with my molecular biologist daughter.

The difference between me and the molecular biologists, of course, is that they know what they're talking about, whereas I know only how to talk. It is a difference basic to the life of the mind in our time—a time that can usefully be thought of as going back to Goethe, who didn't like Newton's theories about colour. Goethe had good humanist reasons for his dislike but didn't have the maths to back them up. Science was already off on its own; there were already two cultures. It could be said— it should be said, in my view—that only one of these, the unscientific one, is really a culture, since the mark of culture is to accumulate quality, whereas science merely advances knowledge. But my view is part of the unscientific culture, and has no weight in the scientific one, which settles its questions within itself, marshalling evidence powerful enough to flatten cities and bore holes in steel with drills of light. If Russell the philosopher had been content to keep his philosophy sounding scientific, his reputation would have remained unassailable, even though, or perhaps because, its published basis was unintelligible. There would never have been any way for the lay critic to get at him.

But, to give Russell his due, he was reluctant to confine his philosophical writings to the safely abstruse. Like most of the great philosophers before him—and unlike many of his successors—he strove to instruct the general reading public in ordinary language. Commendably, and sometimes heroically, he sought the most transparent possible exposition of his ideas, thereby proselytizing for the scientific, critical spirit that would liberate mankind from its perennial irrationality and offer the only hope for reforming a cruel world. Reason was Russell's religion: he believed in it passionately. The question now is not whether this is a self-contradictory position—surely it isn't, unless passion becomes zeal—but whether Russell was equipped by nature to promote it. The evidence provided by this book overwhelmingly suggests that he wasn't. His natural use of language was hopelessly in thrall to high-flown, over-decorated rhetoric. When he wrote passionately, he wrote dreadfully, and he could eschew the ornate only by leaving the passion out. Much of his workaday prose was plain to a fault. The principles he promoted in his voluminous writings on human affairs were unexceptionable—it would be better if people were persuaded by facts instead of myths, loved each other and sought peace—but the language in which he set them down defeats memory. His heart wasn't in it, even if his mind was. His professional philosophy, the hard stuff, all sprang, we are told and must accept, from his conviction that our complex knowledge of the world could be analysed down to its ultimately simple conceptual foundations. But his popular philosophy, the easy stuff that you and I are meant to understand, all too clearly proves that a prose bereft of nuances leaves out the texture of real life. Qualities that Russell entirely lacked were the stylistic density and precision of a writer capable of judging common life in the light of his own most intimate failures and defeats—the density and precision by which a great writer clarifies complexity without simplifying it and intensifies the clarity into incandescence. The last thing Russell could write from was personal experience.

.   .   .

By Monk's account, it isn't any wonder. Russell's personal experience was awful, first of all for himself and later on, crucially, for the women he was involved with. Paradoxically surrounded by the complete apparatus of wealth and comfort, his childhood was all bereavement. In what must have seemed a conspiracy to leave him alone, his parents and everyone else he might have loved departed prematurely, stricken by diphtheria and other then incurable diseases with no respect for rank: in adult life, he would say that he always felt he was a ghost. Nowadays, armed with the knowledge distilled into John Bowlby's great trilogy *Attachment and Loss*, those interested in such things would be able to identify Russell's situation as a casebook example of detachment: undermined from the start by childhood separations of such violent intensity, the victim's relationships in adult life tend to be more controlling than cooperative and much more eloquent than felt. Russell filled the bill to what would be hilarious effect if you could forget that the women who made the mistake of getting involved with him were real, and really suffered. Russell could forget it, but then he had the advantage of having never fully realized it in the first place. In matters of emotion, he was an almost perfect solipsist: a woman could exist for him not as a separate personality but only as an extension of his own personality. Like conscientious objection, free love was a cause he was ready to suffer for, but the freedom was all for him, and the suffering, it turned out, was all for those he loved.

The pattern was set from the start, when he wooed and won Alys Pearsall Smith as his first wife. Russell, a suitor not to be denied, or even interrupted, talked for hours and covered square miles of paper explaining to her that the great thing about marriage would be sex. Alys, by her own admission, distrusted the whole idea, proclaiming for women in general and for herself in particular what Russell described as "an aversion to sexual intercourse and a shrinking from it only to be overcome by the desire for children." Undaunted, the budding ratiocinative genius pursued the courtship with a heat from him that increased with every glint of ice from her. He attempted to persuade her that sex would be the ideal *spiritual* expression of their mutual love. When, in a rare moment of abandon, she allowed him to kiss her glacial breasts, he soared into the stratosphere of prose, declaring in a letter to her that the event was "far and away the most spiritual thing there has yet been in my life." Russell then attempted to convince her that, once the knot had been tied, the proper approach to conjugal bliss would be a plenitude of indulgence, thus to tame in his otherwise elevated soul the disruptive element of testicular agitation. Using the Quakerish "thee" and "thou" familiar form with which the two betrothed conspired to elevate their discourse to the empyrean plane, Russell declared:

It would be a good plan, for me at any rate, to indulge physical feelings a good deal *quite* at first till they no longer have that maddening excitement to the imagination which they now have. I lie in bed and they come before my mind and my heart beats wildly and I begin to breathe heavily and sometimes I tremble with excitement—I feel *almost* sure that when once all the physical feelings have been indulged, this intense and almost painful excitement will subside, and whatever is pure and good and spiritual in them will survive.

The poor schmuck had blue balls, but it would have been a better gag if he had been fooling only himself. Unfortunately, he was also fooling her, and one feels for her even at this range. Dynastically, the alliance of a British aristocratic scholar and a well-connected American blue-stocking looked good on deckle-edged paper. In fact, it was hell, and the partner who suffered its most acute torments was Alys, although Russell, typically, managed to convince himself that *he* was the patsy. Having cajoled her ruthlessly into a cryogenic marriage, he felt within his rights not only to fall for her sexier sister, Mary, during a Continental holiday but to tell Alys all about it: "I am trying to fall in love with her and make these last days pass, and I think I shall succeed enough to avoid too much impatience—she's a fearful flatterer."

Sharing a sitting room in a Paris hotel, Russell and Mary read Nietzsche together by day and wallowed in Wagner by night. Probably they weren't having full sex, because Russell would never have been able to withhold the glad tidings from Alys, thee can bet thy life. He certainly told her about his and Mary's tender goodnight kisses after midnight discussions about the *zeitgeist*. "Why should I mind thee kissing [Mary]?" Alys told him. "Cried most of the morning," she told her diary. She cried most of the rest of her life. The immediate cause of their estrangement, six years later, was Russell's unrequited but spectacular passion for Alfred North Whitehead's wife, Evelyn—a permanently convalescent beauty whose spiritual reluctance to put out was matched by an earthy willingness to soak up Russell's money in the form of gifts, trips and other freebies. Alys had a close-up of the proceedings, because the Russells, fulfilling all the requirements of Strindbergian claustrophobia, were sharing a house in Grantchester with the Whiteheads, where Evelyn faithfully reported to Alys everything Russell was saying—a possibility that failed to occur to Russell even while Evelyn was faithfully reporting to him everything Alys was saying. As Russell's last embers of feeling for Alys chilled to grey, he wrote her a letter that can be said to epitomize his ability to analyze his own emotions:

> Dearest, thee does give me more happiness than I can say—all the happiness I have, in fact. Thee is the only person I know well and yet really and thoroughly admire. I love the absolute certainty that all thy thoughts will be magnanimous and free from all pettiness. Since last winter I have known that life without thee would not be possible.

The writing was on the wall—though backward, like Leonardo's. Life without her became possible two months later. His renowned account of how he got the idea in a flash, as enshrined in his ostensibly frank but deeply self-serving three-volume *Autobiography* (1967–69)—"I went out bicycling one afternoon, and suddenly, as I was riding along a country road, I realized that I no longer loved Alys—turns out to have more truth in it than you might think: there really was a bicycle. But there was no suddenly about it; he was merely bringing to a head what had been festering for years. As Alys went from being miscast to being cast off, she began a slow, limping exit to the wings of the drama, there to await in vain her cue for re-entry, with death a longed-for but elusive alternative. (She despaired when a lump in her breast turned out *not* to be cancer.) She always hoped that he would come back to her. He must have had something.

Mostly, he had a brain, and the ladies went for it, even when they didn't think much of his body. Lady Ottoline Morrell was grandly married but sported an impressive track record of adulterous bunk-ups with *prominenti* of all stamps. Anyone but the great philosopher would have spotted that this was a good reason not to try to get her all to himself. But Russell was so bowled over by an actual, consummated, thrashingly carnal love affair that he went ape. He counselled her to tell her husband, Philip, so as to avoid "deceit and sordidness." Typically, Russell had misread the object of his adoration completely. Ottoline, who, unbeknownst to Russell, was still pursuing long-term affairs with Henry Lamb and Roger Fry, liked her life. She was loyal to her complacent husband. She was a realist. Russell, even though the warm impact of Ottoline's physicality had made him uncertain that he could now maintain contact with the cool world of mathematical logic, was, in emotional matters, still and forever an idealist. For once, the result was less Strindberg than Shaw, with the philosopher Russell spouting high-flown balderdash and the layperson Ottoline talking all the sense. His "morality of passion," he explained to her, demanded the ability "to behave as one might in a grand opera or in epic poetry," and he went on to vaporize about how "rapturous it would be to die together like the people in Rosmersholm." Sensibly planning to die in her comfortable bed like people in real life, Ottoline became more sparing with her favours. "His intellect is supreme, but he lives up there so much that all the rest of him seems to have lost motion," she told her journal. "I feel it exhausting, as I have to keep in step with his intellect all the time, and also satisfy his heart." Russell's intellect was at that time keeping in step with that of his dazzling new discovery, Wittgenstein, so he perhaps found it hard to slow down the pace. Satisfying his heart was not easy, either: satisfaction bred hunger.

When Russell was lecturing in America in his forty-third year, he fell for Helen Dudley, a Bryn Mawr graduate and would-be poet in her late twenties. She was glad to go to bed with him, and Russell responded to that gesture by offering her his hand in marriage, convincing himself that he was doing so principally because of his high esteem for her writing. He was not yet divorced from Alys. Nor was his love affair with Ottoline exactly over, though he filled her in on the news in the confident expectation that she would understand. "My darling," he wrote, "please do not think that this means *any* lessening of my love to you, and I do not see why it should affect our relations."

Ottoline understood, all right. When he got back to England, she refused to see him. When that stratagem failed to reignite his ardour, she saw him and threw him one. This time, she surprised him—and, presumably, herself—by manifesting an unprecedented physical desire. The delighted Russell immediately forgot all about his commitments to Helen. "I am less fond of H.D. than I have tried to persuade myself that I was," he told Ottoline. "Her affection for me has made me do my utmost to respond. This has brought with it an overestimate of her writing." Though Helen was about to set sail for England as had been arranged, she was clearly on her way to the wings. As war approached in Europe, Russell commendably sympathized with a generation's suffering, which he guessed to be forthcoming. But as Helen approached from America his sympathy for her evaporated.

Monk tellingly notes that Russell could think in terms of abstract populations but not of concrete individuals, unless the individual was himself. He knew he was a ghost, but he couldn't see how that fact might help explain why ordinary people were ciphers to him. In particular, he believed that females, as a sex, suffered from "triviality of the soul": they didn't see the big picture, as he did. Helen, with her awkward insistence on arriving as requested, obviously had a bad case of it. "I feel now an absolute blank indifference to her," he told Ottoline, "except as one little atom of the mass of humanity." When Helen arrived in England with suitcases full of pretty clothes she fondly imagined to be her trousseau, he refused to see her.

Blind to the possible consequences, Russell contrived that the desperate Helen should take refuge in the household of none other than Ottoline Morrell. Helen told Ottoline everything and showed her Russell's letters, which the appalled Ottoline discovered to be full of the same exalted flapdoodle that had once been lavished on her. She found Helen's trousseau more tasteless than pathetic, but she had enough heart to be devastated by the revelations of Russell's pettiness and the capacity of his smarm to spread straight from the refrigerator, like margarine. Unimpressed by his reassurances that his "sense of oneness" with her had only increased, Ottoline cooled to him. Soon Russell transferred his affections to Irene Cooper-Willis, with Ottoline playing the go-between. (This is *The School for Scandal* updated by Tom Stoppard. Don't try to figure it out now; just enjoy the flash and filigree as the principals rocket in and out of the parlour.) Irene, a celibate but bewitching young beauty, was ready to be Russell's research assistant but not his mistress. The affair aborted on the pad, but there was enough flame and smoke to bring Ottoline back at full speed. Into the cot with him she duly dived, for one last paradisiacal thrash, inspiring Russell to the whitest heat of his epistolary style:

My Heart, my Life, how can I ever tell you the amazing unspeakable glory of you tonight? You were utterly, absolutely of the stars—& yet of the Eternal Earth too—so that you took me from Earth & in a moment carried me to the highest heights . . . it blended in some unimaginable

way with religion & the central fires . . . the mountains & the storm &
the danger, & the wild sudden beauty, & the free winds of heaven . . . the
depths & wildness & vastness of my love to you . . . a flood, a torrent, an
ocean . . . what the greatest music yearns for, what made the Sunflower
be weary of time, what makes one's life a striving & straining & struggling
after Heaven.

Striving and straining and struggling for a single halfway original
phrase, he sent such letters day after day, like the artillery barrages then
lighting up the Western Front. Everyone writes badly to a lover, but for
specifying Russell's kind of badness—an interstellar bathos ready to gush
at the touch of a button—there are no words in English, although there
is possibly one in German: *Mumpitz*, meaning the higher twaddle. But
not even his prose was enough to turn Ottoline off altogether. As people
would later say in California, she was always there for him: there to be
informed of his latest depredations, incomprehensions and marvels of
self-deceit. On the basis of extensive research, Monk is reluctant to lay
the blame for the madness of T. S. Eliot's wife Vivien on Russell's treatment of her during their affair, but it could scarcely have helped. For this
reader, however, the prize episode of the book is Russell's deep, intimate
misunderstanding of the divinely beautiful twenty-one-year-old actress
Colette Malleson, who should have been one of the great loves of his life.
No doubt he believed she was, to judge from his prose. "I want to take
you into the very centre of my being," he wrote in 1916, "and to reach
myself into the centre of yours." Russell said goodbye to Ottoline all over
again and invited Colette, who was already married to the actor Miles
Malleson, to the peaks of spiritual union: "I love you, & my spirit calls out
to you to come & seek the mountain tops." But the mountaintops, it tran-
spired, held no place for her aspirations to the stage: it wasn't a worthy
ambition for any companion of his, and he did his eloquent best to talk
her out of it. Luckily, she had the strength to read him the news about the
necessity of her staying true to her gift, but you can't help wondering why
he needed to hear it instead of figuring it out for himself. Why was the
philosopher always the most blatant dunderhead on the scene?
The best that can be said for him in this instance is that he was concerned about the sexual temptation that Colette's vocation might put in
her way. He was right to be: a handsome young director won her affections. That development threw Russell into such paroxysms of jealousy

that her husband, a natural philosopher who was clearly better qualified in emotional matters than the professional, very generously worried about Russell's fate more than about Colette's. Russell resorted to composing a long, mordant analysis of Colette's allegedly deficient character, emphasizing her vanity and her inordinate need of sexual adventure. Whether or not this was projection, no term except damnable effrontery can cover the fact that he sent the character study to Colette. She stuck to her guns and went on seeing other men, thereby spurring Russell to a rare statement identifiable as normal human speech: "You said the other day that you didn't know how to repulse people, but you always knew how to repulse me."

Luckily for him, there was yet another young knockout on the scene—the twenty-five-year-old Dora Black, armed with a first-class degree in Modern Languages from Girton and an all-embracing hero-worship for Russell, whom she found "enchantingly ugly." She was the girl in the red dress. Truly desired, Russell responded as might be expected, cranking up his prose style into transgalactic overdrive even as she strove to hold him earthbound with her encircling arms. Colette did an Ottoline, returning to his bed to fill it when it was empty of Dora. Russell, who lied to each of them about the other and told Ottoline the truth about both, was at long last getting all the affection he could take. At this point, any male middle-aged non-philosopher who has become absorbed in Russell's emotional career to the point where the man's requirements have started to seem normal will find it hard to suppress an exhortation from the sideline: Hang in there, don't muck this up, you're doing better than Errol Flynn. But not even Russell could flourish forever in an atmosphere of total unreality. Along with the stars, the storm, the highest heights and the central fires, he wanted children. Dora was ready to give them to him. He ends the book married to her, and we close it with something like relief, as if after watching an unusually obtuse chimp navigate its way through a maze all the way to the bunch of bananas.

.   .   .

None of this, I believe, is a travesty either of Russell's love life or of Monk's account of it: Russell's love life *was* a travesty. The same is true for many men, and perhaps most: sooner or later, sex will make a fool out of any of us, and we are never more likely to talk balls than when they rule our brains. But most of us have not set ourselves up to instruct the world concerning what it should think and feel. Russell did. Fortunately for his memory, there is a parallel tale to be told, and Monk tells it well. All the generosity and forbearance that Russell so conspicuously did not bring to his emotional life he brought to his intellectual one, and there his true magnanimity is to be sought and found. When he learned that his work on the logical foundations of mathematics had been anticipated by the German scholar Gottlob Frege, he was generous to Frege instead of spiteful, and did everything he could to confirm the primacy of Frege's work over his own. Not even Wittgenstein, who shared Russell's proclivity for telling the brutal truth, was able to arouse his enmity. Russell, who arranged for the publication of the *Tractatus Logico-Philosophicus*, and promoted Wittgenstein's career in all respects, had every right to regard the astounding young Austrian as his protégé, but the protégé felt no obligation to protect his mentor's feelings; quite the reverse. Wittgenstein was worse than blunt in undermining Russell's confidence in his own achievement as a professional philosopher, and unrelenting in his contempt for everything Russell did as a popular one. When their friendship was broken off, however, it was at Wittgenstein's instigation, not Russell's. This showed true greatness of soul on Russell's part. It must have been a blow to discover that Wittgenstein did not share his conviction that a scientific philosophy was possible, but worse than a blow—a death threat— to be told that he was a bad writer.

Wittgenstein's qualifications for saying so were impeccable, because he himself was a very good writer indeed. He can be seen as one of the jewels in the glittering German aphoristic tradition that began with Goethe and Lichtenberg and included, in Wittgenstein's own time, Arthur Schnitzler, Karl Kraus and Alfred Polgar. Even in English translation, the habitually terse Wittgenstein inexorably emerged as the artist-philosopher that Russell, inspired originally by the poetic element in Spinoza, had vainly dreamed of being. But Wittgenstein, though a born master of language, was determined not to be seduced by it. Russell was seduced by it every day of his life. Wittgenstein set limitations on philosophy: "What we cannot speak of we should pass over in silence." Russell recognized no such limitations; and there was nothing he could pass over in silence. He gushed even when he turned off the faucet. Talking about ordinary life instead of the heady realm of love, he could leave out the stars, the mountaintops and everything else in the instant-mysticism kit, but his plain language still took off under its own power, clear as crystal and no more yielding, as convinced of its elevated reasonableness as it was unconvincing about the stubbornly unreasonable texture of real life.

There are exceptions, and one of them is likely to remain a great book. A *History of Western Philosophy*, which was published in 1945 and is still the first general book for the layman to read on the subject, shows what Russell's plain prose could do when the subject was safely in the past and some of his earlier exaltation of pure reason was in the past, too. However, abstruse the topic, every sentence is as natural as a breath. For more than eight hundred closely printed pages, the exposition flows without a hitch. "Whatever can be known," he says in its concluding pages, "can be known by means of science; but things which are legitimately matters of feeling lie outside its province." Even this is open to question (there are very few important truths about politics, for example, that can be known by any means except a combination of science *and* feeling), yet at least it shows signs of the old man's having momentarily attained a measure of negative capability. Unfortunately, the bulk of his popular philosophizing was about current events, and was written, even into his old age, with all the overconfident flow of his initial, natural assumption, which was that political and social unreason was most easily to be explained by the mass of humanity's not being as bright as he was. A conviction of his superiority to mere mortals was part of his nature: we know that—know that now better than we ever did—because he was always inviting his latest love to join him on the heights above them.

.   .   .

There is a lot to be worried about in the current vogue for biographies of the great. To find out in advance that Picasso was a monster could be an invitation to underestimate his art, and to wolf down the details of Einstein's infidelity is certainly easier on the nerves and the ego than trying just once more to imagine those lights on the moving trains. Monk must have been aware of the dangers: after all, Russell behaved no worse than Einstein, better than Picasso and a lot better than Matisse. But surely Monk has done the right thing in making Russell's personal life so prominent. Like the creatively fecund but personally unspeakable Brecht, Russell was a great man who used his prestige to back up his political opinions, and when someone does that we want to find out how he treated the people he knew, so as to assess the validity of his exhortations to the millions of people he didn't know. The unsung hero of this volume is D. H.

Lawrence, who put his finger on what Monk bravely calls the central conflict of Russell's nature—or, rather, put his finger painfully *into* it,
because it was a wound. Lawrence pointed out the irreconcilable discrepancy between Russell's ideal of universal love and his alienation from
humanity. The devastated Russell generously declined to withdraw his
lasting admiration of Lawrence, but one can't help feeling that this might
have been partly because he didn't see all the implications of what
Lawrence had said. As the autobiography reveals over and over, Russell
could come to know things about himself after he was told often enough,
but somehow he still couldn't take them in. He was in this respect the
opposite of an artist, since the mark of the artist is to take in more than
he can know.

It shouldn't have mattered, but in the long run it did. While Russell
had no objections to colonialist wars against "primitive" peoples (in his
view, such wars spread enlightenment), he deplored wars between civilized nations. Unremarkable at first blush, this stand required courage in
the war fever of 1914. Having consecrated his vows with a stretch in
prison, Russell unwisely went on to pursue pacifism as part of his religion
of reason. He erected peace into a principle instead of just espousing it as
a desirable state of affairs: if enough people believed in peace, there
would be no more war. The principle started looking shaky when Hitler
came to power and set about incarnating the intractable truth that unless
absolutely everyone believes in peace the few who don't will subjugate all
the others. Einstein, a clear candidate for subjugation, gave up his pacifism straight away: he didn't have to be a physicist to figure it out. But
Russell the philosopher was slow to get the point. And, even when he did,
the principle was never given up. It was there waiting to lead him on to
his biggest absurdity: unilateral nuclear disarmament.

To an issue that he might have helped clarify he added nothing but
confusion. While there was a good case to be made for multilateral
nuclear disarmament, there was none at all to be made for unilateral
nuclear disarmament, since it depended on presenting a moral example
to a regime that was, by its own insistence, not open to moral persuasion.
Russell knew this: he had been one of the first visitors to the Soviet Union
to warn against what was going on there, and when the Americans were
still the only possessors of the atomic bomb he had recommended threatening the Soviets with it in order to change their ways. He knew it, but
somehow he had not taken it in. I myself, as a multilateralist who did my

share of marching from Aldermaston in the early 1960s, well remember the hard-line-unilateralist Committee of 100 and its adherents: talking to them about modern history was like talking to a Seventh-Day Adventist about Elvis Presley. They were fatuous, but with the support lent them by Russell's immense prestige they could believe that they had been granted a vision of a higher truth, beyond the sordid realities of politics. The eventual effect, transmitted through the left wing of the Labour Party, helped to keep the Conservatives in power for a generation, because the public was unable to believe that Labour could be trusted with the deterrent— a distrust that proved well founded when Michael Foot, during his doomed general-election campaign, bizarrely promised to keep the deterrent for only as long as it took to bargain it away.

Russell spoke and thought as if the mass of humanity needed convincing that war was a bad thing. Somehow, he never quite took in the fact that most people already knew this but were genuinely divided as to what should be done about it, and something he never took in at all was that there is no such thing as the mass of humanity—there are only individuals. Failing to grasp that, he was, for all his real sympathy with the sufferings of mankind, paradoxically orating from the same rostrum as the century's worst tyrants. Trying to wake us all up, he could never believe that we were not asleep; that our nightmares were happening in daylight; and that his religion of reason could do little to dispel them. How could he not realize it? In this courageously frank first volume of what could well amount to a classic study of the personality of genius, Ray Monk shows us how—by showing us that no matter how brilliant a mind may be, its stupidity will still break through, if that is what it takes to assuage its solitude. With his eyes on the heights, Russell never noticed that his trousers were around his ankles: but now we know. They're ready for you on the set, Mr. Wilder.

The New Yorker, December 1996;
later included in *Even As We Speak*, 2001

POSTSCRIPT

My idea for a movie about Russell and Wittgenstein was meant to depend for its effect on its manifest absurdity. But a Hollywood producer was on the phone the week after the piece came out, talking large talk about writing a treatment. Since then I've heard nothing, which I suppose is a relief, because it was evident that he wanted to make the kind of comedy that says it's a comedy up front, like *Nuns on the Run*. I probably put him off when I told him the truth: as Russell proved, it isn't funny unless you play it straight.

On reflection, I should have said one thing in favour of Russell's pacifism. There were writers more sensitive than he was who shared the same conviction. One of them was the most subtle essayist of his time, Alfred Polgar, then as famous in the German-speaking countries as he was unknown outside their borders. Even Thomas Mann bowed to Polgar as the living master of German prose. Like Einstein, Polgar was of Jewish background, and well before the Nazis reached power he was aware of what they were after. But unlike Einstein he did not alter his pacifism to fit. He went on writing as if war could be avoided through evoking its cost with sufficient intensity. The first war had so horrified him that he thought a second war unthinkable, and he went on declaring his aversion as a principle even as it became clear that it was only a wish, because Hitler was thinking of nothing else. Polgar was still a pacifist when he was forced into exile by the threat of death. In so rational a man, the tenacity of so irrational a view raises the question of whether it is really a view at all. It might be better appreciated as a kind of pre-emptive panic reflex, like the strange, strained serenity with which we go on failing to open a letter from the tax office. Russell understood everything about the belligerent force of totalitarian power, but he was still speaking against rearmament when Hitler had already declared war in all but name. Russell's message was that the war would be a disaster for human values, and therefore should not be fought. The first part of the message was too true to be interesting. The second part made no sense at all, because Hitler had removed the choice. Whether this utter deficiency of ordinary logic on the outstanding political issue of the day retroactively undermines the validity of Russell's symbolic logic is for symbolic logicians to decide. One guesses that it doesn't: the two mental processes are different in kind. But social commentators should certainly keep in mind Russell's public performance before World War II when they try to assess his public performance after it. Presumably for the benefit of anyone who though that atomic bombs were toys, he correctly said that they were terrible things: so terrible that that the Soviet Union should be left to possess them on its own until shamed into abandoning them by the example of more enlightened nations. Once again, the first part of the message was a commonplace, and once again the second part was ludicrous. The fact that he had had been one of the pioneers in detecting the real nature of the Soviet regime made it more ludicrous still. He didn't even have the excuse of being a dupe. One of the most intelligent men alive, he could scarcely be diagnosed as lacking the capacity for reason, so the answer to the conundrum must be sought in his personality, in which his superior knowledge reinforced his narcissism instead of chastening it. As so often when contemplating the political follies of great minds, we are forced back to the definition of democracy bequeathed to us by Camus. Democracy is the regime conceived, created and sustained by people who know that they do not know everything.

2003

PART
IV

VISUAL

IMAGES

43

———

THE NEW DIAGHILEV

Discreetly increasing itself a few titles at a time, the "MGM Classic Collection" (MGM/UA) has already reached the point where you need a month to take it all in. But unless your first allegiance goes to Elizabeth Taylor modelling lingerie for the fuller figure in *Cat on a Hot Tin Roof,* there can be no doubt that the musicals are what validate the word "classic" in the collection so far. Just follow the dancing feet.

Not that even MGM had a sure-fire formula. Musicals could be either mechanical or successful, but not both. What MGM had was an inspired producer, Arthur Freed. Opinions differ about which was the very best musical with his name on it, *Singin' in the Rain* or *The Band Wagon,* made in 1952 and 1953 respectively.

Those with ambitions towards forming a library will have already purchased or stolen a video of the former, but they should note that the latter is also there for the asking, at an advertised playing time of 108 minutes, which the first-time viewer will find is far short of how long it takes to see once. Some of the numbers will have you lunging for the rewind button before they are half over. The awful, addictive thing about video is that if you can't bear the visual high to end, it doesn't have to. *The Band Wagon* is the video drug in its pure form: cocaine for the corneas.

Freed usually made sure, sometimes too sure, that the numbers, while never clashing with the story, weren't crowded out by it. Fred Astaire is ruminatively crooning "By Myself" only ten minutes into the picture and ten minutes after that he is in full flight with the shoeshine dance routine, which expands into the amusement arcade production number, which in turn ends with a sight gag so good it makes you laugh even when alone. Direction by Vincente Minnelli, screenplay by Comden and Green, choreography by Michael Kidd—everything fits together straight away because of the producer's sense of proportion. Away from Freed, no-one concerned was immune from the self-indulgence that spins things out.

Even Astaire, unless advised to the contrary, would chew his dialogue ten times before swallowing. But he always danced economically even when the routine going on around him limped. *The Band Wagon* never limps, but it does sometimes swan about, especially while establishing Cyd Charisse as a ballerina, so that she can kick over the traces later on. Astaire has to do a lot of standing around flat-footed, and you would be left feeling short-changed if it were not for "The Girl Hunt" production number at the end.

The pre-war musicals usually spaced numbers of even length evenly throughout. The post-war musicals favoured a tease-play approach by which numbers that weren't long enough led up to a flag-waving finale that went on longer than you could believe, or—as happened particularly when Gene Kelly was involved—could bear. But "The Girl Hunt" brings *The Band Wagon* to a blissful climax. Astaire and Charisse finally get to strut their full range of stuff, including a two-minute jump-time jazz dance duet which is the most exhilarating thing of its kind on film.

It's the sequence set in the Dem Bones Café, starting from when Astaire enters with his hat over his eyes. Charisse is perched on a bar stool with her coat done up. She sheds the coat and unfolds that marvellous figure, which would have been poetic even if she hadn't been able to dance—although if she hadn't been able to dance she wouldn't have looked like that. When the film came out I saw it over and over just for those few minutes. When I found out that her real name was Tula Ellice Finklea I only loved her more.

On the Town is earlier and less lush. Freed is once again in charge, but Stanley Donen is keener than Minnelli to cut out the fashion photography and keep things moving. This quality paid off when Gene Kelly was, as here, the star. A Kelly ballet, if left unguarded, would swell to absorb the entire movie. But in 1949 they still had the clock on him.

Since he is one of three sailors on shore leave, and since each sailor has a girlfriend, Kelly gets, theoretically at least, only $16\frac{2}{3}$ per cent of the total screen-time to bare those perfect teeth and/or rise slowly on *demi point* with his bottom tensed. Otherwise Ann Miller bares her perfect legs and Betty Garrett lures Frank Sinatra up to her place—a rare example, for the time, of a lady taking the lead. The way Sinatra's voice comes sidling through the ensembles tells you what tone has that loudness hasn't.

But the producer is the real hero. Five of the six leading characters are wrecking the natural history museum with a song-and-dance routine almost as soon as the picture starts. The sixth character, Vera-Ellen, is an aloof ballerina, but luckily for us she has to earn a secret living as a sideshow dancer on Coney Island, so in the fullness of time she burns the boards with the rest of the gang, and thus obliges Kelly to stop indulging in his least endearing facial expression, shy awe. "Gosh Ivy, I mean Miss Smith, I . . ."

It didn't matter so much if he talked like that, as long as he eventually danced. In *Anchors Aweigh* he is still talking half an hour into the picture and not a dancing foot has been heard, nor has Sinatra sung a note. Freed's name is not on the credits. Once again it is the story of sailors getting liberty, but this time you want them to be deprived of it.

The Barkleys of Broadway ought to be, on paper, a better bet. Freed is in charge, Comden and Green do the script, and Fred Astaire stars with Ginger Rogers. What can go wrong? One tends to conclude that Charles Walters couldn't direct musicals, but it can only have been the producer's fault that when you finally finish waiting for the first number it turns out to be Oscar Levant playing "Ritual Fire Dance." Freed had not yet made *On the Town*, but he was no beginner: *Meet Me in St Louis* was already behind him.

While Homer nods, the two stars cool their heels, no doubt remembering the blessed days of black and white. But it wasn't colour that deprived musicals of their simplicity. It was choreography. The form became so organic that only a producer of genius could keep it under control. In the pre-war Astaire musicals the dances were created by the star himself, with the assistance of Hermes Pan. Together, they knew exactly what was right for him—the routines were balletic only in the metaphorical sense of being light as air, even when he was kicking holes in the floor. Post-war, ballet took over, with *An American in Paris* providing merely the most gargantuan example. Kelly was ballet-prone anyway, but even Astaire got sucked in.

It was Art with a capital A and it spelt death to the screen musical, a tradition which had previously managed to free itself from the cold hand of Busby Berkeley, whose production numbers looked like colonies of bacteria staging a political rally under a microscope. But from ballet there was no escape. Shoes which had worn taps wanted to point their toes. The new energy fell for the only temptation that could kill it—going legit. Strangely enough it was the genius who fell hardest. Arthur Freed was the new Diaghilev until he tried to be like the old one.

The Observer, February, 26, 1984;
later included in *Snakecharmers in Texas*, 1988

POSTSCRIPT

An aspect I left out of the above mini-survey was the impulse of the director to wreck the unity of a dance number unless haunted by a producer with a firm hand. The besetting vice of Busby Berkeley's musicals was that he was in control of them, whereas nobody was in control of him. In the long run, the power of the directors has done far more damage to the form than the balletic pretensions of the stars. Even when the director has a firm hand himself, he tends to loosen it as his prestige grows beyond challenge. An illustrative case is the gifted Australian director Baz Luhrmann. In *Strictly Ballroom*, the movie that made his name, the dance numbers are filmed in takes sufficiently long to show the flow. In *Moulin Rouge* they are pieced together a few frames at a time. In his first phase you are aware of the dancers. In the second phase you are aware of the director. No doubt *Moulin Rouge* was twice as hard to do, but I could bear to see it only once. *Strictly Ballroom* I saw twice in the week it came out. It was as good, and stays as good, as *Dirty Dancing*: which is actually saying quite a lot. Although we undoubtedly lost a reservoir of expertise when MGM shut down its production line, the musical isn't yet dead as a form. It will always be there as long as an occasional movie comes out that makes you want to sing and dance. If it makes you want to be a film director, however, someone has made a mistake.

2003

44

PIER PAOLO
PAIN IN THE NECK

Renaissance man is a description tossed around too lightly in modern times—actors get it if they can play the guitar—but for Pier Paolo Pasolini nothing less will do. From the moment he hit Rome after the Second World War until the moment his own car hit him in 1975, Pasolini single-handedly re-embodied about half the personnel of Burckhardt's *The Civilization of the Renaissance in Italy*. He was poet, novelist, scholar, intellectual, sexual adventurer, reforming zealot, creator of large-scale visual spectaculars—and all these things equally. To make a comparable impact, Raphael would have had to be elected Pope. To make a comparable exit, Michelangelo would have had to fall out of the Sistine Ceiling. Pasolini was a front-page event in every field he entered, including death. A boy he picked up in his Alfa Romeo sports car ran him over with it and left him helpless in the dust. Beat that, Renaissance! Not even Cola di Rienzo got trampled by his own horse.

    Pasolini's sensational demise happened at Ostia, once the port where Julius Caesar took ship and Cleopatra came ashore. The ancient location widens Pasolini's frame of reference still further, to include the whole of Italian history. He was such a national figure that it becomes easy to lose sight of the individual. In a new biography (*Pasolini Requiem*) Barth David Schwartz mercifully doesn't, but his whopping book isn't helped by the bad practice of cramming in all the incidental research to prove that it has been done. European reviewers like to call this an American habit, but really it is a virus with no respect for borders. A more specific stricture to place on Mr. Schwartz might be that a prose style so devoid of verve is no fit instrument to evoke a hero who crackled with energy even when he was being stupid. But Mr. Schwartz, though a plodder, plods briskly enough to make his subject breathe, and some of the specialized knowledge was well worth going to get. In addition to his prodigious archival burrowings and the conducting of interviews on the scale of a door-to-door electoral canvass, Mr. Schwartz seems to have acquainted himself personally with the sexually ambiguous (though unambiguously violent) Roman low life that was Pasolini's stamping ground, or prancing ground. The biographer is to be congratulated not least for coming out alive. The biographee, after all, got killed in there.

As for what he was doing in there, the first answer is obvious: he was cruising, although that word understates his predatory celerity. Better to say that he was pouncing. Quick off the mark and dressed to kill, he was a cheetah in dark glasses. In the *borgata*, the slumland of the Roman periphery, the population was mostly immigrants from the south who had come in search of prosperity and found misery. Petty theft and casual prostitution made up most of their economy. For a well-heeled and voraciously promiscuous homosexual like Pasolini, it was a dream come true. There were boys to be had for a pack of cigarettes or just a ride in his car.

He did his best to have them all. It remains astonishing, when you look at the shelf of books and rack of films signed with his name, that he found the energy to copulate even more prolifically than he created. People who knew him well were astonished, too. On location in North Africa for a film, his colleagues would retire exhausted to their tents after a long day and meet him coming out of his, all set to cruise the dunes.

But the spontaneous and seemingly everlasting abundance of sexual gratification was also the wellspring of his politics. The second and less obvious answer to the question of why he spent so much time in the lower depths was that he found them ethically preferable to the heights. He thought the truth was down there. Unlike other articulate, well-paid enemies of bourgeois society, Pasolini could actually point to an alternative. It wasn't a pretty alternative, but that was one of the things he hated about the bourgeoisie—its concern with mere appearances.

He hated everything else about the bourgeoisie as well, but in that respect he holds little interest except as an especially flagrant example of the modern middle-class intellectual blindly favouring, against common reason and all the historical evidence, a totalitarian substitute for the society that produced him. Valued by the PCI, the Communist Party of Italy, for the publicity he brought it, Pasolini was allowed more latitude than any other mouthpiece. He often spoke against Party doctrines, and used the space given him by the Party's own newspapers to do so. But he was reliable, not to say predictable, in his denunciation of capitalism, neo-capitalism, consumerism, the bourgeoisie, bourgeois consumerism, bourgeois democracy, neo-capitalist democracy, consumerist democracy and, for that matter, democracy itself, which he thought, or said he thought, could never achieve anything more than "false tolerance" so long as it was infected by bourgeois consciousness.

It hardly needs saying that Pasolini had bourgeois origins himself: you don't get that kind of stridency except from someone in a false position. Raised under Fascism in a small town in Friuli—a province in the north-east of the country, where it bends towards Trieste—young Pier Paolo, a natural student, picked up the firm grounding in the etymology of the Friulian dialect which underpinned his lifetime achievement as a scholar and master of the Italian language. But he picked up no grounding at all in the life of the proletariat. He never did a day's manual labour then or later.

This is a standard pattern for revolutionary intellectuals and can't usefully be called hypocrisy, since if there is such a thing as a proletarian consciousness then it is hard to see how any proletarian could escape from it without the help of the revolutionary intellectual—although just how the revolutionary intellectual manages to escape from bourgeois consciousness is a problem that better minds than Pasolini have never been able to solve without sleight of hand. On this point Pasolini never pretended to be analytical, or even consistent. He was content to be merely rhetorical, in a well-established Italian tradition by which political argument is conducted like grand opera, with the tenor, encouraged by the applause or even by the mere absence of abuse, advancing to the footlights to sing his aria all over again, *da capo* and *con amore*.

Another aria Pasolini kept reprising was a bit harder to forgive. Mr. Schwartz could have done more to disabuse the unwary reader of the notion that Pasolini might have had something when he not only awarded himself credentials in the wartime resistance but claimed the resistance as the alma mater of the post-war revolutionary struggle. Pasolini's resistance activities were confined mainly to writing obscure scholarly articles that the censors would have had to go out of their way even to find, let alone interpret. Again, there is no dishonour in this: peo-

ple were shot for less. As in France, there was an understandable tendency in Italy after the war for people who had been helpless civilians
during it to award themselves battle honours retroactively. Pasolini was
just another schoolboy raised under the Fascist system who had the dubious luck to become a questioning adolescent at the precise moment
when Fascism fell apart, and was thus able to convince himself that he
had seen through it.

A more serious piece of mental legerdemain—and one that Mr.
Schwartz doesn't do half enough to point out—was Pasolini's lifelong pretence that the resistance was the prototype of the future Communist state,
and for that very reason had been throttled by the ruthless forces of capitalism, bourgeois democracy, etc. Again as in France, most of the first and
many of the bravest resistance fighters in Italy were indeed Communists.
But the resistance movement soon became too broadly based to be called
revolutionary; a better parallel is with Yugoslavia, Poland or those other
East European countries where not even opposition to the Nazis could
unite the partisan movement, whose Communists regarded its bourgeois
democrats as the real enemy, to be wiped out when the opportunity arose.
This actually happened to Pasolini's brother, an active partisan who was
liquidated by a Communist kangaroo court busily anticipating the post-
war socialist order. In most respects ready to concede that Pasolini was so
cold a fish that even his passions were impersonal, Mr. Schwartz seems
not to have fully grasped that Pasolini was callous about his brother, too,
claiming his death as a sacrifice in an historic struggle that, since it
existed only in the minds of intellectuals, was never truly historic but
always, and only, literary.

It could be that Mr. Schwartz, for all he undoubtedly knows about
Italy now, doesn't know quite enough about what it was like then. He is
especially shaky in the crucial area of Italy's messy emergence from the
war. A reference to German "Junker 25 transports" might just be a misprint for what they ought to be, Junkers 52 transports, but his apparent
belief that a German bomber could be called a Macchi—famously an
Italian aircraft company—undermines confidence in his knowledge of
the period, especially since he is making such a parade of specific references in order to evoke it: "On April 6 [of 1944] Klaus Barbie's Gestapo
in Lyons arrested fifty-one Jews . . ." etc. If this is meant to be an ironic
comment on the terrible bedfellows Mussolini had acquired when he
agreed to set up the Republic of Salò under German tutelage, it scarcely

seems adequate. Why is there nothing about the Nazi assault on the Jews of Italy? It would not only have been more pertinent to the subject; it would have created a more realistic context against which Pasolini's later vapourings about the revolutionary resistance could have been judged. That the Nazi attempt to render Italy *judenrein* was a comparative failure was due at least partly to the historic reluctance of the Italian people to follow fanatics of any stamp further than the parade ground. There were plenty of bourgeois elements, including the rank and file of the Church, who risked their lives to save Jews. Mr. Schwartz might have made more of this, especially since Pasolini himself made so little.

.   .   .

Pasolini's theatrical fantasies about a formative period of his own and his country's history were not casual. Like Sartre's quietly misleading suggestions that he had been a Resistance fighter in the thick of the action, they were fundamental to a political career of posturing histrionics. Pasolini never went as far as Sartre, although Mr. Schwartz is kind to believe his claims of having escaped from the Germans in a hail of bullets. Pasolini's story was that when the regiment into which he had been drafted was ordered by the Germans to surrender its arms he and a friend threw their rifles into a ditch "and then, in a burst of machine-gun fire, dove in after them." The story continued, "We waited for the regiment to march off, and then made our escape. It was completely an instinctive and involuntary beginning to my resistance." Thus Pasolini, quoted by the English journalist Oswald Stack in 1970, and reprinted by Mr. Schwartz without comment.

Well, it *might* have happened: German machine gunners missed, occasionally. A more plausible version is that Pasolini, like many others, managed to desert unnoticed in the confusion. Sartre let people believe that he had escaped from prison camp. In fact he had been allowed to go home. The heroism came later, in the telling of the tale. So it does for most of us. The best reason for not believing that there was any machine gunner, however, is that Pasolini said so little about the incident later on. If it had really happened there would have been essays, epic poems, movies, operas. A fabulist on Pasolini's scale could never leave unexploited a fact that had actually occurred.

Pasolini respected facts. He just didn't respect their context. You couldn't take his word about the meaning of things. But in his early days

in Rome he was unbeatable at pointing out things that other people—
bourgeois people—preferred to ignore. For a while, he had the only game
in town. Propelled by the post-war economic recovery, Roman high life
regained all its old extravagance. Out at its edge, in the *periferia*, Roman
low life grew ever more malodorous, and for the same reason: the wealth
that fuelled the party had drawn the poor people to the glowing window.
Pasolini's mission was to remind the high life that the low life existed, to
tell the *dolce vita* about the *malavita*.

He did it first as a novelist. His 1959 novel *Una Vita Violenta* has just
been republished, by Pantheon, as *A Violent Life*, in the 1968 translation
by William Weaver, of whom it should be said that the international reputation of modern Italian literature wouldn't be the same without him.
Like Max Hayward with Russian, Weaver has been vital to the job of
transmitting the cultural force of an off-trail language into the world's
consciousness. (It remains a terrible pity that Weaver didn't find time to
translate all of Primo Levi's books instead of only a couple of them.) But
not even Weaver could translate the full impact of *Una Vita Violenta*,
because the book depends on the shock effect of being written ugly in a
beautiful language. Through Weaver's translation is rendered in the most
faithful squalid English, it is not more horrifying than *Last Exist to Brook-
lyn*, whereas it ought to turn the mind's stomach like the invective of the
damned in Dante's Hell. Pasolini went searching for boys among the rubbish dumps and came back with picture of how they lived. His Roman
borgata was like a Rio *favela* without the flowers. In *Black Orpheus*, Marcel Camus's film about Rio, which was a worldwide art-house hit at about
the same time, unquenchable poetry steams out of the garbage to meet
the rising sun. In Pasolini's novel there is just the garbage, and human
begins are part of it. When a flood comes, one of the characters finds it
within himself to punctuate a career of theft by acting selflessly. But that
is the only note of hope. The book was designed as a kick in the teeth for
Pasolini's hated bourgeois enemy. It worked. His reputation as a teller of
the awkward truth was rapidly established, and not only among the radical intelligentsia. After all, the awkward truth was true. You didn't have to
be a Marxist to spot it.

Pasolini, however, did have to be a Marxist. Though never much
concerned with elaborating a coherent social analysis, he never gave up
on the class war. That became part of his tragedy, because the class he
championed finally realized its only ambition, which was to be absorbed

by the class he attacked. But at the time he was a recognized type of radical intellectual, valued even by the non-radical because of his dazzling verbal bravura, forgiven his excesses because he was such an adornment to the scene—a word hard to avoid, considering the theatricality of Italian political discussion. Again, Mr. Schwartz might have made more of just how much forgiveness was required: "He knew nothing about Stalin's purges" is a needless concession to Pasolini's wilful obtuseness. Italian Communist intellectuals knew all about Stalin. The best of them were trying to establish a brand of communism that left him out—the hope that we later learned to call Euro-Communism, or Socialism with a Human Face. The best possible construction to put on Pasolini's polemical writings is that he was trying to do this, too. He had a promising model to follow—Gramsci, about whom Pasolini wrote the most sustained of his many remarkable poetic works, *The Ashes of Gramsci*.

Later on, in the flower-power phase of the 1960s, Gramsci became a hero to thousands of young revolutionaries scattered all over the world; some of them even read a few selected pages, usually from the letters he had written in a Fascist prison. Pasolini got in early and read everything Gramsci wrote. Pasolini promised his hero's shade that the struggle would continue. What he couldn't promise was a solution to the problem posed by the fact that communism in practice had turned out to need as much coercive apparatus as Fascism. At least part of Gramsci's undoubted charm was that he had died in jail without ever having to take part in the application of those theories he had elaborated with such humane subtlety. There was no guarantee that had he done so he would not have turned out like George Lukacs, Hungary's visionary turned cultural commissar—or, to go back to the beginning, Lunacharsky in the Soviet Union, who in 1929 was obliged to crack down on the same avant-garde artists he had previously encouraged.

Gramsci's seductive vision of justice could not have been brought about without unlimited state power. Neither could Pasolini's, and with him there was even less justification for believing it could. But plenty of Pasolini's admirers knew that. They knew him to be wrong but still they marvelled. *The Ashes of Gramsci* told them that they were dealing with a prodigy. Mr. Schwartz forgets to mention one of the things that made the message clear: *Le Ceneri di Gramsci* is written in a version of *terza rima*, the same measure as the *Divine Comedy*. Pasolini cast his wild revolutionary document in the most hallowed of strict forms as a guarantee of national continuity. There is more truth than the author seems to realize in Mr. Schwartz's solemn assurance: "At poem's end, poet and Italy are one." ("Poem's end" is an erstwhile *Time*-style construction that our author has unfortunately resurrected, employing it not quite often enough to reduce the reader to tether's end, just often enough to arouse the dreadful suspicion that a tin ear for English might be hearing Italian the same way.)

.   .   .

Pasolini the writer had established himself beyond question, if not beyond criticism. Bourgeois intellectuals who knew that his politics were nonsense still knew that he was a prodigy. He had ample evidence for his theories about a bourgeois conspiracy against spontaneity and social justice: busted on a morals charge, he was hounded for his perversity by Christian Democrat politicians and their attendant newspapers. Neo-Fascists joined in with delight. But the more awkward truth, for him, was that there was such a thing as an independent, middle-of-the-road intelligentsia, which was perfectly capable of recognizing that he was a classic case in the best sense as well as the worst. He himself was no faddist when it came to critical allegiances. When the name of Roland Barthes came up, Pasolini said that although he admired Barthes's work he would give it all up for a page of Gianfranco Contini or Roberto Longhi. As a student in Bologna, Pasolini had sat at Longhi's feet when the great teacher of art history made a case for the historical continuity of inspiration beyond the reach of any ideology. As for the philologist Contini, he was Pasolini's true conscience, as he was for a greater poet, Eugenio Montale, and for almost every other prominent artist in the post-war period. In the first marvellous years of his career, Pasolini reported to Contini by letter like a truant son to the father he had never had. Contini, the least radical of men, a true cultural conservative for whom learning was the world—and who mastered more of the world's learning than any other scholar—understood the tension in Pasolini between the irreconcilable forces of social rage and creative ambition. But so did many people less qualified. Pasolini was so obviously a star, and stars are on fire.

.   .   .

Pasolini loved stardom, which for a champion of the common man is always bound to present a contradiction. It can be reconciled, but it takes humour, and humour was not conspicuously among his gifts. It it had been, he might have been funnier about his need for an ever bigger stage. He preferred to believe that it was a political necessity. The movies reached people who couldn't read. While his literary reputation was still building up, Pasolini was already preparing to compromise it by contributing to the screenplays of the famous directors, which in Italy have traditionally been group efforts. In 1957, he wrote scenes for Fellini's *Le Notti di Cabiria*. Fellini gave him his first car, a Fiat 600, as part payment. The tiny *macchina* can be seen as the germ of a dangerous taste, but Pasolini didn't really need much encouragement beyond the thrill of being in on the most glamorous artistic activity available. The lowlife scenes of Fellini's *La Dolce Vita* were also written by Pasolini. In that so wonderfully, so *easily* symbolic moment when Marcello Mastroianni and Anouk Aimée are shown by the prostitute across the plank in her flooded basement room Pasolini's harsh knowledge of the periphery underlies Fellini's humanity.

Having so resonantly played backseat driver, Pasolini was bound to grab the wheel. *Accattone*, his début movie as a director, in 1961, was the world of *Una Vita Violenta* made noisomely accessible to all, with no punches pulled, even in the casting: the bad teeth on display were the genuine article. The only star associated with the movie was Pasolini himself. The result was a triumph. Condemned out of hand by all the right people, it was a scandalous artistic success that was widely seen to spring from an even more scandalous reality. By a paradox whose consequences he would never cease trying to talk his way out of, Pasolini gained immediate and universal acceptance as the first fully authenticated multimedia genius ever to wear dark glasses indoors and a silk shirt undone to the third button.His subject matter was life beyond the margin; he himself was no more marginal than the Pope. How to reconcile this anomaly?

He couldn't, but he made a great try. If Mr. Schwartz had gone lighter on inessential detail he might have found room for a few paragraphs pointing out what a continuous thrill it was to be in or near Italy when the film directors were all living in each other's pockets, poaching each other's personnel and turning out movies that struck you even at the time as memories to be kept, partly because the people who made them so obviously had memories of their own. The glaring difference between the Italian cinema and the French New Wave was that the Italians hadn't sent boys to do a man's work. Quite apart from the international big guns like Fellini and Visconti and Antonioni, there was a whole row of domestic household names who could get the tragic recent history of their country even into their comedies. Anyone who wanted to know what really happened to young Italian deserters who ran away from German machine guns could have found out from Comencini's *Tutti a Casa*, a comic vehicle for Alberto Sordi which nevertheless brought out the full tragedy of the collapsing Fascist farce. Most of these directors were social democrats—moderates, if you like, or bourgeois liberals, if you insist— but they could produce a socially responsible cinema, and there was at least one Marxist, Gillo Pontecorvo, who left Pasolini's Marxism looking like the caprice it was. Pontecorvo's *The Battle of Algiers* was a political film in the way Pasolini's films never were.

But everyone at the time knew that Pasolini's role was to remain unpredictable by refusing to mature. He carried a licence to shoot his mouth off out of season, forever making statements because he could never make sense. Italian cinema had room for just one Godard-style head case, and Pasolini was it. The special exemption he held in the literary world also applied, on a larger scale, in the more spectacular world of the movies. Almost every film he made was indicted, sequestered, banned from the festival, reinstated, fought over, laughed at—above all, talked about. If he hadn't scandalized them, people would have been disappointed.

He was a spoiled child given a camera for his birthday, who made home movies about what had spoiled him. *Oedipus Rex* was an obvious love poem to his mother, played by Silvana Mangano at her most iconically beautiful, with Pasolini's alter ego Franco Citti in the title role. Starring in *Medea*, Maria Callas was his mother all over again: statuesque, mad about Jason, ready to kill anyone for him, including her own sons. In *Teorema*, Terence Stamp played Pasolini himself, the sexually omnipotent stranger who penetrated the bourgeois household and everyone in it, as if the plot of Jerome K. Jerome's play *The Passing of the Third-Floor Back* had been given a monkey-gland injection. Stamp, looking more beautiful than Mangano and Callas put together, was almost credible as the avatar before whom the whole household lined up seriatim to be ravished and transfigured. An earlier choice for the role, Lee Van Cleef, might have made disbelief harder to suspend. The early choices for the role of Jesus Christ in *The Gospel According to St. Matthew* were similarly unpromising. Jack Kerouac was one, Allen Ginsberg was another, and there was even a dizzy moment when Yevtushenko was considered. But Pasolini saw sense, cast a strikingly good-looking unknown and made his best film, the one that shocked even the Marxists. It took the Gospel straight. Under the influence of Pope John XXIII, the Curia had decided that the occasional venture into the mass media need not be ruled out. The Franciscans put up the money for the movie on the sole condition that Pasolini's script stuck to the book. Pasolini might have done so anyway. Matthew's Christ comes with a sword. It was the way Pasolini saw himself: the man from nowhere, speaking authentic speech, potent beyond containment, loving the poor, transfiguring them by his touch. Authenticity was aided by the contractual and temporal impossibility of Christ's castigating the bourgeoisie, consumerism, American-style false tolerance, etc. All He was allowed to do was cleanse the temple, which will always need cleansing. As a Biblical film, *The Gospel According to St. Matthew* has no peers and only one plausible emulator I can think of— Bruce Beresford's 1985 *King David*. That film, much derided even by Beresford himself, has something of the same startling, self-contained feeling of being there where it all began, away from here where it all ends. Recast and given the budget to finish the big scenes that were cut short when bad weather chewed up its shooting time, *King David* might have come even closer to the Pasolini film Beresford so admired when it came out, in 1964. But Hollywood was a bad place for Beresford to start from. To that extent Pasolini was right about American consumerism. He was just wrong about the Italian bourgeoisie, from which came the independent producers who backed his movies not just because they hoped to make money—always a gamble with a director out to get banned if he could—but because they respected his gift. The Franciscans respected it, too. Modern Italian society was more complex and fruitful than Pasolini ever allowed. He wasn't sufficiently impressed by how it had given rise to him. He was too busy being impressed with himself.

It did him in, in the end. History caught up with him in the late 1960s, when the student rebellion outflanked him. His reaction to the student revolutionaries was the same as de Gaulle's. *Vi odio cari studenti*: I hate you, darling students. Pasolini cheered the police for hitting them. At least the police were poor, whereas the students were *figli di papà*, sons of daddy—in a word, bourgeois.

But by then it was becoming evident even to Pasolini that the class war was over and the bourgeoisie had won it. Belief in the socialist state was draining away in the West because it was already dead in the East. The only course left was to clean up democracy. Pasolini didn't take defeat gracefully. Using the regular front-page platform given him by the country's leading newspaper, the *Corriere della Sera*, he railed against every aspect of the new reforming spirit. He condemned abortion, divorce, even gay rights. He could have been preaching from the Reverend Criswell's pulpit in Dallas, except that he still considered himself the true Left. All this new stuff was just "the American type of modernist tolerance." The bourgeoisie was just boxing clever.

This was foolish, but there was worse to come. He condemned the poor, too. They had failed him, the way the Germans failed Hitler. Like many social commentators who love people by the class, Pasolini had never been much good at loving them one by one: apart from his sainted mother, he froze out everybody in the end—he was the authentic Brechtian iceman. But in the last phase he did the same thing even to his collective paragon, the poor people of the *borgata*. His undoubted passion for their way of life had always been riven by a contradiction. He thought they were authentic, speaking a tongue unspoiled by suave hypocrisy, honest in their animal lust. If all this had been true it would have been a good case for keeping them poor. But he also said that the slums they lived in were capitalism self-condemned, "truly and really concentration camps." (Pasolini also habitually trivialized the word "genocide," thereby pioneering the unfortunate current practice of squandering the language appropriate to an absolute evil on a relative one.)

The tension between these two attitudes was fruitful for him as long as they could be held in balance. When it became evident, however, that the only wish of the poor was to join the consumers he despised, Pasolini could find no recourse except to enrol them among his enemies. In his three, increasingly dreadful last movies, his ideal pre-bourgeois world of freely available sex is successively discovered in Boccaccio, Chaucer and de Sade. The trilogy makes painful viewing. Escapism is too dignified a word. Pasolini was fleeing into a past that never existed from a present he couldn't face. In a notorious front-page piece for the *Corriere* he dismissed his once beloved Roman sub-proletariat as having succumbed to "a degeneration of bodies and sex organs." Pasolini even had the gall to suggest that education was ruining them. For the admirer of Gramsci it was a sad betrayal. Gramsci had always been delighted by any evidence of his proletarians' improving themselves. Pasolini wanted them to stay the way they were. When they showed signs of independent life, he lost interest in them.

Perhaps too kindly, Mr. Schwartz doesn't make much of the possibility that they were losing interest in Pasolini. One of the most famous men in the country, recognizable at a glance, he still drove by night into the territory of the Violent Life. But time was ticking by. Once, the car and the clothes would have been enough. Now he needed his fame. What next? Charlus with his rouged cheeks? Aschenbach with his rinse? Rage, rage against the dyeing of the hair. Luckily, Pasolini never had to face the sad, slow twilight of the predator gone weak in the hams. He died the way he had lived, dramatically.

He had always thought that life was like that: drama. It was the belief that made him the kind of Communist who sounds like a Fascist. His politics were an insult to his intelligence. But there was a saving grace. The Italians are cursed with a language so seductive it can gloss over anything; Pasolini could always make it reveal more than it concealed, even when he talked tripe. He cut through the mellifluous uproar to speak the unspeakable. Pasolini's matchless ability to be irritating in every way meant that he was also irritating in the ways that count. Beneath Pasolini's politics lay his perceptions, and some of those remain permanently true. Free societies feel free to waste human lives, pushing them to the edge and calling them part of the landscape. The better we are at telling ourselves that this is inevitable, the more we still need telling that it won't do.

The New Yorker, December 28, 1992, and January 4, 1993;
later included in *Even As We Speak*, 2001

POSTSCRIPT

When I was at Cambridge in the mid-1960s, my other seat of education was Florence, where my future wife was enrolled for a doctorate at the university. I was never enrolled anywhere except at a bar near the Bargello, but I learned the language, read in it hungrily and loved the life. This piece and the next were two of the long-term fruits. There is nothing like submission to another culture for getting a handle on one's own. At the time, the brightest foreign scholars in Florence were American graduate students. I was lucky enough to make friends with several of

them, and was always impressed by how they could range in their talk
from Pontormo to U.S. foreign policy during the course of a single flask
of chianti. But when they went home they were claimed by the university system that had paid for their time abroad, and their civilized knowledge was soaked up by the learned quarterlies. What was good for academic learning was bad for literary journalism until the advent of the
New York Review of Books, which gave the scholars who had something
extra to say a chance to go moonlighting, with excellent results.

2003

45

MONDO FELLINI

Asanisimasa is a seeming nonsense word that crops up early in Fellini's $8\frac{1}{2}$. Later on you find out that it isn't nonsense at all, but a real word expressed in a children's code, like one of the language games Mozart played with his sister. Simpler even than pig Latin, the code works by inserting an "s" after each vowel and then repeating the vowel before moving on to the next consonant. Take out the padding and *asanisimasa* contracts to *anima*, the Italian for "soul." At the heart of Fellini's greatest film, one of the greatest works of art of the century, is a single word.

To get to it, though, you have to do more than crack a childishly simple code. You have to follow the director down a long corridor in an old-fashioned luxury hotel. It is late at night. Along the corridor comes Marcello Mastroianni in the role of Guido Anselmi, a renowned Italian director buckling under the strain of starting work on his latest, make-or-break film before the script is really finished. Guido is wearing a black hat with its sides curled up, he has hangdog bags under his eyes and his overcoat is draped over his forearm. Surely this is the studied sartorial insouciance of Fellini himself—a clear confession that the director is his own hero. We know who this is. We know what must be going on in his head: anguish, remorse, panic. But without breaking step in his forlorn march he suddenly twists and flicks one foot sidewise while it is in midair, as if he were momentarily attacked by the memory of a dance. Why does he do that?

I first asked myself this question in Florence, in 1963, when $8\frac{1}{2}$ came out. Even in the delighted shock of that first viewing, it was clear that $8\frac{1}{2}$

had dozens of such apparently self-contained moments, enigmatic yet instantly memorable: the squeaky crackle of Guido lying back with languorous angst on a bed heaped with the eight-by-ten glossies of actresses from whom he has to choose the supporting cast; the sheeting that shrouds the scaffolding of the uncompleted rocket ship flapping in the sea wind at night; Guido's father going down into his hole in the ground; the ancient cardinal's face inhaling the steam in the sauna at the spa; Sandra Milo, Guido's airhead mistress, trying to walk in two different directions at once when she spots Anouk Aimée, the terrifyingly poised wife; Guido slumped in the preview theatre in front of the intellectualizing screenwriter who has nagged him beyond endurance and who, in the beleaguered director's imagination, has just allowed himself to be hanged. If you could have stopped the film from moment to moment, it might have looked like any film in which a visually gifted director lights fireworks that will illuminate the darkness of an unilluminating script. But the film established its coherence in the first few minutes and unfolded inevitably. It was a film about an unfinished film—about a film that never even started—and yet it looked and sounded more finished than any film you had ever seen. About a director who didn't know what to do next, it always knew exactly what to do next. It was a cosmic joke.

That much I got, though I couldn't understand all the dialogue. At the time, I knew barely enough Italian to follow the story. My future wife, who spoke Italian fluently, was sitting beside me: she disliked having her concentration broken but provided whispered explanations when asked, filling in the details about the lying, cheating husband, who is insufficiently consumed by guilt for having granted himself romantic privileges on the strength of his creative gift, while his classy wife faces yet another crisis in the endless process of deciding whether to put up with him or walk away. The film should have functioned as a pre-emptive counselling session—an advertisement for the advisability of filling out the divorce papers before signing the marriage register. But the aesthetic thrill overwhelmed everything. Long before the lights went up on the stunned audience, everyone in it knew that this was a work to grow old with—one that, as T. S. Eliot once said about Dante's poetry, you could hope to appreciate fully only at the end of your life. You couldn't expect, then, to tease out the meaning of the film's single moments. First, you had to absorb the impact of its initial impression, as authoritative and disabling as that created by the two great widescreen Botticellis in the Uffizi—only a few hundred yards away from the cinema where $8\frac{1}{2}$ was playing *in prima visione*—which slowed your step and kept you at a distance while you strove to refocus your brain along with your eyes.

In the subsequent three decades, growing older if not wiser, I have seen $8\frac{1}{2}$ every time it was re-released. Now there is a video of it: not a perfect way for a newcomer to see the film but, for anyone who knows it well, a handy *aide-memoire* to the order of its events—an order that, though precisely calculated, is inherently bewildering, because the chronology of the immediate narrative sometimes includes scene-long figments of Guido's self-serving imagination and is continually intersected by divergent ripples spun out from his underlying memory. On the whole, "personal" films are to be distrusted, if by personal it is meant that they are personal to their authors. (After the *auteur* theory took hold, no director could make a film bad enough to be dismissed: a kludge on the scale of John Ford's *Seven Women* was discovered to be personal instead of lousy.) But $8\frac{1}{2}$ is the kind of film that becomes personal to its viewer. Whether $8\frac{1}{2}$ is really about Fellini is a question raised by the film itself—a question answered, in part, by the uncomfortable certitude of any married man who watches it that it is really about *him*. Men, we're all in this together. Fellini had us figured out.

Until almost the eve of the start of production on $8\frac{1}{2}$ the Guido Anselmi character wasn't a film director. We know this because Deena Boyer, a journalist born in America but raised in France, was trusted enough by Fellini to be given unprecedented access to the preparation of this film about the preparation of a film. Even the best movie books are usually more entertaining than indispensable; hers breaks the rule. It was first published in French, as *Les 200 Jours de $8\frac{1}{2}$*, but I have never seen it except in German, as a tatty second-hand Rowohlt paperback called *Die 200 Tage von $8\frac{1}{2}$*. There is no point in trying to be omniscient about a work of art whose stature depends upon its knowing more about life than you do, but Boyer's supply of first-hand information is handy for dispelling illusions, and the illusion that Fellini set out to make a film about a film director is a crucial one to have dispelled. Woody Allen's *Stardust Memories*, in part a copycat of $8\frac{1}{2}$, could hardly work if it were not about an artist in a crisis. But Fellini's ur-hero was *l'homme moyen sensuel* in a crisis. At first, he was "just anyone," or, as Fellini told Boyer, "a man who goes to a watering place and starts thinking about his life."

Guido graduated from being just anybody after Fellini decided to give him a career, so that the audience could get a handle on what his immediate crisis was about. Guido graduated from being just anybody to being a writer, Boyer records. If $8\frac{1}{2}$ had actually been made on that basis, it would have provided an interesting parallel to Antonioni's masterpiece of two years earlier, *La Notte*: same leading man, same professional anguish, same lustrous camerawork by Gianni Di Venanzo. But, as the start of production drew near, Fellini, with Mastroianni already cast, opted for the calling whose nuts and bolts he and his star could most easily show. Thus, very late in the game, $8\frac{1}{2}$ acquired the solid-seeming foreground that snares your initial attention while the psychological background sends out tendrils through its interstices to gather you in. All the fascination, all the *fun* of the Italian film world, the *mondo del cinema*, is right up front working its charm: the randy production manager getting off with bimbo bit players, the producer carrying on like a prima donna, the prima donna melting down like a maniac, the deals, the double deals, the chaos, the creativity.

.   .   .

Above all, the creativity. It's getting hard for younger generations to grasp, as time goes by, but in the 1950s and 1960s Italy was the true centre of the film world. Before the *auteur* theories promoted by *Cahiers du Cinéma* in France, by the magazine *Movie* in Britain and by critics such as Andrew Sarris in America forced the movie-mad intelligentsia all over the globe to reassess the Hollywood heritage instead of just enjoying it— a vital preparatory step in the development of the Planet Hollywood we all so uneasily inhabit now—the lesser nations produced the films that seemed to matter most, and of the lesser nations Italy led the pack, ahead of France, Sweden, Poland, India and Japan. It was as if Italy had risen reinvigorated out of the ashes of the war, a phoenix with a body by Farina and the Klaxon voice of Giuseppe Di Stefano: sexy, strident, attention-getting, bung-full of tradition yet terrifically up-to-date. Italian movies were a worldwide art-house attraction even before *La Dolce Vita* came out, in 1960. After that, they were a sensation. Fellini, with his big hat and loosely slung coat, was in all the photo magazines. Apparently, he lived at a table in the Via Veneto, looking tolerant but reserved while being mobbed by students and *paparazzi*. (Actually, he never went there or anywhere else in public except to be photographed, and he put up with it only so that his face could pull in money with which to make movies—

but we couldn't tell that from looking.) He wasn't alone. Film artists of impeccable intellectual credentials lived in coronas of personal publicity. Everybody had just worked with everybody else or was about to. The general effect was to make Italy look like an updated opera, with props and costumes shipped in from the future: *Cavalleria Rusticana* with a Ferrari onstage instead of a horse, *Tosca* on a Vespa. The effect, in short, was magnetic.

Australians of my generation on their way to Britain stopped off in Italy to absorb an atmosphere they had correctly divined to be a magic compound of culture and hedonism. Those of us who stuck around long enough to pick up the language found that the film world was even more effervescent than we had guessed. In Florence there was an unending supply of American Fulbright scholars who were supposed to be studying Mannerist painting but still found time to keep up with all the gossip of the Rome-based industry, as if Pasolini were as important as Pontormo, Bolognini as Bronzino. They didn't have to haunt the library to get the facts. It was all in the papers. Producers, directors, cameramen and actors were getting married, divorced, sued, betrayed, killed, buried and born again in a pattern constant only in its unrelenting turbulence. Everyone was a star.

Essentially, each Italian film was a collaboration, usually involving three or more writers, two or more of whom would be directors next week and one or more of whom was a producer last week, but the money ran out. All those egos, however, were born to clash: hence the fizz, and hence the air of dedication, detectable in comedies and serious films alike. It is unfair to Antonioni to read his career backward—from the disaster of *Zabriskie Point*, through the awful, wilful obfuscations of *Blow-Up* to the brain-curdling deterministic lethargy of *Red Desert* and *The Eclipse*—and to decide that the spaced-out pacing of his high-impact central movies *La Notte* and *L'Avventura* was a bogus claim to seriousness. You didn't have to be mad about Monica Vitti (and we all were, even the women) to decide that those films were definitive treatises on the loss of love, all the more convincing for moving no faster than a snail's funeral. They retain their integrity when seen now, if we can suppress our awareness of how the director himself fell to pieces. Seen at the time, they looked monumental, but they didn't stand alone: bustling at their feet was a metropolis of the imagination.

On the subject of the mature Italian male's sexual dilemma, the comedies of Pietro Germi looked at least as thoughtful as any dirge by Antonioni, and packed in a lot more incident. (In Germi's *L'Immorale*, Ugo Tognazzi runs around frantically to keep three fully fleshed female characters happily out of touch with one another until he finally conks out—not from guilt but from an overtaxed heart.) Watching the comedies of Germi, Salce, Comencini, Monicelli and a half-dozen others as they appeared, we got an education in just how comprehensive and satisfying a popular art form could be without ceasing to be either popular or artistic. The entire national life was up there on the screen, with an interval for drinks.

Over and above the comedies, there was the straight stuff. Post-war neo-realism had evolved into something even better: realism, with a fact-based imaginative scope that could take in anything, even the deep-seated, dangerously retaliatory corruption of the country that had given rise to it. In 1963, Francesco Rosi's *Le Mani sulla Città* (*Hands over the City*) helped to light a fuse under the Italian political system which finally burned its way to the dynamite more than two decades later. In 1966, Gillo Pontecorvo made *The Battle of Algiers*. A radical film of such power that it remains compulsory viewing even for conservatives, it put the dazzling first features of Bertolucci and Bellocchio into sober perspective, making them look childishly hipped on their own anger. In short, the Italian cinema of those years was a lush field for someone to stand out from. Fellini did, head and shoulders.

· · ·

Even more than *La Dolce Vita*, $8\frac{1}{2}$ is a clear demonstration of how Fellini became Italy's national director and its ambassador to the world—the ambassador who never left home. The totality of his films is more than the sum of its parts, but all his films are contained, at some degree of compression, in $8\frac{1}{2}$: they all lead up to it or lead on from it. Rich even by his standards, his supreme masterpiece first conveys its wealth through its sumptuous visual texture. Since *Nights of Cabiria*, for which the designer Piero Gherardi joined his entourage, Fellini had already put more of his country's visual excitement into his movies than any other director except perhaps Kurosawa. In $8\frac{1}{2}$, with Di Venanzo lighting Gherardi's sets, Fellini excelled even his own previous efforts at pulling his tumultuous homeland into shape.

The lustre isn't just the look of Italy; it's the look of Fellini. Compared with him, the world's other great national directors hardly cared about what the camera could do. Buñuel never moved the camera unless he had to. Renoir called for a bravura set-up only if there was no other way to make a narrative point: that much-studied, Ophuls-like long exterior tracking shot in *Le Crime de Monsieur Lange* is there just so you can see exactly how far the hero has to run along corridors and down flights of stairs. And you can't imagine Bergman actually enjoying what in his case you feel inclined to call the physical side of it. But Fellini, even in his maturity, is like Orson Welles playing with the toy train set for the first time. In $8\frac{1}{2}$, through sets built by Gherardi to look real and real locations lit by Di Venanzo to look like sets, the camera sails and swoops weightlessly yet without a flutter, as if following grooves in space. As Boyer's book reveals, there was no question of Fellini's standing aside and letting Di Venanzo make all this happen. Fellini was with him behind the camera: the instructions given to the operator, Pasquale de Santis, were their joint work, with Fellini always in the ascendant, specifying every aspect of a black-and-white *mise en scène* gorgeous enough to make colour look famished. Fellini was so sure of getting what he wanted that it didn't bother him if he was unable to check his work. He almost never looked at rushes, although for much of the shooting of $8\frac{1}{2}$ he couldn't have even if he had wanted to: the laboratories were on strike.

Not only were there hardly any dailies, there were practically no scripts. Only two complete copies of the script existed anywhere near the production. Fellini had the picture in his head. To a large extent, it happened the way you feel it happened: like a marvellous, fluent improvisation, with a freedom of expression which extended to the actors—even to those who were amateurs and needed dozens of takes to get a tricky scene right. According to Fellini's usual practice, the players, whether professional or amateur, were cast for their faces. For Fellini, *la faccia* was everything. In a little book of 1980, *Fare un Film*, Fellini said that he would have preferred not to decide on his cast until he had seen every face in the world. Fellini had always taken delight in casting untrained faces and getting precise performances out of them, but until *La Dolce Vita* he mainly confined them to the lower ranks of the cast. In $8\frac{1}{2}$ they are up among the leading figures. The role of Guido's increasingly apoplectic producer (clearly modelled on Fellini's real-life bagman, Angelo Rizzoli) is played by an industrialist, Guido Alberti. Physically ideal in his pampered rotundity, he uncorks a performance that a trained actor would be proud of. (Alberti went semi-pro afterwards: he'd got the bug.) Similarly, the screenwriter is played by a real screenwriter, Jean Rougeul. Possessing a face that begs to be slapped, he, too, is physically ideal, but it is remarkable how good he is at the lines, or how good Fellini makes him. Contrary to legend, in Italy it does matter if an actor can't say the lines properly: though Italian films are post-synched, the lips have to match the words in anything except a long shot. Rougeul, a Frenchman, had to work hard. He does an amazing job of being repellent. When he gets strung up, the audience laughs.

In a TV interview given by the late Alexander Mackendrick to Stephen Frears, Mackendrick said he had always found mixing untrained actors with trained ones doubly fruitful, because the untrained caught discipline and the trained caught naturalness. This effect can be seen working at a high pitch in $8\frac{1}{2}$. The principal players have no star mannerisms: they are just people. Mastroianni and Anouk Aimée, playing Guido's wife, Luisa, aren't on-screen together for much more than fifteen minutes, but the way they connect across distance burns at the centre of the film: these are the embers of a long love, too spent to keep either party warm yet still too hot to handle. As his mistress Carla, Sandra Milo pulls off the impossible trick of being a nitwit angel that a smart man might like to know almost as much as he would like to lay. To fatten her up for the role, Fellini made her eat until she groaned. In *Fare un Film* he calls the character a *culone*, which more or less means that her brain is in her behind. Milo convinces you that it's a good brain anyway. Purely physical, ecstatically devoted to her exciting lover—he is the White Sheik from one of Fellini's early films, but in a black hat—she is not to be blamed that he is bored with her almost as soon as she steps off the train. It isn't her fault: it's his. This is about something deeper than adultery. If it was just the story of a man caught between wife and mistress and satisfied with neither, it would be *La Dolce Vita*. But $8\frac{1}{2}$ isn't about the melodrama in the life of its protagonist, it's about the psychodrama in his mind.

"Didn't you know the devil is Saraghina?" The question that rings through $8\frac{1}{2}$ rang through Fellini's life. In $8\frac{1}{2}$ the young Guido, making an appearance in the mature Guido's memory, hears that question from the priests and doesn't know how to answer. Saraghina is an enormous, blowsy, barefoot madwoman who lives on the beach and dances and exposes herself for Guido and his fellow inmates of a church school. After a flagrant exhibition by Saraghina, the young Guido gets caught, led off by the ear and made to kneel on dried peas while the priests put him to the question. In real life, Fellini never made a secret of Saraghina. Fellini commonly told interviewers anything that would get rid of them, but on the subject of Saraghina he either always told the same lie or else it was a fact. In *Fare un Film*—cobbled together from a baker's dozen interviews and articles by other people, but reprocessed by Fellini and bearing his signature—the Saraghina story is given neat. He says that while he was at the church school in Fano, the only period in his childhood when he spent much time away from his native town of Rimini, he visited Saraghina often and paid the price for inciting her to her revelatory routine. (She was cheap: her name meant "sardines" and she would do her number for a few of them as payment.) Refusing to believe that Saraghina was the Devil was obviously the essential early decision of Fellini's emotional life. He preferred to believe that she was an angel.

Whether or not the Saraghina episode ever happened to Fellini, or merely something like it—or, still more merely, numerous and diverse episodes scarcely at all like it but he synthesized them later in the way that artists do—for $8\frac{1}{2}$ Saraghina is one of the elements that help to dramatize Guido's memory as a convincing determinant of his imagination. The memory of Saraghina is the gross, unfrocked and irrepressible guarantee that Guido's imagination can't be a thing of refinement: the most he can hope for is to make refined things from it, but his imagination itself must remain primitive, shaped incorrigibly by the initial impact of her uncorseted oomph. Guido is unsettled by the knowledge that his memory should dominate his imagination in such a way. He still half-regrets that he can never give the priests a satisfactory answer, still hopes that the cardinal in the steam can show him the true path. But Fellini himself, judging from the sum of his films, seems to have been glad enough, if not exactly grateful, to have a story in his mind that would help him to script and shoot the male sexual imagination as a divine comedy.

The mind is the house of the Lord, and in the house of the Lord there are many mansions, and one of them is a honky-tonk. Fellini's central boldness is to embrace that fact and body it forth without shame, but without any knowing pride either—just the embarrassment necessarily involved in being consciously human. Self-revealing without being self-exculpatory, he is not offering *carte blanche* for adultery, a concrete act that needs excusing at the very least and is often a crime. Besides, there

are married men who have never committed adultery, and one or two of
them have even reached the White House. But there is no married man
who has not, like President Carter, committed adultery in his heart—
meaning, of course, in his imagination, which grows out of his memory,
and has been with him always.

This interior imbroglio is $8\frac{1}{2}$'s real subject. In real life Guido is
merely entangled. In his mental life he is tied to time: the rope that
threatens to drag him by the leg from the sky back down to the beach is
a doubly exact metaphor, because the beach is where Fellini's imagination began its life. Saraghina was as meaty, beaty, big and bouncy as all
the world's women rolled into one and that's what Guido has wanted ever
since—all the women in the world. Not every woman he wants is an
uncomplicated *culone* like the one played by Sandra Milo. There is also
the young, vital ideal of fructive beauty, played in $8\frac{1}{2}$ by Claudia Cardinale, whose looks and personality made a unique contribution to Italian
movies in the early 1960s before she went international later in the
decade and rather dissipated the effect. Silvana Mangano, Sophia Loren
and Monica Vitti could all act better. Even Virna Lisi could act better,
although few ever appreciated her as an actress because she was so beautiful. But Cardinale wasn't just beautiful, she had the knack of incarnating a dream type, the aristocratic peasant. Visconti used her for that quality, twice and at length, in *Vaghe stelle dell'Orsa* (hardly seen outside
Italy, it had a title from Leopardi—*Beautiful Stars of the Bear*—and a plot
from hell, but she looked unputdownably scrumptious) and his much-
mangled international blockbuster *The Leopard* (she was the gorgeous
upmarket earth girl that Burt Lancaster and Alain Delon both cherished
as the personification of authenticity, a judgement which received ironic
reinforcement from the film as a whole, camped as it was somewhere
between Sicily and the abstract outworld we have since come to recognize as Planet Hollywood). In $8\frac{1}{2}$ Fellini got the same charge out of her
as a glorified walk-on, a bit part with billing. Practically all she does is
turn up. But she triggers Guido's mixed vision of carnal purity and we
believe it. Dante's Beatrice on the cover of *Vogue*. Petrarch's Laura with
an agent, an unblemished spirit in perfect flesh, she is infinitely desirable:
we know he'll be longing for her on the day he dies, if only because he
has never touched her. As a token of her power to stir his imagination,
even her appearance in the actual now has a tinge of the altered, heightened pseudo-reality of the hero's wish world, whose bridal candour, we

come to realize, doubles as white mourning. When she and Guido are for a little while alone together, in the empty piazza in Filacciano, the authentic architecture around them, built long ago by other hands than Gherardi's, is the only setting in the film that looks artificial, and the breeze that stirs Cardinale's black feather boa blows only for her, rather in the way that the envoys from the beyond in Cocteau's *Orphée* are contained in their own micro-climate. Cardinale is Guido's dream walking, but when she realizes that he is idealizing her she laughs, and he realizes that she is right.

Another version of breathtaking unavailability is played by Caterina Boratto, as the guest at the spa who does nothing but descend the staircase of the grand hotel and cross the lobby. Statuesque in a personal cloud of white chiffon, she is a poised blast from the past of the Italian cinema. Boratto was a diva of those escapist movies, made at Cinecittà in Fascism's heyday, in which the protagonists indicated their luxurious lives (*Vivere!* was the title of her big hit of 1936: *To Live!*) by talking into white telephones. To present a white telephone star as a womanly ideal is Fellini's indication that in Guido's sexual imagination even the ideals of subtlety and refinement have something cartoonlike about them. The women in his brain are all caricatures. He knows they are, but he's stuck with it. His mind is in poor taste.

All the caricatures get together in one of the film's most elaborate sequences. When he hears the word *Asanisimasa* pronounced by his old friend the vaudeville mind-reader, Guido is propelled back in his memory to a favourite place of his childhood, the barn fitted out as a small wine factory—a *fattoria*—where he was teased, tucked up, looked after and generally spoiled by older women. Guido goes back to the same *fattoria* in his imagination, to stage a wish-fulfilment scene in which all the women in his life, along with all the women whom he would like to be in his life, live together in harmony: united, instead of divided, by their common desire for him. They all take their tune from the old peasant women who teased him and tucked him up. Their only role is to spoil him. They compete in nothing except subservience. His wife is there, smiling in acquiescence: she understands his needs. Every woman he has even fleetingly noticed in the course of the film's real-time story turns up as a worshipper. Women we have never seen before are there too: this place has been in business for a long time. A black girl dances through, flashing an open-mouthed white smile before snapping it shut. (I can still remember, from the first time I saw the movie, how a single American male groan outsoared the collective Italian male whimper in an audience whose females has already audibly made it obvious that they found the whole scene a *sciocchezza*—a foolishness.)

But this isn't just the place where Guido's dreams come true. It is also where they go sour. An early love, an exuberant soubrette, has out-lived her desirability. Desperately she tries to interest him again but she stands revealed as just a not very good singer and dancer. Guido is ruth-less with her: she has to go upstairs, where he consigns the women he no longer wants. (In real life, Fellini might have been ruthless with the actress who plays her: Boyer reports that the actress sang and danced too well, so he made her repeat the number until she was exhausted and in tears. However it happened, pathos certainly got into the scene.) Guido is suddenly recast as a monster. His dream women rebel, having realized that the same thing might happen to them. He has to get his whip out and drive them like animals. It is a clear confession, on Guido's part, that his sexual imagination is an unrealizable, incurably adolescent fantasy of banal variety and impotent control.

Just as clearly, it is Fellini's confession too. This is really why he made Guido a film director: not just to give him a believable role, but to show him cracking his whip over his tumultuous desires—to show him marshalling fantasies. Fellini is assuming that in this respect a film direc-tor is just everyman writ large, or at any rate writ more obvious. It is a big assumption, which will provide ammunition to condemn him if it is rejected as an excuse. Fellini's real-life wife, the distinguished actress Giulietta Masina, was on the set to witness the filming of $8\frac{1}{2}$'s key scene. It was her dubious privilege to watch her husband's surrogate setting about his harem with a whip to bring them back into line. Masina had no doubt long before been made aware of Fellini's belief that what goes on in a man's mind he can't help, so he had better be judged on his conduct. What she thought of that belief is one of the many secrets of their long marriage. What Fellini thought of his wife is brought out explicitly in *Fare un Film*, where he ascribes their marriage to a decision of fate and would obviously, had he been a believer, have ascribed it to a decision of God. But you don't need to read his book to know what she meant to him. All you have to do is look at the films, which from *La Strada* onwards are about their marriage even when she is not in them. Sometimes, indeed, they are at their strongest on that subject when she isn't there. In $8\frac{1}{2}$

Anouk's face, *la faccia*, is enough to establish that this wife is no willing victim but a strong, independent woman with as much class and style as her famous husband, if not more.

Anouk's incandescent performance shows why a director needs his prestige. Able to persuade her that she was participating in a serious project, Fellini talked her into acting against her charm and in line with her magnificent bone structure. Fully exposed by a boyish hairstyle, those knife-edged facial planes that kept her beautiful for decades could take on overtones of a hatchet when she was angry, and Fellini made sure that anger was almost the only emotion she was allowed to register. We are obliged to conclude that if this is a long-suffering wife, it isn't because she's a patsy. The film's moral edifice pivots on this point, because if it isn't accepted then the whole thing looks self-serving. The plot provides Luisa with a young, handsome, adoring admirer. She can't get interested in him. Is Fellini saying that she forgoes mere devotion because her faithless husband is more fascinating? Most feminists would say yes. They would have half a point, but only by hindsight. Fellini was a feminist *avant la lettre*: he had already proved that much with his early films, all of which feature, and some of which focus on, men's manipulation of women.

God knows he had enough to go on. In the early 1960s Italy was still in the grip of a chest-beating male supremacy stretching back to the Borgias, among whom Lucrezia probably took up poisoning just to get some attention at the dinner table. The first week I was in Rome, the papers were running editorials about a young Italian male whose Dutch girlfriend had told him she wanted to break off their affair because her real boyfriend was about to arrive from Holland. The Italian boy stabbed her sixteen times with a carving knife. The editorials daringly suggested that this sort of thing was giving Italy a bad image abroad. It was still a bold innovation to suggest that the crime of honour was unforgivable. From Sicily as far north as Naples, if a girl refused a man's hand in marriage he could still get her by raping her, because then no other man would want her. (Scandal arose only when *he* didn't want her either, on account of her being no longer a virgin.) As for men pestering young women in the streets, there was no north and south: Milan was as bad as Messina. Foreign women suffered most. They were assumed to be whores just for being there. In Florence I used to get so angry at what I saw that it would spoil the visit. After the Florence flood in 1966 there was a startling change, which hit the other big cities not long after. Suddenly the women's magazines, which had previously been almost exclusively preoccupied with the mysteries of the trousseau, started carrying articles about how to divorce a sadistic husband without getting killed. Women's rights got a look in at last.

But anyone interpreting Italy then from the vantage point of now should realize that feminism was starting from a long way behind. Looking at Fellini's wide screens full of big breasts and accommodating thighs, it is easy to decide that he was part of the problem. The truth is that he was part of the solution. He was saying that men should be held responsible for what they did, not for how they felt. It was an especially important message for a country in which what men did could beggar belief. Trying to change the way a man felt who had just stabbed his girlfriend sixteen times, you might possibly persuade him to stab his next girlfriend only fifteen times. The trick was to call his outburst of passion by its proper name, murder. And to do that, you had to argue that passion was every man's property, and the management of it his responsibility.

Feminism was one of Fellini's touchstones of liberty. The anger he aroused in feminists later on was because of his other touchstones, one of them being the liberty to express the full squalor of the male mind. He did it with such bravura that it struck the censorious eye as a boast. It wasn't, though: it was an abasement, and Anouk's tight-lipped fury is there to prove it. *"Vacca!"* is the word she spits at the *culone*, Carla. It means "cow" and in Italy it is a harsh word for one woman to use about another—the last word, the fighting word. Luisa is insulted by the banality of her rival. For Guido to take a mistress might have been forgivable. But if this is what he dreams of, what sort of man has she been living with?

If Fellini had not driven a wedge between how Guido thinks and how he acts, Guido would stand condemned, and Fellini along with him. But the wedge is there, in the beautiful form of Luisa. Guido once dreamed of her, too, and he is still involved with her even though she has become real—the best evidence that she must have been the most powerful dream of all. Luisa is what the German socialists used to call a *Lebensgefährtin*, a lifetime companion. Strong in her anguish, graceful even in despair, she is the true Felliniesque womanly icon. Anouk looked the part. Masina's misfortune was that she didn't. When it came to the crunch, she didn't have the right face to play herself.

In *La Strada* and *Nights of Cabiria*, Masina played the waif. She could be funny, resilient and even tough, but with a face like a doll she just couldn't transmit flintlike fury. You always wanted to pity her, and the point of Luisa is that she finds her husband pitiful, and hates him for it. Fellini followed $8\frac{1}{2}$ with *Juliet of the Spirits*, the all-colour extravaganza which is nowadays the most neglected of his major films. This time Giulietta Masina plays the wife. With the inexorable proviso that her face is borrowed from a Cinderella who will never get to try on the shoe, the film is an opulent, radiant, unmanningly reverent tribute to her stature in Fellini's life. This was the last film Fellini made with Gherardi and Di Venanzo. They both excelled themselves. The sets are a cumulative marvel from an unsung opera and the photography makes colour film look as if it were being invented all over again. Giulietta's imagination and memory are explored like Guido's in $8\frac{1}{2}$. In addition, there are layers of Jungian analysis, parapsychology, voodoo and drug-induced hallucinations. Fellini subsequently told *Cahiers du Cinéma* that he didn't need LSD to have visions, but there can be no doubt that he was willing to try anything in order to give his votive offering to his wife the depth, weight and splendour he felt she deserved. The inescapable problem was that it was all within his gift. The idea was to show her liberating herself from her psychological burden. But it was his idea, not hers. In *Fare un Film*, Fellini movingly looked forward to the day when women would give us their view of the world. There could be no question of his generosity. But that day hadn't yet come, and for the meantime he was stuck with his own stuff.

.   .   .

He still had plenty more, but first he had a crisis to get through. *Juliet of the Spirits* tanked in a big way, he broke with Gherardi, lost Di Venanzo, swapped Rizzoli for Dino de Laurentiis, sailed straight into a real-life $8\frac{1}{2}$ situation with a film he couldn't start, and wound up suffering from what seemed like terminal depression. Most directors would have quit at that point and gone off to give lectures, but Fellini was on the verge of a string of films that are, at the very least, all interesting sidelights on $8\frac{1}{2}$, and some of which, in one aspect or another, actually supersede it. Peter Bogdanovich once pointed out that Fellini's first few movies, the ones we rarely see, would have been enough to establish him as an important director. It should also be said, but rarely is, that the films after *Juliet of the Spirits* would have been sufficient to work the same trick. A few weeks ago, on a plane between London and Bangkok, I watched videos of *Fellini Satyricon* and *Fellini's Roma*. I still didn't enjoy *Satyricon* very much: except for the scene where the patrician married couple commit suicide to get away from the moral squalor—a clear echo of Steiner's unexpected yet inevitable exit from *La Dolce Vita*—it just doesn't offer enough relief from its own all-consuming animality. The people in it behave like pigs, but not even pigs behave like pigs all the time; sometimes they just lie there. (Fellini was too decent to be any good at decadence, and even if he had been, decadence dates: this is the reason some parts of *La Dolce Vita* now look *passé*.) *Roma*, however, came up fresh as paint. The traffic-jam scene is a far more effective comment on modern barbarism and insanity than anything in *Satyricon*, which was supposed to reflect our own age but made it look good by comparison. In *Roma*, the threat of industrial society's inhumanity is made real by the intensity of the humanity. The *trattoria* on the street, with the tram clanging past, looks like the way of life we all want but suspect that only the Italians have ever had. It was probably never quite that folksy in Rome: Fellini is remembering Rimini.

When I got back to London, *Amarcord*, the film that actually does remember Rimini, was showing on television as part of a memorial season. I had always recalled it as a delight, but now it looks like a masterpiece. It hasn't changed; perhaps I have. *Amarcord* (in the dialect of Rimini, the word means "I remember") is like all the childhood flashbacks in $8\frac{1}{2}$ condensed into one. Saraghina is there again: a nameless tobacco vendor this time, but with breasts bigger than ever. Our young hero, appropriately called Titta, gets his head caught between them, and this counts as a big adventure. Everything here is small-time: the cinema, the bar, the square. The cars of the Mille Miglia automobile race howl through town, but they are going somewhere else. The big, lit-up liner sails away. The citizens remain, eating, drinking, having families and occasionally dressing up as Fascists. It takes a while for the viewer to realize that this is a film about Fascism, and longer still to realize that this is *the* film about Fascism. Especially in the late 1960s, Fellini was accused of having said nothing about politics. He defended himself by saying that he saw politics purely in terms of personal liberty, and in *Fare un Film* he explains that the life led in *Amarcord* was the soil from which Fascism grew and can always grow: a life of arrested adolescence, narrow horizons, mean dreams, easy solutions and—saturating everything—ignorance. The film bears out his analysis in every respect. He shows the disease with a clarity that defines the cure: Fascism is undisciplined nostalgia, a giving in to childish wishes, the cuddle continued, the tantrum in perpetuity.

Fellini's Casanova is the film he should never have made. Artistically, it has some interest; strategically, it was a disaster. Some critics decided, on the strength of its weakness, that he had been an erotomaniac all along. But *Casanova* is a dud precisely because Fellini was no pornographer. If he had been, his films would be running continuously on Eighth Avenue and making a lot of money. Casanova the seducer is the wrong hero for a man who wanted to submit to his women, not dominate them; Fellini craved their individuality, not their similarity. (So did Casanova, incidentally, but the statistics made it look otherwise.) Fellini had nothing but contempt for Casanova and wanted to prove it—a bad plan for an artist whose forte was his range of sympathy. The film was such an unequivocal stiff that you wept for Donald Sutherland, who must have felt honoured to be in it and devastated when it didn't work out. (Sutherland had previously starred in Larry Tucker and Paul Mazursky's *Alex in Wonderland*, a now forgotten but considerable homage to $8\frac{1}{2}$, in which a young American director has trouble starting a movie.)

Casanova is in Fellini's next big film and last masterpiece, *La Città delle Donne* (*The City of Women*, 1980)—only this time he is called Dottore Sante Katzone. (Since *cazzo* is the Italian word for "cock" and *-one* is the enlarging suffix, the name means that he has a big one.) Katzone, like Casanova, is really just another version of Don Juan, and must suffer the same fate: to find his own endlessly repeated excitement an endless disappointment, to suffer the built-in let-down of the permanent hard-on. Katzone, though not on-screen long, is probably the best stab at Don Juan's pitiable doom since Mozart's. Bergman, in *The Devil's Eye*, gave his Don Juan too much finesse: his punishment is to have the woman disappear at the moment he embraces her, whereat he gently recoils with a polite sigh. Katzone gets what he wants, and it eats him up. He can feel himself coarsening even as he thickens, turning into one of the phallic sculptures that decorate his room, a petrified forest of dildos in which he is the only flexible component, and only just. Snaporaz, the film's hero, has no desire to be Katzone. Played by none other than Marcello Mastroianni in full panic mode, Snaporaz (the name seems to be one of Fellini's many code names for a liar) is, like Guido in $8\frac{1}{2}$, a married man battling his sexual imagination, but this time it's in colour, and the women of his desires come on in choruses, in kick lines, in cabarets with Las Vegas lighting effects: they slide down poles and go up in balloons. At the beginning, he gets off a train, and he spends the rest of the film trying to get back on. (It sounds like the same train scene that was cut from the end of $8\frac{1}{2}$ when Fellini realized that the circus finale was the only possible wrap-up.) He is trying to hide out in his own fantasies, but the militant feminists are in there, too, and they want his guts for garters and his scrotum for a handbag.

Mastroianni's brilliantly conveyed helplessness didn't save the film's reputation. An unflinching portrayal of a man at bay was widely condemned as a conscienceless parade of unreconstructed male chauvinism. By this time, Fellini was routinely being called sentimental, even by critics who conceded the historical importance of his central films. Sentimentality was supposed to be his weakness. His case wasn't helped by *E la Nave Va* (*And the Ship Sails On*, 1983). The ship-of-fools format is a certain loser unless the ship makes landfall: we are given no tangible social life for comparison, so the artificial one on the ship has to refer to itself, with cramped results. But faces, as always with Fellini, stick in the memory: Pina Bausch playing a blind woman, staring straight out of the screen with eyes like those of the dead sunfish on the beach at the end of *La Dolce Vita*, when Mastroianni sees the girl who incarnates his lost innocence. . . . Even at the end of Fellini's career, there was something in each new movie to remind you of all the others—something to remind you that there was a man behind the film, and that he had a woman beside him to whom he felt bound to explain himself. The explanation was always about the difficulty of marriage and the emptiness of the alternatives. It was always about Fellini and Masina. *Ginger and Fred* was charming, but unworthy of them: the story of a couple of old hoofers who couldn't really dance that well, it gave Masina and Mastroianni all too many opportunities to be cute. But Fellini and Masina *could* dance that well: they were people of majesty, not puppets of fate. Pathos was inappropriate.

.   .   .

I called some friends in the Czech Republic recently, who said they were looking forward to seeing $8\frac{1}{2}$ the next evening on a satellite movie channel. Fellini distrusted television. In the later part of his life, when big movies were harder to finance, he made films for television, but he always disliked the restrictions: the TV screen didn't have enough information in it; the shot could never go deep; the lighting had to be too even. Above all, he disliked the atomization of the audience—one, two, or, at most, a few people in front of the set, eating, drinking and talking. He thought that the movie house as he had known it for most of his life was the last church. He valued its sacred aspect. Well, TV screens will get bigger, and the resolution will get better. It doesn't take a clairvoyant to envisage the day when all you can see in the cinema you will be able to see at home, without some lout behind you laughing through his popcorn at all the wrong moments. Every movie of any consequence that has ever been made will be there in front of you at the touch of a button. But *l'aspetto sacrale* probably won't be coming back. On the information highway, each of us is going to be alone in the middle of a hundred lanes of traffic. It will be a lot like trying to walk out of Los Angeles on the freeway system.

In any case, most of the entertainment that people all over the world touch their telephones to get will be manufactured somewhere in the San Fernando Valley. And I suppose a more horrible fate for the world can be imagined: American films at their most mindless have seldom been as toxic as any totalitarian country's films at their most sophisticated. On the whole, back in the 1960s, we were right to restate our enjoyment of the old Hollywood as admiration, to turn fandom into scholarship.

But this development had one lasting deleterious consequence. The attention that had been focused on the great national directors of other countries began to lapse. Renoir, Bergman, Ray, Wajda, Kurosawa, Ozu, Fellini: we had been preoccupied with them for a long time; we had grown bored with endorsing their obvious eminence; and, anyway, they could look after themselves. So we sort of let them go. Yet they had something that their successors didn't always have—we could see that Truffaut might be another Renoir, but Godard obviously wasn't anything of the kind—and that the American directors didn't have at all. To begin with, the earlier masters were mainly true filmmakers, not just directors who were nothing without the right producer to bring them the right script. They developed a project from the beginning and got the whole of their country's life into it, and they went on doing this until they were old and grey. In America, Orson Welles might have done that if his personality had been different. Peter Bogdanovich might have done it if his life had been different. But it has always been hard to avoid the conclusion that what really needed to be different was America itself.

Not that Hollywood lacked a sense of history. Contrary to what foreign intellectuals usually thought and had such fun expressing, Hollywood always expended huge energy on getting the historical details right, right down to the buttons on the costumes. Where history went missing was in the people. Even today, when some of the cleverest people in the world are writing and directing Hollywood films, the characters on the screen are usually present only in the present. They haven't got a past, except as a series of plot points. They might say wise things, but not from experience. They are happily married until they love someone else, and then they leave the person they were with and go off to be happy with the other, as if love were some kind of moral imperative. And if one of the miracles of modern Hollywood is the energy that is lavished on these sleepwalking ciphers, another is how the people doing the creating often end up behaving like their creations.

Too many of the people busy with their careers in Planet Hollywood are just boys and girls, whereas a man like Federico Fellini was a man. Called "sentimental" by those for whom his emotions were too big and too pure, he was really the enemy of sentimentality, which he had correctly diagnosed as being only a step away from cynicism. The typical aria of sentimentality is from an operetta: it breathes the perfumed atmosphere of *Leichtsinn*, that dreadful Viennese word which makes the heart heavy the moment it is sung. In $8\frac{1}{2}$, Mastroianni at first glance looks like a refugee from an updated production of *Die Fledermaus*. But there is no *Leichtsinn* here, no glibly wry tolerance of other people's suffering, no easily borne betrayals. Instead, there is melancholy. It comes from the self-examination without which life is not worth living. Fellini's is the tragic view of life, the gift of the old countries to the new ones where people think their life is over if they are not happy. It is the view of life formed in that aspect of the mind which, even when all the religions are dead, dying or preaching holy war, we still feel bound to call the soul. *Anima*: the word denotes a thing.

Fellini was by no means a perfect man. He was not an ideal man. He was a real one. His individuality resided in his being able to see what was universal about himself; he had a scope, within and without, that made him in post-war Italy what Verdi had been for the Risorgimento: the great cultural figure of Italy's recuperation, and, beyond his own country, one of the great men of the modern world.

Fellini was even beyond the cinema as a specific art. Though he was the master of all its techniques, he pursued it not as one art form among others but as if it were art itself. The last scene of *Les Enfants du Paradis* is magnificent, but it is just cinema. Its director, Marcel Carné, would have been lost without Jacques Prévert's screenplay, and Baptiste and Garance were only symbolically separated by the crowd flowing past the Théâtre des Funambules—they could have met again around the corner. The last scene of $8\frac{1}{2}$ is often compared with Carné's flag-waving finale, but the difference is the difference between substance and stylishness, between a revelation and mere flair. Fellini's outburst of exuberance has a grief in it that leaves the children of paradise looking like the children they are—patronized by their parents, the makers of the film. Fellini patronizes no one. He knows himself too well. When Guido joins the circle with his wife and all the people he lives and works with, the spectacle is no pretty ring out of an Arcadia by Poussin. It is an acknowledgement of a truth that the most prodigious artists realize with their souls, even if they sometimes deny it with their mouths: that, despite their uniqueness, they are not alone, that they live and work for the people, of whom each of them is only one.

The evidence suggests that Fellini, for all his mighty ego, was a man with no vanity (except about his thinning hair), and that he experienced his talent as a responsibility to be lived up to as long as his life lasted, even when his best collaborators were gone, the money had run out, the young directors who had hoped to emulate him had given up or gone abroad and Italy's *mondo del cinema*, stripped of its atmosphere by the voracious gravity of Planet Hollywood, was reduced to a lifeless satellite. As long as the art prince Fellini was alive, the Italian film industry had a face.

But though *la faccia* is gone, *l'anima* yet lives. Fellini's films are already popping up everywhere, even out of the armrests of airline seats, and at least one of them will be watched in awe when human beings live in spaceships and have at last grasped that the longest voyage is inside the mind. $8\frac{1}{2}$ will transmit the distillation of a national culture to an international, homogenized future that might well be condemned to have no other source of such qualities except the past. It is the work of a man who could realize his gift because he realized what a gift is. A gift comes from Heaven, as an elation of the spirit. For its recipient not to enjoy it would be ungracious, despite the grief it might bring—which is why Fellini told Marcello, before he began his long, weary walk down the corridor, to flick that foot.

The New Yorker, May 21, 1994; later included in *Even As We Speak*, 2001

46

WHO *WAS* THAT

MASKED MAN?

Peter Bogdanovich doesn't need a career, because he has a destiny. The same once applied to his hero Orson Welles, and it is a tribute to Bogdanovich's mind, soul and stature—all increasingly rare attributes in modern Hollywood—that the comparative powerlessness of his mature years should remind us so much of how Welles's exultant precocity came unstuck. In at least one dimension, the comparison works to Bogdanovich's advantage: his opening moves, though uncannily assured, might not quite have ranked with Welles's for their lasting impact, but his endgame, despite a private life undeniably baroque in some of its salient aspects, is showing a lot more class. Welles wound up narrating commercials for social-climbing brands of mid-price wine, and one of the reasons for his inability to get a film financed was that he was a spendthrift: prodigal even with peanuts, he was the enemy of his own best gift. Bogdanovich, though he might never be allowed to direct another movie, looks admirably determined to keep at least one side of his best gift well tended and fruitful.

Right from the jump, he could write about the movies with a cogency that placed him in the top flight of critics, and as an interviewer he has always been without peer. His latest book, *Who the Devil Made It*, is just further confirmation of a quality he seems to have had since the cradle. When it comes to movies, the master of the medium is often a buff but rarely a scholar—he hasn't the time, even when he has the inclination—yet Bogdanovich somehow always managed to service his debt to the creativity of his past masters while he was busy with his own: articles and interviews, slim monographs and fat books were all done with manifest love, despite his being in a tearing hurry. Here, from the new book, is Bogdanovich on the Lubitsch Touch. First he defines it as "a miraculous ability to mock and celebrate both at once." Then he gives an example.

In *Monte Carlo*, alone in her train compartment, Jeanette MacDonald sings "Beyond the Blue Horizon" in that pseudo-operatic, sometimes not far from ludicrous way of hers, and you can feel right from the start that Lubitsch loves her not despite the fragility of her talent but *because* of it: her way of singing was something irrevocably linked to an era that would soon be gone and whose gentle beauties Lubitsch longed to preserve and to praise, though he would also transcend them.

When a critic can quote so creatively, his criticism becomes a creation in itself. Among Bogdanovich's previous volumes, *Pieces of Time* remains a model of how a miscellany of pieces can add up to a lodestone, and *This Is Orson Welles* rivals Truffaut's mega-colloquy with Hitchcock as an example of how a sufficiently instructed disciple can get his master to talk revealingly about the nuts and bolts in the mechanism of his miracles. Bogdanovich was, and remains, the kind of star student who goes on studying after he graduates.

Being a star student was how he got into movies in the first place. He started off as an enthusiastic young archivist, putting retrospective screenings together for the Museum of Modern Art in New York. Catalogues for the retrospectives would include interviews with veteran directors, conducted *in extenso* by Bogdanovich himself. His licence to pester gained him entrée to the Hollywood studios, where in time he was allowed to try his hand as a director, perhaps because it was less trouble than showing him the door. After proving his competence with a low-budget effort called *Targets*, he was off and running like Craig Breedlove. But when his run of hits—*The Last Picture Show* (1971), *What's Up, Doc?* (1972), *Paper Moon* (1973)—was wrecked by the failure of the musical *At Long Last Love* (1975), his wunderkind's privilege of creative freedom was brutally withdrawn. (The memory of that deprivation must surely have been rekindled by the recent success of Woody Allen's *Everyone Says I Love You*, another musical full of people who can't sing, but this time with the sour notes meeting critical approbation.)

Bogdanovich, his career as a director already in irretrievable trouble, was then stricken by tragedy on a Greek scale. In 1980, his muse and mistress, a twenty-year-old *Playboy* centrefold named Dorothy Stratten, was murdered by her lowlife husband: *The Killing of the Unicorn* was what Bogdanovich titled his subsequent book about the event. On any objective scale, the Unicorn was not greatly talented as an actress, but Bogdanovich can be forgiven for thinking otherwise, because she was greatly beautiful. Unable to get over his loss, Bogdanovich began looking after her thirteen-year-old sister, whom he married seven years later; the dream lived on. But his fame faded, to the point where his name is now starting to sound foreign. Perhaps he never was a typical American in the first place. The tradition behind his work was American, but the way he *thought* of it as a tradition was European. Now that the work has dried up, the thoughtfulness remains, and might well be his lasting contribution.

Extraordinarily concerned in his films with the integrity of his technique and the burden of what he was saying with it, he has shown in his publications where he got that concern from: his predecessors. He was Hollywood's Mr. Memory even while he was its golden boy. Now that he has become the Man in the Iron Mask, he is free to cultivate the archives at his leisure. Executives who played a part in condemning him to strangle in his own beard might be in for an unpleasant surprise. What makes them pygmies is that there once were giants: it's a cliché, but on the strength of the documentation assembled in *Who the Devil Made It*, Bogdanovich looks as if he might raise it to the status of an axiom.

The book comprises interviews with veteran filmmakers—Allan Dwan, Howard Hawks, Alfred Hitchcock, Fritz Lang, Sidney Lumet, Leo McCarey, Otto Preminger, Don Siegel, Josef von Sternberg, Raoul Walsh and others less famous though sometimes even more ready with illuminating war stories of their craft. These were (and sometimes are: a few yet breathe) men rooted in history as much as in Hollywood. Their collected memories make the past look fearfully rich beside a present that is poverty-stricken in everything except money. "Whoever invented spending millions of dollars has absolutely ruined the picture business," Allan Dwan told Bogdanovich in the late 1960s. It might have sounded like an old man's bitterness then. Said today, it would simply sound accurate— except, of course, for the amount of money. For "millions" read "hundreds of millions." A mere million buys you one pout from Val Kilmer in *The Saint* and maybe two drops of sweat from Tom Cruise in *Mission: Impossible* as he hangs there reprising the heist scene from *Topkapi* at a hundred times the outlay for a tenth of the impact. Today's blockbusters, despite the technical bravura of their components, rarely strike us as being very well put together: the tornado twists, the mountain blows up, the dinosaurs eat the scenery, and you are supposed to be lost in wonder, but instead you are left wondering why you are meant to care, because the characters risking death have never been alive and there would be no story without the scenes that interrupt it. The special effects leave NASA looking underfunded, yet the general effect, despite oodles of expertise, is one of a hyperactive ineptitude—of the point missed at full volume, as in the unstoppable monologue of a clever, spoiled child. Mountains of money in labour give birth to ridiculous mice. There's a reason, and this book's radiant bullion of reminiscence illuminates what it is.

To put it bluntly, the old guys had to tell a story because they couldn't blow up the world. There were limitations you couldn't spend your way out of, and in overcoming them lay the essence of the craft, its economy and brio. Don Siegel says it for all the others when he unveils the secret of shooting on the back lot: "For instance, if there's an area which looks weak, I decide that I'll pan down to the feet of the guys walking and then come up where the area's good. . . . At the moment where it's weak, I'm closest to the feet. This is no hard and fast rule, just an example." When you remember that one of the main reasons that *Heaven's Gate* nearly bankrupted United Artists was that Michael Cimino couldn't live with the idea of a background that looked weak for even a single square yard, you realize that there is a whole aesthetic, and hence a morality, embodied in Siegel's attitude. To accept and transcend limitation can be a source of creative vibrancy, whereas to eliminate it with money almost always leads to inertia. On his seventeenth, and last, day of shooting *Baby Face Nelson*, Siegel did fifty-five separate camera setups, and they're all in the picture. ("It cost $175,000 to make," Siegel told Bogdanovich, "and it took a lot of bookkeeping to make it *up* to $175,000.") Warren Beatty, given the choice, would have gone on editing *Reds* forever, but no amount of editing could lend tension to the footage, in which only Jack Nicholson behaved as if he owned a watch. *Reds*, a pioneering effort in the annals of modern wastage, was made in order to indulge the creative whims of its maker. *Baby Face Nelson* was a cynical, cost-conscious piece of exploitation. Which was the work of art? All right, which would you rather see again tonight?

Reality is a useful brake on megalomania. Besides this key point (continually and hearteningly endorsed by almost everyone in the book), there is plenty of other stuff that merits thoughtful attention from the current generation of moviemakers, who so often not only can't do anything small but don't even want to, except as a career move on the way towards doing something big. Leo McCarey took credit for very few of the hundred or so Laurel and Hardy films that he was effectively responsible for, but his vision shaped that of his actors. "At that time," he says, "comics had a tendency to do too much." (There has never been a time when they had any other tendency, but let that pass.) In *From Soup to Nuts*, Hardy as the *maitre d'* came in to serve a cake. He tripped, fell and buried his head in the cake. It was McCarey who shouted (in 1928 the audience couldn't hear him), "Don't move! Just don't move! Stay like that!" Seeing it now, all you get to look at is Hardy's back, stock-still as you rock back and forth with the best kind of laughter—the kind you bring to the joke, participating in it with your imagination.

.   .   .

The movies are a collaborative art, then—or, rather, they were a collaborative art *then*, back at a time when the audience didn't feel left out. But this is to talk like a curmudgeon. Actually, there are more good, solid, humane, well-plotted and well-acted movies being made now than ever before. Compare a densely textured political thriller like *City Hall* with the average FBI gang-busting melo of the 1940s—one of those movies in which the agents sneak up on the spies while a yelping commentator on the soundtrack tells you what they are doing (sneaking up on the spies). But there is no comparison. The movie business now is immeasurably more sophisticated than it used to be. Sophistication, however, is a two-edged sword. It abrades the innocent delight necessary for the making of, say, a screwball comedy. (Bogdanovich's triumphant latter-day contribution to the genre—*What's Up, Doc?*—is the surest testimony that we should put the best possible construction on everything that has happened to him since the death of Dorothy Stratten: only a man capable of deep love could celebrate a wild girl's pilgrim soul with so much joy.) And, above all, it erodes the concept of a modest sufficiency. It ought not to—in almost any other field, the sophisticated rein themselves in—but in the movies it somehow does. People who have made small, intelligent movies dream of making big, dumb ones, persuading themselves that if all values except production values are left out some kind of artistic purity will accrue.

So the creators get carried away. And they want to carry us away with them, but without giving us anything to hold on to except a train being chased by a helicopter through a tunnel. To adapt the famous words of Gertrude Stein, it is amazing how we are not interested. The hero could-n't be doing that, even if it looks as if he were, so the only point of interest is how they worked the trick. Whereas in the old days, even if he didn't especially look as if he were doing that, he *could* have been doing that. So we were with him, and we didn't care how they worked the trick. We let them care. That was their job. They didn't expect to have articles written about it, or to be interviewed—least of all in advance, before the movie was even finished. They worked from pride, but the pride was private. Somewhere in there is the difference between then and now. Then we participated in the movie without participating in its making. Now it's the other way around, and now will pretty soon become intolerable if we don't remember then. This book will help, like all of Bogdanovich's other books.

It might even help us remember his movies, which were marked from the beginning by a rare compassion for those blasted by fate. The great scene in his first great success, *The Last Picture Show*, was when Ben Johnson told the normal boys off for their "trashy behaviour" in humiliating a halfwit. In one of his later movies, *Mask*, the director's challenge, met with subtlety and grace, is to transmit the awful self-consciousness of a superior mind as its grotesque containing skull closes in on it. Bogdanovich's understanding of fate's unbiddably cruel workings is rare among filmmakers anywhere in the world and almost unheard-of in America. He seems to have been blessed with it from birth. But the blessing brought a curse with it. Fate came for him, too. The killing of the Unicorn left him inconsolable. Since then, he has been living a story so sadly strange that not even he could plausibly make a movie of it. One would like to believe that he doesn't want to, since without a deep, literate conviction that the movies can't do everything, he would have less of a gift for celebrating everything they have done.

The New Yorker, July 7, 1997; later
included in *Even As We Speak*, 2001

POSTSCRIPT

Out of respect, and because he was already suffering enough, I soft-pedalled the common knowledge that Bogdanovich had arranged plastic surgery for the Unicorn's sister in order to make her look even more like the prize he had lost. For one thing, I didn't know if the common knowledge was true, and I thought it incumbent on me not to find out for sure. One of the virtues of *The New Yorker* was that it could understand such reticence and did not insist that the personal stuff be jemmied into the piece. Other magazines would have been less forbearing. Though short of back-up by that stage, Bogdanovich had further film projects on his mind and could scarcely have relished my tones of valediction.

Nevertheless he got in touch the next time he came to London and we went out to lunch in Notting Hill. I had already interviewed him on television and knew him to be an entertaining man, but this time, with no clock ticking and nothing at stake, I found out just how entertaining he could be. In the studio he had been sparing with his powers of mimicry. Now he let rip. The mimic's gift is extravagant anyway, but Bogdanovich has an extravagant gift to an extraterrestrial degree, as if he had be been sent here to docket the voice patterns of the human race. Nor is there the problem that was undoubtedly raised in the case of Peter Sellers, of finding the real man among the many adopted personalities. Bogdanovich might have been talking in the voice of Gary Cooper, Cary Grant or Boris Karloff, but the brain driving the supernaturally adaptable muscles of the mouth and vocal cords was all his.

So amused that I starved, I found it hard to believe that a man who could do all that could have lost control of his career. He had, though. A film director has to be a general before he is an artist, and when they take away his army, he has to fight his battles in a sand tray. If things had been going well, Bogdanovich, although always a courteous man, wouldn't have had time for lunch with a writer. I tried to be sorry about that, but I was too glad to have heard him in the full flight of his fancy.

2003

47

THE GENTLE SLOPE
TO CASTALIA

The very first book illustrated with photographs, William Fox Talbot's *The Pencil of Nature* (1844), carried as an epigraph a quotation from Virgil. Talbot, who was a learned classicist as well as a chemist clever enough to invent photography, enlisted Virgil's aid in declaring how sweet it was to cross a mountain ridge unblemished by the wheel ruts of previous visitors, and thence descend the gentle slope to Castalia—a rural paradise complete with well-tended olive groves. The gentle slope turned out to be a precipice and Castalia is buried miles deep under photographs. A subsidiary avalanche, composed of books about photographs, is even now descending. In this brief survey I have selected with some rigour from the recent output, which has filled my office and chased me downstairs into the kitchen.

. . .

In her book *On Photography* (1977) Susan Sontag darkly warned the world that images are out to consume it. Books about images are presumably also in on the feast. Hers remains the best theoretical work to date, although competitors are appearing with startling frequency. Gisèle Freund's *Photography and Society*, now finally available in English, is half historical survey, half theoretical analysis. Her own experience as a celebrated photographer has obviously helped anchor speculation to reality. When the argument takes off, it takes off into a comfortingly recognizable brand of historical determinism. Thus it is made clear how the early portrait photographers served the needs of the bourgeoisie and wiped out the miniaturists who had done the same job for the aristocracy: hence the collapse of taste. Baudelaire, who hated the bourgeoisie, consequently hated photography too. These reflections come in handy when you are looking at the famous photograph of Baudelaire by Nadar. That baleful look must spring from resentment. Sontag makes greater play with such historical cruxes but Freund gives you more of the facts.

Janet Malcolm, the *New Yorker's* photography critic, has produced a worthwhile compilation of her essays. She thinks "discomfit" means "make uncomfortable," but such lapses are rare. More high-flown than Freund, although less self-intoxicatingly so than Sontag, Malcolm is an excellent critic between gusts of aesthetic speculation. *Diana and Nikon* is grandly subtitled "Essays on the Aesthetic of Photography." Whether there is such a thing as an aesthetic of photography is a question which critics should try to keep open as long as possible, since that is one of the things that good criticism always does—i.e., stops aestheticians from forming a premature synthesis. In her essay on Richard Avedon, Malcolm assesses the April 1965 issue of *Harper's Bazaar*, the one edited by Avedon, as a "self-indulgent mess." But she insists on being charitable, against what she has already revealed to be her own better judgement, about his warts-foremost portraits of the mid-1950s. "Like the death's-head at the feast in medieval iconography, these pictures come to tell us that the golden lads and lasses frolicking down the streets of Paris today will be horrible old people tomorrow . . . Avedon *means* to disturb and shock with these pictures, in the way that the young Rembrandt . . . the ageing Swift . . ."

Whatever its stature as aesthetics, this is low-grade criticism. Every artist who shoves something nasty in your face *means* to shock. When Rembrandt portrayed the decay of the flesh he was saying that ugliness, too, is a part of life, and even part of the beautiful. By using such a phrase as "horrible old people" Malcolm unwittingly proves that she has caught something of Avedon's crassness, even while taking him to task. A photographer might be permitted to think in such coarse terms if he is inventive enough in his work, but it is a ruinous habit in a critic and can't be much of an advantage even to an aesthetician, who should be above making her older readers feel uncomfortable, or discomfited. *Cras mihi*— tomorrow it is my turn—remains a useful motto.

Malcolm calls photography the uppity housemaid of painting. Not a bad idea, but like her range of reference it shows an inclination to worry at the phantom problem of whether photography is an art or not. Sontag does better by calling photography a language: nobody wastes time trying to find out whether a language is an art. But Malcolm, between mandatory bouts of ratiocinative fever, stays cool enough to give you some idea of the thinner book she might have written—the one subtitled "Critical Essays about Photography." She shows herself capable of scepticism—a quality not to be confused with cynicism, especially in this field, where an initial enthusiasm at the sheer wealth of stimuli on offer can so easily switch to a bilious rejection of the whole farrago.

On the subject of Diane Arbus's supposedly revolting portraits of freaks and victims, Malcolm makes the penetrating remark that they are not really all that revolting after all—the reason for their popularity is that they are reassuringly in "the composed, static style of the nineteenth century." Such limiting judgements are more useful than dismissive ones, and more subversive too. Similarly, when she says that Edward Weston, far from being the "straight" photographer he said he was, was simply copying new styles of painting instead of old ones, she isn't trying to destroy him—just to define him.

.   .   .

A vigorously interested but properly sceptical tone is the necessary corrective to the star system promoted by John Szarkowski. Operating from his command centre at New York's Museum of Modern Art, Szarkowski has conjured up from photography's short past more geniuses than the Renaissance ever knew. Szarkowski's passion would be infectious even if he lacked discrimination, but in fact he is a first-rate critic in detail and an admirably cogent thinker within his field. The Museum of Modern Art booklet *Looking at Photographs* (1973) continues to be the best possible short introduction to the entire topic. In it he draws the vital distinction between self-expression and documentary, and draws it at the moment when it is least obvious yet most apposite—with reference to a photograph by Atget of a vase at Versailles. Other photographers, according to Szarkowski, had been concerned either with describing the specific facts (documentation) or with exploiting their individual sensibilities (self-expression). Atget fused and transcended both approaches. Szarkowski's gift for argument manages to convince you that Atget's artistic personality is somehow present in a picture otherwise devoid of living human content. In an earlier Museum booklet, *The Photographer's Eye*

(1966, reprinted this year), he declared himself aware that the "fine art" and "functional" traditions were intimately involved with each other— another vital critical precept.

So there is nothing simplistic about Szarkowski. It will be a rare aesthetician who matches his analytical capacity. There is not much wrong with his prose either, apart from his conviction that "disinterested" means "uninterested." What disturbs you about his writings is how they make photography so overwhelmingly significant. For Szarkowski, photography is the biggest deal since the wheel. If he did not feel that way he would never have got so far as a curator and showman, but when the same fervour smites his readers they can be excused for succumbing to a mild panic. Surely photography isn't everything.

It isn't, but it isn't nothing either. One can be sceptical about just how great Szarkowski's great artists are, but there is no reason for deciding that they are anything less than a remarkable group of people. Just how remarkable is now being revealed by a swathe of plush monographs. The hard work of the archivists and curators is paying off in a big way. Only in a climate of acceptance could these sumptuously produced books come to exist. The late Nancy Newhall's *The Eloquent Light* is a new edition of her biography of Ansel Adams, first published by the Sierra Club in 1963. It traces Adams's career from 1902 up to 1938, by which time Alfred Stieglitz had given him—in 1936, to be precise—the one-man show that helped establish him as a master photographer.

The book has plates drawn from Adams's whole range, although the Yosemite photographs inevitably stand out. The text gives due regard to the emphasis he placed on cleanliness. The washed prints were tested for any lingering traces of hypo. Adams was not alone among the American photographers in taking himself so solemnly: with monklike austerity they acted out the seriousness of their calling. That its seriousness was not yet unquestioned only made it the more necessary to keep a long face. In the case of Adams the results justified any amount of pious rhetoric about the Expanding Photographic Universe. Published last year, *Yosemite and the Range of Light* contains the finest fruits of Adams's long obsession with the Sierra Nevada. The quality of the prints is bewitching. They are so sharp you can taste the steel. Blacks, grays and whites look as lustrous as the skin of a Siamese cat.

Walter Benjamin thought a work of art could have authenticity but a photograph could not. He said so in the famous essay whose title is usually translated as "The Work of Art in the Age of Mechanical Reproduction," although really it should be translated as "The Work of Art in the Age of Its Mechanical Reproducibility," since Benjamin's point was that mankind had always produced everyday things in multiple copies but it was only lately that the work of art had become subject to the same rule. Since a given negative could yield any number of prints, Benjamin argued, to ask for an "authentic" print made no sense (*"die Frage nach dem echten Abzug hat keinen Sinn"*). Sontag, who in other respects might have subjected Benjamin's great essay to a less awe-stricken scrutiny, realized that on this point at least the sage was exactly wrong. Negatives can be damaged, prints can be made from prints, paper and methods of reproduction can fall short of a photographer's wishes. Obviously some prints are more authentic than others and you can't have greater or lesser degrees of nothing. These prints of Adams's Yosemite photographs are so *echt* they sing. El Capitan looms through a winter sunrise. Half Dome shines clean as a hound's tooth under a thunderhead or fills with shadows as the moon, filled with shadows of its own, plugs a hole in the sheet steel sky.

Suppose Paul Strand had taken pictures of the same chunks of geology: could a layman, however knowledgeable, tell the difference? Even the most distinctive photographers tend to be defined more by subject matter than by style. If a photographer's any and every photograph were immediately identifiable as his he would probably be individual to the point of mania. Good photographs look better than bad photographs but don't often look all that much different from one another. Some of Paul Strand's photographs in *Time in New England*, a book devised in collaboration with the much-missed Nancy Newhall (she died in 1974), look as if Adams might have taken them, yet it is no reflection on either man. The book was first published in 1950 but is now redesigned, with the prints brought closer to the authentic state. Adams's senior by twelve years, Strand likewise profited from an association with Stieglitz. These connections of inspiration and patronage are very easy to be impressed by, but it is worth remembering that just because half the Florentine sculptors were all born on the same few hills did not make them blood brothers. The life of art lies in what makes artists different from one another—the individual creative personality. The main difference between a clapboard church by Paul Strand and a clapboard house by Harry Callahan is that in Strand's lens the church leans backward and in Callahan's the house leans forward.

In *Brett Weston: Photographs from Five Decades* there is more than enough clean-cut shapeliness to recall his father Edward's predilection for "the *thing itself.*" The air of dedication is once again monastic. "For Brett, the struggle has been a long, unhurried process of refining an uncompromising, inborn vision. He did not acquire it: it was simply granted to him, like grace." There is no reason to doubt the intensity of Brett's inborn vision. What niggles is the fact that a beach photographed by Brett Weston and a beach photographed by Harry Callahan look like roughly similar stretches of the same stuff—sand.

.   .   .

Water's Edge collects the best of Callahan's black-and-white Beach Series (always capitalized) from 1941 until now. The light, the sand patterns, the reeds and the frail water could not be more delicately caught. When they *are* more delicately caught, the result is the kind of abstraction that leaves you striving to admire. But generally Callahan photographing is good at what Lichtenberg said was the most important thing about think-ing—keeping the right distance from the subject. The text, a deeply rhythmless poetic concoction by A. R. Ammons ("I allow myself eddies of meaning") is in the hallowed tradition of overwriting for which, with his accompanying prose to Walker Evans's photographs in *Let Us Now Praise Famous Men*, James Agee unfortunately gave an eternal sanction. For crazy people, there is a deluxe limited edition priced at $1,500. Presum-ably it is bound in platinum. *Harry Callahan: Color* has some of the Beach Series in colour and a lot more besides: clapboard houses, bill-boards, store fronts and, most importantly, his wife Eleanor. Callahan composes exceptionally pretty scenes but human beings keep stealing them.

The same applies to the old Czech master Sudek, who was born in 1896 and is apparently still alive. Not much of his work has been seen outside Czechoslovakia until now. Sonja Bullaty and Anna Farova have compiled and introduced their monograph in a manner befitting his unarguable stature. The amber haze of the early prints proclaims his affinity with Steichen, whose symbolist nudes in *Steichen: The Master Prints 1895–1914* might have been signed by Sudek. The wily Czech's still lifes and surrealist fantasies are enough to keep aestheticians happily chatting, but once again the people, when they are allowed to appear, infallibly upstage the settings.

The same is doubly true for Lotte Jacobi, whose people are not, like Sudek's, anonymous. Jacobi was also born in 1896. Kelly Wise's book on her, called just *Lotte Jacobi*, was published in the U.S. in 1978 but English readers might like to note that it has only lately succeeded in crossing the Atlantic. In New York for ten years after World War II Jacobi busied herself with abstract effects called "photogenics." Like all art inspired by its own technique, they dated instantly and are now of little interest. But her portraits, mainly taken in pre-war Germany, are of high value. The high value becomes especially high when the sitters are world famous, but there is no way around that. Weill, Lorre, Walter, Furtwängler, Piscator, Lang, Kraus, Planck, Zuckmayer, Grosz and many more are all preserved in *echt* condition. She did a whole, fascinating sequence of Einstein portraits both in Germany and in American exile. There are also multiple portraits of Thomas Mann, Chagall, Frost and Stieglitz. The cover girl is Lotte Lenya.

Jacobi also did a portrait of Moholy-Nagy. If Moholy-Nagy had done more portraits himself, Andreas Haus's book on him, *Moholy-Nagy: Photographs and Photograms*, might have been of more than historical interest. The volume is well kitted out for study by aestheticians, but even those up on Moholy-Nagy's theories of perception could well find that the photograms no longer thrill. Herr Haus speaks of Moholy-Nagy's "attempt to solve his problems as a painter (the penetration of planes, the elimination of individual handwriting) by means of a new technique. . . ." Unfortunately Moholy-Nagy's chief problem as a painter, shortage of talent, could not be solved by technical innovation, despite an abundant output of compensatory aesthetic sloganeering. Moholy-Nagy talked about "the hygiene of the optical" and announced that "everyone will be compelled to see what is optically true." (I once heard Pierre Boulez, at a lunch thrown for him in London by my newspaper the *Observer*, promise that the general public would be made familiar with contemporary music "by force.") Moholy-Nagy's real contribution lay not in abstract doodling but in his knack for shooting reality from unexpected angles so as to reveal forms and textures previously unlooked for. Everybody has since appropriated these technical advances, with the result that most of his once startling photographs are no longer immediately identifiable as being by him. Such is the fate of the technical innovator.

.   .   .

But Moholy-Nagy's people are vivid enough. From a balcony in Dessau (datelined "1926–1928") a woman looks down at a pretty girl stretched smiling on a parapet. Moholy-Nagy was a tireless organizer of forms but the most interesting form, that of the human being, comes ready made. Cecil Beaton, to his credit, never doubted that his career as a photographer owed something to the human beings he was pointing his camera at. *Self-Portrait with Friends*, the selection from his diaries which appeared last year, now receives its necessary supplement in the form of *Beaton*, a collection of his best portrait photographs, edited by James Danziger. Raphael, Berenson was fond of saying, shows us the classicism of our yearnings. Beaton gave famous and fashionable people the look they would have liked to have. In many cases they had it already. Lady Oxford, photographed in 1927, may have been a battleaxe, but she was a regal battleaxe. Beaton wasn't a sentimentalist so much as a dandy who believed in glamour as a separate country. Until the 1950s he was almost the only mainstream British photographer the young aspirants could look to. (Bill Brandt was a dropout.) From the technical viewpoint he was awesomely capable—he snatched candids in Hollywood that look as uncluttered as the best official studio portraits.

Beyond technique he had a sense of occasion. At times this might have been indistinguishable from snobbery, but it served him better than the routine compulsion to record documentary truth. His book *New York* (1938) is painfully weak when it goes up to Harlem. ("These people are children.") In *Far East* (1945) he is plainly more interested in Imperial Delhi than in the air-raid casualties. In *Time Exposure* (1946) his "Bomb Victim" is merely cute, whereas the portrait of John Gielgud "in a Restoration role" slips straight into immortality with no waiting. These books and several more lie behind the present compilation, which loses little from being deprived of the original text. (The "DeHavilland fighter, 1941" depicted on page 42 is, however, clearly a Spitfire, which was manufactured by Vickers Supermarine. How old is Mr. Danziger? Eight?) Beaton was a social butterfly who wrote the higher gossip. But the circles he moved in provided him with human subjects who were, in many cases, works of art ready made. With Beaton's beautiful socialites, as with Baron de Meyer's, it is hard to avoid the conclusion that they had no other reason for existence than getting into the picture. Beaton has, if anybody has, a clearly defined artistic personality. But once again the self-expression is largely defined by the field of documentation. His exquisite drawings, which he left like thank-you notes in the grand houses, are far more characteristic than his photographs.

Mainly by shading his eyes with a wide-brimmed hat and allowing his feet to take him in congenial directions, Beaton found the world seductive. He wasn't out to shape reality, even by photography, which he rated, perhaps jokingly, fifth among his interests. With Diana Vreeland seductiveness becomes Allure. In a folio called just that, Ms. Vreeland collects some of her favourite twentieth-century photographs. Equipped with a stream of semi-consciousness text emanating from DV herself, the book (which I see the latest number of *Manhattan Catalogue* calls "absolutely historic," not just historic) has been thrown together with such abandon that some of the captions have landed on the wrong photographs—in my copy, at least. The picture dubbed "Baron de Meyer / *The New Hat Called Violette Worn by the Honorable Mrs. Reginald Fellowes—Alex, 1924*" should almost certainly be entitled "Louise Dahl-Wolfe/*Balenciaga's white linen over-blouse, 1953*" and vice versa. In later copies, I understand, such anomalies have been put right. The model for the Balenciaga is, unless my eyes are giving out under the strain, Suzy Parker. Even at this late date, Ms. Vreeland continues *Vogue's* queenly habit of always crediting the fashionable ladies but rarely the models. In effect this quirk has helped to glorify the photographers, who get kudos not only for the way they make the girl look but for the way she looks anyway.

The most striking pictures in Vreeland's book are by Anonymous, who snapped the British royal women at George VI's funeral. By the time these prints, probably duped off other prints, have been blown up to fit the squash-court-sized pages of *Allure*, there is not much left to say about authenticity. Yet aura—the many-layered immanence which Benjamin said photography deprived things of—is present in large amounts, possibly because Allure has been banished.

Not that it stays banished for long. On most of Vreeland's pages it seems fighting to get in somewhere. In the context of Vreeland's unbridled prose, Eva Perón becomes a figure of moral stature, since she cared how she looked to the bitter end. Vreeland is a place where appearance is everything. But the occasional big-name photographer manages to look timelessly unfussy. Some of the cleanest plates in *Allure*'s pantheon are by George Hoyningen-Huene, this year the subject of a retrospective exhibition, called "Eye for Elegance," at the International Center of Photography in New York. The catalogue gives a taste of his work, although really he is too protean to sample. Among other activities, he set the standard for pre-war French *Vogue*'s studio photography and was colour consultant on some of the best-looking Hollywood films of the fifties and early sixties, including Cukor's wildly beautiful *Heller in Pink Tights*. No fashion photographer ever had a wider range. The shadows on his reclining swimsuit models are calculated to the centimetre, yet some of his celebrity portraits of the 1930s look natural enough to have been done today. His 1934 Gary Cooper, for example, seems to be lit by nothing except sunlight. The profile is almost lost in the background and every skin blemish is left intact. Yet the result has aura to burn.

.　　.　　.

The Hollywood studio photographer retouched as a matter of course. In his splendidly produced *The Art of the Great Hollywood Portrait Photographers*, John Kobal gives us the rich benefit of his archival labours. Based in London, Kobal has built up a peerless collection of the original negatives. Kobal knows everything about how the studios marketed their property. Some studios assessed the daily output of their photographers by the pound. The stars were expected to cooperate and the smarter of them realized that it was in their interests to do so. Lombard, it seems, was particularly keen. Garbo was nervous, but Clarence Sinclair Bull never made the mistake of saying "hold it"—he just lit her and waited. One key light, one top light, and a long lens parked some way off so she wouldn't notice. There are stories by and about, among others, Ruth Harriet Louise, Ernest Bachrach, Eugene Robert Richee, George Hurrell and Laszlo Willinger. Sternberg knew exactly how he wanted Dietrich to look but otherwise it was a conspiracy between the studio and the photographer, with the star in on it if she was powerful enough. Before and after shots show how drastically Columbia rearranged the accoutrements of

Rita Hayworth's face. One of the after shots, by A. L. "Whitey" Schaefer, is surely an image for eternity.

But the studio photographers were not engaged in making something out of nothing, even though the lead used for retouching formed such a significant proportion of their daily poundage. The stars might have been helped to realize their ideal selves, but the ideal self was not, and could not be, too far divorced from the real appearance. When the silver transcontinental trains pulled in at Dearborn Station in Chicago, a man called Len Lisovitch used to be lurking in wait. He was an amateur photographer who wanted the stars all to himself. Len collected, among others, Hedy Lamarr, Betty Grable, Merle Oberon and Greer Garson. His candids of Hedy Lamarr are not decisively less enchanting than the portraits turned out with such labour by Laszlo Willinger at MGM. Admittedly Lamarr had flawless skin and always photographed well as long as she was not allowed to become animated, but the point is hard to duck: the stars were already well on their way to being works of art before the hot lights touched them. They were simply beautiful human beings—if there is anything simple about that.

.   .   .

In *Mrs. David Bailey*—called, in the UK, *Trouble and Strife*, cockney rhyming slang for "wife"—David Bailey celebrates the extraordinary beauty of his wife Marie Helvin. Bailey, Terence Donovan and Brian Duffey became such famous photographers in London during the sixties that they have been faced ever since with the requirement to astonish. This book is not wholly free from the strained compulsion to dazzle, but it is still Bailey's best effort since *Goodbye Baby and Amen*, mainly because Marie Helvin is so bliss-provokingly lovely that she takes the sting out of the naughtiest poses Bailey can think up. There is an admiring prefatory note by J. H. Lartigue, who would have done at least one thing Bailey hasn't—caught her smiling. *Avoir pour amour une femme aussi belle, jolie, charmante et troublante que Marie, quelle inspiration pour un artiste*. At eighty-four Lartigue still has an eye for a pretty foot.

Bailey has graciously allowed his model to retain her name. Helmut Newton takes that away and a lot more besides. *Special Collection 24 Photo Lithos* comprises big, slick prints of photographs you might have seen before in *White Women* (1976) and *Sleepless Nights* (1978). Rapturously introducing *Sleepless Nights*, Philippe Garner, billed as the photographic curator of London Sotheby's, unintentionally pinned Newton to the wall. "There is, surely, an added spice in having the talent to present a subject as blatant as this in such a way that the spokespersons of a society which should, in theory, deplore such an image as shocking actually pat one on the back for taking it and reward one handsomely." There was also a lot about Newton's alleged humour.

Mercifully his new book is deprived of textual accompaniment, leaving those who have a taste for these things free to indulge their fantasies of exhibitionism, bondage and flagellation. Apologists have explained that Newton loves women so much he wants to show how they retain their dignity no matter what you do to them, or pretend to do to them. So here they are in a variety of neck braces, trusses and plaster casts. For men who want to be in the saddle, there is a spurred and booted beauty wearing a saddle. Famous in the trade for his technical skill, Newton will take endless pains to find the right props and setting. I suppose he is trying to make us question our own desires, but I always find myself questioning his. It can be argued that Newton's sado-masochistic confections pale beside what can be found in hard-core pornography, yet the question still arises of why he thinks he is engaged in anything more exalted than a fashionable triteness already going out of date. He gives you the impression of somebody who has had his life changed by an Alice Cooper album. How his dogged prurience makes you long for Lartigue.

But what Newton does to girls is a sweet caress compared with what girls do to girls. *Women on Women* gave a broad hint at what was on the way. Women covered with cream, women with skulls in their twats, women flaunting six-foot styrofoam dicks, women solemnly feeling each other up in the backseats of limos. At first glance, Joyce Baronio's *42nd Street Studio*, with an introduction by Professor Linda Nochlin of CUNY, is the same scene, folio size. One's initial impulse, when faced with the spectacle of a naked girl attached by ropes to a blond stud in black boots plus obligatory whip, is to burst out yawning. But Baronio's pictures are laudable for their quality and most of the fantasies count as found objects. They litter the Times Square district where she works. She is performing a certain documentary service in recording them, even if you doubt the lasting value of her self-expression. For myself, I'm bound to say I'm at least half hooked, and would like to see what she does next. I don't *think* it's just because of the pretty girls, although I could certainly do without some of the guys, especially the one in the leather jockstrap and the hat.

A photographer who interests himself more in documentary than in self-expression is nowadays likely to remain anonymous until such time as his unassertive vision turns out to have been unique all along. For most photographers that time will never come no matter how arresting their photographs. *The Best of Photojournalism 5* enshrines some of the year's most riveting shots. You can flick through it and decide if reality is being consumed. I was particularly impressed by L. Roger Turner's three pictures of a Down's syndrome boy hefting a bowling ball in the Special Olympics. Perhaps I am congratulating myself on my own compassion, which has in fact been reduced to a stock response by too many images. There is also a chance that my aesthetic sensibility is being blunted instead of sharpened when I admire Bill Wax's study of Chris Snode preparing to dive into a heated Florida pool on a cold winter's morning. Crucified in steam, Snode looks like a Duccio plus dry ice.

Eve Arnold's new book *In China* raises the question of veracity. Sontag argues persuasively that the beautifying power of photography derives from its weakness as a truth-teller. It is indeed true that a photograph can tell you something only if you already know something about its context, but the same applies to any other kind of signal. Here are some extremely pretty coloured photographs of China. They inform you of many facts, including the fact that there is at least one bald Buddhist monk still in business at the Cold Mountain monastery in Suchow. What they can't tell you is just how long those children singing in the classroom will be obliged to go on believing in the divinity of the man with his picture on the wall. The same kind of stricture, if it is one, applies to *Photographs for the Tsar*, which collects the astonishing pre-Revolutionary coloured photographs by Sergei Prokudin-Gorskii, a forgotten pioneer now destined to be clamorously remembered.

Prokudin-Gorskii employed a triple-negative process of his own devising. Nicholas II commissioned him to perpetuate anything that took his fancy. The results fell short of those Eve Arnold is accustomed to obtaining but not by far. Prokudin-Gorskii was necessarily limited to photographing stationary objects but took care to pick the right ones. The book takes its place beside Chloe Obolensky's indispensable *The Russian Empire*, published last year.

Across the Rhine is the latest in the Time-Life corporation's admirable series based on its own World War II archive. Once again the text, contributed this time by Franklin M. Davis, Jr., but with the usual assistance from "the editors of Time-Life Books," is a sane corrective to the revisionist theories now rife among more exalted historians. The photographs do what photographs best can—they give you some idea of what the reality you already know something about was like in detail. Some of the pictures taken in the liberated concentration camps are included. Sontag tells us that her life was changed by seeing these very pictures—a moment in her book which I appreciated from the heart, since it was an extensive reading of the Nuremberg transcripts, with due attention to the horrific photographic evidence contained in Volume XXXI, that did more than anything else to shape my own view of life.

Sontag might agree that whatever else images had done to take the edge off reality, they rubbed her nose in it in that case. These photographs are hard to respond to adequately but then so might have been the reality. The brave documentary photographer Margaret Bourke-White, after taking her pictures in Buchenwald, told her editors that she would have to see the prints developed before she believed what she had witnessed. It is a point for an aesthetician to seize, but too much should not be made of it. She was speaking metaphorically. The thing had happened and she could tell that it had happened. Her photographs helped, however inadequately, to tell the world.

There is a case for photographing horrors, since not all torturers are as keen as Hitler's and Pol Pot's to keep their own pictorial record of what they get up to. Snapping celebrities with their pants down is harder to justify, but in his preface to *Private Pictures* Anthony Burgess does his best to convince us that the *paparazzi* are engaged in something valuable. From the photographs you can't find out much beyond a few variously startling physical facts about the firmness of Romy Schneider's behind, the pliancy of Elton John's wrist and the magnitude of Giovanni Agnelli's virile member. It is also sensationally revealed that Orson Welles has a fat gut and Yul Brynner a bald head. Burgess is pretty scathing about Brigitte Bardot's breasts, but to me she looks in better shape than Burgess was when I last saw him.

Apparently Burgess shares the gutter press assumption that those who achieve fame should be made to suffer from it. But many of this book's victims are famous only as a side-effect of pursuing honourable careers. "This book," growls Burgess, "in bringing stars down to the

human level, is a kind of visual poem on the theme of expendability."
One night before a Cambridge Union debate I saw Burgess get angry
because Glenda Jackson had not turned up to lead the opposing team.
Burgess made it clear that to meet her ranked high among his reasons for
being in attendance. Not even such unexpendable philosophers as
Burgess are always entirely innocent of the star-fucking impulse. *Private
Pictures* supplies additional evidence for the already well-documented
theory that those who fuck the stars are the same people who enjoy sticking it to them.

The grinding triviality of the *paparazzi* retroactively makes the dedication of the documentary photographers sound less like solemnity and
more like high seriousness. Karin Becker Ohrn's *Dorothea Lange and the
Documentary Tradition* takes you back to the days of the Farm Security
Administration, when a photographer could feel that she was helping to
open the world's eyes. Lange believed that it took time for a photographer's personality to emerge. Some photographers can't wait that long,
but even if the wrong people sometimes get famous it is generally true
that only the right ones stay that way. *Dialogue with Photography*, edited
by Paul Hill and Thomas Cooper, is an absorbing compilation of interviews with the big names, including Strand, Brassaï, Cartier-Bresson,
Beaton, Lartigue and Kertész. The simplicity of true artistic absorption
comes shining through even the murkiest rhetoric about Art. According
to the late Minor White, Stieglitz asked him if he had ever been in love.
When White said yes, Stieglitz told him he could be a photographer. Lartigue makes the same point. "First, one must learn how to look, how to
love." It probably sounds better in French.

Brandt, the perpetual loner, is not present. On BBC radio recently
he described how Cartier-Bresson, when they met in Paris in the 1950s,
wouldn't speak to him, because he had sinned against photographic
purity by cropping the negative and using artificial light. At the time of
writing, Brandt is all set to unleash on London an exhibition of his recent
work in which the girls are reportedly weighed down with more chains
and leather straps than Helmut Newton ever dreamed of. Cartier-Bresson
would doubtless not approve. The photographers have always been quite
capable of ideological warfare. Ansel Adams said that Walker Evans's
work gave him a hernia.

Peter Tausk's *Photography in the 20th Century* tells you how the Western photographic tradition looks from Czechoslovakia, for whose art and photography students this book was originally written. Tausk has his nose pressed to the glass but is not unduly dazzled. He has a useful way of pointing out that the reporters are as worthy of attention as the name photographers—the kind of thought which would occur to you with special sharpness if you lived in a country where there are no reporters. The best encyclopedia of the name photographers is still *The Magic Image* by Cecil Beaton and Gail Buckland (1975). One had always suspected that Gail Buckland must have done most of the work. The suspicion is confirmed by the high quality of *Fox Talbot and the Invention of Photography*, the authorship of which is claimed by her alone. Etymology, philology, mathematics, crystallography—his interests were endless, and all pursued at the highest level. On top of all that, he set the standards for the intelligent use of his invention. His photograph of volumes from his own library is a necessary reminder, bequeathed to us by the progenitor, that the apparent divorce between word and image is really an indissoluble marriage. One closes the book more astounded than ever at Talbot's achievements. It was a genius who started it all.

Whether all those famous names that have cropped up since should be thought of as geniuses is open to doubt. The Americans are more vexed by such questions than the Europeans, who better understand that some arts are minor and that it is more satisfactory to be an accomplished practitioner of a minor art than a third-rate exponent of a major one. Enjoying a less coherent social and intellectual life, the Americans have understandably either clung together for warmth or been strident in isolation. The consequent rhetoric should not too quickly be dismissed even when it is patent moonshine. The impure applied and minor arts are often accompanied by dumb talk, off which it is easy for the critic to score points. He does best, however, when addressing the thing itself. Photography, despite the attendant cacophony of promotion, remains, after all, a miraculous event—almost as interesting, in fact, as Szarkowski says it is. Castalia still has its attractions. As for the higher thinker, he must sooner or later discover that the aesthetic of photography, like the aesthetic of the novel or the aesthetic of the ballet, is a snark. The best contribution a critic can make to aesthetics is to aim for consistency, argue closely and be wary of big ideas.

Sontag's notion that images consume reality counts as a big idea.

Intellectuals should speak for themselves in the first instance. Obviously images are not consuming *her* reality. So she must mean the rest of us. Nor was Benjamin being as penetrating as he sounded when he said that people flooded with images would not know how to read a book. My own children watch television for half a day at a stretch and still read more books than I did at their age. Benjamin thought of photography as one of the means by which Fascism would allow the masses to express themselves without posing any threat to the social order. At that time everyone had a theory about the masses. Benjamin had already died his lonely death before it was generally realized that the masses do not exist. There are only people—so many of them that the aesthetician can be forgiven for finding their numbers meaningless. But the critic's job is to maintain what the best photographers have helped define—a discriminating eye.

New York Review of Books, December 18, 1980; later included in *Even As We Speak*, 2001

48

PICTURES IN SILVER

Camera Lucida: Reflections on Photography by
Roland Barthes, translated by Richard Howard

The flow of photographic images from the past suggests that what we are already experiencing as a deepening flood in the present will seem, in the near future, like a terminal inundation. Most of the theoretical works purporting to find some sort of pattern in the cataract of pictures only increase the likelihood that we will lose our grip. But occasionally a book makes sense of the uproar. Appearing in the author's native language just before his death, Roland Barthes's *Camera Lucida*, now published posthumously in English, will make the reader sorrier than ever that this effervescent critic is no longer among the living. Barthes was the inspiration of many a giftless tract by his disciples but he himself was debarred by genuine critical talent from finding any lasting value in mechanized schemes. By the end of his life he seemed very keen to re-establish the personal, the playful and even the quirky at the centre of his intellectual effort, perhaps because he had seen, among some of those who took his earlier work as an example, how easily method can become madness.

Whatever the truth of that, here is a small but seductively argued book which the grateful reader can place on the short shelf of truly useful commentaries on photography, along with Walter Benjamin's *Das Kunstwerk im Zeitalter seiner technischen Reproduzierbarkeit*, Susan Sontag's *On Photography*, John Szarkowski's promotional essays and the critical articles of Janet Malcolm. Also asking for a home on the same shelf is the recently published *Photography in Print*, edited by Vicki Goldberg and including many of the best shorter writings about photography from its first days to now. As well as the expected, essential opinions of everyone from Fox Talbot to Sontag, there are such out-of-the-way but closely relevant pieces as a reminiscence by Nadar which suggests that Balzac pre-empted Benjamin's idea about photographs robbing an object of its aura; a stunningly dull critique written by one Cuthbert Bode in 1855 which shows that photography has always generated, as well as a special enthusiasm, a special intensity of patronizing scorn; and a brilliantly turned *Hiawatha*-metre poem by that fervent shutterbug Lewis Carroll.

> From his shoulder Hiawatha
> Took the camera of rosewood
> Made of sliding, folding rosewood;
> Neatly put it all together.
> In its case it lay compactly,
> Folded into nearly nothing;
> But he opened out the hinges,
> Pushed and pulled the joints and hinges,
> Till it looked all squares and oblongs,
> Like a complicated figure
> In the second book of Euclid.

There is, of course, a much longer shelf, indeed a whole wall of long shelves, packed with commentaries which are not particularly wrong-headed. But they are platitudinous, and in the very short run it is the weight of unobjectionable but unremarkable accompanying prose which threatens to make a minor art boring. The major arts can stand the pressure.

Barthes at his best had a knack for timing the soufflé. The texture of *Camera Lucida* is light, making it suitable for a heavy message. The message is heavy enough to be called subversive. Barthes finds photography interesting, but not as art. An awful lot of would-be artists are going to be disappointed to hear this. But before they smash up their Nikons in frustration they should hear the argument through, because if Barthes is disinclined to treat photographers as artists he is uncommonly inclined to examine what they do with an intelligently selective eye. "A photograph is always invisible," he writes, "it's not it that we see." Barthes says that what we see is the subject matter: "the referent adheres." Barthes airily dismisses all talk of composition. Indeed he goes a long way towards saying that a photograph hasn't got any formal element worth bothering about. He claims for himself, where photography is concerned, "a desperate resistance to any reductive system"—pretty cool, when you consider the number and aridity of reductive systems his example has given rise to.

Barthes says that what he brings to the average photograph is *studium*—general curiosity. What leaps out of the exceptional photograph is a *punctum*—a point of interest. In Kertész's 1926 portrait of Tristan Tzara (unfortunately not reproduced in this book), the *studium*, says Barthes, might have to do with a Dadaist having his picture taken but the *punctum* is his dirty fingernails. In William Klein's photograph "Near the Bowery" (1954), you and I might have our attention drawn by the toy gun held to the smiling boy's head, especially if the scene arouses an echo of the Viet Cong prisoner being summarily executed in one of the most famous pieces of news film footage to have come out of Vietnam. But Barthes can't help noticing the little boy's bad teeth. Barthes is not always startled by what the photographer finds startling and is never startled by what the photographer rigs to be startling—abstract and surrealist concoctions leave him cold.

A photograph, says Barthes, does not nostalgically call up the past. Instead it shows the past was real, like now. Photography proves the past to be a reality we can no longer touch. Instead of the solace of nostalgia, the bitterness of separation. Photography is powerless as art but potent as magic. Thus his little book concludes as it began, with a confident emphasis on subject matter.

When John Szarkowski, in his 1966 critical anthology *The Photographer's Eye*, showed that for every master photographer's laboriously created definitive statement there was at least one amateur snapshot equally interesting, the photographic world had the choice of inferring either that the artists weren't artistic or else that the amateurs were artistic too. On the whole the latter course was taken, mainly because Szarkowski so persuasively extended the range of what it was possible to discuss about a photograph, so that the mere business of selecting what to shoot stood revealed for what it is—an artistic choice at some level, however diffident.

Similarly Barthes's potentially devastating re-emphasis is mollified by his willingness to concede that the selectivity involved is not just his own unusually receptive eye for the *punctum*. The photographer is allowed the faculty of selectivity too. Barthes does not seem to allow even the best photographer much more, but perhaps he just never got around to developing his argument, which nevertheless is an attractive one as it stands. If one famous American classical photographer's photograph of trees has ever worried you by looking indistinguishable from another famous American classical photographer's photograph of trees, here is a way out of your dilemma. The identity of subject matter tends to render the alleged compositional and tonal subtleties nugatory in each case. There is no reason to feel guilty just because we have got one of the Westons mixed up with one of the others.

The composition of a photograph can be analysed usefully, but not as long as it can be analysed uselessly. As with a literary work, there is a line to be drawn between the critical remark that yields meaning and the analytical rigmarole which tells you little beyond the fact that some ambitious young academic has time on his hands. Barthes's thesis is a refreshing simplification. But a fresh look doesn't always simplify. In *Before Photography: Painting and the Invention of Photography*, the catalogue for the Museum of Modern Art exhibition which will next be seen in Los Angeles and Chicago, Peter Galassi cunningly advances the deceptively simple thesis that some paintings prepared the way for the invention of photography by manifesting "a new and fundamentally modern pictorial syntax of immediate, synoptic perceptions and discontinuous, unexpected forms."

Galassi's argument has already been examined at some length by Charles Rosen and Henri Zerner. I will not rehearse their analysis beyond saying that they find Mr. Galassi's achievement as impressive as I do. They argue that Mr. Galassi gives an incomplete account of perspective. Galassi says that over the centuries the original pictorial strategy, to make a three-dimensional world out of a flat medium, gradually reversed itself, and became the new pictorial strategy of making a flat picture out of a three-dimensional world—at which point photography, which might have been invented much earlier if anyone had really wanted it, finally showed up in order to answer the new need. Rosen and Zerner recommend that Galassi should take into account the implications of the empirical representation developed by the fifteenth-century Flemish painters. No doubt they are right, but I can think of someone else who might fit Galassi's theory even more instructively—Velázquez.

As Ortega explains in *The Dehumanisation of Art*, Velázquez was the first to look into the distance with a dilated pupil and so blur the focus of things near. That is why foreground figures in some of his pictures—one thinks particularly of *Las Meninas*—look so strange. They are strange because they are the unexamined familiar. They look the way things look when we are looking past them, as if they were floating, *converdidas en gases cromáticos, en flámulas informes, en puros reflejos.* Converted into chromatic gases, into formless flames, into pure reflections. (Ortega's writings on aesthetics are so poetic that they constitute an aesthetic problem in themselves.)

Unless I have got it hopelessly wrong, Ortega uncovered in Velázquez a concern with focus and depth of field which presages just those aspects of the photographic vision. No doubt Velázquez developed these perceptions out of a desire to mimic how the eye actually sees, but Galassi seems to be saying that the photographic pictorial strategy developed out of just that impulse, away from conceptual ordering and towards the randomly inclusive. Ortega, who said that you could see a Velázquez in one gulp, even has a vocabulary that seems ready-made for Galassi's thesis. Ortega says that the closely focussed analytic vision is feudal and that the distantly focused, synthetic vision is democratic.

Doubtless other readers of Galassi's essay will have their own ideas, not just because his argument is the kind that makes us recognize something we already suspected, but because so many of us have a head full of references. By now Malraux's *musée imaginaire,* the Museum Without Walls, has transferred itself from books of reproductions into our own skulls. But a brain which already has a few hundred of the world's great paintings arranged inside it is likely to panic when asked to take in several thousand of the world's putatively great photographs as well. Yet we can retain the notion of the photographer as artist without feeling obliged to accept his every creation as a work of art.

By and large that is what John Szarkowski does in his excellent introductory essay to *The Work of Atget,* Vol. 1: *Old France,* the magnificently produced and highly desirable catalogue volume for the first of what will be four Museum of Modern Art exhibitions devoted to Atget's work, the cycle being due to complete itself in 1984. The material will take a long time to show and took even longer to get ready. Berenice Abbott gave the museum her collection of about 5,000 Atget prints in 1968. Maria Morris Hambourg, Szarkowski's co-scholar on the project, has been occupied with nothing else since 1976. Together they have performed prodigies of research, but one expects no less. Less predictable was the way Szarkowski, while diving around among all this visual wealth like Scrooge McDuck in Money Barn No. 64, has managed to keep his critical balance, something that a man with his capacity for enthusiasm does not always find easy.

Echoing the useful distinction he established in 1966 between documentary and self-expression, Szarkowski is able to divide Atget's work up into the large number of photographs which are of historical interest and the smaller number in which the historical interest is somehow ignited into an aesthetic moment—in which, that is to say, the *studium* acquires a *punctum*. But the viewer who finds his attention not only attracted but delighted by some of these pictures will be hard-pressed to decide where the *punctum* is. Is it in the plough or the well, the overhanging tree or the doorway in the wall?

It soon becomes clear that the best of Atget's photographs, while they are unlikely to hold your interest as long as paintings might do that are nominally of the same subject, nevertheless owe their aesthetic authority to much more than an isolated piquancy. They really do imply some kind of controlling artistic personality, however attenuated. The notion of *punctum*, while necessary and welcome, is too limited a critical criterion to be sufficient. On the other hand, Barthes's other and larger notion, the one about the thereness of the past and the lost reality which rules out nostalgia, is underlined with full force. Leaving aside the soft tones of the albumen process, here is Old France looking close enough to touch and as irrecoverable as the Garden of Eden—an effect only increased by Atget's reluctance to include human beings even when the exposure time would have allowed it.

On a smaller scale but still good to have, *The Autochromes of J. H. Lartigue* shows us an unfamiliar side of another indisputable artist—his work in colour. The autochrome process has the effect, when the prints are reproduced today, of making everything look like a pointillist painting. Since Lartigue's sensibility was so like Seurat's anyway, the echo effect is often uncanny, but in fact Lartigue was no more likely than his predecessor Atget to ape painting. In his late teens when he started shooting autochromes, he kept it up from 1912 to 1927. The best surviving results are given here, prefaced by a typically charming interview with the master himself.

It is a small book but makes a substantial supplement to his indispensable *Diary of a Century*, which chronicles his work in black and white and proves him to have been the first great lyrical celebrator of human beings at play. In black and white the relatively short exposure time enabled him to capture movement. In autochrome he couldn't do that, but his joyous personality still comes bubbling through. He had an inexhaustible supply of pretty girl acquaintances trying out new scooters, dashing brothers who built flying machines, etc. Perhaps other photographers were similarly blessed, but Lartigue knew exactly what to include in the frame and when to press the button or squeeze the bulb. Highly endowed with a knack for what Cartier-Bresson was later to call the guess, Lartigue could see a *punctum* a mile off. He could see *puncta* in clusters. In other words, he had a self to express.

As time increases the total number of photographers and it becomes increasingly obvious that there is no room for all of them to express themselves, it may become permissible to suggest that documentary interest is a sufficiently respectable interest for a photographer's work to have, and that if a photographer can go on getting good documentary results for a long time then he is artist enough. To have such a point conceded would make it easier to save some of the masterly but less than outstanding photographers of the past from an otherwise inevitable public revulsion against the indigestibly strident claims made for their seriousness.

The Photography of Max Yavno, for example, is a book well worth having. Yavno has been taking thoughtful photographs since the 1930s. Not all of them are as striking as his famous 1947 picture of the San Francisco cable car being swung on the turntable by its balletically swaying attendants. The picture adorns the jacket of this book, is superbly reproduced in a plate within and features in just about every anthology of photographs published in the last thirty years. It should be possible to allow a man a few such happily sought-out and taken chances without trying to find the same significance in the rest of his work, which the law of averages dictates will be more *studium* than *punctum*. Luckily, the mandatory prose-poem captions (once again it is hard to suppress a blasphemous twinge of regret that James Agee and Walker Evans ever got together) are largely offset by an appended interview with Yavno in which he reveals himself to be admirably, indeed monosyllabically, unpretentious. Except when generously reminiscing about his fellow veteran practitioners, he keeps things on the yep-nope level, Gary Cooper style.

Much the same applies to *Feininger's Chicago 1941*, in which Andreas Feininger, in a lively introduction written forty years later, keeps his ego perhaps excessively within bounds. Forgetting to inform us that he was a Bauhaus-trained intellectual who personally invented the super-telephoto camera, Feininger gives humble thanks that he was obliged to view Chicago with the fresh eye of the displaced European. Here are parking elevators at a time when cars were just about to lose their running boards, Union and Dearborn Stations when the silver trains still ran, Lake Shore Drive before Mies van der Rohe built his apartments and the kind of skyscraper that Stalin copied and that now exists nowhere except in the Soviet Union. Feininger presents his lost city without any accompanying verbal elegies.

The Weston family tends to be less taciturn. *Cole Weston: Eighteen Photographs* enshrines the colour work of one of Edward Weston's sons. Like Brett Weston, another son, Cole seems to have inherited from his father a deep sense of mission. As is recounted in Charis Wilson's introduction to this volume, Edward Weston had Parkinson's disease and young Cole had to help him work the camera. It's like reading about Renoir *père et fils*—an apostolic succession. On the other hand it is not like that, since the painter and the filmmaker each had a separate, fully developed artistic vision which makes their blood kinship remarkable, whereas one suspects that for photography to run in the family is no more startling than for carpentry to run in the family, as a craft to be learned rather than an inner impulse to be bodied forth. Nonetheless, here are sumptuous colour prints of California surf, Nova Scotia fishing coves, Utah aspens and similar Americana. A close-up of rust on a water tank looks like abstract expressionism, showing that painting still has its pull despite all the disclaimers. Also a nude lady seen from the same angle as the Rokeby Venus reclines on an old stone staircase in Arizona. She looks exactly like a confession that the staircase would not be very interesting without her.

Cole and Brett Weston take you back to Edward Weston, to Paul Strand, to Minor White, to Ansel Adams—to every master photographer, in fact, who has ever gone out into the American landscape and tried to isolate a clean piece of nature within his metal frame. Some of the results are collected in *American Photographers and the National Parks*, edited by Robert Cahn and Robert Glenn Ketchum. The pictures are arranged chronologically, starting with a William Henry Jackson study of Yosemite Falls in 1898. Jackson got a terrific action shot, in colour, of the Yellowstone Great Geyser in 1902. Edward Weston's Zabriskie Point picture of 1938 reminds you of just how good the old man was at waiting for the right shadows. The Ansel Adams pictures will be familiar to most readers but still stand out. They don't stand out so far, though, as to convince you that subject matter is anything less than very important. Even for Adams, to pursue too closely the light patterns on a cactus was to court inanity. In Barthes's terms, the referent adheres. If it doesn't, you've got nothing.

Adams deserves our lasting respect for the reverent skill with which he photographed a mountain, even though a modern amateur with up-to-date equipment might fluke a picture not entirely risible by comparison. After all, Adams knew what he was doing, and could do it again. So could Paul Strand when taking pictures of clapboard houses. Nevertheless *New England Reflections, 1882–1907* features, among other things, enough clapboard houses, photographed with more than enough verve, to set you wondering whether that particular form of architecture ever needed Paul Strand to bring out its full beauty. All the pictures were taken by the three Howes brothers, who formed themselves into a commercial outfit and toted their tripods around New England persuading people, obviously with profitable results, that great moments in life should be permanently recorded. The glass-plate negatives having miraculously survived to our own day, here is the permanent record. It is a fascinating little book which Richard Wilbur honours with a foreword that you might wish were longer, since Wilbur's distinguished, visually fastidious sensibility is exactly what such material requires to give it a proper context. But Gerald McFarland provides a useful historical introduction and anyway the pictures are so rich themselves that you would be drowning in *puncta* even if you didn't know where and when they came from.

All seems in order, even the home for the handicapped, whose inmates have formed up for a serene group shot as if Diane Arbus did not exist—which, of course, she as yet didn't. Here is the irrecoverable past only a few inches away. Some of the buildings are still intact, so that inhabitants of New England who buy this book will be able to stand in the right spot and look through time. Paradoxically, the Howes brothers were just going about their everyday business, with not much thought of preserving a threatened heritage, whereas Atget, who had a Balzacian urge to register his epoch, saw much of what he photographed destroyed within his lifetime, and if he were to come back now would find almost nothing left.

If a photographer wants to express himself but fears that his personal view might be short on originality, originality of subject matter is one way out of the trap. The only drawback to this escape route is that the number of subjects, if not finite, is certainly coterminous with the known universe. Already most topics are starting to look used up. In *Man as Art: New Guinea*, Malcolm Kirk has persuaded an impressive number of New Guinea natives to pose in full warlike and/or ceremonial make-up and drag. Thus we are able to observe, in plate 74, that a Western Highlands warrior male called Nigel resembles, when fully attired for battle, Allen Ginsberg in blackface with a Las Vegas hotel sign on his head.

Some of the pictures are stunning, or at least startling, but there is no denying that the natives have shown at least as much invention as the photographer, whose skill in lighting them and pressing the button can scarcely be compared to theirs in caking their skins with clay, inserting bones in their noses, and pulling on their grass skirts. Nor, more damagingly, is there any denying that we have already seen most of this in the *National Geographic*, albeit on a smaller scale. Much of the justification for these big picture books is that they give you big pictures, but there is also the consideration that what looks appropriately dramatic when bled to the edges of a full page in a magazine starts looking emptily pretentious when pumped up to folio size. Not only is it bigger than the negative, it's bigger than the reality. In real life you would learn all you need to know about Nigel without going quite so close.

Still on the *National Geographic* beat, *Rajasthan: India's Enchanted Land* comprises pictures by Raghubir Singh which suggest that its title might not be a complete misnomer, although for at least this viewer the *puncta* which are obviously meant to be bursting out of such a picture as "A Gujar Villager, Pushkar" remain defiantly quiescent. Far from being amazed that a man with a turban is wearing a watch and smoking a cigarette, I'd be amazed if he were not. More exciting, or less unexciting, is another shot in which all the village males, after a hard day's work supervising the women, are rewarding themselves by sucking popsicles. There is a foreword by Satyajit Ray to remind us that for Indian artists of all kinds Rajasthan is a fairly resonant part of the subcontinent, but you can see how a foreign photographer with a reputation to make might want a more jazzy angle.

In *Falkland Road: Prostitutes of Bombay*, Mary Ellen Mark shows how this can be done. She moved in with the eponymous hookers, became part of the scenery and ended up by reaching such a level of acceptance that the girls and their clients allowed her to photograph them *in flagrante*. The results are unlikely to put you off sex, with which the activities in Falkland Road seem to have only a parodic connection, but they might well put you off India. The girls work in cubicles the size of packing crates and perform their ablutions in a bucket. Hepatitis hangs in the air like aerosol spray. For the alert customer the whole deal would be a bit of a downer even if Ms. Mark were not poised in the rafters busily snapping the action. The intrepid photographer contributes her own introduction, in which she spends a lot of time conveying her deep affection for the girls without ever raising the topic of whether she, too, might not be said to be drawing sustenance from the sad traffic, and in a much safer way. Still, Cartier-Bresson photographed whores in Mexico in 1934.

Already responsible for nine books, Ms. Mark was born in 1940 and graduated from the University of Pennsylvania. Susan Meiselas, author of *Nicaragua*, is a Sarah Lawrence graduate who does not give her age but can safely be adjudged even younger than Ms. Mark. Both women are getting well known fast, not because either of them is Gisèle Freund or Lotte Jacobi reborn but because they both know how to get in and get the story. Ms. Meiselas's story is the Nicaraguan version of with-Fidel-in-the-Sierra, down to and including the berets, Che moustaches and .45 automatics triumphantly raised in adolescent fists. "Yet unlike most photographs of such material," says an accompanying note from John Berger, "these refuse all the rhetoric normally associated with such pictures." Not for the first time one wonders how Berger, inventor of the purportedly illuminating concept "ways of seeing," actually does see. His eyes certainly work differently from mine, which find Ms. Meiselas's every second picture laden with rhetoric. But despite more recent reports from Nicaragua, one concedes that the rhetoric might be, in this case, on the side of the angels. Nor can it be gainsaid that people calling on themselves to be courageous often behave rhetorically. Who looks natural when nerving himself for battle?

Photographs, according to Barthes, never entirely leave the world of words. In *Visions of China* Marc Riboud's photographs taken between 1957 and 1980 constitute, even more than Eve Arnold's recent volume on the same subject, a reminder that if we know nothing about the background we might well make a hash of interpreting the foreground. Orville Schell's introduction makes much of Riboud's supposed ability to see past the rhetoric to the reality beneath. Certainly Riboud got off the beaten track and managed to hint that not all was harmony, but it should not need saying—and yet it does—that he got nowhere near recording the full impact of the Cultural Revolution, which we were allowed to see nothing of in the form of pictures and have since had to hear about in the form of words. Most of these words were emitted between sobs, since those victims who survived are often unable to recall their sufferings with equanimity.

This fact should lend additional significance to such a photograph as plate 89, "Student Dancer, Shanghai, 1971." It shows a radiantly happy girl being inspired by the mere presence of Mao's little red book. But in this case the *punctum*, instead of crossing from the photograph to the viewer's mind, travels in the other direction. Today's viewer will have heard that the Chinese ballerinas were sent by Mrs. Mao to have their muscles ruined in the fields. The dancers were already suffering at the time when Shirley MacLaine, a dancer herself, was wondering, in her television documentary about China, why the Chinese looked so happy. The viewer haunted by these considerations is unlikely to look on Riboud's photograph of a Chinese dancer as being anything more edifying than a pretty picture.

But where any pictures are hard to get, all pictures have some value, even if they seem to point in the wrong direction until interpreted. So it is with China and so it will probably always be with the Soviet Union. Vladimir Sichov's *The Russians* deserves immediate notice, since the standard of photography in the Soviet Union is so blandly low that any attempt at realism looks like a sunburst. Sichov was born in 1945 and in 1979 was permitted to leave for the West. He brought 5,000 rolls of film out safely—his whole archive. The full effect is of a dowdiness so comprehensive that it becomes almost enthralling. Unfortunately Sichov seems to have concentrated on the routine dowdiness of old women in shapeless coats rather than the more interesting dowdiness of young ones in the latest fashions from GUM. The true visual squalor in the Soviet Union resides in what is thought to be chic, a fact which Sichov has subsequently had ample opportunity to realize, because he is nowadays an ace catwalk photographer for the Paris fashion shows, a task to which he brings the hungry eye of a man raised during a famine. Photographers brought up on a visual diet in which swimsuits look as if they have been cut out of motel shower curtains tend to be especially grateful for what Yves Saint-Laurent hangs on Jerry Hall.

William Klein makes America look almost as scruffy as Russia but in the case of his collection *William Klein* much of the flakiness is due to inky printing. Klein has issued a protest about how his publishers have treated him and if later copies look like my early copy then he is right. Some of the pictures look like action shots of a black cat in a coal bunker. In the ones you can see, however, *puncta* proliferate. The snap Barthes liked of the little boy with the toy gun to his head is here spread over two pages, making the bad teeth more attention-getting than ever. But most viewers will probably still take the gun, rather than the teeth, to be the main point. Mainly because he runs forward to involve himself instead of hanging back to be objective, Klein is very good at catching the vivid moment. There are also pictures taken in Italy, Russia and elsewhere, but really Manhattan, where he was born, is Klein's precinct. He can see the casual calligraphic symmetry of window signs offering breaded veal cutlets for $1.05. So could every American urban photographer back to Weegee and beyond, but the thereness never fails to grip.

More involved even than Klein, more involved even than Hemingway, almost as involved as the soldiers themselves, Don McCullin gets his camera into the war. An Englishman, McCullin started by photographing his own country's dark underside, but he was not alone. Covering Cyprus in 1964 he discovered his own bailiwick, up where the bullets were flying. Since then he has been in all the wars, most notably Vietnam, where his work was on a par with that of Philip Jones Griffiths. But his eye is not so spoiled by the adrenaline of action that it refrains from dwelling on the aftermath. Dead soldiers in every variety of contortion and civilians in every stage of starvation are duly recorded.

Scanning the worst of McCullin's horrors, you find yourself wishing that Barthes were less right about the past really having been there. But anyone not capable of realizing that these things happen will not be much struck by the photographs anyway, so John le Carré's introductory exhortations about McCullin's mission to "appall the comfortable" are themselves somewhat cosy. It is a characteristic of the English intellectual middle class to believe that the mass of the public is uninstructed in the world's grim realities and needs waking up. McCullin is too bravely independent to share so smug an attitude but it has helped make him famous — the most dazzling current example of the photographer singled out by subject.

Not many photographers would have the nerve to follow reality as far as McCullin does in search of their own territory, even supposing that there were any territory left. The alternative has always been to take the reality nearby and fiddle with it. By now I think it is becoming clear that for photographers abstraction and surrealism are a dry well, partly because, *pace* Galassi, painting always seems to exert at least as strong a pull on photography as photography does on painting. The moment the photographer starts treating the objects of experience symbolically, the referent ceases to adhere, and what he composes gravitates seemingly inexorably towards something already made familiar by the painters.

Herbert List: Photographs 1930–1970 collects the best work of a photographer with an impressive intellectual background. Trained by Andreas Feininger, List consorted with the visiting English writers in the Germany of the early 1930s and after leaving Germany in 1936 he became the leading purveyor of surrealist-tinged photographs to the slick magazines. But in this collection it is precisely the portrait photography which looks permanent and the surrealist compositions which seem to have been overtaken by time. Barthes should give us the courage to confess our difficulties about getting interested in the artificially arranged *punctum.*

Most of List's cleanly lit and composed surrealist confections flare to life only when they include a couple of strapping young men standing around in G-strings. Immediately you get interested in the life going on off camera. Stephen Spender evokes some of it in the introduction, which like everything he writes about the Germany of the time makes you sorry not to have been there. He is much better than Isherwood at giving you some idea of the mental excitement. Isherwood, even today, concentrates on the physical excitement.

Drawing on their memories, writers can pursue their own tastes into old age. For photographers it is not so easy. List gave up after the war, feeling that once he had explored the limits of his own technique he was through as an artist, always supposing he had ever been one. Some of the portraits are good enough to make you think he judged himself too harshly, but there is no getting away from the fact that even with them the interest resides at least partly in the identity of the sitter. It is Morandi, Cocteau, Chirico, Picasso, Montherlant, Auden and Somerset Maugham who lend List renown, and not vice versa.

Anyone who finds it hard wholly to admire List is going to make heavy weather of admiring Robert Rauschenberg. *Robert Rauschenberg Photographs* shows what he has been up to in a medium to which he is not new, since he started off as a photographer. Having achieved fame, and presumably fulfilment, as a painter, he has recently revisited his first passion.

Rauschenberg's chief trick in any medium is to juxtapose ready-made images. I can remember wondering, when I saw his exhibition of paintings at the Whitechapel Gallery in the East End of London in the early 1960s, why he didn't juxtapose them more tightly, suggestively—in a word, wittily. I liked what he was doing but didn't think he took it any distance, and resented the suggestion, made on his behalf by eager commentators, that the grubby white space left in each of his large canvases was meant to give my own imagination room to work. My own imagination was already *at* work, wondering how much of Rauschenberg's allegedly selective creativity was doodling.

All the same doubts go double here, where there are not even a few swipes of paint to indicate personal intervention. In plate 45 a Mona Lisa tea towel hangs over the back of a canvas chair which is also variously draped and decorated with discarded clothes and a folded newspaper. If you buy the theory that a pure response to the Mona Lisa is no longer possible, here is food for thought. But for anyone to whom the Mona Lisa is still the Mona Lisa whatever happens, the inevitable reaction is a fervent wish that Rauschenberg would paint his own pictures and leave Leonardo's alone.

"So what?" is not necessarily a philistine reaction. Sometimes it is required for the preservation of sanity, especially when one is presented with the intentionally meaningless and told to find it meaningful. John Pfahl's *Altered Landscapes* shows us how a competent photographer can beautifully photograph landscapes in the same way as any other equally competent photographer can beautifully photograph landscapes, but pick up extra, reputation-making acclaim by "altering" them, hence the title. A picture taken in Monument Valley includes a piece of red string squiggling along the ground, which enables it to be called "Monument Valley with Red String." Some of the pictures generate a sufficient frisson to make record album covers. Rock groups with metaphysical proclivities often favour the sort of album covers in which a line of large coloured spheres marches across the Sahara: altered landscapes for altered states.

Sam Haskins, it hardly needs saying, is better than competent, especially when photographing pretty young girls, for whom he has a hawk eye. But *Sam Haskins/Photo graphics* reveals a desire to be something more than the kind of craftsman whose output the uninitiated might mistake for soft porn. The term "photo graphics" calls up Moholy-Nagy's photograms. Think of a Moholy photogram, add colour, focus the composition on the exquisitely lit, plumply swelling pantie-cupped crotch of a young girl lying back thinking pure thoughts about a sky full of roses, and you've got a Haskins photo graphic. You have to take it on trust that the picture bears no relation to a hot paragraph by Terry Southern. This is a meticulously produced book by whose technical accomplishment Haskins's fellow-photographers will no doubt be suitably cowed, but the sceptical viewer could be excused for wondering whether a picture of a rainbow shining out of a pretty girl's behind might not be a more direct indication of the artist's state of mind than the circumambient surrealist trappings.

With *Bill Brandt: Nudes 1945–1980* we are in another, less ambiguous, part of the forest. The model and inspiration for the young British photographers of the 1960s, the one home-grown loner they could admire without reserve, Brandt dedicated his career to photographing Woman in a way that would resolve her sensual appeal into a formal design. Hiding the lady's face and applying every device of elongation, distortion and convolution, he pushed the formal design towards the abstract. But it approached the abstract asymptotically, as if Brandt were aware that when the referent ceased to adhere the result would be not just no woman but no anything.

Brandt's hermetic commitment cost him a great deal and won him deserved admiration. Looking at these pictures, even the most clueless viewer will sense himself in the presence of a rare concentration of thought and feeling. But it is still possible to say, I think, that in treating the human body as a sculptural form Brandt was unable to avoid the gravitational pull of sculpture itself. Warm bottoms become cold Brancusis. Hips turn into Arps. Finally, in his most recent phase, Brandt unexpectedly and shockingly starts to load his nudes down with ropes and chains, as if it were his new ambition to take a studio on Forty-second Street or set up in partnership with Helmut Newton. It looks like a despairing confession that whereas a painter can significantly change the woman in front of him and make her part of something more significant, a photographer can't significantly change her without destroying her significance altogether. But with all that said, nobody should mistake this book for anything less than the work of a unique isolated master photographer.

In the long run the photographers who glorified women individually, rather than rendering them all symbolically impersonal, stood a better chance of being called artists. The Hollywood portrait photographers rarely thought of themselves as much more than craftsmen, but John Kobal's essential book *The Art of the Great Hollywood Portrait Photographers* has no doubt given the survivors a higher, and well-merited, estimation of themselves. Likewise assembled by Kobal from his unrivalled archive, *Hollywood Color Portraits* is the colour supplement to the black-and-white standard work. Less weighty than its predecessor, it is still well worth having. Not only was colour less adaptable than black and white to subtle lighting; it was also much harder to retouch, so in this book you see some of the stars as they really looked, right down to the enlarged pores and—in Burt Lancaster's case—the five o'clock shadow of Nixonite tenacity.

Theories of the hunger towards realism suffer a setback when faced with this order of evidence. Black and white was the ideal, colour was the real, and the ideal looked realer. Bob Coburn's colour picture of Rita Hayworth in 1948 is just a pretty girl. "Whitey" Schaefer's 1941 black-and-white portrait of her is an angelic visitation. Yet surely the black and white is the more true to the way she was. Not many of us who are grateful for her talent can look at such a photograph without feeling the bitterness of the irrecoverable reality that Barthes talks about. There was a day when supreme personal beauty was impossible to capture fully and so could fade without its possessor being too forcibly reminded of its loss. That time is past—one certain way, among all the conjectural ones, in which photography has changed the world.

For reasons of space and self-preservation I have had to leave many current books out of this survey. Nor are all the books I have included likely to prove essential in the long run. But *A Century of Japanese Photography* I can confidently recommend to any institution concerned with photography and to any person who can afford the price. Compiled in Japan and presented for Western consumption by John W. Dower, the book is a treasure city, a Kyoto of the printed image. Barthes would have been so shot through with *puncta* that he would have felt like Saint Sebastian, or Toshiro Mifune in the climactic scene of *Throne of Blood*. Peter Galassi will find his theory simultaneously borne out and borne away, since so much of Japanese painting led up to photography (what else did Hiroshige and Hokusai do with their winter landscapes but

bleach out the inessential?) and so many of the Japanese master photographers are drawn back into the established pictorial tradition.

Since the Meiji restoration the Japanese have been photographing
one another and the inhabitants of every country they have invaded.
They seem rarely to have decapitated anyone without getting some carefully framed before-and-after shots. The level of violence in the book is
made even more terrifying by the degree of delicacy. You feel that you are
at a tea ceremony with Mishima and that he might behead you and dis-
embowel himself at any moment and in either order.

The photographs of war put McCullin's work in its proper perspective. McCullin might be trying to awaken our dormant psyches but for
the Japanese the gap between everyday tranquillity and stark horror seems
always to have been only a step wide. And just as readily as they photographed the violence they inflicted, they photographed the violence
inflicted on them. Elegantly judged, Pompeii-like photographs of the
charred bodies after the Tokyo fire raids may be edifyingly compared with
similar studies obtained in Nagasaki and Hiroshima. Proudly saluting
from the cockpit, a kamikaze pilot taxis past a class of schoolgirls waving
cherry branches in farewell. Words are needed to tell us where he is flying to, but once we know that, the picture tells us that he was there. Probably some of the schoolgirls are still alive and can pick themselves out in
the picture. They were there too. Reality is the *donnée* of photography
and sets the limit for how much the photographer can transform what he
sees into a personal creation. For the artist photographer the limit is high
but it still exists. To think it can be transcended is to be like Kant's dove,
which, upon being told about air resistance, thought it could fly faster by
abolishing the air.

New York Review of Books, December 17, 1981;
later included in *Snakecharmers in Texas*, 1988

POSTSCRIPT

Like writing about television, writing about photography was a chance to
talk about everything. If someone had taken a photograph in China, I
could talk about China. Doing a round-up of all the world's books about
photography in the past and present, I could go on for pages about time,
space and the history of the world. But I couldn't go on for long about

photography itself, because apart from the technicalities there isn't much to discuss, and criticism based solely on technicalities is doomed to famine. It can sound impressive, but so can an actor pretending to be a doctor. The specialist photography magazines are full of articles specifying shutter speed, focal length and what have you. No doubt it all means a lot to the adept, but it leaves the layman facing the same void as he always does when an aesthetic event is discussed in mechanical terms. A solo by Darcey Bussell, for example, can be registered on the page as a set of steps and poses with French names. Unfortunately every member of the *corps de ballet* can do them too. So the writer has evoked precisely nothing. In the case of photography the problem is exacerbated by the remorseless industrial effort to get all the relevant expertise into the camera itself, and out of the fallible hands of the goof holding it. There is indeed a miracle of creativity involved, but it is all inside the mechanism: more than a hundred and fifty years of intense technical development, none of which, if it were all forgotten tomorrow, even the most gifted photographer could begin to recapitulate.

Making a television programme about a safari in Kenya, I was supplied by my producers with the very latest Nikon. All I had to do was point it and twist the bit that stuck out until something I could see through the little window was in focus—anything. I can't even remember if I had to press a button. Perhaps it pressed its own button and told me afterwards. Anyway, I got a close-up of an angry lion's face. The lion was angry because the car I was in woke it up, and some idiot human sticking out of the top of the car was pointing a sinister-looking box of tricks at it. When the photograph came back from the chemist's, I was as open-mouthed as the lion. Cartier-Bresson would have swallowed his hyphen with envy. The photograph was as sharp as a tack, impressive as the crack of doom, frightening to chill the mind. It could have gone straight into a glossy magazine, full page, bled to the edges. There is a lot I could say concerning that photograph. I could talk about my fear and the lion's nobility, Africa's tragedy and the pathos of civilization. But there is almost nothing illuminating to say about the technique with which I secured it. With a camera like that, the lion could have taken a photograph of me.

Art is safe from such developments. We aren't, but it is. At once primitive and infinitely protean, art wasn't born of consciousness: consciousness was born of it. As long as human life lasts, art will go on being the one activity for which no amount of calculation can provide a substitute, and the job of the critic will be to explain why this is so. The ability to realize that he can never attain to an exhaustive analysis of the thing he loves best is the indispensable qualification for signing on. What he has to offer is his life, of which his learning can only be a part: the more he knows the better, but if he thinks that nothing else counts then he will count for nothing. *Primum vivere, deinde philosophari* is a rap that nobody can beat.

Reliable Essays, 2001

INDEX

ABOUT THE AUTHOR

Clive James was born in Sydney, Australia, in 1939 and educated at Sydney Technical High School and Sydney University, where he was literary editor of the student newspaper *Honi Soit* and also directed the annual Union Revue. After a year spent as assistant editor of the magazine page of the *Sydney Morning Herald* he sailed in late 1961 for England. Three years of a bohemian existence in London were succeeded by his entry into Cambridge University, where he read for a further degree while contributing to all the undergraduate periodicals and rising to the presidency of Footlights.

His prominence in extracurricular activities having attracted the attention of the London literary editors, the byline "Clive James" was soon appearing in the *Listener*, the *New Statesman*, the *Review* and several other periodicals, all of them keen to tap into the erudite verve which had been showing up so unexpectedly in *Varsity* and the *Cambridge Review*. Yet the article that made his name was unsigned. At the invitation of Ian Hamilton, who as well as editing the *Review* was assistant editor of the *Times Literary Supplement*—which was still holding at the time to its traditional policy of strict anonymity—the new man in town was given several pages of the paper for a long, valedictory article about Edmund Wilson. Called "The Metropolitan Critic" in honour of its subject, the piece aroused widespread speculation as to its authorship: Graham Greene was only one of the many subscribers who wrote to the editor asking for their congratulations to be passed on, and it became a point of honour in the literary world to know the masked man's real identity.

Embarrassed to find himself graced with the same title he had given his exemplar, Clive James rapidly established himself as one of the most influential metropolitan critics of his generation, but he continued to act on his belief that a cultural commentator could only benefit from being as involved as possible with his subject, and over as wide a range as opportunity allowed. The Sunday newspaper the *Observer* hired him as a television reviewer in 1972, and for ten years his weekly column was one of the most famous regular features in Fleet Street journalism, setting a style which was later widely copied.

During this period he gradually became a prominent television performer himself, and over the next two decades he wrote and presented countless studio series and specials, as well as pioneering the "Postcard" format of travel programmes, which are still in syndication all over the world. His major series *Fame in the Twentieth Century* was broadcast in Britain by the BBC, in Australia by the ABC and in the United States by the PBS network.

But despite the temptations and distractions of media celebrity, he always maintained his literary activity as a critic, author, poet and lyricist. In 1974, his satirical verse epic *Peregrine Prykke's Pilgrimage* was the talk of literary London, many of whose leading figures were disconcerted by appearing in it, and more disconcerted if they were left out. In the same year, *The Metropolitan Critic* was merely the first of what would eventually be six separate collections of his articles, and in 1979 his first book of autobiography, *Unreliable Memoirs*, recounting his upbringing in Australia, was an enormous publishing success, which has by now extended to more than sixty reprintings. It was followed by two other volumes of autobiography, *Falling Towards England* and *May Week Was in June*.

In addition there have been four novels, several books of poetry—a complete edition is planned—and a collection of travel writings, *Flying Visits*. His literary journalism became familiar in the United States through *Commentary*, the *New York Review of Books* and *The New Yorker*. His fourth novel, *The Silver Castle*, the first book about Bollywood, was published in the United States in 1996.

Collaborating with the singer and musician Pete Atkin, he wrote the lyrics for six commercially released albums in the early 1970s, and the partnership resumed with two more albums after the turn of the millennium, culminating with a hit appearance for their two-man song-show on the Edinburgh Fringe in 2001 and a tour of Britain in 2002. Extended tours of both Britain and Australia are planned for 2003. After helping to found the successful independent television production company Watchmaker, Clive James retired from mainstream television to become chairman of the Internet enterprise Welcome Stranger, for which he now broadcasts in both video and audio on www.welcomestranger.com, the first webcasting site of its type. He is currently completing a long study of cultural discontinuity in the twentieth century, under the title of *Alone in the Café*, and has begun work on a dance operetta based on his passion for the Argentinian tango. In 1992 he was made a member of the Order of Australia, and in 1999 an honorary Doctor of Letters of Sydney University.